ALISON WEIR

Alison Weir lives and works in Surrey. Her non-fiction books include *The Six Wives of Henry VIII*, *Children of England*, *Eleanor of Acquitaine*, *Henry VIII: King and Court*, *Mary, Queen of Scots*, *Katherine Swynford* and *Elizabeth of York*. Her novels include *Innocent Traitor*, *The Lady Elizabeth* and *A Dangerous Inheritance*.

ALSO BY ALISON WEIR

Non-fiction

Britain's Royal Families: The Complete Genealogy
The Six Wives of Henry VIII
Richard III and the Princes in the Tower
Lancaster and York: The Wars of the Roses
Children of England: The Heirs of Henry VIII 1547–1558
Elizabeth the Queen
Eleanor of Aquitaine
Henry VIII: King and Court
Mary Queen of Scots and the Murder of Lord Darnley
Isabella: She-Wolf of France, Queen of England
Katherine Swynford: The Story of John of Gaunt and His Scandalous Duchess
The Lady in the Tower: The Fall of Anne Boleyn
Mary Boleyn: 'The Great and Infamous Whore'
Elizabeth of York: The First Tudor Queen

As co-author

The Ring and the Crown: A History of Royal Weddings, 1066–2011

Fiction

Innocent Traitor
The Lady Elizabeth
The Captive Queen
A Dangerous Inheritance

Quick Reads

Traitors of the Tower

ALISON WEIR

The Lost Tudor Princess

A Life of Margaret Douglas,
Countess of Lennox

VINTAGE

1 3 5 7 9 10 8 6 4 2

Vintage
20 Vauxhall Bridge Road,
London SW1V 2SA

Vintage is part of the Penguin Random House group of companies
whose addresses can be found at global.penguinrandomhouse.com

Penguin
Random House
UK

First published in Vintage in 2016
First published in hardback by Jonathan Cape in 2015

www.vintage-books.co.uk

A CIP catalogue record for this book
is available from the British Library

ISBN 9780099546467

Printed and bound by CPI Group (UK) Ltd, Croydon CR0 4YY

MIX
Paper from
responsible sources
FSC® C018179

Penguin Random House is committed to a sustainable future
for our business, our readers and our planet. This book is
made from Forest Stewardship Council® certified paper

To Tracy Borman
and Tom Ashworth
to mark their marriage

Contents

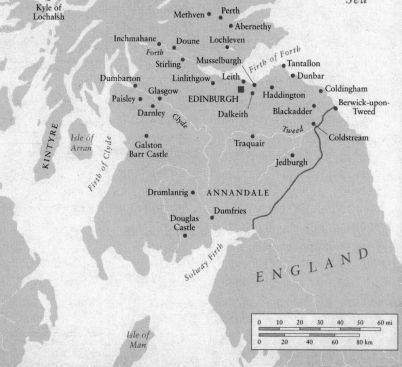

Margaret's Scotland

Margaret's England

SCOTLAND

North Sea

Berwick-upon-Tweed
Norham
Flodden
Harbottle
Morpeth
Newcastle
Carlisle
Durham
Whorlton
Darlington
Richmond
Scarborough
Bolton
Hunmanby
Jervaulx
Settrington
Bridlington bay
Leeds
YORK
Pocklington
Smallwood
Temple
Newsam
Wressle
Doncaster
Sheffield
Lincoln
Chester
Chatsworth
Rufford
Newark
Grantham
Yarmouth
Grimsthorpe
Kenninghall
Fotheringhay
Thetford
ENGLAND
Westhorpe
Waltham
Ipswich
Enfield
Hunsdon
Harwich
Hatfield
Beaulieu
Islington
Hackney
Thames
Chiswick
Stepney
Reading
Syon
Rochester
Windsor
Greenwich
Guildford
LONDON
Dover
Winchester
Sheen
Hampton
Court
Richmond
Southampton
Titchfield
Portsmouth

Isle of Man

Irish Sea

WALES

St Georges Channel

Bristol Channel

Bristol

English Channel

Scilly Isles

N
W   E
S

0   20   40   60   80 mi
0 20 40 60 80 100 120 km

HOUSE OF STEWART (SCOTLAND)

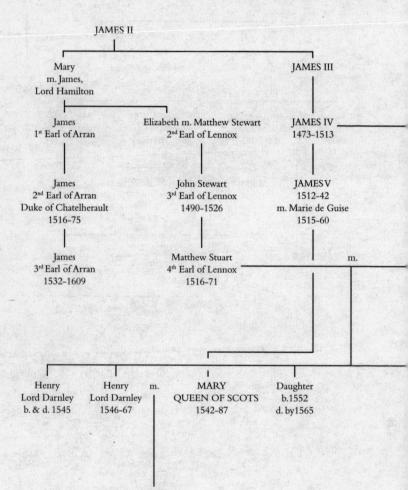

JAMES II

Mary
m. James,
Lord Hamilton

JAMES III

James
1st Earl of Arran

Elizabeth m. Matthew Stewart
2nd Earl of Lennox

JAMES IV
1473–1513

James
2nd Earl of Arran
Duke of Chatelherault
1516–75

John Stewart
3rd Earl of Lennox
1490–1526

JAMES V
1512–42
m. Marie de Guise
1515–60

James
3rd Earl of Arran
1532–1609

Matthew Stuart
4th Earl of Lennox
1516–71

m.

Henry
Lord Darnley
b. & d. 1545

Henry
Lord Darnley
1546–67

m.

MARY
QUEEN OF SCOTS
1542–87

Daughter
b.1552
d. by1565

JAMES VI
(JAMES I OF ENGLAND
AND GREAT BRITAIN)
1566–1625

Stuart Dynasty

HOUSES OF YORK AND TUDOR (ENGLAND)

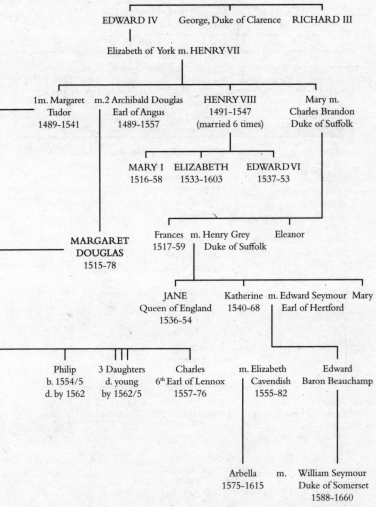

EDWARD IV   George, Duke of Clarence   RICHARD III

Elizabeth of York m. HENRY VII

1m. Margaret   m.2 Archibald Douglas   HENRY VIII   Mary m.
Tudor   Earl of Angus   1491–1547   Charles Brandon
1489–1541   1489–1557   (married 6 times) Duke of Suffolk

MARY I   ELIZABETH   EDWARD VI
1516–58   1533–1603   1537–53

MARGARET   Frances   m. Henry Grey   Eleanor
DOUGLAS   1517–59   Duke of Suffolk
1515–78

JANE   Katherine m. Edward Seymour Mary
Queen of England   1540–68   Earl of Hertford
1536–54

Philip   3 Daughters   Charles   m. Elizabeth   Edward
b. 1554/5   d. young   6th Earl of Lennox   Cavendish   Baron Beauchamp
d. by 1562   by 1562/5   1557–76   1555–82

Arbella   m.   William Seymour
1575–1615   Duke of Somerset
                     1588–1660

THE HOUSE OF ANGUS

Archibald 'Bell-the-Cat' Douglas m. Elizabeth Boyd
5th Earl of Angus   (second wife)
1449–1513

George Douglas m. Elizabeth   Mariot m. Cuthbert
Master of Angus   Drummond   Cunningham
1469–1513   Earl of Glencairn

Archibald Douglas m. 1. Margaret   Sir George of   William
6th Earl of Angus   Hepburn   Pittendreich   Prior of Coldingham
1489–1557   d. 1513   d.1552   d. 1528
                            m.Elizabeth
          2. Margaret   Douglas of
            Tudor   Pittendreich
            1489–1541

          3. Margaret
            Maxwell   David Douglas   James Douglas
                          7th Earl of Angus Earl of Morton
                          1515–58   1516–81
                          m. Margaret   m.Elizabeth
                          Hamilton   Douglas

                            Archibald
                         8th Earl of Angus
                           1555–88

MARGARET   James   Sons   Janet m. Patrick   George
DOUGLAS   Master of Angus d. young d.c. 1552   Lord Ruthven Bishop
1515–78   1520–66   of Moray
                                                           d.1589

Sir William
Douglas
d. 1513

Gavin Douglas
Bishop of Dunkeld
1474–1522

Elizabeth

Sir Archibald Douglas
Laird of Kilspindie
1475–1540
m. Isobel Hoppar

Elizabeth
d. 1573
m. John Hay
3rd Lord of Yester
d. 1543

Janet
d. 1537
m. John Lyon
6th Lord Glamis
d. 1528

Margaret
m. James Douglas
7th Lord of Drumlanrig
d. 1578

Sir Archibald
Douglas
of Glenbervie
1513–70
m. Agnes Keith

William Douglas
9th Earl of Angus
d. 1591

THE HOUSE OF LENNOX

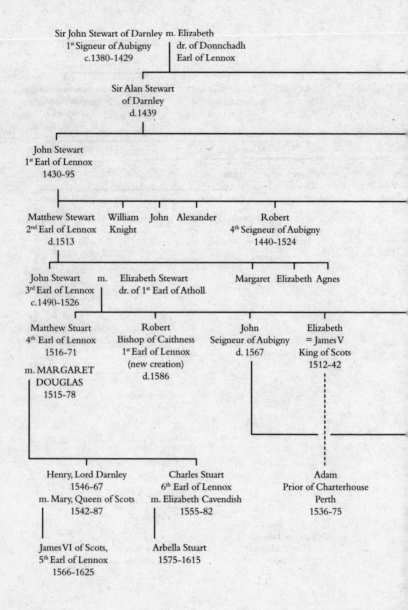

Sir John Stewart of Darnley m. Elizabeth
1st Signeur of Aubigny   dr. of Donnchadh
c.1380–1429   Earl of Lennox

Sir Alan Stewart
of Darnley
d.1439

John Stewart
1st Earl of Lennox
1430–95

Matthew Stewart   William   John   Alexander   Robert
2nd Earl of Lennox   Knight   4th Seigneur of Aubigny
d.1513   1440–1524

John Stewart   m.   Elizabeth Stewart   Margaret   Elizabeth   Agnes
3rd Earl of Lennox   dr. of 1st Earl of Atholl
c.1490–1526

Matthew Stuart   Robert   John   Elizabeth
4th Earl of Lennox   Bishop of Caithness   Seigneur of Aubigny   = James V
1516–71   1st Earl of Lennox   d. 1567   King of Scots
m. MARGARET   (new creation)   1512–42
DOUGLAS   d.1586
1515–78

Henry, Lord Darnley   Charles Stuart   Adam
1546–67   6th Earl of Lennox   Prior of Charterhouse
m. Mary, Queen of Scots   m. Elizabeth Cavendish   Perth
1542–87   1555–82   1536–75

James VI of Scots,   Arbella Stuart
5th Earl of Lennox   1575–1615
1566–1625

John Stewart
2nd Seigneur of Aubigny
d.1482

Alexander Stewart
Laird of Galston
d.1450

Bernard Stewart
3rd Seigneur of Aubigny
1452–1508

Elizabeth m. Archibald Campbell   Marion   Janet   Margaret   Alan Stewart
2nd Earl of Argyll   Laird of
d.1513   Cardonald
                                                                   d. after 1496

James Stewart
Laird of Cardonald

Helen
m. 1 William Hay
6th Earl of Erroll
1521–41

James Stewart
Laird of Cardonald
1512–84

2. John Gordon
11th Earl of Sutherland
1525–67

Robert Stewart
Laird of Galston
d. c.1505

Esmé Stuart
1st Duke of Lennox
1542–83

Alexander Stewart
Laird of Galston

Thomas Stewart
Laird of Galston
d.1542/5

Ludovic Stuart
2nd Duke of Lennox
1st Duke of Richmond
1574–1650

Thomas Stewart
Laird of Galston

List of Illustrations

Probably Katherine Willoughby, Duchess of Suffolk, artist unknown, sixteenth century. (Photographic Survey, The Courtauld Institute of Art, London. Private collection)

SECTION 2

Elizabeth I, miniature by Nicholas Hilliard, c.1572. (© National Portrait Gallery, London)

William Cecil, Lord Burghley, artist unknown, seventeenth century. (© National Trust Images)

Robert Dudley, Earl of Leicester, attributed to Steven van der Meulen, c.1560–5. (© The Wallace Collection, London)

The former Charterhouse at Sheen, pen and ink with watercolour by Antonis van der Wyngaerde, 1562. (WA.C.LG.IV.12b, detail from: Richmond Palace from across the Thames, © Ashmolean Museum, University of Oxford)

Henry, Lord Darnley, and Charles Stuart, by Hans Eworth, 1563. (Royal Collection Trust/© Her Majesty Queen Elizabeth II 2015)

Henry, Lord Darnley, and Charles Stuart, attributed to Hans Eworth, 1562. (Royal Collection Trust/© Her Majesty Queen Elizabeth II 2015)

Margaret's unnamed daughters, from her tomb in Westminster Abbey. (© Angelo Hornak/Corbis)

The Lennoxes' house at Whorlton, drawing by Samuel Buck, 1725. (By permission of the British Library, MS.914 Lansdowne MS)

The Lennox Jewel, obverse and reverse. (Royal Collection Trust/© Her Majesty Queen Elizabeth II 2015)

Mary, Queen of Scots, artist unknown, c.1569. (Reproduced by permission of Blairs Museum)

Henry, Lord Darnley, artist unknown, 1567. (© Alan Spencer Photography)

The Lieutenant's Lodging (now the Queen's House) in the Tower of London. (© Sebastian Wasek/LOOP IMAGES/Loop Images/Corbis)

The murder scene at Kirk O'Field. (The National Archives, MPF 1/366)

Coldharbour, London, from Walter Thornbury's *London, Old and New*. (Digital Collections and Archives, Tufts University)

Somerset Place, Strand, London. (© Look and Learn)

The Darnley Memorial, by Livinius de Vogelaare, 1568. (Royal Collection Trust/© Her Majesty Queen Elizabeth II 2015)

The Lost Tudor Princess

Introduction

Royal Tudor blood ran in her veins. Her parentage was of 'high renown'.[1] Her mother was a queen, her father an earl, and she herself was the granddaughter, niece, cousin and grandmother of monarchs. Lady Margaret Douglas, Countess of Lennox, was an important figure in Tudor England, and yet today, when her Tudor relations have achieved almost celebrity status, she is largely forgotten.

Her story deserves to be better known. It is of an extraordinary life that spans five Tudor reigns, and is packed with intrigue, drama and tragedy. In an age in which women were expected to be subordinate to men, and to occupy themselves only with domestic concerns, she stands out as a strong, capable and intelligent character who operated effectively, and fearlessly, at the very highest levels of power. The sources for her life are rich and varied, and many of her letters survive. In writing her biography I am building on research I began in 1974, when, wishing to rescue Margaret from obscurity, I started work on a book about her. But my tale of a forgotten Tudor princess remained untold.

In 2010 I attended a lecture on Margaret Douglas by a good friend, Siobhan Clarke, a Tudor historian who guides in costume as Margaret at Hampton Court. Hearing Siobhan revived my interest at a time when the field of Tudor biography was becoming crowded. It reminded me that Margaret Douglas deserved to be better known. Siobhan Clarke was the ideal person to write her biography, and I tried to persuade her to put pen to paper, but she very generously urged me to tackle the project myself. When I put the idea to my publishers, they realised immediately that the life of Margaret Douglas provides many missing links in the story of the Tudor and Stuart dynasties.

As always, I do my research first from original sources, and evolve theories from that. When I come to look at the secondary sources, I sometimes find that other historians have reached the same conclusions. Where they have come up with valid theories different from my own, I have credited them in the notes.

Paragraphs were not used in sixteenth-century letters, but where I have quoted extensively from contemporary letters here, I have broken them up so that they are easier to read. I have used the National Archives Currency Converter to determine the approximate present-day values of sums quoted in the text; these appear in brackets. Please note that values could change from year to year.

I should like to express my warmest appreciation and thanks to my British editor, Anthony Whittome, and my American editor, Susanna Porter, for their expertise and their wonderful creative ideas, which have enriched the book in so many ways. Thanks are also due to Dan Franklin at Jonathan Cape for so enthusiastically commissioning the book; to Clare Bullock at Cape for her excellent picture research and support; to Jane Selley, for being such an observant and accomplished copy-editor; to Alison Rae, for great proof-reading; to Neil Bradford for his inspired work on the illustrations sections; to Darren Bennett for his superb maps; and to Ceri Maxwell for being such a great publicist. Special thanks go to Dr Josephine Wilkinson for preparing the indexes for both the British and American editions of the book; to Nicola Tallis, who came to my rescue as I was racing to a deadline by searching out and transcribing crucial documents in the National Archives and the British Library; to the historian Linda Porter, for thoughtfully offering to lend me Sarah Macauley's thesis on the Earl of Lennox, which has proved very helpful.

I wish to acknowledge the huge support I have received from my agent, Julian Alexander, and from my husband Rankin. As the French writer, Antoine de Sainte-Exupery once wrote, 'One man may hit the mark, another blunder; but heed not these distinctions. Only from the alliance of the one, working with and through the other, are great things born.'

Readers may find it helpful to refer to the Dramatis Personae on page 417.

Prologue

In 1515 the Palace of Linlithgow, future birthplace of Mary, Queen of Scots, was a magnificent royal residence overlooking one of Scotland's most beautiful lochs. A favoured residence of the Scottish kings, it had been built by successive monarchs around a great courtyard and boasted a fine hall and princely chambers.

It was to this tranquil setting that, in September that year, Margaret Tudor, Queen Dowager of Scotland, Countess of Angus and sister of Henry VIII of England, came to bear her seventh child.

We have no record of her going into confinement – or taking to her chamber, as it was known – but it is likely that she followed the ceremonial observed by her mother, Elizabeth of York, and attended a service in chapel, where she and her household prayed for a safe and happy delivery; after this she would have been served spiced wine and comfits before bidding farewell to the lords and officers in attendance and disappearing with her women beyond the traverse, the heavy curtain that hung over the door to her bedchamber. Here she would remain secluded until after her child was born, and it was assumed that she would rest and take good care of herself in preparation for the birth.

But Margaret Tudor did no such thing. She remained in her chamber for just forty-eight hours, convinced that she was in danger and determined to flee from her enemies. At midnight on 13 September, accompanied only by her second husband, Archibald Douglas, Earl of Angus, his brother, George Douglas, and four or five servants, she left Linlithgow by stealth. It had been agreed with Thomas, Lord Dacre of Gilsland, Henry VIII's warden of the northern border Marches, that the sympathetic Alexander, Lord Home, would meet Queen Margaret a few miles from Linlithgow with forty 'hardy and well-striking fellows', and escort her south to Blackadder Tower, a castle in the Scottish Borders whence she could easily make her escape into England.[1] At the rendezvous, it was decided that, rather than go straight to Blackadder, over sixty miles away, Home should escort the Queen's party to Angus's great castle of Tantallon, a spectacular stronghold high on the cliffs overlooking the Firth of Forth, near North Berwick. That still involved a ride of fifty-five miles, and Margaret Tudor, who was nearly eight months pregnant, must have been exhausted when she got there.

But there could be no respite. On 16 September, the party continued on its way south to Blackadder Tower. The regent of Scotland, the Duke of Albany, who was ruling for Margaret's infant son, James V, had learned of the Queen's escape and sent a large force in pursuit – and it was not far behind her. Fearful that her flight would undermine his support in Scotland, or that she would return with an English army, he was intent on bringing her back, and ready to offer concessions. But Margaret Tudor later formally complained that he had already declared her and her husband traitors.[2] Fearing that Albany would besiege Blackadder Tower, she continued south towards Berwick, which lay just across the border with England. Sir Anthony Ughtred, its English governor, had no authority to receive her, so she and her party had to cross back over the River Tweed to Scotland, where she sought shelter at Coldstream Priory.[3]

Margaret Tudor was now sick and had to be nursed by Agnes Stewart, Lady Home,[4] and it was probably from Coldstream that she wrote to Henry VIII craving 'mercy and comfort'.[5] She had to wait until a messenger had returned from London with express directions from King Henry as to where his sister should be received and made welcome. It would have been a relief when Lord Dacre arrived to escort her into England, because Albany's forces had already captured Lord Home.

King Henry had agreed that Queen Margaret might be received into England on condition that no Scottish man or woman accompanied her. He was determined that, in his kingdom, his sister should be subject to no outside influence. Moreover, she was to stay in Northumberland until she 'knew further of his wishes'.[6] Margaret Tudor therefore had to bid farewell to Angus and the rest of her escort. Before Angus returned north, Dacre made him swear an oath that he would never come to terms with Albany.

The King had designated Dacre's official residence, Morpeth Castle, as Margaret Tudor's temporary abode, but Dacre, concerned about her condition, felt that Harbottle Castle, out in the wilds near the village of Otterburn, was more easily accessible. On Sunday 30 September, like a 'banished person',[7] the Queen crossed into England and so to Harbottle.[8] Her desperate flight ensured that the circumstances of her daughter's birth were as dramatic as her life would be.

Northumberland in the sixteenth century was wild and remote country, a lawless place scarred by centuries of Scottish raids and border warfare. Unlike the peaceful south of England, where castles were no longer built for defence, medieval fortresses still provided security for local nobles and the officers who commanded the English military presence, which was still a necessity in this unsettled region.

Harbottle Castle stood on a high mound at the head of the outstandingly beautiful Coquet Valley, an area known for its healthy air. It was an old royal fortress, first erected in 1157 by Henry II, and rebuilt in stone around 1200. The name derives from 'here-botl', an Old English word for an army building. The rectangular keep was one of Lord Dacre's residences as Warden of the Marches, whence he governed a large and turbulent area and dealt with the constant border warfare between the English and Scots and local clans. Harbottle was essentially a military base and a prison. Surviving records show that the main accommodation was in the keep, and that the castle was kept in good repair at royal expense.[9] But it was ill-prepared for a royal confinement.

In the last weeks of the Queen's pregnancy she 'lay still at Harbottle'. Dacre was an attentive host, and Margaret Tudor had much cause to be grateful to him, especially after her labour began too soon. It lasted for forty-eight hours.[10] According to her own account, she gave birth 'fourteen days before her time', on 7 October.[11] The child was a girl.

1

'A Fair Young Lady'

Margaret Tudor was the eldest daughter of Henry VII, the first Tudor King of England, and his Queen, Elizabeth, heiress of the royal House of York. She had been born in November 1489 and was just thirteen when, in 1503, in the interest of forging good relations with Scotland, England's traditional enemy, she had been married to James IV, King of Scots, who was sixteen years her senior and renowned for his lechery. Four of their six children died in infancy, but in 1512 Margaret Tudor bore a son, also called James, who thrived.

However, the following year James IV invaded England, seeking to take advantage of Henry VIII's absence on a campaign in France. The English were not unprepared, however, and a large force under the command of Thomas Howard, Earl of Surrey, marched north to confront James. The two armies met on 9 September 1513 at Flodden in Northumberland, and by the end of the day King James and the flower of the Scottish nobility lay slaughtered in the field. It was one of the most cataclysmic events in Scottish history, immortalised in ballads such as 'The Flowers of the Forest', in which it is claimed that twelve thousand were slain. Nearly every notable family lost at least one of its sons, and the impact of this disastrous defeat would be felt for generations.

Scotland was now under the nominal rule of an infant, James V, and subject to yet another long minority; such had been its fate for more than a century, as king after king had succeeded in childhood. It was a kingdom dominated by huge interrelated families, notably the Stewarts, the Douglases and the Hamiltons, and this age-old clannish system of kinship groupings had nurtured a fierce sense of family. Allowed virtual autonomy during a succession of regencies, the factious Scottish nobility had come to enjoy great power and pursue deadly rivalries. Alliances and loyalties constantly shifted, and blood feuds could persist for centuries.

The great lords were all hungry for power, and it was rare for a widowed queen to be granted custody of her children; nevertheless Queen Margaret was named regent of Scotland during the minority of her son and given the guardianship of the young King and his infant brother. She had been newly pregnant when her husband was killed, and in April 1514, at Stirling Castle, she had borne another son, Alexander, Duke of Ross.

On 6 August 1514, less than a year after her husband's death, Margaret Tudor secretly married again without consulting the Scottish lords or her brother, Henry VIII. Her bridegroom was Archibald Douglas, Earl of Angus – 'Ard', as he styled himself[1] – a member of her Council and the head of the faction that supported her rule. Handsome, charming, courteous and accomplished in chivalric exploits, he was the son of George Douglas, Master of Angus, and a widower, having lost his first wife, Margaret Hepburn, the year before. Angus, who at twenty-six was the same age as his bride, was 'very lusty in the Queen's sight'.[2] He was a man of mild temper, dry humour and undoubted courage, and although his enemies saw him as treacherous, he was good at building and maintaining friendships. He was ambitious, wholly committed to the aggrandisement of his family, and hungry for power. Although this was a love match on Margaret Tudor's part, it was probably prompted more by self-interest on Angus's.

The Douglas family was an ancient one and could trace its origins back to the Dark Ages. A William Douglas had fought for the Emperor Charlemagne, and Sir James Douglas had carried King Robert the Bruce's heart to the Holy Land; since then the arms of his descendants have borne a crowned heart. Their crest, which Margaret Douglas would also use, was the salamander. They were an ambitious tribe, into which Margaret's strong character fitted well, and 'family envies were strong',[3] leading in 1380 to the clan splitting into two feuding branches, the senior being the Black Douglases and the junior the Red Douglases, to which line the earls of Angus belonged.

The 5th Earl, Archibald 'Bell-the-Cat' Douglas, the most powerful noble in the kingdom, had played traitor against King James IV in 1482, allying himself with Henry VII of England, but he was back in favour a decade later, having established the Douglases as the foremost family in Scotland. He had won his nickname – 'belling the cat' means performing a challenging task – by getting rid of a royal favourite. But his son, George Douglas, Master of Angus, Margaret Douglas's grandfather, had perished at Flodden.

The history of the Douglas clan was a violent one; few of its prominent members had died in their beds, and it looked very much as if Angus, who succeeded 'Bell-the-Cat' as earl in 1514, might be of their number, for it soon became apparent that he was determined to rule Scotland. His marriage to the Queen, and her subsequent advancement of the Douglases to high offices, excited the jealousy of the Scottish nobility and provoked the pro-French party at court, which was headed by James Hamilton, Earl of Arran, a man renowned for his heroic triumphs in the tournament field; it reignited a centuries-old feud between the Douglases and the Hamiltons, and gave rise to a civil war in Scotland. Scotland had long been allied to France, and both countries had a long history of enmity with England; but Margaret Tudor was determined to continue as regent with the pro-English Angus at her side. Her opponents asserted that, under Scottish law, by remarrying she had forfeited the office of guardian ('tutrix') to her under-age children. The Arran-led Council resolved to replace her with John Stewart, Duke of Albany, a grandson of James II and the next royal heir after her sons. Albany was an honourable man and a capable administrator, but he regarded himself primarily as a Frenchman – he had been brought up in France, where he owned vast estates – and was reluctant to take up office in Scotland.

At once the Queen withdrew with her children to the safety of her mighty dower fortress of Stirling, set high on its volcanic crag at the gateway to the Scottish Highlands, against the spectacular backdrop of the Trossachs and the Ochil Hills; whereupon the Scottish lords rose in arms against her. Angus was ousted from power, and Albany, who was still in France, was offered the regency.

Queen Margaret appealed repeatedly to her brother, Henry VIII, for aid, impressing on him that 'all the welfare of me and my children lies in your hands'.[4] Henry threatened Scotland with war, while privately urging his sister to escape with her children to England, but she dared not attempt it because her enemies were keeping her under constant watch.

Margaret Tudor was six months pregnant with her first child by her new husband when, on 12 July 1515, the anti-English Albany was formally installed as regent. He treated her with courtesy at first, but when he learned that Angus, fearing for the safety of the young King and his brother, was plotting to send them to England, he laid siege to Stirling, seized the little boys from the Queen, and made himself their custodian. Margaret Tudor had no choice but to consent; her supporters had either fled or been taken, and she herself was now a captive. In grief at losing her sons, she drew up a long 'remembrance' of her complaints, which she sent to Thomas Magnus, the English ambassador to Scotland, who was then staying in Northumberland.[5]

Thereafter relations between Queen Margaret and Albany grew ever more tense. He made her write to her brother that she was content, and other letters 'contrary to her own mind', and he kept her 'strict prisoner' and under surveillance in Edinburgh, so that she was unable to see her sons, whom Albany had 'in ward'.[6] He had also deprived her of her revenues, leaving her in extreme poverty.[7] She entreated Henry VIII to send someone to mediate between her and the Regent; 'she was in much woe and pain, and besought remedy for God's sake'.[8] But Albany was hostile to England, and for years would make every effort to raise an army and attack it. Effectively forcing Margaret Tudor into a position where she felt the need to flee from Scotland was an insult to Henry VIII, who naturally took her part and responded by offering her refuge.[9]

It was to the Queen's advantage that the birth of her child was approaching, for she was planning to flee to England before it was born. No one would suspect a woman going into seclusion of plotting an escape, for once she had taken to her chamber, she would remain there until she was fit enough for her churching, the ceremony of thanksgiving and purification that marked the end of a woman's confinement and her return to normal life.

On 1 August Margaret Tudor wrote from Edinburgh to Henry VIII: 'Brother, I purpose, by the grace of God, to take my chamber and lie in my palace of Linlithgow within this twelve days, for I have not past eight weeks to my time, at the which I pray Jesu to send me good speed and happy deliverance.'[10]

Knowing that she could count on the aid of her brother, she sent her trusty servant, Robert Carr, to Thomas Magnus and Lord Dacre to ask them to inform the King of her secret plans, and ask for his assistance, which he had already commanded Dacre to extend to her.[11]

Lord Dacre was then forty-eight, fierce, indefatigable and politic- ally astute.[12] In 1485 he had fought for the last Plantagenet King, Richard III, against the future Henry VII at the Battle of Bosworth, but had quickly made his peace with the Tudor victor, who had made him a Knight of the Bath. Dacre had been serving on the Scottish Marches since 1485, and had been made Warden General in 1509 by Henry VIII. He had fought against the Scots at Flodden, but he had been willing to help Margaret Tudor smuggle her sons into England earlier in 1515. At that time she had expressed fears that Scotland was so infested by robbers as to render travelling dangerous, but that seemed the lesser evil now. Dacre and Magnus assured their master that, 'notwithstanding her Grace is within six weeks of her lying down, yet she hath ascertained us she hath good health, and is strong enough to take upon her this journey'.[13]

On 1 September 1515 Lord Dacre wrote to Queen Margaret, urging her to make haste to steal away to Blackadder Tower. Its owner, Andrew Blackadder, had fought and fallen under the Douglas standard at Flodden, and his widow and daughters were loyal. Dacre assured Margaret Tudor that, considering she was near her time, this was the best course of action. She would want for neither household goods nor money, and if all went to plan, her children would be safely restored to her and she herself would be restored as regent. Dacre himself would rendezvous with the Queen and escort her through the marsh where Blackadder Tower stood, 'so that you can resort [there] without any danger'.[14]

But on 3 September Margaret Tudor informed Dacre that she had a strategy of her own.[15] Feigning sickness, she obtained Albany's permission to remove with her husband to Linlithgow Palace for the birth of their child.[16] She and Angus travelled there on 11 September, closely followed by a letter from Lord Dacre informing the Queen that Henry VIII had been advised of her plight, and had confirmed his offer of asylum in England. Everything was now in place for her escape.

After the birth of her daughter Margaret Tudor 'fell into such extreme sickness that her life was despaired of by all'.[17] Given the drama of her flight and the stress she had suffered, that was hardly surprising.

Dacre evidently thought the birth of a daughter of little importance, and it was not until 18 October that he informed Henry VIII that on 'the eighth day after that the Queen of Scots, your sister, came and entered into this your realm, her Grace was delivered and brought in bed of a fair young lady'. He added that 'the sudden time, by God's provision so chanced', took them all unawares. His excuse for not writing sooner was that he had been too busy, and he had not thought it worth sending a letter for the sole purpose of informing the King that he had a new niece.[18]

The Queen's child was christened the day after her birth,[19] on 8 October, the ceremony probably being held in the castle chapel; at the font she was given the name Margaret, after her mother.[20] Cardinal Thomas Wolsey, the minister who was all-powerful at the English court, had been chosen by Queen Margaret as a godparent, in absentia.[21] Dacre was to explain to the King that the baptism had taken place 'with such convenient provisions as could or might be had in this barren and wild country', although everything had been 'done accordingly as appertained to the honour of the same', considering the suddenness of the birth.[22]

Because she was born in Northumberland, the 'fair young lady' started life as an English subject. Her uncle, Henry VIII, had as yet no surviving child to succeed him; his nearest heirs were his sister, Margaret Tudor, and her children, James V and now Margaret Douglas. Although Henry VII, in his will, had not excluded Margaret Tudor's issue from the succession, James V was not an Englishman; since the fourteenth century there had been a common-law rule against alien inheritance,[23] and a majority opinion in England held that that applied to the royal succession. Hence Margaret Douglas was second in line to the English throne after her mother until such time as Henry's Queen, Katherine of Aragon, bore a living child – and Dacre was wrong to regard her as a person of little political importance.

On 10 October, three days after the birth, Queen Margaret was sufficiently recovered to write reprovingly to Albany: 'Cousin, I heartily commend me unto you, and where I have been enforced for fear and danger of my life to depart forth of the realm of Scotland, so it is that, by the grace of Almighty God, I am now delivered and have a Christian soul, being a young lady.' She demanded to be reinstated in the regency, desiring him 'in God's name, as tutrix of the young King and Prince, my tender childer, to have the whole rule and governance' of them and of Scotland.[24]

Albany refused, informing her that 'the governance of the realm expired with the death of her husband, and devolved to the estates' and 'that she had forfeited the tutelage of her children by her second marriage'; if she would not listen to reason, he would be compelled to resort to sterner measures to prevent the disunion between the two kingdoms.[25]

Angus, meanwhile, had entered into a solemn covenant with several powerful, sympathetic nobles to liberate James V and his brother and unite in opposition to Albany. That was sufficiently alarming for Albany to offer the Queen apologies, terms and the return of her jewellery; he said he would even take Angus into favour if she would return to Scotland; but she refused.[26]

When, on 18 October, Dacre informed Henry VIII of Margaret's birth, he asked what was to be done with his royal guest. Her lying-in was proving 'uneaseful and costly' because all necessities had to be carried some distance to Harbottle, so he was 'minded to move her Grace to remove to Morpeth' as soon as she had been churched. Dacre evidently feared that Margaret Tudor would make difficulties about the move, as he suggested to the King that 'it may like your Highness to signify your mind and pleasure unto her, that we may move her accordingly'.

As soon as he had been informed of his sister's imminent arrival in England, Henry VIII had sent one of his gentlemen ushers, Sir Christopher Garnish, north with suitably royal clothing, plate and other necessities for her and her child. Garnish deposited these at Morpeth, then travelled to Harbottle with a letter from Henry that was 'greatly to the Queen's comfort'. Because she was still lying in, and was expected to keep to her chamber for at least three weeks, Dacre advised Garnish to return to Morpeth and remain until she was fit to travel there and receive her brother's gifts.[27]

After Queen Margaret's churching in late October, Henry VIII wanted her to journey south and join the lavish Christmas festivities at his court, but she was too ill to travel, or even to be moved.[28] For weeks she lay bedridden at Harbottle with a 'great and intolerable ache that is in her right leg, nigh to her body', which may have been due to sciatica, a trapped nerve or a fracture. It was not until 26 November that she was well enough to travel. Dacre settled her and her infant in a litter and set off for Morpeth Castle, nearly thirty miles south-east of Harbottle, but 'her Grace was so feeble that all of this way she could not suffer no horses to go in the litter', so it had to be borne by 'honest personages of the country'.[29] On the way they had to rest for four days at fourteenth-century Cartington Castle, a strong fortress of stone. Their next stop, on Sunday 2 December, was five miles away at Brinkburn Priory, and the following morning they came to Morpeth, where Dacre had summoned local dignitaries to greet the Queen.

The castle at Morpeth had been built in the thirteenth century on a steep bank south of Ha' Hill, replacing an earlier eleventh-century structure. Its keep, the Great Tower, stood within a bailey surrounded by a curtain wall.[30] Dacre had spared no expense to welcome the sister of his sovereign. John Younge, Somerset Herald, wrote: 'Never saw I a baron's house better trimmed in all my life: the hall and chambers with the newest device of tapestry, his cupboard all of gilt plate with a great cup of fine gold, the board's end served all with silver vessels, lacking no manner of victual and wildfowl to be put on them.'[31]

When Henry VIII learned that Queen Margaret had borne her child, he commanded all the important gentlemen of Northumberland 'to do them pleasure'.[32] He lifted the ban on any Scot attending upon her, which meant that Angus was now free to join her at Morpeth and meet his new daughter. Lord Home was of his party. When Garnish visited Queen Margaret in December,[33] bringing a letter from the King assuring the Queen and Angus a warm welcome at the English court, she received him lying in bed, and was much cheered by her brother's kindness.

In fact Henry was loudly proclaiming to all how badly his sister had been mistreated by Albany, and accusing the Regent of tearing her from her children, insulting and abusing her, stealing her jewels, forging her handwriting, and forcing her, in late pregnancy, to flee for her life. It was reported in France that 'if the Duke of Albany did not abstain from and make reparation for his injuries to Margaret and her children, Henry would make him do so', and was already planning to invade Scotland.[34] Albany tried to defend himself, protesting that he had had no idea that the Queen had intended to escape, and went on begging her to return to Scotland. The French ambassador added fuel to the flames by claiming that she had been in no danger and had run off in a temper, but no one wanted to listen.

Queen Margaret was still weak on 8 December, when she was carried out of her bedchamber in a chair to inspect the rich gifts the King had sent her. Among them were twenty-two gowns of gold and cloth of tissue, silk and velvet, trimmed with fur.[35] Garnish informed Henry VIII that she was 'one of the lowest-brought ladies, with her great pain of sickness, that I have seen and [es]cape[d death]', and was suffering such agony in her leg that, when she had to be moved or turned in bed, 'it would pity any man's heart to hear the shrieks and cries that her Grace giveth; and yet, for all that, her Grace hath a marvellous mind upon her apparel for her body'.[36] She seems to have been more preoccupied with her new wardrobe than with her baby. Showing off the gowns to Lord Home, she cried,

'Here ye may see that the King my brother hath not forgotten me, and that he would not that I should die for lack of clothes!'[37]

On 17 December Sebastian Giustinian, the Venetian envoy in London, reported that when Queen Margaret was better, she would 'by his Majesty's orders come to the court in London'.[38] But at Christmas, although 'great house' was kept at Morpeth,[39] the intolerable pain in the Queen's leg worsened. The local physician and surgeon having failed to cure her, Dacre wrote to Henry VIII asking that a royal doctor be sent north.[40] Apparently – possibly for want of any word on her progress – it was assumed at the English court that the infant Margaret Douglas had died, for on 2 January Cardinal Wolsey informed Giustinian that Queen Margaret 'is yet most grievously ill, having been prematurely delivered of a daughter, who had subsequently died'.[41] In fact the baby was thriving.

It was not until the end of January 1516 that Queen Margaret began to recover. On 15 March Dacre reported to Henry VIII: 'She amendeth continually and is greatly desirous to be coming towards your Highness.' But, fearing for her health, Dacre was keeping back some tragic news. On 28 December a Scottish delegation had brought word from Stirling Castle that the Queen's favourite son, twenty-month-old Alexander, had died. The cause is not recorded, but in an age long before antibiotics, many children died in infancy, as had four of Alexander's older siblings. Garnish observed, 'If it comes to her knowledge, it will be fatal to her,'[42] and when, in March, Dacre felt that she was sufficiently strong to bear the news, she collapsed in grief. Dacre did not 'suspect any danger or peril of life', but he again asked the King to send a physician from London all the same.

Encouraged by an indignant Henry VIII, Margaret Tudor blamed Albany for Alexander's death, and in her formal complaint against him would state that 'it is much to be suspected he will destroy the young King, now that her son, the young Duke, is dead, most probably through his means'.[43]

Two weeks later she suffered another blow when Angus told her that he would not be accompanying her to the English court. 'More simple than malicious' (as the French ambassador to Scotland described him at this time),[44] he wanted to make peace with Albany and secure the restoration of lands confiscated by the Regent. Without even taking leave of his wife, he left her and their daughter and returned to Scotland with Lord Home.[45] Dacre, who saw this as no less than abandonment, chased the escaping lords as far as Coldstream, but none of his reproaches or pleas could persuade them to return. True to Angus's expectations, Albany pardoned him, received him and Home into favour, and promised to return his lands, and thereafter Angus remained a close associate of the Regent.

Angus's sudden departure 'made [the Queen] much to muse'.[46] She took it 'right heavily, making great moan and lamentation', and looked to her brother for succour, crying that without it, 'the King her son and she are likely to be destroyed'.[47] This is the first evidence of a rift between the Queen and Angus, the first sign of the marital strife and power struggles that were heavily to overshadow Margaret Douglas's childhood.

Meanwhile a temporary peace between England and Scotland had been agreed, and Scottish envoys were on their way to London to discuss terms for Queen Margaret's return to Scotland. The Queen was to follow in their wake. She was sufficiently recovered to leave Morpeth on 7 April 1516, but the litter and horses sent by Henry VIII did not arrive until four o'clock, so she and Margaret, now six months old, set off the next day. They were escorted by Lord Dacre and others as far as Newcastle.[48] Here they were greeted by the city dignitaries and Sir Thomas Parr (father of the future Queen Katherine), before proceeding south the next day to Durham, where there was another civic welcome. From here Henry Percy, Earl of Northumberland, accompanied the Queen's party to York, where Angus, sent by Albany, unexpectedly caught up with them and asked the Queen if he might join a Scottish embassy that was preparing to enter England. Still disgruntled with him, she refused, whereupon he returned to Scotland.

On 27 April Queen Margaret was at Stony Stratford in Northamptonshire, and on 3 May she reached Enfield, Middlesex, where she stayed at Elsyng Palace,[49] the home of Sir Thomas Lovell, treasurer of Henry VIII's household. The next day she rode on to the village of Tottenham, north of London, and it was here, in Bruce Castle, the newly built manor house of a favoured courtier, Sir William Compton,[50] that Henry VIII was waiting to greet her and his infant niece. Brother and sister had not seen each other for thirteen years. When Margaret Tudor had gone to Scotland, Henry, two years her junior, had been a boy of twelve. Now he was a handsome, athletic, talented and egotistical man of twenty-five, and had been ruling England for seven years. Queen Margaret saw before her a tall, broad-shouldered Adonis with flame-red hair and a beardless chin; Henry would not metamorphose into the bearded, overweight colossus of later years for another two decades.

After a short conversation, the King escorted his sister, his niece and their retinue the rest of the way to the City of London, and at six o'clock that evening Queen Margaret, royally attired and riding a white palfrey, passed in procession along Cheapside, preceded by Sir Thomas Parr and followed by many lords and ladies. Thus she came to Baynard's Castle by the River Thames, a royal residence that she would have remembered well from her childhood. Here lodgings had been made ready for her and her daughter.[51] After resting there until 7 May, mother and child joined the court at Greenwich Palace.

Henry VIII and his Queen, Katherine of Aragon, received her there joyfully, and with them was the youngest Tudor sibling, Mary, the widow of Louis XII of France. A year before, Mary, the beauty of the family, had caused a scandal by secretly making a second marriage, for love, with Charles Brandon, Duke of Suffolk. Henry had been furious, and had imposed a crippling fine on the couple before receiving them back into favour. Now there were feasts, revels, jousts and a banquet in the Queen's chamber.

In February 1516 Katherine – whose first four children had died in infancy – had at last presented the King with a healthy daughter, Mary, who now took precedence over Margaret Tudor and Margaret Douglas in the English succession. The two cousins were much of an age, but of course they were far too young at this time to form any friendship. It is likely that Margaret only stayed in the royal nursery at Greenwich while her mother was there, and that after their visit she went to stay with her at 'Scotland', where Queen Margaret was allocated lodgings during her sojourn in England.

'Scotland' was a palatial complex that lay south of Charing Cross. It had acquired its name from being used as a residence for visiting Scottish monarchs, and was convenient for Westminster and Parliament, which they attended in their capacity as English barons. First built by the Saxon King Edgar in AD 959 so that Kenneth III of Scots would have suitable accommodation when he came annually to London to pay homage, the buildings in the complex were called Little Scotland Yard, Middle Scotland Yard and Great Scotland Yard. They were built around a courtyard, enclosed with a brick wall, and had 'large pleasure-grounds extending to the river'. According to the Elizabethan historian John Stow, the palace was 'a very great building', but little else is known about it, and no clear image of it survives. Here Queen Margaret lived quietly, with 'little or no semblance of state'.[52]

In November 1519 an annuity of £10 was granted to Queen Margaret's former nurse, Alice Davy, who had cared for her in her infancy from 1489 to 1491.[53] This was 'for services to the Queen Consort and Margaret, Queen of Scotland'.[54] It was not unusual for royal servants to be rewarded after a lapse of years, but the annuities that Henry VIII had granted to those who had served his mother, Elizabeth of York, who died in 1503, had been assigned by 1515. The fact that Mrs Davy had rendered services to Katherine of Aragon and Margaret Tudor suggests that she had been employed more recently in their nurseries, and that Queen Margaret had called upon her old nurse to look after her baby.

Margaret and her mother remained in England for a year. Angus, despite having been given leave by Albany, had refused to join them. He had also appropriated his wife's rents, so the Queen had little money of her own, and although Henry VIII made occasional payments to her, at Christmas 1516 she was forced to beg Cardinal Wolsey for financial help.[55]

In the summer of 1517 Albany returned to France to tend to his sick wife, leaving James Hamilton, Earl of Arran, as president of the Scottish Council, with Angus and other lords serving alongside him. It was to be a volatile partnership, as Angus was unable to work amicably with Arran, but was bent on pursuing his bloody feud with the Hamiltons.

In the wake of the truce between Scotland and England, Queen Margaret's hopes of regaining the regency flourished anew. On 18 May 1517, furnished with a safe conduct from the young King James and assurances of the restoration of her revenues,[56] she departed from London, taking the eighteen-month-old Margaret with her. Escorted by George Talbot, Earl of Shrewsbury, they set out on the long ride north, the King having summoned various lords and gentlemen to receive them with due ceremony along the route.[57] The Queen fell ill at Doncaster, but pressed on to York, where the Earl of Northumberland waited upon her, and thence to Durham, and Berwick, where she hesitated, reluctant to return to the kingdom where she had suffered so many troubles. 'Her Grace,' Thomas Magnus reported, 'considereth now the honour of England, and the poverty and wretchedness of Scotland, which she did not afore, but in her opinion esteemed Scotland equal to England.' But she had to go back, and on 15 June young Margaret crossed the border into Scotland for the first time.[58]

At Lamberton Kirk, three miles from Berwick, Angus, accompanied by his kinsman, James Douglas, Earl of Morton, and other lords, was waiting to greet his wife and child. He had not come voluntarily but had been sent by the Scottish Council. According to Margaret, he 'behaved right courteously to her',[59] and a reconciliation of sorts took place. Attended by an escort of three thousand men-at-arms, they rode together towards Edinburgh, where, on the evening of 17 June, the Queen was received with some state and lodged in Holyrood Palace, recently vacated by Albany.

But she was still to be denied a share in the government and access to her son, James V. During the succeeding years she made abortive attempts to regain power, but there was no hope of that after Henry VIII made a new truce with the Scots without insisting on redress for the wrongs she had suffered, and she was in financial straits because of difficulties in obtaining payment of her dower revenues. This was the backdrop to Margaret's childhood.

2

'Disdained with Dishonour'

Until she reached the ages of ten or twelve Margaret remained in the charge of her mother. We do not know how much she saw of her, since royal children were normally looked after by nurses and servants; it was a queen's duty to ensure that her offspring were well cared for and educated, sometimes in a household of their own, not to participate in their daily care. But Margaret Tudor, for all that she was preoccupied with political affairs and wrangling for what she believed to be her due entitlements, must have been one of the primary influences on her daughter. Her devotion to the interests of her son, James V, may have had some bearing on the younger Margaret's ambitions for her own sons, and her willingness – in an age not noted for indulging children – to spoil them. We can see in the adult Margaret much of her mother's passionate persistence in fighting for her rights.

Margaret was brought up as a princess, probably spending most of her early years in the nurseries of the various royal palaces in which her mother resided. It is likely that she learned some English from the Queen, but Scots would have been her first language, and even though she would in time learn to speak and write fluent English, her letters in later life – written phonetically, as letters then were – betray a strong Scottish accent. She wrote, for example, 'curt' (court), 'dede' (did), 'erl' (earl), 'borden' (burden) and 'warsse' (worse).[1]

Strictly contemporary sources are for the most part silent on Margaret's childhood, yet shortly after her death a *Commemoration*, in verse form, was published by John Phillips, who had served her and evidently knew her well.[2] It is, predictably, laudatory and reverent, and yet Phillips, a student of divinity, was a Puritan preacher with

no reason to approve of Margaret, who had for years been known –
even notorious – for her strong Catholic faith. The fact that he chose
to hallow her memory with praise says much for the enduring
impression she made on him, and shows that his account was not
mere flattery. The personal details in it strongly suggest that it was
based on her own reminiscences and perhaps those of the people
who served her, so Phillips can be forgiven for getting a little muddled
in places, since he is treating of events that had occurred decades
before. His *Commemoration* was written as if Margaret herself was
looking back over her life, and therefore it has a deeply personal
aspect. From it we know something of the tenor of her early
upbringing and education. Like most high-born girls, she was 'trained
to virtue and grace, in faith and God's fear', in 'obedience and truth.
No lightness in me could any discern. My heart and my hand to
do good was bent, and wisdom to learn I was well content.'

Early in 1518 Queen Margaret discovered that Angus had been
having an affair with the beautiful Lady Janet Stewart of Traquair.
He had been betrothed to her before his marriage to Margaret Tudor,
and had apparently become close to her during his wife's long
sojourn in England; worse still, he was using his wife's revenues to
enrich himself and his mistress. Margaret had forgiven him for allying
with Albany and refusing to join her in England; now she became
consumed with jealousy and a violent, enduring hatred, and decided
to separate from him at once. Margaret, at only three, now found
herself the only child of a broken marriage, for whom the term
'warring parents' would become only too apt.

It was to be a long and complicated affair, drawn out over nine
years, and engendering much bitterness. There were vicious quarrels,
in which the Douglases – and even Henry VIII, who thought it
immoral for Margaret to leave her husband – sided with Angus, and
Angus's enemy, Arran, with the Queen. In October 1518 she wrote
to Henry VIII, 'I am sore troubled with my lord of Angus, and every
day more and more, so that we have not been together this half
year.' He had done her 'much evil' and she was minded 'to part with
him, for I wit well he loves me not, as he shows me daily'.[3] It would
not have been surprising if, under her mother's influence, Margaret
had grown up to have a jaundiced opinion of her father. That would
have been understandable, for Angus seized the Queen's property
and appropriated more of her revenues, obliging her to live 'as a
poor suitor' in Edinburgh. She, in turn, refused to allow him any

share in the regency she hoped to secure, and made secret overtures to Albany for help in obtaining the divorce she desperately wanted. At one point she even alleged – blatantly falsely – that her second marriage was bigamous because her first husband, James IV, had still been alive three years after he had supposedly been slain at Flodden.[4]

But Margaret Tudor needed the support of her brother, Henry VIII, and so in the autumn of 1519 she consented to what proved to be a brief reconciliation with Angus, who agreed to it because he was again engaged in a power struggle with Arran and wanted Henry's backing. Around that time, alarmed at an outbreak of plague in Edinburgh, Queen Margaret took her four-year-old daughter to Stirling Castle. In December the Queen was laid low with a vicious attack of smallpox, and there were fears that she might die. For days she lay prone, unable to move or speak.[5] But she recovered to resume her battles with her estranged husband.

It was the fate of nobly born girls to be the subject of marriage alliances that were advantageous to their parents, and it was not unusual for them to be betrothed in childhood. By reason of her royal blood and her claim to the English succession, and as James V's half-sister and Henry VIII's niece, Margaret was a highly desirable bride – a great prize in the European marriage market. In 1520, when she was not yet five, her mother entered into negotiations with Angus's enemy, Arran, with a view to her becoming affianced to his eldest son, another James Hamilton, then aged about four. Thanks to the ongoing feud between Angus and Arran, affairs in Scotland had deteriorated to the extent that the Duke of Albany was anticipating having to return from France to resume his role as regent. Albany was perturbed by reports of the proposed betrothal, fearing that the Queen and Arran would unite against him. Moreover, in the event of the young King's death, Arran was Albany's rival for the Scottish succession. There was no more talk of the marriage, but later that year Albany formally invited Queen Margaret to assume the regency pending his return. On 15 October she set out from Linlithgow for Edinburgh, having made the pragmatic decision to be reconciled once more with her husband – a decision that cost her the support of some of her party.

Angus and his faction had retained control of the capital, resisting the attempts of Arran to dislodge him from power. He rode forth at the head of four hundred mounted men to receive his wife, offered a cordial welcome and escorted her into Edinburgh Castle. Thereafter

the couple resumed living together, but not for long. Angus continued
to trespass upon the Queen's property, whereupon she lost patience
with him and decided to ally herself with his enemy, Arran. One
night in December she left a dinner hosted by the Archbishop of
St Andrews and stole away to Linlithgow with her daughter and
only six attendants. Leaving Margaret behind, she rode to Stirling,
where she was welcomed by Arran. Angus protested against her
desertion, and Henry VIII castigated her for doing 'much dishonour'
to herself and the King her son, warning that she could not look
for any favour at his hand.[6]

Albany had approached Pope Leo X on Queen Margaret's behalf
about a divorce, but efforts were now made to turn him against her.
When he returned to Scotland late in 1521 and resumed the regency,
the Queen allied with him against Angus, and there were rumours –
probably unfounded – that she was closer to Albany than she should
have been. Albany summoned Angus to answer charges of high
treason, but he failed to appear, whereupon he was sentenced to
death and his estates were once more confiscated. In March 1522,
after Queen Margaret had interceded for his life to be spared, he
was exiled to France, whence, in June 1524, he escaped to England
at Henry VIII's invitation. It has been claimed that Angus took young
Margaret with him into exile, and that she did not see her mother
for the next three years, but this misunderstanding rests on the
incorrect dating to 1523 of a letter that Margaret wrote complaining
that Angus had removed Margaret from her care within the past
three years.[7] The letter was actually written in November 1528 (see
below), and in any case Angus would hardly have welcomed the
risks and practicalities of fleeing into exile with a six-year-old child.

Much to his estranged wife's annoyance, Angus was received
warmly at the English court. He was given a pension, and measures
were taken to bring about his return to Scotland and the mending
of his marriage.[8] Queen Margaret remonstrated with her brother to
obstruct his return, but Henry wanted a pro-English party north of
the border, and Angus was ready to uphold the King's interests. By the
autumn of 1524 Albany had been overthrown and Scotland was 'so
divided, it is hard to say whom to trust. There is no justice, but
continual murders, theft and robbery.'[9] Henry VIII had no time for
the Queen's 'wilfulness towards her husband'.[10]

On 28 October, with the backing of an English alliance, Angus
finally returned to Scotland to find his wife in power and refusing
to have anything to do with him, an attitude that was believed to

have been encouraged by 'one Harry Stewart, a young man about her Grace, which ordereth all causes'.[11] Henry Stewart was eleven years Margaret Tudor's junior, and it was not long before Henry VIII was informed that the two of them had begun an adulterous relationship, one that would cause scandal for several years. Queen Margaret was said to be 'so blinded with folly as to have her ungodly appetite followed; she doth not care what she doth'.[12]

Angus hated his wife's lover, and he was outraged that young Margaret was being exposed to such an undesirable and immoral influence. On 23 November he stormed into Edinburgh, only to have Margaret Tudor's forces open fire on him. Forced to retreat to his stronghold of Tantallon, he proceeded to rally a large contingent of lords to his side.

There is, alas, no evidence of how Margaret, at just nine, was affected by the enmity between her parents. She must have suffered to some extent from conflicting loyalties, and it may be that her mother and Henry Stewart did their best to poison her mind against her father. Nor do we know what she made of the affair between the Queen and Stewart. Fortunately royal children spent more time with those appointed to care for them than with their parents, so she was probably shielded to a degree from the tumult of her mother's life.

Early in 1525, when Margaret was nine, the Earl of Moray asked for her hand. A bastard son of James IV, he was about twenty-six, and an ally of Queen Margaret. The Queen pushed for the match, fearing that her husband might try to marry Margaret to one of her enemies, the Douglases,[13] but Angus was having none of it. In February 1525 he staged a coup, occupying the capital and summoning Parliament, which restored him to power, jointly with David Beaton, the future cardinal and archbishop of St Andrews, and granted him custody of the resentful young King, whom he kept strictly under his control.

Queen Margaret was forced to establish a fragile accord with Angus. Thomas Magnus informed Wolsey that she 'entertaineth the Earl with good countenance and familiar communication, but continually her Grace procureth [him], by all the ways and means she can, to a divorce'.[14] Angus's friends wanted him freed from their marriage, so that he could take another wife and father sons, which would spare him the necessity of having to leave his title and estates to his daughter. The Queen was anxious to ensure that a divorce would not impugn Margaret's legitimacy. She now petitioned Pope

Clement VII on the grounds that before their marriage Angus had entered into a precontract – a formal exchange of promises to marry made before witnesses that was as binding as wedlock – with Lady Janet Stewart; she urged his Holiness to consider that 'by the ignorance of the mother [the daughter] should not suffer any loss, damage or disadvantage'.[15] Normally an annulment rendered the children of an irregular union bastards, but if a marriage had been made in good faith, its issue could be deemed legitimate.

For the next three years Angus enjoyed great power in Scotland, acting as regent for James V; in August 1527 he was made high chancellor. He put Queen Margaret and her supporters to flight, curbed the ambitions of the Hamiltons, and restored order in the kingdom. The young King he kept a virtual prisoner, diverting him with women and dice from learning his kingly duties. The Douglases were now supreme, and it was said that 'none that time durst strive against a Douglas nor a Douglas's man'.[16]

Angus had permitted Margaret's betrothal to Moray to go ahead, and her mother had arranged it, but according to an instrument from the Moray charter chest, dated 10 January 1527, the Queen, when required by Moray to proceed to the marriage, had refused because she had found a more promising bridegroom, ten-year-old Matthew Stewart, Earl of Lennox, whom Margaret would eventually marry nearly sixteen years later.[17] But her plans came to nothing, and we hear no more of either betrothal at this time.

Now came a period of far-reaching change for eleven-year-old Margaret. On 11 March 1527 the Pope granted her mother's petition for an annulment.[18] In accordance with the Queen's wishes, he added a special clause declaring Margaret legitimate.[19] This was endorsed by David Beaton, who declared 'that, the mother being innocent of bad faith in the marriage, the daughter ought not to be disinherited'.[20] Thirty years later it would be asserted by a hostile witness that Margaret 'was openly taken and reputed a bastard in Scotland' after her parents' divorce,[21] and this was no exaggeration, because James V, who hated the Douglases, always referred to her as his 'base sister'.[22] But he had no grounds for doing so.

By 2 April 1528 the Queen had married Henry Stewart, provoking the ire of Henry VIII, who was then seeking the dissolution of his own marriage. He was shocked and indignant on his niece Margaret's behalf, and wrote a letter reminding his sister of 'the divine ordinance of inseparable matrimony first instituted in Paradise', expressing the hope that she would 'perceive how she was seduced by flatterers to an unlawful divorce from the right noble Earl of Angus upon untrue and unsufficient allegations'. Furthermore, the dispensation sent from Rome plainly showed 'how unlawfully it was handled', for judgment had been 'given against a party neither present in person, nor by proxy'.

Thinking of the innocent victim of this 'shameless sentence', and revealing that he had received reports on her daughter's progress, Henry urged the Queen

for the weal of your soul, and to avoid the inevitable damnation threatened against adulterers, to reconcile yourself with Angus as your true husband. Yet the love, the tender pity and motherly kindness towards the fruit of your body, your most dear child and natural daughter, cannot but provoke your Grace unto reconciliation, whose excellent beauty and present behaviour, nothing less godly than goodly, furnished with virtues and womanly demeanours, after such a sort that it would relent and mollify a heart of steel, much more a motherly mind, which, in your Grace, Nature enforcing the same, ought largely to be showed. Moreover, what charge of conscience, what grudge and fretting, yea, what danger of damnation should it be to your soul, with perpetual infamy of your renown; slanderously to distain with dishonour so goodly a creature, so virtuous a lady, and namely your natural child, procreate in lawful matrimony, as to be reputed baseborn, which cannot otherwise be avoided, unless your Grace will (as in conscience ye are bound under peril of God's everlasting indignation) relinquish the adulterer's company with him that is not, nor may be of right, your husband.

This, Wolsey assured the Queen in an enclosing note, was 'the faithful exhortation of my most dread lord and sovereign, your entirely loving brother, with a motherly respect towards your natural child, your own flesh and blood'.[23]

Katherine of Aragon wrote too, sorrowfully reminding Margaret Tudor of the great sin of disparaging 'the fair daughter she had by my Lord Angus'. Margaret replied that she had married him in good faith, so her daughter's legitimacy would not be in question.[24]

Sometime between 1525 and April 1528 Angus removed Margaret from her mother's care. It has been described as a kidnapping,[25] but as a father and a peer of the realm he had every right to the custody of his child. Margaret was approaching marriageable age, which for girls was then twelve, and she could be a valuable political asset in terms of a marriage alliance. We know of her removal from her mother only from a letter written by the elder Margaret on 25 November 1528, in which she recites the evils that Angus had done to her, especially in 'these three years by-past, not having no consideration of our person, honour nor weal, but always putting all in jeopardy; and after would not suffer our own daughter to remain with us for our comfort, who would not have been distressed'.[26]

Some modern accounts have Angus seizing Margaret, literally from her mother's arms on earlier occasions,[27] but this is the first recorded complaint that the Queen made about being deprived of her daughter. The unqualified word 'after' seems likely to refer to the divorce, which suggests that Angus removed Margaret from her mother's care on account of the Queen's notorious relations with Henry Stewart. Probably he took custody of her after news of the Papal judgment reached Scotland in December 1527. She was then twelve, and Margaret Tudor's letter reveals that the change in her circumstances was traumatic for her. She had spent all her life in her mother's care, although the Queen had been much preoccupied with her own personal and political struggles. Margaret Tudor's voluminous correspondence reveals that she was far more interested in her sons, especially James V, than in her daughter, who rarely merits a mention. It was James who was the 'tenderest' of all in the eyes of his mother.[28] Nor is there evidence that she did her utmost to get Margaret back. Any distress that Margaret suffered was probably due to a scene between her parents when she was taken from the Queen.

Angus probably installed her at his mighty stronghold of Tantallon on the East Lothian coast. Tantallon Castle was a magnificent and forbidding fortress, spectacularly situated high on a rocky headland overlooking the Firth of Forth and the Bass Rock, an island in the sea to the east of Scotland. It had been built in the 1350s by William, 1st Earl of Douglas, the son of the Sir James Douglas who had carried Bruce's heart to the Holy Land. Tantallon's great curtain wall of red sandstone encircled a courtyard surrounded by soaring towers, and in the north-west of these, the Douglas Tower, were to be found the lordly apartments. This tower was a circular edifice seven storeys high, with a radius of twelve metres. The chambers on the ground and upper floors were square, with wooden floors and vaulted privies, and there was a prison in the basement, or pit. There were also ranges of buildings erected against the curtain wall; these included a fourteenth-century great hall, which was connected to the Douglas

Tower. The sea provided a natural line of defence and supply on one side of the castle, while the landward wall was massively fortified and surrounded by a huge ditch. The only entrance was a drawbridge to the great gatehouse.[29]

If Angus took Margaret with him when he needed to be in Edinburgh, she would probably have stayed either at court or at medieval Dalkeith Castle, Midlothian, another Douglas property, in a household that seems to have been run by the wives of his brother, Sir George Douglas, and his cousin, Archibald Douglas, Laird of Kilspindie.[30] As the daughter of an earl Margaret was honourably housed and looked after, but not (it was later implied by James V) as well as she had been when in her mother's care.[31]

Margaret cannot have seen much of her father at first because he was much occupied with ruling Scotland, but from now on she became subject to his influence. If she grew up to be a true Douglas, it was thanks to him, and not only because it was in her blood. For it seems that at this time an enduring bond was forged between father and daughter – it has even been suggested that their attachment to each other brought upon Margaret 'the enmity of her mother',[32] although that is more likely to have resulted increasingly from Margaret Tudor's indifference and neglect. Indeed there is no evidence that Margaret ever saw her mother again. From now on, as Angus's letters show, he was far more protective and affectionate towards her than Margaret Tudor had ever been, and those feelings grew and matured until by 1545 he had come to think of his daughter as 'the woman whom [he] loved most in all the world'.[33]

By April 1528 Queen Margaret and her new husband were under siege at Stirling with Angus's old enemy, Arran. Margaret must have been in her father's charge by then, because Angus was to have no other chance to take custody of her. For in June James V, now sixteen, asserted his authority as king. With astonishing speed, he threw off the hateful constraints imposed on him by Angus, escaped to his mother at Stirling, toppled Angus from the regency and forbade him and the Douglases – whom he loathed and feared – to come within seven miles of his royal person. Thereafter he ruled by the advice of his mother and Henry Stewart, whom he created Lord Methven.

Angus was willing to retire from politics, but when the King tried to force him and his kinsfolk into virtual exile and threatened them with imprisonment, he took refuge at the well-defended fortress of Tantallon and fortified it against attack by the royal forces; elsewhere his Douglas relatives were taking similar measures to protect themselves.

Margaret was either already staying at Tantallon, or had fled there from Dalkeith when her father fell.[34] Here father and daughter should have felt reasonably secure – in common parlance, to 'ding doon' Tantallon Castle was to achieve the impossible[35] – but the King now had Angus attainted as a traitor and sentenced him to lose his life and his property, which was forfeit to the Crown. The same sentence was passed on Angus's brother, George, and his cousin, Archibald Douglas of Kilspindie, and both fled into exile. Angus stayed where he was, but he was a marked man, and so feared capture that he had his loyal lords keep watch, in full armour, at his chamber door each night.

Kilspindie's wife, Isobel Hoppar, had taken refuge at Tantallon, and was acting as Margaret's lady-in-waiting and perhaps her governess. Aged about thirty-eight, Isobel was the daughter of a rich Edinburgh merchant of high standing. After her first husband died in 1515 and left her a wealthy widow,[36] she had married Kilspindie, who was Lord High Treasurer and Provost of Edinburgh. While Angus and the Douglases were in control of the government and the King, the couple prospered, and Isobel had been highly influential in Scottish politics.

It was well known that Kilspindie was under his wife's thumb,[37] and through him she had clearly exercised a not always beneficial influence on Angus himself. A contemporary chronicler observed, 'His prideful wife was called my Lady Treasurer, and it is said she was an compositor [arbiter] in the justice eyres [circuit courts].' The 'common voice' was that but for her haughtiness Angus would have been peacefully living in Scotland.[38] Thomas Magnus, the English ambassador, believed that the pernicious influence of Kilspindie, Isobel and George Douglas was responsible for Angus's 'trouble and business'.[39] Isobel and her husband had been among the first to suffer from the toppling of the Douglases: their house and lands were seized by the King and given to his supporters.[40]

This was the strong-minded woman who was now in attendance on Margaret and helped to mould her character. If she also acted as governess she would have been responsible for the virtuous nurturing of her charge, which was seen as more important than any formal education. Margaret was well educated; she grew up to be highly literate and to write lively letters and competent poetry. How far this was due to the tutoring of Isobel Hoppar cannot be estimated, but the example of that strong-willed, ambitious, domineering and

feisty lady, following on from that of Margaret's demanding, troublesome mother, may have had its own impact, because Margaret herself
was to display similar character traits in adulthood.

In this fraught period young Margaret learned what it meant to be
in opposition to the King. Angus was determined to hold Tantallon
Castle against the royal forces, but on 2 October he was obliged
to venture south with two hundred men to Coldingham Priory to
attend the deathbed of his brother William, the Prior. At the same
time James V advanced on the priory with seven hundred soldiers
and laid siege to it. Warned before he arrived that the Prior had
died, Angus and his men escaped and pursued the King to Dunbar.
A furious James mustered eight thousand men, and Angus realised
that he had, of necessity, to take refuge in England, to avoid the
army that the King was bringing against him.[41]

It was announced, by heralds galloping throughout the Borders,
that the King was offering a reward to anyone who could return
his 'base sister', Margaret, to their mother, the Queen, who could
provide her with an establishment suitable to her rank.[42] But it is
unlikely that Margaret, who was now thirteen, wanted to return to
her mother. According to the later testimony of Alexander Pringle,
a Scottish servant of the Douglases, she wanted to marry the Earl
of Bothwell, although Queen Margaret favoured James Stewart,
captain of Doune and younger brother of Harry Stewart, her own
husband.

Patrick Hepburn, Earl of Bothwell, was sixteen, fair-haired, handsome, and a good match.[43] Sir James Stewart of Beath was probably
older, having been born before 1513, but he was landless and well
below Margaret in rank and status, and marriage to him would have
drawn her irrevocably into her mother's faction. Angus was utterly
opposed to that, especially as it appeared that his ex-wife's chief
motive was to secure for her brother-in-law the confiscated estates
of the earldom of Angus.[44] It was this that decided him to get his
daughter to a place of safety, well away from her mother's machinations. He resolved to steal her away into England,[45] anticipating that
her uncle, Henry VIII, would welcome her. She was, after all, a highly
desirable bride and would be an asset to the English King.

Returning to Coldingham, where he had apparently left Margaret,
Angus decided to take her to Norham Castle, seventeen miles away,
just across the River Tweed on the English side. On 5 October 1528
he stole away south to the English border. Shouting from the Scottish

side of the Tweed, he parleyed with Roger Lascelles, steward of the Earl of Northumberland, asking him if chambers could be provided at Norham for the protection of Margaret and Isobel Hoppar, who would wait on his daughter. The steward shouted his assent, and it was also agreed that, if driven to it, Angus himself could seek safety in Norham. Angus sent Margaret to Norham Castle before 9 October.[46]

Many kings and queens had come to Norham in the past. Dating from 1121 and commanding a strategic position on a rocky bluff high above the River Tweed near Berwick, the pink stone castle was one of the foremost border strongholds. Well fortified with walls twenty-eight feet thick, it had been besieged thirteen times, the last, successfully, by James IV just before Flodden, but it had since been returned to English hands and extensively restored and rebuilt. In the inner ward the Bishop's Hall abutted the keep, and there was a kitchen range. Yet Norham was no longer a suitable habitation for the daughter of a queen. Just days before his parley with Angus, Lascelles had complained to Henry VIII that it had not one chamber fit to shelter anyone, and that rain streamed in from the roof to the dungeons.[47]

Here, nevertheless, Margaret would be well guarded. The castle was surrounded by the ravine and the river on one side and a broad moat on the other. Another moat divided the inner and outer wards. The massive twelfth-century keep, built in 1160 and twenty metres high, stood on the large mound in the centre; it had been remodelled in the early fifteenth century, and would be again in the sixteenth. There was a mighty gatehouse on the west face, accessed by a draw-bridge across the moat; an inner gatehouse; and four towers were linked by an outer wall thirty feet high.[48] Lascelles no doubt did his best to ensure that his young guest was accommodated in as much comfort as possible, but he was wondering how long he would have to keep her. This is clear in a letter he wrote informing Henry VIII that Angus 'hath sent unto your Grace's castle of Norham the Lady Margaret, his daughter, who here doth remain until such time as I may know further of your Grace's pleasure'.[49]

But Margaret did not receive an immediate summons south to the English court. At this time Henry VIII was preoccupied with his 'Great Matter', being determined to have his marriage to Katherine of Aragon annulled so that he could marry Anne Boleyn, a dark-haired enchantress with charm and ruthless ambition. With a Papal legate already in England to try the case, and many tensions within the court, it would not have been appropriate for Margaret to go to London.[50] Instead she remained at Norham for eight months, with Isobel Hoppar serving as her gentlewoman.

Angus probably wanted Margaret safe and near at hand, a valuable bargaining counter in case the situation in Scotland changed. During those months he held out against James V's forces. On 18 October James had returned with his army and laid siege to Tantallon. 'Never was so much done in vain to win one house.' But the castle proved impregnable, and on 4 November the King, seeing that the task was hopeless, left for Edinburgh, whereupon Angus sallied forth with his men and appropriated the artillery he had left behind. Then, protesting his loyalty to James, he sued for peace, though the terms the King offered made it plain that he still regarded Angus as a rebel and a traitor.[51]

In December 1528 James V and Henry VIII concluded the Treaty of Berwick, whereby James was to take the Douglas lands on condition that Angus was permitted to seek asylum in England. The treaty was ratified in March 1529,[52] and in April Angus surrendered Tantallon in hope of a pardon that was never forthcoming, and fled into England. At Norham he demanded that Margaret be released to him, and Lascelles had no choice but to agree.

Angus rode eastwards with Margaret along the border to Berwick, where he sought shelter in the castle with Sir Thomas Strangeways, comptroller of the household of her godfather, Cardinal Wolsey. Berwick Castle was a safe haven, being a strong keep on a high mound, surrounded by what became known as the White Wall; it was arguably the most important border fortress, for it commanded the most violently disputed country between England and Scotland. Berwick itself had changed hands thirteen times over the centuries, and had been English since 1482.[53]

In May Angus asked Strangeways to take Margaret into his household while he himself travelled south to seek the support of Henry VIII. He told Strangeways there was a real possibility that Margaret might be 'stolen and withdrawn into Scotland': either the Queen would try to get her daughter back, or James V would seize her, so it was essential that she was well guarded. Angus promised to recompense Strangeways for her expenses and those of Isobel Hoppar and anyone else who would be waiting on her. Strangeways, aware that Wolsey was Margaret's godfather and that Angus had no 'convenient place for her to be in', said he was content to take her 'and to do her the best service' that lay in his power, until he had been advised of the Cardinal's pleasure in the matter. In May Angus departed for the English court with the blessing of Henry VIII.

As Margaret was third in line to the English throne after the Princess Mary and Margaret Tudor, Henry VIII and Wolsey were also concerned about her security. But Wolsey was facing the greatest crisis of his career: the outcome of the legatine court in London, in which, as co-legate with the cardinal sent by the Pope, he was expected to procure a favourable judgment on Henry VIII's nullity suit. He had too much to occupy and worry him to be able to welcome his god-daughter and make provision for her, so he sent a herald, Mr Carlisle, with instructions for Strangeways to keep her securely at Berwick 'and entertain her'; she was to have 'as much liberty and recreation, and rather more, than she hath had'.

Informed of this by Strangeways, Angus was naturally 'very glad and joyous' to hear that Wolsey was concerning himself with Margaret's welfare, and clearly anticipated that the Cardinal would pay for her upkeep.

On 26 July Strangeways wrote to assure the Cardinal that he was keeping a strict eye on his charge, and had been doing so before Wolsey's command arrived. 'And yet,' he added, 'I know well she was never merrier, nor better pleased and content, than she is now, as she oft-times repeats.' He reminded Wolsey that he had now been looking after Margaret, Isobel and a manservant, as well as other friends and servants at times, for three months, and had given Angus bed and board, yet he had not received any payment. He assured the Cardinal that 'what your Grace shall further command me in this matter, or any other, I shall be ready to accomplish the same with the grace of God'.[54] He was evidently hoping that Wolsey would reimburse him.

Margaret remained at Berwick in the custody of Strangeways until the following spring, and was treated well. But no money was forthcoming from Angus, and in August 1530 Strangeways had to ask Wolsey outright for 200 marks (£42,940) 'for the bringing up of the Lady Margaret Douglas, daughter of the earl of Angus'.[55] Given the immensity of the sum, he must have kept his charge in some state. By then the Cardinal, having failed to secure Henry VIII's divorce, had fallen from favour, and he died before he could pay Strangeways.[56]

Angus, meanwhile, had been made welcome at the English court. In exchange for an oath of allegiance, Henry VIII granted him a pension and promised to make any peace with Scotland conditional upon his restoration to favour. James V nevertheless persisted in his policy of crushing the Douglas faction and refused consistently to make any concessions to Angus, so Angus remained at the English court.

It was probably in the early spring of 1530 that Margaret at last received a summons from the King.[57] Escorted south to the capital by Sir Thomas Strangeways,[58] she arrived in London by 6 April, on which date the King ordered various items of clothing for 'our niece' from the Great Wardrobe: gowns of tawny (tan) velvet lined with the same, black damask lined with black velvet, black satin lined with tawny velvet, two kirtles (undergowns) with sleeves, one of black velvet, the other of black satin, and crimson and white satin partlets, or yoke-pieces (chemisettes) worn inside or outside the low-cut, square-necked bodices of the period, sometimes with a stand-up collar, and made of a variety of materials from lawn to velvet. In total these items cost the royal uncle £64.4s.8d. (£20,700).[59] These high-status rich gowns were to befit Margaret for the English court; it is unlikely that she had brought anything of the kind from Scotland.

Margaret would surely have been struck by the contrast between Scotland and England. Henry VIII was popular, rich and envied. England was a peaceful kingdom, not riven by internecine strife between nobles; its people were more prosperous and law-abiding, its court magnificent and decorous, affording myriad pleasures: pageants, disguisings, masques, interludes, gambling at cards and dice, music, dancing and tournaments. In the spacious gardens that surrounded every royal palace there were bowling alleys, banqueting houses and tennis-plays. There was money a-plenty, and hospitality was lavish. These delights must have come as a pleasant surprise after the comparative poverty of Scotland. But Henry VIII's court would also have seemed a world away from the wild, rugged landscapes of Northumberland, the magnificent hills and Renaissance palaces of the Scottish Lowlands and the stark, magnificent fastness of Tantallon, which Margaret would not see again for another twenty-three years.

3

'The Princess of Scotland'

In October 1530 Margaret turned fifteen. She was blossoming into a charming young lady, her good looks crowned with the reddish-auburn hair of her race. Among her contemporaries she became renowned for her beauty and comeliness,[1] and she has been described by modern historians as 'the best-looking Tudor girl' and 'the most beautiful woman of her generation'.[2] Alas, there are no certain images of the young Margaret to bear this out.[3] Her authenticated portraits date from many decades later, but they do show that she had deep-set, heavy-lidded eyes like those of her father, high cheekbones, a slightly retroussé nose, a small, upturned mouth and a prominent pointed chin. If – as seems possible – the famous Somerley portrait is indeed of Margaret,[4] then she was enchantingly beautiful.

There was no hint in 1530 of the dynamic personality that would shortly emerge, although from what we know of the older Margaret, we might surmise that she was a feisty, fearless, independent-minded girl, thanks to her character having been honed by a difficult childhood in a strife-riven land; and that this spiritedness was possibly what Henry VIII liked about his niece. In fact he was much taken with her. She would recall: 'So dearly loved me Henry the King, whose bounty and kindness I may not forget, that by me his Grace so greatly did set.'[5]

She had escaped the tensions of a life overshadowed by feuding parents, only to arrive at a court riven by the Great Matter. The Pope had revoked the case to Rome and matters had reached a stalemate. At court, Queen Katherine was in residence in her apartments, Anne Boleyn in hers. According to John Phillips, Margaret initially went to live with her aunt, Henry's younger sister, Mary

Tudor, Duchess of Suffolk: 'In Scotland my careful Queen Mother I leave to take the guard of King James, her young son; and to France my tale tends, ye may perceive, with the Queen mine aunt.'[6]

Mary Tudor, however, had left France fifteen years earlier. She had not been to her brother's court for three years. Thanks to the financial strain of paying the fine that Henry had exacted as the price of her marriage to Charles Brandon, she could rarely afford to go there. Furthermore she disapproved of Anne Boleyn, who was now riding high at court, waiting impatiently to be made queen of England. It has been asserted that on learning that Anne Boleyn wanted to befriend Margaret, Mary Tudor stoutly objected, and invited her niece to stay with her.[7]

It was not only on account of Anne that Mary Tudor preferred to stay away from court. Since 1525 she had been in failing health, and now she resided mainly at her country seat at Westhorpe, Suffolk. Recently completed, it was a moated courtyard house with corner towers, battlements, chimneys and moulded brick and terracotta ornamentation, including a large statue of Hercules seated beside a lion. Before the house was demolished in 1760, it was noted that 'the hall was of large dimensions and had attached a chapel with cloisters in which existed a fine window of stained glass. The gardens of large extent were kept in the style of the continental pleasure grounds', thought to have been based on those that Mary Tudor had seen during her brief time as queen of France.

In this palatial house, Margaret would have had the company of her cousins, Mary's children: Frances Brandon, who was her junior by twenty-one months, Eleanor, aged nine, and Henry, Earl of Lincoln, aged seven; and it was here that she would lay the foundations of a life-long friendship with Suffolk's eleven-year-old ward, Katherine Willoughby, who had joined the household in 1528.[8] Suffolk was mostly at court; as the King's close friend, he felt obliged to support him in his Great Matter, which cannot have made for harmony between him and his wife. Mary Tudor had long been a friend of Queen Katherine, and sympathised with her plight. She must have made her opinions known to her niece, who imbibed them with her first impressions of England and no doubt came to feel pity for the discarded Queen and her daughter, the Princess Mary, with whom she of all people could identify. Margaret seems to have become fond of her aunt, because after Mary Tudor's death in June 1533 she felt 'bereft'.[9]

★

It was probably before December 1530 that the King decided that, to bring Margaret joy,[10] she should be transferred to the household of his daughter, the Princess Mary.[11] Lady Katherine Gordon, a kinswoman of James IV of Scots, and former wife of the Yorkist pretender, Perkin Warbeck, had served Mary as chief lady of her privy chamber from 1525 to 1530, and Margaret replaced her.[12]

On 14 December 1530, probably in consideration of her new role in the Princess Mary's household, the King paid for more clothing for Margaret: gowns of crimson velvet lined with cloth of gold and black velvet lined with the same, a nightgown of Turkey satin furred with black coney, one kirtle of crimson velvet, another with sleeves of black velvet, a black cloth cloak with black satin vents, a partlet of crimson satin, habiliments (trappings or ornamentation on court dress, probably borders for edging necklines or hoods) of black velvet and crimson velvet, rails (lawn night-shifts), kerchiefs, smocks, and two French hoods of black velvet. This wardrobe cost him £96.17s.¼d. (£31,200). Good black dyes being costly, black was a high-status colour and therefore much favoured by those of high rank; it also afforded a dramatic background for rich jewellery.

Henry paid the wages of Margaret's two gentlewomen and a male servant, and provided the gentlewomen with gowns of tawny camlet lined with tawny velvet, kirtles and sleeves of worsted and tawny velvet, gowns of black cloth with sleeves lined with tawny velvet, and velvet partlets lined with sarcanet.[13] That Christmas, at Greenwich Palace, he gave Margaret a gift of £6.13s.4d. (£2,150).[14]

Early in 1531 Henry VIII demanded that Parliament and the clergy recognise him as supreme head of the Church of England. Already he had determined to break with Rome. That summer he finally separated from Katherine of Aragon – riding off with Anne Boleyn from Windsor without a word of farewell – and the abandoned Queen, who was to maintain till her death that her marriage was lawful, was sent away from court to a succession of increasingly bleak houses. After 1532 she and her daughter Mary would never again be allowed to meet. Mary was sent to Richmond, with Margaret in her train as the chief lady of the Princess's privy chamber, her personal household.[15] The King, who had not yet fallen out with his daughter on account of her support for her mother, may well have felt that the company of a royal cousin of her own age would provide a welcome diversion for Mary at this time.

On 21 October 1531 the King settled accounts for more clothing for Margaret, and paid for the expenses of her two gentlewomen and a servant,[16] and on the 26th, at Waltham Abbey, when ordering cloth and liveries for Mary's household, he provided Margaret with a lavish new wardrobe appropriate to her royal status and her rank in the Princess's privy chamber, issuing a warrant to Andrew, Lord Windsor, Keeper of the Great Wardrobe, to deliver to 'Lady Margaret, daughter of the Queen of Scots', sumptuous gowns of tinsel (taffeta), black damask and black velvet, the latter furred with powdered ermine; kirtles and sleeves of crimson satin, black velvet and black satin; crimson and white satin for making partlets, six lawn partlets, and black velvet and crimson satin for habiliments. She also received thirty ells of Holland cloth, for nightgowns ('rails'), kerchiefs and smocks, and thirty more for sheets, as well as two French hoods of black velvet, a dozen pairs of hose, six pairs of black velvet shoes, eight pairs of leather shoes, ribbon for laces, garters and girdles, twelve pairs of gloves, a hundred needles, thread, pins, two brushes and a standard or banner on which presumably her arms were embroidered.

The King provided Margaret's two gentlewomen with black cloth for gowns, tawny velvet for lining, worsted for kirtles, black velvet for sleeves, partlets and bonnets with crimson velvet frontlets.[17] They also received hose, shoes, lawn and Holland cloth for rails, kerchiefs and smocks, and pins. Her manservant got cloth for a coat, black satin for a doublet, Holland cloth for shirts, hose, shoes and one bonnet.[18] Margaret's two gentlewomen are not named, but one may have been Margaret Maxton, who, having 'dwelt a good season with Lady Margaret Douglas', had licence in August 1546 'to pass into Scotland'.[19]

The cousins, Margaret and Mary, had much in common besides being near in age: Margaret was just sixteen, Mary five months younger. Both had suffered as a result of their parents' marital troubles, and both had been taken by their fathers from their mothers. Both would grow up to be devout Catholics. It followed that Margaret would become Mary's close friend and that they would form a lasting attachment to each other.[20] Margaret was with Mary through much of the suffering that the latter experienced as a result of her father's determination to divorce her mother and marry Anne Boleyn, whom Mary hated, and it would have been natural for her to sympathise and take Mary's part; the influence of her aunt, the French Queen, probably predisposed her to this. Significantly, in the *Commemoration*, Mary is referred to as Henry's 'daughter by right'.[21] Yet Margaret was wise enough publicly to keep a still tongue and not involve herself in controversial matters, and in doing so she retained the King's affection and high opinion, unlike so many swept up in the maelstrom of his Great Matter.

At Beaulieu in Essex and Hunsdon in Hertfordshire, the Princess's principal residences, Margaret shared lessons with Mary, and came under the influence of yet another woman of strong character, the Princess's lady governess, Margaret Pole, Countess of Salisbury, who herself had royal blood, having been born a Plantagenet and been the niece of two kings, Edward IV and Richard III. Margaret Pole was a devoted friend of Katherine of Aragon. A devout Catholic, she represented the old guard at court, the reactionaries who detested Anne Boleyn and her reformist faction. Her sincere piety – Henry VIII had called her 'the most saintly woman in England' – and her loyalty to Mary must have made some impression on the adolescent Margaret, and may even have inspired her to remain true to the Catholic faith.

On 4 December 1531, when the King gave 'my Lady Princess' £20 (£6,440) 'to pass the time in Christmas', Margaret received £6.13s.4d. (£2,150). In January 1532 'Lady Margaret Angwisshe' was listed among the duchesses and countesses who received a New Year gift from Henry.[22] In 1532 the Great Wardrobe paid out £2,261.12s. (£728,460) 'to my Lady Princess and my Lady Margaret, and for the King's stable'.[23] On 23 December 1532 Margaret again received from the King £6.13s.4d. (£2,150) 'to disport her with all this Christmas'.[24] She was clearly living – and being treated – like a princess.[25]

In May 1532 the clergy submitted to the King's jurisdiction over ecclesiastical law, further severing ties between the English Church and the Pope in Rome. The radical Thomas Cranmer was consecrated archbishop of Canterbury in March 1533, and it was he who, on 23 May following, declared Henry's marriage to Katherine of Aragon invalid, and their daughter, the Princess Mary, a bastard. The King had already secretly married Anne Boleyn, who was pregnant. Until her child was born, Margaret was second in line to the throne after her mother, and effectively heiress presumptive, since no one ever considered the volatile Margaret Tudor's claim, and James V was barred because he was Scottish. Anne first appeared at court as queen at Easter that year, and went in virginal white, heavily pregnant, to her coronation on 1 June. Neither the Princess Mary nor Margaret attended.[26] The death of the King's sister, Mary Tudor, on 25 June made Margaret the second lady in the land after the new Queen.[27]

★

On 7 September Queen Anne bore not the long-desired son and heir but a daughter, the future Elizabeth I. The former Princess Mary – the Lady Mary, as she was now known – refused to acknowledge Elizabeth as her father's heir, or her mother as Princess Dowager of Wales, nor would she concede that her mother's marriage was incestuous and unlawful. Her father reacted with anger. At the end of September her establishment was reduced, although it remained under the control of Lady Salisbury. Margaret, who was paid £10 a year (£3,200), stayed on in Mary's household throughout these tense months – on 1 October she is listed as the chief of her nine ladies and thirteen gentlewomen[28] – until the King, exasperated with his daughter's obduracy, disbanded it in December. More than 160 servants were dismissed,[29] including the ladies who had waited on the bastardised Princess. The Countess of Salisbury, one of the richest women in England, offered to support Mary's household herself, but she too was sent away. A distraught Mary was packed off to the Bishop of Ely's palace at Hatfield, Hertfordshire, to wait upon her new half-sister in the nursery household established there that month.

Phillips states that, after the Princess Elizabeth was born, the King 'so tendered [offered]' Margaret that (she later recalled) 'with her in the court I had my chief being'. This was taken by Margaret's nineteenth-century biographer, Agnes Strickland, and others to mean that Margaret was also placed in the household at Hatfield, as first lady of honour to the infant Princess.[30] But Phillips is more likely to have meant that Henry offered Margaret the high honour of waiting upon Elizabeth when the latter was brought to court (which was not very often), because other evidence shows that Margaret was immediately placed in Anne Boleyn's household.[31] Mary was taken to Hatfield on Christmas Day 1533, and Margaret had arrived at court by New Year's Day 1534, as her name is included in the list of the duchesses, countesses and ladies honoured by the King with a gift.[32] Thus she was spared the sight of her former mistress and friend being made to wait upon Anne Boleyn's child, and being herself accorded precedence over Mary. It is apparent from other sources that Margaret was at court in March 1534, and likely that, in deference to her own royal rank, she was appointed first lady of honour to Queen Anne, a role she would retain under all Henry VIII's successive wives. Thus she ended up serving the woman who was the cause of Mary's troubles.

Margaret must have found her loyalties cruelly divided, although she had had little choice in the matter. The Lady Mary certainly did not hold it against her, for it was during these years that the friendship between them was cemented.[33] Mary knew that Margaret was dependent on the King's kindness and charity, and that to retain his favour she had no choice but to show herself amenable to the new Queen. Henry was evidently gratified to see it, especially after the intransigence of his daughter, who was still adamantly refusing to acknowledge Anne Boleyn's marriage as lawful. At New Year he personally gave gifts to Margaret and to his daughter-in-law, Mary Howard, Duchess of Richmond, the wife of his bastard son, Henry Fitzroy, and daughter of Thomas Howard, 3rd Duke of Norfolk.[34] In March 1534 Henry was showing special favour to his niece, 'whom he keeps with the Queen his wife and treats like a queen's daughter'.[35]

In her new post, Margaret was well attended by her own train of servants: a chaplain named Charles, one gentleman, a servant called Harvey (probably the groom who kept her chamber), a groom of the wardrobe called Peter, three maids, and three grooms who looked after her horses.[36] That her mother approved of her advancement and the new régime is apparent from a letter that Queen Margaret wrote to Anne Boleyn that year, saluting her as 'our dearest sister'.[37] To all appearances Margaret got on well with Anne Boleyn, and at court she was 'liked and loved of all'. She was known as Lady Margaret Douglas or 'Lady Margaret Angus', but the Imperial ambassador, Eustache Chapuys, always referred to her as 'the Princess of Scotland', as did other diplomats, even though the title was a misnomer, for she was neither a princess by birth, nor a Scottish one.

No taint of 'looseness of life' sullied Margaret's name[38] in the charged atmosphere of a court in which men outnumbered women by at least ten to one. She could not have afforded to compromise her reputation, for she was a valuable asset to Henry VIII, who meant to bestow her hand in an advantageous political alliance. When, on 16 March 1534, he turned down Alessandro de' Medici, Duke of Florence, as a husband for the Lady Mary, on the grounds that he was not royal, he told the French ambassador, Louis de Perreau, Sieur de Castillon, that if the Duke wished to marry in England, he might have one of the King's nieces, Lady Margaret Douglas or Lady Mary Brandon, Suffolk's daughter by his second wife.[39] He then seems to have thought better of that, for Margaret too was royal, and he hastened to say that, if the French King, Francis I, was seeking a royal bride for his son, he should favour 'his niece, the daughter of the Queen of Scotland; and if any proposition were made for her he would make her marriage worth as much as his daughter Mary's'.

Although Mary had been disinherited, she was still Henry's daughter and he was to use her marriage as a valuable political bargaining tool.

Castillon reported that the King treated Margaret as if she were full sister instead of half-sister to the King of Scots. 'I assure you the lady is beautiful and highly esteemed here.'[40] The Italian marriage proposal came to nothing, but the passing of the 1534 Act of Succession, which vested the crown in Anne Boleyn's heirs, left Margaret effectively third in line to the throne after the Princess Elizabeth and Margaret Tudor, and a most desirable bride.

In November 1534 Parliament passed the Act of Supremacy, which made Henry VIII 'the only Supreme Head on earth of the Church of England'. The English Church was now finally severed from the Roman Catholic Church, although it remained Catholic in doctrine and observances, and the King replaced the Pope as its head. Those holding public or ecclesiastical offices were required to swear an oath recognising him as such, and failure to do so was now misprision of treason.

It was in this climate that, for the next two years, Margaret lived at the centre of the court. Although apparently untouched by the reformist fervour of the Boleyn faction, she was probably not an overt devotee of the old faith, and so evident were her qualities that she attracted the admiration of Catholics and reformists alike.[41] The ladies of the Queen's household were perceived to have some influence, and when Honor Grenville, Lady Lisle, appealed to prominent persons at court for help in securing the release of her niece's husband, Walter Staynings, from debtors' prison, Margaret was among those she approached. The appeal was successful, and Margaret, although only nineteen, may have been instrumental in securing Staynings' release.[42]

On 12 July 1535 we are afforded a glimpse of her in the Queen's service in a letter written by John Husee, the London agent of Honor's husband, Arthur Plantagenet, Viscount Lisle, Lord Deputy of Calais, to Lady Lisle, telling her that Margery Horsman, one of Anne Boleyn's maids-of-honour, and 'my Lady Douglas' had promised him tokens of esteem for her when next he was at court. 'There is no doubt you shall have one of the best kirtles the Queen has.'[43] Margery Horsman worked in the Queen's wardrobe,[44] so it is likely that they had been commanded by Anne Boleyn to select one of her fine undergowns for Lady Lisle.

★

Anne Boleyn presided over a lively circle of courtiers who enjoyed much 'pastime in the Queen's chamber'. Her chamberlain warned gentlemen absent from the court, 'If any of you that be now departed have any ladies that ye thought favoured you, and somewhat would mourn at parting of their servants, I can no whit perceive the same by their dancing and pastime they do use here.'[45] Among those pastimes were making music, jesting, dancing, flirting and writing poetry. The poems these ladies wrote, or enjoyed, were bound into books and circulated at court; one associated with the Boleyn circle, and originating in the Queen's household, survives, the Devonshire Manuscript.[46] Consisting of 124 pages, it still has its original stamped-leather binding and contains 184 poems, most of them in the centuries-old courtly love tradition. These do not all appear in chronological order (and in some cases must have been written down some time after they were composed), and they are in nineteen or twenty different hands. At least two, probably more, were composed by Margaret herself; some are by Mary Shelton, Anne Boleyn's cousin, who was rumoured to have been Henry VIII's mistress for a brief spell early in 1535,[47] and by 1546 had become the wife of Sir Anthony Heveningham; and some by Mary Howard, who, as the wife of the King's bastard son, the Duke of Richmond, ranked equally with Margaret at court.[48]

These three ladies, Margaret Douglas, Mary Shelton and Mary Howard, who were clearly all friends, are believed to have compiled the manuscript in the 1530s and early 1540s. They copied down their own poems and those of others, plagiarised some, wrote responses to others and made notes and corrections. The manuscript contains transcriptions and fragments of verses by Thomas Wyatt, Geoffrey Chaucer, Thomas Hoccleve, Lord Thomas Howard, the younger half-brother and namesake of the powerful third Duke of Norfolk; and Norfolk's heir, Henry Howard, Earl of Surrey. On one page there is an inscription to Margaret and Mary Howard.

Sixteen poems are in Margaret's handwriting.[49] She had evidently learned to write fluently in English during her years at Henry VIII's court, and in the manuscript she marked several verses with the words 'and this', probably as an *aide-memoire*. Against poem 162 she wrote, 'Learn but to sing it.'[50] In ladies, the ability to compose, transcribe and edit poetry was a rare skill much admired at court.[51] The manuscript seems to have been first owned by Mary Howard and then acquired by Margaret, probably after 1537.[52]

Margaret had conducted herself until now with circumspection and wisdom, and, having never given her heart to anyone, thought herself armoured against any grief that life would bring, but now 'from reason, by love, so soon I did fall'.[53] At least a dozen poems – including numbers 41–48, the most discussed and debated verses in the Devonshire Manuscript – treat of real feelings, as opposed to the game of courtly love. Two were probably composed by Margaret, the rest almost certainly by Thomas Howard, and they attest to the couple having fallen deeply, even defiantly, in love. The poems were first linked to them in 1874,[54] and it has been said that the language of courtly love enabled Margaret to 'express a passion for which she was willing to break her duties as daughter and subject' and to protest against a social code that prevented women of her rank from loving and marrying where they wished.[55]

Margaret herself did not copy any of these particular poems into the manuscript; they are written in another hand. They relate to events that happened a year and more after the affair began, and bear witness to the depths of the couple's feelings. Other verses were almost certainly copied into the manuscript because they had a special resonance that echoed those feelings. Taken together, they tell the story of one of the most tragic episodes in Margaret's life.

4

'Suffering in Sorrow'

Lord Thomas Howard, born around 1511–12 and now twenty-three or -four to Margaret's twenty, was the son and namesake of the 2nd Duke of Norfolk by his second wife, Agnes Tilney. He was a competent poet who enjoyed plays on words and conundrums,[1] and it has been suggested that he was educated by the antiquarian and poet John Leland, chaplain and librarian to the King.[2] Thomas and his much older brother Norfolk were uncles to Anne Boleyn, and Thomas had been part of her circle since his arrival at court in 1533,[3] and had helped to carry the canopy at the Princess Elizabeth's christening.[4] It was almost certainly in this hothouse of flirtation and intrigue that was the Queen's chamber that his courtship of Margaret flourished. It had begun in the summer of 1535,[5] and may have been encouraged by the Queen.[6] Anne Boleyn had already been instrumental in arranging the marriage of her cousin, Mary Howard, to the King's illegitimate son; a match between her uncle and the King's niece would further bind her family to the Tudor royal house.

It is not possible to say with certainty that all the poems written by Margaret and Thomas Howard relate to their personal experiences, and in some cases it seems that they wrote verses about imaginary scenarios, or copied out the works of other poets simply because they enjoyed them.[7] But internal evidence in many of their poems, and the emotional intensity of these verses, strongly links them to events in the couple's lives. Three poems by Thomas Howard, numbers 67, 68 and 69, were probably written during the months when he was secretly courting Margaret, and it seems – from poem 67, with its chorus that suggests it was perhaps set to music – that in true courtly tradition she showed herself disdainful, causing her suitor much anguish:

> To joy in pain, my will
> Doth will to, will me still,
> For pain now in this case
> Appeareth joy in place.
>
> Chorus:
> Although my pain be greater
> Than can be told or thought,
> My love is still the better
> The dearer it is bought.
>
> This do I joy in pain,
> Yet I do not obtain
> The thing that I would fain,
> Wherefore I say again: [Chorus]
>
> I have heard say ere this,
> Full many a time and oft:
> That [which] is fetched for ladies
> Far-fetched and dearly bought. [Chorus]
>
> This marvels much to me
> How these two can agree,
> Both joy and pain to be
> In place both twain, perdie. [Chorus]

These poems suggest that the proverbial course of true love did not run smoothly. Poem 68, signed 'T. H.', with its clever plays on words, is about how the writer has been disdained by his passionate lady for valuing friendship as highly as love, and that her friends are siding with her.

> If reason govern fantasy
> So that my fancy judge aright,
> Of all pleasures to man earthly
> The chiefest pleasure of delight
> Is only this that I recite:
> For friendship showed, to find at end
> The friendship of a faithful friend.

If this be true, true is this too:
In all this pleasant evenness
The most displeasure Chance may do
Is unkindness showed for unkindness,
For friendly friendship forwardness;
Like as the one case pleasant is,
Likewise a painful case is this.

These two, approved, approve the third:
That is to say, my self to be
In woeful case. For, at a word,
Where I show friendship, and would see
For friendship, friendship showed to me,
There find I friendship so far fainted
That I scantly may seem acquainted.

By this word friendship now here said,
My meaning to declare truly,
I mean no whit the burning braid [upbraiding]
Of raging love most amorously,
But honest friendly company.
And other love than this, I know
Herself nor yet none other can show.

And since herself no farther knoweth,
Nor I myself, but as I tell –
Though false report as grass doth groweth,
That I love her exceeding well,
And that she taketh my love as ill –
Since I indeed mean no such thing,
What hurt could honest friendship bring?

No staring eye nor hearkening ear
Can hurt in this, except that she
Have other friends that may not bear
In her presence, presence of me,
And that for that her pleasure be
To show unkindness for none other,
But banish me to bring in other.

But since that fancy leads her so,
And leads my friendship from the light

And walketh me darkling to and fro
While other friends may walk in sight,
I pray for patience in that spite.
And, thus fulfilled her appetite,
I shall example be, I trow,
Ere friends show friendship, friends to know.

Underneath have been drawn two barbed arrows, showing that Cupid's darts can have a sting in them.

Poem 69 finds Thomas fretting because something has happened to upset the lovers and made his lady withdraw. Possibly she feared that someone had found them out and would report them. In these verses Thomas makes a rather heavy-handed alliterative play on words, using the word 'hap' as both noun (meaning chance or occurrence) and verb (meaning to happen or chance).

What helpeth hope of happy hap
When hap will hap unhappily?
What helpeth hope to flee the trap
Which hap doth set maliciously?
My hope and hap hap contrary,
For as my hope for right doth long,
So doth my hap award me wrong.

And thus my hap my hope hath turned
Clear out of hope into despair,
For though I burn and long have burned
In fiery love of one most fair,
Where love for love should keep the chair,
There my mishap is overpressed
To set disdain for my unrest.

She knoweth my love of long time meant,
She knoweth my truth, nothing is hid,
She knoweth I love in good intent
As ever man a woman did,
Yet love for love in vain asked.
What cloud hath brought this thunderclap?
Shall I blame her? Nay, I blame hap.

For whereas hap list to arise,
I see both she and other can

For little love much love devise;
And sometime hap doth love so scan
Someone to leave her faithful man,
Whom, saving bondship, nought doth crave,
For him she ought nor cannot have.

Howbeit that hap maketh you so do,
So say I not nor otherwise,
But what such haps, by hap, hap to,
Hap daily showeth in exercise.
As power will serve, I you advise
To flee such hap for hap that growth,
And pardon me, your man, Tom Truth.

Some take no care where they have cure,
Some have no cure and yet take care,
And so do I, sweetheart. Be sure
My love must care for your welfare.
I love you more than I declare,
But as for hap happing thus ill,
Hap shall I hate, hap what hap will.

It has been stated that the King knew of, and even looked kindly upon, the relationship,[8] but this is based on a misreading of a letter sent by Margaret Tudor to Henry VIII in August 1536,[9] in which she says she has been informed that her daughter 'should, by your Grace's advice, promise to marry Lord Thomas Howard, and that your Grace is displeased that she should promise or desire such thing'.[10] The two statements are contradictory, and it may be that Queen Margaret had received conflicting reports and been initially confused herself. The rest of her letter makes it clear that she knew that the King was furious with Margaret. If he had encouraged the relationship there would have been no cause for that, or need for the affair to be conducted in secrecy. The truth was that Anne Boleyn's influence was waning, and it was almost a certainty that Henry VIII would not have approved of such a match for his niece, given that Margaret was third in line to the throne and a valuable counter in the intricate game of diplomacy and power politics. Her marriage – which was of supreme political importance, since there was a chance that her husband might one day end up ruling England beside her – was in the King's gift, to be made to his, and the realm's, advantage. It was not for her to choose the man she would wed: that was her uncle's prerogative, and he would certainly wish to select a suitor with care. Thomas Howard, a younger son with no fortune, no prospects and no influence in any quarter, would not have stood a chance. Henry was already allied to the Howards through his marriage to Anne and his son's marriage to Mary Howard, but with the Boleyn influence diminishing, that alliance was souring.

The lovers ignored these considerations. They managed to arrange many secret trysts, always with the Duchess of Richmond present as chaperone; they would wait until the Queen's aunt, Lady Boleyn, had vacated her chamber and then steal in there.[11] Margaret gave Thomas a portrait of herself and a diamond; in return he gave her a cramp ring blessed by the King on Good Friday 1536;[12] since the time of King Edward the Confessor (reigned 1042–66) such rings were believed to relieve attacks of cramp. According to a poem by Henry Howard, Earl of Surrey, Margaret was Thomas's 'true love', and his own poems suggest as much; but it is possible that he was as hard-headed and ambitious as most of his family and hoped for great things from marrying her. Even so, his feelings appear to have been sincere, and probably compassed friendship as well as passion. In poem 46 Margaret wrote, 'To love me best was his intent.'

The first verse of poem 8 is sometimes attributed (probably incorrectly) to Thomas Wyatt; it reads:

> Suffering in sorrow in hope to attain,
> Desiring in fear, and dare not complain,
> True of belief, in whom is all my trust,
> Do thou apply to ease me of my pain,
> Else thus to serve and suffer still I must.

Next to this verse there is an annotation in Margaret's hand, 'Forget this', beneath which Mary Shelton, whose surname is spelt out in the initial letters of the verses, has written, 'It is worthy.' There is a suggestion in this that Margaret found the subterfuge wearisome and frustrating.

The couple should have known that they were courting disaster. There was even a salutary warning on the first page of the manuscript that Margaret and her friends were compiling:

> Take heed betime lest ye be spied,
> Your loving ways you cannot hide;
> At last the truth will sure be tried,
> Therefore take heed!

The year 1536 was one of unprecedented royal dramas. On 7 January Katherine of Aragon died of cancer at Kimbolton Castle, and on 29 January, the day she was buried at Peterborough Abbey with the honours due to a dowager princess of Wales, Anne Boleyn miscarried of a son.

Anne had never been popular, and her failure to bear the King a male heir laid her open to the machinations of her enemies. The courtly dalliance and frolics she had encouraged proved to be her downfall. On 27 April, as the storm clouds gathered about her unwitting head, she paid £4.13s.7½d. (£1,440) for a gift of 'Venice gold fringe and silk and gold points for a saddle for my Lady Margaret' and '2 round buttons of silk and gold for the bridle'.[13] Already members of Anne's household were being interrogated as to the conduct of their mistress, and Margaret must have been one of those questioned,[14] although no source names her.

She was probably among the ladies in attendance on the Queen at the May Day tournament, from which the King abruptly rose and departed, leaving Anne nonplussed. Like most observers, Margaret would have speculated as to what this portended. And then, sensationally, the next day, in a swift coup masterminded by the King's Secretary of State, the powerful and clever Thomas Cromwell, Anne was arrested at Greenwich and imprisoned in the Tower of London, charged with adultery with five men, one her own brother, and with conspiring to assassinate the King. On 15 May she was tried and condemned to death, and on the 19th she was beheaded by a swordsman. The next day Henry VIII was betrothed to her former maid-of-honour, Jane Seymour, a meek, pale blonde whom nobody thought very beautiful. They were married ten days later.

While the eyes of the world had been focused on Anne Boleyn's swift and sensational fall, Margaret had been living in her fool's paradise with Thomas Howard. For a woman of royal blood to indulge in a clandestine romance was to court scandal and disaster, as the world had just so spectacularly witnessed. All the same, sometime after the court moved to Whitehall Palace on 7 June for the opening of Parliament,[15] Thomas Howard had 'so obtained the favour of the Lady Margaret, then living in the King's court, that some affiancing or privy contract passed between them'.[16]

It cannot be doubted that Margaret dared to enter into a precontract with Thomas Howard[17] in the presence of witnesses,[18] although we do not know who these witnesses were. Thomas later revealed that the next day Margaret had confided news of her betrothal to Margaret Gamage, the wife of his older brother, Lord William Howard.[19] Margaret herself later recalled her betrothal: 'My faith to Lord Thomas Howard I plight; most truly to me his troth did appear.'[20]

Prior to the Reformation (as Margaret had good cause to know, given that her father's precontract had been the grounds on which her mother divorced him) a precontract – a promise to marry made before witnesses – was as binding as a wedding. All that was needed to transform the betrothal into marriage was not the blessing of the Church – although that was considered essential where persons of rank and property were involved – but sexual intercourse. It appears, however, that the couple did not venture so far, as the Imperial ambassador, Eustache Chapuys, was to report that they had not consummated their relationship.[21]

Precontracting herself without royal assent shows how headstrong and reckless Margaret could be;[22] already the 'invincible spirit' referred to in her tomb epitaph was manifesting itself, as well as an alarming talent for dangerous intrigue, character traits that would be evident again and again throughout her adult life. In Margaret 'the ambition and resolution of the Tudors' combined with 'the cunning and courage of the Douglases'.[23] She has been hailed as 'a woman of unusual courage',[24] although one might describe it as impetuosity. This tenacious, articulate, audacious and often outspoken young woman was determined to have what she wanted, and there is plenty of evidence that, a true Douglas, and in many ways the mirror of her formidable great-grandmother and namesake, Margaret Beaufort, she was every bit as combative and determined as the rest of her family. Proud of her royal blood, she has been called 'pathologically ambitious',[25] though that is probably unfair to her, since her close kinship with the monarchs of England and Scotland entitled her to have dynastic aspirations. But she was undoubtedly of an amorous and passionate nature, like her mother, and (it has been said) 'no better than she should be',[26] but that presupposes sexual immorality, and there is no evidence that Margaret ever did anything worse than fall in love with unsuitable men.

She and Thomas must have known that they risked Henry VIII's wrath and worse if their precontract was discovered. Pre-empting the King's prerogative was a serious matter. But the couple were blinded by love, as is evident from their poems, which survive as a poignant memorial to a doomed romance.

Doomed, that is, because secrets like that could not be kept long at court.

Parliament convened on 8 June, and on the 15th, the feast of Corpus Christi, the King rode with his new Queen in procession from Whitehall Palace to Westminster Abbey, with the lords preceding and Jane's ladies following on horseback, Margaret leading them. The bishops and clergy preceded the lords and the King up the nave, followed by the Queen with 'my Lady Marie [sic] Douglas bearing up the train of her gown', and the other ladies and maids-of-honour bringing up the rear. High Mass was celebrated, and afterwards the procession wended its way back to Whitehall.[27]

Jane Seymour's advancement as queen must have been welcome to Margaret. Like herself, Jane favoured the old religion, and she was known to be sympathetic towards the Lady Mary. She was resolved to be the complete antithesis to her predecessor. Even the French hoods that Anne had favoured were banned at Jane's court, and her ladies were ordered to wear English gable hoods. She seems to have liked Margaret. In the 'catalogue of beads' in a book listing the Queen's jewels, some were marked in the margin as given to Margaret Douglas.[28] That must have been soon after Jane became queen, because very soon she would not be able to give Margaret anything.

Margaret's prominent role in the procession was an acknowledgement of her new, enhanced status. Anne Boleyn's marriage had been ruled invalid two days before her death, and her daughter Elizabeth declared a bastard. The probable ground for the annulment was the barrier to the marriage created by Henry's affair with Anne's sister, Mary Boleyn, which rendered it incestuous; and since both parties had known about that at the onset, their marriage could not be deemed to have been made in good faith, and so Elizabeth was illegitimate.

On 4 July Parliament passed a new Act of Succession, which provided that the King could name any heirs he chose, in the event that his marriage was unfruitful. He had not chosen to do so because, according to the Act, any person so named 'might happen to take great heart and courage, and by presumption fall into inobedience and rebellion'.[29] As things stood – his three children, Mary, Elizabeth and the Duke of Richmond, all being bastards, and James V an alien – Margaret was effectively next in line for the throne, and second lady in the land after the new Queen.

But now came exposure. 'Lately, sithen the beginning of this Parliament' – certainly after 15 June, and probably shortly before 8 July – the precontract between Margaret and Thomas Howard came 'to the knowledge of the King's Highness'. We do not know how Henry found out, but almost certainly someone betrayed the lovers.[30]

Henry was not well disposed towards the Howards in the wake of Anne Boleyn's fall; her mother had been Thomas's niece, and the Howards had always been seen very much as major players in her faction. Norfolk himself, presiding at Anne's trial, had wept as he pronounced sentence, but he was out of favour, and had he wished to intercede for his brother, he was in no position to do so.[31] It has been credibly suggested[32] that he exposed Thomas's precontract with Margaret to the King in an attempt to demonstrate that his loyalty to his sovereign was greater than his loyalty to his family. He may also have reasoned that reporting the matter, or his suspicions, would pre-empt anyone else from doing so and implicating him. His daughter Mary was Margaret's friend and had been an accomplice in the affair, and he would have wanted to deflect the King's wrath from her – and himself. Moreover, his family might benefit from Margaret's disgrace, for Mary Howard was married to Henry VIII's bastard son, Richmond, and in the wake of the Princess Elizabeth being disinherited, there was a possibility that Richmond would be legitimated and declared Henry's successor, which might make Mary Howard queen one day. Margaret Douglas, though, indisputably had a better claim, so if Henry could be persuaded to disinherit her, the way would be clear for Richmond – unless, of course, Queen Jane bore a son. But Norfolk, normally no fool, might have anticipated that reporting his brother's folly would put the Howards in worse odour, and give rise to even greater suspicions in the King's mind. It has also been suggested that Henry suspected Norfolk of encouraging the romance to further his own ambitions.[33]

Informed of what had been going on behind his back, Henry VIII was 'much incensed at conceiving that one so joined in blood to him and his nephew, the Scottish King, should not be given nor taken without his consent, especially when she lived so near him'.[34] He was enraged at Thomas's presumption, and not only bitterly disappointed in his niece, having cherished such a high opinion of her, but furious at her for promising herself without his permission and depriving him of the opportunity of marrying her off to his advantage.

But that was the least of it. The clandestine love affair now assumed a sinister significance in Henry's mind.[35] Ever paranoid about treason, especially in the wake of recent events, he conceived 'certain suspicions' that Thomas Howard, uncle of the late executed Queen, had been aspiring to the crown, backed by his powerful family.[36] In the words of the Act of Attainder shortly to be passed against Thomas,

> it is vehemently to be suspected and presumed that the said Lord Thomas falsely, craftily and traitorously both imagined and compassed that, in case our sovereign lord should die without heirs of his body, which God defend, the said Lord Thomas, by reason of marriage in so high a blood, and to one such which pretendeth to be lawful daughter to the Queen of Scots, should aspire by her to the dignity of the imperial crown of this realm, or at the least making division for the same by all likelihoods, having a firm hope and trust that the subjects of this realm would incline and bear affection to the said Lady Margaret, being born in this realm, and not to the King of Scots, her brother, to whom this realm hath nor ever had any affection, but would resist his attempt to the crown to the uttermost of their powers.

Howard was also deemed guilty of 'maliciously and traitorously minding and imagining to put division in this realm', and of deliberately subverting the Act of Succession.[37]

Nine years earlier Henry had castigated Margaret Tudor for compromising her daughter's legitimacy; now – perhaps influenced by Norfolk – he was accusing Margaret of pretending to be Margaret Tudor's legitimate daughter, and was to have her described as the 'natural daughter to the Queen of Scots' in Thomas Howard's attainder.[38] He was making it plain that there was now no question of her deserving a place in the succession.[39]

Henry had good reason for suspecting Thomas Howard's motives, and for wishing to impugn Margaret's legitimacy, because Thomas's betrothal to her looked all the worse for being discovered at a time when the problem of the succession was more pressing than ever. Thomas had entered into the precontract after 17 May, when the Princess Elizabeth had been pronounced a bastard, and upon that pronouncement he would have realised that Margaret now had realistic hopes of the succession. He could also have envisaged his marriage to her as a means of restoring the Howards to power, reviving the Roman faith – the Howards were (and still are) England's premier Catholic peers – and aspiring to the crown, eventualities that would have given the paranoid Henry VIII nightmares. It may be that all these possibilities had occurred to Thomas, although the evidence strongly suggests that his precontract with Margaret was founded upon love as well as ambition. Even so, it was breathtakingly rash of him to venture so far.

It is possible that the King knew about the precontract by 4 July, when Parliament passed the new Act of Succession. His unwillingness to name a successor[40] may have been prompted by his suspicions about Thomas Howard's pretensions.

On 8 July 1536 Thomas was imprisoned in the Tower 'for making a privy contract of matrimony between the Lady Margaret Douglas and him',[41] and examined by Sir Thomas Wriothesley, a clerk of the signet in Thomas Cromwell's service. That day John Husee informed Lady Lisle that 'the lord Thomas [was] examined [on] how long he hath loved the Lady Margaret', and that he had answered, 'About a twelvemonth.' When asked what love tokens he had given her in that period, he replied, 'None but a cramp ring.' What tokens had he received from her? 'None but her physiognomy, painted, and a diamond.' He was asked 'when the first communication was of the contract', and said, 'Only since Easter.' Wriothesley wanted to know who knew of the precontract; Thomas said he had heard that on the day after they had become sworn to each other, Margaret had confided in Margaret Gamage, the wife of Lord William Howard, while he himself had 'lately told it to Hastings, his mother's servant'.[42]

The mention of Lord William Howard, Thomas's older brother, may have led Henry to suspect his sister, Queen Margaret, of encouraging the affair for her own sinister purposes. Up till May Howard had been on an embassy to Scotland to arrange a meeting between Henry VIII and James V, and had been in contact with Margaret Tudor.[43] Had he told her of the affair between his brother and her daughter? No charges were ever laid against him, nor was he even questioned, but the King convinced himself that Queen Margaret had furthered the relationship. He was entertaining a 'vehement suspicion' of her 'traitorous intent', for people were saying that she had plotted to come to England to be reconciled with Angus, intending 'by all vehement presumptions and likelihoods to advance the said Lord Thomas and the said Lady Margaret into the favour of the people of this realm, by reason whereof the traitorous intent of the said Lord Thomas might the sooner be brought to pass'. [44] We hear no more of this, so the King must have persuaded himself that his suspicions were unfounded. It would soon become clear that Queen Margaret knew nothing of her daughter's romance.

Margaret was evidently aware of Thomas's arrest because she told Thomas Smyth, who may have been one of Howard's servants, about the clandestine betrothal and warned him that he might be questioned as to what he knew. [45] But time was running out. Not long after Thomas had been taken there [46] – probably hours later, on 8 July – Margaret too was apprehended and imprisoned in the Tower. This was done so discreetly that no one knew where she had gone; on 23 July Chapuys was to report that 'the Princess [*sic*], however, since the discovery, has entirely disappeared from court, and no one knows whether she is in the Tower, or some other prison'. [47] In August it would be reported in Venice that she was indeed in the Tower. [48]

Her arrest plunged her into turmoil. She later recalled how 'much our fortunes we [she and Howard] both did lament. I mourned that I by fantasy was led, and yet from my love I could not recoil.' Despite her uncle's displeasure, 'true love fought still my days to foil, but love of my love prepared the spoil'. [49]

It is clear from a letter that Margaret wrote to Cromwell in August (see below) that, as the King's niece, she was held in the Tower in some comfort and allowed privileges. It has been stated [50] that she was confined in the Lieutenant's Lodging (the present-day Queen's House), overlooking Tower Green, but that house was in a ruinous condition in 1539 and in danger of falling down, [51] so this is unlikely. Anne Boleyn had been imprisoned in the Queen's lodgings, and it is possible that Margaret was also held there, or – although this is less likely – on the upper floor of the Bell Tower, where her cousin, Katherine Grey, would be imprisoned in the 1560s. The Bell Tower adjoined the Lieutenant's Lodging and could only be accessed through it, so it was ideal for high-security prisoners like errant royals.

Two witnesses were examined by Wriothesley on 9 July. Husee reported that one John Ashley, [52] asked how long he had known of any 'love between the Lady Margaret and the Lord Thomas', said he had been aware of 'love between them' for about three months. Thomas Smyth said the same. This was at variance with Thomas's statement that they had been in love for a year, and testifies to the couple having successfully maintained discretion for nine months. Smyth insisted that he never carried any tokens between them and was never taken into the confidence of either Margaret or Thomas, nor did he know or suspect anyone of being privy to what was going on, except for her women. Asked when he first knew that there was a contract, he said that Margaret had told him 'yesterday',[53] saying she expected to be examined about it. Smyth said he had seen Thomas visit her many times when the Duchess of Richmond was present; Thomas would watch until Lady Boleyn had gone away, then steal into Margaret's chamber. Smyth stated that he had been there with Thomas 'sundry times', but never heard a precontract mentioned.[54] Both Thomas and Margaret made it clear that the Duchess of Richmond knew nothing of their precontract, so she escaped censure.[55]

It was not treason for a man to precontract himself to the King's niece; there was no law forbidding it.[56] That, in the circumstances, needed rectifying. On 18 July the matter was debated in Parliament, in which the Lords and Commons made 'humble intercessions' that the offence be deemed high treason, upon which was passed the Act of Attainder before-mentioned, in which it was laid down that 'the Lord Thomas Howard, being led and seduced by the Devil, not having God afore his eyes, nor regarding his duty of allegiance that he oweth to have borne the King, our and his most dread sovereign lord, hath now lately, within the King's own court and mansion palace at Westminster [i.e. Whitehall], his Majesty being there for affairs of his Parliament, without the knowledge or assent of our most dread sovereign lord the King, contemptuously and traitorously contracted himself, by crafty, fair and flattering words, to and with the Lady Margaret Douglas'. For this he was sentenced to 'suffer such pains and execution of death as in cases of high treason'.

The Act – the first ever to legislate on royal marriages – also laid down

> that if any man of what estate, degree or condition soever he be, at any time hereafter, take upon him to espouse, marry or take to his wife any of the King's children (being lawfully born or otherwise commonly reputed or taken for his children), or any of the King's sisters or aunts of the part of the father, or any of the lawful children of the King's brothers or sisters, or contract marriage with any of them, without the special licence, assent and agreement first thereunto had and obtained of the King's

Highness in writing under his Great Seal, or defile or deflower any of them not being married, shall be deemed and adjudged a traitor to the King and his realm. And be it enacted that the woman so offending shall incur like danger and penalty, and shall suffer such-like death and punishment as appointed to the man offending.[57]

To this Act Henry VIII gave his assent, effectively sentencing his niece to death. She and Thomas stood condemned under a statute that had not been in force when they had committed what was only now legally an offence.

Margaret stood in the greatest jeopardy. On 23 July Chapuys informed Charles V:

Parliament finished on Tuesday, and the appointment of the successor to the Crown has remained in blank, and entirely at the King's will. The same Parliament has condemned to death the younger brother of the Duke of Norfolk for having tried in the presence of witnesses to contract a marriage with the daughter of the Queen of Scotland by the Earl of Angus, a statute having since been made and promulgated condemning to death as traitor whoever should, without the King's sanction, treat of marriage with a lady of royal blood, ordering also that, should the lady herself have consented, she should likewise incur pain of death.[58]

Margaret had some days in which to agonise over the prospect of dying a hideous death, at just twenty years old, for the crime of having fallen in love. She can have been under no illusions as to what she was facing, or that the King would spare her because of their kinship and his former affection for her. That he would send her to the block was all too believable, given that he had recently signed the warrant for his wife, the Queen of England, to be beheaded. And there he had been merciful, for Anne had been sentenced to be burned or beheaded at his pleasure, burning being the statutory sentence for women convicted of treason. In her anguish, Margaret must have prayed that, if it came to it, he would show the same clemency to her.

The scandal was broadcast all over Europe. On 17 August it was reported in Venice that 'the daughter of the Queen of Scotland, the King's sister, has fallen in love with the Duke of Norfolk's son, and he with her, and they promised marriage; this was discovered and pronounced treason. He has been condemned to death and she is placed in a tower where they are accustomed to put those discovered in such errors.'[59] Reginald Pole, Henry VIII's cousin, also in Venice, informed Cardinal Contarini on 31 August 'that a brother of the Duke of Norfolk, for secretly marrying a daughter of the late [sic] Queen of Scotland, the King's sister, has been condemned to death along with his wife, unless the judgment be mitigated by the King's clemency'. Pole rather thought 'that in these cases the King wishes an opportunity of showing mercy, and that is why judgment has been passed on them; for their deaths would be so unjust as to create intolerable hatred' since they had been condemned only on a law passed after their offence had been committed.[60]

It is unlikely that Henry ever meant to execute a niece of royal blood who was close to the throne and could be advantageously married – and of whom he had until now been fond. He had proceeded against her in the white heat of his anger, probably to frighten her, and as a warning to others; but Margaret had no means of knowing how the King's mind worked. Small wonder that she would later recall how deeply 'mine uncle's displeasure did grieve me'.[61] Reginald Pole may have been right in deducing that the King had meant all along to show mercy. There was, after all, no proof that there ever had been a conspiracy. In the end Henry did not demand Margaret's head, or even Thomas Howard's. On 23 July Chapuys reported that Margaret, 'for the present, has been pardoned her life considering that copulation had not taken place'.[62] This had apparently been due to the intercession of Thomas Cromwell,[63] to whom either Margaret or Thomas must have offered this information in their defence. The King contented himself with keeping the couple in prison, having perhaps chosen to see his niece as the passive offender, seduced into making a precontract with an ambitious villain. Now, Margaret would recall, 'Patience gave charge I should be content [and] in my distress with hope did me touch.'[64]

Chapuys observed, with some sympathy, of 'the Princess of Scotland': 'Certainly if she had done much worse, it seems to me that she still deserved pardon; for, after all, she has witnessed and is daily witnessing many examples of that in her own domestic circle, and besides that she is said to have attained marriageable life more than eight years ago.' He added that 'the King is very much annoyed at his niece's marriage, the more so that he has no hope of the Duke of Richmond, whom he certainly intended to be his heir and successor, living long; so fully did he mean this, that, had he [Richmond] not fallen ill, he would have had him proclaimed by Parliament'.[65] This strongly suggests that Henry had been thinking of naming Margaret his successor. Richmond died of an acute pulmonary complaint on the day after Chapuys wrote his report; his death and Margaret's disgrace left the King with no designated heir.

Most prisoners of rank were attended by servants, and had to pay for the privilege, but Margaret was dependent on the King, who was footing the bill for hers; he had also heard that she had too many visitors – another privilege of high-status prisoners – and ordered Thomas Cromwell to write reproving her. On 12 August a thoroughly chastened Margaret – no longer the headstrong girl of a few weeks before – wrote to Cromwell from the Tower. It is the first of her letters to survive:

> My lord,
> What cause have I to give you thanks, and how much bound am I unto you, that by your means hath gotten me, as I trust, the King's Grace his favour again; and, besides that, that it pleaseth you to write and to give me knowledge wherein I might have his Grace's displeasure again, which I pray our Lord sooner to send me death than that; and I assure you, my lord, I will never do that thing willingly that should offend his Grace.
> And, my lord, whereas it is informed you that I do charge the house with a greater number than is convenient, I assure you I have but two more than I had in the court, which, indeed, were my Lord Thomas's servants; and the cause that I took them for was for the poverty that I saw them in, and for no cause else. But seeing, my lord, that it is your pleasure that I shall keep none that did belong unto my Lord Thomas, I will put them from me.

Whatever her inward hopes, she felt it politic to make it plain that there was no risk of her cherishing feelings for Thomas Howard:

> And I beseech you not to think that any fancy doth remain in me touching him, but that all my study and care is how to please the King's Grace and to continue in his favour.
> And, my lord, where it is your pleasure that I shall keep but a few [servants] here with me, I trust ye will think that I can have no fewer than I have, for I have but a gentleman and a

groom that keeps my apparel, and another that keeps my chamber, and a chaplain that was with me always in the court. Now, my lord, I beseech you that I may know your pleasure, if you would that I should keep any fewer; howbeit, my lord, my servants hath put the house to small charge, for they have nothing but the reversion [whatever was left] of my board, nor do I call for nothing but that that is given me; howbeit I am very well entreated.

And, my lord, as for resort [company], I promise you I have none except it be gentlewomen that comes to see me, nor never had since I came hither; for if any resort of men had come, it should neither have become me to have seen them, nor yet to have kept them company, being a maid as I am. Now, my lord, I beseech you to be so good as to get my poor servants their wages[66] and thus I pray our Lord to preserve you, both soul and body.

By her that has her trust in you, Margaret Douglas.[67]

By 12 August slightly garbled news of Margaret's disgrace had been 'brought with speed' to Queen Margaret in Perth, and 'afflicted her much'.[68] That day, horrified to learn that her daughter had been condemned to death, and no doubt remembering that Henry VIII had only recently sent his own wife to the block, the Dowager Queen 'thought fit to write to the King',[69] begging for leniency:

Dearest brother,

We are informed lately that our daughter, Margaret Douglas, should, by your Grace's advice, promise to marry Lord Thomas Howard, and that your Grace is displeased that she should promise or desire such thing; and that your Grace is resolved to punish my said daughter and your near cousin to extreme rigour, which we can no way believe, considering she is our natural daughter, your niece, and sister unto the King, our dearest son, who will not believe that you will do such extremity upon your own, ours and his, being so tender to us all three as our natural daughter is.

She beseeched Henry to 'have compassion and pity of us and of our natural daughter', and to grant Margaret 'your pardon, grace and favour'. She suggested that it might please the King to send her daughter back to Scotland, 'so that in time coming she shall never come in your Grace's presence'. She begged him to grant her 'piteous and most humble request'.[70]

Of course Henry VIII was unlikely to agree to the troublesome Margaret, with her claim to the English throne, going north to join her equally troublesome mother and perhaps making mischief north of the border. She could be of far more use to him in England – when she had had time to repent of her stupidity. He had already shown magnanimity in reprieving Margaret, and presently Margaret Tudor learned of it. On 20 October she wrote to thank him 'for the nobleness you have shown my daughter, who will never have my blessing if she do not all you command her'.[71] On 27 December Henry wrote to assure her that although Margaret had 'used herself so lightly as was greatly to our dishonour and her own great hindrance, yet if she will conform herself to what is convenient henceforth', he would 'be good to her'.[72]

He was certainly thawing towards Margaret, and he did not forget her at New Year. On 31 December 1536 there is a record of parcels of costly silver and crimson silk fringe being delivered to her, with a chair of crimson velvet, Venice silver fringe, crimson silk fringe and two thousand gilt nails, which had been specially made for her at Henry's behest. The total cost for these items was £33.18s.10d. (£10,430).[73] Margaret's spirits must have lifted with the new year of 1537, as it seemed that freedom was in her sights.

5

'Now May I Mourn'

Eight of the Devonshire Manuscript poems (numbers 41 to 48) thought to have been composed by Margaret and Thomas were written during, or about, their captivity in the Tower. None are dated. They read like an exchange of letters written in sequence, and lines in Margaret's poems echo those written by Thomas; for example, where he wrote, 'My love truly shall not decay, for threatening nor for punishment', she responded, 'For me his love will not decay', 'with threatening great he hath been paid, of pain and eke of punishment'.[1] These poems were all written down in the same hand, and the evidence suggests, but does not prove, that Thomas wrote them.[2]

Possibly they were composed by others in his circle who were aware of the couple's feelings, and incorporated into the manuscript later, when it was safe to do so, in which case they are only an interpretation of what they experienced and felt. But it is unlikely that Thomas and Margaret were permitted many visitors, and certainly not anyone who came on a sufficiently regular basis to understand what they were going through. Moreover these poems are deeply personal and minutely relevant to their plight; they contain references to what was happening in the Tower; and the sequence of verses traces an emotional trajectory that relates convincingly to known events. This all suggests that they were composed at the time, and it is even possible that the lovers were able to make contact while in the Tower.

This is not as far-fetched a theory as it sounds. In the 1560s Margaret's cousin, Lady Katherine Grey – who was also imprisoned for making an unsuitable love match – was permitted, through the offices of a kindly gaoler, to receive secret conjugal visits from her husband, and became pregnant as a result. It was only recently discovered that Mary Shelton's brother, Thomas, was a groom porter at the Tower.[3] He may well have been willing to act as go-between. Facilitating contact between prisoners would have been a relatively easy matter.

It would therefore have been possible for the Devonshire Manuscript to have been smuggled by friends into the Tower at Thomas's request, so that he could pass the time in adding to it and recording the poetic exchanges between Margaret and himself, which suggests that those he received from her were crudely written and unfit for inclusion in their raw state. If Thomas did transcribe their verses, he was placing himself in an even more compromising situation, for the poems bitterly criticised the couple's imprisonment and those who had separated them, and if they had come to Henry VIII's notice Thomas and Margaret could have found themselves in serious trouble; it was tantamount to treason to question or criticise the decisions of the King, the Lord's Anointed, who was believed to be invested with a wisdom denied to ordinary mortals. But the poems reveal that Thomas was an angry man; and he had already acted without thought for the future.

In the first of the Tower poems, number 41 in the manuscript, Margaret laments:

> Now may I mourn as one of late
> Driven by force from my delight,
> And cannot see my lonely mate
> To whom forever my heart is plight.
>
> Alas! That ever prison strong
> Should such two lovers separate,
> Yet though our bodies suffereth wrong,
> Our hearts should be of one estate.
>
> I will not swerve, I you assure,
> For gold nor yet for worldly fear,
> But like as iron I will endure,
> Such faithful love to you I bear.

The third verse is has a partly illegible signature at the end, in which the letters 'ma', 'r' and 'h' can perhaps be identified. It could relate to any of the ladies who compiled the manuscript, but perhaps, given its context, it was written by Margaret herself; legally precontracted, she could style herself 'Margaret Howard' as Thomas's wife; the autograph 'Lady Margaret How[ard]' is written on the flyleaf of the manuscript, although the last three letters are missing as the page is torn. The poem continues:

> Thus fare ye well, to me most dear
> Of all the world, both most and least,
> I pray you be of right good cheer
> And think on me that loves you best.
>
> And I will promise you again,
> To think of you I will not let [prevent],
> For nothing could release my pain
> But to think on you my lover sweet.
>   Finis

Poem 42 was clearly written by Thomas, probably in response:

> With sorrowful sighs and wounds smart
> My heart is pierced suddenly.
> To mourn of right it is my part.
> To weep, to fail full grievously.
>
> The bitter tears doth me constrain,
> Although that I would it eschew,
> To wite [the reproach] of them that doth disdain
> Faithful lovers that be so true.
>
> The one of us from the other they do absent,
> Which unto us is a deadly wound,
> Seeing we love in this intent:
> In God's laws for to be bound.

These last two lines make it clear that the couple had resolved not to consummate their love – which they could have done on the strength of the precontract – until they had received the blessing of the Church. Thomas continued:

> With sighs deep my heart is pressed,
> Enduring of great pains among,

> To see her daily whom I love best
> In great and intolerable sorrows strong.

This verse suggests that Thomas could see Margaret each day from his prison. If she was held in the Bell Tower, the Lieutenant might have permitted her to take the air, under guard, in his garden or along the wall walk. If Thomas was held in the Lieutenant's Lodging itself, or in the adjacent Garden Tower (later to be known as the Bloody Tower), from which the wall walk could be accessed, he might have caught sight of her. Possibly Margaret was allowed, under escort, to attend Mass in the Chapel of St Peter ad Vincula. If Thomas was lodged in the Beauchamp Tower, where many high-ranking prisoners were kept, he could have seen her, from his window, walking across Tower Green. On the other hand, his poet's soul could have been imagining what it was like to witness Margaret sunk in daily misery, like himself. He ended:

> There doth not live no loving heart
> But will lament our grievous woe
> And pray to God to ease our smart
> And shortly together that we may go.

He still has hope that the couple have a future. At the end of the poem another hand has added 'Margrt'. It is not a signature, but shows to whom the poem was addressed.

The next poem, number 43, is more optimistic. It could have been written by Thomas, who perhaps felt that his previous offering had been too gloomy, and that he ought to write something to cheer his beloved. It could equally well have been written by Margaret to encourage Thomas out of his despondency and praise him for his devotion and constancy. Of them both, she had the greater cause for hope. The King loved her and had always shown himself an indulgent uncle. He had stayed his hand at sending them to the block, and his displeasure could not last forever. Yes, they did have a future, and must hold to that.

> What thing should cause me to be sad?
> As long [as] ye rejoice with heart,
> My part it is for to be glad:
> Since you have taken me to your part,
> Ye do release my pain and smart,

Which would me very sore ensue
But that for you, my trust so true.

If I should write and make report
What faithfulness in you I find,
The term of life, it were too short
With pen in letters it to bind.
Wherefore, whereas ye be so kind,
As for my part it is but due
Like case to you to be as true.

My love truly shall not decay
For threatening nor for punishment,
For let them think, and let them say,
Toward you alone I am full bent,
Therefore I will be diligent
Our faithful love for to renew,
And still to keep me trusty and true.

Thus fare ye well, my worldly treasure,
Desiring God that, of His grace,
To send in time His will and pleasure,
And shortly to get us out of this place.
Then shall I be in as good case
As a hawk that gets out of his mew
And straight doth seek his trust so true.

Likening their imprisonment to that of a hawk in a mews betrays optimism, as hawks were mewed up so 'that they may be discharged of old feathers, and be so renewed in fairness of youth'.[4] One day soon, it is clear, the writer expects to be freed.

Poem 44 is by Thomas, angry and indignant at the way he has been treated. The implication in the second verse is that he has been questioned in the Tower about his true intentions, and that pressure has been brought to bear, with arguments, fair words and inducements, to make him renounce the precontract.

Alas that men be so ungent [harsh]
To order me so cruelly,
Of right they should themselves repent
If they regard their honesty.

They know my heart is set so sure
That all their words cannot prevail,
Though that they think me to allure
With double tongue and flattering tale.

Alas, methinks they do me wrong
That they would have me to resign
My title [the precontract], which is good and strong,
That I am yours and you are mine.

I think they would that I should swear
Your company to forsake,
But once, there is no worldly fear
Shall cause me such an oath to make.

For I do trust ere it be long
That God of His benignity
Will send us right where we have wrong
For serving Him thus faithfully.

Now fare ye well, mine own sweet wife,
Trusting that shortly I shall hear
From you, the stay of all my life,
Whose health alone is all my cheer.

Thomas's vehemence was the measure of his feelings and his determination. Clearly this was no mere infatuation, but a love that had survived all the obstacles placed in its way. Not even imprisonment in the Tower, or the threat of death, had shaken it.

The next poem, number 45, shows that he was despondent once more. It seems that he had again been pressed to renounce Margaret.

Who hath more cause for to complain
Or to lament his sorrow and pain
Than I which loves and loved again
Yet can not obtain?

I cannot obtain that is mine own,
Which causeth me still to make great moan;
To see thus right with wrong overthrown
Is not unknown.

It is not unknown how wrongfully
They will me her for to deny
Whom I will love most heartily
Until I die.

Until I die I will not let [cease]
To seek her out in cold and heat,
Which hath my heart as firmly set
As tongue or pen can it repeat.

Poem 46 is by Margaret, who was still exulting in her love, and thinking ahead to the day when they would be reunited.

I may well say with joyful heart,
As never woman might say beforn,
That I have taken to my part
The faithfullest lover that ever was born.

Great pains he suffereth for my sake,
Continually both night and day.
For all the pains that he doth take,
From me, his love will not decay.

Her next verse reveals the extent of the pressure that the King had ordered to be put on Thomas. There are many references to pain in the poems, most of them probably to the mental anguish the couple were suffering, but here the threat of pain suggests that torture had been mentioned, while that of punishment may indicate that Thomas had been warned that he was still an attainted traitor and liable to suffer the death penalty if he did not co-operate.

With threatening great he hath been [a]ssayed,
Of pain, and eke [also] of punishment,
Yet all fear aside he hath laid;
To love me best was his intent.

Who shall let [prevent] me then, of right,
Unto myself him to retain
And love him best both day and night
In recompense of his great pain?

If I had more, more he should have,
And that I know he knows full well;
To love him best unto my grave;
Of that he may both buy and sell.

And thus farewell, my heart's desire,
The only stay of me and mine;
Unto God daily I make my prayer
To bring us shortly both in one line.

In poem 47 Thomas mentions Margaret's 'gentle letters', and indeed letters may have passed between them, but in the sixteenth century the word 'letters' meant simply that, not necessarily more than one item of correspondence. Letters could mean a letter or a poem, so Thomas was probably referring to poem 46. In the second verse it appears that he had not only received more threats, but had been offered money as an inducement to repudiate his betrothal. Verse three shows that he was aware that Margaret had chosen a husband far beneath her in rank, and that she had had other admirers.

To your gentle letters an answer to recite
Both I and my pen thereto will apply,
And though that I cannot your goodness acquit
In rhyme and meter elegantly,
Yet do I mean as faithfully
As ever did lover for his part,
I take God to record, Which knoweth my heart.

And whereas ye will continue mine,
To report for me ye may be bold
That if I had lives as Argus had eyen[5]
Yet sooner all them lose I would
Than to be tempted for fear or for gold
You to refuse or forsake,
Which is my faithful and loving make [mate].

Which faithfulness ye did ever pretend [maintain],
And gentleness [noble kindness], as now I see,
Of me, which was your poor old friend,
Your loving husband now to be.
Since ye descend from your degree,

Take ye this unto your part,
My faithful, true and loving heart.

For term of life this gift ye have;
Thus now adieu, mine own sweet wife,
From T. H., which nought doth crave
But you, the stay of all my life.
And they that would either bait or strive
To be tied within your loving bands,
I would they were on Goodwin Sands.[6]

The last poem in the sequence, number 48, reveals that Thomas
was becoming increasingly aware of the hopelessness of his situation and dwelling morbidly on death. He copied almost word
for word lines from Book IV of Chaucer's *Troilus and Criseyde*, in
which Troilus bitterly laments that Criseyde – whom he has loved
secretly – has been sent from Troy as part of an exchange of
prisoners.[7] Thomas evidently saw himself as Troilus, and Margaret
at Criseyde, and from the first couplet we might infer that something had happened to make him compare his plight with that of
the Trojan hero. Had he been warned that he would never see
Margaret again, or that the King would break their precontract
and marry her elsewhere, or that she was being sent away from
the Tower? Whatever it was, he obviously felt that there was
nothing left for him in life but a speedy decline to the grave. It
has been suggested that, when Thomas wrote this poem, he believed
that he had not long to live and may have intended it as his
epitaph,[8] but the central theme of the verses is the departure of
Criseyde. Troilus could do nothing to help himself, and neither
could Thomas. He wrote:

And now my pen, alas, with which I write,
Quaketh for dread of that I must indite.

O very Lord, O love, O God, alas,
That knowest best mine heart and all my thought,
What shall my sorrowful life do in this case
If I forego that I so dear have bought?
Since ye [blank] and me have fully brought
Into your grace and both our hearts sealed,
How may ye suffer, alas, it be repealed?

Where there are blank spaces in Thomas's poem, the name Criseyde appears in Chaucer's original. It was too dangerous for Thomas to substitute 'Margaret', as it could have compromised anyone found with the letters on them.

> What I may do I shall while I may dure
> Alive, in torment and in cruel pain,
> This misfortune or this misadventure
> Alone, as I was born, I will complain.
> Nor never will I see it shine or rain,
> But end I will, as Oedipus [who blinded himself], in darkness,
> My sorrowful life, and so die in distress.
>
> O weary ghost that errest to and fro,
> Why would thou not fly out of the woefullest
> Body that ever might on ground go?
> O soul, lurking in this woeful nest,
> Fly forth out of my heart and [let] it burst
> And follow always [blank] thy lady dear.
> Thy right place is no longer here.
>
> O ye lovers that high upon the wheel
> Been set of fortune, in good adventure,
> God grant that ye find aye love of steel
> And long may your life in joy endure.
> But when you come by my sepulchre,
> Remember that your fellow resteth there,
> For I loved eke [also], though I unworthy were.

Poem 70, signed by 'T. H.', seems also to have been written in the Tower:

> This rooted grief will not but grow,
> To wither away is not its kind;
> My tears of sorrow full well I know,
> Which, will I leave, will not from mind.

There are poems in Margaret's hand in the Devonshire Manuscript that are not of this sequence but may well have been composed in the Tower and copied down later. Poem 86[9] is one of them:

My heart is set not [to] remove,
For whereas I love faithfully,
I know he will not slack his love,
Nor never change his fantasy.

In the next verse she reveals that she has done nothing to compromise her reputation, which is in keeping with Chapuys' statement that the couple had never had sex, and one made in a poem by Thomas that their intent was to marry.

I have delight him for to please
In all that toucheth honesty;
Who feeleth grief so it him ease
Pleaseth doth well my fantasy.

And though that I be banished him fro',
His speech, his sight and company,
Yet will I, in spite of his foe,
Him love and keep my fantasy.

Do what they will, and do their worst,
For all they do is vanity,
For asunder my heart shall burst
Surer than change my fantasy.

The same defiance permeates poem 66:

And this be this ye may
Assure yourself of me,
Nothing shall make me to deny
That I have promised thee.

In poem 61, however, there is a sense of resignation, perhaps born of the corrosive effect of trying in vain to hold out any longer against the powerful forces that were keeping her and Thomas apart:

There is no cure for care of mind
But to forget, which cannot be.
I cannot sail against the wind,
Nor help the thing past remedy.

> If any such adversity
> Do trouble other with suchlike smart,
> This shall I say for charity:
> I pray God help every woeful heart.[10]

Sir Francis Bigod was the son of John Bigod of Settrington, Yorkshire, a place with which Margaret would later be closely associated. Brought up in Cardinal Wolsey's household,[11] Bigod, the son of a staunchly Catholic family, had early on become a secret Lutheran, and on Wolsey's fall he had become friends with Thomas Cromwell and supported the King's religious reforms. In the largely Catholic north, where his estates lay, he was unpopular due to his involvement in the Dissolution of the Monasteries, and when the northern rising called the Pilgrimage of Grace broke out in October 1536, he was captured by the rebels, whose aim was to restore the old faith. Bigod was unwise enough publicly to agree with them that 'the head of the Church of England might be a spiritual man, as the Archbishop of Canterbury or such, but in no wise the King'. The rising was suppressed, but early in 1537, rightly fearing that the King's promise of pardons for the rebels – with whom he was now numbered – was not to be trusted, Bigod raised the East Riding of Yorkshire. However, he could command no support and was forced to flee. He was arrested on 10 February and taken to Carlisle, where he was examined by the Duke of Norfolk before being escorted south and committed to the Tower on 13 March.

Here he made a deposition, and in it some strange assertions about Cromwell's involvement with Margaret and Thomas Howard. He stated that in their council at York, the rebels concluded that Cromwell might be condemned for heresy for procuring the Act of Attainder of Thomas Howard for precontracting himself to Margaret Douglas, for the King had already 'given' her to Cromwell in marriage. They asserted also that the Act of Succession had been passed in order that, if the King died before him, Cromwell would inherit the crown. Cromwell's action was 'determined to be heresy' because it was 'against the laws of God'.[12]

Bigod further asserted, in a letter to Cromwell himself, that Cromwell had procured the Act of Attainder because he wanted to 'have had the Lady Margaret himself'. He claimed that this could be confirmed by Thomas, Lord Wentworth, who had helped to suppress the rebellion, and had said at dinner in Malton Abbey, 'It is reckoned surely that Lord Cromwell hath caused this statute to be made because he would himself have had her to his wife.' One of the rebels' chief fears had been that the King, for lack of other heirs of his body, would name Cromwell his successor; it seems they believed that Cromwell had schemed to marry Margaret to this end, and had manoeuvred Lord Thomas out of the way.[13]

Norfolk, who despised Cromwell as a self-made man, was no doubt gratified to be able to send Bigod's confession to London. The scandals of the previous summer had impacted on his own credit with the King, and he had struggled to reinstate himself in the royal favour. At the same time Cromwell had gained ascendancy, so it must have pleased Norfolk to have been able to report that Cromwell was thought to have aspired to Margaret's hand in order to claim the throne.[14] It was the exact accusation that had been levelled at Norfolk's brother. Of course, there was no corroborative evidence, and almost certainly no truth in the accusations, or in an earlier rumour spread among the rebels that Cromwell had aspired to marry the Lady Mary,[15] but Norfolk may have hoped that his letter was sufficient to plant a seed of suspicion in the King's fertile mind. It did not, and Bigod was found guilty of treason and executed in June.

Queen Margaret had evidently been pressing Cromwell to intercede for Margaret and urge that she be released into her own charge. 'If this is done,' she assured him, 'I will answer that my daughter shall never trouble my brother more.'[16] In May 1537 Cromwell informed her that, further to her 'sundry letters', he had 'travailed with the King, who has of himself been glad to promote her quiet and commodity as the bearer will show'.[17] The bearer probably carried news that Queen Jane was pregnant, and perhaps the assurance that, if she bore a prince, Margaret would be released; or that she would at least be treated more leniently.[18]

James V had never forgotten how Angus and the Douglases had wielded power during his minority, or forgiven them for defying him. Angus, his brother, George, and his cousin, Kilspindie, had remained in exile out of James's reach, and he had forbidden them to return to Scotland. The King's resentment had festered, and now, thwarted of executing sentence on the greater offenders, he exacted a terrible vengeance on Angus's sister, Margaret's aunt, Janet Douglas, Lady Glamis. She was accused of attempting treasonably to communicate with her brothers, but she failed to respond to the summons and her estates were confiscated. James then had her tried for conspiring against his life. Found guilty of witchcraft, without any substantial proof, she was burned at the stake on Castle Hill in Edinburgh on 17 July 1537, her sixteen-year-old son being spared the same fate but forced to watch. News of this dreadful event must have reached Margaret in the Tower, and chilled her to her soul, for she too had been accused of treason. Angus would soon have his revenge by going north and joining the English in hostile forays over the Scottish border, attacks that did not achieve much but were effective in terms of nuisance value.

Soon, however, Margaret would have cause to say: 'And though Fortune did against my bliss grudge, yet Hope at the last her hate did restrain, and to the King's favour did bring me again.'[19] On 12 October 1537, after a long and difficult labour, Jane Seymour presented Henry with the son he had desired for so long, who was named Edward. His birth meant that Margaret was no longer in the perilous position of being Henry's heir presumptive.[20] With her political and dynastic importance diminished, she had ceased to pose a threat to the Crown and was immediately 'pardoned by the King and set again at her liberty'.[21] Long afterwards, she would remember the relief of that moment: 'My fault he remitted and took me to grace; my bondage was past, my hope [of] freedom won.'[22]

It is clear from the account of Charles Wriothesley, Windsor Herald, that she was released in mid-October and Jane Seymour's funeral on 12 November. The news had reached Perth — a journey of at least a week — by 30 October, when Margaret Tudor wrote a letter saying that she had learned of her daughter being set at liberty, and 'that it was a comfort to hear that she was out of the Tower'.[23]

Margaret Tudor might not have felt such relief had she known that, while still in the Tower, both Margaret and Thomas Howard had fallen ill. Thomas was suffering from 'an ague', or fever,[24] possibly typhoid,[25] and Margaret probably had the same complaint, as she was very weak for a long time afterwards. While in the Tower she had been prescribed medicines by Thomas Aske, the King's own apothecary.[26]

It has been stated that Thomas was held in 'atrocious conditions',[27] but as we have seen, prisoners of noble birth, whose families could afford it, were usually lodged in relative comfort in the Tower and allowed servants and food sent in. It has also been suggested that Margaret's sufferings 'told fearfully upon a frame unused to hardship',[28] yet they were almost certainly not due to her being kept in grim circumstances. But suffer she did, on account of her lost love, and stress and misery would have undermined her health still further. Margaret and Thomas had been prisoners for well over a year, and had their accommodation been insanitary they would surely have been afflicted with illness before now. If Thomas were still suffering the malaise in spirits evident in the Troilus poem, he might have been more predisposed to infections.

His condition worsened. Thomas Aske supplied 'certain medicines', which were administered by Dr Walter Cromer, one of the King's own doctors, 'and other physicians, and by the apothecary employed for the relief and conservation of the health of ye Lady Margaret Douglas during the time of her being in the Tower of London, and also since the same'. The King paid out the substantial sum of £14.0s.4d. (£4,310) for these costly medicines,[29] which suggests that there were fears for Margaret's health, and that her illness was of some duration.

In Thomas's case, the unexpected generosity of the King and the efforts of the doctors proved in vain. On 3 November Sir John Wallop informed Lord Lisle that 'my Lord Thomas died in the Tower four days ago of an ague'.[30] The date of his death, 31 October, is confirmed by Charles Wriothesley: 'This year, on All Hallows' Even, the Lord Thomas Howard died in prison in the Tower of London.'[31] An old tradition asserted that he had been poisoned,[32] although there is no evidence for that, and it was also believed that he had expired of a broken heart. Later, his nephew, the poet Earl of Surrey, wrote:

For . . . it is not long ago
Sith that, for love, one of the [Howard] race did end his life in woe.
In Tower both strong and high, for his assured truth,
Whereas in tears he spent his breath, alas! The more the ruth.
This gentle beast so died, whom nothing could remove,
But willingly to lose his life for loss of his true love.[33]

Thomas Cromwell instructed Queen Jane's brother, Edward Seymour, Earl of Hertford, to inform Henry VIII of Howard's passing. Hertford responded: 'My lord, I have showed the King's Highness of my Lord Thomas's death, as Master [Thomas] Wriothesley desired me, as also my lady his mother's request for the burying of him. His Grace is content that she hath him, according to your advice, so that she bury him without pomp.'[34] 'His body was carried to Thetford in Norfolk, and there buried'[35] alongside Henry Fitzroy, Duke of

Richmond, in the priory founded by Thomas's Howard forefathers, several of whom lay interred there.[36]

Margaret, 'that had lyen in prison in the Tower of London for love between him and her', took the news of Thomas's death 'very heavily'.[37] Although she had assured Cromwell in August 1536 that she no longer had any fancy for Thomas Howard, there is evidence in poem 175, in her own handwriting, in the Devonshire Manuscript which shows that she was still devastated by his death a year later. This is borne out by her later remembrance: 'His death with my tears I did often lament', and 'when of my lord I considered the case, and how, for my love, his life was undone, I wept [for] the young wight, that for my love his life did in bonds pay, and yielded his corpse to another in clay'.[38]

There is no record of where Margaret stayed immediately after her release from the Tower, but her illness was still giving cause for concern, for in November the King ordered Cromwell to arrange for her to be moved to the healthier environment of Syon Abbey, where she could be entrusted to the care of the Abbess, Agnes Jordan.

It has often been said that Margaret was placed under house arrest at Syon, but she had already been pardoned and set at liberty, so she was actually sent there only to rest and recuperate. It was evidently a long process, as she was still being treated the following Easter.

On 6 November the Abbess wrote to Cromwell assuring him that, 'according to the will and pleasure of our liege lord and most gracious sovereign and prince, signified unto us by your lordship's letters, as touching the Lady Margaret Douglas, I shall be ready and glad to receive her to such lodgings, walks and commodities as may be to her comfort, and our Prince's pleasure, in our precinct. And what service and pleasure shall be in us to do unto her we shall be ever ready to do, with all our powers. Yet would I require of your good lordship that some person such as you trust may come and see such lodgings and walks as be with us, and to judge which be most convenient.'[39] Wisely the Abbess wanted official approval of what Syon had to offer in comfort and security for her delicate charge. All was evidently in order, and on 24 November 1537 one George Hartwell was paid 11s. (£170) 'for the conveying of my Lady Margaret to Syon by barge'.[40]

Syon stood on the shore of the Thames at Isleworth, Middlesex, and was at that time one of the ten wealthiest abbeys in England. It had been founded by Henry V in 1415, and archaeological surveys suggest that it was almost as large as Salisbury Cathedral.[41] Dedicated to the Virgin Mary and St Bridget of Sweden, it had been built between 1426 and 1431, and was named after Mount Zion in Jerusalem. It housed sixty sisters as well as priests, deacons and lay brothers, all under the rule of an abbess.

There were thirty acres of orchards and gardens in which the convalescent Margaret could take the air, and the ancient mulberry trees under which she may have taken her walks were still be to seen there in the nineteenth century.[42] Most importantly she could benefit from the ethos of Syon Abbey, which was renowned for its piety and learning, its extensive library of over fourteen hundred books and manuscripts, and its preaching. Katherine of Aragon had come here seeking spiritual solace, and thereafter Syon had been associated with opposition to the Reformation. Richard Reynolds, its confessor general, had been put to death in 1535 for opposing the royal supremacy. It would not be long before the abbey was dissolved in the wake of many others in England, but for now, Margaret's life was to be ruled by the bells of the great conventual church calling the community to the divine offices seven times a day.[43]

In 1537 Margaret was included in a list of payments made by Sir Thomas Heneage, Groom of the Stool, to all those 'at your Majesty's wages, exhibition and finding'. She was receiving £40 (£12,300) a year for her clothes and those of her servants.[44] Cromwell's 'remembrances' for April 1538 include a note to settle her charges at Syon,[45] which indicates that she had left the abbey. We do not know where she went to live, but it has been suggested that it was with her old friend, the Lady Mary.[46]

At Easter 1538, which fell on 21 April, and at midsummer, the King paid the wages of Margaret's servants and gentlewomen, totalling £24.7s.10¼d. (£7,500). He also outlaid £20 (£6,150) for 'Lady Margaret Douglas, to the hands of Dr Cromer, for preparations against Easter'. The large sum paid to Dr Cromer suggests that Margaret had been in poor health during her time at Syon, and had perhaps not yet recovered from her illness and grief of the previous autumn. Another sum of £20 was a 'reward, by her to be employed about her necessaries'.[47] In June 1538 Margaret was at Beaulieu, where the Lady Mary repaid her 20s. (£310) that she had loaned her,[48] and on 16 July Henry paid out for clothing for Margaret.[49]

It may have been in this period, when perhaps the Devonshire Manuscript had been returned to her after Thomas's death,[50] that

Margaret, reflecting on her doomed affair with Thomas Howard, transcribed the poems she had composed in the Tower, and wrote in her own hand the word 'Amen' after poem 7:

> I have loved and so doth she,
> And yet in love we suffer still;
> The cause is strange, as seemeth me,
> To love so well and want our will.
>
> O deadly yea! O grievous smart!
> Worse than refuse, unhappy gain,
> I love! Whoever played this part
> To love so well and live in pain?
>
> Was ever heart so well agreed,
> Since love was love, as I do trow,
> That in their love so evil did speed
> To love so well and live in woe?
>
> This mourn we both and hath done long
> With woeful plaint and careful voice.
> Alas, alas, it is a grievous wrong
> To love so well and not rejoice.
>
> And here an end of all our moan.
> With sighing oft my breath is scant
> Since, of mishap, ours is alone
> To love so well, and it to want.
>
> But they that causer is of this,
> Of all our cares, God send them part,
> That they may know what grief it is
> To love so well and live in smart. Amen.

Poem 83, less defiant, may also belong to this period:

> When I bethink my wonted ways,
> How I ere this have spent my time,
> And see how now my joy decays
> And from my wealth how I decline,
> Believe, my friends, that such affrays

Doth cause me plain [pain?] not of the spleen,
But mourn I may those weary days
That are appointed to be mine.

Mary Shelton may have been with Margaret at this time, as Mary wrote another, similar version of poem 83 (poem 87). It was perhaps in response to this that Margaret wrote poem 88:

Lo, in thy haste thou hast begun
To rage and rail and reckon how,
And in thy rage forthwith to run
Further than reason can allow.
But let them leave that list to bow [in defeat],
Or with thy words may so be won,
For, as for me, I dare avow
To do again as I have done.

These were no empty words, in view of what would happen three years hence, when Margaret became entangled with another of the Howards.

6

'Beware the Third Time'

On 19 July 1538 a correspondent of Lady Lisle informed her that he had 'heard say that my lord of Wiltshire will marry Lady Margaret Douglas'.[1] The Earl of Wiltshire was Thomas Boleyn, father of the late Queen Anne; for colluding in his daughter's fall he had never lost the King's favour. He was now sixty-one to Margaret's twenty-two, and had been a widower for only three months, yet such considerations weighed little against the advantages to be gained from an arranged marriage. What benefit could have accrued to the King from bestowing his highly eligible niece on Wiltshire is doubtful, although for an ambitious earl anxious to recover his former high status at court she would have been a great prize. But we hear no more of this marriage, so talk of it was probably mere gossip.

In the summer of 1538 there had been some discussion about the Lady Mary marrying Cosimo de' Medici, Duke of Florence, but by late September Henry VIII was negotiating for her to wed the Infante Don Luis of Portugal.[2] Sir Thomas Wyatt, then on an embassy to Spain, suggested to a Florentine agent, Giovanni Bandino, that Duke Cosimo should still look to England for a bride, and choose from two beauties: either Margaret Douglas, whom his King loved as a daughter, or the Duchess of Richmond, the one being no less beautiful than the other. But Bandino was non-committal.[3]

Henry VIII was thinking seriously along the same lines. On 16 October the Emperor Charles V was informed that 'the King will not stick for pure kindness to bestow his daughter Elizabeth, his niece Lady Margaret and therewith the Duchess of Richmond, by the Emperor's advice, upon such of the princes of Italy meet to be retained in alliance for the conservation of Milan' – which had been conquered by the Emperor in 1525 – 'and for the defence of Naples and Sicily, as shall be thought convenient'. [4]

It is often thought that Margaret had composed poem 175 in the Devonshire Manuscript immediately after Thomas Howard's death, and it is clear that she wrote it – it is in her hand – when she was suffering great distress of mind. Yet evidence in the poem suggests that it was actually written a year after Thomas's death, in the wake of Margaret learning that the King was thinking of marrying her to an Italian prince. It shows that she would rather have died and been reunited with her lover, for whose death she had come to believe herself responsible, and reveals that she was still languishing for him and expected to follow him to the grave very shortly. Indeed, she felt herself to be in such extremity that she had summoned her father, Angus, then still at the English court, to visit her, likewise her friends.

> Now that ye be assembled here,
> All ye my friends at my request,
> Specially you, my father dear,
> That of my blood are the nearest,
> This unto you is my request,
> That ye will patiently hear
> By these my last words expressed,
> My testament entire.
>
> And think not to interrupt me
> For suchwise provided have I
> That though ye willed it will not be.

She had resolved to die, and they could not stop her. Her wording in the next verse suggests that she had read Surrey's poem on the death of Thomas Howard in the 'Tower strong and high':

> This tower ye see is strong and high,
> And the doors fast barred have I
> That no wight my purpose let [prevent] should.
> For to be queen of all Italy
> Not one day longer live I would.
>
> Wherefore, sweet father, I you pray,
> Bear this my death with patience,

> And torment not your hairs grey
> But freely pardon mine offence
> Since it proceedeth of lover's fervence
> And of my heart's constancy.
> Let [forbid] me not from the sweet presence
> Of him that I have caused to die.

It is the reference to Italy that places the poem in October 1538. We do not know where Margaret was living at this time, but certainly she had the freedom to lock her door, which she would not have had in the Tower. Her reference to the 'tower . . . strong and high' could have referred to any tower – many great houses, castles and palaces were built with them – and not necessarily to the Tower of London.

The marriage plans – which Henry clearly took seriously, as the dispatch sent on 16 October is heavily edited in his own hand[5] – came to nothing, and Margaret lived to love another day.[6] In the late 1530s she was back in London and a frequent guest of Anne Stanhope, Lady Hertford, the wife of Jane Seymour's brother, Edward, at Beauchamp Place.[7]

Henry VIII had mourned Jane Seymour sincerely, but that did not prevent him from 'framing his mind' to a fourth marriage for the good of his realm. It was two years, however, before a suitable bride was found in the person of Anne of Cleves, a German princess who, at twenty-four, was the same age as Margaret Douglas. By now Henry was no great catch for any bride: the golden youth, the splendid man, had been superseded by a prematurely aged, progressively immobile invalid with a girth of fifty-four inches and an increasingly maudlin, sanctimonious and tyrannical nature.

The Queen's household had now to be re-established, with the King reserving the senior positions for his female relations and the great ladies of the court. In November 1539 Margaret was appointed chief of the six 'great ladies of the household'.[8] The great ladies serving under her were Mary Howard, Dowager Duchess of Richmond; her friend from Westhorpe, Katherine Willoughby, Duchess of Suffolk, whom the Duke had married after Mary Tudor's death; Mary Arundell, Countess of Sussex; Lady William Howard; and Elizabeth Blount, now Lady Clinton, the King's former mistress and mother of Henry Fitzroy. Among the ladies of the Queen's privy chamber were Eleanor Paston, Countess of Rutland, who had served with Margaret in the households of Anne Boleyn and Jane Seymour; and Jane Parker, Lady Rochford,[9] widow of Anne Boleyn's brother George. She had testified to the incestuous relations between her husband and his sister and helped to bring them to ruin. Margaret and twenty-nine other ladies and maids-of-honour now prepared to accompany the Queen's chief officers to welcome their new mistress at Dartford. 'Doing her due reverence', they were to be presented to her by Archbishop Cranmer, and 'so wait upon her till she approach the King's presence' at an official reception at Blackheath.[10]

Delayed by bad weather, Anne of Cleves did not arrive in England until late December, when an impatient Henry, who had been entranced by Holbein's portrait of her, rode down to Rochester to receive her and 'nourish love'. Alas, she was not as comely as he had expected – the full-face portrait did not reveal her long nose – and he was disgusted by the 'evil smells' about her person. In a fury, the King stormed back to court, feeling most hard-done-by and declaring that he liked her not.

Margaret and the rest of the new Queen's household had been spending Christmas at Greenwich, awaiting the arrival of their mistress. On New Year's Day 1540 Margaret was among the long list of courtiers who received a gift from the King: she got one mark, or 13s.4d. (about £200). The Lady Mary gave 7s.6d. (£120) each to Margaret's chaplain, Charles, and her servant, Harvey.[11]

In January 1540 Margaret is listed among those who had been assigned 'double lodgings' in the Inner, Second and Outer Courts at Hampton Court Palace. 'In the first is the Princess's lodging, and there are lodgings of Mr Heneage, Mr [Anthony] Denny, Lady Margaret, Lady Mary' and, among others, Cromwell.[12] The Inner Court is the present Clock Court.[13] Where the colonnade now stands in Clock Court, there was a range of lodgings built by Henry VIII between 1537 and 1547 and housing new first-floor apartments for the Lady Mary at the west end, extending into the Outer, or Base, Court. The ladies of the Queen's household were lodged on the ground floor of the wing leading from that range to what is now called Anne Boleyn's Gateway, which at the time of writing houses Apartment 36, used as a palace shop. Margaret's lodging must have been in this range, possibly where the shop is, as that was then a large double lodging.[14]

Double courtier lodgings – the most sought-after – consisted of two rooms and a privy, with moulded Gothic mullioned windows and plastered walls that could be adorned with hangings. The floors

were spread with rush matting.[15] Those like Margaret who were
lucky enough to be assigned such privileged accommodation could
bring their own furnishings but had to share the limited space with
personal servants. No doubt Margaret was pleased to be lodged on
the floor below the apartments of her good friend, the Lady Mary.

Desperate efforts were being made to find a loophole in the royal
marriage contract as the magnificent formal reception of Anne of
Cleves went ahead on 3 January 1540 at Blackheath. In a fine pavilion
erected at the foot of Shooter's Hill, Thomas Manners, Earl of Rutland
and Lord Chamberlain to the Queen, was waiting to receive her;
then 'the Lady Margaret Douglas, the Lady Marquess Dorset, being
nieces to the King, and the Duchess of Richmond, and the Countesses
of Rutland and Hertford, with divers other ladies and gentlewomen
to the number of sixty-five, saluted and welcomed her Grace'. Anne
of Cleves alighted from her chariot 'and with most goodly demeanour
and loving countenance gave to them hearty thanks and kissed them
all', then led them into the tents to warm themselves.[16] The King
played his part to perfection, showing his bride every courtesy. But
Margaret, like her uncle, may have been dismayed to find that Anne,
who was her own age, looked 'about thirty years old' and was 'tall
of stature, pitted with the smallpox' and had 'little beauty', not to
mention a 'firm and determined' countenance.[17]

Henry VIII did his best to avoid proceeding with the marriage,
but the contract seemed watertight, so he was obliged to put his
neck into the yoke, as he sourly put it. The wedding went ahead on
6 January, and afterwards he instructed his doctors to make it known
that, while impotent with his new Queen, he was able to perform
the sex act with other ladies. Margaret must have heard the rumours,
and the gossip that Anne remained a virgin.

Unlike Anne Boleyn, this Queen did not lead or instigate court
entertainments; in fact she led a retired life while the King, unknown
to her, desperately cast about for ways to end their marriage. During
these fraught months one of Margaret's pastimes was gambling with
the Lady Mary, who in April 1540 paid her £4 (£1,230) for 'a
frontlet' – a decorative band inset in a gable hood – she had 'lost in
a wager to my Lady Margaret'.[18]

After six months the royal marriage was annulled and Anne, richer
by a very handsome settlement, remained in England as the King's
'dear sister'. By then, Henry had fallen for the charms of pretty
Katherine Howard, a young cousin of Anne Boleyn and niece of

the Duke of Norfolk. On 28 July 1540 – the same day that Cromwell was executed for heresy (although his true offence had been to push the Cleves marriage) – the King married her at Oatlands Palace, Surrey. In August, when the new Queen's household was formed, Margaret, and Katherine's step-grandmother, Agnes Tilney, Dowager Duchess of Norfolk, were summoned to head it jointly as chief ladies of the privy chamber.[19] With them went the duchesses of Richmond and Suffolk and the Countess of Sussex. On 22 August 1540 Edmund Peckham, the King's cofferer, raised with the Privy Council 'matters touching the lodging of the muleteers of the carriage and Lady Margaret's stuff' to the court from Reading, where she had been staying in the former abbey, the remains of which were now used as a royal palace.[20]

That year Margaret and three other ladies of the Queen's household received 13s.4d. (£205) each from the King.[21] An inventory of Katherine Howard's jewels reveals that she gave a pair of beads with pillars (tubular pendant attachments) to Margaret as a New Year's gift.[22] The inventory of the King's jewels taken on 24 April 1542 lists 'all kinds of silks and divers other kinds' that had been delivered to the King, the Queen, the Prince, the Ladies Mary and Elizabeth, Lady Margaret Douglas and others.[23]

Margaret Pole, Countess of Salisbury, the former governess to Margaret and the Lady Mary, was now a prisoner in the Tower of London. A descendant of the Plantagenets, with the royal blood of the House of York in her veins, and a devout Roman Catholic, she had made no secret of her loyalty to the late Queen Katherine of Aragon and the Lady Mary. She was already regarded with suspicion when, in 1536, her son, Reginald Pole, then safely in Italy and pursuing a career in the Church, had written a treatise castigating Henry VIII's marriage to Anne Boleyn, which so damned him in the King's eyes that Pole could never return to England while Henry lived.

Henry had resolved to destroy Pole's family. In 1538 it was made out that they and their friends had plotted to kill the King, and Margaret's eldest son, Henry Pole, Lord Montagu, and his cousin, the Marquess of Exeter, were arrested and sent to the block. There was a round-up of their relations, and even the children were imprisoned in the Tower.

During a search of Margaret Pole's castle at Warblington, Hampshire, a silk tunic had been found bearing the royal arms – undifferenced, as they would be borne by a monarch. Margaret denied that she had ever meant to dispute the right of Henry VIII to the throne, but in March 1539 she too had been taken to the Tower, and condemned by an Act of Attainder to lose her life and possessions. The King seized her lands, and she lay in the Tower for two years, in grim conditions, until the spring of 1541, when there was a revolt in Yorkshire against Henry's rule. The King, as ever, feared a plot to depose him and place someone else on the throne. He remembered that Margaret Pole still lived. She had had nothing to do with the revolt, but he chose to see her as a threat to his safety and ordered that the death sentence be carried out. On the morning of 28 May 1541 the Countess was woken by the Constable of the Tower and told she was to die that morning. Her end was bloody, for the public executioner was a hangman and unskilled at chopping off heads. Faced with this great lady, he panicked and hacked at her head, neck and shoulders until she was dead.[24]

The cruel end of Margaret Pole, whom she knew well, must have shaken Margaret, as it did many people, but that summer and autumn she would have been diverted by accompanying the Queen when Henry VIII made a great progress to Grafton, Doncaster, York – where they stayed at the King's Manor – Pontefract and Lincoln, lodging at the Bishop's Palace. Henry's objectives were to meet his nephew, Margaret's half-brother, James V, and receive the submission of the north after the Pilgrimage of Grace. Queen Katherine was attended by four ladies: Margaret, the Duchess of Richmond, Lady Elizabeth Fitzgerald – the poet Surrey's 'Fair Geraldine' – and Lady Rochford.[25]

It was during this progress that Margaret received the sad news that on 18 October Margaret Tudor, the mother whom she had not seen for at least thirteen years, had died at Methven Castle. The late Queen was fifty-two, and there is little evidence to suggest that she and her daughter had been close. It seems clear that she had always preferred her son, James V, although she had been distressed by Margaret's fall from grace in 1536, and done her best to save her from Henry VIII's wrath. Yet there are no surviving letters or documents to show that mother and daughter had been in regular contact.

As soon as the news reached the court, the Privy Council sent orders to Henry Ray, Berwick Pursuivant, to go to Scotland 'to inquire of the death of the Queen, and whether she died intestate'. He reported: 'She took a palsy [a stroke] upon the Friday before night, at Methven, and died on the Tuesday following before night, but, as she doubted no danger of death, omitted to make her will

until past remembrance for that purpose. She sent to Falkland for
the King, her son, who came not till after she was departed. Seeing
death approach, she desired the friars, her confessors, on their knees,
to beseech the King to be gracious to the Earl of Angus, and asked
God mercy that she had so offended the Earl.'[26] Her thoughts were
with her younger child, and she desired 'her solicitors to solicit from
the King her son, from her, to be good unto the Lady Margaret
Douglas, her daughter, and that she might have of her goods, thinking
it most convenient for her, forasmuch as she never had no thing of
her before'.

But 'the same day, after her decease, the King came to Methven
and commanded Oliver Sinclair and John Tenant, of his Privy
Chamber, to lock up her goods to his use. She left in money but
2,500 marks Scots.'[27] Queen Margaret was buried in the Charterhouse
at Perth. Her widower, Henry Stewart, who had been created Lord
Methven, outlived her till 1552. Margaret was surely moved to hear that
her mother's last thoughts had been of her, and that she had wished
to make up for her neglect, but she never did receive her bequest:
ignoring their mother's wishes, James V appropriated her goods and
gave her jewels to his new Queen, Marie de Guise.[28]

James failed to rendezvous with Henry at York, for he did not
trust him. Margaret may have entertained some curiosity at the
prospect of being reunited with the half-brother she had last seen
in childhood, but any disappointment she felt was probably negligible
compared to the sense of betrayal that struck her uncle the King,
who was furious at James's perfidy. He would have been even more
furious had he known of another betrayal that was going on almost
under his very nose, for during this progress Queen Katherine –
whose upbringing had left a lot to be desired – was rashly carrying
on a secret affair with Thomas Culpeper, a gentleman of the Privy
Chamber, with the connivance of Lady Rochford. And she was not
the only one who was indulging in a clandestine liaison.

Margaret had failed to learn a lesson from the terrible fate of Margaret
Pole, or from the tragic consequences of her earlier involvement
with Thomas Howard. In November 1541, after the court had
returned to Hampton Court, she became involved in yet another
scandal that coincided with the fall of a queen. On 10 November
Chapuys informed Queen Mary of Hungary that Charles Howard,
the Queen's brother, one of Henry VIII's gentlemen, had been
'forbidden the King's chamber'.[29] Charles Howard was the grandson

of the 2nd Duke of Norfolk and nephew to Margaret's late betrothed, Lord Thomas Howard. Little is known of him, save that until now he had been in good favour with the King, who on 8 March had granted him Hurley Priory, Hampshire, the manors of Hurley and Easthampstead, with rectories, tithes and fishing rights, and a licence to import French wines and dyes.[30]

Charles's disgrace coincided with the major tragedy that was overtaking Henry VIII. Some days earlier, the King had been shown proofs that Katherine Howard had been guilty of misconduct before their marriage; and soon there would be evidence that she had probably committed adultery after it. Following a gruelling inter-rogation at Hampton Court, during which she admitted the miscon-duct but denied the adultery, Katherine and the Howard family were poised for a fall. Yet Charles Howard was not forbidden the King's chamber on account of that. His offence had been to involve himself in a love affair with Margaret, which had probably begun during the progress and come to light during the questioning of the ladies of the Queen's household. As Katherine Howard herself was not questioned about the matter, she was probably not thought to have any knowledge of it,[31] and it is clear too that Margaret, unlike several other women in the Queen's household, was not suspected of complicity in her mistress's intrigues. This suggests that the two women were not close, and that not everyone in the Queen's house-hold knew about Katherine's assignations.

The affair between Margaret and Charles had no doubt begun as a flirtation at court. Margaret should have known better, but she seems to have been as impulsive in affairs of the heart as her mother had been.

Poem 62 in the Devonshire Manuscript may reflect her shock at hearing gossip that Howard had been banished, and her fear that he would flee before he had declared her reputation to be unsullied.[32]

> As for my part, I know no thing
> Whether that ye be bound or free,
> But yet of late a bird did sing
> That ye had lost your liberty.
>
> If it be true, take heed betime,
> And if thou may'st honestly fly,
> Leave off and slake this foulest crime
> That toucheth much mine honesty.

I speak not this to know your mind,
Nor of your counsel for to be,
But if I were, thou should me find
Thy faithful friend assuredly.

On 11 November the French ambassador reported that Charles Howard 'is banished from Court without reason given'.[33] Charles fled to Flanders to escape the King's wrath.[34] From there he travelled to France, where in 1543 he participated in a tournament between the English and the French at Therouanne, in which he 'did run well and made very fair courses'. In 1544 he returned to England, which is sufficient evidence that his liaison with Margaret had not been seriously compromising. As further proof of that he was given a command under Edward Seymour, Earl of Hertford, when the latter invaded Scotland; there Charles took part in the sacking of Haddington and Dunbar, and was knighted on 13 May. He is thought to have been killed in France sometime after that,[35] possibly at the siege of Boulogne later in the year.

Poem 95 in the Devonshire Manuscript, copied by Margaret, may reflect her disillusionment with a suitor who had run away and left her to face the King's wrath:

Fancy framed my heart first
To bear goodwill and seek the same;
I sought the best and found the worst,
Yet fancy was no deal to blame,
For fancy hath a double name,
And, as her name, so is her kind:
Fancy a foe, and fancy a friend.

Fancy followed all my desire
To like whereas I had best lust [desire].
What could I more of her require
Than for that thing[36] which needs I must,
And forceth me still for to be just.
In this she showed herself my friend,
To make me lord of mine own mind.

This feigned fancy at the last
Hath caused me for to beware
Of windy words and babbling blast

> Which hath oft times cast me in snare
> And brought me from my joy to care,
> Wherefore I make this promise now:
> To break my fancy and not to bow.

The unfinished poem 101, which Margaret also wrote, perhaps reflects her regret that she had involved herself with Charles Howard:

> Might I as well within my song belay
> The thing I mean as in my heart I may,
> Repentance should draw from these eyes
> Salt tears, with cries, remorse and grudges.

Margaret was very lucky in that, devastated by the truth about his 'rose without a thorn', as he had called Katherine Howard, Henry VIII was remarkably lenient with her. It is not hard to imagine how vexed the King and his Privy Council were at having to be bothered with Margaret's misconduct at such a time, but there were to be no dire consequences as there had been in 1536. That again suggests that the affair with Charles Howard had been little more than a flirtation, as does the fact that Margaret got off very lightly.

When on 11 November Henry commanded that the Queen be sent to the dissolved Syon Abbey (which was now Crown property) pending the laying of her offences before Parliament, he had already resolved that all her ladies were shortly to be dismissed – an ominous sign in itself of what Katherine's fate was to be. 'The King's pleasure is that my Lady Mary be conducted to my Lord Prince's house by Sir John Dudley, with a convenient number of the Queen's servants; and my Lady Margaret Douglas to be conducted to Kenninghall in Norfolk, in whose company shall go my lady of Richmond, if my lord her father [Norfolk] and she [Mary Howard] be so contented.'[37] In the meantime, Hampton Court, where the two ladies were then staying, was closely guarded, 'and none but officers admitted'.[38] This suggests that Margaret, like the Queen, was confined to her rooms.

There is no contemporary evidence to support the frequently made assertion[39] that Margaret had been staying with Mary at Syon Abbey, or was sent there in disgrace and later obliged to vacate her rooms there for Katherine Howard, who was conveyed to Syon on or soon after 14 November; indeed there is no mention in the sources of Margaret staying at Syon at all in 1541. Being sent to Kenninghall was a punishment of sorts; after the Queen's household was disbanded on 13 November, there was no place for Margaret or any other lady at court, but the fact that she was not allowed to accompany the Lady Mary is indicative of the King's displeasure. Yet there is no evidence that she was to be held at Kenninghall under house arrest, and Mary Howard was also her friend, and had been allowed a say in the matter, so it appears that Henry VIII had given some consideration to Margaret's feelings.

Amidst the sensational scandal about the Queen, Margaret's fall from grace rated barely a mention in official sources. The first reference to the affair dates from 12 November, when Sir Ralph Sadler, principal secretary to the King, informed Archbishop Cranmer and others:

> His Majesty's pleasure is that tomorrow you shall call apart unto you my Lady Margaret Douglas, and first declare unto her how indiscreetly she hath demeaned herself towards the King's Majesty, first with the Lord Thomas, and secondly with the Lord [*sic*][40] Charles Howard; in which part you shall, by discretion, charge her with overmuch lightness, and, finally, give her advice to beware the third time, and wholly apply herself to please the King's Majesty, and to follow and obey that [which] shall be his Highness' will and commandment, with other such exhortations as good advices as by your wisdom you can devise to that purpose.[41]

This reprimand and warning was the extent of Margaret's punishment. But she must have been alarmed when Cranmer and the deputation of Privy Councillors arrived to see her on 13 November, and greatly relieved to find that the worst she now faced was a stay in Norfolk in congenial company.

Poem 105, which is also incomplete, suggests that she now saw Charles Howard in his true colours:

> The sudden glance chance did make me muse
> Of him that so late was my friend;
> So strangely now they do me use
> That I well spy his wavering mind.
> Wherefore I make a promise now
> To break my fancy and not to bow.

What could he say more than he did?
Or what appearance more could he show
Always to put me out of dread?[42]

Soon after 13 November Margaret departed with the Duchess of Richmond to Kenninghall. Norfolk was probably grateful to be of service to his royal master by taking Margaret into his house. He had spoken 'with tears in his eyes of the King's grief, who loved [Katherine Howard] much, and the misfortune to his [Norfolk's] house in her and Queen Anne, his two nieces',[43] and no doubt he had feared that Katherine's crimes would redound on him, for several members of the Howard family were already in the Tower on her account.

Mary Howard had now been widowed for over four years. Her marriage to the Duke of Richmond had never been consummated, which was used by the King as an excuse to withhold Mary's dower properties. She had therefore spent her widowhood either at court or at Kenninghall, pursuing her literary interests. There was no second marriage in view for her, after her brother, Surrey, had opposed their father's plan to wed her to Jane Seymour's brother, Thomas, in 1538.[44]

Kenninghall, which derives its name from King's Hall, after the ancient East Anglian kings, had been built by the Duke in 1525–8, to the north-east of the moat of an earlier house called East Hall. Designed in the shape of an H as a compliment to Henry VIII, it was a magnificent brick house that could have served – and later did – as a royal palace; there were fourteen tapestries in the great chamber alone, and twenty-eight portraits of 'divers noble persons' on display in the long gallery. Turkey carpets adorned the floors and tables. In the lofty tapestry-hung chapel there was a large wooden retable and wainscot painted with scenes from the Passion of Christ.[45] Margaret may have been accommodated in 'the great and chiefest lodging' above the great hall, which was reserved for guests.[46]

Margaret probably arrived at Kenninghall with a sense of having been lucky. She might well have guessed that Queen Katherine was about to fare far worse, and that Syon was only a step away from the Tower. During the winter, word would reach Kenninghall that Katherine had been attainted by Parliament and been conveyed to the Tower, where on 13 February 1542 she had been beheaded. The shocking news that the King had sent his twenty-one-year-old wife to the block would have given Margaret and Mary Howard much pause for thought.

Margaret remained in Norfolk's household for most of the next seventeen months. Kenninghall was situated in the middle of a large deer park, bounded to the north by woods and groves. Beneath the broad skies of the Breckland, with its vast dry heaths and numerous warrens, and in the congenial company of Mary Howard, she may have found peace after suffering abandonment, loss and fear. If she came to London with the Duke, she would have stayed at Norfolk House, a red-brick courtyard house near Lambeth Palace. It was the residence of his stepmother, Agnes Tilney, Dowager Duchess of Norfolk, and he lodged there when he was not at court.[47]

In 1542 the King's servant, John Gates, wrote himself a memo to find out the King's answer to a request from Margaret for clothing.[48] Henry apparently responded generously with the first of the many rich fabrics that he would give Margaret over the next five years.[49] On 2 October Angus wrote from Berwick to Norfolk, thanking him for forwarding a letter from Margaret and for his goodness to her, and enclosing a letter for her.[50] It is not often that we see the powerful, self-serving Norfolk in such a sympathetic light.

Norfolk's care for Margaret, her long sojourn under his roof and her association with his daughter Mary show that she remained close to the Howards. Her religious conservatism may well have been encouraged and influenced at Kenninghall. In September 1543 we find mention of her in the postscript to a letter sent by Sir Ralph Vane to Sir Henry Knyvett: 'I wish honour, long life and quiet minds unto my Lady Margaret's Grace, and my Lady Richmond, and no less to my lord of Surrey.'[51] Knyvett's mother, Muriel Howard, had been Norfolk's sister and Surrey's aunt. Again we see evidence of Margaret's affiliation to the Howards. Norfolk must have regretted the fact that his brother and his nephew had both been denied such a great matrimonial prize.

All this time Angus had continued to support Henry VIII against Scotland. In 1542 he took part in English raids on the Scottish border, but the army in which he served was repulsed on 24 August by a force under George Gordon, Earl of Huntly, at the Battle of Haddon Rig. Afterwards Angus made overtures for a reconciliation with James V, using Margaret's hand as a bargaining tool. James agreed that his 'base sister' might be married to the victorious Huntly, but Margaret, offended at the implication that she was illegitimate, declined.[52]

The Scottish victory was overshadowed three months later by a devastating English triumph at the Battle of Solway Moss, and on 14 December, ill and utterly defeated, James V died, aged just thirty, at Falkland Palace, leaving Scotland at the mercy of yet another period of minority rule, for his only surviving child was his infant daughter Mary, born a week earlier at Linlithgow. The lives of Mary, Queen of Scots, and Margaret Douglas were to be inextricably linked, with fatal consequences.

After James V's death, James Hamilton, Earl of Arran, was nominated regent for the young Queen Mary. Aged about twenty-six and a Protestant, Arran was the son of Angus's old enemy, who had died in 1529. His appointment had been opposed by the pro-French Keeper of the Privy Seal, Cardinal David Beaton, who feared that he would ally with Henry VIII, who had broken with the Pope. Arran was rich, affable and tolerant, but unremarkable as a politician, being indolent and infuriatingly vacillating. He was indeed to show himself friendly and amenable to Henry VIII, but he was an untrustworthy ally and increasingly came under the influence of his ambitious bastard half-brother, John Hamilton, later archbishop of St Andrews, who constantly tried to win him around to Beaton's party. But for now Arran was keen to court the friendship of Henry VIII, a desire that was strongly reciprocated.

Arran permitted Angus, who had now been an exile in England for thirteen years, to return to Scotland. It was at last safe for him to do so, for his great enemies, James V and Margaret Tudor, were dead. Henry VIII realised that Angus could be useful to him north of the border, for the King was set on a marriage between Prince Edward and the young Queen of Scots, which would ultimately unite the two kingdoms under English rule. Angus now departed for Scotland, intent upon furthering the marriage.

We know from later sources that Margaret approved of Angus's support for the English cause in Scotland. She seems to have spent the Christmas of 1542 with the Lady Mary, for in January 1543 Mary rewarded her with £20 (£6,150) for bringing her 'a gown of carnation satin of the Venice fashion' as a New Year gift. Their cousin, Frances Brandon, Marchioness of Dorset, was also present, and received the same amount for her gift. Margaret's gift from Mary was a gold brooch made by 'Bush the goldsmith' at a cost of £3.15s. (£1,150).[53]

After the Christmas season Margaret returned to Kenninghall, and she was apparently still in Norfolk's household on 29 April 1543, when Sir Thomas Wriothesley sent William, Lord Parr,[54] his commission as lord warden and keeper of the Northern Marches. Parr was about to ride north and Wriothesley added, 'There be also in the packet letters from my lord of Norfolk and my Lady Margaret Douglas which it may please you to deliver to my Lord Lieutenant to be sent with the next letters that go into Scotland.'[55] One of them was probably from Margaret to her father. In March 1543 Angus's attainder had been reversed; his lands were restored to him and he was appointed a Privy Councillor.[56] In April he had taken a third wife, Margaret, the daughter of Robert, Lord Maxwell.

In the summer of 1543, having decided to marry for the sixth time, Henry VIII summoned Margaret back to court to wait upon his future Queen, the comely, charming Katherine Parr. Margaret was present alongside the Lady Mary, the Lady Elizabeth, Katherine Willoughby, Duchess of Suffolk, Anne Stanhope, Countess of Hertford, and a select company of courtiers at the wedding, which took place on 12 July 1543 'in an upper oratory called the Queen's Privy Closet' at Hampton Court. Margaret was Katherine's trainbearer.[57]

Thereafter she was one of her chief ladies-in-waiting, several of whom were closet Protestants like their mistress. But despite Margaret being a Catholic and Katherine a reformist, they became good friends, and both were close to the devout Lady Mary. Among the great ladies serving the Queen were Margaret's old friends, the Duchess of Richmond, her former sister-in-law, Elizabeth Stafford, Duchess of Norfolk, and Katherine Willoughby, Duchess of Suffolk, who was a fervent Protestant yet remained friends with Margaret for several decades – which suggests that Margaret was no bigot.[58] Margaret and the King's daughters all accompanied the King and Queen on their summer progress.[59]

Margaret was now twenty-seven, and old to be unmarried in an age in which girls could be wedded and bedded at twelve and the average age at which upper-class women married was about twenty. There is no evidence that she was 'rather unhappy' at still being unwed, as has been suggested,[60] but if she did feel that way, she was soon to have cause for hope. Before she had witnessed the King and Katherine Parr making their marriage vows, someone had offered for her own hand.

7

'A Strong Man of Personage'

That summer Margaret learned that she had a new suitor, one of Scotland's foremost nobles and a man not a year younger than herself. Matthew Stuart, 4th Earl of Lennox,[1] had been born on 21 September 1516 at Dumbarton Castle, and came from one of the greatest noble houses in Scotland, whose extensive lands centred upon Glasgow, Dumbarton and the west of the kingdom north of the River Clyde, as well as large parts of Stirlingshire. More importantly, he was descended from James II, King of Scots, through whom he had a claim to the Scottish throne via the female line.[2] The Lennox crest was a bull's head, and the family motto was *To achieve, I endure*; it was to prove apposite in Matthew Stuart's case.

With Lennox came the prospect of marrying into a long-standing feud, one that was fatally to dominate his life and cast a long shadow over Scottish politics. When Matthew was nine, his father, John Stewart, 3rd Earl of Lennox, had been murdered by a bastard of the powerful Hamilton clan, and ever since there had been bad blood between the Lennoxes and the Hamiltons. Because of this it had been deemed safer for Lennox and his brother, John, to live in France, where King Francis I was happy to offer them his protection. In 1532, having publicly, but unwillingly, forgiven his father's murderer, the young Earl accepted an invitation to stay in the Loire valley with his childless uncle, Robert Stewart, Seigneur of Aubigny, whose ancestors had been rewarded with lands in Berry, in central France, for supporting the French against the English in the Hundred Years War, and had been held in high esteem by French monarchs ever since.[3]

Lennox stayed in France for ten years. Thanks to Aubigny's influence and patronage, he grew up to be well educated and imbued with the culture of the northern Renaissance; he spoke fluent French and was a skilful player on the lute. He also received a thorough military grounding, which was then regarded as a sound basis for a gentleman in royal service. As captain of the *Garde Ecossaise* (the Scots Guard), the French King's elite personal bodyguards, Aubigny was close to Francis I, and it had been through his influence that Lennox joined their ranks as soon as he arrived in France, and – at fifteen – was given command of eight hundred men.[4] He fought for Francis I in Provence and Italy, and in 1537 the King granted him the right of denizenship under the French Crown, an honour he did not often bestow upon foreigners.[5] While in France, Lennox adopted the French spelling of his surname, Stuart, and enjoyed a pleasant life at court until 1542, when James V unexpectedly died.

Lennox was determined to counter the power of his hereditary foes, the Hamiltons, in Scotland. The Regent Arran was the head of the powerful Hamilton clan, and the half-brother of the man who had murdered Lennox's father. He claimed to be Mary, Queen of Scots' heir, for he was descended, like Lennox, from King James II,[6] but there was some uncertainty as to whether his parents had been lawfully married. It was Arran's chief purpose in life to establish the legality of their union and the supremacy of his claim to the throne, yet his indolence and instability alienated many lords who might otherwise have backed him.

Cardinal David Beaton, Arran's opponent, now invited Lennox to return to Scotland, and King Francis appointed Lennox to act as his ambassador there, hoping to counteract the influence of the pro-English, Protestant Arran.[7] Thereafter, for so long as Arran favoured the English, Lennox would protect and further French interests and feather his own nest in the process. Although he himself would later recall that he had done 'good and faithful service' to the little Queen in her minority,[8] he was a great intriguer and dissembler, aspiring and duplicitous, and, as many would discover, unreliable, treacherous and driven by self-interest, but he had one great and useful virtue: perseverance.[9]

Lennox was also ambitious. He insisted that he was Mary, Queen of Scots' heir-presumptive, even asserting that James V had named him thus, and as soon as he arrived in Scotland in April 1543 he contested Arran's claim, and his right to the governorship of Scotland during the regency; all his life he would maintain that Arran had usurped his right to that office. In opposing Arran, Lennox tried to enlist the support of the Queen Dowager, Marie de Guise.

Queen Marie, a member of the powerful noble French House of Guise, was then twenty-eight, a tall, charming and attractive woman who had now been twice widowed. Having been made to leave her children behind in France when she married James V in 1538, she had suffered acute homesickness, yet had quickly learned to speak Scots and taken a lively interest in her new country, while at the same time encouraging French Renaissance influences at court. She was always to remain politically pro-French and a devout Catholic, and was now focusing her efforts on ensuring that her daughter would rule a kingdom where these viewpoints predominated – a policy that would soon see her loyalties called into question by the Protestant party in Scotland. But she was an adept political player with a talent for diplomacy and dissimulation, and indefatigable in protecting the little Queen's interests.

Before Lennox's return to Scotland there had been a French-backed plan for his marriage to Marie de Guise,[10] and he now saw it as a means of overthrowing Arran and gaining control of the young Queen. Marie, believing Lennox to be an ardent Francophile, encouraged him. In return for his allying with her and Beaton against Arran, she undertook to support his claim to the succession. Lennox now began competing with her other suitor, Patrick Hepburn, 3rd Earl of Bothwell, for her hand. 'They daily pursued the court and the Queen Mother with bravery, singing, dancing and playing on instruments, and prided who should be the most gallant in their clothing.'[11] Yet Marie gave them only 'fair words', for 'she had been a king's wife' and 'her heart was too high to look any lower'.[12] It is clear that she meant to use Lennox only to oust Arran from the regency and had no interest in supporting his claims; nor did anyone else on whose support he had counted.

Lennox was in a strong position, however. Francis I needed him to bolster the 'Auld Alliance' between Scotland and France; Henry VIII hoped that he would transfer his allegiance to England.[13] Henry was now bent on the marriage of five-year-old Prince Edward to the infant Queen Mary. Angus backed the plan, as did the pro-English Arran, and Margaret was vigorously to support it.[14] Eager to secure the English King's support for his claim to be heir presumptive in the event of the little Queen of Scots' death, Arran agreed to his proposal, and on 1 July 1543 the marriage treaty was concluded at Greenwich. Mary was to go to England when she was ten, and be married the following year. Many Scots found this unacceptable, fearing that Scotland would thereby lose its independence and end up being ruled from England.

Kept at arm's length by the Queen Dowager, Lennox was beginning to realise that no support for his claim would be forthcoming from that source. On hearing an unsubstantiated rumour that Marie was to marry Bothwell, he took the first step towards defecting to the English, which was calculated to push his rival Arran into the arms of the French. By July Lennox had conceived the idea of allying with the Anglophile Angus, and asked him formally for Margaret's hand in marriage. Lennox would have been aware that Margaret had a claim to the English throne, and that marriage to her would assuredly strengthen his claim to be Queen Mary's successor. Margaret was also a member of the ancient, distinguished and powerful Douglas clan, and, should any children born of her father's new marriage fail to survive, potentially a great heiress.[15]

Having received a favourable response from Angus, and been made aware that he needed also to secure Henry VIII's consent to the marriage because Margaret was one of the heirs to the English succession, Lennox approached Sir Ralph Sadler, the English ambassador in Scotland. On 2 July Sadler reported to Henry VIII that Angus had 'lately said that Lennox would gladly make alliance with him [Angus], and marry his daughter, the Lady Margaret Douglas, which marriage he referreth wholly to your Majesty'.[16] The proposal appealed to Henry VIII, who saw it as a means of securing the support of a powerful Scottish noble for his own dynastic ambitions; and it must have intrigued Margaret greatly.

But Sadler was not sure where Lennox's loyalty really lay. That month Cardinal Beaton and Marie de Guise resurrected the Earl's hopes of marriage with the latter and the governorship of Scotland in Arran's place.[17] On 13 July Sadler informed Henry VIII that he had not been given 'any hope of Lennox being induced from France to the King's devotion'. Sadler had canvassed the opinions of those who knew Lennox, of whom Sir Hugh Campbell, Sheriff of Ayr, 'thinketh that Lennox would be content to marry Lady Margaret Douglas, yet whether for her he would leave France [i.e. his French allegiance] and adhere firmly to your Majesty, he is in great doubt'.[18]

The Catholic party in Scotland, led by Marie de Guise and Cardinal Beaton, was vehemently opposed to the treaty that Arran had signed, and Lennox, seeing a pretext for overthrowing his rival, now gave them his support. Late in July, backed by a force of ten thousand men, he confronted Arran at Linlithgow and emerged supreme, removing the little Queen from Arran's custody and triumphantly escorting her and her mother to Stirling Castle, where Mary was crowned in the Chapel Royal on 9 September 1543. Lennox was present, carrying the sceptre. Arran remained in office, but Lennox was not prepared to work with him, although he was active on the regency Council, championing French interests.

Sadler had been right to doubt Lennox's intentions. Lennox had for the moment abandoned his plan to marry Margaret, for his hopes of marrying the Queen Dowager had been revived. Marie, however, remained evasive, and when, in mid-September, an angry Lennox left Stirling without permission and she rebuked him for his 'strange' departure, he replied that he found it strange that she should find fault with him.[19] Her interest, he was realising, had been merely a ploy to keep him sweet; she and Beaton had used him. Disillusioned and alienated, he left Stirling to join Angus.[20]

Henry VIII was now wary of agreeing to the marriage of Margaret and Lennox. He was all too aware of Margaret's dynastic importance, and felt threatened by the prospect of her being united with the ambitious and powerful Lennox. On the other hand, Lennox could prove useful to him in Scotland, and he had a claim to the Scottish throne that might be prosecuted, should any ill befall the young Queen Mary. But could he be trusted?

Lennox knew that Henry VIII's support would be advantageous. On 20 September Sadler informed Henry that Lennox's ally, William Cunningham, Earl of Glencairn, had 'sent word that Lennox would leave his affection to France and gladly ally with Angus, by the marriage of the Lady Margaret, in which case he hopes for the King's aid in the recovery of his title to this realm, which (he says) the Governor [Arran] usurps'. As Sadler was writing his dispatch, a servant of Lennox brought him two letters from Glencairn, one for Margaret and one for himself. The servant told him that Lennox 'is now become a good Englishman, and will bear his heart and his service to your Majesty, and very shortly intendeth to despatch a servant of his to your Highness, and to the said Lady Margaret, with his full mind in all behalfs'.[21] On 30 September Sadler reported that Lennox was at Angus's 'devotion' and plotting to march on Arran in Edinburgh.[22]

Francis I had naturally supported the French party in Scotland. On 6 October six French ships had sailed up the Clyde with money and firearms for the Queen Dowager. Lennox intercepted them, appropriating all the money and most of the artillery.[23] That day

Hugh, Lord Somerville, who was with Lennox and Angus, informed Sadler that Lennox 'hath his mind so set on the marriage of the Lady Margaret Douglas that he will not now slip from the party of the King's Majesty's friends here, notwithstanding the arrival of the said aids from France'. Sadler, who had doubts about Lennox's sincerity, could 'hardly believe' it. 'This he saith, but what he will do knoweth God.'[24]

Yet it was now crucial to English interests that Lennox remain tied to Henry VIII, and it did seem that he was in earnest. At Glasgow, in October, he complained to a French envoy about Arran's misgovernment, and asked if it was any wonder that he was tempted by the English King's offers to make him governor in Arran's place, and to marry him to his niece.[25] Warned that he could, as a French subject, be prosecuted for treason for intercepting the ships, Lennox hastened to Stirling and made a diplomatic peace with the Queen Dowager.[26] But he held on to most of the money.[27]

On 11 October Sadler was informed by the Privy Council that Henry VIII wanted possession of the strongholds of Dunbar and Dumbarton, to cut off access by water from their enemies. Lennox had been granted a nineteen-year tenure and governorship of Dumbarton Castle in 1531. It was the strategically sited gateway to the west of Scotland, and Henry, with some justification, regarded it as the key to that kingdom. He let it be known that, 'if Lennox has such desire to serve the King and so fervent love for the King's niece, Lady Margaret Douglas, he will not stick to deliver Dumbarton'.[28] Thus it was made clear to Lennox from the start what the terms of any marriage alliance would be.

Two days later Sadler reported to Henry VIII that he had discussed the matter with Angus and others, but not with Lennox, who had gone back to Dumbarton. Angus and the rest appeared willing to agree to Henry's terms, but made it clear that they would wait and see what transpired at Dumbarton. Angus's brother, George Douglas, had visited Sadler and expressed the view that 'Lennox, although young, was more constant than the Governor [Arran], but that he would require two things of the King, viz. the marriage of Lady Margaret Douglas, with a convenient living in lieu of that which he will lose in France, and assistance in attaining his title to this realm, which the Governor now usurps the government of.'

George Douglas, fearing the consequences of Lennox gaining too much power, thought that Henry VIII should consent to the marriage, but that Henry himself should invade Scotland the following summer. Lennox, he advised, 'should be entertained, because he is of great power here, and if assured to the King will do good service'. Several lords were riding west to join him 'to establish his good determination towards the King' and to ensure that the money and munitions sent by the French to Dumbarton were not seized by the Governor. 'They intend to persuade Lennox to repair to the King to see Lady Margaret.'[29]

But Lennox was still clinging to the remote chance that the French party would abandon Arran in favour of his own claim to the governorship, and was not willing to commit to Henry until he was forced to abandon that hope.[30] Courted by both sides, he knew he was in a strong position and stood to do well out of it. On 16 October the English Council were informed that he was now demanding to be acknowledged as joint heir with Margaret to Angus's earldom, 'to which Angus will not agree'.[31] Should there be no children of her father's marriage to Margaret Maxwell, Margaret would be his lawful heiress, destined to be countess of Angus in her own right.

The seizure of Dumbarton was now crucial to both the English and the Scots, but on 22 October Sadler expressed the opinion that 'Lennox would as lief depart with his right hand as with Dumbarton Castle, and to move it to him were the next way to make him revolt to the adverse party, with the French money and munition'; therefore his advice was 'not to be over hasty for that till it be seen whether he will repair to the King'.[32] The next day he heard from Angus's father-in-law, Lord Maxwell, that Lennox did desire 'the marriage of Angus's daughter and the government of this realm, but would not be induced to repair to the King, until assured of the King's mind towards him in these things, as he would lose the French King and all his profits in France'. But Maxwell had no great confidence in Lennox, and he was not alone in thinking that Lennox would 'hold in on both sides till he perceives the King's mind in his desires'.[33]

Angus and the other lords could not make Lennox budge. He still professed himself keen to marry Margaret, but was unwilling to travel down to London until assured of sufficient funds from King Henry to compensate for what he would lose in France and Scotland if the marriage went ahead.[34] Even now he had not given up hope of marrying Marie de Guise, whose hand he again demanded in November.[35] But she and her party were keen to be rid of him. On 29 November Chapuys reported from London that Lennox 'had half revolted against the French, and practises a marriage with this King's niece'.[36]

Lennox was away gathering forces against Arran when, in December, the Catholic-dominated Scottish Parliament repudiated Queen Mary's betrothal to Prince Edward and began looking towards renewing Scotland's ancient alliance with France. Henry VIII, incensed, and more determined than ever to unite the two kingdoms under Tudor rule, declared war on Scotland.

Lennox now temporarily cooled towards Henry. Chapuys wrote: 'The Earl of Lennox was about to take this King's part because of the good treatment offered him, together with the marriage of the King's niece', but had 'broken off his practice with this King and turned against him once more'.[37] But when Arran froze Lennox out of the Council, Lennox retaliated by giving his full backing to Angus and others who supported the English marriage alliance.[38] He helped Angus and his party to raise troops and marched with them on Edinburgh, bent on compelling Arran to agree to their terms; but they found themselves critically outnumbered. Forced to agree to a humiliating treaty,[39] they slunk off to their estates. Margaret was probably concerned about her father; she wrote to him before 15 January, her letter being enclosed with a dispatch sent by the Duke of Suffolk to George Douglas.[40]

In November the Lady Mary had given Margaret a gift of £4 (£1,230) and rewarded her with 3s.4d. (£50) for 'bringing cheese to my lady's Grace'; she also paid Margaret's servant Peter for embroidering a pair of sleeves for her. Margaret, Mary and the young Elizabeth all kept Christmas at Whitehall, and at New Year 1544 Margaret 'delivered herself' a gift to Mary, who gave Margaret's three gentlewomen a sovereign (£380) each.[41]

Margaret was now in high favour at the English court. In February 1544 Juan Esteban, the Spanish Duke of Najera, visited Whitehall, and after he had been received by the King 'the Duke came forth and was accompanied to the Queen's chamber, where were also the Princess Mary and many attendants, including a daughter of the Queen of Scotland. The Duke kissed the Queen's hand and was then conducted to another chamber to which the Queen and ladies followed and there was music and much beautiful dancing.' Resplendent in a gown of cloth of gold and scarlet velvet, 'the Queen danced first with her brother, very gracefully, and then Princess Mary and the Princess of Scotland danced with other gentlemen, and many other ladies [who] were dressed in different silks with splendid head-dresses also danced. After the dancing had lasted several hours, the Queen returned to her chamber, first causing one of the noblemen who spoke Spanish to offer some presents to the Duke, who kissed her hand. He would likewise have kissed that of the Princess Mary, but she offered her lips' – the customary way in which women were greeted in England – 'and so he saluted her and all the other ladies.'[42]

The birth of a son, Francis, to the Dauphin Henry of France in January 1544 brought with it the prospect of a great marriage for the young Queen Mary, and hardened the Scots' resolve never to allow her to wed Prince Edward.[43] But Henry VIII was determined to have his way, and by February 1544 he had decided to send an army into Scotland.[44] That month he gave his assent to a new Act of Succession that Parliament had drawn up the previous July.[45] Margaret, along with the other Scottish heirs of Margaret Tudor, was excluded, probably because Henry was bent on undermining the claim of Queen Mary to the English crown, intending that she would only become queen of England if his plans to marry her to Edward came to fruition. That way he could pre-empt the Scots from ever ruling England. Of course he had to exclude Margaret too, and in doing so he was also pre-empting any future claims by Lennox in right of his wife that might trouble Henry's successors and threaten the union of England and Scotland under Tudor rule. It has been suggested that another consideration was Margaret's staunch Catholicism, the King perhaps fearing that she would return England to the Roman fold,[46] but there is no evidence that she had provoked him by showing any signs of allegiance to the Pope, and indeed there is no significant evidence of her attachment to the Catholic cause in this period.

Disillusioned and disaffected by affairs in Scotland, Lennox and his allies – Angus, Glencairn and Gilbert Kennedy, Earl of Cassilis – looked to the friendship and support of Henry VIII, just as Henry was seeking to build a strong party in Scotland in support of the marriage of Edward and Mary.[47] In negotiating with the English King, Lennox was committing treason, but, given his grievances, he no doubt considered his actions justified.

In February Angus sent his chaplain, Sir John Penvan, to meet Sadler and two English Privy Councillors, Hertford and Cuthbert Tunstall, Bishop of Durham, at a place called Darnton[48] to treat of the marriage of Margaret and Lennox.[49] Lennox sent with them his secretary, Thomas Bishop, a notary public and former sheriff clerk of Dumbarton, and a man who was to loom large and dangerous in Margaret's story. He was there to lay down Lennox's terms for her hand. What Lennox had to offer was invaluable to Henry, since few Scottish nobles favoured the English alliance, and the King was gratified to have two of the most powerful, Lennox and Angus, working on his behalf. Lennox's affinity of fighting men, the money and arms he had covertly commandeered from the French, his knowledge of France and his military experience would all be exceptionally useful to Henry, who saw this splendid marriage with Margaret Douglas as a means of keeping Lennox firmly in the English camp.

On 8 March Penvan told the English deputation that Thomas Bishop was 'repairing to court to see the Lady Margaret, with whom (Penvan says) Lennox is far in love, and only refrains from coming himself because he would first convey his brother out of France, whom he intends secretly to call home, and for whom he desires safe-conduct to Calais and through England'.[50] Lennox had never met Margaret, so his claim to love her can only have proceeded from his eagerness for the match and conventional custom. But the duplicitous Lennox was keeping his options open. Even as he was declaring his devotion to Margaret, he was still making overtures to the French faction in Scotland and pressing his suit to Marie de Guise. In a letter sent on 7 March he assured Marie that he would be loyal to her eternally,[51] and on 21 March he met with her in secret.[52] It would be for the last time, however, for she told him that she would never marry him.[53]

Angry as he was at being rejected, Lennox was nevertheless aware that Margaret was a highly covetable substitute. Notwithstanding his pursuit of Marie de Guise, Thomas Bishop had 'made suit' to Henry on Lennox's behalf 'to have in marriage the Lady Margaret'. On 26 March Henry VIII commissioned Thomas, Lord Wharton, Warden of the Marches and victor of Solway Moss, and a lawyer and soldier, Sir Robert Bowes, to treat with Lennox at Carlisle. The commissioners informed Lennox and his allies that, 'reputing them to be men of honour, the King will show what he desires of them and what he will do for them in return, and has devised certain articles, which if they perform (and for that purpose presently lay hostages), he will send in his army to daunt their enemies, and also do for them as hereafter expressed'.

Henry's terms were as follows: Lennox and his allies were to 'cause the Word of God to be taught and preached' in Scotland 'as the only foundation of truth'; this has been interpreted as an instruction to Lennox to turn Protestant, but the King regarded the Protestant faith as heresy, and what he intended was that Lennox and the rest should enforce the Catholic faith throughout Scotland and establish Henry himself as the head of the Scottish Church. They were forever to 'remain perfect friends to the King and to England, and shall never consent to any league to the contrary, and shall renounce all leagues between France and Scotland, and all other private pacts which they may have made to the French King or other to the prejudice of England'; they were to ensure that 'the young Queen is not conveyed away; and shall do their utmost to get the keeping of her and deliver her to the King until of age to be married to his son'; they were to assist Henry in gaining possession of various border towns and strongholds; and 'with all their force' they were to help him to become protector of Scotland during the minority of his great-niece.

If they agreed to these articles, and to giving hostages, Henry VIII undertook in return to send an army into Scotland 'to defeat their common enemies, with charge to devastate nothing that belongs to the said earls'; to make Lennox governor of Scotland 'under the King, with a council of the King's appointment, provided he accept the King as Protector, and call no Parliament without the King's express consent; Lennox, as Governor, shall have a reasonable portion of the revenues to maintain that estate, leaving sufficient for the entertainment of the young Queen'; and to maintain Lennox's claim to the succession against Arran's. If Lennox fulfilled his part of the bargain, and Mary died without issue, Henry would 'aid him to obtain his title'.

Finally – and Henry was afterwards to make it clear that he was bowing to pressure from Lennox, Bishop, Glencairn and others[54] – Wharton and Bowes were empowered to discuss Lennox's marriage with Margaret Douglas. They were to say that, if Lennox 'should perform the said covenants' according to the King's expectations, Henry would be 'contented' for the marriage to take place. Yet he imposed a condition, unusual in royal marriage negotiations, 'forasmuch as we have promised unto our niece never to cause her to marry any but whom she shall find in her own heart to love, and that, they never having one seen another, we know not how they shall like one another when they see together; and for that also, though we were never so well pleased with the matter, and they also like each other never so well, yet the thing cannot be perfected with the honour of all parties until it also be agreed on either side, both what shall be given with her, and also what she shall have again assured unto her by the said Earl for her dower'. Because Margaret and Lennox had not yet met, the 'covenant cannot be easily now treated', so Wharton and Bowes were to tell Lennox that, when he had 'done some notable good service unto us, and shall, upon the sight of our niece, like her, and she again like him, we shall, upon his overture in that matter, make him such a reasonable answer as he shall have cause to be contented'.[55]

On the surface it was exceptionally enlightened of Henry VIII to make such a promise to Margaret, whose hand, after all, could prove so politically advantageous to him. She had already found it 'in her own heart to love' two men, and yet, fond of her as he was, he had punished her for it and made it absolutely clear that she must wholly apply herself to please him and obey his will and commandment. Had he repented of his severity since then? It should be remembered that in 1514, when marrying off his reluctant sister Mary to Louis XII of France, he had promised her that she could choose her second husband, but later erupted in wrath when she did so. Maybe he had made a similar promise to Margaret, for what it was worth – or, which seems more likely, he had done no such thing, but invented this story as a pretext for retaining the advantage over Lennox until the last possible moment.

Henry's invasion force was poised to march into Scotland. On 10 April he instructed its commander, the Earl of Hertford: 'Put all to fire and sword, burn Edinburgh, so razed and defaced when you have sacked and gotten what ye can of it, as there may remain forever a perpetual memory of the vengeance of God lightened upon [the Scots] for their falsehood and disloyalty.'[56] Hertford knew that Lennox's position in Scotland had become precarious. 'He is now brought to such a strait as I think he must needs condescend to such covenants as your Highness will appoint, for he knoweth the French King cannot trust him, and the Governor and he will never agree,' he wrote to Henry VIII on 12 April.[57]

On 16 April Hertford informed Henry that Thomas Bishop, now back in the north, was pressing 'for the conclusion of the marriage with Lady Margaret as the knot of all the rest; wherein his master refers all conditions to the King'. Hertford had told him that the King, 'as a prince of honour', would not 'promise the marriage without the consent of the parties, for which they must see each other. Bishop was not fully satisfied, but said, however, that if his master had a good ship or durst venture by land, he would come to the King, as they meant to have done and to have returned with the army into Scotland.'[58] It was a most perfunctory way to refer to the celebration of a royal marriage.

Early in May Henry's forces invaded Scotland by land and sea, an offensive that became known as the 'Rough Wooing'. Hertford's army was mercilessly to sack and burn scores of towns, villages and abbeys in south-eastern Scotland, leaving a trail of destruction in its wake, which served only to harden the resolve of the Scots to stand firm against English bullying tactics. Angus's lands were among those that Hertford ravaged, and that sufficed finally to turn him against the English and drive him into the arms of Arran, who was now negotiating for Queen Mary to marry the Dauphin of France. Thereafter, as lieutenant of southern Scotland, Angus would fight valiantly for the Scots against the forces of England, which left him and his daughter on opposing sides, and ultimately estranged, for Margaret was about to align herself irrevocably with English interests. For now, however, Angus tricked Henry VIII into believing that he was still willing to support him.[59]

Wharton and Bowes met again with Lennox at Carlisle, where on 17 May 1544 he signed a formal alliance with Henry VIII, acceding to the English King's terms. It was agreed that, 'where Lennox has made suit to marry Lady Margaret Douglas, the King's niece, the King's pleasure is that, if Lennox perform the covenants according to the King's expectation, and Lady Margaret and Lennox on seeing one the other shall agree and well like together for that purpose, he will both agree to the marriage and further consider Lennox's good service'.[60]

Lennox now led a naval expedition along the west coast of Scotland, aiming to seize strategic fortresses, kidnap Queen Mary and send her to England. It failed, and while Arran was defending Edinburgh against Hertford's onslaughts, Lennox mustered a small fleet, put his affairs in order and, on 28 May, sailed from Dumbarton for England to obtain support from King Henry and claim his bride.

On 7 June Lennox's ship put in at Chester, whence he rode to London, joining the court at St James's Palace[61] on 13 June. Chapuys had requested an audience with the King on that day, but thought it best to excuse himself 'on account of the arrival at court of Count [*sic*] Lennox'.[62]

At last, after nearly a year of negotiations, Margaret, now twenty-eight, came face to face with her bridegroom. Having no doubt heard of his reputation as one of the foremost gallant gentlemen of the Scottish court, she must have been delighted to find Matthew Stuart handsome and charming. 'Being well bred in the wars of France, he excelled in ability of body and dexterity of exercise. He was of strong body, well proportionate, of lusty and manly visage, straight in stature and pleasant in behaviour, wherefore at that time he was very pleasant in the sight of gentlewomen.'[63] 'He was, for manly courage and other virtues, as well of body as mind, inferior to none of his time.'[64]

The Royal Collection owns a full-length portrait, dating from the 1530s–40s, of a high-ranking gentleman wearing a splendid scarlet gown, doublet and hose, and a shirt with rich black-work embroidery. He stands against a mountainous landscape and cloudy blue sky. The painter is thought to have been a Netherlandish artist working in England. No one has ever successfully identified the sitter, although it has been suggested that he was Henry Fitzroy, Duke of Richmond, or Henry Howard, Earl of Surrey. But on the hilt of his sword there is a thistle, a symbol used as the emblem of Scotland since the thirteenth century, and on Scottish coins. The landscape in the background is perhaps meant to be a Scottish one, painted by an artist who had never seen Scotland. Thus it follows that the man in red was probably a Scot. His sumptuous costume, the rare (for its time) full-length outdoor pose and the quality of the painting show that he was of very high, probably noble, rank. His features compare closely with those of the older Lennox in his portrait at Hardwick Hall, notably the pointed chin, partly concealed in the latter by a sparse beard. It has been suggested that the sitter is quite young, but there is a strength and maturity in the jaw compatible with a man in his mid-twenties. Thus it is possible that this is a portrait of Lennox, painted in England to mark his marriage to Margaret.

His good looks aside, Margaret was probably already well disposed towards Lennox, for there was a possibility that he might yet become king of Scots and place a crown on her head. And this was the marriage her mother had wanted for her many years ago. Small wonder she felt it would 'banish my cares and my bliss augment'.[65]

It was said that, having seen Margaret, Lennox was so set on her that there was no question but that he would be true to the alliance.[66] Henry was now satisfied that the match could go ahead, and in June 1544 Sir Thomas Wriothesley, Chancellor of England, Charles

Brandon, Duke of Suffolk, Great Master of the Household, and Sir William Paget, one of the King's principal secretaries, were granted a commission 'to treat with Matthew, Earl of Lennox, touching the realm of Scotland and the marriage between him and the King's niece, Margaret, daughter of the late Queen of Scotland'.[67]

Lennox had been a little indisposed, for on 13 June the King's apothecaries supplied pills for him and special water for his eyes.[68] His ailments had presumably improved when on 26 June he met with the appointed Privy Councillors at Whitehall to sign the marriage treaty. In it were enshrined most of the articles of the Carlisle agreement, but Lennox now made over to Henry VIII his rights to the crown of Scotland[69] and promised to serve as his subject 'against all who impugn his right, title and authority in Scotland'. He also renounced 'all pacts contrary hereto with any of his own countrymen or others, and [to] serve the King against all princes and potentates, without exception'. Seeing that he was still a Scottish subject, this was a gross act of treachery.

Nevertheless he had evidently made a good impression on Henry, whose attitude towards him seems to have undergone a change: in the treaty Lennox was praised for his 'faithful and royal affection to his Majesty', and as he had made 'humble suit unto his Majesty for marriage with his Highness's niece, Lady Margaret Douglas, it hath pleased his Highness, for the good opinion he hath conceived of the said Earl's faithful loyal affection to his Majesty, upon an assured hope that the said marriage shall be an indissoluble knot-band of the said Earl's and his posterity's love towards his Highness and his most noble successors, to grant his suit therein'.

Lennox further bound himself to Henry by endowing his bride with lands within the earldom of Lennox, the sheriffdoms of Dumbarton,[70] Renfrew and Perth, and the lordship of Darnley, his subsidiary title, 'all which lands the Earl promises to be clearly worth yearly 500 marks [£102,470]'. Arran sneeringly valued these lands at less than £10,000 Scots (£768,900).[71] However, unless Lennox succeeded in all that he had promised Henry VIII to undertake, he was unlikely ever to be in a position to give Margaret those lands, so for 'more ample assurance of the said lands to the said Lady Margaret Douglas', he bound himself 'to do all and every such thing and things from time to time as shall be required by his Majesty or his Highness' heir'.

The King, in turn, was pleased to grant Lennox 'the marriage of Lady Margaret Douglas and, in recompense of the loss he will sustain in France by this submission, to give the Earl and her, in tail, lands to the clear yearly value of 6,800 marks Scots, which amounts to 1,700 marks sterling [£348,520]'. The bridegroom signed himself 'Matthew, Orle of Levinax', his phonetic spelling betraying a strong French accent.[72]

The treaty made it very plain that Henry VIII intended to play a prominent role in Scottish affairs.[73] The Scottish government was, not surprisingly, enraged by the betrothal and its terms, although in England there were those who thought that Margaret should be kept unmarried in case the young Queen Mary should die, in which case she might be married to her cousin, Prince Edward, and rule Scotland with him, rather than that the King had chosen to 'gratify' Lennox and 'put a perpetual obligation on him'.[74] In France an angry King Francis threw Lennox's unfortunate brother John into the Bastille, where he languished for three years.

On the day the treaty was signed, the King celebrated the betrothal with a feast at Whitehall Palace in Lennox's honour, attended by Henry's three children and 'divers other lords and ladies'. Five courses and a 'void' (a private banquet for select guests) were served. The day's festivities came to a climax with a 'supper at Hyde Park', at which, as at the feast, there were five courses.[75] No mention is made of Margaret herself being present, or of the Queen, although they may have been. There was no custom that precluded a woman attending her betrothal celebrations, but with the wedding only three days hence, both ladies perhaps had to forgo the pleasure in the interests of making their preparations.

8

'This Happy Match'

Margaret Douglas and Matthew Stuart were married on 29 June 1544 at St James's Palace, built by Henry VIII for Anne Boleyn between 1531 and 1536 on the site of a leper hospital. The red-brick gatehouse with its octagonal turrets survives today, adorned with Tudor roses and the initials of Henry and Anne, as do three rooms and the Chapel Royal, in which Margaret was married.

The date of the wedding is sometimes given as 6 July.[1] The confusion has seemingly arisen because on 10 July Chapuys reported that Lennox had 'arrived here [in London], and married this King's niece',[2] but on the morning of 29 June Chapuys had come to the court with letters from the Emperor to Henry VIII, 'without previously applying, as usual, for an audience, lest there should be delay in the granting of it owing to this King's many occupations, and principally to the solemnity of the marriage about to be celebrated of Count [sic] Lennox and Dame Marguerite [sic] Douglas, the King's niece. I found that the King was not yet ready to receive me in his chamber, owing principally to the solemnity of the marriage about to be [performed].' Later that day Chapuys informed the Emperor that 'the marriage of the Count [sic] of Lennox and Dame Margaret Douglas took place this morning at Mass, the King and Queen being present; and it is said that the King has promised the bridegroom and lady 3,000 or 4,000 ducats a year'.[3]

Margaret would have gone in procession from the Queen's apartments, which lay to the east of Friary Court, then down to the Great Court (now Colour Court) and so to the beautiful Chapel Royal, which still stands to the west of the gatehouse. She and Matthew exchanged their vows under the magnificent ceiling – thought to have been designed by the King's painter, Hans Holbein – that had been decorated with royal initials and coats of arms to mark the King's marriage to Anne of Cleves.[4]

Jousts followed the wedding, for which many soldiers had gathered in London.[5] The Lady Mary gave lavish gifts to Margaret 'at her marriage': a balas ruby with a table diamond and three pendant pearls, a pendant depicting St George and the Dragon set with diamonds, one gold brooch with a balas ruby depicting the story of Susanna and the Elders, another gold brooch with an emerald portraying 'the story of Solomon', a third set with a little diamond showing the history of Moses, and a fourth 'of the history of David' set with a diamond and a ruby; a brooch portraying Noah's flood 'set with many little diamonds and rubies', and one portraying 'how Christ healed the man of the palsy, a table diamond in the same'. Sometime afterwards Mary gave 'my cousin Margaret Lennox' two brooches of gold with large sapphires, another with an emerald with the story of Solomon – presumably Margaret had so liked the first that Mary had another fashioned for her – and a brooch with 'a helmet of mother of pearl standing in a touchstone garnished with gold'.[6]

'This happy match', as the antiquary William Camden called it, was successfully consummated, and a child was conceived almost immediately. Happiness in marriage was never a given in an age in which most unions were arranged for profit or advantage, but Margaret was exceptionally lucky, for the evidence shows that she and her bridegroom were soon lovers in every sense. 'He was in my power, and I his true bride.'[7]

Margaret was a Catholic, while Lennox, ever the pragmatist looking to his own advantage, bent with the wind. Having re-embraced the Catholic faith of his youth at Henry VIII's behest, he was never as committed to it as his wife, and would later turn Protestant, demonstrating that religion was ever a matter of expediency for him. Yet the couple were always to be happy in their marriage and devoted to each other, managing to surmount the difference in religion that could have divided them. This is evidenced by their letters, in which Margaret called her husband 'Mathieu' (the French version of his name, which was probably how he spoke it), while he called her his 'own sweet Madge', or 'Meg', told her she was his 'chiefest comfort', and signed himself 'your own Mathieu and most loving husband'.[8] She was always to behave towards him with the 'matchless steadfastness' mentioned in her tomb epitaph, and he seems to have been so 'far in love' with her that he became 'wholly governed by his wife'.[9] It is clear that Margaret was the stronger character of the two, and the driving force and the dominant – if not domineering – partner in the relationship.

On 10 July Lennox became a naturalised Englishman.[10] This should have set the seal on his allegiance to England, but there was to come a time when the Crown would have cause to distrust him, for he had once become a French citizen, yet had betrayed Francis I. And now he, a claimant to the Scottish throne, was married to the King's niece, who had a claim to the English one. It was a formidable alliance, and for the couple themselves a match made in dynastic heaven – but others, in the years ahead, would have good reason to fear its consequences.

At Whitehall, on 12 July, in accordance with the marriage treaty, and to compensate Lennox for his losses in France and Scotland, the King issued Letters Patent granting him and Margaret property and estates in Yorkshire, Lancashire and Durham to the value of 1,700 marks (£340,780) per annum. The greater part of these lands had come to the King when Jervaulx Abbey was dissolved, and they mostly comprised estates on the north-eastern border of the Yorkshire Dales. The rest – including two great houses, Temple Newsam and Settrington House – had been confiscated from Thomas, Lord Darcy, Sir Francis Bigod and Sir James Strangeways, all of whom had been attainted for their involvement in the Pilgrimage of Grace,[11] or made over to the King by the childless Henry Percy, Earl of Northumberland, who had died in 1537. Almost certainly Henry VIII hoped that Lennox would create a strong and loyal affinity in the Papist north, or would at least put a brake on subversive activity in the area. This argues that up till now, Margaret had followed the King's lead in religion, remaining Catholic in her observances but displaying no loyalty to the Pope. In fact, for all her piety, this seems to have remained her stance throughout her life, for there is scant evidence of her having any dealings with Rome, and no Pope ever properly espoused her cause.[12] Yet Henry miscalculated badly in establishing Margaret in Yorkshire, the heartland of the old religion, as time would prove.

The properties given to the Lennoxes were granted 'in tail'; in other words, they were to be directly inherited by the heirs of the bodies of the recipients, and could not form part of Margaret's jointure were she to be widowed. That meant that all she would then have to support her would be the Scottish lands settled on her by Lennox, but as they remained confiscated, she could never receive them unless Lennox emerged victorious in Scotland.[13]

The Lennoxes did not have houses in all the estates granted them by the King. Most of these lands were a source of rents that would provide them with 'a convenient living', or income. For example, forty-six tenants are recorded at Settrington, paying a total of £57.6s.5d. (£17,630) in rent annually. Their names – and Margaret clearly came to know them all – recur again and again in the records: Dodsworths, Fothergills, Nesbits, Bells, Hungates, Blenkoes and a Thomasina Percy, among others. Simon Dodsworth was bailiff 'long before' Margaret's death. Thomas Fowler of Settringham was to play an important role in Margaret's life, and served her for years, rising from clerk of the kitchen to become her secretary and later her treasurer, and he would remain faithful to her until she died.[14]

The Lennox estates were administered by stewards on the Earl and Countess's behalf. In 1598 Robert Dolman was to state that he and his father had served the family as stewards and receivers for sixty years.[15] In the 1560s there would also be two other stewards, Richard Norton, a former captain of Berwick, and Sir Marmaduke Constable.[16] All were Catholics, and Constable's great-uncle Robert had been executed by Henry VIII for his leadership of the Pilgrimage of Grace.

Lennox's secretary, Thomas Bishop, would later assert that 'my lady and he [Lennox], to the evil bruit of the country, hath defaced castles and manors, and sold away the lead, timber, brick and stones, and as I think never in their days spent one hundred marks in building'.[17] The contentious Thomas Bishop, who was in time to incur the enmity of the Lennoxes, was a hostile observer, and he was probably exaggerating; what he later said about them was almost certainly a tissue of truth, half-truths and lies. This was an age in which much of the fabric of the dissolved religious houses had been appropriated for local building, and the Lennoxes not only had monastic properties to plunder but also several houses of their own; and they were inveterate builders, as will be seen.

There seems to have been mutual animosity from the first between Margaret and Thomas Bishop. He has been called vicious, treacherous, and 'the most determined mischief-maker'.[18] He himself insisted that he was 'of honest nature', but the Lennoxes later laid to his charge – and he did not deny it – that Henry VIII came to repent of giving him a living for 'the faithful service which [the King] supposed [Bishop] had done for the Earl, understanding that he went about to set dissension and debate between the Earl and his lady'.[19] They claimed that the King was enraged to hear that Bishop had tried to come between them.[20] There is plenty of other evidence that Bishop was a troublemaker, but he was to insist that Margaret had been out to disparage him all along. Much of his ill-feeling seems to have sprung from his resentment at her having undermined his influence with Lennox, 'seeking the rule of her husband' and urging him to dismiss Bishop from his service.[21] Since his association with Lennox was his likeliest route to preferment at court, that threat was enough to make Bishop hate Margaret, the interloper in a hitherto satisfactory partnership, and in time he would exact a terrible revenge.

As well as great estates, Henry VIII gave the Lennoxes lavish gifts of costly clothing. Between 1542 and 1547 Margaret received over 1,040 yards of rich fabrics from his silk store at Whitehall, and 248 ells of linen, in equal amounts to similar items given to the King's daughters, which served to underline her high status. At various dates she received cloth of tissue; cloth of gold in crimson, incarnate (red or rose), purple and blue; cloth of silver; velvet in black, crimson, incarnate, purple, russet, tawny and yellow; satin in black, crimson, incarnate, purple, tawny and white; damask in black, blue, crimson, murrey (mulberry), tawny, white and yellow; taffeta in black, crimson, incarnate and purple; sarsanet in black, crimson and red, murrey, purple, blue, violet, russet, tawny, white and yellow; 'bridges satin', or Satin de Bruges, a combination of silk and wool; Holland cloth (unbleached linen); Normandy cloth (used as a base for embroidery); and cambric. Lennox received a total of sixty-eight yards of materials: crimson cloth of gold, cloth of silver, crimson satin, crimson damask and white sarcanet. Some may have been for his wedding clothes.[22] Purple was reserved for the use of the King and his family, so none was issued to Lennox, although Margaret was permitted to wear it. Blue was the colour of royal mourning, and these fabrics were probably given to her early on in her marriage, for the saddest of reasons.

Through her marriage to Lennox Margaret immediately became involved in Anglo-Scottish politics, and she was loyally to support all the causes taken up by her husband. That must have been hard to begin with, because almost immediately Henry VIII expected Lennox to fulfil his side of the marriage treaty by returning to Scotland and taking Dumbarton. In July 1544 he was given command of sixteen ships and six hundred soldiers,[23] and early in August, unaware that Margaret was already pregnant, he was obliged to leave her in attendance on the Queen and sail north from Bristol. During these early years of her marriage she 'was always honourably entertained in England, as both her birth in respect of her kingly blood, and her calling in respect of her place, did worthily deserve'.[24]

Lennox began his campaign by making an alliance with the Irish, laying waste the shores of the Firth of Clyde and the Isle of Arran, and initially trying fruitlessly to win back the support of Angus, whose disaffection was now obvious. In leading this campaign, he was not acting solely as Henry VIII's puppet; as he wrote to Francis Talbot, Earl of Shrewsbury, in March 1545, he wanted 'revenge upon the King's enemies, and those who slaughtered my father and oppressed his house'.[25] The Scottish lords, outraged at Lennox's defection, expressed to Francis I the opinion that he had lost his senses.

King Henry, who was himself on campaign that summer, besieging Boulogne, was pleased with Lennox's progress. On 8 August he appointed him lieutenant of the north of England and southern Scotland, although they were empty titles since Lennox did not have the power bases to support them. The next day Queen Katherine, now acting as regent of England, wrote to the King that the good speed that Lennox had made was because 'he hath given himself to serve such a master whom God doth aid and support in all things. He might have served the French King, his old master, many years, and not attained such a victory of his enemies.'[26] But she was being over-optimistic.

On 8 September Henry wrote to Katherine: 'We pray you to give in our name our hearty blessings to all our children, and recommendations to our cousin Margett [sic] and the rest of the ladies and gentlewomen.'[27] The misspelling of Margaret's name was probably deliberate, for 'Margett' may have been Henry's pet name for her.

By the time she received this message Margaret must have known that she was expecting her first child. In Lennox's absence she had remained with the Queen, but later that year, when her pregnancy grew more advanced, she bade farewell to Katherine and to her friends at court and retired to Stepney Palace, east of London.

There had been a village at Stepney,[28] two miles east of the City, since Saxon times. During the sixteenth century suburbs grew up along the north bank of the Thames beyond London's walls; by 1548 the parish population numbered more than 1,700, and in the fifteenth and early sixteenth centuries it became fashionable for courtiers, knights, gentlemen and wealthy merchants to build houses in Stepney.

'The Old Palace' stood on Stepney Green, near St Dunstan's Church.[29] Commonly known as 'King John's Court' or 'King John's Palace', it had no connection with King John but had been built between 1450 and 1550 and boasted an impressive early Tudor gatehouse. Like Temple Newsam, it had been the property of Lord Darcy.[30] Margaret's aunt, the French Queen, had visited several times and dated letters there.[31] It was a twelve-roomed building described as 'standing on a kind of terrace, with elaborate chimney-pieces and a large oaken staircase'.[32] In 2013 the ditch, the walled moat, the boundary walls, the foundations of the gatehouse, and indications of a bridge across the moat were excavated, and fine sixteenth-century glassware in the fashion of Venice was uncovered. Other finds included a fashionable man's shoe with cuts, such as Henry VIII himself wore, and Tudor bowling balls, suggesting that the house had a bowling alley.[33] There is no record of Stepney Palace ever having been in royal ownership, and it does not feature on the list of properties granted to Lennox, so he or the King must have leased it for Margaret. Katherine Parr is known to have visited her there.[34]

Margaret did not see her new husband for many months. Lennox 'was not so fortunate as he might have been' and achieved neither the King's objective, Dumbarton, nor his own, which was to be revenged on Arran and the turncoat Angus.[35] In fact, having landed at Dumbarton and claimed it for England, he and his men had had to flee for their lives. In Scotland his 'shameless conduct' was deplored,[36] and much later Thomas Bishop, who was with him at Dumbarton, would assert that, rather than fight, Lennox chose to 'return with shame to England',[37] but that was somewhat unfair, not least because of the treachery of his former ally, Glencairn. Lennox did succeed in taking Stirling, but was ejected when the garrison learned that his intention was to surrender it to Henry VIII. His ship was shot at when he sailed down the Clyde towards Dumbarton. In the late autumn of 1544, after invading Kintyre and raiding the coasts of Kyle of Lochalsh and Carrick, he returned briefly to Bristol. The season for campaigning was now over, and the taking of Dumbarton would have to await the spring. If he had not succeeded in his military objective, he had at least aided King Henry's cause by stirring up dissension in Scotland.[38]

Possibly Lennox saw Margaret during his brief visit to England, but early in November he was ordered by the King to go north again to Carlisle to negotiate with the Scots and press them to agree to the marriage of their Queen and Prince Edward; he was also enjoined to try once more to win back his father-in-law Angus to Henry's cause. Lennox spent the winter in Carlisle. During his absence he wrote to Margaret whenever he could. On 15 November 1544 the Earl of Shrewsbury, Cuthbert Tunstall and Ralph Sadler wrote from Darnton to the Council about their suspicions of one James Colquhoun, a Scotsman 'who pretends to be Lennox's servant and for his sake banished out of Scotland', and who had 'arrived with letters from Angus to Lady Margaret, and others to Lennox from the captain of Dumbarton'. William Murray, the Laird of Tullibardine, who was there when he arrived, 'seemed to suspect him to be a spy about Lennox', perhaps in the pay of Angus, so to be on the safe side Shrewsbury and Sadler sent Colquhoun's letters on to the Council.[39]

Lennox was instructed on 9 December that if Angus finally broke with him 'touching the King's affairs', 'out of regard for his honour, having married his daughter', he was to charge him with ingratitude to the King; if Angus offered to uphold the marriage of the Queen of Scots to Prince Edward and make peace with Henry VIII, Lennox was to say 'he cannot move in that matter' as the Scots had 'so little regarded their promises'; but if they wished to be trusted they should deliver the young Queen into the King's hands. Margaret was furious with what she saw as her father's treachery, and the fact that the recent birth of a son to him had displaced her as his heir, and the writer noted approvingly that 'it were well that Lennox took with him letters from his wife to her father complaining of his unkindness to the King and her and her husband, and requiring him to redub [make reparation for] the past'.[40]

Margaret suffered various ailments during her pregnancy. In January 1545 Thomas Alsopp, the royal apothecary, supplied her with liquorice (used to treat chest problems, migraines and constipation), boxes of powders for the breast, 'almond milk restrictive' (used as a substitute for cow's milk on fast days) and a conserve of quinces; it was believed that quinces strengthened the stomach and aided digestion. On 5 February she was prescribed a vial of 'aqua composita' – a preparation used to relieve stomach problems – and an ounce of 'worm-seed',[41] which kills off parasitical worms or treats dysentery and sickness, but would not nowadays be given to pregnant women because it is poisonous. It can cause foetal abnormalities and vaginal bleeding, and increase the risk of miscarriage. Margaret's use of it may have led to tragedy.

For a decade and more she was to be continuously occupied with bearing and rearing children. According to her tomb epitaph, she and Lennox had eight, 'to make our hearts glad':[42] the kneeling effigies of four boys and four girls can be seen on her tomb in Westminster Abbey. The first to arrive was a boy, born around the end of February 1545, probably at Stepney Palace. As proof of how far his father had identified himself with the English cause, he was given the name Henry, after the King, who was probably his godfather, and the English courtesy title Lord Darnley, rather than the Scottish title 'the Master of Lennox', traditionally borne by the heirs to the earldom. The lordship of Darnley, south-west of Glasgow, had been granted to Lennox's forebears in 1356.

Margaret's son was born prematurely at seven to eight months – he cannot have been conceived earlier than late June 1544.[43] It is possible that Margaret's ingestion of wormseed may have brought on a premature labour. It has been questioned whether an infant born at seven months would have survived in those days,[44] but there are instances of premature babies surviving in the Tudor period.[45] The Lady Mary gave 'to my cousin Margaret Lennox's son a lace of goldsmith's work set with little sparks of diamonds and rubies and xxi small pearls'.[46] This was probably a habiliment to edge the baby's cap or robe.

In the three years following his marriage, Lennox led five expeditions to harry the western coast of Scotland, all in attempts to take Dumbarton, 'in time of which journeys I was in displeasure with my lady', he later revealed,[47] showing that Margaret resented the long separations. He was obliged to remain in the north until the spring of 1546, so they were apart for more than a year.[48]

While Lennox was away in Scotland, Margaret seems to have stayed either at Stepney or at Wressle Castle, Yorkshire,[49] a once-magnificent moated stronghold of the Catholic Percys, substantially modernised in the early sixteenth century and acquired by the Crown on the childless Earl of Northumberland's death in 1537. In 1540 Leland had called it 'the most proper beyond [the River] Trent. The hall and chambers be fair, and so is the chapel and closets; so were the gardens within the moat and the orchards without', where there was fine topiary.[50]

On 8 February 1545 Angus, having been charged by Lennox with ingratitude to Henry VIII, let it be known that, 'whereas he was called the King's foe, he loved the King best of all men and if Lennox would obtain a truce for two months to commune with his friends in Scotland, he should be made chief ruler in Scotland, for, having married the woman whom Angus loved most in all the world, Angus loved him entirely'.[51] But it was merely a ploy to neutralise Lennox, for on 27 February, under the command of Angus, the Scots decisively defeated the English at the Battle of Ancrum Moor, near Jedburgh.

In September 1545 Henry VIII temporarily abandoned the plan to take Dumbarton, and sent Lennox to assist Hertford, who was still holding out against the Scots and French in the east. But in Lennox's absence, his army in the west disintegrated. He was now the most hated man in Scotland. On 1 October 1545 the Scottish Parliament attainted him and his brother Robert, the unconsecrated Bishop of Caithness, for treason, seized his lands – which were given to Arran and other lords – and deprived him of his earldom, although he continued to use the title 'Earl of Lennox'. Thus for the second time in her life Margaret, the Countess of Lennox, was styled by a title that was not rightfully hers.

Even though Lennox's Scottish lands and honours amounted to far less than those he held in England, their loss financially compromised the Earl and Countess for two decades, as they had to rely on the rents from the properties that Henry VIII had given them; moreover, Lennox's attainder was seriously to undermine his claim to the Scottish succession. Margaret, who had been deprived of the lands with which her husband had endowed her, stoutly supported him in his efforts to get back what he had lost.

In November Lennox made another futile attempt to take Dumbarton. Banished from Scotland as a traitor, he remained in the north, directing operations from Carlisle. He and Margaret both knew that if he attempted to enter Scotland, his life would be forfeit. Only by successfully bringing to fruition Henry VIII's plans could he return to the land of his birth.

In these years Margaret was chiefly occupied with domestic matters. On 2 April 1545 she received an ounce of spermaceti wax from the royal apothecary, Thomas Alsopp; this wax was used as an ointment or a cosmetic or to make candles. On 7 June Alsopp supplied her with 'mastick', an aromatic gum used for varnish or flavouring food. On 26 July she was given two plasters for her shoulders and an ointment, and a month later she got treacle for her pet monkey and two glasses of 'water of virgin's milk' for a skin blemish or blister. Early in August she visited Titchfield Abbey, Hampshire, the home of the Lord Chancellor, Sir Thomas Wriothesley, where Alsopp had left her 'with Mr Cromer' a box of quince conserve.[52] On 22 April Lord Wharton enclosed 'a letter from my lord of Lennox to my lady his wife' with one to the Earl of Shrewsbury.[53] Margaret may have been the 'Lady Douglas' who bought goods from the executors of Cromwell's nephew, Sir Richard Williams (who had adopted the surname Cromwell), on 20 November.[54]

Just over a week later, on 28 November, Margaret's infant son Henry died at Stepney, aged nine months. Prematurity may have accounted for his early demise, or the wormseed his mother took in late pregnancy. He was buried in St Dunstan and All Saints, Stepney, an ancient church dating from the tenth century and rebuilt largely in the fifteenth, which still stands. The memorial raised by the grieving parents to their firstborn has now disappeared, but in 1631 the antiquary John Weever described it as a slab in the floor of the upper end of the thirteenth-century chancel, situated east of the font and adorned with many small coats of arms. The brass inscription read: 'Here lieth Henry Stuart, Lord Darnley, of the age of three-quarters of a year, late son and heir to Matthew, Earl of Lennox, and the Lady Margaret his wife, which Henry deceased the twenty-eight day of November in the year of God 1545, whose soul Jesus pardon.'[55] In 1786 the church wardens recorded that there were 'many monuments, tombs and vaults in the church and chancel of St Dunstan's Stepney in a ruinous state'. Little Lord Darnley's was probably one of them, and since there was no one interested in restoring it, it was irrevocably lost.[56]

Undoubtedly Margaret had vested her dynastic hopes in her firstborn; she allegedly 'at the death of her first son' consulted 'prophesiers', who told her that 'her son should be king both of England and Scotland'.[57] If this is true, she must have been desperate to know whether she would have other sons who could fulfil her ambitions, but the source is Thomas Bishop, so it is hostile and therefore suspect.

There is no evidence to support the assertion that Margaret was at Temple Newsam when her son died.[58] It was probably at this time that the royal wardrobe issued her with cloth of gold, damask and sarsanet, all in blue, the colour of royal mourning. The grief of bereavement may have affected her health, for in December she was prescribed several medicines by Thomas Alsopp: a fomentation, or poultice, ointment, a plaster for stomach ache, a plaster for her back, two sponges, sugar candy (then regarded as an aid to digestion) and 'lozenges of diadragantum', used for diarrhoea or coughs. In January and February 1546 more lozenges, pills and sugar candy were supplied by the apothecary, as well as 'pills for my lord' and medicaments 'for two of her women, one a powder, another a purgation and liquorice'.[59] Margaret conceived again soon after Lennox's return home, probably in the middle of March.

It was around this time that Queen Katherine is known to have written letters to Margaret, who was still at Stepney, and several other people.[60] At a time when the King was clamping down on heresy, the Queen was becoming nervous about her secret adherence to the new faith and, fearful that the Catholic party at court might move against her, was seeking support.[61] She may even have been warning her friends to hide or destroy any compromising books. Margaret, as a Catholic, would not have needed such a warning, but Katherine may have been asking her not to betray any secrets.

By May 1546 Lennox had mustered more ships and men, and again he moved on Dumbarton, demanding that its governor surrender it. The governor admitted Lennox into the castle, but Arran laid siege to it, and Lennox was forced to abandon the project and flee back to England, knowing that he faced a long exile and a fight to regain his inheritance. It did not help that Angus's brother, Robert, had gone over to Arran, seduced by the return of his confiscated revenues.

In May 1546 'my Lady Margaret Douglas' is listed after the Lady Mary and the Lady Elizabeth as one of 'the ladies ordinary [customary] attendant at the court'. She was also one of 'the Queen's ordinary accustomed to be lodged within the King's Majesty's house'.[62] She was at court in July for the official reception of Claude d'Annebault, Admiral of France, the new French ambassador. A host of lords, ladies and courtiers were summoned to attend on him at Greenwich and accompany him to London and thence to Hampton Court. The Ladies Mary and Elizabeth, Anne of Cleves and the duchesses of Richmond and Suffolk were also present. The ladies of the Queen's privy chamber are listed separately, so Margaret was evidently not one of them at this time.[63]

That summer the religious conservatives at court persuaded the King to agree to an investigation into the Queen's household and her religious beliefs. Warned in time, and seeing herself facing death at the stake, Katherine Parr threw such a fit of hysterics that Henry came to see her and she managed to convince him of her innocence.[64] Margaret was not implicated in any way; her compliance in religion seems not to have been in doubt.

That year she and Lennox continued to suffer from intermittent minor ailments. In April he was prescribed more pills, after which his complaint seems to have gone away, but her health issues may have been connected with pregnancy. In April and May she was given oxirodium, 'an ointment, a glass with diaciton', used to cure melancholy and other distempers in the brain, a plaster for her stomach, and a box of '*manus Christi*' – sweet boiled candy made with gold leaf. Between June and September she received various other remedies including senna 'cods' for the relief of constipation, and kidney plasters. At various times during the period 1544–6 Thomas Alsopp supplied glass containers used for the examination of urine, a common diagnostic practice in those days.[65]

On 29 September Henry Whitreason, 'receiver to the right noble Matthew, Earl of Lennox and Lady Margaret his wife', petitioned the King to pay for a whole host of expenses incurred by his employers during the past year. These open a few windows on the Lennoxes' daily life at this time. 'Money delivered to my lady' amounting to £280 (£56,140) on 23 and 31 December 1545 was probably for Christmas celebrations and gifts. Two London mercers received 'by my lord's warrant' a total of £70 (£14,000) for supplying rich fabrics.

Among those who received fees were the Lennoxes' stewards and bailiffs, and those responsible for 'the game and wood in Wensleydale'. Margaret's devotion to her faith is evident in the annuities, stipends and other charges paid to eight chantry priests, all – as was customary Catholic practice then – styled with the courtesy title 'Sir': Sir John Cancefeld, Sir Peter Glentham and Sir Martin Wardman at York Minster; Sir John Kay at Leeming, Yorkshire; Sir Richard Waddell and Sir John Wilde at Lazenby; and Sir Thomas Swadale and Sir Thomas Middelton at Bedale. William Knockes, 'my lord's falconer', who bought Lennox a goshawk, was on the list, as was Margaret Maxton, the Countess's former attendant, who was paid 'a whole year's annuity' of £10 (£2,000).

William Mompesson got a 'half year's fee, for keeping the house or manor at Temple Hirst', a former preceptory of the Knights Templar, now owned by the Lennoxes. A bricklayer of York had received a fee for viewing 'the faults at Temple Newsam', and two plumbers had been paid 'to value the lead' at another of the Lennoxes' Yorkshire properties, Whorlton Castle, and 'for taking down and melting the lead'.

A baker of York had been paid for 'baking a red deer that went to London', likewise the man who conveyed 'a barrel of fresh sturgeon from York to London', and two others for barley, beans and peas. A Mr Bates was paid 'for a gelding bought of him for my lord'. Edmund Andrews, fishmonger, of London, received £9.11s.8d. (£1,921).[66]

By December 1546 Margaret had taken up residence at Temple Newsam. This imposing mansion was situated five miles east of Leeds in the West Riding of Yorkshire, and the surrounding estate comprised about four thousand acres, extending east from Leeds to Swillington, and south from Whitkirk to Rothwell. There had been a property on the site since Saxon times, and 'Neuhusam', meaning 'new houses', was recorded in the Domesday Book as the former property of two thanes, Dunstan and Glunier. It was granted by William the Conqueror to Ilbert de Lacy, but from c.1155 until 1308 it was in the possession of the Knights Templar, hence the addition of the name Temple; it was this fortified preceptory that was immortalised as Templestowe in Sir Walter Scott's *Ivanhoe*.[67]

After the Templar Order was suppressed in 1307, Temple Newsam was confiscated by Edward II, whose son, Edward III, granted it to Marie de St Pol, Countess of Pembroke and foundress of Pembroke College, Cambridge. When she died in 1377 it passed to the Darcy family. Around 1517–35, on the site of the older building, Thomas Darcy built what has been called 'the Hampton Court of the north': a palatial square Tudor house of pink diaper-patterned brickwork with stone quoins, projecting rectangular bays and tall mullioned windows. He did not enjoy it long, for he was executed in 1537 for his involvement in the Pilgrimage of Grace, and the mansion reverted to the Crown. The great house that survives today, which partially replaced Darcy's, is an E-plan one dating mostly from the first half of the seventeenth century and later, and it was much restored in Victorian times.[68]

Archaeological excavations and an inventory made in 1565 have shown that the quadrangular house Margaret knew was built on a collegiate plan around a courtyard, with a porter's lodge and gatehouse (on the site of the present North Hall) in the north wing. There were two galleries, probably in this gatehouse wing, described as 'the gallery' and 'the new gallery', which suggests that the Lennoxes added the latter. In 1565 it contained a pair of old organs (small portable musical instruments) worth 40s. (£350). There was a chapel, of which the small Tudor doorway survives, where the family would have attended Mass. Next to it was the chapel chamber and a 'low wardrobe' containing (in 1565) an old dripping pan, a lute, a crossbow and arrows.

In the south wing was a great hall with an 'outer entry' from the courtyard at the eastern screens end and a dais at the west end. Almost certainly the hall soared to the full height of the house. Beneath were vast cellars, which can still be seen. In 1565 they contained 'four empty hogsheads, one cupboard, one pail and the gantries [wooden stands for barrels]'.[69]

Recent excavations made beyond the hall suggest that a polygonal tower housed a staircase leading into the western range – the only range that survives today from the Lennoxes' house, with its interior much remodelled, and rooms added at either end. The first floor of this wing housed the couple's private apartments, the chief of which was their great chamber, accessed through an antechamber. Here too were the ladies' chamber and the gentlewomen's chamber (used by Margaret's attendants), the nursery, a closet and the Earl's bedchamber. The present 'Gothick Room' was then a high-status chamber, for it extended to the whole width of the building, had bays at either end, and was hung with tapestries. A pencil sketch of Lord Darcy's crest survives in the stonework to the left of the bay window, where a moulded sixteenth-century arch is covered by eighteenth-century decoration. This may have been Lennox's bedchamber. A perpendicular Tudor fireplace and ribbed ceiling survive in another first-floor room.

The 'high wardrobe' was probably on the top floor; here were stored clothes, personal effects and unused furnishings. There was a chamber on its south side, and others leading off from that. In the present-day Tudor Room on the second floor, a perpendicular stone fireplace and doorway arches remain from Lord Darcy's time. The ground floor probably provided lodgings for the household officers, while the rest of the servants would have bedded down in the 'retainers' wing'.

That wing – the service range – stood on the eastern side of the courtyard. It contained the musicians' chamber, the steward's room (the steward being in charge of the 'downstairs' household), another nursery, the tailors' room, the schoolmaster's chamber, 'the Langstroppe chamber',[70] and a new chamber – again, probably one of the Lennoxes' improvements. The service range was connected to the eastern end of the hall range, where there were kitchens, a wet larder, a dry larder, a buttery, a pantry, a brewhouse and a patisserie.

The inventory shows that there were about as many rooms in the Lennoxes' house as there are in Temple Newsam today, and that they were arranged on a similar plan, although the level of the courtyard has been raised since their day.[71]

The 1565 inventory lists little in the way of furniture apart from beds, but several paintings. There were nine in the great chamber, 'some very small and some bigger', and they included portraits of Margaret herself, her husband, their second son, Lord Darnley, Margaret Tudor, Henry VIII, Mary I, Philip II of Spain and Lennox's brother, John Stuart, Seigneur of Aubigny. That room also contained six 'hangings of old imagery' and a tester (cloth of estate) of cloth of gold and silver 'with the arms of the Earl and his wife embroidered, and curtains of yellow and white sarcanet'. In Lord Darnley's chamber there were six tapestries depicting hunting and hawking, a bedstead with gilt posts, twelve feather beds and fourteen bolsters. Lennox's magnificent bed in the Earl's chamber was decked out with a tester of cloth of gold and purple velvet, on which were embroidered the royal arms of England, and crimson damask curtains. It was valued at £70 (£12,170). No separate bedchamber is designated as the Countess's, so this great bed, with its emblems of sovereignty, was Margaret's marriage bed, and a fitting place for the conception of potential heirs to the throne.[72]

Temple Newsam was to come to mean more to Margaret than just another grand house. Its links with the Catholic Darcy family and the Pilgrimage of Grace perhaps had resonance with her, and in a region where the Pilgrimage was vividly remembered and many nursed bitter grievances against the King's religious reforms and the Dissolution of the Monasteries. Margaret, who was to become identified with the Catholic cause, would in time make Temple Newsam a major centre for the old faith in the north.

If Margaret had indeed consulted a seer, it may have seemed to her that the prophesier's words looked very much like being fulfilled with the birth of the second Lord Darnley. It was perhaps because she had hopes of his one day wearing two crowns that she named him, as she had named his brother, after her ageing uncle, Henry VIII, who was probably godfather to both. This longed-for child was born on 7 December 1546 at Temple Newsam. In 1715 Ralph Thoresby, the Leeds antiquarian, stated that 'the identical apartment in which Lord Darnley was born remained in his time, and was distinguished by the name of the King's Chamber'. By the time Thomas Whitaker published his edition of Thoresby's work in 1816, that room could not be identified.[73]

There has been some debate over the year of Lord Darnley's birth. According to the continuator of John Knox's history, he was not yet twenty-one when he married in July 1565, placing his birth in 1544, which is impossible, since his parents only married in July that year and his brother, born in 1545, had been styled Lord Darnley as Lennox's heir. A 1563 copy of a portrait of Darnley executed in 1562 states that he was seventeen, implying a date of birth in 1545–6; and Margaret's epitaph too dates his birth to 1545–6. Given this evidence, it has often been stated that he was born in December 1545. But Margaret had given birth to the first Lord Darnley in late February that year, which means that she would have had to conceive and bear a child within nine months. Moreover, at the time when she would have conceived, Lennox was still in Scotland. In March 1566 a messenger sent by Mary, Queen of Scots, to her uncle, Charles de Guise, Cardinal of Lorraine, stated that Darnley was nineteen years old.[74] Thus he was born in 1546.

Six of Margaret's eight children died young, and the names of her four daughters are unrecorded. Given that she bore her last child in 1557, when she was forty-one, and that a study of aristocratic births in the sixteenth century shows that most women had their menopause in their thirties, it is likely that the daughters were all born before 1556. The fact that their effigies, and those of the two sons who were lost in infancy, show them as grown children does not necessarily mean that they survived babyhood; they may have died before baptism. The effigies of the daughters are of different sizes, possibly for architecturally aesthetic reasons, but perhaps suggesting that some lived longer than others. One was born in 1552, and two are recorded as being alive in 1562; the slender evidence we have suggests that they died that year. The other two daughters were probably dead by 1565. The Temple Newsam inventory records crimson velvet and satin bearing cloths trimmed with ermine, in which Margaret's infants were wrapped for their christenings.[75]

This dismal obstetric account echoes those of other members of Margaret's family. The Tudors had a poor record when it came to producing heirs. Margaret's mother had had six children by James IV, of whom one lived beyond infancy. Her grandparents, Henry VII and Elizabeth of York, had had seven children, but only three survived into adulthood. Her uncle Henry VIII had fathered fifteen children by his wives and mistresses, seven of them sons; of these, only five daughters[76] grew to maturity.

The loss of her little ones had a heavy impact on Margaret and her husband. 'But Death unto life found daily a foe: six of our children away from us bent; in tender youth he laid them down low, whose loss with tears we did much lament; but yet with God's will we stood well content, Whose divine working we could not withstand, Who maketh and killeth in turning a hand.'[77]

Towards the end of 1546 Henry VIII's health deteriorated. Later Thomas Bishop would claim that the King and Margaret had a bitter dispute, which allegedly took place in Henry's final months, for Bishop refers to a grant of land he received 'a little before [the King's] death, and after the breach with my Lady Lennox'.[78] It has sometimes been assumed that the King objected to Margaret's attachment to the Church of Rome,[79] but Bishop later stated that the King was so angered by false accusations made by the Lennoxes about him that Margaret 'ever after lost a part of his heart, as appeared at his death'.[80] This tells us much about Bishop's over-inflated sense of self-importance, since Henry VIII is hardly likely to have fallen out with Margaret on account of her unspecified allegations against a servant[81] – unless Bishop wasn't telling the whole story, and had in fact been the cause of trouble between her and her uncle. The latter is a more plausible explanation, since Bishop's statements are suspiciously vague and doubt has very rightly been cast on their veracity.[82] Certainly between 1546 and 1553 Bishop was dismissed from the Lennoxes' service, which would account for his enmity towards them, and it may have been to justify that dismissal that Margaret made accusations against him to Henry VIII – although whether they were false or not is another matter.

Bishop also claimed that the breach with Margaret became apparent at the King's death, and so it may have seemed, because when Henry came to make his will in December 1546, he excluded Margaret Tudor's heirs from the succession: the Queen of Scots, not just because she was an alien, but because he was determined that she should marry his son; and Margaret, perhaps on the grounds that she was of dubious legitimacy, but more likely because Henry did not want the Scots or the duplicitous Lennox ruling England. Some writers have accepted that there was a breach, and that that was the reason why Henry passed over Margaret in his will,[83] but far too much has been made of this alleged quarrel,[84] and there were more compelling reasons for her exclusion. It should be remembered that Henry had never once named Margaret as his heir.

Possibly Henry's true reason for excluding Margaret was the same reason why he had excluded her from the Act of Succession, which was to remove a dynastic threat to his son.[85] Lennox's claim to the Scottish throne could only be pressed if the little Queen of Scots died, and then he would have had Arran to contend with, for each claimed a prior right. It would not have suited Henry to have his subject ruling autonomously north of the border, and he would have been aware that Lennox had turned his coat to serve his own interests before and was not to be trusted. Once King of Scots, Matthew's ambitions might extend to the throne of England, to which his wife had a claim, although it is highly unlikely that the xenophobic English would have rejected Henry VIII's heirs in favour of Margaret and her Scottish husband. Almost certainly Henry's chief considerations were to prevent England coming under Scottish rule, and to smooth the way for the two kingdoms to be united through the marriage of Edward to Mary, Queen of Scots.[86] Whatever his reasons, his exclusion of the Lennoxes from the succession must have been devastating for them.[87]

Having thus passed over the line of his elder sister, Henry left the throne – failing any issue of his body – 'to the heirs of the body of the Lady Frances, our niece, eldest daughter of our late sister, the French Queen', and failing those to the heirs of her younger daughter, Eleanor.[88] The King's will had legal force, since the 1544 Act of Succession had provided for him to leave the throne to his children, in turn, and then to whomsoever he chose.

On 28 January 1547 Henry VIII died at Whitehall Palace. Giving the lie to Thomas Bishop's calumnies, Phillips's *Commemoration* reveals that Margaret mourned him deeply: 'My griefs did increase, my plaints did abound, and with me all England themselves did bestow to wail for his want. A Mars was he named, such was his power, not Hector could gain more honour in [the] field.' While Henry lived, she had had a strong advocate and generous protector; now that he was dead, she would be cast adrift into a very different world.

9

'Great Unnaturalness'

Henry VIII was succeeded by his nine-year-old son, Edward VI, and England, like Scotland, became subject to a regency council. It was headed by the new King's uncle, Edward Seymour, now Duke of Somerset, who was determined to carry on the war against Scotland. That spring Margaret visited Hampton Court with the infant Darnley, and there the Scottish ambassador, Sir Adam Otterbourne, saw her present her son to the young King.[1] She was obviously hoping for great things for him. Several noble boys were being brought up and educated with Edward, and Darnley, with his royal Tudor blood, was an obvious choice.

But her reception was cool.[2] The court – and the religious climate – had changed. Henry VIII had remained a Catholic all his life, but he had appointed reformers to the Council who would govern for his son. The young King had long been under the influence of reformist tutors, his uncle, Somerset, and Queen Katherine Parr, all of whom had been secret Protestants in Henry's reign. The boy was ready openly and fervently to embrace the reformed faith, and under the governance of the Council the kingdom officially turned Protestant.

It must have been early in the new reign that the Lennoxes moved against one John Hume, who is described by John Foxe in his *Acts and Monuments* ('The Book of Martyrs') as Lennox's servant. They had him arrested for denying the Sacrament to be the real flesh and blood of Christ, and for saying that he would never doff his bonnet to it, even if he were sentenced to be burned at the stake for it, and that if he heard Mass he would be damned. The Lennoxes sent him 'with special letters' to Archbishop Cranmer, demanding that Hume be punished for his offences, which legally still amounted to heresy. But Foxe could find no record of his execution,[3] probably because neither the new government nor Cranmer was willing to proceed against a man whose views corresponded with their own.

As a Catholic, Margaret was out of place in Edward's court. The new Protestant regime must have been inimical to her, and the pious young King – England's 'new Josiah' – was a cold, distant child who, while he might show courtesy and refer to her as 'my cousin Marget',[4] stood much on ceremony and did not approve of her beliefs. His sister Mary was to spend the years of her brother's reign at her country houses, fighting for the right to hear Mass, which had been declared illegal. Margaret engaged in no such dispute, and seems – outwardly at least – to have complied with the law.

As the young King was unmarried, there were no places for women at his court anyway, save on official occasions when they were required to accompany their husbands. Katherine Parr, to whom Margaret had been close, had left court and retired to the royal palace at Chelsea. In the spring of 1547 she secretly married the Protector's brother, Thomas, Lord Seymour, which caused a great scandal as Henry VIII had been dead for less than three months. The Lady Elizabeth went to live with her stepmother, but after Seymour made improper advances to her she was sent away for her own protection. Later, after Katherine's death in childbirth in September 1548, Elizabeth came under suspicion when Seymour was tried for treason, for it was believed that she had treasonably intrigued to marry him. Following his execution in March 1549 she too stayed away from court, making every effort to retrieve her tarnished reputation.

Thus there was no more than an occasional ceremonial role for Margaret in the new order, and little hope of preferment for Darnley. She retired to Yorkshire and remained there for most of the six years of Edward's reign, running her household, bearing the girl babies who were to die young, and supervising Darnley's education. Rarely did she go to court.

Lennox, who was pragmatic in matters of religion, remained in favour with the regency government. He was useful to Somerset, for he funded, from his own pocket, an army of spies whose purpose was to infiltrate the Scottish government and supply their master with valuable information, which he passed on to the English Council. Thus Somerset learned what the Scots and their French allies intended, and much about the rugged Scottish topography, which had long confounded the English. Indeed the maps that Lennox acquired were still in use in the 1590s.[5] Lennox was prepared to serve Somerset, but with the 'sole motive' of revenging himself on the Hamiltons, which happily coincided with the Protector's objective of establishing an English presence on the Clyde.[6] In the early autumn of 1547 he even supported Somerset's campaign to force the Scots to marry their Queen to Edward VI and stand with England against Rome. Stationed at Carlisle with Lord Wharton, he led a diversionary assault on western Scotland while Somerset invaded the east. Lennox ravaged the western Marches and Annandale, captured Dumfries, and sustained wounds.

His father-in-law, Angus, was fighting on the opposing side. His defection had angered Margaret, and left no question as to where her loyalties lay, but his years in exile had strengthened his character, and he had now proved his loyalty, his ability and his wisdom to his countrymen, which did much to improve the popularity of the Douglases in Scotland. When the Scots, led by Arran, were bloodily defeated at the Battle of Pinkie Cleugh, near Musselburgh, on 10 September 1547, Angus won fame for his brave command of the van. But the English were now entrenched in south-eastern Scotland, and the Scots were obliged to hasten the young Queen away to Inchmahome Priory, which stood on an island in the Lake of Menteith, near Stirling, more than fifty miles north-west of Edinburgh.

By 7 October Lennox had rejoined Margaret at Wressle Castle, where he raised troops from his local tenants and followers.[7] By December he was back at Carlisle,[8] and early in 1548 he and Wharton invaded Scotland. Angus's brother-in-law, Robert, Master of Maxwell, promised to join them at Dumfries with two thousand men, and sent ten hostages to Lord Wharton as sureties for that; but when Lennox appeared before Dumfries, Maxwell's force was nowhere to be seen. Wharton, meanwhile, had tried to ambush Angus's forces at Drumlanrig, intent on capturing him and punishing him for his treachery, but Angus defeated him and escaped to Edinburgh. According to a later report by the malevolent Thomas Bishop, Lennox had failed to go to Wharton's aid because he was sixteen miles away 'sleeping in his bed'.[9] By 3 January Lennox and Wharton had retreated to Carlisle, where Lennox, enraged at Maxwell's treachery, convened a court to deal with the hostages. Four were hanged.[10]

That January Lennox was gratified to learn that Arran had abandoned a plan to marry his son, another James Hamilton, to Queen Mary, yet was dismayed to hear that Arran was negotiating for her to be sent to safety in France, where she was to marry the Dauphin

Francis. In February 1548 the Scottish Parliament formally approved the match, in return for which the French had promised to send troops to expel the English from Scotland.

Late in February, after Angus had attempted to entrap him at Drumlanrig Castle, Lennox, having failed to take Dumfries, was forced to flee south into England, and by 6 March he had returned to Margaret at Wressle.[11] He had lost any support that had remained to him in Scotland, and Wharton found it 'displeasant to see the small estimation he hath with those which are of his own blood in that realm'.[12] Somerset, in recognition of his efforts in Scotland, bestowed on Lennox the office of castellan of Wressle Castle, a paltry reward commensurate with his achievements.[13]

Lennox took no further active part in the war, which dragged on ineffectively for another year. In the spring he was at Carlisle, poised for instructions, but he had returned to Margaret at Temple Newsam by the middle of June. Thereafter the Lennoxes had leisure to enjoy their great estates, and they resided mainly at Temple Newsam, their chief seat in the late 1540s and 1550s.[14]

Living in palatial splendour in Yorkshire, at a safe distance from London, the Lennoxes were able to intrigue in secret, as they were to do for the rest of their lives. Margaret discreetly opened their house – which already had strong associations with the old religion thanks to its connection with the Pilgrimage of Grace – to her fellow Catholics, and made it the most important centre for the old religion in the kingdom, much to the irritation of the government, which remained suspicious of the Lennoxes' activities. Yet the couple never did anything overtly to arouse censure.[15]

Lennox corresponded with his brother, Robert, Margaret with her Douglas connections and occasionally with her father, Angus, with whom her relations were marred by bitterness at what she clearly saw as his disloyal support of the French faction in Scotland. It had placed her in an embarrassing position. And there was bad blood between Lennox and Angus because of what had happened at Drumlanrig, which put paid to the appeals that Lennox had made to his father-in-law for aid in securing the restitution of his Scottish estates.[16]

Margaret's cousin, the flame-haired James Douglas, Master of Morton, was the second son of George Douglas, Angus's brother. Contemporaries remarked on his majestic countenance, yet his character belied that, for he was boorish, illiterate and greedy. Seduced by a pension from Henry II, the new King of France, Morton had abandoned his alliance with Somerset and come out for the French party in Scotland. In June 1548 a French army succeeded in cutting a swathe through the occupied territories and capturing Haddington, but the forces of William, Lord Grey de Wilton, had driven Morton, his kinsmen and his adherents out of Dalkeith Palace; they had been taken hostage and were now being escorted south on their way to the Tower of London. From Edinburgh, on 20 June, Angus, who had been obliged to give up his bastard son, George Douglas, as one of the hostages, urged Margaret to aid her relations:

Dearest daughter,

After my most tender commendations and heartly blessing, this is to advertise you that, through mischance and undertrust, as I believe, the house of Dalkeith was destroyed, and taken forth of it our cousin [Archibald Douglas], the Laird of Glenbervie, the Master of Morton, George my son, David Home of Wedderburn [Angus's brother-in-law], and Alexander his uncle. Praying you, with the advice of your husband, to see if ye can get them, or part of them, put in friends' hands and gently treated there; and specially the Laird of Glenbervie, that is one sickly, tender man and has nine motherless bairns. Let George lie in pledge for him as your wisdom thinks best. And make my hearty commendation to my lord your husband, and give credence to the bearer, my servitor, David Stewart, as to myself. And God preserve you.

Your father, Ard, Earl of Angus.[17]

Angus's messenger, David Stewart, arrived at Temple Newsam on 27 June and gave Margaret her father's letter and one from her uncle, Sir George Douglas. Lennox forwarded both, with one of his own, to Somerset on 27 June, telling him that Angus 'has desired my wife and me to sue your Grace for our having the custody of the gentlemen named in their letters, and if not all of them, at least of the Master of Morton and the Laird of Glenbervie, which last the Earl esteems more than his own bastard son George, which he did deliver in hostage ere yet all the rest'. Lennox was very clear that Angus and his brother would have done better to have approached others 'to have been suitors for them than either my wife or me, for we have received no such benefit at either of their hands, but rather to desire your Grace to keep fast when you have them, as always my poor opinion has been'. This belies the popular assumption that Margaret had put pressure on Lennox to aid her kinsman.

Lennox did offer to have Morton and Glenbervie in 'sure keeping' in his house, but only because he wanted 'to prove what fruit might follow on the fair words' of Angus and his brother. Angus had said that when Lennox was next in Carlisle, he would then 'well perceive' the goodwill of them both to Edward VI, and also towards Lennox's advancement and the recovery of the lands he had lost in Scotland. Lennox assured Somerset that whatever the Protector decided in regard to their plea, as in all things, he would 'be ready to accomplish [it] to my power: and as I am shortly to repair to Carlisle, I shall be glad to know your pleasure in the premises'. He added: 'My wife hath desired me to make her humble recommendations unto your Grace, and saith that she will make answer neither to father nor uncle until she know your Grace's pleasure therein.'[18]

Somerset sanctioned the removal of Morton and Glenbervie to Temple Newsam, but it was only a short stop on the way to the Tower, where Morton was to spend the next two years. Glenbervie recovered his health and lived until 1570.

On 7 July a treaty was signed at Haddington, providing for the marriage of Queen Mary and the Dauphin and guaranteeing Scotland's future autonomy. Arran was to remain regent for six more years, during which the Queen Dowager, Marie de Guise, would steadily gain power and prove a formidable opponent, for she was determined to protect her daughter's interests and preserve her Catholic kingdom intact. But the Church in Scotland was lax and corrupt, and the Protestant reformers had already begun to make an impact. Religious affiliations had become identified with political factions: the Catholics who favoured the 'Auld Alliance' with France, and a growing body of Protestants who wanted closer ties to Protestant England.

Still wishing to retain Arran's support, Marie de Guise persuaded Henry II of France to grant him the French dukedom of Châtelherault (and it is as Châtelherault that he will be referred to subsequently in this narrative). She also secured the appointment of his dissolute bastard brother, John Hamilton, as archbishop of St Andrews and primate of Scotland, hoping that he would be the saviour of the Church in Scotland.

In July 1548 Lennox again journeyed north to Carlisle to await orders from Somerset, but they never came, and by the middle of the month he had gone south to Wressle Castle,[19] having directed Wharton to inform the Protector that he was ready to do any further service in the English cause.[20] On 7 August 1548 Mary, Queen of Scots, now five years old, left her kingdom and took ship for France.

Leaving Margaret at Wressle, Lennox, eager to secure his restitution in Scotland, travelled north in the winter of 1548–9 hoping that Angus would cross the border into England to meet with him and demonstrate the goodwill he had talked of in his letter of the previous summer; Lennox, of course, risked arrest if he entered Scotland. Angus, however, refused to see him, probably because he was unable to offer the help he had promised.

Margaret Maxwell had borne Angus at least three sons.[21] The eldest, James Douglas, Master of Angus, who had displaced Margaret in the succession to the earldom, had died in February 1548, and his younger brothers had recently passed away too. These bereavements may have prompted Angus to seek a reconciliation with his only surviving child.

He extended an olive branch by sending his falconer, James Lindsay, to inform Lennox 'that he had a promising cast of hawks for his mews, if his lordship would send [to] him across the Border for them'. Lennox dispatched his Scottish servant, William Paterson, to Douglas Castle in Dumfries to fetch the hawks, and on 23 February 1549 he informed William Parr, Marquess of Northampton, a Privy Councillor and the brother of Queen Katherine, what had transpired.

Paterson had met with Angus on the green outside his castle, and Angus 'kindly asked how my lord of Lennox, his son, did, and his daughter and their young son, for he would be glad to hear of [their] good welfare'. He asked what Lennox 'intended to do. Is there no secret thing th'hath bidden thee show to me?'

Paterson answered, 'His lordship commanded me in no things in special at this time but to bring his hawks, and if I saw your lordship to commend him to his father, the Earl of Angus, and would be glad he were in good health, and more kind to him nor he hath been in times past.'

'Well,' Angus replied, 'seeing he hath sent no thing else to me, I will break a little of my mind to thee, for I trust thee well enough, and hath given the servants of my lands charge to receive thee at all times. Thou shall declare my daughter is [the] thing in the world that I love best, and my lord her husband, and that young boy there [Darnley], for my children are dead. And if they [the Lennox family] be at hom[e and] well then

I am in comfort, and yet I am as strange to their doi[ngs] and proceedings, or how they intend to pass over the world as any enemy they have; nor I can not see them, nor they me, which breaks my heart. Trowest [thinkest] thou that I would see any man above, but that man [Lennox], and that boy [Darnley] which is my blood? And he hath been of a noble house and I have seen him like a man. An will he do my counsel, I shall wear these old bones of mine [Angus was then about fifty], but I shall make him a man yet. The world is very strange; I have seen many changes, yet hath it been said in old times that a[n] earl of Lennox and an earl of Angus could have ruled some thing upon this side of [the Firth of] Forth.'

He asked Paterson to warn Lennox of a plan to bring 'a great man' from France to take command of the French party in Scotland, which would pose a threat to the English commander, Lord Grey, then entrenched in the eastern Lowlands and already holding off French troops. 'Therefore desire my son to get leave and my daughter to come down to Carlisle that I may see her ere I die, and that I may know his mind. An his way be better nor mine, I will use his counsel, and if mine be better nor his it is natural for him to take it, for I will give him advice in no thing but that which shall be for the weal of both the realms, and shall not be for the hurt of any thing he brooks in that realm. What care I [for] all the rest of the world if they [the Lennoxes] be in honour? Thou may tell him there was bonds between us afore this, but now there is greater bonds of flesh and blood.'[22]

Angus, emotional in the wake of his recent losses, had offered everything the Lennoxes could have wished for: declarations of love and loyalty, the hint of the earldom of Angus for Darnley along with his grandfather's vision of a glorious future, and a willingness to work amicably with Lennox, even to the extent of betraying his own government, proof if any were needed that his loyalty to his daughter and her husband came before all other considerations. It was this new intelligence that prompted Lennox to make his report to Northampton.

But Lennox did not trust Angus, and would do nothing without the approval of the English government. On 11 March he informed the Council that because 'the Earl of Angus, according to his accustomed fashion, hath often sent me fair words without deeds, and having experience of his untruths to the King's Majesty, and unnaturalness always to me in Scotland as in this realm', he had passed his new offer of friendship 'lightly over'. He forwarded with his letter an importunate 'hot message' that Angus had sent him on 23 February, 'and if it stand with your pleasure that I shall repair to Carlisle, either to allure him to the King's Majesty's service or to put him in greater suspicion within that realm of Scotland, or rather the regency thereof, I shall obediently accomplish the same'.[23]

Margaret was not yet aware of the deaths of her infant half-brothers, or of Angus's meeting with Paterson. She was still angry with Angus for refusing to see Lennox, and could not forgive his refusal to support the marriage of the Queen of Scots to Edward VI. In one of Wressle Castle's five towers there was a study called Paradise,[24] and it was probably from here that on 15 March Margaret wrote a scathing letter to her father, which reveals a strong sense of self-worth:

My lord,

After my humble commendations and desiring of your blessing, this shall be to signify unto you the great unnatural-ness which you show me daily, being too long to rehearse in all points; but in some I will declare. Now, last of all, my lord, being near you and so desirous to have spoken with you, yet ye refused it and would not; wherein ye showed yourself not to be so loving as ye ought to be, or else so unstable that any one may turn you. For divers times you have said you would be glad to speak with your son [Lennox]. My lord, remember he hath married your own daughter, and the best child to you that ever ye had, if ye call to remembrance your being here in England; howbeit your deeds showeth the forgetfulness thereof, insomuch as ye are so contrary to the King's Majesty's affairs that now is, his father being so good and so liberal a prince to you, which ought never to be forgotten.

But now, my lord, I hear say that ye have professed never to agree with England, for so much as the most part of your friends are slain. But whom can you blame for that, but only your self-will? For if you would agree to this godly marriage,[25] there needed not Christian blood to be shed. For God's sake remember yourself now in your old age, and seek to have an honourable peace, which cannot be without this marriage. And what a memorial should it be to you for ever, if you could be an instrument for it.

If I should write so long a letter as I could find matter with the wrong of your part, and the right of mine, it were too tedious for you to read. But, forasmuch as I purpose, God willing, to come to Carlisle shortly after Easter, I will keep it in store to tell you myself, for I am sure ye will not refuse coming to me, although my Uncle George [Douglas] and the Laird of Drumlanrig[26] speak against it, whom I know would be glad to see you in your grave, although they flatter you to your face. My Uncle George hath said, as divers Scotchmen have told me, that though you had sons, he would be heir and make them all bastards; but, my lord, if God send you no more sons, and I live after you, he shall have least part thereof, or else many a man shall smart for it.

Thus, leaving to declare further of my mind till I may speak with you myself, I commit you to the keeping of Almighty God, who send you long life with much honour.

From the King's Majesty's castle of Wressle, the 15th day of March, by your humble daughter,

Margaret Lennox.[27]

The tone was anything but humble; it was hectoring and angry, with only a nod to the conventional courtesies, and unsurprisingly it scuppered all chances of a reconciliation for the present.

Somerset now believed Lennox to be a spent force, and he was not recalled to fight the Scots. In 1549 the occupying English forces were finally driven out of Scotland and the pro-French Catholic party emerged victorious. From 1550 Lennox lived the life of a country gentleman with Margaret in Yorkshire, focusing on local concerns, such as trespassers on his land, rather than matters of national importance. On 8 September that year the Council wrote to John, Lord Conyers, 'with all convenient speed' about letters from Margaret complaining of people hunting on her husband's land.[28] On 18 September the Council asked the Lord Chancellor to look into the matter,[29] and it appears that it was resolved to her satisfaction as we hear no more of it.

On 9 May 1551 King Edward recorded in his journal that a Scotsman called Robert Stewart, a member of the elite Scots Guard, the personal bodyguard of the King of France, had planned to poison the young Queen of Scots in the hope of winning favour in England.[30] In June Jehan Scheyfve, the Spanish ambassador, reported that Stewart had made an offer to the Council to poison not only Queen Mary but also King Henry II of France. The councillors had cross-examined him as to ways and means and made him set it all down in writing. When he had done that, they arrested him and had him imprisoned in the Tower and Newgate. At Henry II's insistence, Stewart was deported to Calais and handed over to the French with his written statement, to be punished 'according to his deserts'.[31] Stewart was immediately executed, but there was speculation in England that Lennox himself was behind the plot to kill Mary so that he could seize the Scottish throne.[32] However, no proceedings were taken against him, so it was almost certainly unfounded.

In that June of 1551 England finally conceded defeat and concluded a peace with Scotland, sealed by the Treaty of Norham. It left Lennox in an anomalous position: he could not return to Scotland because of his attainder,[33] yet after John Dudley, Duke of Northumberland – he who had escorted Margaret to Kenninghall ten years earlier – ousted Protector Somerset from power in October that year, Lennox was also regarded with suspicion by the English government, probably because he had been an associate of Somerset.

There was no diminution in Margaret's standing. In November 1551 she was among the privileged courtiers chosen to play a prominent role when Marie de Guise came to Whitehall during a state visit to England. Marie had been visiting her daughter in France, and wanted to meet with Edward VI on her way home. The English government, eager to cement the peace, granted her a safe-conduct and prepared a warm welcome. Lennox, of course, could not be present, for he was still an attainted traitor in Scotland and its Queen could not receive him. For Margaret, this was a chance to meet the woman whom Lennox had once schemed to marry.

On 4 November Margaret and her cousin, Frances Brandon, Duchess of Suffolk, led the great ladies who accompanied Frances's husband, Henry Grey, Duke of Suffolk, and 'many other lords and gentlemen' when they went to welcome Marie de Guise at the Bishop's Palace by St Paul's Cathedral. Followed by the duchesses of Richmond and Northumberland, Lady Jane Grey, the Suffolks' fifteen-year-old daughter, and over a hundred other high-ranking ladies, they conducted the Queen Dowager through London to Westminster, where she was received by the Duke of Northumberland and the great officers of the household.[34]

'She was most honourably and princely received and welcomed by the King's Majesty in the hall, and led up to her chamber on the Queen's side, where his Majesty dined with her, and in the afternoon departed; she taking her leave of him with most hearty and earnest thanks for the kingly usage of her and hers.'³⁵ In his journal Edward records that 'the court, the hall and the stairs were full of serving men; the presence chamber, great chamber and her presence chamber was [*sic*] full of gentlemen. She dined under the same cloth of estate at my left hand. At her reward [favour] dined my cousin Frances and my cousin Marget [*sic*]. At mine sat the French ambassador. We were served by two services of sewers, cupbearers, carvers and gentlemen. There were two cupboards brought in, one of gold four tiers high, another of solid silver six tiers high. After dinner, when she had heard some music, I brought her to the hall, and so she went away.'³⁶ Neither Margaret nor Marie de Guise could have foreseen at this time that their children's fates would be inextricably linked. In fact it cannot have been a comfortable experience sitting next to the Queen Dowager when you were the daughter of one traitor to Scotland and the wife of another.

Two days later Northumberland, and the earls of Pembroke and Wiltshire, attended by their liveried retinues, with many ladies, including – as the King recorded – 'my cousin Margaret and the duchesses of Richmond and Northumberland, accompanied the Queen to Shoreditch, through Cheapside and Cornhill, and there she was met by the gentlemen of Middlesex, a hundred horse, and so she was conveyed out of the realm'.³⁷

By the spring of 1552 Margaret and her father had become reconciled – the circumstances are not recorded – and on 7 April Northumberland informed the Secretary of State, Sir William Cecil, that 'Lady Margaret Douglas wishes to return home [to Scotland], being pregnant', and wished to be back in England in time to be confined in her own house.³⁸ She was expecting one of her unnamed daughters, who was almost certainly born within the year. But Northumberland did not trust Angus, or Margaret, and after sounding out Cecil's views, he refused her permission to cross the border. In December Angus invited her to stay with him at Tantallon, saying he wanted to see her once more and had something important to tell her,³⁹ but still Northumberland would not allow either her or any of her family to go, although it appears that she had intended to travel alone for what Angus had insisted would be a private visit. In a letter to Cecil about the 'affairs of Lady Lennox and her husband', written on 11 December, Northumberland expressed his concerns:

I pray you, remember what I showed you concerning the Lady Lennox, you and I seeming to be of one mind. Nevertheless, forasmuch as I hear no word mentioned of her husband, who, if he mind to remain here, and also keeping her children within the realm, and circumspectly looked to in her absence, the danger can be nothing. And further I remember that her husband dare not come within the realm of Scotland because of a deadly feud between the Governor's [i.e. Châtelherault's] blood and him; and also that he pretendeth a title for lack [of] issue of the young Queen, before the Governor, and hath offered to prove the Governor to descend of a base line. All which considered, I cannot think so much danger in her going to her father as I did when you and I did commune of it. And so it may hap that he would open some matter to her worthy the hearing. Wherefore it is to be considered by the great wisdom of the lords what is to be done in it.

Touching her father's inheritance, I am sure she cannot have no [any] profit except she would refuse her habitation here and remain there, as I doubt not but all my lords do know it to be likely and true. Wherefore it museth me to think what occasion should be that moveth her father to seek to have her come so far only to speak to him, but some mystery there must be in it, whatsoever it be, as knoweth the Lord.[40]

Possibly Northumberland feared that, through Margaret, Lennox would stir up trouble in Scotland by allying with Marie de Guise against Châtelherault. Certainly he was perturbed at the prospect of Margaret's children, with their royal blood and Catholic claim to the English throne, being taken into Scotland. It is clear from his letter that the family were under surveillance, and also clear that if Margaret were to inherit the earldom of Angus, she would not be able to stay in England. Interestingly the reference to her children in the plural indicates that at least two were living at this time, Darnley and probably the daughter born that year.

Someone – either Margaret or Angus – continued to put pressure on the Council to allow the visit. On 7 April 1553 Northumberland suddenly ordered Cecil to expedite the issue of a passport with such convenient speed as possible, stressing the necessity for Margaret to ask the King to sign it; he himself would be at court the next day to authorise its issue.[41] On 8 April the Council wrote to Lord Wharton, Deputy Warden of the Marches, 'touching the Countess of Lennox's repair into Scotland',[42] and sent a letter to Margaret 'touching the same matter'. Finally, 'after a long suit', a licence was granted to her to see her father for two months, while her husband and children remained in England.[43]

There was a compelling reason for Northumberland's change of heart. It was now clear that Edward VI was dying of tuberculosis, and that the Duke's power was under threat, for the King's next heir was the Catholic Lady Mary, who had long battled with Northumberland for the right to celebrate Mass. There was no doubt that Mary would overthrow the Protestant faith in England and the Duke with it. So he was plotting to marry his son Guildford to the devoutly Protestant Lady Jane Grey, the daughter of Frances Brandon, and set Jane up as queen. Under the terms of Henry VIII's will, failing the heirs of his body (who were now to be set aside), the crown was to pass to the heirs of the Lady Frances. Margaret, a Catholic descended from a senior line, might well contest that, so it would be politic to have her out of the way, safely in Scotland, with her family in England as hostages for her good behaviour.

Marie de Guise had granted Margaret leave to enter Scotland,[44] and she journeyed alone to visit her father at Tantallon.[45] There is evidence to suggest that she stayed with Angus until the autumn of that year,[46] so she was probably at Tantallon when Edward VI died on 6 July 1553, and therefore she missed the dramatic coup that ensued. On his deathbed Edward drew up a Device for the Succession, in which he designated Lady Jane Grey as his heir. He made no mention of the claims of Mary, Queen of Scots, Margaret and Lord Darnley, his nearest male heir. All, of course, were Catholics.

Jane's reign lasted for only nine days because the people rallied in force to the Lady Mary, the rightful heir, and she was proclaimed queen on 19 July. This news, reaching Tantallon, must have brought joy to Margaret's heart.

10

'The Person Best Suited to Succeed'

Queen Mary was crowned at Westminster Abbey on 1 October 1553, and it is likely that Margaret had hastened back from Scotland to be present,[1] no doubt rejoicing that a Catholic monarch, her good friend, once more sat on the throne.

Margaret could now practise her religion openly, and showed herself to be a staunch Catholic like the new Queen, who would have applauded her steadfastness in the faith in King Edward's time. 'There was a special love [felt for her] by Queen Mary in the beginning of her reign',[2] and from the first Margaret found herself prominent and in high favour at court, for Mary regarded her as indisputably legitimate, the Pope having pronounced her so.[3] Indeed, she would give every appearance of wanting Margaret to succeed her instead of the Protestant Elizabeth, the bastard half-sister whom Mary disliked and feared. When her first Parliament met on 5 October, she expressed her desire to repeal the 1544 Act of Succession that named Elizabeth as her heir but was warned that Parliament would not co-operate. After all, Mary's own claim to the throne derived from that Act.[4]

Margaret was present at a banquet hosted by the Queen on 17 October in the great hall of Whitehall Palace for the new Spanish ambassador, Simon Renard, and some departing envoys. The Lady Elizabeth and Margaret – to whom Renard refers as 'my Lady Doubley [sic],[5] who has come hither from Scotland' – were standing 'at a window'. The four envoys sat at the Queen's right, 'and during supper the music of hautboys, cornets, flutes, harps and dulcimers ceased not to play'.[6]

Bolstered by the knowledge that Margaret was high in Mary's favour, Lennox (according to two reports of Antoine de Noailles, the French ambassador) was plotting to seize the regency in Scotland from Marie de Guise. Apparently his plan was for Margaret to return, ostensibly on another visit to her father, but in reality to pave the way for his success. However, Queen Mary scuppered the scheme by insisting that she could not part with Margaret, who must stay with her at court.[7]

On 25 November the Queen, undaunted by Parliament's response, summoned Renard to advise her, and told him that 'for the kingdom's tranquillity' she had to consider the question of the succession in case she were to die without heirs. She named the rival claimants: Mary, Queen of Scots, who had 'the best right' by descent, but might be excluded because she had been born abroad; Frances Brandon, Duchess of Suffolk, although her legitimacy was dubious, given her father's complicated marital career; and the Lady Elizabeth, who was the next heir under the terms of the 1544 Act of Succession and Henry VIII's will. But 'the Queen would scruple to allow her to succeed because of her heretical opinions, illegitimacy and characteristics in which she resembled her mother; and as her mother had caused great trouble in the kingdom, the Queen feared that Elizabeth might do the same, and particularly that she would imitate her mother in being a French partisan. The Queen thought that if God were to call her without giving her heirs of her body, the Lady Margaret Douglas would be the person best suited to succeed.'[8]

Apparently no one agreed with Mary. Like Lady Jane Grey, Margaret was not well known in England.[9] The Lord Privy Seal, William, Lord Paget, warned the Queen that 'as Parliament had accepted the Lady Elizabeth as proper to succeed, it would be difficult to deprive her of the right she claimed without causing trouble. It would be very hard to take her claim from her without having the Act of Parliament repealed, which would be very difficult of accomplishment, although the Queen's arguments were compelling and Elizabeth was notoriously illegitimate.'[10]

By 30 November Mary, heedless of Paget's advice, was making her intentions clear, for Antoine de Noailles reported: 'Now the Princess [Elizabeth] has sometimes to give place to the Countess of Lennox, who is called my Lady Margaret here, and to my Lady Frances.'[11] Mary was openly treating Margaret as her heir presumptive. She assigned the Lennoxes rooms at Whitehall,[12] and furnished them with twenty-one pieces of tapestry and ten beds, Margaret's being hung with royal purple velvet and cloth of gold, 'with St George figured on it in sundry places'. The Queen also ordered that they and their servants be provided with free food and drink from her own privy kitchen.[13] She lavished gifts on them: for Margaret, two gowns of gold tissue and a large pointed diamond, once the property of Anne Stanhope, Duchess of Somerset; for Matthew, Edward VI's best horse; and for Darnley, his lutes (including one of ebony from Venice) and three suits of his clothing, which may have been seen as evidence that she regarded Darnley as her ultimate successor, and Edward's.[14] Lennox was appointed to the Privy Council for the first time,[15] and made Master of the Hawks.[16] It was probably at this time that the Lennoxes were granted possession of the demesne lands of Syon Abbey in Isleworth, and of lands in Heston, Middlesex, belonging to the Crown.[17] Unsurprisingly people began to believe that, failing issue of the Queen's body, Margaret would succeed her.

Mary went on showing favour to Margaret. At Christmas 1553 she presented her with 'a fair table diamond, a girdle of gold set through with diamonds and rubies, and a painted diamond of great value'. The girdle alone was worth £500 (£100,250). Jewels like these complemented the costly gowns that Margaret wore to Mary's court; some were of taffeta, worn over embroidered kirtles,[18] and others must have been made with the black velvets and bright satins that Margaret had hitherto favoured.

Serving alongside her in the Queen's Privy Chamber were Mary Howard, Duchess of Richmond, and Anne Stanhope, Duchess of Somerset, old friends of Margaret and the Queen. Like Margaret, both had remained loyal to Mary in the dark days of her brother's reign. But the Duchess of Richmond did not remain at court for long, for she had embraced the Protestant faith and was soon out of favour, which cannot but have affected her friendship with Margaret. Thereafter the Duchess lived quietly in retirement and died in 1557.

The Lady Elizabeth – twenty-five years old, tall, slender, red-haired and potentially a formidable enemy – seems to have made no secret of her ill will towards Margaret, which is hardly surprising. Margaret had evidently long shared Mary's dislike of Elizabeth, and both regarded her as a bastard and a heretic who was not to be trusted. As Elizabeth gave further proof of that by making protests about attending Mass, Mary's initial flowering of goodwill towards her withered and died. She began to voice doubts that Elizabeth was not Henry VIII's child, but Anne Boleyn's bastard by a musician, Mark

Smeaton, and she became ever more convinced that Margaret should succeed her. As Elizabeth's star waned, Margaret's rose ever higher.

Everyone expected the Queen to marry and have heirs of her own. A small, spare spinster of thirty-eight, snub-nosed with a heavy brow, she had been prematurely aged by the troubles she had suffered, and was painfully modest. But she had fallen in love with the portrait of a man eleven years her junior, Philip of Spain, son and heir of the Emperor Charles V, and there were compelling political reasons for the match, for Philip was already known to be a staunch champion of the Catholic faith, which Mary was determined to restore in England. Her insular subjects, especially the Protestants, were against the marriage, and early in 1554 a Kentish gentleman, Sir Thomas Wyatt, led a rebellion against it. He was joined by, among others, the Duke of Suffolk, the father of Lady Jane Grey, who had been imprisoned in the Tower since Mary's accession, and had had a death sentence hanging over her head since November; it was only the mercy of Queen Mary that had so far spared her. Rashly Suffolk now proclaimed his daughter queen once more. The Lennoxes were at court and lived through the frightening days when Wyatt marched on London and there was panic and hysteria at Whitehall. But Queen Mary showed great courage in going to the Guildhall and rallying the people.

When the rebellion was suppressed, both Suffolk and Wyatt were executed, and Lady Jane's fate was sealed, even though the Queen had earlier resolved to spare her. On 12 February 1554 Jane and her husband, Lord Guildford Dudley, were beheaded. The Lennoxes played no known part in these events.[19]

Mary strongly suspected that her half-sister Elizabeth had been involved with Wyatt, and Elizabeth was brought to London under guard and lodged in a ground-floor chamber in Whitehall Palace, immediately beneath Margaret's apartments. Margaret had no time for the Protestant Elizabeth, and almost certainly shared Mary's view that she had committed treason. Thomas Bishop, who seized every opportunity to denigrate Margaret, was later to assert 'how that innocent lady [Elizabeth] cruelly by her was handled is well known'; how 'unfaithfully', when Elizabeth was sick, Margaret deliberately had her servants remove the hangings in the room above where she lay and bade them use it as a kitchen, with much 'casting down of logs, pots, and vessels', to Elizabeth's annoyance.[20] Bishop may have been exaggerating, but he would have been aware that his statement might be read by Queen Elizabeth, who could have corroborated it or not; and it is true that, after Elizabeth became queen, she took care to ensure that her apartments were nowhere near any kitchens.

According to Bishop, who had his own axe to grind, Margaret did worse than create an annoyance for Elizabeth. She wasted no opportunity 'of putting in the Queen's head that it was a quietness for the time to have her [sister] shut up'. She made reports against Elizabeth 'and others, to procure her going to the Tower'.[21] Margaret herself was vehemently to protest that 'none alive is able to justify this false and untrue report, as therein I will be sworn, if I were put to it, that never in all my life I had, or meant to have, any such words with Queen Mary touching [Elizabeth], nor I, for my part, bare no such stroke to give any advice in any such weighty matter'.[22] But even if she did not traduce and torment Elizabeth, at the very least, being aware of the Queen's wishes in the matter, and disapproving of Elizabeth's religion, she was hoping that Elizabeth's claim to the succession would be set aside in favour of her own.

However, when Queen Mary brought Katherine Grey, Lady Jane's sister, to court, granted her a handsome allowance and treated her and her hunchbacked younger sister Mary with great favour, people began to speculate that the Queen might choose Katherine as her successor. Of undoubted legitimacy, she had been reared as a Protestant, but now, unlike Elizabeth, she was willing to convert to the Roman faith. Many Catholics voiced their opinion that they would prefer Katherine to the other Catholic heiresses, Margaret and Mary, Queen of Scots, because they feared the intervention of the Scots and the French in English affairs.

Soon, however, Margaret had another crown in view. Since the peace of 1551 Scotland had witnessed a power struggle between Châtelherault and Marie de Guise for the regency. Châtelherault was a spent force, and real power now lay in the hands of the Queen Dowager, although that was not apparent to outsiders, for on 3 April Renard assured the Emperor that Châtelherault was 'daily gathering strength against the Queen Dowager, and is resolved not to allow the French to get the upper hand in the kingdom'. But Queen Marie, 'feeling her own weakness', had exploited the feud between Châtelherault and Lennox to her own ends, proposing to Lennox that, if he wished to return to Scotland and support her, she would have his property restored to him and treat him as befitted his rank. Thus she hoped 'to gain him over to the party hostile to the Regent, as he is an important personage and has some chance of succeeding to the Scottish crown'.[23]

Lennox had now been an exile in England for almost ten years and was naturally eager to return to Scotland and recover his honours and estates. Anticipating the fulfilment of his ambition to be acknowledged as the Queen of Scots' heir presumptive, he began scheming accordingly. In this he had the Queen of England on his side, for rather than have a pro-French party in power in Edinburgh, and the young Queen in the clutches of the French, she much preferred the prospect of a Catholic ruler who was married to her beloved cousin and friendly to England. That would be advantageous to Spain as well, France and Spain being established enemies. Mary wanted Lennox to go to Scotland and secretly enter into communications with Châtelherault against the Queen Dowager, with a view not only to driving her from the country, but to making himself king if possible, and throwing Scottish affairs into confusion. 'If he is able to do this, the Queen will help him with money, to the best of her ability.'[24] Such was the depth of his ambition that Lennox was prepared to intrigue with his enemy, Châtelherault, against the woman who was ready to receive him back into favour.

But that April Marie de Guise, offering huge financial inducements, persuaded Châtelherault to step aside and assumed the regency of Scotland herself. With French influence restored, it seemed for a time as if the country would remain Catholic, although the tide of Protestantism was sweeping in stealthily. Determined to stem that, Queen Marie immediately revived Scotland's ancient alliance with France, and strengthened her position by importing French advisers and French troops. But this served only further to alienate the proud, independent Scots, who already feared that their country would become a satellite state of France. Since Lennox was hated in Scotland, and the Queen Regent's policies were proving unpopular enough, she could not afford to show favour to one who was widely reviled as a traitor; and as Lennox was now unable to go to Scotland, Queen Mary's plan also came to grief.

On 25 July 1554 Queen Mary was married to Philip of Spain in Winchester Cathedral, amidst great splendour. Margaret, as the chief lady of honour, bore the train of the Queen's magnificent cloth-of-gold wedding gown, assisted by Elizabeth Capel, Marchioness of Winchester; together they walked behind her in procession from Wolvesey Palace to the cathedral, entering at the great west door.

William Paulet, now Marquess of Winchester, gave the bride away, then 'all the people gave a great shout, praying God to send them joy'. When the wedding ring was 'laid upon the book to be hallowed', Philip also laid there 'three handfuls of fine gold', symbolising his worldly goods, whereupon Margaret opened the Queen's purse and Mary, smiling, placed them in it. The trumpets sounded, the royal couple's titles were proclaimed, and then Mary, her new consort and their guests walked to Wolvesey Palace for a magnificent feast.[25]

Margaret remained at Winchester with Mary and Philip and the court until 31 July, then moved with them to Windsor, Richmond and Suffolk Place in Southwark before the Queen and her new King made their state entry into London on 18 September, passing in procession through streets packed with crowds and enlivened with tableaux and pageants, to Whitehall Palace.[26]

After the wedding Mary had given Margaret more jewels, money and plate.[27] Thereafter Margaret served as the Queen's chief gentle-woman and keeper of her privy purse. She was pregnant at the time of Mary's wedding, and when her third son was born, probably in the winter of 1554–5, she named him Philip in honour of the new King.[28] In 1565 a portrait of Mary I with Philip of Spain was on display in the great chamber at Temple Newsam.[29]

Margaret was one of several aristocrats who patronised Mary's favoured painter, Hans Eworth,[30] and in 1555 she commissioned him to paint a portrait of the nine-year-old Lord Darnley,[31] inscribed *Aetatis IX, MDLV Henricus Stuardus Dominus Darnley*.[32] Eworth was to paint Darnley at least twice, and one of these works may have been the portrait recorded at Temple Newsam in 1565.

Time would show just how much Margaret adored her oldest child, and Lennox later wrote of 'the paternal love and steadfast affection he bare unto his dear son Henry'; always, fatally, he saw him as an 'innocent lamb'.[33] The Lennoxes' ambitions were now invested in Darnley, a handsome boy, tall – he grew to be six foot three – and fair; one ambassador said that 'it was not possible to see a more beautiful prince'. In being fiercely ambitious for her son, Margaret was typical of many aristocratic mothers of the period.[34]

She brought Darnley up in the Roman faith. In 1554 Lennox had appointed as tutor their household chaplain, the learned John Elder, originally a staunch Protestant from the Scottish Highlands, who had been a member of the collegiate church at Dumbarton and probably came to England with Lennox in 1544. He had converted to Catholicism when Mary I ascended the throne, thus escaping the persecution of heresy unleashed by the government in 1555.[35] An excellent man of letters and a sound linguist and Latinist, Elder had published an account of the Queen's marriage ceremonies in 1554, in which he refers to Darnley's 'noble parents' as his 'singular and good patrons'. That year he is recorded as being with Darnley at Temple Newsam.[36]

Darnley, like Margaret, had been born in England, and therefore had a sound claim to the throne, of which he was doubtless early on made well aware. There can be no doubt that Margaret – perhaps seeing herself emulating her great-grandmother and namesake, Margaret Beaufort, who had schemed to place a crown on the head of her son, Henry VII[37] – was grooming him as a claimant to the English throne who might, on account of his gender and his charm – and the fact that his parents, although of different faiths, lived together harmoniously – be acceptable to both Catholics and Protestants. Darnley was being imbued with culture, learning and courtly manners. He was taught languages – French, Latin and even Scots – and grew up to be skilled in penmanship. He sang and danced well, excelling, like his father, on the lute, as well as in physical exercises and horsemanship. Above all, he was being indoctrinated with the dynastic ambitions of his parents.

Tradition has it that Darnley translated the works of the Roman historian Valerius Maximus into English. Certainly he inherited his mother's talent for writing poetry, for when he was 'not full nine years of age' John Elder sent Darnley's uncle, the Bishop of Caithness, some verses that the boy had composed at Temple Newsam;[38] and he also wrote short plays known as interludes. When Darnley was just eight he sent one to Queen Mary, asking if she would accept 'a little plot of my simple penning, which I termed *Utopia Nova*'; she rewarded him with 'a rich chain of gold'. On another occasion he wrote to her that he wished that his 'tender years' had not prevented him from fighting against her rebels led by Wyatt.[39]

But Darnley had a weak character; as an adult he was arrogant, stupid and wayward, and displayed little moral sensibility. In other words, he was spoilt. This is hardly surprising seeing how precious he was to a father who doted fondly on him – one of Lennox's later letters to his son has been described as 'fawning'[40] – and a mother who was to lose six other children, and who invested all her hopes in him. Of his parents, she was the more dominant, and he respected her more than he did Lennox.[41]

Lennox had never given up hope of regaining his Scottish lands. Early in August 1556 he sent his servant, Laurence Nesbit, to France to resolve his 'matter' with Mary, Queen of Scots.[42] Nesbit was away for months. That year John Elder also left for France with letters for Aubigny, asking him to make suit to the young Queen of Scots to relieve the Lennoxes' financial problems.[43] He was replaced as schoolmaster by Arthur Lallard, a native of Cambrai, which was then part of the Holy Roman Empire.[44]

The year 1557 was to be a momentous one in Scotland. The Protestant faith had grown so far in popularity as to become widely associated with an injured sense of national identity, born of resentment against French interference and garrisons. Châtelherault and four other leading Protestant nobles now banded together and, calling themselves the Lords of the Congregation, united in solidarity with militant preachers and signed a bond, or covenant, undertaking to establish the reformed faith as the official religion of Scotland.

There is no record of how often Margaret was in contact with her father during the last years of his life. She seems not to have returned to Scotland after 1553, so it was at least three years since she had seen him when, shortly before 22 January 1557, Angus died of erysipelas in the arms of his priest, Sir John Dixon, whom Margaret afterwards took into her service as her secretary.[45] That day the French ambassador in Edinburgh, Henry Cleutin, Sieur d'Oysel, reported 'the death of the Earl of Angus, of whom Lady Lennox is the principal benefactress. I much think that the Queen of England will favour as much as she can the claims of that lady to the succession, and that she will do all she can, by one way or another, for that purpose. I have had the boldness to advise this Queen [Marie de Guise] to seize a strong place called Tantallon, which pertained to the late Earl.' Margaret had been planning to visit Angus there to rally support for Lennox in Scotland. Oysel urged Marie de Guise to seize the earldom of Angus for her daughter, lest the Queen of England should insist on Margaret being admitted to it.[46]

The ambassador was mistaken: Angus left Margaret nothing in his will.[47] 'There was a[n] entail upon the lordship of Douglas, parcel of the earldom of Angus', and both, with their vast estates, were left to his male heirs. Sir George Douglas having died in 1552, the earldom now passed to his son, David, but he followed his father to the grave in June 1557, leaving a minor, Archibald Douglas, as his heir.

The ruling that the earldom of Angus should go to Archibald Douglas, Angus's great-nephew, left Margaret unfairly (as she saw it) dispossessed, but she did not go down without a long fight. From now on she defiantly signed her letters 'Margaret Lennox and Angus',[48] and to her death would maintain that she was her father's sole heir, as she was described in the inscription on her tomb.[49] But the Scottish Parliament did not look favourably on her claim because her husband, Lennox, was still an attainted traitor whose lands and title were forfeit. Margaret's persistence in styling herself countess of Angus also prejudiced her claim, and there was the added complication that she needed her husband's permission to pursue it. Nevertheless, she had the support of Queen Mary, who, at her request, sent Dr Laurence Hussey to Scotland to plead on her behalf, and Lennox's.

This request further compromised Margaret's case. Hussey was received by Marie de Guise on 5 April, but it was not until 24 May that she wrote to Queen Mary – deliberately omitting to refer to Margaret as countess of Lennox – that she had 'given Dr Hussey favourable audience in that matter' and commanded that the Scottish Chancery look into Margaret's claim to the earldom of Angus. But in the next sentence, referring to Hussey's plea for her to 'dispense with the rebellion of the Lady Margaret's husband, sometime earl of Lennox', she said that she 'could not meddle therewith', for it was a matter for her 'dearest daughter herself'.[50] Thus it was made plain that Margaret's case would get short shrift.

King Philip, having, as he thought, left Mary pregnant (although she had already suffered one phantom pregnancy and this turned out to be another), had spent the winter abroad, but in March 1557 he returned to England, and on the 21st he and the Queen were reunited at Greenwich. On 24 March they travelled to London by barge, landing at the Tower, and thence through the city to Whitehall. A few days later the duchesses of Lorraine and Parma arrived in London. It is recorded that 'the Countess of Clidact [sic], the Admiral and other lords and ladies came by water',[51] and it has been suggested that this Countess was Margaret, but it was probably Mabel Browne, Countess of Kildare, because around April or May 1557, Margaret gave birth to her youngest son, Charles,[52] at Temple Newsam.[53] He was almost certainly named after the Emperor Charles V, the father of King Philip, which suggests that his brother Philip, born the previous year, was still alive, otherwise – given the fact that the Lennoxes' second son had been given the same name as their deceased first son – he too would probably have been christened Philip.[54] Charles was almost certainly Margaret's last child, given that she was forty-one when she had him. He was raised as a Catholic, and, like his elder brother Darnley, grew up to be spoiled and arrogant.

Marie de Guise had now relented somewhat towards Margaret, and on 14 November 1557, with her sanction, Sir William Kirkcaldy of Grange met Lord Wharton at Berwick to discuss Margaret's claim to the earldom of Angus. During the meeting Wharton asked 'whether it would not be a great matter to bring back the Lady Margaret and her lord, requiring a strong and influential party in their favour among the nobility of Scotland'.

Grange agreed. 'They ought first to have the castle of Tantallon given them, which is in the keeping of the Laird of Craigmillar and in the Dowager Queen's power,' he said.[55] But nothing came of this summit.

Queen Mary, never robust in health, and now an ailing and embittered woman, hated more than ever the idea of Elizabeth succeeding her, and had tried once more, in vain, to have her removed from the succession. In March 1558 Renard made notes on the subject for a letter to King Philip. Assuming that Mary died without issue, Elizabeth would be queen, under the terms of Henry VIII's will, 'in spite of the taint of illegitimacy'. That was the last thing the Spanish wanted. Elizabeth had been 'brought up in the doctrines of the new religion, she was formerly of the French faction, she hates the Queen and has many supporters who are suspect from the point of view of religion. If she succeeds, and marries an Englishman, religion will be undermined, everything sacred profaned, Catholics ill-treated, churchmen driven out, those monasteries which have been restored will again suffer, churches will be destroyed . . .'

Renard feared that the friendship between England and Spain would 'disappear altogether', since 'the French faction will prevail'. Some months earlier the Queen had tried to have Elizabeth debarred from the succession. Had her efforts not been in vain, Renard believed that the next heir would have been Mary, Queen of Scots, but if she were ruled out as a foreigner, 'the wife of the Earl of Lennox or her children would come next', and then Lady Katherine and Lady Mary Grey, the younger sisters of Lady Jane.

Renard was being a realist when he stated, 'In none of these cases do I see the succession being firmly established. The realm would fall a prey to civil strife. And it is doubtful whether any of these persons would be more deserving of confidence than Elizabeth herself.'[56] The English would not tolerate a foreigner on the throne, and Margaret and her cousins could never hope to command popular support.

Mary nevertheless considered changing Henry VIII's will and leaving the crown to Mary, Queen of Scots, who had married the Dauphin Francis in Paris in April, but King Philip would not hear of it, as Spain and France were traditional enemies, and he did not want a French-dominated queen on the English throne. He feared that leaving the throne to Margaret or Frances Brandon would provoke coups and civil war, which might even open the door to a French invasion of England, something that would be contrary to his interests. Mary was forced to recognise these obstacles too, and had to come to terms with the fact that her successor was a bastard heretic who would undoubtedly undo all her work in restoring the Catholic faith.[57]

Not content with making it appear that Margaret had lost the favour of Henry VIII because of her false accusations against himself, Thomas Bishop later alleged that towards the end of her life Queen Mary came to distrust Margaret too, also on his account. In the end, 'perceiving my lady's inclination' to press her claim to the earldom of Angus, Mary would grant a safe-conduct for Nesbit, Lennox's servant, for only two months, 'which the Earl and my lady refused'.[58] Bishop would also assert that 'Queen Mary, though Lady Lennox told her I was an heretic, gave me (unknown to her who would have had me forsaken) my pension anew, and to the end of her Majesty's days, in the affairs of Scotland, trusted me where she did not her dear cousin of Lennox.'[59]

Bishop may have acted as he did out of resentment at Margaret's understandable failure to help him recover what he believed to be his property. As lord of the manor of Pocklington, Yorkshire, he had claimed ownership of a holding in Waplington, but sometime after July 1553 he complained that his former steward, Thomas Dolman – whose family also served the Lennoxes as stewards and receivers – had dispossessed him of it, and secured it by royal grant. Thereafter Waplington was held in dispute until at least 1628.[60]

It is clear that most of Bishop's allegations were nonsense and that the Lennoxes did not lose the Queen's favour. On 19 December 1557 she had assigned them revenues from twelve sacks of wool from a shipment at the port of Southampton, amounting to nearly 3,000 marks (£401,000) per annum.[61] And Nesbit did go to Scotland in 1557, his mission being to sue for the return of his master's estates. In that he failed, but he made the acquaintance of Lennox's distant cousin, James Stewart, Laird of Cardonald near Glasgow, who wanted Lennox's support against the Queen Dowager's rule. But Lennox would not commit himself.[62]

Marie de Guise was beleaguered enough as it was. In 1558 the Lords of the Congregation increased in strength, and they were joined by Margaret's nephew, the Queen of Scots' bastard half-brother, James Stewart, Earl of Moray, a natural son of James V. Ruthless, clever and opportunistic, he cherished a deep-seated grievance because he had not been born legitimate, and may have had designs on the throne. Yet he was sincere in his Calvinist convictions, a model of moral rectitude, and would soon be the richest man in Scotland.

In the summer of 1558 Lennox fell ill. He and Margaret were staying in the north at the time. On 27 July the Queen, much concerned to hear that he was 'sick unto death',[63] and perhaps doubting his fervour for the Catholic faith, asked the devoutly conservative Thomas Robertson, Dean of Durham, to visit him, trusting that Lennox 'might be much eased and relieved by the presence of some good, virtuous and learned man'. Robertson was instructed to give Lennox 'godly and learned counsel, advice and comfort', in which he was to 'travail to the best of your power, and to advertise us in the end what you have done in this behalf, wherein you shall administer unto us acceptable pleasure and service'.[64] The Queen also sent her personal condolences to her 'dear Mathieu' and recommended a physician.[65] It may have been his remedies that were efficacious, as Lennox recovered.

John Stuart, Lennox's youngest brother, had succeeded their uncle as seigneur of Aubigny in 1544, and in the wake of the alliance of England and Spain had been a means of communication between the Lennoxes and the French court. Aubigny had been captured by the Spanish after the Battle of Saint-Quentin in August 1557 and later ransomed, thanks to the good offices of Lennox, the Count of Feria, who had served as Philip's ambassador in England since 1554, and the schoolmaster Arthur Lallard, who acted as go-between. In January 1558 Aubigny had been in the French army that took Calais, the last remaining outpost of England's French empire, a cataclysmic disaster for England that would haunt Queen Mary until her death.

The Catholic Aubigny favoured the succession of Mary, Queen of Scots, to the English throne. He worked as an agent of Marie de Guise, and in the autumn of 1558 took part in a border raid into England, during which he was captured. Lennox secretly sent him money, but also wrote to Queen Mary expressing his opinion that his brother might be persuaded to abandon the Scots, and might 'tell much if he but list'. Margaret asked Queen Mary to send her copies of the dispatches of the Count of Feria, who was ordered to London in October 1558 after King Philip learned that the Queen was ill. These dispatches were conveyed to her by Lallard. But Aubigny escaped back to France, and when the Queen learned of this she began to look upon Lennox with grave suspicion.[66] It may have been to this that Bishop was referring. Yet there were to be no adverse consequences, for Mary died at St James's Palace on 17 November. In the end it was not Margaret who succeeded her, but Elizabeth, whom she had finally acknowledged as her heir on 6 November.

11

'The Second Person in the Kingdom'

As soon as Elizabeth had been proclaimed queen, Margaret and Lennox hastened to her court at Hatfield, making sure that they were among the first to congratulate her. Elizabeth's welcome was gracious,[1] which seemed to augur well for the future, and Margaret rode immediately behind the new monarch when she made her state entry into London.[2]

On 13 December Margaret was chief mourner at Queen Mary's funeral in Westminster Abbey. Mounted on horseback and followed by several great ladies, 'riding all in black trailed to the ground', she followed the chariot, which bore a wooden effigy of the late Queen, crowned and robed, from St James's Palace to the Abbey, where the Abbot and four bishops received the coffin for the first of the liturgical offices for the dead. Margaret was present the next morning for the Requiem Mass and the interment in the side aisle of the Henry VII Chapel, at which the officers of the late Queen's household symbolically broke their staves of office and cast them into the grave. Then the heralds cried, 'The Queen is dead! Long live the Queen!' and the mourners went to dinner.[3] This was to prove the last funeral of a reigning English sovereign to be conducted with Roman Catholic rites, and Margaret must have been aware that religious change would soon come.

Henry II of France did not recognise the Protestant, illegitimate Elizabeth as her sister's lawful heir, and on learning of her accession he ordered that the arms of his daughter-in-law, the Queen of Scots, be quartered with the royal arms of England, effectively acknowledging

Mary Stuart as the rightful, Catholic queen. It was an act that would colour all future relations between the two women, and of course to Elizabeth it represented a serious threat to her throne.

To counteract French influence in Scotland, she made clear her intention of allying herself to Lennox's enemy, Châtelherault, and his cohort Moray, who was at that time contesting Margaret's claim to the earldom of Angus.[4] Marie de Guise, desperately trying to preserve her daughter's Catholic kingdom intact, now turned to Lennox. On 20 December Châtelherault's son, James Hamilton, now Earl of Arran, and Moray informed Cecil, who had been reappointed secretary of state, 'that the Dowager has desired the Earl of Lennox to come home in this country, promising him both his own lands and the Earldom of Angus, to which he has agreed. Desiring you to stop his coming.'[5] The Lords of the Congregation wanted no interference from a man who had identified himself with the Catholic cause.

On 14 January 1559 Margaret took part in the celebrations marking Elizabeth's state entry into London prior to her coronation. In the great procession that advanced from the Tower through the gaily bedecked, crowded streets of the City, Lord Robert Dudley, as Master of Horse, followed immediately behind the Queen's chariot, then after him came Margaret at the head of thirty-nine ladies; she and the duchesses of Norfolk, Suffolk and Northumberland rode with twenty others on palfreys, the rest travelling in three chariots. The next day Margaret and the other ladies followed the Queen as she walked from Westminster Hall along a blue carpet to Westminster Abbey to the joyous sound of fifes, drums, organs and all the bells of London pealing. Yet it was not Margaret who was given the high honour of carrying the Queen's train, but Margaret Audley, Duchess of Norfolk. Margaret followed with 'the duchesses, marchionesses, countesses, etc., dragging their trains after them, going two by two, and being exquisitely dressed, with their coronets on their heads, and so handsome and beautiful that it was a marvellous sight'.[6] The entire peerage, including Lennox, was present in Westminster Abbey when the Queen was crowned. One can only imagine Margaret's thoughts at such a moment.

Afterwards, doubtless to her dismay, she and Lennox were given leave to return to Yorkshire. The Queen had offered no place or office at court, yet on bidding them farewell she told Margaret she had appointed Sir William Cecil to look to their affairs, and that they should contact him if they needed any assistance from her.[7]

The Lennoxes could not have mistaken the cold draught emanating from the throne. Excluded from the succession she might have been, but Margaret was still the second lady in England and remained a dynastic threat to Elizabeth, who hated and distrusted her, as she did all her female heirs, although in Margaret's case she had more reason, given how unkindly Margaret had behaved towards her. Elizabeth would have identified Margaret strongly with the late Queen's reign and policies,[8] and had good reason to believe that she shared Queen Mary's antipathy towards her. She had not forgotten how Margaret had been given precedence before her, and she was aware that the Act of Succession could be repealed in response to political and popular opinion; indeed, time would show that many believed the Scottish line to have the prior right to the English succession. She was also aware that Margaret had sons with strong claims to the crowns of England and Scotland, and that the Catholic Lennoxes had the potential to enlist support in Scotland, France and Spain; she knew too that Margaret would not hesitate to reinstate the Counter-Reformation, should sovereign power ever be hers.

In Phillips's *Commemoration*, Margaret praises Elizabeth to the skies, extolling her as 'a Princess of Peace' who excelled the Muses and the Graces, advanced God's truth and put down falsehood – sentiments she can never have entertained in the early years of the Queen's reign. But this was written many years later, when much had been forgiven, if not forgotten, and when she knew she must not go to her Maker with hatred in her heart, or offend the one person who could protect the interests of her grandchildren.

At the outset, Margaret spared no thought for Elizabeth's insecurities. The hatred was mutual. Margaret had cherished hopes that she herself might succeed Mary. It has been shrewdly observed that 'no Stuart, before or after, was so hypnotised by the crown as this Stuart by marriage, [who] understood herself to be the pure and living chalice of the blood royal'. Margaret was, after all, a great-granddaughter, granddaughter, niece, cousin, sister, mother and grandmother to kings of Scotland, England and France, and on the distaff side she was 'in equally close relationship to seven queens'. Probably 'she found it hardly endurable that she herself should be denied the sweets of majesty'.[9]

In the Protestant Edward VI's reign, Margaret had had no grounds for opposing the legitimacy of the King's title, but like most Catholics she regarded Elizabeth as a bastard, a heretic and a usurper, and seems never inwardly to have accepted her as the rightful queen of England.

In her own eyes, it was herself, Margaret, who was the true inheritor of the kingdom,[10] and her sons who should come after her. Under Queen Mary, Margaret had had the freedom to practise her religion openly, and clearly she felt that she should not now be prevented from doing so by one who had no right to royal authority. From now on she would have no compunction about undermining the claims of the usurper Elizabeth whenever she could, and advancing the Catholic cause. It is easy to believe Thomas Bishop's assertion that in the privacy of her house, 'she openly said that either Queen Mary or Queen Elizabeth was a bastard, and all the world knew that Queen Mary was lawful; and for herself she desired nothing but her rights, which she trusted to have one day. By open talk [she] many times usurped the name of second personage to the crown of England, and [said] that in default of the Queen she would give place to none. Her servants have made like boasts.'[11]

It has been credibly suggested that, descended from the same grandfather, Margaret and Elizabeth had been 'forced very probably by heredity into similar trains of thought' and come thoroughly to distrust each other, 'probably because each understood, and so could be prepared for, the other's wiles'.[12] Elizabeth could never count on Margaret's loyalty, and Margaret could never trust Elizabeth to give her what she believed to be her rightful due as a close heir to the throne.

It is now, with her rival in power, that the real Margaret emerges, a strong, 'masterful, ambitious woman' of forty-three 'with more than a dash of Tudor spirit',[13] whose ambitions and prejudices had hitherto been fed, or kept in check, by circumstances, and who had been denied her rights to a great earldom and a crown. It would not be surprising if she felt angry and wronged, especially now that she found herself in opposition to a powerful enemy who represented everything she despised. Margaret had already demonstrated that she had an audacious, passionate nature and a talent for dangerous scheming, and it was at this time that her relentless ambition and determination came into evidence. She did not shrink from what Elizabeth would certainly have seen as treasonable activities, although Margaret would not have regarded them as such. Two forces now drove her: her fierce ambition for her sons, and a burning desire to see England and Scotland united under Catholic rule. And so, in the words of the Victorian historian James Anthony Froude, she embarked on 'a restless life of feverish intrigue',[14] working to her uttermost to advance her house and exploit every political opportunity that came her way,[15] emerging in the process as a serious political operator, the true successor of her ancestors on both sides. Fearlessly she would risk all, and for many years, as a leading Catholic with royal blood, she was to prove a powerful force in Elizabethan politics.

Even though they still treated Temple Newsam as their chief seat,[16] from 1558 – as Lennox's letters show – the Lennoxes resided mainly at Settrington, a great house remotely situated in Ryedale, not thirty miles from Bridlington Bay on the Yorkshire coast, where ships from Dieppe came to trade.[17] It was therefore well placed to facilitate communications with France and its Queen, Mary Stuart, and it was far distant from London. Another advantage was that it lay in an area well populated with old Catholic families, and came with strong Catholic connections. It had been the home of the Bigod family from the thirteenth century until Francis Bigod had involved himself in the Pilgrimage of Grace and paid with his life and his estates. He had rebuilt the medieval house.

There is no surviving image of Settrington, but a survey carried out by John Mansfield in 1599–1600, when it was 'damnified by decay', lists its rooms, offices and outbuildings: the Low Parlour, with a chamber above and a little room next to it; the Great Chamber; the stair head by the Great Chamber door; a small room called the Tailor's Chamber; another little chamber and an entry next to it; a corner chamber on the west side of the house; the hall, wet larder and dry larder; the kitchen; the buttery and hall porch; a room called Paradise, then 'fallen down and clean gone', which had measured three yards by six, with a ceiling three and a half yards high, covered with lead. It may be significant that Margaret had a room called Paradise, as Queen Elizabeth had the famed and opulent Paradise Chamber at Hampton Court, and Margaret was perhaps trying to emulate her rival.

Outside were the gatehouse and a granary store, or 'garner', the 'places of ease' (latrines), a dovecote, a stable, the barn, the larder house, the bakehouse, the brewhouse and the laundry house. Pipes and cisterns of lead supplied the kitchen and brewhouse with water. Beyond the house were yards, orchards and fishponds.[18]

The Lennoxes also spent time at their manor of East Witton near Leyburn in Wensleydale, seventy miles east of Settrington. It incorporated the ruins of Jervaulx Abbey, dissolved and dismantled under Henry VIII. A 1997 survey of the surrounding earthworks revealed evidence of a 'totally unsuspected but short-lived great house and formal garden on the site, probably built by the Earl of Lennox in the second half of the sixteenth century, but demolished or abandoned by 1627', for no sign of it, or the grand formal gardens, appears on a 1627 map of the estate.[19] The survey showed that the house was massive and stood in the abbey precinct, in the southeastern corner of the inner court. A rectangular area of mounds and hollows adjoining the monastic buildings and measuring twenty-five by thirty metres was perhaps the end part of a southern range, but the northern range had disappeared under later landscaping. Surviving monastic buildings were probably incorporated into the main part of the house.

This lost house of the Lennoxes was of great status. It had up to fourteen formal gardens with paths, terraces and watercourses. There were two pavilions and possibly a gazebo, situated so as to afford views over the gardens. The monastery's water supply system and fishponds were adapted for ornamental water features, and its watermill was made into a picturesque ruin. On the eastern side of the gardens there was an embankment to divide the formal area from the hunting park. The remains of what might have been a coach house were located in the field to the south of Mark Hill.[20]

At a time when Parliament was establishing the Protestant Church of England, and the Queen was working for religious unity in her realm, Margaret's houses once again became lodestars for those of the Roman faith. Her household was not only effectively a northern court, but also a focus for Catholic intrigues that might encourage disaffection and undermine the new Anglican settlement, which was initially to make very little impact in the predominantly Catholic north. For the first time we hear that Margaret was 'one who is beyond measure hostile to [the Protestant] religion, more violent even than Queen Mary herself',[21] and, according to Miles Coverdale, the translator of the Bible into English, 'more stiff in her Poperies' than Mary.[22] Her hatred of the Protestant faith had doubtless been fuelled by the grim news that her mother's tomb had been desecrated, her corpse burned and the ashes scattered when the Charterhouse at Perth was attacked and destroyed by a mob of Calvinist reformers on 11 May 1559.[23] Soon it would become clear that she was ready to use her faith as a political weapon and exploit it in order to bolster the claims of herself and Darnley to the throne. Thus it is not hard to see why the activities of the Lennoxes, and of Margaret in particular, came to be regarded as threats to the security of the state.

The reports of government informers reveal that Margaret was the chief champion of the old religion in the Lennox household. This was more or less the norm in recusant circles, with the husbands outwardly conforming to the established Church, and the wives contriving in the domestic sphere to instruct their children and preserve the old ways.[24] Much of what we know of Margaret's religious practices comes from the later testimony of Thomas Bishop, who had now rejoined the Lennoxes' household. At the beginning of Elizabeth's reign, he and his wife Janet were living in extreme poverty in the Sanctuary at Westminster, where he had probably sought refuge from his creditors. His wife, who had visited Elizabeth's court at the same time as Margaret, possibly hoping for a post in the latter's employ, died in the Sanctuary. Bishop, unable to afford to bury her, and ill himself, asked charity of Lennox, who took him back into his household. No doubt he used all his persuasions to get Margaret to agree. But when Bishop was cured, 'he returned to his dogged nature', sowing dissension in the household, slandering the gentlewomen and plotting vengeance on Margaret, for there was still no love lost between them. Bishop would later testify that, 'to pleasure the hearts of the Papists to regard her true title [to the throne], she hath contemptuously and openly declared her religion under colour of her conscience, uses her beads, auricular confession, pinning of idols and images within and about her bed and that of Lord Darnley, whom she has grafted in that devilish papistry'. She had also employed a priest, 'one little Sir William, besides Malton', to celebrate Mass 'at sundry times in her bedchamber' for herself, her husband and Lord Darnley. Bishop also alleged that 'by mediate persons she uses witches and soothsayers, and has one within her house'. As has been noted, one had allegedly prophesied in 1546 that her son should wear the crowns of England and Scotland.[25]

Bishop was a hostile witness and may well have exaggerated, or even fabricated, his evidence. Yet there was widespread interest among the Elizabethan aristocracy in astrology, palmistry and other occult practices, so Margaret's preoccupations were not unusual for her time, although the assertion that she resorted to witches may have been an invention. Even so, it was dangerous for her to dabble in such things, especially as the government was becoming increasingly concerned that supernatural practices might be used to undermine the State.

Margaret could also have been prosecuted for hearing Mass, which was now illegal. From June 1559 Catholics who failed to attend

Anglican services were fined, but there is no record of that penalty being imposed on Margaret, which suggests that she, or Lennox, as head of the household, conformed outwardly, although evidently the government remained suspicious.

Being of royal blood, Margaret was infinitely more of a threat to the State than most Catholic wives, and the government knew that she was the dominant force in the Lennox marriage. She could also count on considerable local support. In March 1559 the Venetian ambassador reported that, although the Queen's Protestant subjects were increasing in number, 'they are not so powerful as the Catholics, who comprise the chief personages of the kingdom, with very great command in their estates, having also many followers'.[26] He was almost certainly referring not only to the Lennoxes, but also to several other great lords in Yorkshire, among whom were Lord Wharton, and the earls of Northumberland and Westmorland.

Thomas Percy, 7th Earl of Northumberland, the greatest landowner and a Catholic, was like a king in the north. Henry Neville, Earl of Westmorland, has been called a 'boisterous' character. In 1546–7 he had been imprisoned for plotting to murder his first wife and his father by witchcraft. Having confessed and been pardoned, he had since served as a Privy Councillor and Lieutenant of the North, but in 1558, when his second wife was found dead in bed and he immediately married her sister, causing a great scandal, outraged rumours had it that they had colluded to poison her.[27] It would later be asserted that Westmorland cherished feelings for Margaret: 'of all women [he] bears her his heart'.[28] Strickland called it 'a deep and enduring passion',[29] but that is probably what the Earl cherished for his third wife rather than Lady Lennox. He was ten years Margaret's junior, and the most he probably felt for her was admiration and loyalty.

Sir Richard Chamberlain, the keeper of nearby Scarborough Castle, was a Lennox man and a good friend of the Earl and his wife. Likewise his successor, Sir Richard Cholmeley, Sir William Babthorpe, a local Justice of the Peace and a 'misliker' of the new religion, and several others in Yorkshire.[30] It has been estimated that about three quarters of the population in the North Riding was Catholic.[31] There were three priests in the Lennox household: Thomas Robertson, William of Malton and John Dixon, who also acted as Margaret's secretary, and they and the Earl's Catholic stewards were known to the authorities.[32] The Lennoxes' solicitor, Peter Vavasour, was described by the government as another 'misliker of religion', 'a Papist of the worst sort', and a counsellor to Lennox, Margaret and Northumberland.[33]

IN SEARCH OF PORTRAITS OF MARGARET DOUGLAS
(*Above left*) Unknown woman by Hans Holbein, once thought to be Katherine Howard.
(*Above right*) The intriguing Somerley Portrait. (*Below left*) Unknown woman by William Scrots,
*c.*1544–55. (*Below right*) The only authenticated portrait of Margaret; detail from the
Darnley Memorial painting of 1568.

Margaret's warring parents, Archibald Douglas, Earl of Angus, and Margaret Tudor.

The ruins of Harbottle Castle, Northumberland, where Margaret was born in 1515.

The spectacular remains of Tantallon Castle, East Lothian, where Margaret lived with her father during her childhood.

Norham Castle, where Angus sent Margaret to safety in 1529. It had 'not one chamber fit to shelter anyone'.

Henry VIII was fond of his niece 'Margett', and generous, but did not hesitate to condemn her to death when he found out about her secret betrothal.

'The Queen mine aunt': Mary Tudor, Duchess of Suffolk, with whom Margaret lived when she first came to England in 1530, before joining the household of Henry VIII's daughter, the Princess Mary, later Mary I (*above right*), who became a life-long friend.

The Lady Heveyham.

The Lady of Richmond.

PASTIME IN THE QUEEN'S CHAMBER
(*Above left*) Mary Shelton. (*Above right*) Mary Howard, Duchess of Richmond.
These ladies collaborated with Margaret in transcribing the poems in the Devonshire Manuscript.
(*Below left*) Queen Anne Boleyn, in whose household Margaret first served at the English court.

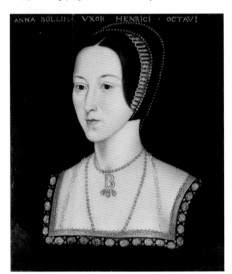

ANNA BOLLINA VXOR HENRICI · OCTAVI

(*Right*) Verses copied by Margaret into the
Devonshire Manuscript. Many relate to her
doomed love for Lord Thomas Howard.
'For whereas I love faithfully, I know he will
not slack his love, nor never change his fantasy.'

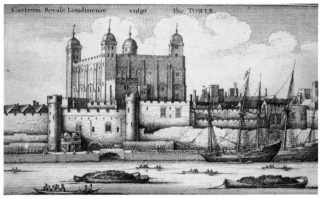

'The Tower of London. Alas! That ever prison strong should such two lovers separate…'

(*Above left*) Syon Abbey. Ill and in grief, Margaret stayed here for five months in 1537–8.

(*Above*) All that remains of Norfolk's great house at Kenninghall, Norfolk. In her seventeen months' stay Margaret may have found peace, after suffering abandonment, loss and fear.

Thomas Howard, Duke of Norfolk. Angus was grateful for his goodness to Margaret.

(*Left*) 'He was very pleasant in the sight of gentlewomen.' The mysterious 'Man in Red'. Is this a portrait of the young Matthew Stuart, Earl of Lennox? (*Below*) Marie de Guise, Queen Dowager of Scotland. Lennox had sought her as a bride. Even as he was declaring his devotion to Margaret, he was still pressing his suit to Marie.

(*Left*) St James's Palace, London, showing Henry VIII's gatehouse, with the window of the Chapel Royal to the right. (*Below*) The Chapel Royal at St James's Palace, where Margaret and Matthew were married in 1544. The ceiling was installed for Anne of Cleves, but the rest of the Chapel has been much remodelled.

THE LENNOX RESIDENCES

(*Above left*) Stepney Palace, or King John's Court, where Margaret lived in the early years of her marriage. (*Above right*) Wressle Castle, where Margaret often stayed when Lennox was campaigning in Scotland. (*Centre left*) Temple Newsam in 1707. (*Centre right*) The west wing of Temple Newsam, all that remains above ground of the Lennoxes' great house.

(*Above left*) A view over Settrington, Yorkshire. Nothing survives of the Lennoxes' house, the scene of so many intrigues. (*Above right*) Jervaulx Abbey. The Lennoxes built a large house and extensive gardens within its precincts.

KATHARINE PARR

(*Above left*) Queen Katherine Parr, Henry VIII's sixth wife. Margaret attended their wedding in 1543.
(*Above right*) Miniature of an unknown woman, possibly Margaret Douglas.
(*Below left*) Anne Stanhope, Countess of Hertford and Duchess of Somerset.
(*Below right*) Katherine Willoughby, Duchess of Suffolk.

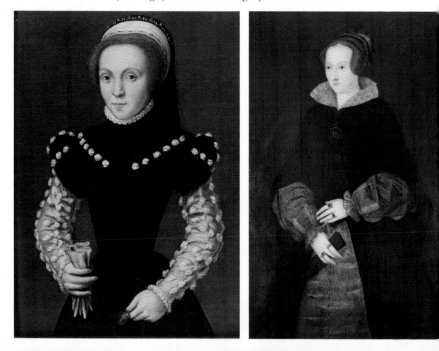

John Elder was strategically placed in France, and the tutor Arthur Lallard made himself useful by translating letters written in French.[34]

Elizabeth's policy towards her Catholic subjects was conciliatory – to begin with. But the Lennoxes were clearly not prepared to lie dormant. It is impossible to keep track of the many messengers and agents who worked for them, secretly disseminating information at home and abroad, furthering the preservation of the old faith, the return of Lennox's Scottish lands, and, as time went by, the couple's dynastic ambitions. What stands in stark contrast to all this activity is the enduring love between Margaret and her husband, which has been described as 'an element of purity and gentleness in a household credited with dark political intrigues'.[35]

It was not long before that household was infiltrated by government agents whose presence Margaret clearly did not suspect. At least one of the Lennoxes' servants was informing on them to Sir William Cecil, the Queen's chief minister, and another, William Forbes, was a spy in the pay of Lord Robert Dudley, who was close to the Queen.[36] Through them, Elizabeth would learn of Margaret's animosity. Speaking later of her royal cousins, she told Sir William Maitland of Lethington (now Lennoxlove), the Scottish Secretary of State, that some 'had made declaration to the world that there are more worthy of [the crown] than either she [the Queen of Scots] or I'.[37] It was clear whom she meant, so it is hardly surprising that she had Margaret and Lennox kept under surveillance.

The new Queen's councillors feared that Margaret would make a bid for the throne, supported by the might of Spain and the Catholic lords in the north. For more than two years Margaret was to have covert dealings with Alvaro de Quadra, Bishop of Aquila, the Spanish ambassador, a man with considerable diplomatic skills and social graces, who came from a family with a long tradition of service to the Spanish Crown. She 'had her factors [agents] about him'.[38] One, called Brinklow, was later hanged for robbery; another was Francis Yaxley.

A former protégé of Cecil and servant of Queen Mary, Yaxley had worked for the Privy Council and as a diplomat, and was now a Member of Parliament and clerk of the signet, and described as a member of the Queen's Privy Chamber.[39] Margaret employed him to obtain information from Quadra, and used him from time to time to send her word by a go-between, Hugh Allen, of anything that might serve her interests. Yaxley's letters to her do not survive because she burnt them.[40] Hugh Allen was a Lennox agent based in

London, who sent his employers messages from abroad and from two informers at court, a Scottish woman and a mysterious lady in attendance on the Queen, both of whom used Arthur Lallard as another channel of communication,[41] but only by word of mouth, as none of them dared write anything down.[42] Thus Margaret could keep abreast of what the Queen was saying about her.

According to Quadra, Yaxley had too great a love of intrigue and was incapable of keeping secrets – in January 1561 he would be imprisoned for having 'babbled' about the Queen's notorious affair with Lord Robert Dudley[43] – but he was a 'good Catholic'[44] who would willingly serve as an agent for Mary, Queen of Scots, later on.[45] His family, whose seat, Yaxley Hall in Suffolk, still stands, was of the old faith and allied to the Howards, and its members were to appear on official lists of recusants.

Aside from the religious settlement, there was one pressing matter on the government's agenda, and that was the Queen's marriage. But although Elizabeth was willing to be courted by many foreign suitors, rampant gossip had already linked her name to her Master of Horse, Lord Robert Dudley, the son of the traitor Northumberland, who had been executed after Queen Mary's accession in 1553. Their affair was soon the talk – and the scandal – of Europe, and many believed that they were lovers. Margaret was apparently ready to vilify Elizabeth and besmirch her reputation. The spy William Forbes was to report: 'She loves not the Queen,' citing as proof the fact that for two years she had allowed her fool to make barbed jokes about her and never reproved him.[46] But Forbes may have been lying.

Scotland was now in turmoil. The Queen Regent was involved in a bitter conflict with the Lords of the Congregation, horrified at the escalating violence and iconoclasm of their movement. To prevent further desecration of abbeys and churches, she sent in her French troops, an unpopular move that served only to harden Protestant resistance, which gathered momentum when the fiery and charismatic preacher John Knox, a former chaplain to Edward VI, returned from exile in May and joined the Lords of the Congregation, whipping up support for them in impassioned sermons.

On 21 June Sir Nicholas Throckmorton, Elizabeth's ambassador in Paris, reported that the French King intended to prosecute Mary, Queen of Scots' title to the English throne, and that Aubigny, Lennox's brother, was hand in glove with him in those matters and had said that Queen Elizabeth 'had not so much right to England as the

Queen Dauphine; and if [Mary's] title was not good there was another nearer than the Queen'.[47] He was clearly referring to Margaret. But King Henry had no opportunity to press Mary's claim. On 6 July 1559 he died of agonising wounds after a lance pierced his eye and throat in a tournament. Fifteen-year-old Francis II, who was plagued by skin eruptions and dizzy spells, now ascended the throne, and Mary, Queen of Scots, sixteen, six feet tall, beautiful and accomplished, became queen of France.

At Aubigny's invitation the Lennoxes sent the twelve-year-old Lord Darnley to the French court to congratulate the new King and Queen and to give them a letter asking for their support in securing the restoration of Lennox's Scottish estates. The boy was received with 'great distinction' by Francis and Mary.[48] With him was his former tutor, John Elder, who brought letters for Mary from the Lennoxes, his purpose being to make further overtures to the young Queen on behalf of them and their son.[49] Sir Nicholas Throckmorton warned Elizabeth that Elder posed a 'dangerous' threat to England's security, and urged that anyone associated with him be kept under surveillance.[50] Queen Mary refused to restore the Lennox estates, but she did give Darnley a thousand crowns and invite him to attend the coming coronation, which took place at Rheims on 18 September.[51]

Margaret had had another agenda in sending her son to France. For many years, according to Thomas Bishop, she had dreamed of Darnley marrying the Queen of Scots.[52] This is credible, for she would have been aware that Francis was sickly and not likely to live long, and was probably looking forward to the day when Mary would be free to marry again and unite her claim to the English throne to Darnley's. Not only would that make him king of Scots, it would also strengthen his claim to the English succession – and, in Catholic eyes, to the throne itself. Because Margaret's ambitions encompassed more than the crown matrimonial of Scotland: she envisaged – more than forty years before it actually happened – a day when the thrones of England and Scotland would be united.[53]

A marriage between Mary and Darnley would almost certainly be assured of the support of the Lennox and Catholic factions in England,[54] and it would be a focus for Catholic resistance to Elizabeth's rule. It was imperative therefore that Darnley catch the Queen's eye and impress her with his charm, so that she would remember him in the future when she was seeking a new consort. Lennox too was hot for the marriage, having probably abandoned his own hopes of the Scottish throne and invested them in his son, and Margaret knew that she could count on the support of the Catholics in the north. The time was now ripe, for Lennox's rival Châtelherault was out of favour, and had been deprived of his French dukedom as punishment for opposing Marie de Guise, although he would continue to use the title.

The Lennoxes still deemed it important to court Elizabeth's favour, for, pursuing her policy of conciliation, she had agreed to support the Earl's quest for restitution of his Scottish lands and titles. But that, inevitably, would mean his deeper – and potentially dangerous – involvement in Scottish politics. Already Lennox was becoming enmeshed. On 14 December, at Settrington, he received a letter from his brother, the Bishop of Caithness, brought from Scotland by Captain Sir John Borthwick, and Lennox's cousin, Thomas Stewart, Laird of Galston, who was later to serve Mary, Queen of Scots. Borthwick, a Scottish reformer who had defected to the English in Henry VIII's time, had been sent by Elizabeth to the Borders with a force of a thousand men; but now he was contemplating abandoning the Queen and joining the party of Marie de Guise against that of Châtelherault, and he wanted Lennox to support him. He had been sent by the Queen Dowager to tell the Earl that now, if ever, was the time to 'prosecute his affairs' with Châtelherault.[55]

Margaret feared that this was not the way to recover Lennox's estates, and she knew that supporting the Queen Dowager was against Elizabeth's policy, but she and her husband made Borthwick welcome and showed off Lord Darnley to him. The Captain was much impressed. 'Young Darnley is the nearest person in the regal succession to both realms,' he wrote to the French ambassador, de Noailles, 'by right of his father in Scotland, if Queen Mary has no issue; likewise he is next heir to the throne of England through his mother.'[56] But in private Margaret prevailed upon Lennox not to embroil himself further with Borthwick, prompting the latter angrily to complain later to de Noailles that he could not fathom Lennox's intentions because he was 'wholly governed by his wife'.[57]

Lennox's priority was to secure the restoration of his lands and the Scottish succession, and he felt it his 'bounden duty' immediately to forward his brother's letter to Cecil, so that he might show it to the Queen, whom he desired 'most humbly to be my good and gracious lady, as her progenitors hath been to me heretofore. And that which her Majesty doth for us for the recovery of our living in Scotland, I trust, God willing, shall redound to her Grace's own commodity, and shall be more able to do her Highness better service there than here.'[58]

But Lennox was playing a duplicitous game. He sent Laurence Nesbit to London with a twofold mission: to ask Cecil to request Elizabeth's permission for Lennox to prosecute his claims in Scotland; and secretly to show de Noailles a genealogy showing the Lennoxes' claim to the Scottish throne, and ask him to write to Marie de Guise to express 'the anxiety of his master to serve the Queen Dowager against the disloyal and ungrateful house of Arran'.

Margaret's own instructions to Nesbit contravened Elizabeth's foreign policy, and it is hard to believe that she would not have known this, or the risk she was taking. She told him he must urge Cecil to persuade the Queen neither to support Châtelherault's claim to the Scottish succession, nor enter into a war with the French, who still had great influence in Scotland and were keen to enlist Lennox's support against the Lords of the Congregation and their leader, Châtelherault. In December de Noailles informed Marie de Guise that the pedigree showed that Lennox's claim was superior to that of the Hamiltons,[59] an opinion he repeated two days later.[60]

On Christmas Day Sir Ralph Sadler informed the English Council that Lennox's cousin, the Laird of Cardonald, was now asking him to lead a new faction against Châtelherault and the Lords of the Congregation.[61] Cardonald had written to remind the Lennoxes how in 1557 he had pressed the Earl to move against Marie de Guise, which had then seemed 'the best remedy that I could find touching your lordship's affairs in this country', but had had no response. Yet now, 'the occasion presents that your lordship may with great honour come to your own', and in so doing might gain, 'besides money, other great preys', including 'the great revenge that ye might have of your enemies'.[62] It was a tempting offer, but Lennox resisted it.

Cecil, however, feared that Lennox would succumb to Cardonald's persuasions, and that the Earl's blood feud with the Hamiltons would interfere with Elizabeth's determination to support the Reformation in Scotland.[63] If Lennox fought a private war with the Hamiltons and emerged victorious, the Lords of the Congregation and the Protestant cause might be fatally undermined, and the French – who might yet pursue the Queen of Scots' claim to the English throne – would gain the upper hand and a foothold in Scotland.

That same Christmas Day Cecil gave secret instructions to Thomas Howard, 4th Duke of Norfolk, the Queen's Lieutenant General in the north, 'to have regard to the Earl of Lennox and the Queen's cousin, his wife', for there was cause to fear that the French and the Catholics might lure them into subverting English policy in Scotland.[64] From now on Norfolk and his agents would be watching the Lennoxes.

On 13 January 1560 the Council informed Norfolk that Nesbit had approached Cecil with Lennox's letter requesting licence from the Queen to allow him to send his people to Scotland from time to time to negotiate with his friends there in regard to his restitution. Cecil communicated this to the Council as a matter of 'no small moment', because he believed that the French were using Lennox.

Having learned that Nesbit had secretly visited de Noailles, the Council 'hauled him before them'.[65] Under questioning he rashly quoted de Noailles as saying that Lennox did well to pursue 'the title that he had to the crown of Scotland, failing the Queen of France and Scotland and issue of her body, as we are all mortals'.[66] He confessed that his master had required de Noailles to write to Marie de Guise in favour of his claim to the Scottish throne. The councillors regarded this as 'very dangerous' and committed Nesbit to the Tower, where he was to be 'further examined'. They wrote a letter informing Lennox of his servant's imprisonment, which Norfolk was to deliver to him 'without appearing to him or to his wife to have any knowledge of the cause', but presumably watching his reaction. Norfolk was also ordered to be even more vigilant on all fronts, and to prevent any Scotsman from crossing the border without his knowledge.[67]

When Lennox found out that Nesbit had been sent to the Tower, he wrote at once to Cecil to say that he marvelled at it, as Nesbit's mission had concerned only Châtelherault's right to the Scottish throne. He trusted that the Queen would still support him and Margaret in the recovery of his lands in Scotland, considering how gracious her forebears had always been to his wife and himself, and how 'upright' the Lennoxes had been 'from the beginning to this hour'. He prayed 'that he may know the offence of his servant'.[68]

According to Thomas Bishop, the soothsayer whom Margaret kept in her house told her, when Nesbit was in the Tower, that the latter would not cause trouble for her, but that she would face a greater trouble yet all would be well in the end. Bishop asserted that she and Lennox did not cease to say 'that they would set all upon six and seven'[69] – meaning that they would risk everything to achieve their aims.

On 15 January the Council explained to Lennox that Nesbit's 'strange conduct' and the genealogy they had found on him were the reasons why he was in the Tower. They were sorry that Nesbit's 'lewd handling' of Lennox's affairs had been injurious to the Earl's causes, but assured him that they could not have done otherwise.[70]

A week later Lennox replied that he in turn was sorry that his servant Nesbit's conduct 'should be the occasion of his own punishment and the hindrance of his [own] suit'. Lying in his teeth, he assured them that Nesbit's mission had solely concerned Châtelherault, and desired them, 'as the poor man has perhaps overshot himself in words, and considering the service that he [Lennox] has done to the Queen's progenitors, that his servant may be set at liberty'. He also sent 'his wife's commendations to their lordships, with thanks for their remembrance of her'.[71]

But the interrogation of Nesbit continued, and it is clear that he talked. On 3 February 1560 Quadra informed King Philip that the Queen herself had ordered Nesbit to tell the Council what Margaret had instructed him to say to de Noailles. Immediately, they had him rearrested and sent for his mistress.

As soon as she arrived at court, Margaret herself was brought before the Council. She would only say that, as she was the nearest relative to the Queen of Scots and her husband was next in succession to the Scottish crown, she had sent to beg Elizabeth not to favour Châtelherault or his sons, and not to enter into a war with the French on this account, as she was sure that if the Queen of Scots were to die without sons, the French would certainly put Margaret herself on the Scottish throne. As Elizabeth was already under threat from the French in regard to Mary Stuart's claim, the last thing she would have wanted to hear was that they had another claimant in mind, and the prospect of a new French-backed government in Edinburgh would have been anathema to her.

But Quadra did not believe that Margaret had any treasonable intentions, and thought that the interrogations of her and Nesbit were all part of a plot by the government to discredit Catholics. 'These people are cleverly making sure of all the Catholics of whom they have any suspicion by summoning them hither on various excuses.'[72]

But Queen Elizabeth was suspicious, indeed paranoid, about the female cousins who might pose a threat to her crown. She had demoted Lady Katherine Grey, her next heir under the 1544 Act of Succession, from Lady of the Bedchamber to Lady of the Presence Chamber. In January 1560 Quadra reported: 'The Queen calls Lady

Katharine her daughter, although the feeling between them can hardly be that of mother and child. She even talks about formally adopting her. On the other hand Cecil tells me that neither she nor any other woman will succeed, in order to exclude also the Countess of Lennox.' If Margaret's son Darnley were taken to France, that would really discountenance the English government.[73]

To pre-empt any French designs on Darnley, and because of the dangerous pretensions of his mother, Elizabeth took steps to obtain evidence that Margaret was illegitimate. The Queen's allies, the Lords of the Congregation, led by Châtelherault, were also keen to see Margaret declared a bastard, as the young Queen Mary's health was poor and they could not stomach the thought of the Lennoxes succeeding in Scotland.[74] But all that could be found was evidence that Angus had been precontracted to another lady when he married Margaret's mother, which was well known and had not prevented the Pope from declaring Margaret legitimate. Elizabeth was nevertheless determined to put an end to French influence in Scotland. On 27 February, at Berwick, her representatives and the Lords of the Congregation concluded a treaty whereby she agreed to send a force to overthrow the Queen Regent and drive out the French.

On 28 February Lennox, in a letter sent to Cecil from Settrington, marvelled 'at his servant Nesbit's crime, knowing his own uprightness'. He explained his dealings with the French ambassador, said he was determined to support his claims in Scotland against Châtelherault's base birth, and again refused to recognise Châtelherault as governor. Nevertheless, asserting 'his [own] innocence in all his transactions', he assured the Queen that he would not undermine her efforts to support the Protestant Reformation in Scotland.[75]

Lord Darnley was clearly seen as a viable contender for the English crown as well as that of Scotland. On 7 March Quadra wrote: 'I understand that, if any disaster happens to the Queen's life or estate, the Catholics will raise to the throne a son of the Countess of Lennox, and this talk, according to what Paget tells me, is well founded. Both the lad and his parents are strong Catholics, and they say he is very promising.' Elizabeth was determined to counter that, and signified her intention of declaring Lord Hastings, a distant cousin who was descended from the Plantagenets,[76] as her successor, although Hastings himself was 'quite of a different opinion and goes in constant dread of being sent to the Tower'.[77] Yet according to Quadra, writing on 15 March, 'the people in the country are so anxious to have Lady Margaret's son for king, that not only would he be universally accepted if the Queen were to die without issue, but I am told that at the first opportunity, even now, many Catholic lords would proclaim him king. In any case they will not have any more women to rule them as they are so afraid of foreign influence. He has the best right of any of the claimants, and is the best in every way, but it is feared that the French want to get hold of him.'[78]

In April 1560 an English army laid siege to Leith, the port of Edinburgh, which was held by French troops of the Queen Regent. The last years of Marie's regency had seen her fighting a losing battle against the increasingly powerful Lords of the Congregation, who overthrew her later that April and set up a Protestant Great Council to govern on behalf of the absent Queen Mary. Châtelherault was its figurehead, but real power was held by Moray and Knox. On 11 June Marie de Guise died of dropsy at Edinburgh Castle, leaving the way clear for the new government to implement a Protestant reformation and drive out the French. Hostilities now ceased and a new treaty, signed at Leith, brought to an end Scotland's 'Auld Alliance' with France.

On 6 July, at Edinburgh, another treaty, negotiated by Cecil, was concluded, providing for closer relations between England and Scotland, and for the recognition of Elizabeth as the rightful queen of England, a clause that the Queen of Scots consistently refused to ratify. In August the Scottish Parliament, in defiance of its lawful Catholic sovereign, and without her assent, passed the legislation that would establish the Protestant Reformation in Scotland. The Catholic faith was outlawed and the celebration of Mass became a capital offence.

In September Margaret's red-haired cousin, James Douglas, now Earl of Morton, rode south, as ambassador for the Lords of the Congregation, to express their gratitude for Elizabeth's support. On the way he visited his cousin Margaret at Settrington, Lennox then being away. Morton was now on the opposite side of the religious divide from Margaret, having become a reformer in 1557 and a founder member of the Lords of the Congregation.

Both Margaret and Morton would probably have heard how Robert Dudley's wife, Amy Robsart, had recently been found dead, her neck broken, at the foot of a flight of stairs at Cumnor Place, Oxfordshire, and how Dudley had been forbidden the court pending the outcome of an inquest that would clear him of murder. It would have been around this time, according to the spy Forbes, that Margaret allegedly allowed her fool to disparage Dudley and his family by calling them 'traitor's birds', saying Dudley had had his wife killed, and using 'more odious words' than it was fit to repeat. Forbes also claimed that Margaret had said to Hugh Allen that a man of good reputation had told her that Dudley had syphilis.[79] But Forbes's testimony is suspect.

Margaret had continued to contest the right of Morton's ward, Archibald Douglas, to the earldom of Angus, but Morton must have been very persuasive as he now prevailed upon her to relinquish her claim. However, because Lennox was not present to give his consent, her agreement held no force in law,[80] and in fact Lennox refused to sanction it, for which Margaret was grateful, having regretted capitulating to Morton.

Thanks to Cecil's brilliant diplomacy in negotiating the Treaty of Edinburgh, Elizabeth now stood high in the estimation of the Scots, and in August 1560 Moray proposed that she marry Châtelherault's son, the Earl of Arran. Naturally it seemed to the Lennoxes that the Queen was favouring their rival for the Scottish throne, and soon afterwards, to add insult to injury, she snubbed them by overlooking Lennox and appointing several prominent Protestants to the Council of the North.[81] The couple had compromised themselves by their dealings with de Noailles, and that autumn they were summoned to court, where Elizabeth could keep an eye on them.

Lennox still wanted the Scottish throne, yet he feared that Elizabeth was doing her best to undermine his ambitions. On 15 October he and Margaret complained to Bishop de Quadra 'that not only did the Queen treat them as prisoners because they were Catholics, but she was trying to injure their claim to the succession by helping the Duke of Châtelherault'. They begged King Philip to help them, as they were sure, with his favour, to recover what rightly belonged to them and restore Catholicism in Scotland with the aid of their friends. Quadra thought they were referring to what might happen if the Queen of Scots died, but they explained that they did not mean it in that way, but would attempt to overthrow her at once. What they were effectively asking Philip to do was send an armed force to support them in a coup.

Quadra was aware that the French ambassador had secretly been treating with the Lennoxes, but the Lennoxes had made it clear that they did not trust the French, and he feared 'that they may be led by passion to do something rash'. Intriguing with the French had been rash, and they evidently knew it because they asked Quadra if, in the event of their being in danger because of it, King Philip would allow them to go to Flanders. He said he would write to his master and ask him, and urged Philip to answer without delay. He also sent him a genealogical tree of the kings of Scotland, 'with a statement of the rights of the various claimants to the succession'.[82]

On 20 November, having heard that the intention of Cecil and the Protestant Council was to make Hastings king, Quadra reported to Philip that the Lennoxes were worried about it and had begged leave from the Queen to go home to Yorkshire.[83] Permission was evidently granted, because ten days later Lennox wrote from Settrington to Cecil, complaining that copies of the letter and genealogy he had sent him had been sent to the Hamiltons and his other enemies in Scotland. His friends there had seen them. He demanded that, since Morton was unjustly keeping the earldom of Angus from Margaret, and Glencairn was a traitor for deceiving Henry VIII and Lennox, his own affairs be kept secret. 'And I hope in God that, if I and my wife prosper in our matters,' he added, it would contribute more to the Queen's profit than anything his enemies could do. He desired pardon 'for writing thus plainly' and concluded 'with my wife's hearty commendations to you and my lady your wife'.[84]

Margaret had brought back with her to Settrington a new servant, Mabel Fortescue, who on 30 November wrote to Francis Yaxley to thank him 'for having placed her with my lady's Grace, who as yet is very gentle and gracious'. Yaxley had also recommended his cousin, Mary Silles, to Margaret. Mabel's letters deal only with domestic matters, not intrigues, but they reveal that Margaret kept in her household several young girls who were royal wards – the orphaned heirs to landed estates. Cecil had been appointed Master of the Court of Wards in January 1561, and it was his responsibility to ensure that the estates of each ward were properly administered during his or her minority, and to arrange for the care, upbringing and marriage of every ward in his charge. Wardships were granted by the court and could be a lucrative source of income, since the guardian gained control of the ward's lands and could use a third of their revenues to his own advantage; he could also marry them off to his own profit. Needless to say, it was a system that was open to abuse, but Mabel had been lucky. In letters she addressed Yaxley as 'My good Governor', a term used to address a guardian, who would call his ward his 'charge', as Yaxley did. Probably both these girls were his wards, and the Lennoxes had agreed to them living in their household.[85]

Early in December Cecil laid down strategies for dealing with Lennox. If he caused further trouble, he was to be reminded that he had fulfilled none of the undertakings he had made in his marriage treaty, and that the Crown had had no benefit from him; and that he had sworn allegiance to the Queen as her naturalised subject and promised that he would never have any private dealings with a foreign power without her licence. Cecil thought that Lennox's pursuit of his restoration in Scotland was 'but a colour' for something greater. Elizabeth had been unusually forbearing. 'The Queen is good lady to Lord Lennox and his wife in suffering them to enjoy those great livings without disturbance, considering what faint hearts they bear her, and against their own commodities [welfare, benefits] seek to be her enemy. He enjoys more of the Queen's liberality yearly than he thinks. The Queen's usage of him has been more gracious than that of other Princes, and his liberty not so liberally overseen as he reports.'

Cecil also referred to Lennox having in the past been in negotiations with Lucy Somerset, Lady Latimer, with a view to marrying one of her daughters – all co-heiresses – to Darnley. However, since the death of Henry II, there had been no more talk of that, and the friendship between Lennox and Lady Latimer had cooled more than a year before.[86] The Lennoxes now had bigger fish to fry, and the event they had been anticipating occurred on 5 December 1560, when Francis II died in agony due to complications arising from an abscess in the ear, leaving Mary, Queen of Scots, a widow at eighteen.

12

'Her Son Should Be King'

Margaret wasted no time in putting her long-cherished plans into action. Local tradition has it that she was residing at Whorlton Castle on the North Yorkshire moors[1] when she wrote to Mary proposing a marriage with Darnley. This is said to have been in the autumn of 1561, but Margaret had broached the matter long before then. Lennox was already cherishing hopes that, if the widowed Mary returned to Scotland, she would reverse his attainder and restore his estates. On 30 November, at Settrington, he had written to Elizabeth telling her that Galston and his friends in Scotland had advised him to sue for pardon and his lands to the Queen of Scots, 'always with your Majesty's advice. I intend still to follow your Majesty's pleasure as in time past before that of my friends, trusting to have comfortable answer.'[2]

Mary's marriage to his son would render Lennox's restoration a certainty. But Darnley was Elizabeth's subject, and both Lennox and Margaret must have known that she would not approve of the match. Indeed, she had already made it clear that anyone who stood in the line of succession must not marry without her express permission; as the law stood, to contravene that was to commit treason – and Margaret had good cause to know it, for the law had been passed as a result of her own folly in precontracting herself to Thomas Howard. But she, like her cousin, Lady Katherine Grey, seems to have taken little account of that.

What happened to Katherine served as a chilling example of what could befall royal heirs who dared to marry without the Queen's permission. In December 1560 Katherine went through a secret ceremony of marriage with the man she loved, Edward Seymour,

Earl of Hertford, son of the late Protector Somerset. It was a rash act on the couple's part because Katherine was the Queen's legal, if unacknowledged, heir. Katherine quickly conceived, and when, in the summer of 1561, she could conceal her pregnancy no longer, she appealed to Dudley for help, but he informed the Queen, and Katherine was sent to the Tower. Her child, a son, Edward, was born there the following September – another potential threat to Elizabeth's throne.

Cecil was keeping a wary eye on the Lennoxes. By 12 December 1560 he had in his possession a document sent by the Earl's friends in Scotland through Galston. They belived that if Queen Elizabeth helped the couple, Lennox would recover his earldom and Margaret the earldom of Angus. But they feared his 'great sloth' in the matter; if he was to be more diligent, he would find more friends in Scotland.[3]

Three days later Cecil informed Lennox that Elizabeth, on hearing of the French King's death, had postponed her appeal to Queen Mary on the Earl's behalf. 'I am sorry for this stay of your matters,' Cecil wrote, adding that he thought it likely that the delay would be to Lennox's advantage, and sending his 'humble commendations to my lady's Grace', assuring them both of his good intentions towards them.[4]

Elizabeth had already anticipated that the Lennoxes might try to marry Darnley to Mary, which was naturally an alarming prospect, given that it would unite two strong claims to the English throne. No one knew what Mary would do now, and until the Scottish Queen's future was settled, Elizabeth realised that it was imperative to keep the family in England, and abandoned all thought of helping Lennox to recover his Scottish estates.

On 16 December she wrote to Lennox: 'We are sorry, in respect of your particular cause, that the death of the French King does so alter the time, or suspend the judgment of what is meet, that it seems requisite for a season to forbear for your causes, and yourself also to stay, not doubting but that it will give us better occasion to further the same.' Cleverly she implied that this disruption to her efforts on Lennox's behalf was merely temporary, 'as surely for our cousin your wife's sake, nature shall duly move us, and for your own sake, being our subject' – a timely reminder, this – 'we will not neglect nor predetermine any thing that reasonably we may do'. She ended by sending her 'most hearty commendations to her dear cousin, the Earl's wife'.[5]

Thomas Randolph, Elizabeth's agent in Scotland, had also guessed that the Lennoxes would try to marry Darnley to Queen Mary. On 23 December he told Cecil he wished that Darnley could be summoned to court to pre-empt anyone trying to lure him to Scotland or any other place.[6] Randolph, who admired Châtelherault, had no time for Lennox, and regarded him as a traitor to his country.[7]

By now the Lennoxes had had enough of the troublesome Thomas Bishop, and it may have been around this time that 'the Earl discharged him his house'. Bishop evidently saw in this the hand of Margaret, and now, cast out and in need of money, he saw an opportunity of being revenged on her and of recovering his disputed manor. By the end of the year he had agreed to act for the Privy Council as an informer against the Lennoxes.[8] Clearly his loyalty to Lennox had been suborned on account of Margaret's antipathy and his own desire for royal favour and preferment, and possibly, aware of the couple's hopes for Darnley, he had approached the Council himself. That December, having apparently heard his employers complaining about the Queen, he wrote for his new masters a tract against the Lennoxes in which he claimed that they thought Elizabeth ungrateful for their service.[9] That was followed, on 9 February, by another tract written for Cecil, in which Bishop himself bragged of his manifold good services to England.[10]

It is important to remember that much of the information laid against the Lennoxes in this period came from Thomas Bishop. He was a clever man, and the detail in his statements argues some basis in fact, but he had an agenda. He had long hated Margaret, who had probably poisoned Lennox's mind against him, and he was out for preferment at court. Bishop's information tallies closely – sometimes word for word – with that of the man who was probably one of his informants, the spy William Forbes, which suggests collusion, either to supply false information, or to ensure that there were no discrepancies that might cast doubt. Therefore the statements of both should be treated with caution, and we should look elsewhere for corroborative evidence, which does not always exist.

On 23 February 1561 Quadra informed his master that 'Lady Margaret Lennox is trying to marry her son, Lord Darnley, to the Queen of Scotland, and I understand she is not without hope of succeeding.' But the Scottish Parliament was recommending that Mary marry Châtelherault's heir, Arran,[11] which in itself was enough to spur the Lennoxes onwards with their plans.

It was probably during the winter of 1560–1 that Margaret commissioned the court artist Levina Teerlinc to paint a miniature of

Darnley,[12] which was almost certainly destined for Queen Mary. In February Margaret arranged for Darnley, now fourteen, to go to France with Francis Russell, Earl of Bedford, who had been sent to offer Mary Elizabeth's condolences on the death of the late King.[13] Darnley carried with him a letter from his mother to the widowed Queen, which he delivered to her personally at Orléans.[14] Margaret wanted her son to make an impression on Mary, and inevitably people drew their own conclusions.

By now it was clear that Elizabeth, wishing to keep the Lennoxes in England, had no intention of helping the Earl to recover his Scottish estates, so in 1561, at Lennox's behest, Galston appealed to Queen Mary, which served only to cast a further cloud of suspicion over Lennox in England.[15] On 16 March Galston wrote from Edinburgh to inform Lennox that he had spoken with the Earl's friends, who were going to capitalise on their favour with the Queen of Scots for obtaining his pardon, and had written to her urging that Lennox and his Countess should enjoy their inheritances in Scotland.[16]

That same day Galston also wrote to Margaret, saying he had intended to visit her and her husband, but his friends had asked him to stay in Scotland to aid them in their appeal. He told her that 'the common bruit' in Edinburgh was that Darnley had gone to France to be a suitor to the Queen of Scots. Many people had asked him if it was true, but he had said he did not know. He hoped to see her soon, and sent his 'hearty commendations to Lord Darnley and Master Charles'.[17]

According to Bishop, Margaret continued secretly to build support for the marriage of Darnley to Queen Mary. After Easter, which fell on 6 April, she covertly sent her servant, Ralph Lacy,[18] with letters of credence from herself, Lennox and Darnley to Aubigny in France, and thence to Spain to the Count of Feria, the former ambassador to England, and his English wife, Jane Dormer, who had devotedly served Mary I.[19] In May, Bishop revealed, Margaret persuaded Lennox to ask Galston to carry letters into France. Lennox wrote them in French, at her behest, and Darnley handed them to the Queen of Scots at Orléans.[20] But Mary was not interested in marrying Darnley, and he came away with just two letters from her to his mother.[21]

Margaret was placing herself in a perilous position, because in the wake of a recent supposedly Catholic plot to murder Elizabeth by witchcraft, the Queen – who had enlightened religious views but feared Catholic activists – had reluctantly authorised Cecil to bring the full force of the law to bear on recusants suspected of intriguing against her.[22]

If Bishop is to be believed, Margaret was now intriguing behind the scenes with Scottish nobles, spurred on by the news that Queen Mary was planning to return to Scotland to take up the reins of government. With Mary just north of the border, it would be far easier to arrange a match with Darnley. Around Whit Sunday (25 May), after Galston's return to Settrington, Margaret sent him and William Forbes to Lennox's brother-in-law, the Earl of Sutherland,[23] and other noblemen, to 'prove their good minds and affection towards the marriage of her son, the Lord Darnley, with the Queen of Scots'. Forbes brought their answers to Margaret at Temple Newsam; one, Lord Seton, had said 'that he would not only spend his living, but would also spend his blood for that purpose'.[24] Margaret was to have cause to regret entrusting William Forbes with such a mission.

In the summer of 1561 Yaxley warned her he had received word that Thomas Bishop had been passing on information about the marriage that was being plotted. This was probably the first indication she had of Bishop's treachery, and of course she could have had no idea how far he had already betrayed her and Lennox. Quadra had revealed the information to Yaxley so that Margaret 'might provide remedy for the same', and arrange for one of his contacts, John Stewart, Laird of Minto and Provost of Glasgow, to take Bishop captive if his nefarious activities took him into Scotland.[25] Bishop would later allege that Lennox wanted Minto to murder him.[26]

On 15 August Sir William Maitland warned Cecil that he had heard that the Queen of Scots intended to 'draw home the Earl of Lennox and set him up against the Duke of Châtelherault'. He trusted that Queen Elizabeth would be on her guard.[27] But Elizabeth had more reasons than that to fear Mary's return to Scotland. Mary had never signed the Treaty of Edinburgh, which had renounced on her behalf her claim to the English crown, vested the regency in the Lords of the Congregation and sealed a friendship between Protestant Scotland and Protestant England. She had also made clear her intention of marrying Don Carlos, the son and heir of Philip of Spain – and Elizabeth had no desire to see a threatening Spanish presence north of the border.

The Lennoxes, of course, held a very different view. When Queen Mary returned to Scotland in August 1561, having avoided an English fleet sent by Elizabeth to intercept her, Margaret's joy – according to Bishop – knew no bounds. 'Hearing that the Queen of Scots had passed through the seas, she sat down and gave God thanks, declaring to those by how he had always preserved that Princess at all times, especially now, for when the Queen's ships were almost near taking of the Scottish Queen, there fell down a mist from heaven that separated them and preserved her.'[28] Now it would be easier for Margaret to bring her plans to fruition.

Lennox had high hopes of regaining his lands. Bishop was to state that, after learning of Mary's arrival in Edinburgh, he and Margaret sent Arthur Lallard, Darnley's schoolmaster, ostensibly to meet with Aubigny, but secretly to give Mary letters from Lord Darnley. One morning the Earl of Sutherland brought Lallard to the Queen's chamber at Stirling so that he could deliver the letters. She walked up and down with him, out of earshot of everyone but her women, and then sat down on a coffer and talked of Darnley, 'his stature, age, qualities, ability', and of Margaret's friends in Scotland. Lallard thought that Darnley had been 'well accepted'.

He then spoke to Mary of Lennox's request to have his appeal heard before the Scottish Parliament. Her reply was evasive: 'she was but newly returned into her realm, therefor she could not give me such an answer as she would; but all she might do for my lord and my lady her aunt, she would do at a proper time all that they of reason could demand, desiring my lady to be always her good aunt, as she knew her for to be', and sending 'remembrances to them both'.[29] Mary was stalling. She must have been aware that few of her lords would welcome Lennox back to Scotland,[30] and that he was a potential focus for trouble.

But Margaret was encouraged by Mary's message. Soon she had various agents – Forbes, his man, her falconer Wat Nepe, Thomas Kelly and Rigg, her footman – 'continually passing with letters into Scotland', assisted by Galston. Bishop alleged that she became a spy for Mary against the English government, devising that in all the letters that passed the Queen of Scots should be referred to as 'the Hawk', and insisting that those missives should all be burnt. He asserted that she enjoined Mary to warn her powerful Guise uncles that any information she confided to them should remain secret. Mary's replies to Margaret were written in her own hand.[31] Forbes was to say that Margaret informed Mary 'of all the things she had intelligence of',[32] and that her secret dealings were known to Nesbit, Yaxley, Hugh Allen, Lallard and Thomas Fowler, the clerk of her kitchen, who had recently killed a poor stranger in circumstances that are unknown, and subsequently fled.[33]

At the end of September Margaret sent Galston to ask the Queen of Scots whether she would keep her promise made in France or not, 'and by plain and open words [he] made suit in the Earl and Countess's names to the Queen for her marriage to Lord Darnley'. Mary commanded him to write to the Lennoxes telling them that he had received a 'gentle answer' that she considered the matter to be of great importance, and that she would advise them of her decision, whereupon Galston told William Forbes that all would be well for Lord Darnley.[34]

Bishop later claimed that Margaret openly spoke of what a good thing it would be to have both the realms in one through the marriage of the Queen of Scots to Darnley, who would then be king of both England and Scotland, 'as her prophesiers at the death of her first son told her'.[35] Later Margaret would say much the same thing in a letter to Quadra, and Mary was to inform Elizabeth that, from the time she arrived in Scotland, Margaret had never ceased urging her to marry Darnley. She herself, she would protest, had never given him a thought, or heeded his mother, for she had far greater suitors in her sights. But Margaret had inundated her with messages, letters and tokens pressing her son's suit, and repeatedly reminded her that he was of the royal blood of England and Scotland, a Stuart, a Catholic and her rightful heir, and that he would always treat her respectfully.[36]

The French were unlikely to back any claim by Margaret and her sons to the English throne. On 8 October Sir Nicholas Throckmorton reported to Elizabeth that Mary's uncle, Francis, Duke of Guise, had insisted that his niece was Elizabeth's lawful heir. Although Mary was excluded from inheriting the crown because she was not born in England, he cited the cases of King Stephen and Richard II, who had both been born in what was now France. As to Margaret's claim, the question of her legitimacy would prove a greater obstacle. However, people were saying that Katherine Grey and the sons of 'Madam Lennox' should be recalled to court, 'as they ought to be'.[37]

The Lennoxes still did not know that Elizabeth's spies had been planted in their household and were reporting their activities, but Bishop stated that they went in fear of Elizabeth finding out about their intrigues with Mary. They told their friend John Lockhart, the Laird of Barr, that 'Queen Elizabeth loved them not, and that they looked every day for a pursuivant to come to their gates'[38] with warrants for their arrest. Barr was an associate of Galston, and Barr

Castle still stands in Galston, Ayrshire. From 1561 he was active on behalf of the Lennoxes in pursuing Queen Mary's marriage to Darnley.

Lord Grey, now governor of Berwick and warden of the Scottish Marches, was evidently unaware of Forbes's true role. On 3 November he informed Cecil that a servant of Lennox, William Forbes, had been waiting in Berwick for a fortnight to receive intelligence from Châtelherault's son, Arran, and should have crossed into Scotland with errands from Lennox, but had been commanded by his master to remain till letters came to him from Scotland. Grey was content to let him stay there, because he hoped to intercept his letters. In the meantime he would be offering him 'courteous entertainment' to pre-empt Forbes becoming suspicious. But Grey was concerned that if he found reasons in the letters to arrest him, Forbes's informants would go to ground. Grey asked Cecil what he should do,[39] and Cecil probably told him that Forbes was in Dudley's employ. He certainly ordered him to arrest any of Lennox's genuine messengers, which Grey did.[40]

On 27 November Quadra reported:

> The Queen has sent a summons to Lady Margaret Douglas to come hither [to London] with her husband and children. It is said publicly that the reason of this is that she shows favour to the Catholics in the province of York, and that consequently the Bishop dares not visit his diocese or punish any Papist. This reason, however, is a pretended one, and has been made public to deceive the people as to the reality, which is that the Queen hears that Lady Margaret is trying to marry her son to the Queen of Scots. This has been divulged by one of her servants whom the Queen has taken into her service and rewarded for the information, and inquiries are now being made as to those who may have taken part in the matter. The earls of Northumberland and Westmorland and the Duke of Norfolk have been brought hither at once with the excuse that the Queen wished them to pass Christmas with her.

Norfolk had long been keeping Margaret under surveillance, and it was known that the earls were her friends. Margaret, probably warned by Quadra that a summons was on its way, had evidently written to the ambassador, for he continued:

> I understand that Lady Margaret is much distressed, as she thinks she will be thrown into the Tower, and that her son's life is in

danger. I am told that she is resolved not to deny the allegation about the marriage of the Queen of Scots as she says it is no crime, and as that Queen is her niece, the daughter of her brother, she thinks she has done no harm in advising her to do what she believes would be the best for her, namely, to marry her son, by which the succession of this kingdom would be secured to the Scotch Queen, and all reason for strife would be avoided in case of the Queen of England dying without issue.

In other words, Margaret was doing her patriotic best to avoid the prospect of a war over a disputed succession.

If the English should allege that the Queen of Scots could not succeed in consequence of her being a foreigner, she would nevertheless reign over the kingdom by right of this youth, the son of Lady Margaret, if she married him, as he is an Englishman and beyond doubt the nearest heir to the crown after her. This Queen, however, bases her security on there being no certain successor to whom the people could turn if they were to tire of her rule, and I understand she is in great alarm about this business, and determined to obtain possession of the persons without the reason being made public, as she fears that if the people were to understand the business it might please them and cause a disturbance if Lady Margaret were free. In order to summon her without turmoil they have taken the pretext of finding fault with her about religion, which will make her unpopular with London people. This gives great pain to the faithful, as they had placed all their trust in this woman and her son, and if they dared I am sure they would help her, and forces would be forthcoming in the country itself if they had any hopes of help from without.[41]

Margaret had panicked prematurely. What Quadra assumed was a summons with sinister import was probably an invitation to spend Christmas at court,[42] so that the Council could keep her under observation. Moreover, it seems highly unlikely that Margaret did go to London at this time; as will be seen, she was still expected there at the end of January.

That December Elizabeth began pressing for a meeting with Queen Mary, a matter that was to remain under discussion for some months. But – again this is Bishop – 'Lady Lennox was a let [hindrance] to the Queen of Scots coming through England.' Fearing that Mary might inadvertently let slip something about their secret dealings, she did her best to persuade her not to agree to coming to England for the meeting. She sent word to the Queen of Scots 'to have her most trusty friends about her, and to keep herself near the castles of Edinburgh and Stirling, declaring that if she came here, England would have them all'.[43]

On 14 December Lord Grey had to inform Cecil that he had been about to apprehend messengers of the Earl of Lennox, but they had given him the slip and gone south to Northallerton, where they had been arrested.[44] One was John Lockhart, the young Laird of Barr, who was taken with letters that John Knox described as 'the cause of his and [the Lennoxes'] trouble', as their content led to accusations that they had been 'trafficking with Papists'.[45]

Lennox, hearing of Barr's arrest, immediately went up to London 'of his own accord', as Cecil later divulged.[46] Margaret probably did not accompany him.[47] Lennox knew that the letters found on young Barr were compromising and clearly wanted to limit the damage. He must have given a satisfactory explanation, otherwise the government would quickly have moved against him, which it did not.

For some weeks prior to Christmas, Elizabeth was very ill with dropsy.[48] Thomas Bishop would claim that, during the festive season, hearing of the Queen's sickness, Margaret's servants at Settrington 'said their mistress should rule as long, and that they should have the ball at their foot'.[49] The implication was that they were hoping that Elizabeth would die so that Margaret could ascend the throne – but of course this could have been a malicious invention on Bishop's part.[50]

On 2 January 1562 Randolph informed Cecil that 'nothing will be done touching the Earl of Lennox', and that the Queen of Scots 'will make the Queen privy to all his intention'.[51] On the 15th, Maitland told Cecil he trusted 'that Lennox's practices here will do no great harm', and said that Queen Mary had assured him they would not.[52] That day Randolph confirmed that Maitland had spoken to Mary 'touching the Earl of Lennox. She said that whatever he intends she will advertise the Queen.'[53]

Despite the gathering storm clouds, Margaret remained hopeful. It must have been early in January 1562 – she would not have been free to do it later in the year – that she commissioned a full-length double portrait of Darnley and his younger brother Charles, who was still in long skirts and not yet breeched; the brothers stand in front of a battened wall. Unusually the picture was painted on linen, probably so that it could be rolled up and transported easily to Scotland to be viewed by Queen Mary. It was inscribed: *These be the sons of the right honourables the Earl of Lennox and the Lady Margaret's Grace, Countess of Lennox and Angus, An. Do. MDLXII [1562] Henry Stewart, Lord Darnley and Douglas, aetatis svae X; Charles Stewart his brother, aetatis svae VI.*[54] Although the inscription states that they were respectively in their tenth and sixth years, Darnley was actually fifteen and Charles not quite five.

As we see below, Margaret was expected daily in the capital at the end of January. It has been stated that, after spending Christmas at court, she must have left with her children early in the new year and gone back to Yorkshire,[55] but Quadra makes it clear that in the first half of January she had sent a messenger to the Queen asking if she could visit her.[56] She had no doubt been worrying how Lennox was faring at court.

On 17 January Quadra reported that William Rastell,

one of the judges at Westminster, has secretly gone to Flanders, which has caused great sensation here. The cause of his going, although it is publicly said to be on account of religion, I am told by some of his friends is to avoid signing an opinion which seven or eight lawyers are to give on the succession to the crown, declaring as it is suspected that there is no certain heir. All this is to exclude the Scotch Queen and Lady Margaret and declare that the selection of a king devolves upon the nation itself. I do not know whether it be true that Rastell has fled for this reason, but I am quite sure that it is a scheme of Cecil and his friends, as he himself has told me several times. The plan of getting these lawyers to sign the opinion is to make sure of them at a time when they will not dare to say what they think so as not to appear attached to the cause of the Queen of Scotland, Lady Margaret, or the Catholic religion.

What Quadra had to report next was ominous:

Notwithstanding Lady Margaret's message recently to the Queen that she wished to visit her, to which a very civil answer was sent, they have arrested a servant of her husband, and have commenced proceedings against them [the Lennoxes]. I think this must be in order to make sure of my lady's son one way or another, as they certainly have reason to fear him seeing the large number of adherents the youth has in this country.[57]

On 28 January Arran asked Randolph – hopefully, one imagines – if it was true 'that the Earl of Lennox and his lady are both put in ward'.[58] It was not. Two days later Randolph asked Cecil 'what he had heard of the Earl of Lennox, of whom it was reported that he was sent for to court'. Cecil told him that Lennox had come of his own accord as soon as he heard that Barr had been arrested. He added that the Council were taking 'no great account' of Lennox, for Maitland believed that Mary would not marry anyone of Darnley's age.[59] Mary was then nineteen, four years older than Darnley.

Soon Margaret had devastating news. On 31 January Quadra reported talk 'that Lady Margaret wants to marry her son to the Queen of Scotland, which has given rise to much suspicion here, and the Earl her husband has been arrested with three or four of his servants and others'.[60] Lennox was being held under house arrest in Rolls House, Chancery Lane, the official residence of Sir William Cordell, Master of the Rolls.[61] When state prisoners were being investigated or under house arrest, the Crown often asked loyal, high-ranking subjects to take charge of them.

At the end of January Margaret was expected in London daily with her sons. Elizabeth and her government recognised her as a greater threat than Lennox. Quadra reported:

> The Queen wishes to take this opportunity of getting Parliament to declare that there is no certain heir to the crown, and giving her the power of nominating whom she pleases to succeed her. This would have the effect, they tell her, of making her more respected in and out of the country, and would ensure her living more securely; but Cecil's scheme, and he rules all, is only to exclude the Queen of Scotland and Lady Margaret, who are Catholics, and keep the kingdom in the hands of heretics.[62]

Quadra added that his letter 'did not go as the post was stopped at Dover. The ports were closed as it was suspected Lady Margaret's son wished to escape, and the Queen herself gave me to understand that it was for reasons of great importance.' She did not, however, say what these were, for she did not trust Quadra, who was intriguing with too many of her enemies. However, he did not put much weight on her words, explaining that many people had expressed the opinion that the closure of the ports

> was only an artifice to give them time to raise a sum of money in Antwerp on exchange here, the exchanges having risen greatly as they believed there that the value of money had fallen.
>
> The statement that Lady Margaret's son has fled to Scotland is thought to be false. If it were true the Queen would not be so calm as she is, and the young man may be expected here with his mother any day. I hear they have sent to arrest two or three of the principal gentlemen in the country on suspicion of their favouring the cause of this youngster.
>
> They have thought well also to inquire whether I have any understanding with Lady Margaret, and have asked all those who have been arrested on this account if I know anything of the matters they confess.

But Quadra had covered his tracks.

> The truth is they can hear nothing of me but what the Queen should be pleased at, but these heretics so dislike my stay here that they cease not to plot how they can place me in her bad graces. What they are doing with me now in Lady Margaret's affair they did last year when the Abbé Martinengo's coming was under discussion, but they have never dared to go so far as this before, not even the Queen herself.

Abbé Ascanio Martinengo, the Papal Nuncio, had been sent to England to establish friendly relations between the Vatican and Elizabeth I, but she would not allow him to enter England, and had indeed ordered the arrest of several prominent Catholics. Quadra himself had once been accused of complicity in a Papist plot – and now he was under suspicion again. He told Elizabeth he 'was very tired of these inquiries and investigations every year about me and their taking note of those who went in and out of my house, which was so notorious that I could not avoid advising your Majesty about it. She answered me with all the amiability in the world.'[63]

On 7 February John Jewel, Bishop of Salisbury, reported the gossip about Darnley marrying the Queen of Scots in a letter to the Italian theologian Pietro Martire Vermigli:

There is a certain noble lady called the Lady Margaret, a niece
of Henry VIII, and one who is beyond measure hostile to [the
Protestant] religion, more violent even than Queen Mary herself.
The crown, it is surmised, will descend to her son, a young
man of about eighteen, should anything unhappily happen to
Elizabeth, which God forbid. The husband of this woman has
within these few days been committed to the Tower. The son,
they say, is either spirited away by his mother, or has taken
refuge in Scotland. There are, as is usually the case, various
reports concerning him. The Queen of Scotland is, as you know,
unmarried, so that a matrimonial alliance may possibly be
formed between them.[64]

Jewel's letter shows that people were taking the prospect seriously.

On 9 February 1562, as part of the mounting investigation into the
Lennoxes' activities, Thomas Bishop was examined by Cecil. Knowing
him to be their enemy, one who either knew their secrets or would
act out of sheer malice, both Margaret and Lennox had laid complaints
against him, accusing him of bearing false witness against them. In
retaliation, Bishop made an extraordinary self-aggrandising statement,
which makes very clear the enmity between him and Margaret, and
shows him to have been cunning and manipulative. He told Cecil
that, having been charged by her 'with slanderous and untrue instructions against the rule of honesty', he had sent one of his servants to
Settrington to retrieve letters that would 'answer that infamy'. He
said he would consider himself well rewarded if Cecil and 'one or
two of the Council' would hear his answer, 'not for my vain glory,
but to declare my demeanour'. He would then 'study' to serve the
Queen without fear of reprisals from Margaret.

Manifesting astonishment that anyone should suspect him of
intriguing on behalf of the Lennoxes, Bishop proceeded to enumerate,
in many points, how he had served the Queen, under the heading
'My special services in England'. He was prepared to go back a long
way to disparage the Lennoxes and show himself loyal beyond the
ordinary to the Crown. During the fighting at Dumbarton Castle
in the 1540s, 'openly I willed the Earl of Lennox take a pike and
fight rather than return with shame'. Bishop's 'good policy' after that
'betrayal' had been to preserve Henry VIII's power on land, for which
the King had been suitably grateful. After Bishop had showed bravery
at the siege of Boulogne in 1544, he had been 'embraced in the

King's Majesty's arms, with words of comfort, before his whole Privy Council in his privy chamber', and been given many rewards including a £25 annuity. In 1544, in gratitude for Bishop's efforts in negotiating Margaret's marriage treaty, Henry had granted this 'well-beloved servant' the manor of Pocklington, and in 1546 'his Majesty, besides all this (a little before his death), and after the breach with my Lady Lennox, gave me and my heirs 20 marks [of] land'. But all that Bishop had received since the King's death 'had been but trifles'.

He gave a long account of his exceptional service and 'notable exploits' under Edward VI, Somerset and Northumberland, and the paltry rewards he had received. Somerset had 'understood my knowledge and intelligence' and 'to his dying day ever used me in all affairs for Scotland, like a counsellor'. The advice Bishop had given to Somerset and the Duke of Northumberland had stopped Lord Grey entering Scotland at a dangerous moment with six thousand men, 'the flower of England'. Bishop recalled how Queen Mary had restored his pension, despite Margaret telling her that he was a heretic, and how Mary had trusted him in regard to Scottish affairs, whereas she had not trusted Lennox.

Bishop reminded Cecil that he and some of the Privy Councillors had in their possession plans, books and speeches of his, all written in support of 'suppressing the French in Scotland'; these had been sent to Marie de Guise 'to damage me', and possibly he was implying that Margaret had done that. As for his allegiance to England, he had been 'most earnest, most inventive, most cruel and careful to subvert that realm of Scotland [and] let our trumpet be blown upon the Marches, requiring any Scot or Frenchman to charge me!' Whenever Lennox, in return for intelligence, had given a crown to a spy, Bishop had given fourscore. He had been out of pocket 'above a thousand pound' protecting himself because of Margaret's enmity, and he knew that lately Lennox had planned to have him slaughtered in Scotland, 'where he knows I dare not go and no money will save me', and had heard that the Earl had laid a similar trap in England. And now, 'with infamy', Lennox 'by his wife's procurement' had lied about Bishop and tried to compass his ruin by complaining to the Council about him. In an injured tone he trusted that 'in my honest trial the Queen's Majesty will be as good sovereign to me as her gracious father my master was, and her predecessors have been: whom without fear of my Lady Lennox or others I shall truly serve'.

In a postscript Bishop stated that Darnley's tutor, John Elder, had told him he had in his possession letters from Aubigny to Lennox,

Darnley and (Bishop thought) Margaret. 'I know the man,' he added, insinuating himself into Cecil's service, 'and have gone no further with him yet.' Elder 'might be traited [drawn out] a little' on what he knew.[65]

In his postscript Bishop did his best to disparage the Lennox claims to the throne by insisting that, under the terms of her original marriage treaty – the Treaty of Perpetual Peace of 1502 – Margaret Tudor's descendants 'should not claim, enjoy nor inherit any patrimony, lands, dignities, honours, titles nor possessions within the realm of England'. Henry VII had indeed been concerned that, failing male heirs in England, the succession would fall to a Scottish ruler, yet the treaty of 1502 had been broken when James IV invaded England in 1513, and in the end did not prevent the succession of Margaret Tudor's descendants to the throne of England. But Bishop further pointed out that the line of Margaret and her sons had been 'corrupted by meaner blood of subjects', and alleged that, although she had been born in England, she could not be considered English because her mother had not been officially invited into England.[66]

In his efforts to ingratiate himself with his interrogators, Bishop had raked up every damning detail that he could to discredit the Lennoxes. But in mentioning the succession he touched a raw nerve, prompting the Council to commission Alexander Pringle, a former adherent of the Douglases, to examine Margaret's pedigree, and her claim, with a critical eye.[67]

By so vigorously stressing his record of loyal service, and by cleverly showing his employers in the worst light, Bishop apparently exonerated himself from the Lennoxes' complaints. Despite his animosity towards them, he had given little away. But he had not finished with them yet.

No succour would be forthcoming for the Lennoxes from Scotland. On 12 February Randolph informed Cecil that in Edinburgh 'it is not lamented that I can hear of any that the Earl of Lennox is prisoner'. Few knew about Arthur Lallard's visit to Queen Mary at Stirling, and Lennox's friends had 'little hope that he or his shall get great good here'. Despite all his scheming to marry his son to Mary, she did not like the Lennox Stuarts and had determined never 'to match with that race'.[68] Not long afterwards Randolph again informed Cecil, 'The Queen likes not the marriage with the Lord Darnley.'[69]

★

Francis Yaxley was now hauled in for questioning. Bishop had told the Council that if Yaxley was 'well handled, he can tell other matters, and at whose back door he hath had recourse'.[70] The Queen was informed that Yaxley had been spying on her for the Lennoxes, and that Margaret had also employed him to extract information from the Spanish ambassador and to help further Darnley's marriage to Queen Mary.

On 14 February 1562 Yaxley petitioned the Queen's favourite, Robert Dudley, for help, as he had been summoned to appear before the council. Why he thought Dudley would look sympathetically on him seems inexplicable, as he had been imprisoned a year earlier for slandering Dudley, but Dudley had once written to him promising his support if he came to court and saying he would be 'very welcome always unto me'. Evidently that was no longer the case, for by 22 February Yaxley was a prisoner in the Tower,[71] and at some stage during these proceedings he made a confession that incriminated the Lennoxes. He admitted that Quadra had fed him information about matters at court that would be useful to Margaret, and that Quadra had used him and Hugh Allen to pass on messages and tokens to her. Margaret had deployed him as her agent to further the marriage of Darnley with the Queen of Scots, he declared. She and Yaxley had discussed 'the title of my lady and her son' to the throne, and during the past year she had ordered him to canvas her friends in the north and 'bring the matter in head', so that she might learn how much support she could command.[72] Upon this testimony the Council resolved to summon Margaret to London to answer for her conduct.

Around March, Bishop drew up for the government a 'note of gifts made to Lady Margaret Lennox and her husband in the days of Queen Mary, and of her ill treatment of Queen Elizabeth, when Princess'.[73] Elizabeth, already nursing a sense of grievance against the Lennoxes, was now to be reminded of past wrongs to hold in account against them.

Quadra reported on 6 March that Elizabeth and her ministers were 'full of suspicion', having heard that many English Catholic gentlemen, 'tired of what is going on here', had offered their services to the Queen of Scots and were in communication with her. They were also suspicious of Margaret, believing her to be somehow involved. 'They have not done much against her yet, but perhaps when they have despatched ships and placed them between England and Scotland and occupied the land passes they may lay hands on her and on some others with whom they are now temporising.'

Quadra had also heard that there was to be a meeting in Lancaster, under the pretext of a hare hunt, of gentlemen 'who are not favourable to the Catholics, the duke of Norfolk amongst others'. Norfolk, who had been ordered to keep watch on Margaret, was to take with him William Parr, Marquess of Northampton, the earls of Huntingdon (the former Lord Hastings) and Rutland, and the Queen's cousin, Henry Carey, Lord Hunsdon. Quadra was not deceived. 'It is suspected that this meeting may be to fall unawares on some of the Catholics who are most feared, but whom they dare not arrest without some such precaution, for fear of a disaster.' He was almost certainly referring to Margaret and, worried that her arrest was imminent, warned that 'it is quite certain that five or six ships are being fitted out which are to be despatched next week in the direction of Scotland, and which will very soon cause trouble there'.[74]

Norfolk and his colleagues did not make for Lancaster – that had probably been false information fed to Quadra – but instead for York, 'to ensure the province against any rising that might take place'.[75] Norfolk's purpose was almost certainly to close in on Margaret and her associates. It may have been he who arrested 'four gentlemen neighbours' of Lennox's in York – among them Sir Richard Cholmeley, Sir William of Malton and George Chamberlain (probably a kinsman of Sir Richard, the keeper of Scarborough Castle) – and sent them to London. Shortly before 13 March Lennox and these men were questioned.[76]

Lennox, who had not been informed of the reason for his imprisonment, rashly said the one thing calculated to alarm his interrogators and increase their severity. 'Before the Council, being examined, he said his wife was the next heir to the crown.'[77] Quadra told King Philip that he did not think there was much against Lennox, 'but although they gave him hope of speedy liberation, they sent him to the Tower the day before yesterday [11 March]'. Yet still no charges had been laid against him. The real target of the government's campaign was his wife.

Given what had befallen Lord Thomas Howard in the Tower, and her memories of her own long durance there, Margaret must have been horrified when she heard that Lennox was now a prisoner in that same place, and to realise that she herself might very soon be joining him. Quadra continued:

They have sent for Lady Margaret and her sons, and will treat them in the same way as the Earl, and will then declare Lady

Margaret a bastard on the ground that her father was already secretly married when he wedded Queen Margaret. It appears that this evidence was obtained two years ago, at the time the last war began between this Queen and the King of France in Scotland. These heretics both here and in Scotland are much afraid that, if this Queen and the Queen of Scots were to die, Lady Margaret would succeed, and in view of the illness of the Queen of Scots at the time they ordered certain proceedings to be taken to prove the illegitimacy. However this may be, the inclination of the people of this country is strongly in favour of Lady Margaret's son, both amongst Catholics and others of the highest standing. Two of them recently asked me if your Majesty would be willing for this lad to take refuge in Flanders or in some place in this country where help could be given to him. I could only say that your Majesty was not yet aware of what was going on here, and I did not know what your answer would be in such case, but I was convinced of the goodwill your Majesty bore to Lady Margaret on account of her virtue and goodness.[78]

On 13 March Quadra complained, 'This business of Lady Margaret will doubtless do harm to some and is not harmless to me, as the heretics have spread amongst the common people that I had a hand in it, although to me personally they dissemble. The imprisonment of this good lady cannot fail to trouble many Catholics and others.'[79] A week later he wrote:

I have much greater reason to complain of the suspicion with which I am treated. Not a man dares to enter my house because of the distrust that is publicly shown of all those who associate with me, and not a person is arrested for state reasons without his being asked whether he has any conversation with me. They have done this in Lady Margaret Douglas's affair, but have never found what they seek.[80]

In fact Quadra was involved up to his neck, having been often in contact with Margaret herself and her servants and friends. Moreover, the evidence – even without the damning testimony of Thomas Bishop – proves that Margaret had intrigued to marry Darnley to Queen Mary. She had admitted it herself to Quadra in November.

13

'Indignation and Punishment'

Around the middle of March 1562 Margaret was arrested at Settrington. It is likely that Norfolk and his lordly colleagues came to apprehend her, for she was, after all, of the blood royal. They would have brought with them the Queen's warrant, issued by the Court of Star Chamber, and been accompanied by armed guards, who would escort Margaret, her children and her principal servants to London.[1] At this nerve-racking time Margaret focused on practicalities. 'Money was needed for on all sides, for the travelling expenses of my family and servants, and for their maintenance as prisoners.'[2]

Taking with her Darnley, Charles and at least two of her daughters, Margaret set out, no doubt full of apprehension. It was her intention to leave her sons in a safe place and to take the younger children with her, for she had no idea how long she would be away. It was not long since the Queen had sent Katherine Grey to the Tower for marrying without her permission, and that knowledge must have haunted Margaret on her way south.

In a list of 'Intelligences' compiled on 2 April 1562, Quadra wrote, prematurely, that 'Madame Margaret, wife of the Earl of Lennox, has been sent here to prison, her husband being likewise imprisoned; it is suspected that they desired to marry their son to the Queen of Scotland. The prison will soon be full of the nearest relations of the Crown.'[3] But on 3 April he corrected himself, saying that 'Lady Margaret will arrive here during the week, a prisoner, with her two sons.[4] It is thought that after they have examined her she will be cast into the Tower like her husband. The Tower is already full of prisoners, and the suspicions of the Queen increase daily.'[5]

Later that day Quadra received fresh news.

Lady Margaret will arrive here to-day or to-morrow. Her sons remain at York in safe hands, and the going of the Duke of Norfolk with the other hunters in that direction was only to ensure the province against any rising that might take place on this account. The lawyers here are still busy about the question of the succession, and I hear they are much in favour of Lady Margaret. When they have made up their mind who is the rightful heir they will discuss how they shall publish it or if at all. I am sure it will all end by the Queen obtaining power to select her own successor or leave the crown by will, and that Lady Margaret will thus be excluded, and the succession fall into the hands of some heretic, such as the Earl of Huntingdon or the Earl of Hertford.[6]

It may have been with Margaret's connivance that Darnley escaped from his lodging at York, then circumvented the security measures in place at the ports and stole abroad. As a consequence of his brother's flight, Charles was made to stay in York while Margaret was escorted on to London; parting from her sons, leaving one in the hands of strangers, the other facing exile, only added to her anxieties. On arriving at Whitehall, her servants were lodged in the Gatehouse prison at Westminster Abbey, where Lennox's servants were probably already being held, and Margaret and her daughters were confined to apartments in the palace.[7]

Here, almost immediately, she was apprehended on the very serious charges of treason and witchcraft, and conveyed with her daughters to the former Charterhouse at Sheen in Surrey,[8] where she was to remain under house arrest in the custody of the Queen's cousin, the wealthy lawyer and Chancellor of the Exchequer, Sir Richard Sackville, and his wife, Winifred Bridges. Sackville was a first cousin of Anne Boleyn, and therefore related to the Queen; the great scholar Roger Ascham, in *The Schoolmaster*, describing him as 'that worthy gentleman of worthy memory', praised his enlightened views about education,[9] and he was a capable man who would surely have proved a cordial and fair gaoler.

The Carthusian monastery of Sheen had been established by Henry V in 1413. After its dissolution in 1539 it had been granted by the Crown to Henry Grey, Duke of Suffolk, and his wife, Frances Brandon,[10] Margaret's cousin; they had converted the priory buildings into a mansion. After Suffolk was executed in 1554, the property had been declared forfeit. In 1557 Mary I had restored Sheen to the Carthusians, but after Elizabeth's accession they had been evicted and it reverted to the Crown. Sir Richard Sackville had leased a suite of rooms there from 1559. The house lay on the south bank of the River Thames, opposite Syon Abbey and half a mile from Richmond Palace.[11] Here Margaret was allowed to keep a small household of servants, among whom was the faithful Thomas Fowler, now back in her service, having probably been cleared of murder.[12]

On 7 April Randolph informed Cecil: 'It is bruited here that the Lord Darnley is conveyed into France.'[13] How relieved Margaret must have been to hear that.

Elizabeth was now determined to overturn Margaret's claim to the throne as well as her claim to the earldom of Angus. On 2 April 1562 Alexander Pringle, who had been looking into the matter since February, was examined by the Privy Council 'concerning the illegitimacy of Lady Margaret Lennox'. He told Cecil that a servant of Lennox had stated that the priest Dixon had found among Angus's papers proof that 'old Earl Archibald, who died after Flodden Field, broke the [entail], leaving the whole earldom to heirs general', which included females. Dixon had also discovered a copy of the letter written by Angus to Sir John Bellenden, the Justice Clerk of Scotland, which affirmed that there was no entail. But this letter had been 'stopped', or destroyed, by Dixon, to prevent Margaret's cousin Morton from succeeding. This sounds suspect, because evidence that there had been no entail would have validated Margaret's claim. Dixon was her priest, so it is unlikely that he would have deceived and betrayed her so cruelly. One might wonder if Pringle himself had got rid of the letter. Whoever it was, the end result was the same: 'no right remaineth to my Lady Lennox, but insufficient upon the divorcement of the Queen her mother'.[14] In other words, she was a bastard, and barred from inheriting anyway.

Pringle rehearsed the hoary tale of Angus's precontract, saying he had seen Margaret Tudor's bill of divorcement 'under seal' at Berwick. He omitted to mention that the Pope had specifically pronounced Margaret legitimate, but told the Council that 'my Lady Lennox was openly taken and reputed a bastard in Scotland'.[15] However, this was not sufficient evidence to declare Margaret a bastard or overturn her dynastic claims.

Elizabeth had good cause to be uneasy about that, because it now emerged that Quadra, with the might of Spain behind him, had been plotting on Margaret's behalf. On 28 April his confidential secretary, an Italian called Borghese Venturini, in return for a bribe from Cecil, revealed that he himself had recently accompanied a priest called Dr Turner to Flanders to appeal to King Philip to support a bid for the throne by Margaret. Turner had with him a list of the disaffected lords and other Catholics who were ready to back her, and details of their proposed plans to show to Philip. But he had died in Flanders, leaving his papers in Venturini's hands. Venturini had made copies and given the originals to Bishop de Quadra. Among the papers was a letter in which Quadra strongly recommended Philip to give aid to Lady Lennox and her son, informing him that eight or ten lords would rise in her favour and overthrow Elizabeth.

Venturini added: 'A declaration has been made respecting the succession to the crown, of which the next heir is said to be the Lady Margaret, the Queen of Scotland having been declared to be disqualified as a stranger and an enemy. Lady Margaret has been committed to prison, and the Queen wishes to be enabled to settle the succession.' He anticipated that she would nominate 'a heretic like herself', but if King Philip would agree to help Margaret and Darnley, 'the Catholic religion would be restored, and that this could easily be done, the majority of the nobles being of that faith; and eight or ten of the nobility would rise in favour of Lady Margaret and her son. But until he move they must keep quiet, and his long delay has much dismayed them.'[16]

It is not clear how far Margaret was involved with this scheme, but Venturini's evidence gave the government grounds to fear that she was in it up to her neck.

The Council now had good reason to broaden their inquiries into the activities of the Lennoxes. Thomas Bishop was especially helpful. He had no compunction about throwing Margaret to the wolves, and on 7 May drew up a list of fifteen articles 'to be laid against my Lady Lennox', which he gave to the Council.[17] Whatever ills Margaret had done to him, he was now to repay in full measure in an extraordinary document in which he itemised under numbered headings what he considered to be her crimes.

First, according to Forbes, Yaxley and Hugh Allen, she had secretly communicated with the ambassadors of France and Spain, 'as at the siege of Leith and other places'.[18] The former allegation was undeniably true. But had Margaret 'practised' to subvert the siege of Leith in 1560? For twelve years from 1548 French troops had maintained a presence in the port, but in 1560 English forces and those of the Lords of the Congregation had combined to rid the kingdom of this pro-Catholic force and laid siege to Leith, which fell to them that summer after a bitter struggle. Possibly Margaret had assured the French or Spanish ambassadors in England of her support, but it is hard to believe that she actively involved herself. If she had – although there is no proof of that – she would have been guilty of high treason.

Second, she had corresponded secretly with the Queen of Scots. 'The Laird of Barr proveth these, as also will Mr Forbes.'

Third, she, Lennox and Darnley had sent letters to Aubigny in Paris, and to the Count and Countess of Feria in Spain. Forbes, Lallard and Elder could testify to this.

Fourth, she and Lennox had sent William Forbes with letters to the lords of Scotland to sound them out on the prospect of a marriage between their Queen and Darnley.

Fifth, they had sent Arthur Lallard to Mary with a letter from Darnley.

Sixth, at Michaelmas last they had sent the Laird of Galston to Mary to treat of the marriage 'by plain and open words'. According to Barr, Margaret had pressed Mary for an answer.

Seventh, Margaret had reminded Mary of the latter's claim to the English throne, and pressed upon her the desirability of uniting England and Scotland under one sovereign, and of burning all her letters. Barr had told Bishop that Margaret had set forth her claim to the throne, and Darnley's, as inducements to Mary.

Eighth, Margaret had persuaded Mary not to agree to any meetings with Queen Elizabeth. Barr had said that, because the Lennoxes feared Elizabeth, Margaret had undermined the plan for the queens to meet.

Ninth, she had received by Hugh Allen communications about the Darnley marriage from Francis Yaxley in Spain.

Tenth, Margaret had spoken many times of her claim to the English throne, and had claimed to be the second person in the realm. Forbes had heard her claiming to be the Queen's successor, and Bishop had seen for himself that she had 'blinded' her adherents in Yorkshire, who were in hope that 'their mistress should rule as long, and they should have the ball at their foot'.

Eleventh, she had called the Queen a bastard, and declared that all the world knew that the Queen of Scots was legitimate, that she, Margaret, looked to have her rights one day, and that the Earl of Pembroke and Lord William Howard had sworn that they had heard her say that she would challenge the crown one day, with or without an insurrection of Papists. Forbes had declared that she would not have stopped at 'an insurrection of Papists', but would have 'usurped if power had served her', despite being a bastard.

Twelfth, she had allowed her fool to rail at the Queen without reproach, and encouraged him to mock Elizabeth's relationship with Robert Dudley; and she had let her servants call Dudley a 'pox-ridden wife-murderer'. She had praised God when Mary returned safely to Scotland, claimed that He 'had always preferred' Mary to Elizabeth, and warned Mary that Elizabeth was not to be trusted.

Thirteenth, she had sent messengers to Scotland, the names of whom Bishop helpfully listed.

Fourteenth, Nesbit, Yaxley, Allen, Lallard and Fowler were all thought to be concealing more of Margaret's secrets.

Fifteenth, Margaret used Catholic practices, soothsayers and witches, and kept one in her house, who had abetted her in her pretensions. Forbes and Barr had testified to this, and Bridget Hussey, Countess of Rutland, had told Bishop that after Easter 1562 she had heard from Lucy Somerset, Lady Latimer – no friend to the Lennoxes – that Margaret had allowed her fool to disparage the Queen. Forbes had recounted how Margaret had given thanks for Mary's safe return to Scotland, and Bishop thereby managed to raise suspicions that Mary owed her preservation to Margaret's witchcraft, Margaret having conjured up the mist that had hidden her ships from Elizabeth's.[19]

All these things Bishop knew either by virtue of his privileged position in the Lennox household, or, latterly, from informers. It was all pretty damning, and some of it was evidently true. But it was clear that he had gone even further and conducted his own investigations, questioning everyone he believed to be involved, and no doubt using bullying tactics where necessary. Probably he had feared that he would be dragged down with the Lennoxes, and was making a pre-emptive strike, but there can be little doubt that he relished having his revenge on his former employers.

The spy Forbes had furnished Bishop with much of his information. It was he who revealed the names of servants who had been complicit in Margaret's activities, enabling Bishop to question them.

Bishop stated that one of the Lennoxes' servants had expressed the opinion that Elder 'hath wit to play the spy where he listeth'.[20] Elder and Yaxley seem to have been intimidated by Bishop into giving away the Lennoxes' secrets, as both would later return to Darnley's service, Elder after spending time abroad in Flanders. Lallard too was probably a reluctant witness. Lallard had 'confessed' to Bishop that he had gone to Scotland and spoken with Mary.

Cecil endorsed Bishop's articles, and the Council authorised them to be 'published in the Star Chamber, by authority, or by Statute'.[21] That same day Cecil, having listened to Bishop's earlier diatribe, and wishing to establish the Lennoxes' financial position and how far they were obligated to the Crown, had Bishop draw up a list of 'Remembrances to answer the Earl of Lennox for my Lady his wife'. He left nothing out.

'If the Earl and Countess, upon strait handling, may brag upon the covenants made with Henry VIII,' he began, Cecil should answer that the government had fulfilled its obligations under the couple's marriage treaty, and given the couple 100,000 crowns more, but Lennox had never kept his side of the bargain. Margaret, Bishop pointed out, should no longer benefit from Henry VIII's settlement: as Lennox's wife, and an English subject, she was bound to keep the promise her husband had made never to 'enter into any private bond' with a foreign power, but she had broken that promise.

Bishop asserted that Lennox 'has had wrongfully from the Queen 200 marks [£22,700] of land for these 17 years past'. He informed Cecil that the Earl received 6,000 marks Scots (£51,000) in rents annually, which was more in rents of assize than the earls of Angus and Morton had between them. Bishop thought that, as Lennox had the equivalent revenues of three Scottish earldoms, he should surrender Settrington to the Queen. He added that the Earl had no right to pursue his claim to Scotland as he had surrendered 'all right and title' to Henry VIII. There was more, mostly trivial and malicious, or things that Cecil already knew.

Margaret, Bishop claimed, had had a loan of £200 (£34,000), but had treated it as a gift. As a parting shot he insisted that she had 'no right to the earldom of Angus'.[22]

Two days later, on 9 May, in the presence of Cecil, William Forbes made a fourteen-point deposition – a statement of witness testimony – which corroborated much of what Bishop had said. It is this that proves – if other proof were needed – that he had been employed

as a spy in the Lennox household, because the Council's other informants – Yaxley, Lallard and Lacy – would make confessions to the
Council rather than depositions.

In her thesis on Lennox, Sarah Macauley has observed that the
information given by Forbes was in parts worded very similarly to
that laid by Bishop, and cites two passages in particular. One refers
to Margaret's reaction on hearing that Queen Mary had returned
safely to Scotland. Bishop wrote: 'She sat down and gave good thanks,
declaring to those by how God had always preferred that prince at
all times.' Forbes's version is: 'She sat herself down, held up her hands,
and gave God thanks for preserving the Scottish Queen, saying how
God preserved that Princess of all times.' Bishop wrote elsewhere:
'As for Queen Mary, she said all the world knew that she was lawful,
and for herself she desired nothing but her right, which she trusted
to have one day.' Compare with Forbes: 'As for Queen Mary, all the
world knew that she was lawful, and for herself she desired no thing
but her right, which she knew God would send her one day.' It is
possible to imagine Bishop and Forbes checking their stories with
each other and perhaps even making them up.

In his deposition Forbes stated that he knew of 'the despatch of
letters sent to the Queen of Scotland from Lord and Lady Lennox
and Lord Darnley', and 'heard in all the house that the Countess is
next the crown'. Forbes too hinted that Margaret had practised
witchcraft. In June 1561 the steeple of St Paul's Cathedral had burst
into flames and crashed through the roof into the church below.
The cause was probably a lightning strike, but both Protestants and
Catholics had attributed it to God's displeasure. Forbes, however,
implied that Margaret had set her occult forces to work, deposing
that 'on the day that Paul's steeple was burnt, six of Lord Robert's
men, and divers of the Queen's guards, were struck with sudden
death in St James's Park'.

Forbes echoed Bishop word for word when he stated that the
Earl of Westmorland loved Margaret more than any other woman.
He said that Lallard had made 'a commentary upon the prognostica-
tions of Nostradamus, to the pleasure of my lady, with which he
wrote to my lord of Westmorland, who gave him ten crowns with
great entertainment and thanks'. Michel de Nostradamus, who
enjoyed high favour at the French court, had published his book of
prophesies in France in 1555, but the English edition would not be
published until 1572, so probably John Elder and Darnley had brought
a copy back with them from Paris.[23] Margaret had searched Lallard's

commentary for a prophecy 'that the highest should have declined', meaning that Elizabeth would die or be dethroned, but Forbes took it to refer to the collapse of St Paul's steeple, which she herself had supposedly brought about by witchcraft.

Developing that theme, and referring to the witch who lived in the Lennoxes' household, Forbes stated that Margaret had said that 'she hopeth for a day the which I trust she shall never see, her doings being espied betimes'. The implication was deadly, for to compass or imagine the death of the monarch, by sorcery or other means, was high treason.

In testifying to Sir William of Malton celebrating Mass in Margaret's bedchamber, Forbes was further incriminating her, for from April 1561 the government had cracked down on Mass being celebrated in private chapels, and in that month twenty-four members of the gentry had been arrested for that crime.[24] However, there may have been some truth in Quadra's statement that the local authorities had been fearful of challenging Margaret.[25]

Forbes concluded, 'I know that my Lady Margaret loveth neither God nor the Queen's Majesty, nor yet your Honour, and that Francis Yaxley should have gone into France this year for her affairs. The said Yaxley sent her word of all things by Hugh Allen, and wrote at sundry times letters, which she hath burnt, and also he did send my Lord Darnley a fair turquoise in a token,' a gift from his mother.[26]

Margaret was in mortal peril. In imagining the Queen's death, branding her a bastard, trumpeting her own claims, and possibly plotting to become queen, she had committed treason, no less, and the punishment was death by burning, unless the Queen mercifully commuted it to decapitation. She might also be charged with witchcraft. Henry VIII had passed a law against witchcraft, repealed under Edward VI, but increasing public concern had led to a new Act being drafted in 1559 in Elizabeth's first Parliament. Although it would not be ratified until early 1563, its provisions had been actively in force since 1560, and launched a wave of persecution. Under them, if harm had been caused by a witch, the penalty was death; otherwise it was imprisonment; and it could be argued that Margaret's dabbling in witchcraft had led to harm. In 1561 Parliament, fearing that Catholics might resort to sorcery against the Queen, had passed another Act forbidding 'fond and fantastical prophecies'.[27] Margaret's soothsayers had predicted two crowns for Darnley.

Margaret was not as yet aware of the evidence laid against her, and being kept in suspense as to what was going on must have been nerve-racking. Any day she might be summoned for trial or to the Tower, and she was no doubt haunted by thoughts of the bloody fates of other royal ladies accused of being traitors. She was also concerned about her husband, and began bombarding Cecil with letters. Her tone was righteous, her stance throughout that she and Lennox were innocent of the charges, it was wrong of the government to imprison them, and she herself was a good friend to the Queen, who ought not to treat her so badly. The first was sent from Sheen, on 14 May, 'To my very friend, Sir William Cecil, knight, Chief Secretary to the Queen's Majesty, Master of her Wards, and one of her Highness's most honourable Privy Council.'

Good Master Secretary,

After my right hearty commendations, this is to require of you some comfort concerning my husband's liberty, either to be clearly out of the Tower, which should be most to my comfort, or else at the least some more liberty within it. I have stayed in troubling you for that my hope was to have had some good news, for that I myself do know the Queen's Majesty to be of so gracious, so good and gentle nature that, if her Highness had been moved for my lord and me, she would have had some pity on us ere now, considering the long time of trouble we have had, which has been since Christmas. Wherefore I shall beseech you to move her Majesty in this my humble and lowly petition, and that my lord may come to his answer again, for that ye sent me word by Fowler that he stood to the denial of all things laid to his charge. I trust he will not contend or deny anything of truth, and in so doing my hope is her Majesty will be his good and gracious lady, for he never meant to willingly deserve the contrary, as knoweth God, who have you in His keeping.

From Sheen, the 14th of May, your assured friend to my power,

Margaret Lennox and Angus.[28]

A week later, on 21 May, having had no reply to a letter, now lost, that she had sent to the Queen, and having heard from Cecil that there was new evidence against her and Lennox, perhaps arising from Forbes's deposition, Margaret wrote again:

I have received your answer by my man Fowler, but nothing touching the petitions in my letter, for that ye say there is new matter both against my lord and me, which, when it shall please the Queen's Majesty, I shall be glad to understand, not doubting, with God's grace, but both my lord and I shall be able to acquit ourselves, if right may take place [and] that our accusers may be brought before us. I assure you I am weary of this life and would fain receive some comfort from her Majesty, for, as methink, we have had punishment enough for a great offence.

I cannot but choose to trouble you with this letter for that I have no kin and not many friends to sue for me; for if I had, I should have received some comfortable answers ere now. Wherefore I shall desire you to be my friend in being some means to the Queen's Majesty of yourself, for my lord and me, for that I think her Highness will give better ear to you than to my letter.

Good Master Secretary, God knoweth my innocency and uprightness, and my lord's also, toward her Majesty and her realm, howsoever our doings is otherwise taken. But my sure trust is that her Majesty will have remorse of me, her poor kinswoman, who, never meaning to offend her, thinketh myself not worthy of this, her Majesty's indignation and punishment. Notwithstanding, as her Highness' pleasure is, I am content; but I shall pray to Him Who is the champion and defender of the innocent, to inspire her Majesty's heart towards me according to the good nature I know her Majesty to be of. Declaring this unto her shall bind my lord and me to be yours assuredly.[29]

Asking to be confronted with her accusers was a bold move on Margaret's part, for she could have had no means of knowing what evidence had been laid against her.

She had been at Sheen for nearly eight weeks when she was finally interrogated. Cecil's notes 'for the Examination of the Countess of Lennox', made in his own hand on 25 May, still survive. She was to be asked 'what communication hath she had of the bastardy of Queen Mary and the Queen that now is [Elizabeth], and what words hath she uttered thereon against the Queen. When Paul's steeple was burnt, what report was made to her of a certain number of men struck with sudden death in St James' Park? What moved her to say that touching the right to the crown she would give place to none of the rest? What message was brought to her from the Lord Seton concerning his furtherance in setting forth of Lord Darnley?' The document ends with a list of people about whom Margaret was presumably to be questioned: Galston, Lallard, Lacy, a fool in the house, the Scottish Queen and Hugh Allen.[30]

Cecil and other Privy Councillors visited Margaret and questioned her, but she declared that she was innocent. She was to maintain steadfastly that she had been falsely accused and was being held unjustly, and would keep pressing to be brought face to face with her accusers, and to justify herself to Elizabeth in person. She acted throughout as if she and Lennox were the injured parties.

On 30 May she wrote to Cecil:

At your last being with me at Sheen ye opened so many new and strange matters that I am, as I told you, desirous to see them that made the same; and if, in case it be that they may not come so far as Sheen, I pray you let me take the pains to come to some of your chambers in the court, where I may answer for myself. Being so far off, I find the old proverb true, 'Long ways, long lies'. And in that her Majesty will in no wise I come into her presence, ye shall be sure I will not seek to displease her therein, but shall content myself to be a suitor among you, my lords of the Council. For being there, so far off, and in her Highness' displeasure, as all men know, no doubt but I shall have some of the worst sort to speak like themselves against me, in hope to win reward whereof they stand [in] need. Otherwise ye may keep me here still with new inventions every day, which would redouble the wrong I have already.

I assure you, Master Secretary, it is a great grief to me, and the greatest that I ever had, to perceive the little love and affection that her Majesty bears me, and especially in this one matter [obtaining permission to see the Queen and plead her case in person] that I thought that her Majesty would rather have fortified and strengthened me in, than to have given hearing or sufferance to such a manifest wrong and injury against her poor kinswoman.

Cecil, who does not appear to have taken the accusations of witchcraft too seriously, had also informed Margaret that her legitimacy was still subject to an inquiry by the Court of Star Chamber. At this she waxed vociferous:

Even as God hath made me so I am lawful daughter to the Queen of Scots and the Earl of Angus, which none alive is able to make me otherwise without doing wrong.

Master Secretary, I do perceive that Fowler, my man, has commandment from the Star Chamber not to come out of London. I trust he hath not offended, but in his absence I shall have want of him in my household, such as it is, for I have no other here to look to it. Wherefore I shall both thank you for your gentle using of him, and desire you that he may be coming and going, and he shall be always ready at commandment.[31]

That same day Arthur Lallard made a 'confession', in which – at variance with the testimonies of Bishop and Forbes – he gave a rather different version of his mission to Edinburgh in the late summer of 1561, in which there was no mention of the Darnley marriage. Nor did he refer to Margaret sending him, but stated that Lennox, hearing three weeks before Michaelmas that Queen Mary was to return to Scotland, had instructed him to ride north with a message to the Queen asking if he could renew his suit for the restitution of his estates. 'This was the chief cause of his sending.' He admitted that he had spoken with Queen Mary and made 'his lord's and her aunt's commendations to her'. In response to Lennox's plea, she had told him 'that she was but newly and rawly come into her country, and that she could not give him such an answer as she would, but all that she might do for Lord and Lady Lennox, her aunt, for their right, she would with time and place; desiring his lady to be always her good aunt, with her commendations to them both.' Lallard insisted to the Council: 'And this, my most honourable lords, is the very truth of both my journeys.'[32]

It may be that Lallard's instructions had been as he stated, but they were perhaps not the only reason for his journey. Lallard had testified that Lennox had also given him a message for Aubigny, but Forbes was adamant that Lallard had known before he set out that Aubigny would not be in Scotland;[33] if that was true, the Lennoxes and Lallard had been lying.

Hugh Allen was also interrogated on 30 May, to discover 'what gentlemen and commoners in Yorkshire and other places beareth their hearts and assistance to my lady'. He revealed that foremost among Margaret's friends were Westmorland, Constable and Cholmeley, who was 'a secret father to her and all her causes'.[34] Cholmeley had already been questioned by the Council of the North earlier that month, without being penalised;[35] he was more fortunate than George Chamberlain and Arthur Lallard, who were clapped in the Tower in June.[36]

Quadra knew that he too was under suspicion. On 6 June he found out that Venturini had betrayed him, and informed King Philip that he was 'greatly troubled about a disaster that has happened in my house. It is a case of a servant of mine who has been bribed by the Queen's ministers and has divulged a host of things prejudicial to private persons and, even in public matters, has laid more on to me than he could truthfully do. I could satisfy the Queen about it if she would hear me, but, being a woman and ill-informed by the leading men in her Council, she is so shocked that I do not know to what lengths she will go.'[37]

On 8 June Sir Henry Sidney informed Sir Nicholas Throckmorton, 'The Earl of Lennox remains close prisoner in the Tower, and his wife at Sheen; she was very obstinate in her answers to the Council sent to her.' In the same letter he wrote that 'the match between my Lord of Hertford and my Lady Katherine [Grey] as I hear is judged adultery, and the punishment thereof left to the Queen, as chief governor of ecclesiastical matters'.[38] The treacherous misconduct of one female cousin cannot have left Elizabeth feeling well disposed towards another who had apparently committed worse crimes.

That day Cecil reported to Sir Thomas Challoner, England's ambassador in Spain: 'At home all things are quiet. The Earl of Lennox remains in the Tower.' Charles Stuart must have been brought south from York to join his mother in captivity, as Cecil mentions that 'Lady Lennox and her son are at Sheen, in the household of Sir Richard Sackville. They [the Lennoxes] are charged with two things, one with secret intimation that she has a right to the crown of England next to the Queen, and the other with secret compassing of marriage betwixt the Scottish Queen and her son, which matters they deny, although there are many proofs.' Cecil did not think that 'any extremity is intended towards them'.[39] But Margaret, of course, did not know that.

On 12 June Margaret was feeling ill with a pain in her head and a 'rheum',[40] and bade a servant write to Cecil to say that she understood 'by his answer that the Queen would not grant the Earl of Lennox any more liberty in the Tower while he used himself as he did, which is strange and grievous to me, considering thereby that such wicked and envious reports are now credited' and he was suffering from ill health. 'He will not deny anything laid to his charge which is true.' She could not 'perceive any way in which he offends, unless, perhaps, you, Master Secretary, with the rest of the lords of the Council, would have him agree to false matters by him never known, meant, or thought, when you may long keep him as he is to the encouragement of his enemies'.[41]

A week later (19 June) she was complaining 'of being kept here as a prisoner, and put off with delaying answers, that so long as my lord uses himself as he does and will not confess things manifestly known he shall have no more liberty than he has, nor shall I come to the Queen's presence'. She said she would 'again humbly beseech the Queen to release us out of our miserable trouble, and suffer my lord and me to come together; or at least let him have the liberty of the Tower for his health'.[42] We know that she did send such a petition.[43]

Elizabeth was in a bad mood when she gave an audience to Quadra sometime between 6 and 20 June. He told King Philip that she 'could not refrain from telling me that she was going to complain to your Majesty of me for the bad offices I did in always writing ill of her and her affairs. She tried to convince me by citing particular cases, and at last said I could not deny that I had sent Dr Turner to Flanders to try to get her turned off the throne and substitute others (meaning Lady Margaret).' We can deduce from this that Elizabeth did not suspect Margaret herself of complicity in the plot, and Quadra took care to exonerate her. He insisted that he had sent Turner 'to arrange my private affairs', and took the opportunity of his going to tell him to give an account to the Duchess of Parma[44] of a plan mooted by the English Council to secure 'the adherence of Lady Margaret to their side' by finding a French bride for Darnley. Then, if the Queen of Scots, who was then in bad health, were to die, Margaret and Darnley would still have a claim to the English succession, but would be prevented from gaining a foothold in Scotland.[45] We hear no more of this plan.

Lennox had been questioned several times by the Council, and on 20 June, in the Tower, he made a written statement, saying he had 'been oftentimes before them' and 'answered to many matters untruly charged against him'. He declared his innocence, and complained of the methods of his accusers. He could not 'declare more than he had already done, which he intends to rest upon during his life'. He 'hears that there is more matter against him, which may very well be true, so long as he remains in captivity, his enemies in favour and at liberty, and their exploiters, hired men, and other fantastical persons allowed as his accusers', and he 'desires to know what the new matter is'. He wished 'that the Queen would consider that he came not hither as a vagabond, or for lack of living, as some of his accusers did, but to serve her father'. As his livelihood had been granted only as part of his marriage settlement, and not as recompense for his lost inheritance in Scotland, he wished that the Queen would take it back and permit him 'to depart her realm quietly, as he came into it, and not to receive this wrong and undeserved punishment'.[46]

On 27 June Lennox wrote again to the Council from the Tower, saying he 'hoped to have received some comfort from the Queen'. The Lieutenant of the Tower had told him that the councillors greatly disliked two points in his letter: 'the one, that he should offer to deliver again his living into the Queen's hands; the other, that he wrote that he sustained wrong in his imprisonment'. Their reply was that 'he shall be judged by the laws of the realm. This answer is very grievous to him, which he supposes happened by some negligence in his writing. To the first he meant that rather than remain thus in the Queen's high displeasure he would willingly yield up all such lands and livings as he has received, so that he trusts to recover her favour and to enjoy the lands quietly. To the second, if anything passed more than was seemly, it came from the pen and not the heart.'[47]

That same day Margaret sent yet another plea to Cecil.[48]

A marriage between Queen Mary and King Philip's unstable heir, Don Carlos, was still under discussion, and Elizabeth remained determined to prevent it, for she had no intention of allowing the Spaniards to gain a foothold north of the border. Her alarm was shared by Catherine de' Medici, the Queen Mother of France, and this was to Margaret's advantage as it brought the marriage of Darnley to Mary once more into prospect. Margaret had been able to keep in touch with Quadra, who, on 4 July, reported that Queen Catherine 'fears the marriage of the Queen of Scotland with our Prince as much as the Queen of England does', and 'they think that jointly they can hinder it'. Catherine thought that a good plan would be to marry Mary to Darnley. Quadra believed that Moray was of the same opinion. 'This brother of the Queen is all powerful now and, in consequence of his enmity to the Duke of Châtelherault and his sons, would be glad to hand over the country to the Earl of Lennox, who is the foe of Châtelherault and his rival for the succession.'

Quadra was unsure how Elizabeth would feel about Mary marrying Darnley, 'as she is displeased with Lady Margaret', but she was so fearful of her marrying Don Carlos that 'she may well consent to it'. Elizabeth believed that Darnley might in time be persuaded to turn Protestant, which Quadra thought 'quite possible', and thereby she would not 'lack means to ensure herself against the Queen of Scots and Lady Margaret'.

Quadra could not help thinking that there was 'a closer under-standing' between Mary and Margaret on the subject of the Darnley marriage than he had hitherto been informed, judging from the last words of a note he had received from Margaret:

The whole cause of the Queen's anger with my lord and with me, and the sole reason of our imprisonment and trouble, is the Queen of Scotland's business. The basis of all charges against us is that we have tried to promote a marriage between the Queen of Scotland and our son, and are attached to the said Queen, which of itself is considered a great crime here, and that my lord and I have dared to send a simple recommenda-tion to the said Queen, she being, as the members of the Council said, an enemy of her Majesty. They would have it that my lord and I had confessed to the charge about the marriage, but we never put forward such a thing and never confessed it.[49]

On 10 July Margaret complained to Cecil:

I have no answer of my last petition to the Queen's Majesty, which were that it might please her Highness to be so gracious as to suffer my lord and me to come together, or at the least he to have the liberty of the Tower. My lord's sickness comes only by close keeping and lack of comfort, so that, if it might please her Majesty to suffer him to come to Sheen and be kept here as I am, we should think ourselves much bound to her Highness, for otherwise I know he can not continue without danger of his life, which to her Majesty should be small pleasure.

In the meantime she begged that he be allowed freedom to take exercise within the Tower.[50]

The Council's investigations into the Lennoxes' activities were still ongoing. On 18 July Cecil sent instructions to Henry Manners, Earl of Rutland, to examine Ralph Lacy 'as to the cause of his absence [overseas], and his dealings whilst he was abroad. If there shall appear any good matter against him, detain him in ward, or take bond for his appearance.' The Queen also wanted Rutland and Thomas Young, Archbishop of York, to closely question the priest Sir William of Malton about his celebration of Mass.[51]

Margaret was becoming desperate. On 22 July she again wrote to Cecil:

Good Master Secretary,

This is great grief to me always to have such deferring answers, much like unto the first, as that my lord shall know his offence and shall have no more liberty as yet. For offence, I must say, as I have said, that neither my lord nor I have willingly offended her Majesty; but her pleasure is to take our doings not in so good part as other princes hath heretofore, in respect whereof we have received punishment, wherewith her Highness may be satisfied.

Beseeching the Queen to have some consideration of me, her poor kinswoman, and of my husband (the rather for my sake), who is in close prison without comfort, far unmeet to his nature and, as her Highness knows, not very healthful, having a disease which solitariness is most against, as heretofore, to my comfort, her Majesty hath willed me to cause him always to be in company.

Beseeching Her Highness, for the honour of God and for nature's sake, to mollify and appease her indignation against us, who is and shall be, during our lives, her Majesty's true and faithful subjects; desiring you, Master Secretary, to participate to her Majesty the same, and to be a mean that I may have some more comfortable answer than as yet I have had; in the which doing I shall find myself much bound unto you, and shall not forget the same if it lies in my power. And thus, with my very hearty commendations to you, I bid the same likewise farewell.

From Sheen, this Wednesday, your assured friend to my power,

Margaret Lennox and Angus.[52]

There has been some speculation as to why Lennox feared being alone to the extent of having, as Margaret described it, 'a disease which solitariness is most against'. This mention in her letter is the only reference to it. Strickland[53] suggested that the remembrance of his cruel 'deed of blood' in hanging child hostages in 1548 had haunted him ever since, and left him with a superstitious fear of being left alone with his conscience. But Strickland heavily embellished the facts, and her account was undermined by Sir William Fraser as far back as 1874.[54] Nowadays the fear of solitude is recognised as autophobia, which may arise from a fear of being abandoned or neglected. Like other phobias it can be triggered by a traumatic event, particularly at an early age, so the murder of Lennox's father, when he was ten, is more likely to have accounted for the condition. If that is true, he had even more cause to hate the Hamiltons. The symptoms can be both physical and psychological, and in an age that did not understand phobias might have appeared alarming, even life-threatening. Possibly Margaret was exaggerating Lennox's condition in a bid for sympathy, but it is clear from her letter that the Queen knew about it and had suggested a way of dealing with it.

On 24 July Margaret received a most unsatisfactory response from Cecil, and replied in frustration:

Good Master Secretary,

I have received answer from you by my man Fowler that my lord must acknowledge an offence and submit himself to the Queen's Majesty, wherein ye know for my lord I am not able to say anything on his behalf unless I might speak with him, and so to give my best advice, or else have leave to send to him.

As for my part, except it were for the schoolmaster's going into Scotland without the Queen's Majesty's leave, I can remember no offence, and for that I do most humbly submit myself to her Majesty, and trust that my lord will so do, if he have not done the like already, being well assured, knowing his good nature as I do, that no man doth more lament the Queen's Highness' displeasure than he, or would more willingly submit himself in all things to have her favour, which I pray God to send us shortly, beseeching you, as I did before, to be a mean to her Majesty that my lord may have his liberty, wherein we shall think ourselves most bound during our lives, and shall pray for her Majesty's most noble estate long to reign over us. And thus, beseeching you of answer with my most hearty commendations, I commit the same to the tuition of Almighty God.

From Sheen this Friday. Your assured friend to my power, Margaret Lennox and Angus.[55]

★

On 2 August the Earl of Rutland questioned Ralph Lacy. He had
received further instructions from Cecil five days earlier by the
indefatigable Bishop. Lacy, who had travelled in Europe on many
errands for the Lennoxes, confessed that he had carried letters of
commendation from Lennox and Darnley to Aubigny and the
Countess of Feria. Lennox had funded his trips and Margaret had
given him £4 (£680) for a horse. In Paris Lacy had met the Scottish
ambassador and Aubigny. He had sent letters from Paris to Lord and
Lady Lennox, Arthur Lallard and Lennox's servants. He had met
Elder in Paris and they had both attended Queen Mary when she
supped in her chamber. Lacy had then taken ship for Scarborough,
and Rutland suspected that he had made contact with the Lennoxes'
adherents in the area. All that Lacy would admit was that he had
visited Settrington twice, and that, over a drink in the hall, three of
the tenants had informed him that the master and mistress were in
prison in London. None of this was particularly incriminating.

The next day, 3 August, Rutland questioned Lacy again, and asked
him if he had heard talk of 'my lady's pretence in succession'. Lacy
professed ignorance, but during the course of this and a third interrogation, he did reveal the names of several agents working for the
Lennoxes abroad, among whom were Lallard and Fowler. Despite
having got very little of substance from Lacy, Rutland committed
him to prison in York Castle.[56]

Margaret's plea to speak with Lennox before he answered the
charges against him prompted a terse response from Elizabeth.
Margaret was stung by this, and on 5 August she wrote again to Cecil

> for that he sent word by Fowler that the Queen said that my
> lord's submission must come of himself and not by his wife's
> teaching. As to that, my lord needs not to learn at my hand
> how to use himself to the prince [sovereign], wherein he was
> expert ere he came into England; and since his coming here
> he has needed no such schoolmistress.
>
> And for suing to any other of the Council save to yourself,
> I know not the pace, neither have I been accustomed to write
> to a council, but to assign one of them, of which it pleased
> the Queen's Majesty, when my lord and I took leave of her
> Highness to go into Yorkshire when she was first queen, to
> appoint us yourself in our affairs, which we have hitherto
> observed. Besides that, I know my imbecility and weakness of
> brain far unmeet to indite [write] to such councillors, but only

that I am traded with you already, praying you not to weary of my troublesome letters, and to have me in remembrance as ye see cause, which I pray God may be shortly, to my comfort, after these my long troubles.[57]

On 11 August Rutland informed Cecil that he and the Archbishop of York had had the priest, Sir William, before them, but had allowed him 'to depart upon a bond for his appearance when called for'.[58]

Lennox had now made a formal submission to the Queen – but in vain. On 12 August Margaret raged to Cecil that she had 'received many answers, whereby it seemed that her lord's liberty rested only upon his submission', but Lennox had tried throw himself on Elizabeth's mercy 'and now it pleases the Queen not to accept it, which submission she accounts very slender for such a fault'. Since Margaret was sure he had made it 'as largely as the fault required', she had taken Cecil's advice and written in protest to the Lord Keeper, Sir Nicholas Bacon, and the Earl of Pembroke, both Privy Councillors.[59]

By 22 August the long months of confinement and anxiety had begun to take their toll, and Margaret was becoming deeply distressed about her and Lennox's financial situation, since prisoners were required to pay for their own upkeep and any comforts they required, and the bills and debts were mounting up. The fact that she felt she could turn yet again to Cecil suggests that he had shown patience, and perhaps some sympathy, towards her. She wrote to him:

Good Master Secretary,
    I can not cease but trouble you still till I may receive some comfort, praying you to remember my intolerable griefs, which ariseth divers ways, as well by my lord's imprisonment and mine, being there thereby separated, as also by impoverishment, which daily increaseth, to our utter undoing: as first, being in great debt before the beginning of this trouble, and then coming up [from Yorkshire] upon the sudden, having nought but upon borrowing to sustain my charges of travelling; leaving all goods, though small they be, as well cattle as household stuff and grounds, without order, which now goeth to ruin and decay for lack of looking to; having not any trusty person spare to redress the same, certain of the servants being in prison, and the rest few enough to attend our business here besides.
    Then the great charges we are at in these parts, one way with my lord and his servants' imprisonment, another way with

mine own and children's, and those attending on me and them.[60] That having naught but upon borrowing to suffice the ordinary charges since my coming up from Settrington to London, which shift I have so long made that now it faileth. And for the small portion of living my lord and I have, the revenue thereof is far unable to suffice the half of the ordinary charges we be now at, besides that we were beforehand of divers of our bailiffs, as occasion enforced us unto.

All which considered, making my moan to you, my trust is that ye will be a mean to shorten the time of my lord's trouble and mine, beseeching ye, so soon as ye may, to participate the premises to the Queen's Majesty, having confidence that her Majesty's good nature is such that she will not see me utterly impoverished now in my old age [she was forty-six], being her Majesty's poor kinswoman. And thus, leaving to trouble you any further, save with my hearty commendations, I commit you to the tuition of Almighty God.

From Sheen this Saturday. Your assured friend to my power, Margaret Lennox and Angus.[61]

In the Tower, Lennox, shut up with his fears, was furious to learn that another prisoner, Katherine Grey's husband, the Earl of Hertford, was allowed certain freedoms. On 20 September Sir Edward Warner, the Lieutenant of the Tower, told Cecil how greatly he was 'annoyed by the extreme passions of the Earl of Lennox, who has been more unquiet since the Earl of Hertford was allowed his small liberty'.[62] It must have made Lennox feel even more desperate.

At the beginning of October Cecil informed Margaret that her Majesty had cherished resentful feelings against her ever since she herself had been imprisoned in the Tower by her late sister, Queen Mary, it having been reported to her by Thomas Bishop at the time that Margaret had advised that measure. On 2 October Margaret vehemently denied this, and complained again of the injustice of all the other accusations that had been laid against her and Lennox. 'If my lord and I might find the Queen's Majesty so good and gracious to us as to hear our accusers and us, face to face, I would be out of doubt to find shortly some part of her Highness's favour again.'[63]

But now it looked as if Elizabeth would never have a chance to permit that, even if she were so inclined. That October, while staying at Hampton Court, she contracted smallpox and became so ill that she was not expected to live. Her councillors, gathered together in anticipation of the worst, urgently debated the complex question of who was to succeed her. 'Out of the fifteen or sixteen of them, there were nearly as many different opinions about the succession. It would be impossible to please them all.' The Marquess of Winchester put forward Margaret's name, saying he thought it should be her or Darnley. When this was suggested to the Queen, she would not – or could not – comment, but Quadra was sure that in the end the councillors would form two or three parties, and that the Catholic party would have on its side a majority of the country, 'although I do not know whether the Catholics themselves would be able to agree, as some would like the Queen of Scots and others Lady Margaret, who is considered sensible and devout'.[64] Robert Dudley, knowing it was unlikely that Katherine Grey would ever be queen, and looking to a future in which Queen Margaret reigned, urged that Lady Lennox be set at liberty.

But no one dared take that decision, so Margaret remained confined at Sheen, no doubt wondering if her moment of liberation and triumph was at hand. If the Queen died, there was a good chance that the Catholics, backed by Dudley and Winchester, would declare for Margaret or her son. But by 25 October Elizabeth had rallied a little, and on that day Margaret dutifully wrote to Cecil: 'Thanks be to God of the Queen's amendment, which is no small comfort to me, and I shall pray God daily to increase her Majesty's health and strength, long to reign over us.' It seems she hoped that knocking at Death's door would have softened Elizabeth's attitude towards herself and Lennox, for she continued:

> Beseeching you to bear my lord and me in remembrance to her Highness, hoping by your good means that she will consider the long time of my lord's imprisonment and mine, and our absence one from the other, specially he being in the Tower, the winter come, and that house both unwholesome and cold. I shall most humbly and lowly beseech her Highness, first for God's cause, and next for nature's sake, to suffer my lord my husband and me to come together.[65]

Her plea was from the heart, and she had more cause than most to make it, for she could not have forgotten that her long-lost love, Thomas Howard, had succumbed to sickness and died in the Tower twenty-six years earlier to the month. The Queen was too ill to give

heed to Margaret's plea, nor did she do so when, against all expectations, she recovered soon afterwards.

Margaret now had a fresh cause for complaint. Her letter of
12 November to Cecil has an injured tone:

> At the time of her Majesty's sickness, which (as before to you
> I have written) I did much lament (God be the judge), and
> being so near[66] where her Highness lay, could not be suffered
> to show myself to her, according as both by nature and duty
> I am bound, it cannot but augment my grief. And now, her
> Highness being recovered, thanks be to God, therefore I, being
> most glad to hear the same, yet otherwise that I am restrained
> from her Majesty's presence, the sight whereof would be most
> to my comfort, that I might, with the rest of her servants,
> rejoice at her restoring to health, I am enforced in my heart
> to think it rare and grievous.

Again she complained to Cecil of the long imprisonment of Lennox,
'how indisposed her husband was, and how unfit for his recovery
the Tower was, likewise the ill air of the place, and the cold time
of the year'. Once more she desired Cecil 'to be a means with the
Queen to procure the liberty of my lord and myself', but if nothing
further was to be granted, 'I pray that he may be imprisoned with
me and my children, and I shall be content'.[67]

This time her plea bore fruit, for besides Cecil there were others
at court – opponents of Katherine Grey – who were in a position
favourably to influence the Queen and persuade her that Lennox really
was no threat to her, and that Katherine and her supporters should
be discountenanced. Soon afterwards Margaret received the long-
hoped-for, welcome news that he was at last to be freed from the
Tower and allowed to join her at Sheen, although both were to remain
under house arrest. This, Quadra reported on 30 November, was

> by the favour of the Earl of Pembroke and Lord Robert, who
> are much against Lady Katherine. I think that the liberation of
> Lennox has two objects, first, to hinder Lady Katherine by
> providing a competitor, and secondly, to give a little satisfaction
> to the Catholics who are desperate at Lady Margaret's misery,
> and place all their hopes in the Queen of Scots and the husband
> she may choose. By giving them some small hope that the
> succession may fall to Lady Margaret and her son they may

cool somewhat towards the Queen of Scots. All this is convenient for the Queen, who wants to have the power to declare her own successor when she likes.[68]

Lennox had left the Tower and been reunited – one imagines most joyfully – with Margaret by 24 November, when, in her twelfth letter to Cecil, she thanked him 'for exertions in behalf of her husband, and for the liberty which he now enjoys', and expressed the hope that he would 'vouchsafe to be like means to the Queen for the restoration of her favour'. She expressed her love for Elizabeth and earnestly desired that, with her lord, she be permitted to 'pay her duty to the Queen's person, as usual'.[69] Cecil, in his reply, intimated that the time was now ripe for her to write to her Majesty, and Margaret duly did so.

In December – possibly because Sheen needed to be cleansed – the Lennoxes were temporarily moved across the Thames to Syon, where Margaret had sought a refuge in 1537 after the death of Thomas Howard. On 6 December Quadra reported that 'the Earl of Lennox is at Syon House with his wife, and it seems that his release from the castle was rather a change of prison than a liberation'.[70] Lennox no longer had to endure the horrors brought on by solitude, but he became ill sometime in December or January, which Margaret attributed in her next letter to Cecil to Elizabeth's unkindness. This letter was sent on 8 January 1563, when the couple were back at Sheen. It was the first she had sent him for six weeks, for he had made it clear in his last response that her constant importuning was wearisome to him. But now the couple were not only thoroughly demoralised but also in financial extremity.

Good Mr Secretary,

Having rested all this time not sending to you in attempting my suit to the Queen's Majesty as before, perceiving in the answer you sent me by Fowler that my oft sending hath been a trouble to you, and being loth to be troublesome to any (so near as I can so long as I may) I have forborne till very need and necessity enforceth me to utter my grief, which oftentimes I have done to you; in especial, and last of all, writing so humble to the Queen's Majesty, whereof I was put in hope to have ere now some comfortable answer; but in place I received from, by my said servant, an extreme and grievous answer.

I impute the same to be the only cause of my lord's sickness at this time.

Mr Secretary, considering how we have continually begged and craved, in most humble wise, her Majesty's favour, together with the punishment my lord in especial hath received, and thereby so extremely impoverished, and yet so remaining must needs make me account that I am but unnaturally used, being her Majesty's poor and next kinswoman of her father's side, who neither hath, nor willingly will deserve, such lack of her Highness' favour, as God and the world knoweth.

And now, seeing we cannot as yet obtain her favour, which thing is most to our grief, we are constrained to enter into another suit to her Majesty, which our poverty driveth us unto, beseeching you most heartily to move her Majesty therein, that whereas I ever since my coming to Sheen (being before far in debt), I have bought all things with ready money, for the furniture of our family and household, travelling and other necessaries; which money having not of our own, I was driven to borrow it of Lady Sackville and others, the most part. And now, the same being spent, not knowing where to get any to support our needful charges upon being here – at more charges than if we lay in the City, by almost the third part – I shall therefore most humbly beseech her Highness to appoint us something to live upon in the country, or else to allow us other ways, as to her Majesty shall seem good, for our farther relief; for that in our present necessity is such as, without the same, we are not able to continue.

And if her Majesty will not grant us one of these suits, we shall be forced to require her Majesty's licence (which we would be most loth to do) to repair into the country where our poor living lieth, till such time as it may please God we may have her Highness' favour, without which, if we might otherwise choose, we should be loth to go or abide in any place.

And thus, with my most hearty commendations, desiring you of answer, I commit you to the tuition of Almighty God. Your assured friend to my power,

Margaret Lennox and Angus.[71]

To press home her point, Margaret wrote another letter along the same lines to her servant, William Robinson, whom she instructed to carry both to Cecil.[72] This tried the Secretary's patience too far, and he vented his anger on the unfortunate Robinson. In a letter sent on 17 January Margaret apologised, assuring Cecil that she did not blame him 'for the slow progress of my suits to the Queen's Majesty; on the contrary, I have just cause to thank you for your advocacy and am grateful for your good offices'. She made it quite clear whom she thought was responsible.

> Marry, I must needs think I have some back friends [backbiters], but I can judge none, or I must otherwise account that it proceeds from the Queen's Majesty's self, which I trust not. I assure you that my lord and I have so many injuries arising by her Highness' displeasure, as first by the grief it is to us, then our necessity for money, and every evil-willer of ours in the country [of] Yorkshire encouraged thereby to encroach upon the small living we have there, as even at this present our servant, being coming from thence, declareth that matters of traverse [obstruction] is newly grown in seven several lordships of ours. Half the revenue we have will scant defend our right, having quietly enjoyed the same nineteen years without trouble, saving the Strangeways lands.[73] I trust your wisdom will consider whether we have occasion to be weary of this life or not.[74]

Yaxley was again examined by the Privy Council on 14 January 1563. It is not known how long he was imprisoned in the Tower, but he had been freed by August 1565.

That January Parliament again debated the problem of the royal succession. One of its members, John Hales, was moved to publish a tract, *A Declaration of the Succession of the Crown Imperial of England*, which controversially advocated the succession of Lady Katherine Grey. Margaret, Hales argued, could not succeed because she was an alien, nationality deriving from the father. Hales's crime in pronouncing an opinion on so dangerous a subject was considered to be so serious that he was incarcerated in the Fleet prison for four years.

But Katherine Grey now disgraced herself again. In February 1563, still a prisoner in the Tower, she gave birth to another son, Thomas, after the sympathetic Lieutenant had allowed her husband two illicit conjugal visits. This made Elizabeth more determined than ever to discountenance Katherine, and that meant showing favour to the Lennoxes. It was probably this, rather than her being convinced of their innocence, that prompted her decision to free the couple in February, when she sent word to them 'that she had forgiven and forgotten their offence, yet she would not see them'.[75]

Their release was conditional upon Margaret swearing a solemn oath that she would not allow her son to marry without the Queen's consent.[76] It has been stated that the Lennoxes were not formally pardoned,[77] but in fact they had never been convicted of a crime. Nor were they now in a position to commit any, for their intelligence network had been exposed and neutralised.

It is a measure of Elizabeth's tolerance – in later years she would recall that in her time she had 'winked at so many treasons'[78] – and her pragmatism that the Lennoxes were set at liberty, given the evidence against them.[79] Margaret's reported remarks about her right to the throne could have been construed as treasonable, but the Council was probably shrewd enough to know that Bishop was a hostile witness and that Forbes had perhaps been suborned. Witchcraft had not been proved, nor had Margaret's part in Quadra's intrigues. She had schemed to marry her son to Queen Mary, but Darnley did not come within the compass of the Act of Succession of 1536, so she could not be prosecuted for that. As she had told Quadra in November, she thought it no crime, as Mary was her niece, and that there was no harm in advising her to do what was best for her. So there was no real evidence of a treasonable conspiracy.[80]

The last of Margaret's letters to Cecil was written on 3 February from Sackville Place, Sir Richard Sackville's town house, which lay to the south of Fleet Street. Built in the fifteenth century as Salisbury House, the London residence of the bishops of Salisbury, Sackville Place would become known as Dorset House after the Sackvilles became earls of Dorset in 1604. The Lennoxes stayed here temporarily after their release, but what Margaret now wanted was to be fully restored to the Queen's favour and back at court where she should be. She told Cecil that she and Lennox could not 'reckon themselves fully restored to the Queen's favour, unless they be admitted to her presence', and she requested him to intercede with the Queen to that effect.[81]

On 7 February 'a well-known Catholic gentleman, a member of Parliament', confided to Quadra 'that some of the nobles would like to set aside all these pretenders such as Lady Katharine, Lady Margaret, the Earl of Huntingdon and all these folks, and give the kingdom to the person to whom it rightly belongs, namely the Queen of Scotland', especially if she married Don Carlos and restored the Catholic faith.[82]

The Privy Council would not have agreed, but they certainly wanted to set aside Margaret's claim to the throne, and were secretly taking steps to undermine it. But someone talked, because on 28 March Quadra reported that 'the Queen's council are occupied in proving Lady Margaret to be a bastard, and are taking evidence on the matter, though with great secrecy'.[83] They had obtained a statement from William Barlow, Bishop of Chichester, that on an embassy to James V of Scots in 1534–5, he had been instructed to persuade Margaret Tudor to renounce Lord Methven and be reconciled to Angus. Methven had protested that the Queen was lawfully married to him, and shown Barlow 'an authentic instrument of divorce made at Rome', which showed that 'the cause of the divorce was grounded upon allegations and proofs that before the Earl married the Queen he was married to another gentlewoman'.

Lord William Howard, who had accompanied Barlow on this embassy, had told him he had a special command from the King's Majesty 'diligently to inquire' about Margaret Tudor's marriage, and he and Barlow had obtained from Angus's first wife a letter in her own hand, as proof of her marriage with the Earl.[84]

On 21 March Cecil wrote a memorandum summing up this information[85] and sounded out Maitland on the issue of Margaret's legitimacy.[86] But there could be no arguing with the well-known plea of Margaret Tudor that she had been ignorant of any precontract entered into by Angus, or the confirmation of that in the dispensation granted to her, and so Margaret's legitimacy had to be upheld.[87]

14

'Lady Lennox's Disgrace'

After a short sojourn at Sackville Place the Lennoxes returned to Settrington to sort out their troubled affairs,[1] but Margaret did not stay long, and on 14 May 1563 it was reported that 'Lady Lennox lies at St John's' of Jerusalem,[2] the old priory of the Knights Hospitallers in Clerkenwell, where Mary Tudor had stayed in some state in Edward VI's reign. Having reverted to the Crown at the Dissolution, it was one of several properties that the Queen had at her disposal to make available to Margaret.

Elizabeth was now in negotiations to marry the Archduke Charles of Austria, who was the son of the Holy Roman Emperor Ferdinand I and also a suitor of Mary, Queen of Scots, but Quadra reported that 'the Catholics of this country are dead against the match with the Archduke'. They had told him clearly they would rather have Darnley as king than the Archduke, 'as they are dissatisfied with the latter in the matter of religion'.[3]

Margaret was making efforts to get into the Queen's good books, and found that Elizabeth, eager to discountenance the supporters of Katherine Grey, was now full of goodwill towards her and her husband and ready to receive them back at court. In June she agreed to write to Queen Mary in support of their appeal to have the attainder on Lennox reversed, which was now a matter of the most urgent necessity, given his desperate financial situation. On 16 June she informed Mary that, 'having sundry times been requested by our dear cousin, the Lady Margaret, and her husband, the Earl of Lennox, to recommend their several suits, which have continued long in Scotland', and 'having spoken to him, and considered the nearness of her blood' to herself and to Mary, 'we thought neither we could deny this for our part, nor you mislike our request for your part'. She urged Mary 'to give their causes such consideration as in honour and reason they shall merit'.[4] This was not a wholly altruistic gesture, as Elizabeth was well aware that Lennox's Scottish estates were worth far less than the property he owned in England, and that, if they were restored to him, his best interests would still remain in England, so he was unlikely to jeopardise them by trying to marry his son to the Scottish Queen.

It may be that Elizabeth supported Lennox's suit because she saw it as a means of being rid of him and his troublesome wife. Queen Mary was unlikely to tolerate Margaret's pretensions to the English throne, since she wanted it for herself. Moray, who had shunted aside Châtelherault, was ready to welcome back the Duke's rival as a counterbalance to the Hamiltons.[5]

Apart from making her position clear in regard to Katherine Grey, there was another reason why it now pleased Elizabeth to show favour to the Lennoxes. For four years now she had been carrying on a very public affair with her Master of Horse, Lord Robert Dudley, and there had been endless speculation as to whether they would marry. But Elizabeth had now conceived the idea of proposing Dudley as a husband for the Queen of Scots. His loyalty was undoubted, and he could be trusted to promote England's interests in Scotland; he would be a link between the two queens, a means of smoothing relations between them. As Elizabeth did not wish to marry at all, she was giving him the opportunity of making another royal marriage and fathering an heir to both kingdoms.[6] But this was also part of a strategy to deflect Mary from pursuing a marriage with Don Carlos, the son and heir of Philip of Spain. It was not yet public knowledge that Don Carlos was insane.

Dudley was against the plan from the first, and horrified at the prospect of having to abandon his ambition to be king consort of England. But Elizabeth was adamant, and told Maitland that if Mary would allow her to choose a husband for her, she might proclaim her her heir. The astute Maitland soon guessed that she was referring to Dudley, but could hardly believe it, since Dudley was so far below Mary in rank and had a dubious reputation. Even Randolph, who had been instructed to pave the way for public acceptance of Dudley in Scotland, was praying that he would not have to disclose to Mary the identity of the husband Elizabeth was proposing for her. Elizabeth wanted to keep Mary guessing; it was all apiece with her plan to delay her rival marrying as long as possible. Marriage to Dudley was

to be the price of Elizabeth naming Mary her heir, and to demonstrate that she was looking favourably upon the Scottish line, she
was happy to show a smiling face to the Lennoxes.

Margaret misread the signs. She had every reason to think that
the husband intended for Mary was Darnley. On 19 June Quadra
wrote that 'Lady Margaret is now in the palace, apparently in high
favour and entertains some hope, as I believe, that the Queen of
Scotland will marry her son with the Queen of England's consent.'[7]

A week later he reported: 'Many people think that if the Queen
of Scotland does marry a person unacceptable to this Queen, the
latter will declare as her successor the son of Lady Margaret, whom
she now keeps in the palace and shows such favour to as to make
this appear probable.'[8]

On 19 July Sir John Mason informed Sir Thomas Challoner that
'Lord and Lady Lennox are continual courtiers, and much made of'.
Darnley was waiting daily on the Queen and often played on the
lute before her, 'wherein it should seem she taketh pleasure, as indeed
he plays very well'.[9] It pleased Elizabeth to make Darnley welcome
at court and to treat him like a prince; he was, after all, not yet
sixteen, and her nearest male relation. That might well keep his
mother sweet, but beyond that he was useful to the Queen, and no
doubt she wanted him under her eye. Above all it would do no harm
for Queen Mary to realise that there was one with a prior claim to
the English throne who stood well with Elizabeth.

In August the Queen went on progress to Northampton, and on
9 September it was reported that 'the Lady Lennox, her husband
and son, have waited [on her] all this progress, and now have leave
to go into the north'.[10] Doubtless Elizabeth hoped that the favour
shown to the Lennoxes would earn her credit with the Catholics
and pre-empt any further intrigues in Yorkshire. Unknown to her,
on 27 September Pope Pius IV wrote to Lennox and other Scottish
lords congratulating them on their loyalty to Queen Mary, and
exhorting them to persevere.[11] This may well have given impetus
and weight to Margaret's ambitions.

Despite the oath that she had made to Elizabeth, she had not
given up on her ambitions for Darnley, and her hopes were riding
high. Sometime in the latter half of 1563 she commissioned from
Hans Eworth a smaller, wood-panel version of the double portrait
of her sons, which bears a similar legend but a different date: *These
be the sons of the right honourables the Earl of Lennox and of the Lady
Margaret's Grace, Countess of Lennox and Angus. 1563: Charles Stewart/*

his brother/aetatis 6. Henry Stewart, Lord Darnley and Douglas, aetatis 17 – meaning that the boys were in their sixth and seventeenth years. In this version they are shown standing in the long gallery of a great house, probably Temple Newsam. Presumably the picture was intended for Queen Mary.[12]

Cecil and the authorities were not so naïve as to think that Margaret had given up hope of marrying Darnley to Mary. On 21 February 1564 Randolph expressed to Cecil doubts that Mary would take Darnley's suit seriously, although some Scots saw him as the obvious choice on account of the earldoms of Lennox and Angus that might, through him, become vested in the Scottish Crown. Predictably Châtelherault was against the idea, hating the prospect of his enemy's son becoming king.[13]

In March 1564 Elizabeth formally offered Dudley as a husband for the Queen of Scots,[14] and Mary immediately refused, saying that it could not be compatible with her honour to take such a subject.[15] Indeed, she was much offended at the notion that she should wed the Queen's 'horse-master', yet she did not want to jeopardise her chances of being named Elizabeth's successor, so she instructed her lords to arrange a meeting to discuss the proposal.[16]

Margaret seized her chance. She sent Thomas Fowler, now her secretary, to Scotland on the pretext of looking into Lennox's affairs there in preparation for his return.[17] That may indeed have been part of his remit, but he almost certainly had further instructions. In 1573 it would be observed in a report from Scotland that the full circumstances of the negotiations for the marriage of Mary and Darnley 'are not fully known, and of all those involved left alive only Margaret could best explain them'.[18] Obviously she was deeply involved.

Fowler's movements did not go unnoticed. On 6 April a concerned Randolph reported to Cecil 'that there came and is gone to Scotland a servant of my lord of Lennox; I believe he will be an evil welcome guest. Pardon me, though somewhat suspicious. I have a favourable letter by him from my lady's Grace.'[19] It appears that Margaret was doing her best to keep everything above board, but Randolph was still not convinced.

Until now Mary had evaded the issue of Lennox's restoration, but that month, leaning at last towards the idea of taking Darnley as a husband, and perhaps persuaded thereto by Margaret, through Fowler (who had not gone home, as Randolph thought), she agreed to restore his father's honours and invited Lennox to return to Scotland to be reinstated in his estates and property. She did this with the full backing of Moray and Maitland, who remained desirous of countering the influence of the Hamiltons.[20]

Ten months earlier Elizabeth had asked Mary to look kindly on Lennox's plea, but since then she may have heard rumours of Don Carlos's insanity, and realised that Mary would see Darnley as a viable alternative. Elizabeth may have guessed from Randolph's reports that there was more to the Lennoxes' interests in Scotland than they were giving her to believe, so she was now suspicious of Lennox's going there, and initially refused to allow it; she raged at him for wanting to return to Scotland, to which he protested that he was merely 'travelling for his right'.[21]

Fowler may have been awaiting an opportunity formally to offer Darnley as a husband for the Queen. It has been suggested that he did so, on Margaret's instructions, on or shortly before 14 April 1564,[22] because on that day Randolph reported to Cecil that 'a friend of good knowledge and judgement wrote unto me [that Mary] will at length let fall her anchor between Dover and Berwick, though perchance not in that port, haven or road that you wish she should'.[23] Around 30 April Sir William Kirkcaldy of Grange warned Randolph that Mary had agreed to Lennox's restoration because she was thinking of marrying Darnley. Much disconcerted, Randolph immediately relayed this information to Cecil.[24] On 3 May Knox – who was at one with the Lords of the Congregation in opposing the marriage – informed Randolph that 'the Earl of Lennox's servant is familiar in Court, and it is supposed that it is not without knowledge, yea, and labour of the English Court. Some in this country look for the lady [Margaret] and the young Earl [Darnley] ere it be long. It is whispered to me licence is already given to them [i.e. Margaret and her son]. God's providence is inscrutable to man, but, to be plain with you, that journey and progress I like not.'[25]

By 5 May Randolph had learned that Elizabeth had agreed to allow Lennox to return to Scotland and make his own appeal to Queen Mary. 'Some suspect she shall at length be persuaded to favour his son.'[26] Elizabeth also authorised Margaret to accompany her husband.[27]

Early in June rumours were rampant that Elizabeth was 'to meet the Queen of Scots to arrange for her to marry the son of Lady Margaret'.[28] That was credible in view of the favour now being shown to Darnley, as on 22 June a Spanish envoy, Diego Guzman de Silva, arrived at Richmond Palace to find that young man in high favour, and delegated to receive Silva. 'Presently there came to me, on behalf of the Queen, Lord Darnley, the son of Lady Margaret Lennox, who led me to the door of the presence chamber, where I was met by the Lord Chamberlain, who entered with me and accompanied me to the Queen.' When Silva took his leave of Elizabeth, the Lord Chamberlain conducted him 'to the door of the antechamber, and thence Lady Margaret's son' and two other gentlemen accompanied him to the jetty where his barge awaited.[29] In July the Queen and Margaret both acted as sponsors at the baptism of Cecil's newborn daughter, Elizabeth, and attended the celebratory feast at Cecil House on London's Strand, which rather gave the impression that the Queen considered Margaret to be the second lady in the land and her likely successor.[30]

In July Fowler returned to face an interrogation by Cecil about his visit to Scotland. Which of the Scottish lords were friends or enemies to England? Did he know the names of any English informers who were passing on information to them? No mention was made of Darnley, and it has been suggested that Cecil was not yet aware that secret negotiations for his marriage were afoot.[31] However, he cannot but have inferred as much from Randolph's letters.

Elizabeth remained uneasy about Lennox going to Scotland, fearing that he might stir up religious strife by reviving his old feud with the Hamiltons. When the Lennoxes 'asked leave to take with them a son of theirs, who is an amiable youth, the Queen was angry at this and revoked the licence she had given them'. This was on 5 July.[32] That day she wrote secretly to Mary, urging her to forbid Lennox entry to her kingdom.

Moray reported to Cecil on 13 July that 'some of Queen Elizabeth's best friends here mislike the home-coming of the Earl of Lennox, and would have me persuade my mistress that Lennox might be stayed for this year'; but Moray was not overly concerned 'as to the factions that the coming of Lennox might make for the matters of religion'; he thanked God that 'their foundation is not so weak that they have cause to fear'.[33] Mary (who had found it hard work persuading Châtelherault that Lennox would not pose a threat to him)[34] was of the same mind, and refused to retract her invitation. She had no wish to offend the man whose son she was thinking of marrying.

That same day Maitland, having received a protest from Cecil about Moray's support for Lennox, expressed surprise, seeing how earnestly Elizabeth had 'recommended Lennox's cause and his lady's to me at my being in the court of England. I never had acquaintance or intelligence with the lord of Lennox or his lady before the time that Queen Elizabeth spoke unto me in their favour.' It was Elizabeth's recommendation that had moved Moray – and, as Moray thought, Mary – to favour Lennox. If Mary was now to prevent Lennox from coming, it 'would somewhat touch her honour, having permitted him licence. To be short, she sees no danger in this matter.'[35]

On 3 August Bedford, the Governor of Berwick, had heard that 'Lady Margaret shall come into Scotland with the Earl her husband', and asked for Cecil's advice, 'or rather Her Majesty's pleasure, herein, as peradventure some gentlemen of Yorkshire would accompany them into Scotland'.[36] This must have set alarms ringing in Cecil's head.

Elizabeth knew that Mary, averse to marrying Dudley and aware that a match with Don Carlos was no longer viable because of his insanity, was now seriously considering marrying the seventeen-year-old Darnley. She was well aware that the Lennoxes had plotted to bring about the match, and she must have known that, once in Scotland, Lennox would be well placed to negotiate it. Yet by 12 August, in response to a bitter complaint from Mary, and fat bribes offered by Lennox,[37] Elizabeth had relented and agreed that he might return there, but only on condition that he did nothing prejudicial to England's interests. Dudley, a reluctant suitor, hoping that Mary would choose Darnley over himself, had added his persuasions. He told Maitland later that month that he had upheld Lennox's pleas. 'No man more wished his going than I, or furthered it more at her Majesty's hands.'[38] But did Elizabeth really believe that such an ambitious man as Lennox would not seek to marry his son to the Queen of Scots?

Lennox departed without further delay, doubtless lest Elizabeth repent of her decision, but Margaret did not go with him. On 12 August Silva reported that the Queen had 'given leave for the husband alone to go, and he is already on the road with his licence, if they do not take it away again. I know it has cost him a good deal of money to get it.'[39] It is likely that Elizabeth had insisted on Margaret remaining at the English court with her son as sureties for her husband's loyalty, and although after Lennox had ridden north there were rumours that she was to follow him with Darnley, she remained in England.

The couple had no idea of how long they would be separated, and Margaret may have had concerns as to how her husband would fare without her. Lennox later told the Scottish diplomat Sir James Melville that 'my lady his wife, at his coming from her, had willed him' to take counsel of Melville and the latter's brother Robert 'in all he did, as that of her friends and kinsmen'.[40]

Margaret lost one of her greatest supporters when Bishop de Quadra succumbed to the plague in August. On the 26th it was reported that he had died 'in great grief that he should drop from his work just when he hoped to succeed'. He expired with the words, 'I can do no more.'[41] Guzman de Silva succeeded him as ambassador.

Speculation that Elizabeth would marry Dudley was still rife, even though she continued to insist that he wed Queen Mary. Now Dudley, following the Queen's lead and showing himself friendly to Margaret – in which he was not insincere – made her his confidante, and on 4 September Silva informed King Philip that 'Margaret Lennox, one of the pretenders to this crown and a strong Catholic, has sent word to me that I may be sure that the Queen's [Elizabeth's] marriage with Lord Robert will not take place. She says he is undeceived and has told her so himself. I should not be at all surprised if it did take place or did not, so constantly are things changing.'[42]

Probably Dudley had been instructed to tell Margaret that he would never be able to marry Elizabeth, so that she would believe that the match with Mary was likely to take place. But for their different reasons, both Margaret and Dudley were working to overturn it, and in so doing made common cause together. Dudley had shown himself sufficiently sympathetic and kind to Margaret in the past for her not to think it unusual that he should confide in her; she probably knew that he had urged her release from Sheen the previous year. Thus were laid the foundations of an enduring friendship between them, which argues that Dudley had given little credence to Bishop's allegations that Margaret had disparaged him. The auguries were in her favour, and Dudley's. On 19 September Kirkcaldy of Grange informed Randolph that the Scots would not accept Dudley as king, but 'if ye will earnestly press it, ye may cause us [to] take the Lord Darnley'.[43]

Lennox had arrived in Edinburgh by 23 September, and Margaret would have rejoiced to learn that, at Queen Mary's command, he had been welcomed by the Scottish nobles in Parliament, which had rescinded the sentence of outlawry on him. No longer was he a fugitive traitor but a nobleman in high favour with his Queen, who had promised to reverse the attainder passed on him twenty years earlier. Margaret surely saw this as a strong indication of Mary's growing resolve to marry Darnley, for the Queen could not contemplate marrying a man whose father was an attainted traitor. Lennox's restoration would also alleviate the financial problems that he and Margaret continued to suffer.

That week there was 'nothing but banqueting of Lennox and the ladies'.[44] On 28 September Mary wrote to Elizabeth that she perceived how her sister monarch 'entirely tendered the causes of him and our right well-beloved cousin, his wife', and to say that she herself had 'shown him her good will in favourably receiving him and hearing his petitions'.[45] On 30 September Lennox, now installed in a fine apartment in Holyrood Palace, informed Elizabeth that Mary had 'shown him such graciousness that he must think himself bound to her [Elizabeth] more than ever he was' for aiding him. He asked her 'to extend the like favour to his wife, your poor kinswoman, who has no refuge in my absence but you only'.[46]

The next step was to persuade Queen Elizabeth to allow Darnley to join Lennox in Scotland. That September Mary sent Sir James Melville, a Lennox adherent, as ambassador to England. He came with 'instructions out of the Queen's own mouth, to deal with the Queen of England, the Spanish ambassador, and with my Lady Margaret Douglas and sundry friends she had in England of different opinions'.[47] Mary had entrusted him with 'a secret charge to deal with Lady Lennox to procure liberty for [Darnley] to go to Scotland under the pretext of seeing the country and conveying his father back again to England'[48] – as if Elizabeth would be taken in by that.

Again we have evidence that Margaret was working behind the scenes to bring the Darnley marriage to fruition – and that Mary was now seriously interested. During the nine days Melville spent at the English court he arranged a covert meeting with Margaret to discuss the possibility of a match, and would later observe, 'She was a very wise and discreet matron, and had many favourers in England.'[49] Margaret, ignoring her oath to Queen Elizabeth, made it clear that she would do everything in her power to further the project.

When, on 29 September, Elizabeth created Robert Dudley earl of Leicester at St James's Palace, with a view to befitting him to marry the Queen of Scots, Darnley was conspicuous in the ceremonies, carrying the sword of state before the Queen as she went in procession to the presence chamber. After the ceremony Elizabeth asked Melville, 'How do you like my new creation?' He gave a courteous answer but she pointed at Darnley, declaring, 'And yet ye like better of yonder long lad!'

Melville evidently thought Darnley effeminate. 'No woman of spirit would make choice of such a man, that was liker a woman than a man, for he is very lusty, beardless and lady-faced,' he wrote later. 'I had no will that the Queen of England should think I liked Lord Darnley or had any eye or dealing that way.'[50] Elizabeth told him that Darnley 'was one of two that she had in her head to offer our Queen, as born within the realm of England',[51] which no doubt raised Margaret's hopes when it was reported to her.

When Melville returned to Scotland, 'my Lady Lennox sent many good advices to the Queen [Mary], to be followed according as occasion offered', and 'tokens', including 'a ring with a fair diamond'. Margaret also sent inducements to win over Mary's chief lords: a diamond for Moray and a watch set with diamonds and rubies for Maitland. There was a ruby ring for Melville's brother Robert, and for Lennox an emerald, a stone then believed to be a powerful talisman against the lures of the Devil, and symbolising purity, faith and immortality. These gifts must have come out of Margaret's own jewel casket, for it is unlikely that she could have afforded to buy such costly pieces. She was no doubt happy to sacrifice them, 'for she was still in good hope that her son, my Lord Darnley, would come better speed concerning the marriage of our Queen than the Earl of Leicester'.[52] But in sending these tokens, she was again breaking her oath to Elizabeth.

It has been suggested that it was around this time that Margaret sent her husband the famous Lennox, or Darnley, Jewel, a richly enamelled, intricate pendant locket in the shape of a heart, which survives in the Royal Collection.[53] This jewel is mired in controversy. Some have postulated that it was of considerable significance in the Darnley marriage negotiations, and even that it contained coded symbols that would convey to Lennox plans that were too dangerous for Margaret to entrust to a letter or messenger. It has also been asserted that it was commissioned by Margaret as a *memento mori* of her husband, and dates from after his death.[54] But two historians have cast credible doubt on that, as the Jewel contains no memorials to him or any reference to events in his life.[55]

The Lennox Jewel has been dated to the 1560s.[56] The complex symbols that adorn it suggest that it was commissioned by Lennox around 1564–5. It has also been suggested that it is to be identified with a 'marvellous fair and rich jewel' he gave to Queen Mary, which was much admired at court,[57] yet its imagery relates very personally

to the union between himself and his wife and their dynastic aspirations, and the likeliest theory is that it was commissioned by Lennox
for Margaret to mark the imminent fruition of their hopes. The
imagery in the Jewel is as much of a key to understanding their
relationship as the letters they exchanged. Heart jewels, it has been
pointed out, were invariably gifts between lovers or married couples.[58]
It is not known where the Jewel was made, but it has been suggested
that it came from Edinburgh.[59]

The Lennox Jewel is of fine workmanship, three inches in length,
and decorated with translucent enamel over a textured gold base
(*basse taille*). On the outer face is a crown set with Burmese rubies,
an Indian emerald and other precious stones, and surmounted by
three *fleurs-de-lis*, the royal arms of France, which appear on an azure
shield in the first quarter of Lennox's arms; the right to bear these
arms had been granted to his forebear, Sir John Stewart of Darnley,
by Charles VII.

Beneath the crown is a heart made of a single great sapphire,
Lennox's birthstone, which symbolised wisdom, purity and steadfastness; its feathered wings are enamelled in ruby, emerald and gold.
The crown and the heart together were the ancient emblems of the
Douglases, and the protective wings symbolise the soaring aspirations
of the family; they may also represent Lennox's love winging its way
to Margaret.

Supporting the crown and the heart are four allegorical figures:
Faith, with a cross and a lamb, for Christ, the Lamb of God; Hope,
with her symbol, the anchor, which also stood for constancy and
fidelity, and again for Christ, the soul's anchor; Victory, with an olive
branch; and Truth, with a mirror. These symbols, like others in the
Jewel, embody not only the love and fidelity between Margaret and
Matthew and her deep Catholic faith, but their dynastic ambitions
and their hopes for their son, Darnley.

The Jewel bears twenty-eight emblems, some of which can only
be seen properly with a magnifying glass, and six inscriptions in old
Scots. On the white enamel border is an inscription: 'Who hopes
still constantly with patience shall obtain victory in their pretence
[claim]', which refers to the couple's pursuit of crowns for themselves
and their offspring, and their confident conviction that their hopes
will be realised.

The crown on the Jewel opens up to reveal two hearts joined by
a blue buckle – buckles featured in both the Lennox and Douglas
arms – and a gold true love's knot pierced by two feathered arrows

with gold barbs, presumably shot by Cupid. Below are the initials M. S. L. for Matthew (or perhaps Margaret) Stuart Lennox; these devices represent the couple's marriage and Lennox's deep and enduring love for his wife, and they are crowned with a chaplet of leaves, the symbol of victory, and also of Christ, whom St Paul called the 'wreath that will never die'.

The winged heart opens to reveal two joined hands holding by a ruby filet a green hunting horn, then a symbol of aristocratic status. Underneath this device is a *memento mori*, a skull and crossbones, a reminder of mortality. This links to a motto in the crown compartment, 'What we resolve', which is completed by that in the heart compartment: 'Only death shall dissolve'. This inscription also refers to the undying love between Margaret and Matthew. Another inscription in the inner heart, 'Tym gares al leir', is an anagram of 'Margaret is leil', which means true and affectionate.

Partially encircling the reverse of the Jewel is the inscription: 'My state to these I may compare for you, who are of rare goodness.' Again, it is probably a tribute from Lennox to Margaret. The words surround the sun in splendour – a symbol of royalty and glory – amidst azure clouds (symbolising the unseen Divine Presence) studded with stars (spiritual light piercing the darkness), with a crescent moon to one corner, having a man's face in profile: the moon symbolises humanity, the Roman Catholic Church, and, in its monthly rebirth, the Resurrection.

Beneath the sun is a 'pelican in its piety', a crowned bird feeding its young with blood from its own breast until it dies, a symbol of the sacrificial maternal love felt by Margaret for her children. The pelican was also a symbol of charity and of the Eucharist, symbolising Christ's sacrificial love for mankind.

Under the moon is a salamander – Margaret's emblem – ascending unburned from the fire, reflecting her determination to rise above the difficulties that had befallen her and triumph in the end. Generally a salamander represents a righteous soul who remains calm when beset by enemies. Some accounts of the Jewel describe it as a phoenix, in which case it may allude to Margaret's protectiveness of her son. The phoenix was one of Elizabeth I's devices.

In the lower corner of the heart is the figure of a man lying on the grass, who has been identified as Lord Darnley but is more likely to have symbolised Lennox. The image probably refers to a line in Psalm 23: 'He maketh me to lie down in green pastures.' Beside him lies a crown, a symbol both of royal authority and of Christ, and from it sprouts a sunflower, which stands for God's love and for a soul directing its thoughts and feelings to the Deity; the sunflower opens up its radial petals to the sun, which also symbolises divine love. On the flower rests a lizard, a symbol closely associated with light and sun, and often representing a soul longing for Christ. Behind the recumbent man stands a laurel tree, a symbol of victory and immortality, in which a gaudy little bird is perched; he stands for a saved soul. In these symbols we see Lennox's ambition on the way to being fulfilled, justified and sanctified by his faith.

The back of the Jewel also opens, to reveal martyrs burning at the stake, with roses in the flames, probably representing how much Margaret had suffered for her religion. Nearby a crowned queen is enthroned with the motto 'Cause tell my release'. She may represent Margaret having been released from prison and the machinations of her enemies, and triumphing in the end – or the prospect of Queen Mary being freed from the tutelage of the Protestant lords through her marriage to the Catholic Darnley.

Standing on a celestial sphere representing the heavens (on which appear the words 'You seem all my pleasure') is the figure of Time, his upper body shown with a forelock, wings and an hourglass, his feet cloven like those of the Devil. In the sixteenth century Time was regarded as a malevolent figure: since ancient times he had been associated with the god Saturn, who in turn had become identified with Satan, hence the cloven hoofs. Here the phrase 'take time by the forelock' seems apposite, for the Lennoxes now needed to act quickly and decisively, being aware that time flew on wings, and that life was finite, according to Time's hourglass.

But Time was not all bad. To one side he pulls the naked figure of Truth out of a well; the concept of 'the naked truth' was prevalent in Renaissance culture, and a well represented a womb; thus the fruit of Margaret's womb was the true Catholic heir who would prevail in time. On the other side of Time two black jaws representing the gates of Hell vomit flames and demons. Above is the legend 'Time causes all to learn'. It may be an observation on what would befall those who persisted in heresy and did not acknowledge their rightful ruler.

In the lower section of the Jewel is a soldier, perhaps Lennox, about to kill his opponent – Châtelherault? – who points to a red shield bearing a face, possibly Darnley's, surmounted by a crown; and a crowned warrior – who may again be Darnley – with a drawn sword, holding a lady by the hair. Possibly she symbolises Mary, who

Darnley will capture and defend, or more likely Queen Elizabeth deposed, loose hair being symbolic of virginity and a virgin queen.

This reading of the iconography of the Lennox Jewel strongly suggests that it was made after Lennox's restitution and before Darnley's marriage. It is a moving testimony to Lennox's love for his absent wife and his hopes for their son, and to Margaret's invincible faith.[60]

It may have been in consequence of Margaret's pleas, conveyed by Melville, that soon afterwards Mary asked Elizabeth to permit Darnley to join his father. But Elizabeth refused; she was still insisting that Mary should wed Leicester, even though he had no liking for the match. Both Cecil and Leicester knew very well that Mary would never agree, and put pressure on the Queen to allow Darnley to go to Scotland, arguing that he would not risk the confiscation of the Lennox lands in England by outstaying his licence or marrying Mary without Elizabeth's consent.[61] Margaret added her pleas, assuring Elizabeth that Darnley would be back within a month, yet to no avail.[62]

On 4 October, the day on which Queen Mary formally restored Lennox to his lands, Sir Thomas Smith, Elizabeth's ambassador in Paris, reported that the French believed the Darnley marriage to be a fait accompli.[63]

Lennox's heavy investment in gaining Mary's favour was paying off. On 16 October his restitution was proclaimed at the market cross in Edinburgh 'in presence of the lords'. Then 'by blast of trumpet' it was announced that the Parliament that would ratify the Queen's clemency would sit on 4 December. 'The lords rode up the gait [road] in pairs, Argyll and Lennox together, and down the gait Lennox and the Chancellor. All the lords dined that day with Lennox.'[64]

On 24 October Randolph himself was Lennox's dinner guest.

> The house where he lodges is well hanged, two chambers very well furnished, one specially rich, and a fair bed, with a passage made through the wall to come into the court when he wills. [Randolph] saw him honourably used of all men. The Queen liked his behaviour. His cheer is great, and his household many. He finds occasions to disburse money very fast, and of his £700 [£119,200] he brought with him is sure that much is not left. He gave the Queen a marvellous fair and rich jewel, whereof there is made no small account, a clock and a dial curiously

wrought and set with stones, and a looking glass very richly set with stones. The bruit is here that Lady Lennox and Lord Darnley are coming. There is here a marvellous good liking of the young lord, a fair, jolly young man.[65]

On the 27th, to gratify the Queen, Lennox went through a ceremony of reconciliation with Châtelherault, his old foe, although their enmity would continue to simmer.

Randolph reported on 3 November that Mary had spoken no word about marrying Darnley, 'though here it is in the mouths of all men that it is concluded in this Queen's heart'. Still 'Lady Margaret and Lord Darnley are looked for' in Scotland, but Randolph expressed doubts whether Margaret would 'be as soon restored unto the earldom of Angus, as her husband was to Lennox, for there depends more matter thereon, which if proved true, will disappoint her farther than anything she looks for here'.[66] Morton, acting for his nephew, Archibald Douglas, was doing his utmost to prove Margaret illegitimate.

On 4 November Silva informed Philip II that Lennox had written to Elizabeth 'informing her that, as his relatives and lawyers are of opinion that the presence of his son is necessary for the preservation of these estates, he begs her to give him leave to come and take joint possession with him. The Queen replied to Lady Margaret, congratulating her on the restoration of her husband's estate, and said she would be pleased to give her son the licence requested. This was repeated to her also by Cecil and Leicester.' But then, Silva went on to explain, Elizabeth's mood changed.

After the licence was granted, the next day the Queen said to Margaret that she was very vexed and offended at her husband for having asked for the licence for the son with all this caution, saying that his lawyers had advised him that his son's presence was necessary to take possession of the estate, when such was not the fact. For this reason she had decided not to give him leave to go, as she would have done willingly if she had been asked in a straightforward way.

Margaret explained the matter in such a way that the Queen again said she would give the licence and would answer her husband's letter. Notwithstanding all this it has been decided not to give the licence. This is the way with everything – absolutely no certainty.

This Lennox, Margaret and her son are Catholics, and profess attachment to your Majesty. I do what is requisite to entertain them, although with great caution and secrecy. As Margaret is one of the claimants to the succession, and a Catholic, the Queen and her ministers attach a great deal of importance to her and are so suspicious, so excited and so anxious that Margaret says they conduct themselves as if they were frantic, and certainly she is not far wrong.[67]

The English and Scottish commissioners had met at Berwick on 18 November to discuss the proposed marriage between Mary and Leicester even though the matter was virtually moribund. But since Elizabeth insisted that she would never willingly consent to any subject save Leicester marrying Mary, an impasse was reached.

Lennox's attainder was reversed by the Scottish Parliament on 9 December.[68] He now set about re-establishing his influence at the heart of Scotland's political elite, and began by raising a following of lords and lairds, many of whom had been excluded by Moray and the Hamiltons from government. He also set himself to convince Queen Mary of the desirability of marrying his son.

But now, inexplicably, Elizabeth seemed to be having a change of heart. On 3 December the Scottish lords had pressed her to make concessions to render the Leicester marriage acceptable to Mary,[69] but Elizabeth failed to do so, which suggests that the continuing Dudley negotiations were a bluff, and that she had for some time been planning to dangle Darnley as a carrot before Mary.

At Berwick, around 14 December, Bedford and Randolph met with Moray and Maitland 'on behalf of the respective queens'. Astonishingly, Elizabeth had proposed to Mary 'that she should choose between the following three Englishmen: the Earl of Leicester, the Duke of Norfolk and the son of Lady Margaret Lennox; and in the event of her marrying either of them she will declare her heiress to the crown'. Mary responded 'that she was willing to marry an Englishman if the succession was declared, but not the Earl of Leicester'. Not one word was spoken of Darnley, but Mary wrote to Elizabeth 'asking her still to give leave for Lady Margaret's son to come to his father in Scotland'.[70]

It seems strange that Elizabeth should suddenly have offered Darnley as a husband for Mary. She must have anticipated that Mary would see marriage to Darnley as a means of uniting their claims to the English throne and thereby strengthening her own. On the face of it, Elizabeth was courting disaster. If she was hoping, by suggesting suitor after suitor, to prolong negotiations so that Mary remained unmarried for as long as possible, she was taking a perilous risk. On the other hand, as a Catholic king consort, Darnley would be anathema to the Calvinist Scottish lords. If Mary married him she would be summoning up a tempest in her kingdom.

Certainly the Scots came to believe that Elizabeth's aim in allowing Darnley to go to Scotland had been to ruin Mary, which was exactly what happened. A dispatch from Randolph to Cecil, written on 14 December, reveals an awareness of the likely consequences of a marriage between Mary and Darnley and the influence of the Catholic Margaret. 'There has been more thought of Lord Darnley before his father's coming than is at present. The father is now here well known, the mother more feared a great deal than beloved of any that know her.'

Morton was one who had good reason to fear Margaret, as did the Lords of the Congregation and those who were enemies of the Douglases. Randolph continued: 'To think that Lord Darnley should marry with this Queen, and his mother bear that stroke [influence] with her that she bore with Queen Mary, which she is like to do, as you can conjecture the causes why, this would alienate as many minds from the Queen's Majesty, my sovereign, by sending home as great a plague into this country, as that which, to her honour, and perpetual love of the faithful and godly, she drove out of the same when the French were forced to retire themselves.' The plague to which Randolph referred was the Catholic religion, and anyone could have foreseen that Queen Mary, being of that faith, would be susceptible to the influence of a strong-willed mother-in-law. Yet it looked as if the marriage really would come about. 'Within these four days Lord Darnley's father told Mr John Leslie, Lord of the Session, that his son should marry this Queen.'[71]

It is not surprising that the Lennoxes were keeping closely in touch at this time. On 16 December Bedford forwarded to Cecil a letter from Lennox to Margaret,[72] and another was dispatched on 4 February;[73] given the couple's ability to facilitate secret communications, there would almost certainly have been more that bypassed official scrutiny.

There was cause for Margaret to feel triumphal elation when, in January 1565, Queen Elizabeth, ostensibly at her request and Mary's, finally gave Darnley permission to go to Scotland. Again she had bowed to Leicester's persuasions, and to Cecil's.[74] Darnley was granted licence to stay in Scotland for three months. Possibly Elizabeth thought that sufficient time for him to woo Mary but not to marry her,[75] yet surely she must have guessed that Darnley would seize the golden opportunity now presented to him. She must have been aware that, encouraged by his parents, he was greedy for a crown, and that all that was required for him to achieve that was permission to go to Scotland.

Melville thought that Elizabeth allowed Darnley to go to Scotland because she and Cecil believed that he would not risk his English inheritance by marrying Mary without her permission.[76] It has been stated that she and her advisers made a grave error of misjudgement,[77] but she may have calculated that the benefits of sending Darnley north might well outweigh the risks. The Protestant lords were unlikely to accept him, and if Mary married him in the face of their opposition, she might be overthrown or neutralised. Crucially, the marriage would prevent Mary allying herself with a great Catholic power. Furthermore, Elizabeth probably had the measure of Darnley, and knew him to be weak, vicious and arrogant; given enough rope, Mary might hang herself by marrying such a liability.

As well as Randolph's letter quoted above, there is good evidence to support the theory that Elizabeth favoured the marriage. A French ambassador, Michel de Castelnau, Sieur de la Mauvissière, asserted that Elizabeth had 'cast her eyes on the young Lord Darnley to make a present of him to the Scottish Queen, and found means to persuade the Queen of Scots that there was not a marriage in Christendom which could bring her [Mary] more certain advantages'. That was true, but the uniting of two claims to the English throne would be very much to Elizabeth's disadvantage – and peril. Castelnau was adamant, however: 'Her Majesty did outwardly show the joy and pleasure which was in her heart when I told her that this marriage was advancing apace', yet 'she affected not to approve it, which did rather hasten than retard it. And yet I am assured she used all her efforts and spared nothing to get this marriage a-going.'[78]

He was not alone in his view. Margaret herself had written to Mary that 'the Queen of England's displeasure against the marriage was full of affectations'.[79] Silva was to report that 'there is a suspicion that the match has been arranged with the concurrence of some of the great people here' in England.[80] In March 1565 Cecil was to tell the French ambassador, Paul de Foix, that the marriage of the Queen of Scots was an affair in the hands of his mistress.[81] In April Randolph would report from Scotland that it was 'here spoken to my face that the sending him [Lennox] home was done of purpose to match the Queen meanly and poorly, rather than live long in amity'.[82]

It was probably with highly mixed emotions that Margaret bade Darnley farewell as he left on the journey that was to end with the fulfilment of all her hopes. Forced to remain in England with young Charles, she was doubtless well aware that her movements were closely watched, while separation from her husband and beloved elder son for an indefinite period must have been hard to bear. Yet it was in the best of causes, and hopefully it would not last long.

On 3 February an English intelligence report – drawn up at Cecil's behest for Sir Nicholas Throckmorton (who was now ambassador to Scotland), and written in a Scottish hand, probably that of Thomas Bishop – listed Lennox's enemies and friends in Scotland, showing that the enemies outnumbered the friends. Among them were the Douglases, but only 'if my Lady Lennox do not relinquish her title to the earldom of Angus, which I suppose in respect of their greater advancement she hath already promised'. The report also revealed that Queen Mary intended to discountenance Châtelherault by advancing Lennox as her heir apparent. 'If Darnley hit the mark, then careth my lady [Margaret] neither for the earldoms of Lennox, Angus nor lands in England, having enough that way.' If the Queen married Darnley, division would follow and 'the overthrow of religion'. Once the Lennoxes and their son were in Scotland, whatever 'flourishing words' they used, in their hearts they had only enmity to Elizabeth and wished division to her realm. It appears that Bishop had been sent to Scotland by Cecil to spy on Lennox.[83]

The last poem to be copied into the Devonshire Manuscript, number 82, was a love poem composed by Darnley, probably for Mary, Queen of Scots, and he may have sent it to her at this time, in advance of his arrival:[84]

> My hope is you for to obtain,
> Let not my hope be lost in vain.
> Forget not my pains manifold,
> Nor my meaning to you untold.
> And eke with deeds I did you crave,
> With sweet words for you to have.
> To my hap and hope condescend,

> Let not Cupido in vain his bow to bend,
> Nor us two lovers, faithful, true,
> Like a bow made of bowing yew.
> But now receive by your industry and art
> Your humble servant, Harry Stuart.

Darnley arrived in Edinburgh on 13 February. When Mary, now twenty-two, saw this tall, fair youth of eighteen, she pronounced him 'the lustiest and best-proportioned long man that she had seen'.[85] On 21 February Lennox wrote to Queen Elizabeth, acknowledging 'her goodness in furthering his cause here, and the comfort he has by the proof of the continuance thereof by her licensing his son to come to him'.[86]

Darnley made a good beginning in Edinburgh. 'His behaviour is liked, and there is great praise of him.'[87] 'There resorted divers unto him,' Randolph reported. 'They like well of his personage.'[88] Around this time Margaret assured Mary that she would have the allegiance of both the English and Scottish Catholics if she and Darnley would unite their claims in marriage and come forward as the King and Queen of Great Britain. Elizabeth would have regarded this as treason.

On 8 March Lennox wrote to Elizabeth asking for 'licence to abide here [in Scotland] for three months more, in order to proceed in the assurance of my lands to my son, the laws here requiring three or four months at the least'.[89] That was not the only reason. Nine days earlier Randolph had reported that there was 'now less talk of anything intended by the Queen' towards Darnley,[90] and Lennox needed time to revive Mary's interest in the marriage project. Two more letters for Margaret were forwarded by Bedford on 15 March,[91] and on 6 April Bedford would pray Cecil 'to desire the Lady of Lennox's pardon for the slack conveyance of letters to her'.[92]

On 24 March Elizabeth told Silva 'that Margaret's son had been very well received and treated in Scotland, and that he and his father would return in May'. But Silva had been told – possibly by Margaret – 'that he has no such intention'.[93] A week later Silva wrote to Philip II that Margaret had informed him

of the kind treatment her son has received at the hands of the Queen of Scotland and that the French ambassador here sent to her in great secrecy to offer and promise all his support for the marriage of her son and anything he might require. She says she knows the French way of dealing and thinks this is for the purpose of discovering whether there is anything afoot, and, perhaps even on the advice of this Queen [Elizabeth].

She repeats that she and her children have no other refuge but your Majesty, to whom she and they will always remain faithful, and begs me address your Majesty in their favour so that in case the Queen of Scotland should choose to negotiate about her son, or in the event of the death of this Queen [Elizabeth], they may look to your Majesty.

Silva had sent Margaret 'as kind an answer as I could'. He told her he had heard that the French were trying to arrange a marriage for Mary with Henry, Duke of Orléans, the younger brother of Charles IX, and asked her to find out through her friends where Elizabeth stood in this, and to advise him of what she heard. He told King Philip he would do the same for her 'as a proof of the great affection your Majesty bears her for many reasons and especially for her high Christian character'.[94]

Again Margaret was venturing into dangerous waters, for it was treason for an English subject to profess an allegiance to the King of Spain.

The Lords of the Congregation, under the leadership of Moray, remained opposed to the Darnley marriage, well aware that the Lennoxes were aligned with the English Catholics. Elizabeth appeared to be doing her best to prevent the marriage going ahead. Darnley had been given leave to stay in Scotland for three months, and it was only with a great deal of difficulty that in the middle of April Margaret finally prevailed upon the Queen to grant him licence for three more.

On 14 April a courier arrived from Scotland with news that 'the son of Lady Margaret Lennox has been ill of small-pox'.[95] It was actually measles, and on 18 April a scandalised Bedford informed Cecil that 'Lord Darnley, all the while he was sick and since, has been almost continually visited by that Queen [Mary], and well near at all hours, few excepted. It appeareth by her tenderness over him that she feared not whether the sickness were infective. This he [Bedford] had of Lennox's man,' who brought him a letter from Mary to Maitland 'and one of her lady's Grace [Margaret's]'.[96] Darnley's illness had accomplished what months of diplomatic manoeuvring had failed to do: Mary was now infatuated with him.

According to Lennox, Mary was 'struck by the dart of love' with the 'comeliness of [Darnley's] sweet behaviour, personage and virtuous qualities as well in languages and letters, sciences, music, dancing and playing on instruments, and especially she also considering the blood he was come of both by the father and mother'.[97]

On 15 April Randolph had informed Cecil that the matter of Darnley 'is now grown to further ripeness. The Queen's familiarity with him breeds no small suspicion that there is more intended than merely giving him honour for his nobility, or for the Queen's Majesty's sake, by whom it is said he was so well recommended. It is now commonly said, and I believe is more than a bruit, that this Queen has already such good liking of him, that she can be content to forsake all other offers and content herself with her own choice.'[98]

Margaret was in high favour. When, in March, Leicester had played host to Elizabeth, Margaret, the French ambassador and 'other of the principal ladies [had] supped with the Queen, as is usual on similar occasions'.[99] On the night of 17 April Elizabeth visited Margaret in her chamber at court, and her manner was kindly and respectful. But the next day everything changed. Maitland arrived in London to seek Elizabeth's consent to Mary's marriage to Darnley and to press her to name Mary her heir, requests Elizabeth was adamantly to refuse. Indeed, she was angered by them, for it was up to Darnley, as her subject, to seek her consent for his marriage, and Mary was presuming too much. Elizabeth now seized her chance of exploiting the situation to her own advantage and neutralising her old adversary. That morning her demeanour towards Margaret suddenly changed, and from then on Margaret was out of favour. Many felt sorry for her.[100]

On 21 April Margaret sent to tell Silva of the arrival of Maitland at court, 'and that her son was well again'. She asked Silva to inform Maitland that King Philip 'desired to favour her, as she believed it would help considerably in her son's business. She thinks very possibly he may marry the Queen [Mary],' and assured Silva that Mary rested her claim to England more on the support of King Philip 'than on anything else, especially as the Queen Mother of France is very much against her'. Silva promised to 'try to keep this matter in hand, showing sympathy, as I have done, until I receive orders from your Majesty'.[101] Margaret wanted Philip to see Darnley, the putative champion of Catholicism in England and Scotland, as the perfect match for Mary.

On 22 April Margaret was commanded by the Queen to keep to her chamber at Whitehall.[102] Effectively she was under house arrest. Four days later she got word to Silva, who informed Philip II that she

> had gone to the Queen's chamber and that her Majesty refused to speak to her, and afterwards sent an order that she was not to leave her apartments, giving her to understand that she was to consider herself a prisoner, as she had received letters from a foreign prince without her permission, and without conveying the contents to her.
>
> Lady Margaret answered that it was true she had received a letter from the Queen of Scotland by her secretary, and had gone to the Queen's chamber for the purpose of showing it to her Majesty, who had refused to speak to her, and conse-quently it was not her fault. An answer came from the Queen to the effect that, although she was detained in her apartments, there was no intention of preventing her friends from visiting her, as is usually done here in cases where persons are placed under arrest.
>
> Lady Margaret also advised me that the negotiations for the marriage of her son with the Queen of Scotland were progressing favourably, and asked me, in case Lethington [Maitland] said anything about it to me, to assure him that your Majesty was favourable to it as they were, and always had been so faithful to your Majesty.[103]

Elizabeth had sent orders to Randolph that Lennox and Darnley must now return to England, but on 23 April Cecil informed Bedford that 'her Majesty had commanded to stay the order of proceeding for calling home the Earl and his son, whereupon he despatched a post after Randolph'.[104] The next day Elizabeth issued instructions to Throckmorton: 'After your arrival in Scotland, you shall do all to understand how far forward the intention of marriage is between the Queen and Lord Darnley – how begun, how liked, how to be stayed, with all necessary circumstances thereto belonging. Thereafter you shall proceed (1) for stay or dissolution thereof and (2) to procure the Queen's acceptance either of Leicester or some foreign prince agreeable to her honour, and meet to nourish the amity betwixt us both, and our two countries.'

Throckmorton later informed Mary that Elizabeth had heard 'fond and strange rumours' that so touched Mary's honour and reputation that she herself was 'grieved and sorry', and had sent him to Scotland to tell Mary so. He was to inform the Queen of Scots 'how it is reported by Darnley's friends that she has so far proceeded in love of him' that, although he was infectious with measles, she could not stay away from him, and much desired to marry him.

Elizabeth was 'heartily offended' because, despite Maitland's assurance that these 'unseemly tales were false', she had since heard more of them, 'and to show they were not true, we did command the Lady Lennox, to whom we had of late time showed singular favour, to forbear from our presence, and could, but for some other respects, have showed more tokens of our displeasure towards her'. As for marrying Darnley, Throckmorton was to tell Mary that there were 'many just causes' why Elizabeth did not think it suitable.[105]

On 26 April Silva heard from the French ambassador that Queen Elizabeth had said that pressure from her subjects, and 'the inconvenience' of Mary remaining unmarried, had caused her to listen to 'certain proposals and conversations with the son of the Earl of Lennox and Lady Margaret. Besides being related to her on both his father's and his mother's side, he was not a foreigner.' It seemed as if Elizabeth was thinking about naming Darnley her successor, in which case, if he married Mary, the two crowns would be united on Elizabeth's death. It sounds like an inducement, but of course Elizabeth would not commit herself. Later that day Silva told Maitland that Darnley seemed the most suitable match for Mary, 'both on account of the promise displayed by himself, and on account of his parents, for whom, and particularly for Lady Margaret, my master has an especial regard'. He impressed this on Maitland 'because I knew he would communicate this to Margaret'.

Silva had heard from various people 'that this marriage [of Mary and Darnley] has actually taken place'. Maitland had mentioned a man saying that one of Margaret's servants had been in Scotland and acted as a witness, but that was not what Margaret herself had said. From what Silva had learned, Elizabeth was 'greatly incensed about the affair, as she thinks the Queen of Scotland's party in this country will be strengthened greatly by it'.

Elizabeth was playing a double game. Although she had rescinded her order for the return of Lennox and Darnley, Silva had heard that she was endeavouring to get Darnley to come back, and had even written hinting that she would marry him herself if he would do so. But Silva did not think he would 'loose his hold' in Scotland.

Silva had also heard that Throckmorton was to go to Scotland for the purpose of trying to stop the marriage, 'which will somewhat console the Catholics', as they had given up hoping that Mary would marry Don Carlos, 'upon which they had set their hearts. They thought that would remedy all evils, but as this gentleman [Darnley] and his parents are held in esteem by them they see in the marriage some glimmer of hope.'

As Silva ended his long dispatch, Margaret sent to say that 'she considers her son's affair an accomplished fact that admits of no doubt'.[106] Two days later he reported that 'Lady Margaret looks upon the business as done'. Silva discovered that during the previous twenty-four hours, Elizabeth had sent 'secret orders that no one is to be allowed to pass the Scotch frontier without being searched to see whether he bears letters. So far as I can gather from conversation and observation, I believe this marriage with Darnley must already have been effected.'

Margaret had remained under house arrest in the palace of Whitehall, and on 28 April Silva asked Maitland 'if he had spoken to the Queen respecting the imprisonment of Lady Margaret, and he told me he had done so, and believed they would release her from her confinement to her rooms today to the extent of allowing her to go all over the palace so long as she did not see the Queen'.[107] That day Bedford forwarded to Cecil 'a letter from the Earl of Lennox to his wife. It cannot be but there is some news therein; you may use your wisdom in retaining or delivering thereof.'[108] Probably he suspected that it concerned the Darnley marriage.

On 29 April Randolph reported that he had 'stayed' the Queen's orders for the recall of Darnley and Lennox. But he expressed the opinion that, if she had thought it good to have them implemented, 'she might have been void of that suspicion that is now almost universal of her, that the sending of Darnley [north] was done of purpose to worse end than he is willing to write'.[109] It was what people in Scotland, who had now had time to learn more of Darnley, were increasingly beginning to suspect.

On 3 May Randolph informed Cecil that Moray and other Lords of the Congregation were bitterly opposed to Mary's marriage plans, not least because Darnley had claimed that the wealthy Moray was over-endowed in landed estates. 'The speech of this marriage to any of them is so contrary to their desires that they think their nation dishonoured, the Queen's Majesty shamed, and their country undone. A greater plague to her there cannot be, a greater benefit to the Queen's Majesty [Elizabeth] could not have chanced than to see this dishonour fall upon her. Such pride is noted in the father and son that there is almost no society or company amongst them.' Lennox was 'saucier than ever', and 'the young lord, being sick on his bed, boasted that he would knock the Duke's [Châtelherault's] pate when he is whole'. Morton, however, was hedging his bets: he was 'more in hopes that the lady's Grace [Margaret] will give over her right of Angus, and so will he become a friend to her side'.[110]

On 4 May Bedford informed Cecil that Thomas Fowler, now back in Scotland, 'has filled the court full of talk of Lady Lennox's disgrace'.[111] Fowler had recently travelled north on sufficient occasions on his employers' business for Randolph to nickname him 'the Flying Post'. He was now to stay at the Scottish court in Darnley's service, and his growing influence would come to be resented by Scots and English alike.

On 15 May, the day Throckmorton arrived at Stirling, Mary created Darnley earl of Ross, a title he unhesitatingly accepted without seeking Elizabeth's consent, which, as her subject, he was bound to do; worse still, he swore fealty to Mary, despite owing allegiance to Elizabeth. 'The Queen in her love is transported,' Randolph wrote on 21 May, 'and Darnley grown so proud that to all honest men he is intolerable.'[112]

Elizabeth may not have intended that things would have progressed so far so soon. She might have been hoping that Darnley and Lennox would make sufficient trouble in Scotland to discredit Mary and the Catholics before any marriage took place. But it is hard to escape the conclusion that she did feel it was worth the risk to herself to let Mary go ahead and marry Darnley, then face a backlash that could well be to her own advantage. A memo written by Throckmorton to Cecil and Leicester on 21 May makes it plain that Elizabeth and her Council were resolved to 'make it appear to all folks that the proceedings of the Queen of Scotland with Darnley are so misliked that she must chasten the arrogance of her subjects, and avenge the indignity offered by the Queen of Scotland'. Darnley, who had behaved treacherously to Elizabeth, was out of reach, so it was upon his mother that Elizabeth's wrath would be vented.

Margaret had 'many favourers' in England,[113] and on 27 May Throckmorton, having realised that Mary was bent on marrying Darnley, and fearing the consequences, warned that a vigilant watch should now be kept on the Catholics in the north of England. The Catholic Earl of Northumberland should be kept in London and orders should be sent to the Council of the North at York to 'have good eye to the doings of Northumberland and the Lady Lennox faction, by no means suffering the Papists through the realm, either in or out of court, to think themselves in credit or estimation'. To that end Throckmorton urged the Privy Council 'to put greater restraint upon Lady Lennox, and harder sequestration than now, that she may have no conference but with those appointed to her, nor any means left for intelligence with the French ambassador, but chiefly none with the Spanish – which imports most'. He advised 'that the Queen's Majesty lie in good wait that Lady Lennox directly or indirectly have no intelligence of her doings or speech other than that severity is intended. It shall be to very good purpose, that both from her Majesty and [Cecil and Leicester], cunningly, Lady Lennox shall know they all marvel that Lethington [Maitland] – a man of judgment – can be so blinded as to further this marriage so earnestly, which they did so well espy by his last legation.' Throckmorton concluded by suggesting that more favour be shown to Lady Katherine Grey.[114]

Margaret had continued to manoeuvre on her son's behalf. She knew that the Scottish lords were hostile to his coming marriage, and was determined to enlist support for him. In the middle of May she finally renounced her claim to the earldom of Angus. As a married woman she did not herself sign the contract, but endorsed it on the back, 'To the Earl of Lennox, my husband.'[115] As she had anticipated, conceding the victory to Archibald Douglas persuaded Morton to abandon Moray and support Darnley's marriage to Mary; and it removed the risk of Margaret being declared a bastard, which would prejudice her hopes for her son.

Elizabeth now took steps that would seemingly limit the damage resulting from what must have begun to look to many like a serious error of judgement. On 27 May she commanded the immediate return of Lennox and Darnley to England. Neither obeyed her summons, and Mary gave them leave to remain safely in Scotland. Elizabeth was enraged when she learned that Darnley had allowed himself to be betrothed to Mary without asking leave of herself, and had sworn allegiance to the Scottish Queen. 'The Queen, finding the intended marriage of Queen Mary with Lord Darnley strange, has communicated the same to certain of her Council, who with one assent thought that it would be unmeet and directly prejudicial to the sincere amity between both the queens.'[116] On 4 June the Privy Council held a conference to debate 'what perils might ensue to the Queen or this realm of the marriage' and 'what were meet to remedy the same'. There were two main causes for alarm:

> The first, that a great number in this realm might be alienated from Queen Elizabeth to depend upon the success of this marriage as a means to establish the succession of both crowns in the issue of the marriage, and so favour all devices that should tend to the advancement of the Queen of Scots. There was a plain intention to further the pretended title of the Queen of Scots, not only to succeed to the Queen's Majesty, but to occupy her estate, as when she was in power she did declare. The second was that hereby the Romish religion should be erected and increased daily in this realm.

It was exactly what Margaret had schemed for.

The Council devised a list of remedies, but three were of prime importance: 'it was necessary that the Queen [Elizabeth] should marry with no long delay'; action must be taken 'to advance the profession of [the Protestant] religion in Scotland and in England, and to diminish and weaken the contrary'; and the English government must 'proceed in sundry ways either to break the intended marriage, or at least thereby to procure the same not to be hurtful to this realm'. It was agreed 'that Lady Lennox be committed to some place where she may be kept from giving or receiving intelligence'; that 'the Earl of Lennox and his son be sent for, and required to be sent home by the Queen of Scots according to the treaty, failing which, his English estates to be forfeited'; and that 'Master Charles, the younger son of the Earl of Lennox, be removed [from Settrington] to where he may be forthcoming'.[117] It was not thought unusual that a child of eight could be questioned about the activities of his parents.

On 6 June, having learned of Mary's betrothal, King Philip wrote to Silva that he had noted the information passed on by Maitland

> respecting the state of the match of the Queen of Scotland with Lord Darnley, and also the intelligence you obtained from Lady Margaret, and from the Earl of Leicester, to the effect that the marriage had taken place. Your news on this head has been very pleasing to me, and, on the presumption that the marriage of the Queen and Darnley has really gone so far, the bridegroom and his parents being good Catholics and our

affectionate servitors, and considering the Queen's good claims to the crown of England, to which Darnley also pretends, we have arrived at the conclusion that the marriage is one that is favourable to our interests and should be forwarded and supported to the full extent of our power. You may convey to Lady Margaret Lennox the sympathy and goodwill I bear towards her son and the successful accomplishment of the project, in order that they may be satisfied and may know that they can depend upon me in matters concerning this business, and so be able to entertain and encourage the Catholics and their party in England.

Philip then raised the matter of the English succession.

The most prudent course will be for the Queen of Scotland not to press the Queen to appoint her, but leave the question of declaration of a successor in suspense for the present, because failing the Queen, there is no doubt that people would all flock to the Queen of Scotland and Lord Darnley, and this must be the object to which all energy must be directed. You will make Lady Margaret understand this, and that not only shall I be glad for her son to be king of Scotland and will help him thereto, but also to be king of England if this marriage is carried through.[118]

Margaret could not have hoped for more, but according to Silva,

the Queen of England and her Council are much troubled and perplexed by the marriage of the Queen of Scots with Lord Darnley, both of them being next heirs to the Crown of England, and their respective claims thus consolidated. The rivalry between them, therefore, ceases, and the Queen of England had always looked for her security to the maintenance of this rivalry by delaying the nomination of her successor. The second cause of anxiety is the dissensions in the country, many people favouring Darnley in the belief that by his means they may get rid of the Queen and her Government.

'The Queen appears to be daily more annoyed at the Queen of Scotland's marriage,' Silva reported. 'She has summoned Darnley hither under threat of punishment for high treason, and in consequence of his disobedience has thrown his mother, Lady Margaret, into the Tower of London.' In fact Margaret was still under house arrest at Whitehall,[119] and the next day, 9 June, Silva corrected the information in his previous dispatch: 'It was determined yesterday to send Lady Margaret to the Tower, where she is expected to be lodged tonight or tomorrow.'[120]

Not only had Margaret broken her oath to the Queen, but she had also 'deceitfully asked leave for her son to go to Scotland', knowing his true intentions. Elizabeth was 'justly indignant',[121] but for a few days she stayed her hand. It was not until 16 June,[122] the night before the arrival of Maitland, who had been commanded by Mary to return to England,[123] that the Queen sent Cecil and the Vice-Chamberlain, Sir Francis Knollys, to tell Margaret that she had delayed sending her to the Tower 'until the coming of the Scotch Ambassador, but seeing that he did not arrive she should not avoid any longer sending her thither, and told her to be ready by the time the tide rose. Lady Margaret asked them to tell the Queen from her that she did not know the cause of such an injury being done her, and begged her to suspend the order at least until the next day. They said they would convey the message, but that she was to be prepared, as they had already told her.'[124]

15

'Strait Imprisonment'

On the evening of 16 June 1565, 'at the hour appointed, the Vice-Chamberlain, with six of the guard', arrested Margaret and 'took her to the Tower in one of the Queen's barges with two or three women, knowing very well that the Scotch Ambassador was to arrive on the morrow'. Silva observed: 'This imprisonment has not given general satisfaction, as Lady Margaret is held in high esteem here, and is very popular. The Protestants, knowing that she is a Catholic still, are strongly attached to her. The affair has been so public and her claims on us are so strong that I should have taken some step in her favour but that I do not want to arouse the suspicion of these people, and I have therefore not said a word.'[1] The timing of her imprisonment was finely calculated: Maitland would arrive at the appropriate moment and could be counted on to warn Darnley off.[2] Elizabeth probably knew Darnley well enough to guess that he would always put his own interests before those of anyone else, even at the risk of his mother's well-being and safety.

When the barge conveying her to the Tower arrived at Traitor's Gate (then known as the water gate),[3] Margaret must have been thinking of Lennox, who had been immured within the fortress, and, remembering her earlier sojourn here, nearly thirty years ago now, maybe wondering if she would escape with her life this time. It made little difference that, as a prisoner of high rank, she was to be imprisoned in reasonable comfort in the Lieutenant's Lodging; Anne Boleyn had been held in some splendour in the Queen's apartments in the royal palace, yet she had lost her head.

The Lieutenant's Lodging survives today as the Queen's House. Located in the corner of the Inner Ward, facing Tower Green, it had been built in 1540 on the site of its decayed medieval predecessor, and was the substantial and well-appointed residence of the Lieutenant of the Tower. The house had a first-floor hall, a dining hall and parlour leading off it, a great kitchen and accommodation for the Lieutenant and his family, his guests and, occasionally, prisoners; Katherine Grey had been held here a couple of years earlier with her infant son and eight servants. There was a fenced garden accessed from the house, but the door to it was locked at night.[4] Margaret's chamber was on the third and top floor of the house, adjoining the Bell Tower, a high-security prison that was part of the Lieutenant's Lodging and could only be accessed through it.[5]

Like so many prisoners in the Tower, Margaret and her servants were to pass the tedious hours in carving an inscription, above the stone fireplace in her chamber: *Upon the twenty day of June xx in the year of Our Lord a thousand, five hundred, three score and five, the Right Honourable Countess of Lennox Grace committed prisoner to this lodging for the marrying of her son, my lord Henry Darnley, and the Queen of Scotland. Here is their names that do wait upon her noble Grace this place: Elizabeth Husey [Hussey], John Baily, Elizabeth Chambrlen [Chamberlain], Robert Portynger [Portinger], Edward C. Veyne [Vane]. Anno Domini 1566.*[6]

The inscription dates Margaret's imprisonment from 20 June 1565, but it is clear that she was taken to the Tower on the 16th. Either she got the date wrong, or the Tower officials had not had sufficient time to prepare for their important prisoner, and had to accommodate her elsewhere for the first four days.

Next to this inscription is another: *As God preserved Christ His Son in trouble and in thrall, so when we call upon the Lord he will preserve us all.* This too has been attributed to Margaret.[7] Today this chamber is called the Lennox Room.

Katherine Grey had been allowed to furnish her prison with tapestries, curtains, Turkey carpets, a handsome bed with a feather mattress and a chair upholstered in cloth of gold and crimson velvet.[8] Margaret's room was specially decorated and furnished for her, probably as splendidly, which might account for the four days' delay in her occupying it; and she was allowed a staff of five servants: two ladies, a gentlewoman, a gentleman and a yeoman.[9] The Privy Council may have accorded her the special privilege,[10] sometimes extended to distinguished prisoners, of dining at the table of the Lieutenant, Sir Francis Jobson, a diligent public servant in his late fifties with a long career in administration and politics behind him; he had been appointed lieutenant in 1564.

The room in which Margaret was imprisoned may have been at the front of the house and had a view of Tower Green, a sobering and frightening reminder of the fate of royal women who had fallen foul of the Crown, for it was here, in front of the House of Ordnance, that Anne Boleyn, Katherine Howard and Lady Jane Grey had all been beheaded.

Margaret had not been abandoned. On 14 June Queen Mary had sent her Master of Requests, John Hay, to Elizabeth's court with instructions to complain of the severity with which her mother-in-law was being treated. He was to express the hope that Margaret would be relieved of her present troubles, if only to disabuse rumour-mongers who were spreading the word that she was being badly used on Queen Mary's account. Hay was also to make representations on behalf of Lennox, whose affairs now required him to spend time in both England and Scotland. Mary was proposing that, as sureties for his loyalty to herself and Elizabeth, Margaret and Charles be kept as hostages in England when he was in Scotland, and in Scotland when he was in England.[11]

On 18 June Elizabeth wrote to Mary: 'For divers good causes we have expressly commanded the Earl of Lennox and Henry, Lord Darnley, as our subjects, to return hither without delay, and we require you to give your safe-conduct to pass through your countries, for their speedier coming.'[12] There was now no question of Mary complying. On 25 June Maitland told Silva that

he had conversed with the Queen [Elizabeth] on the subject of the marriage of his Queen with Lord Darnley, and that she flew into a rage directly the subject was introduced. She said she was greatly displeased at the match because it had been arranged without her consent, and for other reasons, and he asked her that these reasons might be handed to him in writing, that he might show them to his Queen, but she refused.

He asked permission to visit Lady Margaret and handed her a letter which he had from the Queen for her, and another from her husband, to which the Queen replied that she was greatly astonished that the Queen of Scotland should think she would allow Lady Margaret to receive visits, seeing that she was imprisoned for so grave a crime. When she was in prison before, she was let out by her on her solemn oath that she would not allow her son to marry without her consent, and she had deceived her. The letters, [Elizabeth] said, might be handed to her, but she must see them first.

[Maitland] asked permission to hand to her Majesty a letter from the Earl of Lennox, but she refused to receive it, saying that she would not accept letters from a traitor, as she should very soon proclaim him to be, and his son as well.

Maitland concluded that there was nothing more he could do but return to Scotland.[13]

On 23 June the Privy Council sent instructions to Thomas Young, Archbishop of York, who was president of the Council of the North and active in trying to reconcile the north of England to the Protestant religion. He was to draw up a list of names of 'the Friends and Servants to the Earl of Lennox and the lady his wife'.[14] Margaret's younger son, eight-year-old Charles, was still at Settrington, and there had been some talk of the Archbishop removing him, it being hoped that he would wean young Charles from the Catholic faith instilled in him by his mother; but Cecil had not wanted that because Charles was reputed to be sickly, so Young let him be, reporting: 'Here he is in health and at Settrington, where he has thirty servants.' He expressed doubts as to the wisdom of leaving Charles there, as some of those servants had been selling the Lennoxes' corn, sheep and other commodities, presumably to pay for their living expenses in their mistress's absence, and it was 'uncertain how long they intend to stay'. Furthermore, 'the house is in the open country, ten or twelve miles from the sea, where the Earl and Sir Richard Chamberlain have boats, by which Charles could easily be carried to Scotland, so this is not the place to keep him safely'.[15] Cecil took heed, and the boy was taken into the Archbishop's household at Bishopthorpe Palace near York.

Elizabeth expressed fury against Mary. She raged that the Queen of Scots had 'so manifestly broken the treaty in maintaining and keeping the Earl of Lennox, Lord Darnley, and other of her subjects there contrary to her will'.[16] She voiced her determination that 'steps should be taken to bring back both the Earl of Lennox and his son to this country, and if this was not effected they should be proceeded against as rebels'.[17]

Lennox was incensed to hear of his wife's imprisonment, and told Randolph bluntly that he would not return to face similar ill-treatment.[18] Both he and Darnley sent letters protesting that Margaret had been ignorant of developments in Scotland, and was wholly innocent.[19] But on 2 July Randolph reported that some people there 'that already have heard of my lady['s] Grace's imprisonment like very well thereof, and wish both her husband and son to keep her company'.[20]

By 2 July Silva told King Philip that he had been able to arrange a channel of communication with Margaret, who had 'been advised by secret and suitable means in the Tower of your Majesty's interest in her affairs'.[21] A week later he reported that 'Lady Margaret is still confined in the Tower, well guarded, but I have means of learning how she is, and of conveying words of encouragement to her. Her son Charles is in the keeping of the Archbishop of York.'[22] Silva's was not the only channel of communication open to Margaret. On 13 July she informed him 'that the French ambassador makes her many offers of service on behalf of his master, and makes similar offers to the Queen of Scotland. I tell her to thank him and beware.'[23] But Margaret, indomitable as ever, was to use any means she could to keep in touch with the outside world. Heedless of the possible consequences, she would continue intriguing for the benefit of Darnley and herself, difficult and dangerous though it must have been. On 23 July Margaret wrote to Cecil and Knollys:

I have earnestly desired the Lieutenant [of the Tower] that I might write to those that first I was committed to in my trouble, who, with much ado and persuasion, hath given me leave. I beseech you, my Lord Chamberlain, and you, Master Secretary, to be means to the Queen's Majesty not to continue my heavy [severe] lady, having not deserved it: indeed, my greatest imprisonment is her Highness' displeasure.

You both are fathers: consider then in God's cause what I suffer, besides as not hearing from my lord my husband and son there [in Scotland], nor yet from my child, being in Yorkshire, family nor officers, lacking wherewith to buy my necessaries and to pay some part of the great debt that I am in by many occasions this year past, as seldom being suffered to be at home, whereby I spent, and got little. Yet of that I never complained, so long as I had my prince's [Elizabeth's] favour, which God inspire her heart I may have again, beseeching you to be petitioners therefor.

Thus I cease to trouble you this time, save with my hearty commendations, committing you both to the keeping of Almighty God.

> From the Tower, the xxiii July, your friend to her power,
> Margaret Lennox and Angus.[24]

That day saw Margaret interesting herself in the case of a minor aristocrat, Thomas Cobham, who had been condemned to death for piracy, as Elizabeth wished to make a diplomatic example of him for attacking Spanish ships (which she herself was all too willing to plunder). Margaret asked Silva to intercede for him 'in order that his family, who are her adherents, may be confirmed in their friend-ship' to her. Many others were adding their pleas to hers, moving the Queen to show mercy. Her beneficent mood extended to Margaret too, and Silva was pleased to report that her imprisonment had been 'somewhat moderated, and her son, who was detained in the keeping of the Archbishop of York, is released'.[25] Charles was now back home at Settrington.[26]

Silva's optimism was premature. On 30 June King Charles IX of France had written to Elizabeth, praying that she would be pleased to release Margaret.[27] But his letter reinforced Elizabeth's suspicions that Margaret had intrigued to secure the backing of the great Catholic powers of France and Spain for herself and Darnley. As Silva was writing his dispatch of 23 July, he 'received advice that Lady Margaret's imprisonment, which I had just written had been moderated, is now again been made hourly more severe. The changes here are constant.'[28]

On 28 July a gentleman sent from Scotland by Queen Mary saw Silva and told him that Moray, 'thinking that when she is married he will not have so large a share in the management of affairs as hitherto', had allied with Châtelherault and demanded that Mary abandon the Mass. 'This gentleman says the Queen will be married to-morrow, and that any harm that may happen to her from her subjects will be in consequence of the action of this Queen [Elizabeth] as there are otherwise a good ten Catholics for every heretic in that country. He also begs me from his mistress to try to get Lady Margaret released.'[29]

By 29 July the French ambassador had spoken to Elizabeth 'respecting Margaret's imprisonment'. He too 'begged that she might be released and that her son should not be proceeded against as was intended'. Elizabeth gave him 'an account of the reasons she had to be aggrieved against the Queen of Scotland and Margaret'. She was, however, expecting an envoy from the Queen of Scots, 'and when he arrived an answer on the whole matter would be given'.[30] But it was soon to be made plain to her that the time for giving answers was past, for between the hours of five and six in the morning, on that very day, 29 July 1565, Mary married Darnley.

It was Lennox himself who triumphantly entered the chapel of Holyrood Palace with the bride on his arm, then returned with the Earl of Argyll to lead in Darnley, who had been created duke of Albany for the occasion and was resplendent in a sumptuous suit that glittered with jewels. Mary wore a voluminous black mourning gown and a large white hood and veil – similar to the *deuil blanc*, the white widow's garb of French queens that she had donned for the funeral of her first husband, and worn for several portraits. Darnley placed three rings (representing the Trinity) on her finger, kissed her after the nuptials, and left her to hear Mass alone, as he did not wish to offend the Protestant establishment. Presently Mary joined him in her chamber, where she was ceremonially divested of her widow's weeds and attired in wedding finery. The marriage was consummated that night.

The next day Mary had Darnley proclaimed 'King Henry' by the heralds, without waiting to have his title ratified by Parliament. It was noted that not one Scottish lord said 'Amen' apart from Lennox, who cried, 'God save his Grace!'[31] It has been said that the Darnley marriage was his finest achievement,[32] and so it must then have seemed, to him, to Margaret and to others; but ultimately it was an achievement only in terms on its dynastic impact, the fruition of which Lennox would not live to see. In other respects it was a disaster that would rebound horribly on him, Margaret, Mary and many others. But at the time it looked as if he had succeeded in uniting two Catholic claims to the thrones of England and Scotland, and that the issue of this marriage might well bring about a counter-reformation in both realms.

No one seems to have paused to think of the possible consequences for Margaret. Lennox and Darnley probably knew that she desired the marriage so greatly that she was willing to suffer in her son's interests; but while Darnley appears not to have been too concerned about what happened to his mother, Lennox was to endure great anxiety on her behalf, not least because the danger in which she stood was very soon made explicit. On 30 July Elizabeth and her Council – who did not, of course, yet know about the marriage – sent an envoy, John Tamworth (or Thornworth), to Scotland. Chiefly he was to protest against the 'craft' used by the Lennoxes in compassing the marriage of their son to Queen Mary. 'If the Earl of Lennox or Lord

Darnley shall desire to speak with him, he shall in the end not refuse utterly to hear them, without saying anything to them as from [Queen Elizabeth], but shall use them with such strangeness as their cause requires. And yet he may, as of himself, advise them to use themselves otherwise than is reported they do; and to move them the more, he may remember to them the hard case of the Lady Margaret, now in the Tower, whose wellbeing must depend upon their behaviour there.' If Mary required Tamworth 'to direct his speech to Lord Darnley as to her husband, he shall refuse so to do'.[33] It would be a long time before Elizabeth would acknowledge Darnley as king of Scots.

The Scottish lords were definitely not rejoicing about the marriage. They hated Darnley because he was a Catholic and an Englishman, and they feared his influence and that of Lennox, whose power, as father to the new King, was now ascendant.[34] Roused by Moray, they rose in a rebellion that became known as 'the Chaseabout Raid'.

News of the Darnley marriage provoked fury and alarm in Queen Elizabeth. For Margaret, this should have been a time of rejoicing, since all her years of scheming had paid off, her ambitions had been joyfully fulfilled, and one day, if God willed, her grandson would wear a crown, possibly two; but here she was, shut up in the Tower, with the Queen threatening vengeance. She could take comfort only in the remembrance that Elizabeth had not sent Katherine Grey to the block — but then Katherine had only borne a son with royal blood, not married him to Elizabeth's rival.

By 6 August the French ambassador had received a reply 'to his remonstrance on behalf of his King in the matter of Lady Margaret'. Elizabeth asked King Charles 'to consider, if he had a subject who had left his country under an artful pretext for the purpose of deceiving him, and had married against the King's will, and had done other similar acts, whether he would be offended with him or not. She therefore requested that the King would not take it amiss if she took further time to consider what she had better do.'[35]

On 12 August Mary saw Tamworth and told him 'it cannot be found strange for her to detain within her realm that person with whom she is joined in marriage'. She desired 'that the Queen will not meddle with any matters within the realm of Scotland', declared that she did 'not mean to make any innovation in religion', and prayed

> her good sister to consider how moderately she has used herself in a case wherein she had good occasion to have meddled more earnestly: that is, in the cause of her mother-in-law, the Lady

Margaret, Countess of Lennox, being also so tender of blood to her Majesty – whom, being induced by her example, she does most earnestly and effectuously request her good sister to relieve forth of captivity and restore her to her lands, &c., and former favour, wherein as she shall neither offend against justice nor her own honour, so she shall do her Majesty most acceptable pleasure.[36]

The next day Queen Mary and King Henry assured Elizabeth that they would never do anything to the prejudice of her title, meddle with her subjects, enter into alliances with foreign princes against her, or – if called to the throne of England – make changes to the established religion, on condition that 'their good sister', among other things,

> shall by Act of Parliament establish the succession to her crown, failing herself and the lawful issue of her body, in the Queen's [Mary's] person and the lawful issue of her body: failing which, in that of Lady Margaret, Countess of Lennox, mother to the King, her Majesty's husband, and [the] lawful issue of her body, as the persons by the law of God and nature next inheritable to the crown of England; and that she shall not procure anything prejudicial to her Majesty or Lady Margaret and their heirs aforesaid.[37]

Nothing could have been better calculated to arouse Elizabeth's fury than this high-handed letter with its implicit threat. But by 13 August Silva had cause to hope that she had relented somewhat towards Margaret.

> The Queen is not at all pleased with Scotch affairs. I told her I had heard that the King of France had written to her about Margaret's imprisonment, which she said was true, and told me her answer. She said the King had written at the request of the Queen of Scotland and he had not been able to refuse, giving me to understand that he had done it simply out of compliment. I told her it was a thing in which I thought she might show clemency if rightly considered, as I had heard that the Queen of Scotland had always obeyed her as if she was her younger sister and had married one of her subjects. The Queen seems more pliable in this matter than I was led to expect.[38]

Again Silva's hopes were premature. On 27 August he had to report: 'They have sequestrated Lady Margaret's property in addition to her imprisonment, and she will now suffer need.'[39] Lennox's auditor was ordered to make an inventory of the contents of Temple Newsam as well as a record of the rents from all the couple's estates.[40] On 23 September letters were issued to the Crown's commissioners, Sir Thomas Gargrave, Henry Gates and a Justice of the Peace, John Vaughan of Sutton-on-Derwent, Yorkshire, 'for seizure and management of the Earl of Lennox's lands'.[41] That day Gargrave reported to the Lord Treasurer, William Paulet, Marquess of Winchester, that Lennox had taken half of his plate to Scotland, while the rest was either with Lady Lennox or 'here at Settrington, where Mr Charles, the Earl's son, lives, and the house is kept for him by the servants; but it is only a little salt, two bowls and certain spoons'. If these items were to be sold, what was to be done about Mr Charles and the housekeeper? Gargrave awaited the Queen's pleasure in the matter.[42]

Burdensome debts were often the punishment of those who offended the Crown. With the income generated from rents and other dues suddenly cut off, Margaret found herself with no money at all, and of that she had immediate need, since prisoners in the Tower had to pay for their food, servants and comforts. However, the Lennoxes were not in fact formally dispossessed of all their lands. It has been pointed out that the sequestration was merely a pretext to search their property for incriminating evidence. Some of the estates were sold off by the Crown in 1567, but most, including Temple Newsam and Settrington, were allowed to remain in the couple's possession, and continued to be called the Lennox lands until long after Margaret's death.[43] But it would be some time before it became clear that the Lennoxes were not to be dispossessed and impoverished after all.

Hugh Allen, who had resumed his duties as courier after the couple's release from Sheen in 1563, was now imprisoned in the Gatehouse at Westminster. He was to languish there for two years before pleading with Cecil for his release. Margaret would do nothing for him, for she believed that he had betrayed her, but the government's treatment of him gives the lie to that.[44]

It was probably Margaret who, late in August, arranged for Francis Yaxley to travel to Scotland from Flanders, to be welcomed by Darnley and appointed ambassador to Spain. Yaxley's role was to be a bridge between Darnley and the English Catholics.[45] He furnished

Darnley with a list of persons who were ready to assist Philip II in 'the alteration of religion' in Britain. At the top was Jane Dormer, Countess of Feria.[46]

On 1 September the French ambassador, Michel de Castelnau, informed Queen Mary that he had 'asked for the deliverance of the Countess of Lennox, but the Queen refused, though she is well treated, which is all he can say'.[47] That same day Elizabeth wrote to her commissioner, Judge John Vaughan, and his wife, commanding

> that the second son to the Earl of Lennox, named Charles Stuart, now remaining at Settrington, near to you,[48] should be looked unto, as well for his health, being of tender years, as for his surety, considering that the said Earl, his father, remaineth in Scotland, and his mother in our Tower of London; and because we know none thereabouts meeter than yourself, and the Lady Knyvett, your wife,[49] to take charge of him. We require you to make your repair to the said house of Settrington, or else where the said Charles is, and, declaring this our pleasure to such as have charge of him, to receive him into the custody of you and your wife; and that such care be taken of him as be meet and agreeable for his health and safety; and that which shall be convenient for the charges of him, and one or two to attend upon him, as his years shall require, shall be allowed unto you, as reason is. If cause shall require to have more to attend upon him than two, it is left to your discretion.[50]

Charles appears not to have remained long in the care of the Vaughans in Yorkshire, for at some point he was brought south to London, where he was placed in the charge of Gabriel Goodman, the Dean of Westminster, at Cheyneygates, the former Abbot's house, now the Deanery, within the abbey precincts.

'Lady Margaret is still in prison and has been unwell,' Silva wrote to King Philip on 10 September. 'They have refused permission for a doctor to visit her, and have taken away and sequestered all her property. She sends me word that her only hope now is in God and your Majesty. I have not ventured to speak to the Queen about her business as I thought it might cause some inconvenience, as will be understood.'[51]

When Silva saw Elizabeth on 17 September, he would have spoken of 'certain things about these Scotch matters if I had not noticed her stiffness to me on the subject'. He had wanted to say that not only foreigners but her own people blamed her for three things. The first was that, considering that the Queen of Scotland had married one of her subjects and relatives brought up in her own house, she ought rather to be thankful to her for it than angry and offended. The second was the imprisonment and harsh treatment of a person of such high position as Lady Margaret, simply because she had wished to marry her son well, which was only natural for a mother to desire. The third was the help she [Elizabeth] gave to the Scottish rebels against their Queen, a most pernicious example for other kings and for her.

But these reproofs went unsaid. 'The news was flying about the world, and I had been much astonished that she had not mentioned the matter to me, as it was of the utmost importance that what she was doing and negotiating should be known.'

Elizabeth herself raised the matter of Margaret's offences.

During this period, she said, Lady Margaret deceitfully asked leave for her son to go to Scotland to take possession of his father's estates. She had given her this licence, telling her at the same time to take care she did not deceive her and let her son do anything else, or she would find herself the person deceived; and then as soon as he arrived the Queen of Scotland made up her mind to marry him, and sent to ask her advice about it when the thing was as good as done, demanding at the same time the declaration of the succession, this being the first information she had received of it all. She was therefore justly indignant with the Queen, and especially with Lady Margaret, as they had both deceived her. She then again returned to Margaret's imprisonment, greatly exaggerating the deceit she had practised on her, although she had formerly released her from prison and entertained her in her house, and had given her leave for the son to go, so that she could not avoid being very angry with her and exacting ample reparation. She asked me what I thought of it. I said I should have expected quite the reverse from her great and customary clemency. She had always shown a valiant spirit, and only the timid were cruel. She replied that I was right and spoke the truth, giving me to understand that in the end she would do as I suggested.[52]

Elizabeth did take Silva's remonstrations seriously, and kept her word. That September the Council drew up 'A note of such things as the Lady Margaret Lennox hath great need of for her apparel and furniture in the Tower, and of the wages of her attendants.' Several items were supplied to her from the Royal Wardrobe: two petticoats, of scarlet and crimson silk; a gown of black velvet and a nightgown of satin, both lined with coney fur; a round kirtle of black velvet; Holland cloth for kerchiefs, smocks and partlets; a French hood; a cornette[53] or white cap, and a habiliment; twelve pairs of hose; six pairs of velvet shoes; two pairs of slippers; two pairs of mules and a farthingale.[54]

For furnishing her chamber Margaret was provided with a rug, a quilt, 'a pair of fustians',[55] two pairs of sheets, a dining table, a chair for herself, six joint stools and two small covered stools for her attendants, a side cupboard, four cupboard cloths,[56] a table on which to brush clothing, a green table-cover, four tablecloths, two dozen napkins, eight platters, eight dishes, eight saucers, four porringers,[57] a salt cellar, two silver spoons, a cup for drinking, a basin for washing hands at table, a ewer, 'a great basin for the chamber, a pair of creepers',[58] a fire-pan, a pair of tongs, a pair of bellows and candle snuffers.[59]

The three female servants who lodged with Margaret were paid livery and wages of £12 (£2,040) each, due at Michaelmas 1565, and 'Christian, my lady's woman', who had lodgings outside the Tower, received the same. Margaret herself paid the gentleman waiting upon her wages of 53s.4d. (£455), while her yeoman got 26s.8d. (£227). Her servant, William Robinson, was paid more than £13 (£2,214) at Michaelmas.[60]

This list provides interesting insights into how a lady of Margaret's rank fared in captivity. The clothes provided were appropriate to her high rank. The eight stools and dinner service for eight show that she dined with her servants. There was a fireplace in her room, so she could keep warm – unlike less privileged prisoners – and her bed was adequately made up. Thus she did not lack essential creature comforts. But the Queen was to insist that Margaret pay for all the items provided, and for the expenses incurred during her imprisonment,[61] and the cost was ruinous to one who was already burdened by debt and had no income.

Scotland was now in turmoil. Darnley was alienating people with his posturing and his insolence, and it was clear that Lennox, reportedly his 'master in all things', actually had no control over him.[62] Margaret had been the dominant influence in Darnley's life, and after that influence was removed there was no one to curb his behaviour.

Determined to settle old scores, Lennox had used the rising as a pretext to 'ruin' the Hamiltons, but in the end it was his lands in western Scotland that were plundered by Châtelherault's ally Argyll.[63] Eventually Mary's forces routed her rebel lords, and Moray and his adherents were outlawed and forced to take flight into England. On 19 September Bedford informed Cecil that Moray's pregnant countess, Agnes Keith, had been arrested by the royal forces and kept prisoner in similar conditions to Margaret's,[64] but the next day Randolph reported that 'Lady Moray has been sought and cannot be found. Some say she has been imprisoned for the relief of Lady Lennox, whose husband leaves no man unspoiled of whom he likes to take.'[65] Both Bedford and Randolph had been misled by rumours, for the Countess proved to have been at St Andrew's Priory, her own home, all the time.

On 7 October Margaret turned fifty. Nothing more had been done to ease her plight, and on 20 October King Philip wrote to Silva: 'We have been much grieved at the imprisonment and ill-treatment of Lady Margaret, and the reason for it, and I shall therefore be glad if you will encourage her and tell her what is best to be done on all occasions as you have hitherto, and you will try to keep on good terms of understanding with her, but always in such a way as to give no cause for the Queen to take offence.'[66]

In instructions issued to her ambassadors in Scotland on 24 October, Elizabeth commanded them 'to endeavour to restore the amity, to complain of the strange conduct of the Queen of Scots regarding her marriage' and to 'do what they can to procure the restitution of the lords, particularly the Earl of Moray', by promising an 'inquisition into Mary's title' to the English succession. 'As it is certain that she will require Lady Lennox to be released [and] the Earl restored to his lands in England, Elizabeth will agree, if in other things Mary accords with her.'[67] But when, soon afterwards, Mary wrote a long letter to Paul de Foix, the French ambassador in London, begging him to secure Margaret's liberty, Elizabeth remained deaf to his appeal.

On 24 October Francis Yaxley arrived at Philip's court at Segovia with letters of accreditation from Mary and Darnley, informing Philip of 'their zealous desire to establish and reform their kingdom under the Christian religion', and begging him for aid. They also asked him 'to be pleased to write affectionate letters to the Queen of England with two very necessary objects; first the release of Lady Margaret, and secondly that the said Queen should desist from helping the Scottish rebels either publicly or privately.'

Philip was reluctant to provoke Elizabeth. He wrote to Silva that his intervention 'would do harm rather than good, but when an opportunity arrived we would not miss it and would send instructions to you'. He added that he approved of the way Silva had 'introduced the subject of Lady Margaret' to Elizabeth. 'You will continue in the same style whenever you see a chance, taking care however, not to arouse the suspicion or jealousy of the Queen.'[68]

Silva thought that Philip's caution was prudent and his answer 'the most fitting, as your Majesty's intercession would do [Margaret] no good, but would rather arouse greater suspicion against her, even if there were not other reasons against it'.[69] And Mary would not agree to pardon Moray, so Margaret had to remain in prison.

16

'In Great Trouble'

Within five months the marriage of Mary and Darnley had broken down. Lennox dated the rift to the collapse of the rebellion,[1] and whatever had gone wrong was made worse by the Queen pardoning Châtelherault on 1 December, arousing Darnley's fury.[2] Mary was beginning to realise how shallow and vicious he could be, and he grew even more so when she continued to deny him the crown matrimonial, which would have given him the right to rule autonomously, and to succeed to the throne if she died without issue. Moreover the marriage had failed in its political objective, for the English Catholics had not risen to place Mary and Darnley on Elizabeth's throne.

Mary had lost faith in Darnley, and in Lennox too. She openly wished that her father-in-law 'had not set his foot in Scotland'.[3] Lennox's influence there was now in a steady decline, and henceforth he would spend more and more time on his estates in Glasgow.[4]

In the absence of the exiled lords, Mary was relying more and more on her Italian secretary, David Rizzio, for advice as well as congenial company, and Darnley soon realised that Rizzio was supplanting him in the Queen's counsels – and, some said, in her bed. Bedford would not, for the sake of Mary's honour, write in detail to Cecil of the favour she was showing to the Italian. 'This David, [Thomas] Fowler, and one [Sir James] Balfour rule all.'[5] Balfour was a member of the Scottish Privy Council. Formerly a Protestant, he had reverted to the Catholic faith, prompting Knox to castigate him as an apostate and traitor, and indeed he was a treacherous character, but adept at covering his tracks. It was Darnley who had persuaded Mary to appoint him a councillor.

Fowler's undue influence had been censured by the Scottish Parliament and by John Knox,[6] and in December Darnley made a show of dismissing him from his household.[7] But it was a bluff to provide cover for Fowler, in disguise, to make his way into England on a secret mission carrying letters to Margaret.

By 19 December 1565 Margaret had learned from Randolph that she was to become a grandmother, for Mary and Darnley were expecting a child in the summer. This was the fruition of all her hopes: if God was merciful, one of her blood would sit on the thrones of Scotland and England. Mary was delighted, but the birth of a son would put paid to Darnley's hopes of the crown matrimonial, so he was not rejoicing.[8]

That month a jubilant Lennox wrote a letter addressed 'To my wife, my Lady Margaret'; it was one of those entrusted to Fowler, and it reveals that after twenty years of marriage the couple remained touchingly devoted and close. 'God send us a comfortable meeting,' Lennox began hopefully.

My sweet Madge,

After my most hearty commendations: if ye should take unkindly my slowness in writing to you all this while, as I can not blame you to do, God and this bearer, our old servant Fowler, can best witness th'occasion thereof, it being not a little to my grief now to be debarred, and want the commodity and comfort of intelligence by letters, that we were wont to have passage between us during our absence. But what then? God send us patience in taking all things accordingly, and send us a comfortable meeting, and then we shall talk farther of the matter.

My Madge, we have to give God most hearty thanks for that the King our son continues in good health, and the Queen great with child, God save them all, for the which we have great cause to rejoice more. Yet, of my part, I confess I want and find a lack of my chiefest comfort, which is you, whom I have no cause to forget for any great felicity or wealth that I am in, but I trust it will amend. Although I do not doubt but their Majesties forgetteth you not, yet I am still remembering [reminding] them for your deliverance, to work therein as much as they can, as I doubt not but their Majesties will, else, ere ye should tarry there any longer, I shall wish of God that I may be with you, our life being safe.

Thus, being forced to make no longer letter for want of time, as this bearer knoweth, who will declare unto you all things at more length, being most sorry at his departing out of the King his Majesty's service for sundry respects, I bid mine own sweet Madge most heartily farewell, beseeching Almighty God to preserve you in health and long life, and send us with our children a merry meeting.

From Glasgow, the 19 day of December.

Your own Mathieu, and most loving husband.[9]

Sadly this touching letter never reached Margaret.

Fowler – who had informed Margaret in December that Darnley had thrice attended Mass[10] – had to report that her son had failed to attend Mass on Christmas Day. But Margaret did not cease to intrigue for a Catholic triumph in England and Scotland. On 2 January 1566 Bedford warned Cecil that 'certain bulls are come into Scotland from Rome. It were very good that a good eye were had to this pursuivant, for he bringeth letters to the Papists and to the lady of Lennox.'[11] This is the only hint of any support for Margaret from the Vatican.

Soon afterwards Cecil learned from Bedford that Yaxley's ship had foundered off the Northumberland coast and that he was believed drowned.[12] His death deprived the Lennoxes of a vital link with Spain.

On 28 January Silva informed King Philip that Cecil had told a French envoy

that, when the King of Scotland [Darnley], bearing in mind that he had been an English subject, should write modestly to the Queen saying he was sorry she was angry with him and greatly wished that her anger should disappear, he believed everything would be settled, if at the same time the Queen of Scotland would send an ambassador hither to treat of Lady Margaret's affair. Lady Margaret is still in prison. I have sent a visitor to her to encourage her and urge her to bear her trouble patiently and assure her that God will watch over the affairs of her and her children. She wrote me a letter pressing me much as to her liberation, as her whole trust, after God, is in your Majesty.[13]

Thomas Fowler had now set off on his secret mission. On 26 December he had shaved off his beard, assumed the name Forster, gone to Leith and boarded a ship, *The Aid of Pittenweem*, bound for England. When he eventually arrived in London he had gone into hiding but was discovered, arrested on suspicion of being a spy, and thrown into the Fleet prison, which is why Lennox's letter to Margaret never reached her and ended up filed among Cecil's papers.

Soon afterwards Cecil questioned Fowler, who said he had come 'by sea, on the King's business', landing in turn at Yarmouth, Harwich and Ipswich. He had lodged at the Dolphin inn at Yarmouth, where he burned another letter written by Lennox. At Harwich he changed his name. Asked what persons he had spoken to in London, he said he had met four times with Margaret's servant, William Robinson, at Smithfield, Limehouse and the Black Bell Inn near Fish Street Hill. He had delivered letters to the Black Bell, the Dolphin, St Katherine's Hospital, Limehouse, and his brother-in-law's. He also revealed that he had been at the house of Anthony Standen, a Catholic gentleman, adventurer and later an English spy, who had served Margaret then gone to Scotland with Darnley and been appointed his master of horse.

Fowler was asked if he had had dealings with 'persons belonging to Lady Lennox', but would name only 'Caesar the physician',[14] an old woman and a prisoner called Greville, who were completely insignificant. To further questions he gave away nothing useful.[15] Cecil observed drily, 'He knows of no intelligence the King and Queen of Scotland have but by their servants sent to this court.'[16] He was not satisfied with Fowler's answers, and Fowler was sentenced to death.[17]

By 4 February Silva had heard of the affair, and informed his master that Fowler had come to London 'in order to secretly ascertain the feelings of certain people here towards his Queen. He had lodged in the house of an Italian doctor here called Caesar, and had gone about in disguise to avoid detection, but both he and the doctor and his wife have been taken, the two latter being adherents of Margaret. They have also arrested two of his servants, but released them at once. It is not thought that anything serious will come of it.'[18]

The Lennoxes probably never knew the full extent of Thomas Bishop's treachery, for Bishop had been working undercover for the government, and witness depositions were only revealed if an accused person came to trial. They knew he had passed on some information about them; they must also have had their suspicions that he had been the source of some of the charges laid against them in 1562, but given that other servants and agents of theirs had been questioned, they could not have been certain of that. Bishop had been hostile towards Margaret, yet he had had a long record of service to Lennox, and sometime before February 1566 there had been a rapprochement. But according to an informant of Cecil's, writing in early February, 'though the Earl lately thought [Bishop] had become a new man, yet his lewd behaviour is as bad as ever, grace is past him and no recovery of any goodness in him'. He was 'presently going about to disinherit his own son, keeping harlots' and 'stealing 200 French crowns of the Earl's, at Carlisle'.[19]

This anonymous informant sent Cecil a list of complaints about Bishop, although since most of them concerned the Lennoxes it was not difficult to deduce who had sent it. Possibly Lennox feared that Bishop would make more mischief for him and Margaret, and that it was imperative that the man be discredited once and for all. It may well be that Margaret had secretly communicated with Lennox, reminding him of matters he ought to raise.[20]

On 5 February Bishop was called to answer the charges laid against him, going back over many years. He was accused, amongst other things, of betraying William Stirling, the Captain of Dumbarton, who was murdered in 1534, by running away 'like a coward, leaving his master to be slain'. Henry VIII had given him 'his present living' for his 'supposed service' to Lennox, but the King had 'repented it, hearing that he set up dissension between the Earl and his lady. While in great misery in Edward VI['s] time, by his unthriftiness and whoredom, the Earl and Countess leased him a farm worth £500 [£100,250], provided he lived thereon: but he drew another lease to defraud them, counterfeiting their hands and seals. He had tried to get the Earl to slay his own brother, the Bishop of Caithness, in Stepney.' He had also 'cheated Henry VIII of £400 [£80,200] sent to the Captain of Dumbarton, and persuaded the Earl to open his secrets to Bothwell, then in England'.[21]

In his defence Bishop made a statement:

Albeit the Earl of Lennox and my lady, for my truth to my sovereign and her commonwealth, seek my life: they are not to be credited, and I answer him as follows: [I] being a bareheaded boy of 16 or 17, the Captain of Dumbarton was slain by a band of men laid in wait for him. I so behaved myself, being a child, gave and received strokes, that the Captain on his deathbed declared it before his wife, and left me in his will as he did his children, trusting me with all his evidence, money and keys. This was 31 years since, as I can prove – my age not yet 48. I deny stealing money sent to the Captain of Dumbarton.

The Lennoxes had apparently brought Bishop to trial for this 'at Guildford', but they had withdrawn the charge, and Bishop's enemy, David Murray, was sent to the Tower, and his brother Tullibardine to the Fleet for half a year. Bishop protested that Lennox's brother, Robert Stewart, had 'cowardly surrendered Dumbarton. I deny the charge of getting a false lease, but had £500 from the Lennox tenants for my charges fortifying the town of Ayr.'

He accused Margaret of unkindness:

As for the Earl's cruel charity at London: when my wife died after coming with her to court, I asked Lady Lennox to let her gentlewomen attend the burial: she would not let a boy come! For the burial my Lord Paget, like a father, took order by his steward and receiver. As for disinheriting my son: I know not his meaning. I bring him up in the fear of God at Cambridge, and he has by my Lord Paget all by law, I being but a pensioner to my living. Finally, for rule of my body: I live under two discreet magistrates, my lord President and my lord Archbishop of York. Two noblemen have kept with me one trust and one love these eighteen years – my lords Paget and Wharton, by whom I will be judged.

Signed: Thomas Bishop.[22]

Bishop did not comment on Henry VIII repenting of his generosity because of Bishop sowing dissension between Lennox and Margaret, which suggests that the accusation was true. He failed to address the charge that he had tried to persuade Lennox to kill his brother, apart from hinting that Caithness had deserved it. Nothing came of Bishop's examination, and of course he never served the Lennoxes again.[23]

On 11 February Silva wrote: 'Lady Margaret is kept closer in prison than ever, which she feels greatly. She would like me to speak to the Queen about it, which she thinks would benefit her, and that I might do it, as her ill-treatment is publicly known. I have asked her to have patience, and I will do what is fitting.' Margaret had evidently been kept informed of affairs, for she had heard that Queen Mary, despite having obtained Châtelherault's restoration to his French dukedom, had banished him from Scotland for five years. Margaret was 'greatly surprised' to hear of his restoration, as Mary had written to her 'that she would not return the Duke's rank as he was so great a heretic'.[24]

Having heard that Margaret was ill and in pain, Mary herself wrote to Elizabeth on her behalf on 12 February, charging the messenger 'to move her for her *belle mère* [mother-in-law], who suffers much from her strait imprisonment, which she surely did not merit for merely wishing well to her son'. She also begged Elizabeth 'to have pity on her husband's [Lennox's] servant, Fowler, and defer his execution, whose only offence has been pressing his master's interest'.[25] Elizabeth was graciously pleased to set Fowler at liberty, but she was not in the mood to show mercy to Margaret.

Lennox's ambition was to see Darnley given the crown matrimonial. Offended by Mary's restoration of Châtelherault's title, he encouraged and abetted his son to this end.[26] Randolph informed Cecil on 25 February that Queen Mary had 'knowledge out of England by means of the French Ambassador, [Sir Robert] Melville, and Lady Lennox's friends. I can assure you the chief cause of Melville's being there was to entertain that faction [Margaret's] the most he can.' He added, 'The suspicion of this King towards David [Rizzio] is so great that it must shortly grow unto a scab among them.'[27]

In mid-March Silva reported:

Lady Margaret still remains in prison. From what I hear, this Queen would like the King of Scotland and his father to write to her, asking for Lady Margaret's release. I know that the Queen of Scotland has done so, and a Scotchman named Melville is here to negotiate on the matter. I believe the Queen of Scotland has entrusted this matter to him, as she thinks he will be the most acceptable person, although they will not trust him in other things.[28]

After much deliberation, Mary had made the controversial decision to recall her exiled rebel lords, much to the anger of Lennox and Darnley, who had no wish to see their enemies restored to power.[29] This widened the rift between Mary and Darnley, and further alienated Lennox from the Queen. He, like his son and many nobles, deeply resented the influence of Rizzio. These lords were ready to join forces with the despised Darnley to get rid of the Italian, and they played on his jealousy. In March 1565 Darnley entered into a bond with the lords and willingly undertook to support the establishment of the Protestant faith in Scotland. In return, they promised that they would procure him the crown matrimonial, which brought with it the right of succession, and 'also they will labour with the Queen of England for the relief of the Countess of Lennox and her son'[30] and 'for favour to be shown both to himself and to his mother'.[31]

Lennox signed the bond,[32] thus becoming 'art and part' – as the Scots called it – of a conspiracy to murder Rizzio. Silva was to inform King Philip: 'A good Catholic here tells me that the plot for the murder of the secretary was ordered from here [England], and the Queen helped the conspiracy to the extent of 8,000 crowns [£347,780]. Others have the same suspicion, and believe that the rebels who had fled to this country knew of it, but these are things hard to prove.' Silva also revealed that on 8 March Cecil informed Lady Margaret of Rizzio's murder as an event that had already occurred.[33]

There were a number of reasons why Elizabeth would have wanted Rizzio killed. There was a body of opinion which held that women were weak creatures and unsuited to wielding power over men, and by her suspect relations with Rizzio, Mary was undermining the whole edifice of female sovereignty. Furthermore Elizabeth may have feared that Rizzio, as a Catholic, exerted a subversive influence on Mary. But she may also have meant to upset Mary's standing in Scotland and England in the interests of preserving the Protestant settlements and pre-empting a Catholic succession. Yet it has never been proved that the English government was behind the conspiracy.

On 9 March, as Mary was dining with Rizzio and friends in her closet at Holyrood, Darnley arrived and joined them at table. He was affable enough, and even put his arm around Mary, who was now six months pregnant. Immediately several lords burst in on them, Lennox among them; all were armed.[34] Lord Ruthven, who came in first, told Mary not to be afraid and manhandled her into Darnley's arms. He held her tightly as the intruders engaged in a violent struggle to seize Rizzio. The table was overturned, candles went flying, and the horrified Queen was sure that she herself was being targeted in the assault, and was in great fear that her own life was in danger. Rizzio was clutching at her skirts and crying to her to save him, but he was dragged out and murdered, suffering fifty-six dagger wounds. Darnley had taken no part in the attack, but the lords took care to leave his dagger in Rizzio's side.

Shocked and terrified, Mary was confined to her apartments by the lords. By the next morning it had become clear to Darnley that they had no intention of honouring their promise to him. Contrite and frightened, he begged to see Mary, before whom he fell to his knees, weeping, and confessed that the lords had lured him into their plot to remove Rizzio with the assurance of the crown matrimonial. He assured her he had never intended that Rizzio should be murdered and gave her the bond signed by Moray and others, and told her that if the lords found out he had betrayed them, he would be a dead man. Mary told him just what she thought of him, but when he revealed to her that the lords' plan was to imprison her at Stirling until she died, she persuaded him to help her escape, and soon afterwards they managed this with the aid of the loyal and powerful James Hepburn, 4th Earl of Bothwell, the only Scottish lord who was not in the pay of the English. They fled to the royal castle of Dunbar on the East Lothian coast, one of the mightiest fortresses in Scotland, where Bothwell was custodian and had charge of the kingdom's arsenal of weaponry and its reserves of gunpowder, and soon afterwards, backed by an army he had mustered, Mary was able to re-establish her authority as queen.

Thereafter, although Mary and Darnley still cohabited as man and wife, relations between them were irrevocably fractured, and on 21 March Randolph reported that 'Lennox remains at Dunbar, much offended with his son. The King repents of it, and confesses that he was abused.'[35] But it was not Darnley's behaviour towards Mary that had offended Lennox so much as his betrayal of the conspirators.[36]

The next day Sir Thomas Smith, the English ambassador, wrote from France to say he had heard 'that it is not the Scottish crown which that young King and Queen look for, but a bigger one, and that they have more intelligence and practices in England and in other realms than Cecil thinks for. Both the Pope and the King of Spain's hands are deeper in that dish than he knows.'

Being in prison had not prevented Margaret from intriguing on her son's behalf. A Scottish woman who lived at Westminster and was married to a captain conveyed to her letters that had been brought out of Scotland by trusted messengers.[37] Once a fortnight Margaret was able to smuggle out letters to her husband, and he in turn corresponded with her via Bedford.[38] In January 1567 an agent of Cecil, William Rogers, reported that 'Lady Lennox's letters were conveyed via Flanders to Scotland by one [William] Mompesson, who got them from her ancient gentlewoman, who had access to her', although the Council, knowing this all along, were presumably intercepting the letters.[39] In March 1566 the Council interrogated a servant of Darnley, and asked him what he knew about Margaret's covert activities.[40] Another man was arrested by Randolph at Berwick as he was attempting to enter Scotland. Sewn into his hose was a message instructing an unknown party to crucify a man for whom hanging was too good. Fowler and Standen were mentioned.[41]

By 23 March details of Rizzio's murder were known in London. Silva reported that Moray and his fellow rebels had returned to Scotland 'by order and on the assurance of the King'. Elizabeth was making a show of 'great sorrow at what has happened, and shows a desire to assist the Queen of Scotland. Lady Margaret only knows what this Queen has told her, but she is in great trouble at the news.'[42] Silva did not yet know that Margaret had been aware of the murder – and no doubt been sworn to secrecy – on the day before it took place.

The Rizzio plot and the failure of the Queen's marriage to Darnley irrevocably damaged the Lennoxes' standing in Scotland. On 4 April Randolph wrote that Mary was 'determined the House of Lennox shall be as poor as ever it was'. Lennox, who was still at Holyrood,[43] was sick and 'sore troubled in mind'. Darnley had paid a single visit to Lennox, and Lennox himself had seen Mary once at Edinburgh Castle. Mary had now seen 'all the covenants and bonds that [had] passed between the King and the lords'. She now knew that Darnley had lied to her when he pleaded ignorance of any intention to kill Rizzio, and was 'grievously offended' that he should have sought the crown matrimonial by such means.[44]

By 13 April Darnley had finally bestirred himself on his mother's behalf, sending a Scotsman as emissary to Elizabeth 'speaking of Lady Margaret's imprisonment, in which he had assured the Queen that Lady Margaret was not to blame for anything he had done, and knew nothing of his acts. The Queen refused to reply to this, or even to take the King's letter, although [the emissary] begged her to do so', but she 'asked him if it were true that the King had drawn his dagger in the Queen's presence to stab the Secretary, and he told her it was not. She said that she had not believed it, because all the time he was in this country he had never put his hand to a knife.'

The murder of Rizzio had been 'so much condemned by the Scotch people' that it had been necessary to proclaim 'very emphatically' that the King had no hand in it.[45] Silva heard that Elizabeth had promised not to allow any of those concerned in the conspiracy to remain in England.[46]

On 7 May William Paulet, Marquess of Winchester, asked Cecil 'if the attendants Lady Lennox has with her in the Tower are to be maintained at the Queen's charge', and if her expenses in the Tower were to be borne by herself or the Queen.[47]

Margaret had again been ill. By 18 May Silva had heard 'that the Queen of Scotland will be confined in the month of June at latest. Lady Margaret has sent her some presents, but from Flanders, as she is still in prison and has been unwell. These people have not done badly for their ends in detaining her, because if she had been in Scotland they are sure her son would not have been led astray, nor would these disputes have taken place, as she is prudent and brave, and the son respects her more than he does his father.'[48] That may well have been Elizabeth's intention, and it would prove a tragedy for Margaret and her family that she was unable to bring some influence to bear on Darnley at this time. But she could see no wrong in her son, and she was clearly not pleased with her daughter-in-law or afraid to say so. On 23 May Randolph reported that Mary had 'received a letter from Lady Lennox wherewith she is greatly offended'.[49] Three days later she was still upset, 'letters late come from Lady Lennox' having 'bred great sorrow' in her.[50]

On 8 June Elizabeth gave Sir Robert Melville 'leave to visit Lady Margaret, but in the presence of the keeper of the Tower'.[51] A week later Melville told Silva that he had discussed 'Lady Margaret's business' with the Queen, who had said 'it was grave, but she would make the Queen of Scotland the judge thereof. Not so however with the King and his father, as she would judge them herself.' In regard to Margaret, Silva 'thought that this was merely talk' and that Melville 'should insist upon Lady Margaret's liberation, which however I think difficult, as the Queen and Council know her to be a woman of courage, and if she were free and went to Scotland, she could greatly aid with her counsel, whilst if she remained in this country they would still be in difficulty about her in consequence of her great intelligence and her many friends'.[52]

On 17 June Sir William Drury, Marshal of Berwick, reported that Henry Gwyn, Yaxley's servant, had arrived from Flanders at Leith with two coffers, which contained Margaret's gifts to Queen Mary. Drury thought that Melville had been instrumental in arranging for them to be delivered.[53] Inside were 'dishes of sugar and marmalade', and 'letters from Lady Lennox and Mr [Arthur] Pole, who has given all his right to the King and Queen of Scotland that he had to the crown of England'.[54] Arthur Pole, the grandson of Margaret Pole, was a pretender to Elizabeth's throne, and had been a prisoner in the Tower since 1563. It is possible that Margaret, anxious to pre-empt any claim that might prejudice her grandchild's right to the English succession, had sent a message to Arthur and his brother Edmund, asking them to relinquish their claims to Queen Mary.[55] In June, shortly before taking to her chamber for her confinement, Mary made her will, in which she left small bequests to the Lennoxes: a faceted diamond ring for Margaret and an enamelled diamond ring for the Earl.

On 19 June 1566 Mary gave birth to a healthy son in Edinburgh Castle, and named him James after her father. 'The birth of the young Prince has bred much joy here in general, the Queen in good state for a woman in her case, and the Prince a very goodly child,' reported Elizabeth's envoy, Henry Killigrew, from Berwick. Lennox was not invited to greet his grandson, and in September it would emerge that he had not seen Mary since March.[56] He was out of favour, in indifferent health, and keeping at a safe distance in Glasgow.

Margaret was thrilled to hear of the birth of her first grandchild, but still she remained a prisoner with no hope of seeing him in the foreseeable future. She must have been troubled when she learned that Darnley had refused to attend Prince James's christening, effectively proclaiming to the world his doubts about the child's paternity, which some imputed to Rizzio. He had also threatened to leave Scotland, and was prevented only by illness.

It was not until 23 June that Elizabeth consented to receive the letter that Darnley had sent more than two months earlier, 'but not that of his father. The letter treats of the liberation of Lady Margaret, and the Queen said that she did not well understand it, but would read it at her leisure. She complained somewhat of the style of the letter in the matter of courtesy.'[57] That week a Scottish envoy, come with news of Prince James's birth, 'asked leave to visit Lady Margaret'. Elizabeth told him

that his Queen did not write upon that matter, and she did not know why he asked such a thing, which she refused him.

He replied that he asked it because they heard that Lady Margaret was ill, and he wished to take news of her health. He said he would see her in the presence of anyone the Queen desired, but the permission was withheld from him. The Queen, however, read the Earl of Lennox's letter, which she had refused previously to do. She said that he wrote more politely than his son, and it was easy to see that he was older and wiser. She refused, however, to keep either of the letters, but returned them after she had read them. Four days ago a gentleman of the King of France arrived here, called M. du Croc, who goes as ambassador to Scotland. He was with this Queen the day before yesterday, and asked leave to see Lady Margaret, which was refused him.[58]

Cecil's agent, William Rogers, reported to his master on 5 July that Darnley had declared 'before twenty gentlemen that he was not so ill-loved in England' as in Scotland, 'but that forty gentlemen there would so serve him, and more soon after conveyance of my lady's [Margaret's] letters'. Rogers also drew Cecil's attention to the interest shown by Sir Richard Chamberlain, Captain of Scarborough, in Darnley's affairs, and his placing the castle at Darnley's disposal; and to the interest shown by unnamed persons in the West Country, who had sent Darnley a map of the Scilly Isles off Cornwall. He mentioned his suspicions of Henry Gwyn, Yaxley's servant.[59]

Darnley's boast was no empty one. Margaret, fearful of what might happen to her son in Scotland, had tried, with the aid of her Spanish friends, to arrange his escape to Flanders, and she had probably sought Sir Richard Cholmeley's aid in garrisoning Scarborough to that end.[60] Margaret's aim was almost certainly to secure support from King Philip and her affinity in England for Darnley to press his claim to the English throne.

The government was alarmed to hear what Rogers had to say. If Darnley took Scarborough and the Scillies, Philip II might seize the opportunity to invade England[61] and set him up as a Catholic king. Immediately security around Margaret was tightened up. On 6 July, the day after Rogers had made his report, Silva wrote that Elizabeth had 'again refused to give Melville permission to visit Lady Margaret, whom they keep closer than before. The Queen tells Melville that her liberation is in the hands of his mistress, but no doubt it will be on conditions difficult to accept.'[62] On 15 August Elizabeth did allow Melville 'to speak with Lady Margaret, but in the presence of the keeper of the Tower and others'.[63]

Lennox was not privy to Margaret's plotting, and when he learned something of what was afoot, he did his best to persuade Darnley not to flee Scotland and desert his wife. On 29 September he warned Mary of the plan.[64] Mary questioned Darnley, but he denied any knowledge of it.[65]

On 19 October Silva asked Robert Melville 'whether he had spoken to the Queen about Lady Margaret. He said he had not, as he had no instructions to do so, although he expected to receive them, the reason being that there were disputes between his Queen and her husband which were of no great importance, and did not arise from want of affection, but from childish trifles. His Queen, however, was going to Stirling where the King was, and everything would then be made up.' Silva was concerned because 'the imprisonment of Lady Margaret has been made stricter' and she was 'not allowed to communicate with anybody in order that [she] may not enlist the aid of members of Parliament'.[66] This had the desired effect. In February, when Elizabeth made clear her determination to marry the Archduke Charles of Austria, Silva informed King Philip that 'all the aristocracy apparently desire the match, except Margaret and her party, which is small'.[67]

Despite that setback, Margaret continued to receive news of the outside world. In January 1567 she may have learned that Darnley was at Glasgow with his father and 'there lies full of the small pox, to whom the Queen has sent her physician'.[68] In fact Darnley was suffering not from smallpox but syphilis, which he may have caught during one of his visits to France some years earlier. Lennox, having heard that Darnley was to be 'apprehended and put in ward' for plotting against Mary,[69] had an obvious reason for wanting his son away from the dangers that lurked for him in Edinburgh. He would have been alarmed to hear that Morton, and those other lords who had been betrayed by Darnley and exiled from Scotland for their part in Rizzio's murder, had been summoned home, thanks to the intercession of Cecil.[70] There could be little doubt in anyone's mind that Morton – and his partners in crime – would be out for revenge.

On 3 February Silva wrote:

Margaret is still in prison, and greatly grieved, as she writes me, at the disputes between her son and his wife. She begs me to make every effort to bring them into harmony again, and also to speak to this Queen with regard to her liberation, or, at least, that she shall be taken out of the Tower and placed in some private house in confinement, as she not only suffers now morally, but is in great need, as they have taken all her property. If opportunity offers, I will remind the Queen of it.[71]

Having learned that Darnley had again been plotting against her, and fearing that he would seize Prince James, Mary resolved to go to Glasgow and bring him back to Edinburgh, where she could keep a closer eye on his activities. It was a fateful decision given that the lords who were out for his blood were in the capital, but Mary dared not leave him in the heart of Lennox territory, where he might raise a force to overthrow her. But she found him ill in bed and in a much chastened frame of mind. On the journey to Edinburgh he

confessed that he had failed in some things, but that he was young; he craved her pardon and protested that he would not fail again, and desired nothing but that they might be together as man and wife. She said she was sorry for his sickness and would find remedy therefor as soon as she might. He said, if she would promise him that he and she might be together at bed and board, he would go with her where she pleased, and she answered that her coming was only to that effect. Notwithstanding before they could come together he must be purged and cleansed of his sickness.[72]

On 27 January James Beaton, Archbishop of Glasgow, wrote to Mary from Paris, informing her that Catherine de' Medici had said that Mary's good conduct and rule 'would be a great mean to compass more easily all your designs and enterprises, and in special it would occasion that Madame of Lennox, whom she knew well-favoured by a great part of the nobility of England, would concur with you'.[73]

But already it was too late for Mary and Darnley.

17

'Horrible and Abominable Murder'

It was bitterly cold and snowing in Edinburgh in the early hours of 10 February 1567. To the south of the city Darnley was completing his convalescence in the Old Provost's Lodging at Kirk O'Field. Mary had been visiting him daily, and to all appearances the couple had become reconciled, even affectionate. In the morning Darnley was to return to Holyrood, fully cured, and resume marital relations with his wife. Mary had been at Kirk O'Field the previous evening, but shortly before midnight she left for Holyrood, having promised to attend a masque there in celebration of the wedding of two of her servants. When she and her retinue had departed, Darnley retired for the night.

At two o'clock a mighty explosion reverberated across the city, awakened most of the inhabitants, and initiated one of the greatest murder mysteries in history. Those running to the scene to investigate found that the Old Provost's Lodging had been blown up, undermined – as it proved – by gunpowder. Three hours later the bodies of Darnley and his valet were found lying in a nearby orchard. When Mary learned what had happened she was plunged – according to her own account and the testimony of witnesses – into grief and torment, and appears to have suffered a nervous collapse.[1] On 12 February, two days after the murder, the Scottish government proclaimed a lavish reward for information leading to the arrest of the King's assassins.[2]

The news had reached London by 14 February, when Cecil told Silva that the Queen had been informed 'of the finding of the dead body of the King of Scotland out of doors in his shirt, but without a wound, and with him the dead body of one of his servants; but no news has come as to who had been the author of the crime, nor were any other particulars known. The case is a very strange one, and has greatly grieved the Catholics.'[3]

On 18 and 19 February bills were affixed to the door of the Tolbooth, Edinburgh's Parliament house, council chamber and gaol. One denounced the Earl of Bothwell and his associates as the murderers.[4] Bothwell was certainly at Kirk O'Field on the night of the explosion, and had arranged for the house to be undermined – but he had not killed Darnley. It was not until 1581 that Morton would confess that he had had foreknowledge of the plot, although he had not been 'art and part' in it; but his – and Margaret's – Douglas kinsmen, led by a distant relation, Archibald Douglas, Parson of Douglas, were at the scene. It appears that Darnley and his valet, hearing something suspicious, had fled from the house, climbed over the surrounding city wall and dropped into the orchard below. It was here that they were set upon by the Douglases, who did their evil work then disappeared into the night.

Sir Robert Melville arrived in London on 19 February. He told Silva that Queen Mary was very distressed. Silva 'asked him certain questions to get at the bottom of the suspicions as to who had been the author of the crime, but could get nothing definite'. Melville greatly feared 'that some rising or disturbance will take place in the country.' Silva gained the impression that Queen Mary 'or her followers had some prior notice of the misfortune, although this seems incredible. Even if the Queen clears herself from it, the matter is still obscure.'

Silva reported that Elizabeth had expressed 'sorrow at the death of the King, and she thinks that although he married against her wish, yet, as he was a royal personage and her cousin, the case is a very grave one, and she signifies her intention to punish the offenders'.[5]

By 19 February Elizabeth had received corroboration of the details of the murder, as well as a report that Lennox had been killed too. Now she could no longer delay breaking the appalling news to Margaret. Cecil was moved to write to Sir Henry Norris: 'I hope her Majesty will have some favourable compassion of the said lady, whom any humane nature must needs pity.'[6]

That day Margaret was informed that she had two visitors: Margaret Gamage, the wife of William, Lord Howard, and Cecil's wife, Mildred

Cooke, who had been entrusted by the Queen with the awful task of telling her that both Darnley and Lennox were dead.[7] The shock of learning of the terrible end of her son, who had been just twenty years old, was more than Margaret could bear, and she 'could not by any means be kept from such passion of mind as the horribleness of the fact did require'.[8] 'How may I with tears his death overpass?' she cries in Phillips's *Commemoration*, which contains long reflections on how Darnley was entrapped and betrayed by flatterers and traitors. 'The mother was so grieved that it was necessary for the Queen to send her doctors to her', and Dr Robert Huicke, and Gabriel Goodman, the Protestant Dean of Westminster,[9] who was looking after young Charles Stuart, hastened to the Tower.

For a time it was widely believed that Lennox had been killed alongside his son. On 21 February the Venetian ambassador in France reported that 'the husband of the Queen of Scotland, and his father the Earl of Lennox, had been assassinated'.[10] The next day the Papal Nuncio referred in a letter to 'the news of the death of the King of Scotland and of the Earl of Lennox his father. He and his father were found dead in the public street, both of them stripped, a spectacle worthy of the most profound commiseration.' As late as 20 March it was believed in Paris that Darnley 'and the father of the King both lost their lives'.[11]

In fact Lennox had not been at Kirk O'Field; he had left Glasgow on the night of the murder and gone to Linlithgow, where he was given the dreadful news of his son's death. Immediately he went back to Glasgow.[12] With his enemies – Bothwell, Moray and Maitland – ranged against him, it was the safest place. But by 19 February Mary had summoned him back to Edinburgh.[13]

On 20 February Cecil visited Darnley's 'bereaved mother' in the Tower, and reassured her that Lennox could not have perished in the explosion as he had certainly been at Glasgow when it happened.[14] That was a huge relief to Margaret, but nothing would ever compensate her for the loss of her son, and she was in such grief that Cecil advised the Queen to release her from the Tower.

Elizabeth seems to have felt genuine pity for Margaret. On 21 February she was 'taken out of the Tower, and placed in Sackville's house'.[15] Sackville Place was where Margaret had stayed four years earlier, after her release from Sheen. Her former host, Sir Richard Sackville, had died the previous April, and it was his son, Thomas, Lord Buckhurst, who was now to be her custodian, although the terms of her confinement were not onerous and she was permitted visitors. When Silva saw Elizabeth on 22 February he 'praised her action in consoling and taking Margaret out of prison, and said how it had been approved by all'.[16] Elizabeth had also arranged for Margaret's remaining son, nine-year-old Charles, to be brought to his mother.[17]

Margaret had learned that Mary had left Kirk O'Field for Holyrood two hours before Darnley's murder.[18] With hindsight this looked damning. Melville told Silva that in the first, most terrible, throes of her grief,

> Lady Margaret used words against his Queen, whereat I am not surprised, as I told him, because grief like this distracts the most prudent people, much more one so sorely beset. She is not the only person that suspects the Queen to have had some hand in the business, and they think they see in it revenge for her Italian Secretary, and the long estrangement which this caused between her and her husband gave a greater opportunity for evil persons to increase the trouble. The heretics here publish the Queen's complicity as a fact, but they are helped in their belief by their suspicion and dislike for her. The Catholics are divided, the friends of the King holding with the Queen's guilt and her adherents the contrary.[19]

Margaret could not even find comfort in a funeral service, for already Darnley had been buried in the choir of Holyrood Abbey. It had been a private ceremony, and he had not been accorded the honours of a royal funeral, which drew criticism in London and must have given Margaret further cause for grief. Many years later she would recall how 'thus lingering in woe my dolour increase[d]. Dame Nature constrained me to rush forth my tears; to send forth my woes I no time have ceased; the heavens of my cries just record still bears; the fact of this slaughter blown in my cares, my cares made babble day and night.'[20]

Lennox was as grief-stricken as his wife, and consumed with the desire for vengeance. Honour demanded that he avenge his son's murder, so he resolved to stay in Scotland to gather evidence and bring the perpetrators to justice. On 20 February he had written to Queen Mary complaining that, since she had failed to prosecute anyone, he was 'forced' to give her his 'poor and simple advice for bringing the matter to light'. He reminded her that she was bound to pursue the murderers 'for God's cause and the honour of your Majesty and this your realm', and urged her to summon Parliament to make a 'perfect trial', so 'that the bloody and cruel actors of this deed shall be manifestly known'.[21] The next day Mary informed him that she had already proclaimed a parliament for this purpose.[22] Lennox also appealed to Queen Elizabeth to preserve King James, 'the little innocent, her poor orphan and kinsman'.[23]

On 24 February Elizabeth wrote to Mary of her shock at Darnley's murder. The fact that she addressed her as 'Madame', rather than the customary 'Sister', suggests that she, like Margaret and many others, had her suspicions. She wrote: 'My ears have been so astounded and my heart so frightened to hear of the horrible and abominable murder of your husband, my cousin, that I have scarcely spirit to write, yet I cannot conceal that I grieve for you more than him.' She was concerned about Mary's apparent inertia when it came to pursuing the assassins, and the sinister conclusions that many people were beginning to draw from that. Public opinion was increasingly connecting Bothwell to the murder, and Bothwell was powerful at court and high in favour with Mary, which in itself now looked suspicious. Not knowing that Mary was suffering a nervous and physical collapse, she exhorted her to do something and still the wagging tongues. 'I should not do the office of a faithful cousin and friend if I did not urge you to preserve your honour, rather than look through your fingers at revenge on those who have done you such a favour, as most people say. I counsel you to take this matter to heart that you may show the world what a noble princess and loyal wife you are. I write thus vehemently not that I doubt, but for affection.'[24]

Lennox was also wondering why Mary was not vigorously searching out the murderers. On 26 February, having heard that Parliament would not assemble until 14 April, he expressed his anxiety at the delay, naming Bothwell and others as Darnley's murderers and urging that they be taken into custody and punished 'to the example of ye whole world'. We do not know what evidence he had against Bothwell, but his exhortation to the Queen to consider her duty and her honour, 'for the love of God', reflects a swell of opinion that she was dragging her heels in bringing the murderers to justice. She should act speedily, he urged, so that it should not be said that she was in league with murderers.[25]

Silva later heard, probably from Margaret, that Lennox had written to Mary that he does not think that calling Parliament together is very necessary, as it is not a matter for Parliament to punish such a crime as this. He has written the same effect to his wife, who is still grieving for the loss of her son, and confesses that she, like her husband, has no other object but to avenge his death, although she sees that it would be better for her to be calmer about it than she is. She thinks the end of it all will be that they will murder her husband, as they have murdered her son, and she is in great fear that the heretics will take possession of her grandson, and try to bring him up to their own tricks. She thinks that they have been prompted to this action by some friends here of Catherine [de' Medici], who have found ready compliance in the Scotch, in consequence of their small attachment to the English. Margaret, although she is sensible, is impassioned, as is natural in her position, and believes that the Queen of Scotland is not free from the death of her husband.[26]

Mary responded to Lennox on 1 March, denying that she meant to defer bringing the murderers to justice. She wanted them apprehended 'the sooner the better'. If Lennox could name those he thought worthy to suffer trial, she would approve proceedings against them.[27]

When, shortly before 1 March, Melville visited Margaret, she had calmed down and was more circumspect in regard to Mary. She

told him she could not believe that his Queen had been a party to the death of her son, but she could not help complaining of her for her bad treatment of him. He asked her to write to her, and she said she could not do so without leave of this Queen, who seems to have taken great pity on her, and has sent to her her other son, who was confined in the Dean of Westminster's house.

Every day it becomes clearer that the Queen of Scotland must take steps to prove that she had no hand in the death of her husband, if she is to prosper in her claims to the succession here. The spirit of the Catholics has been greatly weakened by this event.[28]

In Edinburgh there were 'great suspicions' but 'no proof or appearance of apprehension yet'.[29] On 8 March Lennox sent Henry Killigrew to Cecil 'touching this late, unnatural and most cruel murder of the King my son', and urged Cecil to press Elizabeth 'to revenge the shedding of her Highness's own innocent blood'.[30] But it was a month before Elizabeth offered even covert support, and by then it was too late.

On 12 March Winchester, the Lord Treasurer, reported to Cecil: 'I perceive my Lady Lennox is resting now with my Lady Dacre and my Lady Sackville, by the Queen's order, and without money to help herself, and therefore thinketh some unkindness in me that I do not help her.' But he was unable to do so because the money raised from the Lennox estates was at York and the Queen's receiver, who looked after the assets of sequestered properties, was in London. For now Margaret was effectively destitute and reliant on the charity of her hosts. The hardship of her case moved a harrassed Winchester to offer to borrow money for her to pay the Lieutenant of the Tower for the expenses incurred by him on her behalf, and he expressed his wish that 'the Queen's Highness would let her have her land again in her own receipt, and so she would be best pleased, whereof I shall be very glad'.[31]

Margaret's custodian, Cicely Baker, Lady Sackville, was a great beauty, but was to acquire a dubious reputation: in a satire of the period she is thrice damned as a prostitute and called 'my Lady Lecher'.[32] Anne, Lady Dacre, was Thomas Sackville's sister, an imperious woman with a strong character. One might wish for some insights on relations between these two interesting ladies and Margaret, for they were to keep her company for about three more months. In March she was set fully at liberty,[33] but she was to remain at Sackville Place until a suitable lodging could be found for her.

As Queen Mary seemed unwilling to proceed against Bothwell, Lennox wrote to her on 17 March demanding his arrest and trial, and that of half a dozen other suspects – apparently on his own arbitrary assumption that Bothwell was guilty. He could not resist adding that, 'as for ye names of ye persons foresaid, I marvel that ye same has been kept from your Majesty's ears', considering the proliferation of placards naming Bothwell as Darnley's killer. Lennox also asked to be appointed the governor of his grandson, Prince James,[34] in place of John Erskine, Earl of Mar, whom Mary had chosen to have charge of him. It was customary for heirs to the throne to be given their own households and governors, even in infancy.

Six days later Mary authorised Lennox to proceed with a private prosecution of Bothwell and his associates. She informed him that she would command them to stay in Edinburgh for a week, pending the setting of a date for their trial.[35] The next day, 24 March, Lennox officially charged Bothwell with the murder of Darnley.[36] On 28 March the Council decreed that the trial should be held on 12 April, and Lennox was formally summonsed.[37] But most people felt intimidated by Bothwell, who was not only in constant attendance on the Queen and still high in her favour, but could also command a formidable armed following and the royal arsenal at Dunbar. Thus when news of the forthcoming trial spread, what little support Lennox had in Edinburgh began to melt away.[38]

Lennox was worried about Margaret. He marvelled 'what the cause should be that since his wife's liberty she has not let him understand the present state she is in', and on 2 April desired Sir William Drury 'to advertise him what he hears of her'.[39] We do not know the reason for Margaret's silence. Possibly she had been too sunk in grief to write to him, or her letters had been delayed.

There were those in high places in Scotland, the real murderers of Darnley, who had a vested interest in silencing Lennox, and who feared that his persistent demands for justice would lead to their exposure. He knew he was in danger. By 4 April, concerned for his grandson's security, he had resolved with Moray, Atholl and other lords to ask that Prince James be kept in the care of four noblemen, not just one.[40]

But he himself would not be one of them. Before Bothwell's trial even took place, Lennox had already 'procured his leave to depart out of Scotland'.[41] He was fast realising that lack of support and open hostility would hinder his case, especially since Bothwell 'jetteth up and down the street with great companies of men'. On 11 April he wrote to Mary from Stirling, telling her that he was too ill to travel. He asked for a further postponement of the trial, so that he could have time to gather more evidence, and requested that she imprison Bothwell and grant Lennox himself a commission to apprehend anyone whom he suspected of having been involved in Darnley's murder.[42] He sent his servant, Robert Cunningham, to the Queen with this letter and two libels, in the first of which he compared Mary's role in the murder of Darnley, that 'innocent lamb', to Judas's betrayal of Christ.[43] He could not have made it plainer that he considered the Queen a guilty party.

Accompanied by three thousand men of his affinity, Lennox rode from Glasgow to Linlithgow. There he received orders from the Queen that he could take with him to Edinburgh only six of his company, whereupon he 'refused to come in that manner'. Bothwell, on the other hand, was allowed to pack the Tolbooth with four hundred of his armed supporters.[44] Lennox sent Robert Cunningham in his stead, 'protesting that his absence was through fear of his life, and that any judgment by the assize would be in error'.[45] He asked for the case to be postponed, but was refused, and without the only witness for the prosecution the case collapsed. Elizabeth's messenger, come belatedly to urge Mary to postpone the trial, had been halted at the gates of Edinburgh Castle, and was not admitted until the proceedings were over. It was this that hardened Elizabeth's attitude to Mary and earned her sympathy for the Lennoxes. At long last she publicly acknowledged Darnley, her 'nearest kinsman', as king of Scots.[46]

On 21 April Silva reported that Margaret knew nothing of Bothwell's acquittal.[47] Possibly the news had been kept from her for the moment, it being felt that, in her fragile emotional state, it would be too much for her.

Mary had given Lennox licence to leave the country. 'He has the Queen of Scotland's leave for ten years' absence, during which he may enjoy his Scotch revenues.'[48] On 15 April, at Stirling, knowing that he had no choice but to depart from Scotland, Lennox visited the ten-month-old Prince James and asked his friend, John Erskine, Earl of Mar, 'to have earnest regard to his charge'.[49] Disgusted at Mary's apparent inertia, and knowing that he was a marked man, he was obliged to go into hiding in Scotland until a ship could be found to take him to England. On 23 April he wrote to Drury: 'Good Mr Marshal, I shall desire you to dispatch this enclosed letter to my wife by the through post. It is unclosed, that you may see the contents. From my ship at the Gairloch.'[50] He wrote to Margaret: 'The Queen returns this day from Stirling', where she had visited Prince James. 'The Earl of Bothwell hath gathered many of his friends. He is minded to meet her this day and take her by the way, and bring her to Dunbar. Judge ye if it be with her will or no.'[51]

The next day Bothwell effectively seized power in Scotland when he did intercept the Queen near Edinburgh as she was returning from a visit to Prince James at Stirling, and carried her off to Dunbar, where he isolated and later raped her – some said with her consent. No one attempted to rescue her, which in itself indicates how widely it was believed that she had connived at her own abduction. Elizabeth showed herself 'greatly scandalised' when she heard what Bothwell had done, but her ambassador in Paris was saying openly that

Mary had arranged the murder of Darnley so that she could marry Bothwell, so it seems likely that Elizabeth herself believed that Mary had colluded with Bothwell.

On 29 April Lennox sailed from Scotland, and by 10 May he had arrived at Portsmouth. Before landing he sent to Elizabeth for permission to disembark and a safe-conduct. 'She replied that he shall be well treated and may come to her without any need for discussing conditions about it.' She had just received 'letters from Scotland saying that it is publicly announced there that the Queen will be married shortly to Bothwell at Dunbar with all solemnity'.[52] The wedding took place on 15 May at Holyrood Palace, in the same chapel in which Mary had been joined to Darnley, although on this occasion the service was conducted according to the Protestant rite, Bothwell being of that faith – which shows the extent of his power over Mary. Lennox was then still at Portsmouth, awaiting Elizabeth's permission to land, but now a storm drove his vessel across the English Channel to Brittany. When Margaret heard, she 'sent a ship for him'.[53]

On 24 May Silva reported that there was talk of delivering the Prince of Scotland to the English Queen to be brought up by his grandmother, Margaret, who had 'sent to me a few days since to say, that as she heard the Earl of Leicester was coming to consult me as to the advisability of this Queen's receiving the child here, the subject having been discussed in the Council, she begged me to advise that it should be done'. Whoever had the young King in their custody was in the strongest position to influence events in Scotland. Silva told Leicester that

they should make every effort to get the child here, because if it was desirable that he should inherit the crown, they could have him in their own hands, and thus keep in check other claimants in this country, whilst if he were not to succeed they could put him into a safe place, so that in no case would any harm come to them from it. I said it was meet that the Queen should act promptly about it, as it was notorious that the French were endeavouring to get the child. I do not know whether the French will be more artful than they, but they are trying their hardest.[54]

Having been detained briefly by the Governor of Brittany, Lennox had sailed for home and docked safely at Southampton. On 7 June he wrote to Queen Elizabeth seeking forgiveness for his past disloyalty. Killigrew had forwarded a letter from Margaret assuring him that the Queen would be sympathetic, and Lennox told Elizabeth he remembered her

> graciously sending to the Queen of Scots to stay that most partial and unreasonable day of law appointed for the cleansing of him who was the chief persecutor and murderer of the late King of Scotland, my son – I mean the Earl [of] Bothwell. Having a great desire to speak with you, I am now come to Southampton, minding not only to submit me wholly to your merciful hands next to God, but also to serve you, trusting that your highness will remember the murder of your poor kinsman, till upright justice may be had. I await your gracious answer before presuming to depart hence.[55]

Having lost all faith in Mary, the Lennoxes would henceforth direct their appeals for justice to Elizabeth. On 11 June, before Elizabeth left London for Richmond, 'Lady Margaret went to see the Queen. She was well received, and to her prayer that the Queen would help her to avenge the death of her son she obtained a favourable reply.' Her friend Leicester 'made her great promises, and Cecil as well, the latter informing her that all that had been done for her was owing to his efforts, and he would continue to help her. He assured her that she should have her grandson, which proves that they are trying to get hold of him. Lady Margaret thinks the French will not help the Queen of Scots.'[56]

The next day, 12 June, Lennox arrived in London and was reunited with Margaret, probably at Sackville Place. They had not seen each other for the best part of three years, and in that time their lives had been wrecked by tragedy; we can only imagine the feelings that overwhelmed them when they came together. Two days later Silva reported: 'Lady Margaret has news that the Queen of Scotland, having sent word to the Earl of Mar that she wished to see her child, he answered that she might do so, but not Bothwell or any of those who are suspected of the King's murder.'[57]

On 16 June Margaret went to Richmond. 'The Queen treated her well, and told her she could visit her whenever she liked and bring her son with her next time. The following day the Earl, her husband, went to kiss the Queen's hand, and was also received kindly, staying with her over two hours giving her an account of what had happened in Scotland. He asked her aid to avenge his son and for the preservation of the Prince; and the Queen, after assuring him that she was satisfied with respect to the complaints she formerly made against him, said she was willing to help with men, money and all that was needful and in accordance with the Scotch lords, but she could not take any part against the person of the Queen.'[58]

That summer Elizabeth persuaded George Talbot, Earl of Shrewsbury, to let the Lennoxes stay in his ancient and decaying mansion of Coldharbour, since – pending the restoration of their property – they had nowhere to live.[59] Coldharbour stood on the northern foreshore of the Thames, in the parish of All Hallows in the City of London. In 1484 Richard III had granted the royal heralds this ancient house as a permanent home. Dating from at least the early fourteenth century, it had been a great mansion; among its famous residents had been Henry IV, Henry V, Sir John de Pulteney, four times mayor of London and builder of Penshurst Place, and Alice Perrers, Edward III's mistress, who added a tower to the house. The heralds had held the house for only a year when Richard III was killed and Henry VII cancelled the grant of Coldharbour, which he gave to his mother, Margaret Beaufort, Margaret's great-grandmother. In 1553 the house had been given to Francis Talbot, Earl of Shrewsbury, who changed its name to Shrewsbury House. Now it retained only vestiges of its former glory.[60]

By 24 June news of the Queen of Scots' overthrow had reached the English court. Nine days earlier the forces of Mary and Bothwell had been defeated at Carberry Hill. On the promise of the lords to give Bothwell safe conduct into exile, Mary surrendered and was taken prisoner. The lords then paraded her in shame through Edinburgh, where a baying mob howled for her blood. On the face of it, this was good news for the Lennoxes, but the capture of Mary would rebound on their hopes for justice, because Mary was an anointed queen, and Elizabeth, although she sympathised with the couple's frustrations, was to do all she could to secure her sister monarch's release and prevent the Scottish lords from executing her and creating a dangerous precedent. For this she needed the support of the Hamiltons, who were loyal to Mary. At the same time, she was anxious to see a Protestant government in Edinburgh, which would benefit England and bring about a closer relationship between the two kingdoms. None of these policies was acceptable to the Lennoxes.

On 23 June Bedford, hastening southwards, forwarded to Cecil 'letters which he has received from the lords of Scotland', explaining why they had imprisoned their lawful Queen'. He added that the lords did not mean to crown the Prince, but Bedford, thinking that Elizabeth would want them to do so, intended 'to request Lady Lennox to borrow money of the Queen for the furtherance of this action'.[61] He had no doubt that Margaret would want to see her grandson crowned king of Scots in his mother's place.

Mary's fate hung in the balance, as Robert Melville urged Cecil to send Lennox back to Scotland, where he was needed to counteract the influence of the Hamiltons, who were supporting their Queen. Melville also suggested that Thomas Bishop be sent to keep watch on the Earl.[62] On 26 June Silva reported, incorrectly: 'The Earl of Lennox has leave, and even orders, to go to Scotland.' It was true, though, that 'the lords are keeping the Queen of Scotland in a castle on a lake'.[63] This was Lochleven Castle, which stood on an island in the midst of a loch and offered maximum security.

On 28 June Silva informed King Philip that 'a base brother of Margaret' – Angus's bastard, George Douglas, Bishop of Moray –

has arrived here from Scotland, sent by the lords to her and her husband, the Earl of Lennox, to inform them of events, and to press them to ask the Queen for help in their enterprise and in the punishment of those guilty of the murder of the King. They say that they do not need men, but only money to pay them. Bothwell [who had escaped from the lords] is in the north country, raising troops.

Margaret went yesterday to Richmond to speak to the Queen on these matters, and ask her for her decision. She stopped all night, and this brother of hers has gone today to give the Queen a detailed relation of affairs in Scotland. This Queen is sending Throckmorton to Scotland, and has ordered the estates of Lennox and Margaret in this country to be restored to them. She seems to be very sorry for their troubles.'[64]

At the end of June, instructed by Elizabeth to go north and save Mary's skin, Sir Nicholas Throckmorton took leave of the Lennoxes at Coldharbour before departing for Scotland. He reported: 'I have been with my lord and lady of Lennox, and declared briefly her Majesty's honourable intent as to the Queen, the Prince, the lords, and justice on the murderers. They are much troubled with want of

money. My lady wept bitterly, my lord sighed deeply. Surely her
Majesty must needs have some commiseration of them, namely for
her own service!' He added that Lennox was 'desired in Scotland'.[65]

On 1 July Lennox sent his servant, William Mompesson, to Cecil
with a letter begging for leave – and money – to go to Scotland.
He began by praising Elizabeth's magnanimity:

> The Queen's Majesty hath been so gracious unto my wife and
> me, as not only to take us into her favour again, after our long
> troubles, but also, at my wife's last being with her Highness, to
> grant her our living. Mr Secretary, it is not unknown how just
> cause I have with all expedition to be in Scotland, what
> dishonour I receive by my absence there, and how unable I am
> to furnish myself to go as behoveth me, being in such poverty,
> as my wife and I are in debt [to] the sum of £3,000 [£521,670]
> or more.

It is evident that the Crown's officers had not husbanded the Lennox
estates efficiently. Lennox complained: 'Our cattle and our provisions
on our land [have been] sold and dispersed, in a manner, for nothing;
our jewels, with plate, already at gage pawned.' He begged that 'there
may be wherewithal for my wife and child to be maintained', and
asked for a loan of £1,000 (£173,890).[66]

Elizabeth had no intention of allowing Lennox to go to Scotland
at this time; he might upset everything. So he and Margaret remained
in the south, working for Mary's abdication. It did not help that no
one was being brought to justice for Darnley's murder. It clearly ate
at both of them that the killers had got away with the murder of
their son, and they were ceaseless in their efforts to bring them to
justice.

On 12 July it was reported in France that Lennox supported the
rebel Scottish lords, 'having been urged to do so by Queen Elizabeth;
thus she secretly promotes disturbances in Scotland in order to
revenge the death of the late King her relative, or perhaps, as some
think, with an ulterior object; and already many think she desires
to obtain possession of the youthful Prince, who is in the power of
the party which she favours and assists'.[67] That month, when Moray
was in London, he described to Lennox a letter written by Mary
to Bothwell proving her complicity in Darnley's death.

At Lochleven, around the third week in July, Mary was delivered
of premature stillborn twins, probably conceived at Dunbar, and on

the 24th, lying in bed weak from loss of blood, she was forced to abdicate in favour of her thirteen-month-old son, who was crowned five days later as James VI of Scots at the Church of the Holy Rood at Stirling. Margaret had now realised her ambition of being grandmother to a king, although not in the happy circumstances she had envisaged, and she was to dedicate herself to young James's interests for the rest of her life.

Elizabeth was outraged at the Scottish lords' treatment of their Queen. In deposing their anointed sovereign, they had gone too far. She refused to recognise James as king and demanded that he be made her ward and brought to England, ostensibly to be raised by his grandmother, Margaret. Probably Margaret was not too hopeful, for she would have known that the Protestant lords of Scotland would never agree to their King being brought up by a Catholic.

By 2 August Elizabeth was expressing 'a desire to help in [Mary's] liberation, and this is the cause it is believed that she does not treat Lady Margaret so well as she had begun to do'. Margaret, evidently, wanted Mary kept in prison, at the very least. At this time 'she and her husband and son are staying five miles from here [London], and as the Queen has not restored their estates they are in great need'. The Lennoxes had probably moved to Chiswick, where they are recorded as lodging in May 1568. There is no record of their owning or leasing property there, so possibly they stayed at Corney House as guests of the Earl of Bedford, who returned from his northern tour of duty in October 1567.[68] Moray visited Margaret at Chiswick 'and showed a desire to help her, but she is very dissatisfied as she thinks she can never trust heretics'.[69]

At last Elizabeth took pity on the Lennoxes' plight. On 6 August Leicester informed Cecil:

Her Majesty, understanding the needful state of my Lady Margaret Lennox, and of my lord her husband, would that you should confer with the Lord Treasurer and let him understand her Majesty's pleasure is that he should take order that the yearly rents of their living should be from henceforth paid unto my said lady and lord, which her will is in any wise to have performed; and that which her Highness would have said more than before is that the order and government of the whole lands remain in her Majesty's officers' hands, and that all the rents and profits be paid to my lady and my lord's use from time to time.[70]

It was a most unsatisfactory solution from the Lennoxes' point of view, given how inefficiently royal officials had administered their estates over the past two years, and indeed it would be some time before the couple actually received any revenues.

On 30 August Margaret told Silva about the meeting Moray had had with Mary after he arrived back in Scotland: 'He spoke with the Queen, who admitted to her brother that she knew the conspiracy for her husband's murder.' Moray had left Mary 'in hope of nothing but God's mercy, willing her to seek to that as her chiefest refuge',[71] which could only be interpreted as meaning that the lords meant to execute her.

That month Moray was elected regent of Scotland, and the measures he now took to neutralise the Hamiltons, who had opposed Mary's deposition, would have earned Lennox's approval.[72]

In October 1567, when – according to the inscription – James VI was sixteen months old, Margaret and Lennox commissioned a large painting for him, 'The Memorial [or Cenotaph] of Lord Darnley', from the artist Livinius de Vogelaare of Antwerp,[73] which they intended as 'a witness to God's punishment of Mary's complicity in Darnley's murder'. It is a powerful piece of political propaganda, and it has been described as a 'vendetta picture'.[74] According to one of the inscriptions, the Lennoxes had commissioned it because they were now advanced in years: if they did not live to see their grandson and exhort him to bring Darnley's murderers to justice, the picture would serve in their place as a reminder of 'the barbarous murder of the late King, his father, till it should please God to permit him to avenge it'.[75] It was painted on canvas to facilitate easy transportation, and there can be little doubt that every detail was executed according to the Lennoxes' instructions, as a searing testimony to their terrible and vengeful grief.

Finished, according to the inscription, in January 1568 in London, the painting shows the couple – believed to have been sketched from life – with their ten-year-old son Charles, all clad in black mourning, kneeling behind the young crowned and robed James VI on a marble floor before a Catholic altar in a dark church. This was probably meant to be Holyrood Abbey, where Darnley was buried; Margaret would have seen it in childhood and remembered it being adorned with Catholic images, as in the painting, but since the picture was painted in London, the setting is probably to a large extent imaginary.[76] Behind the Lennoxes is a tomb chest on which lies Darnley's painted effigy in golden armour, guarded by the statues of Fame and Justice, with his head supported by two unicorns, and his emblem of a wolf at his feet. Inset into a corner is a scene showing Mary's defeat at Carberry Hill, with a banner portraying Darnley's corpse, and the arms of all the lords present clearly visible.

This was also a dynastic portrait, linking the Lennoxes to their grandson, King James, and underlining their greatness. The inscriptions proclaim that Lennox was of the royal blood of Scotland and Margaret the only daughter of Henry VII's eldest (*sic*) child, and the mother and grandmother of kings. Their arms adorn Darnley's tomb and the banners on the chapel wall.

Scenes inset in the tomb showed Darnley and his valet being dragged from bed by their murderers, and lying dead beneath a bare tree near the ruins of Kirk O'Field. A lengthy inscription on a plaque on the chapel wall told how Darnley was 'cut off, O hard fate!, inhumanly murdered, Queen Mary, his wife, also conspiring his death'. Latin scrolls issued from the mouths of the mourners, driving home the meaning of the picture, including a cry from the young James, 'Arise, Lord, and avenge the innocent blood of the King my father; and me, I entreat Thee, defend with Thy right hand!' His uncle, Charles Stuart, prayed that he may be the instrument of divine vengeance.

A copy of the painting was sent to Lennox's brother, Aubigny; it was probably through Charles Stuart that it later came into the possession of the dukes of Lennox and Richmond, who brought it to Goodwood House in Sussex.[77] In this version several inscriptions accuse Mary of adultery with Bothwell and complicity in the 'ferocious and cruel' murder of her 'affectionate' husband, so that she could marry her lover. In the original these have been scored out and are illegible, and the scenes portrayed on the tomb have also been defaced. It is possible that this was done after 1572, on Margaret's orders, or later, at the instance of James VI.[78]

Around the same time Vogelaare painted a portrait of Lennox wearing mourning, now at Hardwick Hall.[79] A portrait of Margaret is listed in the Hardwick inventory, and may have been a companion piece to the one of Lennox, but it cannot now be identified, and may be lost.

Margaret and Lennox spent the rest of the year 1567 struggling with their finances, and may have travelled north to inspect their properties in Yorkshire. The income that had been restored to them was depleted because some of their lands and goods had been sold off by the government. On 9 November Margaret wrote to Cecil 'touching the great loss which she and her lord have sustained in their estate' and seeking 'to have our own again'. She begged him to 'acquaint the Queen therewith'.[80] That month Cecil ordered the compilation of a list of lands given to Margaret by Lennox before their marriage for her dowry in Scotland, which had a yearly value of 500 marks sterling (£57,960).[81] On 21 December Sir Thomas Gargrave reported to Cecil that 'Lord and Lady Lennox find themselves aggrieved with the late commissioners for the sale of their corn and cattle'.[82]

On 27 January 1568 Margaret, who was ill again, was once more obliged to appeal to Cecil for help in regaining control of her lands:

> Good Master Secretary,
>   I am sorry my hap [fortune] was not to meet you at my last being at court, and although I was not well in health at that time, I am worse at this present of my old colic, or else I had been come in place of my letters, to have spoken with you.

Colic was a name given then to severe lower abdominal pain, and may in Margaret's case have resulted from stress, or a chronic disorder of the womb, such as a fibroid, cyst or polyp, common in women of her age.

Margaret wanted to talk to Cecil 'concerning my lord's great loss and mine in the sale of all our goods, and the increase that should have arisen thereof; our grounds also unstored [unplanted] at this time. All which your wisdom will consider, I trust, and how far behindhand it hath brought us, and unable to keep house in many years.' Her servant had told her that Cecil had been examining the evidence for this mismanagement, where he would have seen that the Queen had authorised the sales. Margaret was sure that Elizabeth had meant the land and goods to realise their proper value; she herself had even offered to buy them back at the price for which they had been sold, if that were possible, and she enclosed for Cecil 'a note of the sale of our goods, and as they were appraised'. She concluded:

> Good Master Secretary, as my trust is in you, show me favour in my reasonable suit, and that her Majesty may understand our wrongs and great loss, and I shall think myself, as I have

done always, bound unto you. And thus scribbled in haste, and so ill I doubt ye can not read it without the help of my man, to whom I have read it.

Your assured friend, Margaret Lennox.[83]

Early in May 1568 Queen Mary made a dramatic escape from Lochleven. The Hamiltons and others rallied to her cause, but on 12 May Moray's forces overcame hers at the Battle of Langside, forcing her to flee south to England with just a handful of supporters and the clothes on her back.

On 22 May Cecil visited Lennox at Chiswick and asked him to supply further details of Darnley's murder. Lennox instructed his servant, John Wood, to write to Moray in the hope of gaining information about the possible involvement of Archbishop Hamilton.[84] It was inevitable that Lennox would suspect his long-standing enemies of abetting Mary and Bothwell.

News of Queen Mary's escape into England arrived at court on 28 May. The Lennoxes heard it too and hastened to see the Queen, fearful that if Mary came to the English court, she would exercise her charm on Elizabeth and persuade her to help her regain her kingdom, which they could never allow. Conspicuous in their deep mourning, they fell to their knees before the Queen and demanded justice on Mary for the death of their son.[85] Margaret, racked with passionate grief, her face 'all swelled and stained with tears', 'grievously complained to Queen Elizabeth in her own and her husband's name, and besought that [Mary] might be called to trial for the murder of her son'. But Elizabeth, 'graciously comforting her, admonished her that she should not charge a crime upon so great a princess, her near kinswoman, which could not be proved by certain evidence, saying that the times were partial, malign and malice blind, which forget crimes against the innocent, but justice clear-sighted, which, being the avenger of wicked facts, is to be expected from God'. She added that 'such accusations must not rest against the good name of a princess without further proof', and that she herself would not condemn Mary without a hearing.[86]

At some point Lennox handed the Queen a 'supplication'. It comprised a long 'narrative' of Darnley's murder ('this most dolorous and woeful matter') that he had written – probably with Margaret's help – during the past twelve days, which is now known as the 'Lennox Narrative'.[87] In this tract, which has been described as 'rambling and emotional',[88] Lennox asserted that 'this tyrant' Mary, 'forgetting her duty to God and her husband, and setting apart her honour and good name', had 'brought her faithful and loving husband, that innocent lamb, from his careful and loving father to the place of execution', having become 'addicted and wholly besotted unto Bothwell', with whom she had first committed adultery in April 1566, just two months before her son's birth. Clearly Lennox was determined to make Mary look utterly depraved. He wanted a full indictment drawn up against her.

On 11 June, in pursuance of the proof Elizabeth required, Lennox sent to Scotland asking for more detailed information about 'the wickedness of that cruel woman, the destroyer of my House and all my friends'.[89] Cecil had already enlisted Margaret's help in tracking down those of Bothwell's supporters who were suspected of being in communication with Mary, and Margaret now found herself in the novel position of assisting with English intelligence, instead of trying to circumvent it. At the end of May Alexander Pringle (who had acted as Cecil's agent three years earlier in trying to prove Margaret illegitimate) wrote to inform her that Bothwell's cousin, Alexander Hepburn, Laird of Riccarton, whom he described as 'the principal deviser of your son's death', was still at large and being entertained by the Bishop of Durham. He urged Margaret to persuade the Queen to order Riccarton's arrest; the Lennoxes' 'special friend', Sir John Foster,[90] was awaiting a commission to take him.[91] Margaret passed on this information to Cecil.

The Queen of Scots' arrival in the north presented Elizabeth with an impossible dilemma. She would not furnish Mary with the troops she wanted because Mary had long claimed Elizabeth's crown and might be persuaded to use them against her. She could not receive Mary at court because Mary's reputation was indelibly stained with suspicions of adultery and murder that would reflect badly on the maiden Elizabeth. She could not allow Mary to remain at large for fear that she would become a focus for Catholic opposition to Elizabeth's rule. In the end, Elizabeth had no choice but to keep Mary under house arrest in the north, far from the court.

For all Margaret's denunciations of Mary, Elizabeth did not trust her. From the time Mary came into England, she had Margaret's movements watched carefully. Margaret was a Catholic and might yet rally to the Catholic Queen of Scots. From July 1568 to January 1569 Mary was held at Bolton Castle, not far from the

Lennox lands in the North Riding of Yorkshire. But Margaret had no intention of helping Mary; on the contrary, she continued to revile her. In a letter probably written in August 1568, Mary complained to Elizabeth that 'the Countess of Lennox, her mother-in-law', had written to 'assure her she will be securely kept from ever returning to Scotland'. Mary felt it deeply unreasonable that she should be barred from Elizabeth's presence, where Lady Lennox and others could accuse her face to face. She protested that Margaret's accusations against her were false, and she would tell Elizabeth so when they met.[92]

Mary continued to press Elizabeth to receive her, but Elizabeth insisted that she could not do that until Mary had been declared innocent of Darnley's murder. At length she determined to have Mary formally tried at York by a special commission, ostensibly to clear her name so that she could come to the English court, but in reality to establish a pretext for keeping her under lock and key.

Lennox was eager to attend the trial. On 18 August he wrote from Chiswick to Cecil:

> As I understand that by the Queen's Majesty's appointment and the estates of Scotland, the murder of the late King my son shall be tried in the beginning of September next: and as my wife and I exhibited a bill of supplication to her Majesty as ye know, requiring justice for that horrible deed, the chief actor thereof being now within her realm: yet being the party whom the matter toucheth nearest, and whose appearance may be thought most necessary, I will no wise determine nor prepare myself for that journey, but as shall stand with her pleasure, which I crave humbly to understand by your mean.[93]

Lennox was referring to the supplication that he had given Elizabeth several weeks earlier, of which he was now writing an updated version, *A Brief Discourse of the Usage [handling] of Henry, the King of Scots, son to me, the Earl of Lennox, by the Queen his wife.* Internal evidence in the surviving draft suggests that Moray had communicated to Lennox the content of the most damning of what were to become notorious as 'the Casket Letters'.[94] The Scottish lords were to allege that they had fortuitously discovered this silver casket of letters, which they claimed had been sent by Mary to Bothwell and contained proof not only of their adultery, but also of their complicity in the murder of Darnley. On 25 August the French ambassador reported that Lennox had new evidence against Mary, and that Moray was going to reward him by re-establishing the Lennoxes in Scotland.[95] But that same day the Queen denied Lennox leave to be present at the hearing.

Mary refused to acknowledge the legality of the commission on the grounds that she was a sovereign queen born out of the realm and not subject to English law, but after much discussion she consented to appear. Moray and other lords who were her enemies attended, and produced a casket of letters. The originals were destroyed in 1584, probably by order of James VI, and the copies that survive contain evidence that genuine letters of Mary's were tampered with or taken out of context, but at the time they caused a sensation, and turned the tide of public opinion against her.

Cecil had written to tell Margaret that he had had Riccarton apprehended and brought south, and then prevailed on the Queen to have him 'stayed'. The Lennoxes were now back at Coldharbour, and it was from there, on 3 October, that Margaret replied:

> Good Master Secretary,
>
> I have received your letter touching the Laird of Riccarton's [arrest], and hath learned what I can of a Scottishman who is, and was, my lord's servant at his being in Scotland, and he says that such report then was that the said Laird was cleared by an assize, but how true it is he cannot tell, and says also that the whole bruit in Scotland was that he carried letters to Bothwell from the Queen since her coming out of Lochleven. This man of my lord's was presently at the last battle between her and the Regent. This is all that I can learn.
>
> I would to God I knew the truth to certify you, but my hope is in God that all those which were guilty there shall be known. If Master John Wood be at court, he can best declare [them]. If he be at London, I shall speak to him. And with my most hearty thanks in this and all other your friendships showed to my lord and me, I commit you to God's protection.
>
> From Cold Harbour, the iii of October.
>
> Your assured loving friend, Margaret Lennox.[96]

Lennox had gone north to York for the trial. He too thought, mistakenly, that Riccarton had been cleared of Darnley's murder. On 9 October he informed Cecil that he had 'received this day by the hands of Mr John Wood, the Regent's servant, a letter from my wife, whereby I see your affectionate mind against all thought guilty of the murder of my son, the late King of Scots, in moving her Majesty to stay the Laird of Riccarton: for though cleansed by an assize, yet he is much to be suspected'. There was an enclosure for Margaret, in which Lennox outlined the grounds of his suspicions of Riccarton, who had been Darnley's 'first household man and familiar servant' and was suspected of the murder, or of being 'at least privy in the counsel' of Bothwell, because he had 'accompanied Bothwell in his enterprises', including his trial, until Bothwell had eventually fled from Scotland to Denmark, and was trying to secure the Earl's release.[97]

On 9 October Guerau de Spes, the ambassador who had replaced Silva, informed King Philip that Margaret had sent to tell him that she thought Riccarton was guilty. He added that Elizabeth wanted to make use of Margaret 'to injure the queen of Scotland'. But Spes had been assured by one Beaton that Riccarton was not involved in the murder.[98] That was the Council's opinion too, and Riccarton was allowed to return to Scotland, although he was apprehended by Moray in Hawick. However, at an assize held on 28 October he was finally 'cleansed of the death of the King'.[99]

When the hearing at York proved inconclusive and was adjourned to Westminster, the Lennoxes hastened south. Mary, for all her protests, was obliged to remain in the north, and would not be allowed to appear in person to defend herself.

On 21 November Cecil drafted a memorandum suggesting ways in which the Queen of Scots might be dealt with. As he saw it, 'the best way for England, but not easiest', was for her to 'remain deprived of her crown, and the State continue as it is'. The second way, which was 'for England profitable and not so hard', was that Mary be induced to accept joint sovereignty of Scotland with James VI, with the government of Scotland entrusted to a council selected by Elizabeth from a list of putative councillors, half to be put forward by Mary, 'and the other half by the Earl of Lennox and the Lady Lennox, [grand]parents to the child: and out of those the Queen's Majesty of England to make choice'.[100]

Elizabeth had relented in regard to Lennox giving evidence, and on 29 November he was permitted to appear at the Westminster tribunal. When Moray and his colleagues departed, Lennox, 'after declaring his grief, and hope of justice only at the hand of God and her Majesty, and his inability to express his cause in words, presented a writing with his charges against the Queen [Mary] for the murder of his son, which he exhibited upon his oath'.[101] That was the extent of his involvement in the proceedings, yet he continued to seek justice, pursuing those persons – chiefly Bothwell's associates, since Bothwell himself was in Denmark – whom he suspected of being involved in Darnley's murder.

On 10 December Elizabeth announced that nothing had been proved against Mary or the lords who had deposed her. But Mary had not been cleared of the charge of murder, and that gave Elizabeth a pretext to keep her in captivity. From the Lennoxes' point of view it was justice of a sort, although not what they had hoped for. Nevertheless Margaret now felt that they could move on: 'Time at the last my cares did exile,' she later recalled, 'and Fortune prepared afresh for to smile' – but 'her pleasant looks did last but small while'.[102]

18

'Business Most Vile'

Queen Elizabeth, wishing to avoid offending the lords of Scotland, now put an end to speculation that the young James VI was to be brought up in England. On 22 January 1569 she issued a proclamation in which she stated 'that there has never been any secret practice betwixt her and [Moray] that the Queen of Scots' son should be delivered to her to be nourished in England. It is true that some motion has been made by the Earl and Countess of Lennox that in case the Prince could not continue in safety in Scotland he might be nourished in England under the custody of such as now have the charge of him.'[1] This must have been a crushing blow for the Lennoxes. In the early weeks of 1569, embarrassed by their creditors in London, they sought and obtained leave to go to Yorkshire.[2] They were now ready to lead a quieter life, spending time on their estates, and venturing when invited to court.

With the Queen of Scots neutralised – or so Elizabeth hoped – the way was now clear for the Protestant government in Scotland to consolidate its rule and make common cause with England. Religion, the need to unite against Catholic Europe, and the increasingly realistic prospect of a united succession had drawn the two kingdoms together as never before. Both Moray and Elizabeth were concerned to preserve the status quo.

To do this Moray needed to destroy Maitland, who had come out in support of the deposed Mary and was working for her restoration. Maitland was arrested at Stirling on 2 September for Darnley's murder, in which he may well have been involved; but he was rescued from his captors by Sir William Kirkcaldy of Grange, who carried him off to Edinburgh Castle, which Grange was holding for Mary. This coalition between Scotland's greatest politician and its greatest soldier was a blow to Moray, who lacked the artillery to take the mighty fortress.

On 26 October 1569 Elizabeth wrote to Sir Henry Norris, her ambassador in Paris. She had no need, she said, to tell him of 'the misfortune of the Queen of Scots to have her husband foully murdered, who indeed was our nearest kinsman on our father's side', or how the 'principal murderer was by her also married and maintained in certain tyranny against the estates of her realm, who sought, as they allege, to have her delivered from such an abominable husband and the country from such a tyrant'. Norris was to impress upon King Charles and anyone else who favoured Mary 'that, by our own means only, her life was saved in her captivity', and that Mary had been treated honourably ever since. Elizabeth had been urged to bring her to justice 'by the father and mother of her husband murdered, whose mother, namely the Lady Margaret, attending upon us in our court, was daughter to our aunt, the Scottish Queen, and sister also to the King of Scots; such circumstances were produced to argue her guilty', but the result of the ensuing enquiry had pleased neither herself nor Mary.[3]

The Lennoxes were back at court by October, when Throckmorton had 'a few words' with Lennox at Greenwich. Lennox said he 'marvelled that the Queen of Scots, a woman so ill thought of heretofore, began now to find friends and to be favoured in England and Scotland'. Throckmorton replied that 'three things moved that; first, her misery; second, her entertainment of such as came to her; and third, the opinion that some had of her title in succession. Both he and the Earl then said that they prayed God to preserve the Queen's Majesty, for neither of them would be glad to live under the Queen of Scots.'[4]

Elizabeth had need of such prayers, for in November the northern earls, Northumberland and Westmorland, and their Catholic adherents rose in rebellion with the aim of deposing her and setting up the Queen of Scots in her place. It was the most dangerous and challenging threat to her rule that she had yet faced, and the rising was ruthlessly suppressed, with more than six hundred men suffering execution and others being forced to flee into exile. The Lennoxes, like many Catholic peers, had not been involved, but they were known to have been friendly with the rebel earls, and this must have been a tense time for them.[5]

Maitland's trial was scheduled for 21 November. On the 13th Drury reported that Moray had forbidden large numbers of Maitland's friends to attend. 'Lord and Lady Lennox and their son have been summoned to compère that day.'[6] But when it came, Maitland, from the safety of Edinburgh Castle, declared he would not 'proceed with the trial at that time',[7] and there was nothing that Moray could do about it.

The ever-present problem of the succession was never far from the minds of those with a vested interest in England's future. On 18 January 1570 Guerau de Spes informed King Philip that, although Elizabeth would not declare a successor, she was 'bringing up with much more state [panoply of rank] than formerly' the two sons of Katherine Grey and the Earl of Hertford. Huntingdon's claim was 'greatly damaged by having no children, and but little following, whilst Lady Margaret, who deserves every good thing, has less still'.[8] The murder of Darnley had left the Lennoxes looking like yesterday's news, but there was still an important part for them to play on the political stage.

On 23 January 1570 the Regent Moray was assassinated at Linlithgow. Whatever else the Lennoxes might have thought of him, they recognised that he had been a strong protector of the young James VI. Shocked and alarmed at the news, their first fear was that Elizabeth might now set Mary free, or James fall prey to the rivalry of the noble factions in Scotland. The only remedy, they felt, was that he be brought to safety in England, to be raised by his loving grandparents.[9]

Five days after Moray's murder the Earl of Mar, James's governor, asked Cecil to forward a letter to Queen Elizabeth, 'firmly looking to your good means to receive her Majesty's favourable answer with some taste of that comfort which this realm and I shall receive at her Highness' hands in this difficult and sorrowful time. I also pray you to deliver this other packet to my Lord or Lady Lennox.'[10]

On 30 January Lord Hunsdon wrote to the Queen, from Berwick, that Morton and other Lords of the Congregation had made it plain that 'the Queen of England would find them ready to run the same course that [Moray] did, so that they might be sure that she would stand with them, and help them in the preservation of their laws. If she will send the Earl of Lennox into Scotland they will make him the head of their faction.'[11] Elizabeth, however, would not commit to recommending Lennox or allow him to go to Scotland.

Margaret was worried about Lennox. The news of Moray's assassination had deeply shocked him at a time when he was not in good health and feeling every one of his fifty-three years. He was not looking to be regent, but to support whoever the Scots might choose. He was even prepared fervently to embrace the Protestant faith. However, his foremost concern, and Margaret's, was the welfare and upbringing of King James, and they hurried south to London to press for him to be brought to England, petitioning Elizabeth, as 'her poor orators and suppliants', that 'she would consider the great danger, Moray being murdered, that your Majesty's fatherless and desolate poor orphan and kinsman remaineth presently in, and take in hand the protection and defence of the said King and his realm, so that his enemies, both those at liberty and those in captivity, may not prevail against him'. They beseeched the Queen, 'of her goodness and pity, to take measures for the safety of that little innocent, that he may be delivered into her Majesty's hands'.[12]

The Lennoxes lodged at Somerset Place, the great Renaissance mansion that Protector Somerset had built on the Strand between 1547 and 1551. It had passed to the Crown on his execution in 1552, and was still unfinished. Elizabeth I had lived here during Mary I's reign; after her accession she had allowed various ambassadors to use the house, and she had made it available to the Lennoxes while they were in London. They remained there until at least the following September, when Margaret dated a letter at Somerset Place.[13]

On 2 February Margaret wrote a long letter to Cecil succinctly outlining her fears for her husband and grandson, and the couple's position in regard to Lennox's role in Scotland and James's welfare:

After my most hearty commendations to you, good Master Secretary, I doubt not but you know partly how many sorrowful griefs I have passed. I thank God of all besides this late chance that hath appeared by the dea[th] of the Lord Regent of Scotland, being not one of the least, but chiefly it toucheth me nearest to see my lord my husband, who and I have been together this twenty-six years, fall into such an extreme heaviness, being very evil at ease since this discomfortable news of Scotland came, so that if he continue any time in the same, I fear he can not long endure, his inward grief is such, and I am not able by any means to comfort him – saying that, only [unless] God of His great mercy and pity put to his helping hand, he sees plainly the destruction of that little innocent King near at hand, wishing of God, that before that day should come, seeing that he cannot be suffered to be there in place, and now in time of need to have been a helper and a strengthening to the said innocent King against his enemies, that God would take him out of this miserable life.

The two principal causes that chiefly grieve and feareth my lord is, that the principal enemies of the said King, and guilty of his father's death, as he is informed, are put to liberty, and he, being the grandfather, to his great grief absent from him, who of right must needs have been the chiefest pillar and strength to the said King in that realm.

Lennox feared that his past record in Scotland had counted against his being considered for a role in the regency Council.

My lord sayeth further, that he thinketh two causes have been, and are the let [prevention] of his going thither – the one for religious cause, and the other for bearing of rule, which, if he had been suffered to have gone [to Scotland], he would have put all that hath such an opinion of him out of that error. As for religion, it should never have fared the worse for him, but rather the better; and for the bearing of rule there as a regent or governor, his mind was never so to do, nor to have troubled himself withal, being of the years which he is of, but to have been an assistant to such noblemen as the Queen's Majesty here, and the state there, should have thought meet to have taken the government of that realm, and my lord to have had but only the keeping of the said King's person, and the nobleman that is in possession thereof already to have joined with him, and thus should the Queen have had good proof of his good service both to the King and state there, and also to the Queen's Majesty here, ere it had been long. But he sayeth that, seeing he cannot perceive that her Highness is willing that he go into that realm, his most humble suit unto her Majesty is to be a means that the said King may be brought into this her Highness' realm, and so to be nourished here under her Majesty's protection and keeping, for the better safety of his person, wherein he most heartily desireth you to be a means unto her Majesty for.

Otherwise my lord most humbly craveth and beseecheth her Majesty, for God's cause, to be a mean that the said King may be delivered into his hands, and with her Majesty's favour he may depart with him to some foreign country for the safety in that realm; otherwise, whosoever bears authority in that realm, as long as he tarries within the same, makes no account of that young innocent's life.

My lord sayeth that he doth not blame her Majesty of his stay here, for he knows right well it is not long of her Highness, knowing the godly and good nature her Majesty is of, but such as have been this long time his back [former] friends, not having deserved it at their hands, wishing of God that they may mean truly and faithfully towards her Majesty as he doth.

Now, good Master Secretary, after I have made the discourse of this my grief unto you as touching my lord, and although her Majesty were willing that he should go into Scotland, and in health and strength of body, as presently he is not yet in, I cannot see how his purse can be able to take that chargeable journey in hand, being in such poor state as presently we are; for lately I have been forced to lay my jewels in gage [pawn] for money to bear the ordinary charges of our house.

Thus leaving to trouble you no further, I commit you, good Master Secretary, to God's holy protection.

From the Queen's Majesty's house of Somerset Place this Candlemas Day.

Your assured loving friend, Margaret, Countess.[14]

On 25 February 1570 an outraged Pope Pius V, learning of the harsh suppression of the Northern Rebellion, excommunicated Elizabeth and charged all true Catholics 'and all and singular the nobles, subjects, peoples and others aforesaid that they do not dare obey her orders, mandates and laws. Those who shall act to the contrary we include in the like sentence of excommunication.'[15] Soon afterwards the Pope made it clear that anyone who assassinated the English Queen would not only receive absolution but would find favour in Heaven. Thereafter the English government would be suspicious of Catholics and treat them as potential enemies of the state rather than religious dissidents. The implications for Margaret were serious.

On 25 February Spes told King Philip that it had been suggested that the English and Scots should agree to the appointment of Lennox as regent, but he feared that might not happen as 'the Queen of England does not like him'.[16] However, there was no other obvious candidate to serve as Moray's successor, and on 26 February Elizabeth let Randolph know that 'if the Earl of Lennox's coming be generally liked by her friends, she will then condescend to it'.[17] Lennox was her subject, and could be expected to look to her interests in Scotland.[18]

Again the Lennoxes faced an indefinite separation, but they had the interests of their grandson at heart, and Lennox wanted to seize the opportunity of putting paid once and for all to the Hamiltons' pretensions. He bade farewell to Margaret and travelled north, but on 16 April he wrote to Cecil from Boroughbridge, Yorkshire, to say he understood 'that the remains of his living in Scotland is gone'. He would 'do any service he can for her Majesty in that country, but cannot proceed any further unless he has some relief of money'.[19] He nevertheless pressed on to Berwick, where, on 22 April, he asked Cecil to forward a letter to his wife.[20]

It has been stated that Lennox rode north with Margaret,[21] who was supportive of his playing an active role in Scottish politics, and that at Berwick Margaret was detained in England, and Lennox had to go on to Scotland without her.[22] But it is quite clear from his letters that Margaret had had to remain at court with Charles, probably as sureties that Lennox would be amenable to Elizabeth's policies. Nevertheless this would work to his advantage, as Margaret very ably continued to represent his interests at Elizabeth's court.[23]

On 27 April Lennox reported that he had fallen extremely ill 'with sickness and hot fevers, and was never so near death as in his last fit, so can neither do service or help his friends, save by a small portion of money, being half the little store he had, which he has sent to Morton and the others for keeping together two hundred soldiers who have done [him] such good service at Glasgow'.[24] In another dispatch to Cecil he wrote: 'I send a letter herewith to my wife to let her understand of my sickness, but not the extremity thereof.'[25] He enclosed another letter for Margaret two days later.[26]

On 1 May, still at Berwick, Lennox informed Cecil: 'Having escaped my fits of this most hot and dangerous fever, I have thought good to advertise my wife thereof by this other letter, which I pray you send to her. It shall not want in me, God willing, to perform that which I have taken in hand as soon as I am able to travel.'[27]

On 11 May, before departing from Berwick, Lennox wrote to the Queen:

I am presently entering into this troublesome country where my fortune heretofore has been very hard. I leave behind me within your Majesty's realm your poor kinswoman my wife, and only son, whom I recommend to your goodness and protection. Although she and I have given but small cause to any to bear us evil will, yet, I know we are not without some back friends, and what cause they have to be so I know not, unless it be in doing your Majesty service, which we do not repent us of, nor ever will so long as your Majesty stands our good lady.

At Windsor, in the beginning of these late troubles, I told your Highness that my wife and I had gotten some enemies in serving you, and if they be such as may hinder us at your hand, I beseech you graciously to consider of it. I am forced at this present to be so bold as to beseech your Majesty that these reports may not take place in your sight, but as the just proof of my doings may bear witness for me, so I trust my proceedings shall be such that, if I mislike the country where I now go, I shall not fear to return to your Majesty's presence again.[28]

Furnished by Drury with an armed escort, Lennox crossed the border into Scotland.[29] Reporting his progress to Cecil, he enclosed his letter for the Queen and one for Margaret.[30] On 5 May Morton and a host of other lords wrote to Elizabeth to say that they would choose anyone she nominated as regent.[31] Her candidate was already on their doorstep. Spes believed she had had an ulterior motive in recommending Lennox to the Scottish lords:

She wishes to make him and his wife, Lady Margaret, her creatures by the appointment, [although] she has kept them always imprisoned and in disgrace for the cause of religion and other reasons. She can do no more against them, and is forwarding his appointment as governor to disarm any future enmity from him. She thinks that because he has his wife, son, and estate in this country, she can be assured that he will govern as her instrument.[32]

On 13 May Lennox entered Edinburgh, as he reported, 'much to the comfort of the nobility here, who are very thankful to the Queen for her supply and aid in this time of need'.[33] On 17 May he was at Stirling, and able to tell Cecil that, at his coming, his adversaries – 'the King's rebels' – had fled. He added, 'As I have no letter to write unto my wife, I desire you to impart the effect of this letter unto her, and let her understand that I have seen the King her oye [grandson], greatly to my comfort.'[34]

The Lennoxes had not supported the aims of the northern rebels, and are not known to have been questioned by the Council, but it appears that at least two of Margaret's gentlemen had been arrested on suspicion of involvement in the rising. Thomas Bishop, who had now allied himself with Queen Mary's supporters, had been questioned several times about his part in it. In March his second son, another Thomas, had been beheaded at York for his part in the rebellion. On 22 May Bishop wrote a deposition for the Council concerning his 'knowledge of the late rebellion'. In September 1569, in London, he had been approached by a servant of the Earl of Northumberland, who had informed him that the Earl was about to take up arms, and asked Bishop to warn them of the anticipated advance of the Queen's forces under the duplicitous Duke of Norfolk. Bishop had left London in October and travelled north. At Topcliffe he met with Northumberland and told him he had heard that Norfolk had been imprisoned in the Tower. One of Northumberland's companions asked Bishop, 'I am sure you have heard by the Earl [Lennox] or his lady since your coming, that there was aid promised us by Spain, what think ye thereof?' Bishop said nothing to that, but advised delaying the rising.

When the north rose in revolt, Bishop had given the earls advice on assaulting York. Now he protested that his concern had been for 'the safety of York', and that, for 'disclosing of the conspiracy of rebellion, and this last saving of York, I ought to have some favour for life at least'. His enmity towards Margaret still festered. He claimed to have one of her gentlemen with him, as well as a servant of the Queen, and stated that, 'as for my knowledge from that lady [Margaret]', he affirmed and stood by what he had said about her.[35] It seems he was somehow trying to implicate her in the rebellion.

His protests and slurs availed him nothing. Bishop spent seven years in the Tower for his dealings with Mary's adherents. After his release in 1576 he returned to Scotland, and died before 1611.[36]

In June Lennox was appointed lieutenant general of Scotland, which gave him overall military command. He wrote from Stirling that he had found 'the nobility and State here very well bent to the Queen of England's devotion, and promises for his part to set forward all that may tend to her service to the uttermost of his power'.[37]

He was in frequent touch with Margaret. On 13 and 22 June he sent further letters to her.[38] On 7 July he thanked Randolph for 'your gentle letter, and the other ye sent from my wife – of no great importance, but I look to hear from her ere long'.[39] The next day he desired Randolph 'that a packet of letters may be forwarded to his wife'.[40] On 13 July Randolph sent on more letters from Lennox to Margaret,[41] and on 5 August Lennox asked Thomas Radcliffe, Earl of Sussex, to 'send this packet to my wife with the first post'.[42]

On 12 July, at the urging of Queen Elizabeth, Morton and Mar elected Lennox regent, and on the 17th he was sworn and proclaimed.[43] Lennox knew he owed his office to Elizabeth and that maintaining her support would be crucial in the face of opposition to his rule. Soon afterwards he wrote to Cecil:

> the Queen's Majesty's advice anent [concerning] the establishment of the regiment [rule] of this realm was to us right comfortable. And although the burden which is laid on my shoulders is weighty and dangerous, yet could I not refuse it, in respect of his [James's] preservation, that is so dear to me. Whereunto I am the more encouraged, and the less fear all perils, by reason of her Majesty's gracious advice given.[44]

Lennox's appointment was bitterly opposed by his foes, the Hamiltons, whose enmity was fatally to overshadow his regency, and by Bothwell's adherents and others who feared his determination to avenge Darnley's murder. There were many in Scotland who still remembered and resented his treachery in deserting to the English during the Rough Wooing. He also faced opposition from the Marian party, who were appealing to Elizabeth to have the deposed Queen Mary restored and refused to acknowledge Lennox as regent. One of their leaders, Kirkcaldy of Grange, resolved to hold Edinburgh Castle on her behalf, and did so for three years. Maitland, whose house Lennox despoiled in the conviction that the former secretary had been instrumental in the murder of Darnley, stood staunchly beside Grange and Mary's other supporters.[45]

On 6 August Lennox was warned of a conspiracy 'made for his slaughter' by Châtelherault's younger son, Lord Claud Hamilton, who had planned to ambush Lennox as he rode from Edinburgh to Stirling.[46] In retaliation, Lennox summarily hanged more than thirty men, provoking howls of outrage from his enemies.[47] On 17 August Spes observed, 'Lennox is not obeyed in Scotland.'[48] But when Queen

Mary's ardent supporter and commissioner at the York conference, John Leslie, Bishop of Ross, complained to Elizabeth of the new Regent's brutality, she answered that 'she never heard anything before of Lennox's cruelty, which she affirmed to be cruelty indeed, but judged the same to proceed rather of the counsel of others than of his own nature, who was but a simple man, and therefore suspected Morton's counsel'.[49]

That August Lennox, 'having some suspicion of his servant, John Moon', had 'caused him to be searched at his departure from Edinburgh, when there was found on him above twenty letters in cipher' from Maitland and others to the Queen of Scots.[50] The defection of Moon meant that Lennox now decided to rely on Margaret to relay his official dispatches and letters to the English government and maintain support for his regency.[51] He sent her a letter via Sussex on 26 August,[52] and thereafter they were in frequent communication. Margaret's opinions carried much weight with Lennox; he trusted her entirely. It could not be said that she was ruling Scotland at one remove, but her influence was undoubtedly felt there.

On 8 September, alarmed to hear that Lennox was perturbed by a report that Elizabeth was thinking of returning Mary to Scotland, Margaret wrote to Cecil from Somerset Place:

Good Master Secretary,

You shall understand that I have heard of some commissioners that shall go to the Queen of Scotland to treat with her of matters tending to her liberty to go hither, of which she herself doth already make assured account; the knowledge whereof being to me of no small discomfort, considering that, notwithstanding the grievous murder which, by her means only, was upon my dear son, her husband, executed, divers persons in this realm doth yet doubt, and a great many doth credit, that since her coming hither she is found clear and not to be culpable of that fact; because, as they say, that since all the conferences had between the nobility touching that matter, it has not been made known that the said Queen was found any way guilty therein. Much more so when they, already displeased, shall see her released to go home at her pleasure, though on some devised conditions to serve the present, their former conceits shall be verified, and they being satisfied, it may appear that she has sustained insufferable wrongs in being restrained so long for no offence. The rest I refer to your wisdom.

My husband being there, whither if she do come, he cannot so well serve the Queen's Majesty's turn as now. Just as nature binds me respecting the state of the young King in his minority, I am enforced to crave your friendship herein, and to impart this my meaning to her Majesty, whose Highness, I trust, will hold me excused, considering whereon I ground my desire for the stay of her who otherwise, I doubt, will stir up such ill as hereafter – all too late – may be repented. If the Queen and her Council think it right that she be delivered, I trust my lord and the nobility there shall be made privy to that order before its conclusion.

Beseeching you to impart this my letter to the Earl of Leicester, whose friendship I assure myself of in this behalf.

Margaret Lennox.[53]

Elizabeth heeded Margaret's request; it suited her policy to do so.

On 16 September Lennox sent a letter 'to the right honourable the Lady Margaret my wife', instructing her to act as his representative at Elizabeth's court. He would henceforth be channelling all information through her, placing her at the very forefront of affairs.

My good Meg, I have considered the letters brought unto me by this bearer, William Stewart, as well from yourself as from the court, with such other things as he reported by mouth, and in respect of the state of matters, both in that realm and here in this country, I have thought meet to return him again with speed unto you, with such information as for the present is meet to be sent, while as I may have the commodity to send a messenger instructed sufficiently in all behalfs to deal as well with the Queen's Majesty as with my lords of the Council in the same matters, and such others as shall occur, and unto that time you must sustain a part of my burden to use the place of a solicitor and agent, as well in delivering of my letters to her Majesty and to my lords according to the directions, as also in declarations of such things as are contained in the memoir and notes herewith enclosed, which behoved to be written apart, being so long. I cannot well commit the handling of those matters, being of such weight, to any other than yourself; neither am I assured if other messengers would be so well liked of, nor if the personages with whom you have to deal would be so plain and frank with others, as they will be with you, and so I thought not meet to commit them to this bearer (although I could well trust him), he being so young. I have also sent unto you herewith two letters written in cipher by Lethington [Maitland], and apprehended with John Moon, which you shall deliver to Mr Secretary, for peradventure he may find the mean to decipher them.

Your own most loving husband, Matthew, Regent.[54]

The enclosures, which Margaret was to hand to Cecil, apparently consisted of lists of noble Scottish partisans of either King James or Queen Mary.[55]

That day Lennox informed the Queen that he had 'instructed his wife to make known to her the state of affairs in Scotland' and report on the welfare of the young King. He beseeched Elizabeth to 'grant her favourable audience' and give credit to what she had to report.[56]

Lennox also wrote to Cecil, asking him to give 'advice for his wife in certain matters which she will impart to him'.[57]

Margaret still enjoyed the friendship of the influential Leicester, who was closer to the Queen than any other. It may have been at her suggestion that on 16 September Lennox wrote to Leicester to say that he meant to serve Elizabeth like 'a very natural born subject', and that his chief reason for accepting the regency was 'the preservation of this young King'. He assured Leicester that he would 'always direct my proceedings principally by her Majesty's advice'.[58]

On 21 September Margaret wrote to Cecil:

Good Master Secretary, such letters as I have received from my lord I send you to peruse, and if I had been at the court, as my lord hoped, I would have imparted them to you myself. My hope is only in God and your wisdoms to foresee the dangers that may happen if that realm should understand the parlementing [parleying] with the Queen of Scots, as by these notes you may perceive. I have sent to you my old and trusty servant, Mompesson, with this bearer, to impart to him your good pleasure. Committing you to God's holy protection. Somerset Place.

Margaret Lennox.[59]

Later that month she wrote again to Cecil, in ironic vein and businesslike fashion:

I thank you for your commendations by this bearer, and also for your lines sent by Mompesson to me, wherein you wrote my prayer would fight with [i.e. support] my lord in his affairs. I assure you I do what I can in that and all other ways. Such as I receive I send you herewith, which are two copies, although I doubt not but you have the one before, which is the principal suit to my Lord Lieutenant.

I sent you a packet by the post to London, in which there were two books of written hand, and one letter to yourself, and another to my lord concerning John Moon – which now I perceive God has caused to be opened – to my lord. God doth much for him. I beseech Him so it may continue.

Margaret Lennox.[60]

On 23 September Elizabeth licensed Lennox 'to remain in Scotland as long as it shall seem to him convenient, except she shall find any reasonable cause for her service to send for him'.[61] Margaret must have been saddened to learn that their separation was to be prolonged, but she would certainly have understood the need for it.

On 4 October John Moon was interrogated and tortured at Doune Castle. He revealed a conspiracy involving several persons, and mentioned that at the persuasion of one Andrew Abercrombie, Margaret had secretly urged Lennox 'to hinder nothing that might hinder the Queen of Scots' cause'. 'After further pains', Moon revealed that Thomas Bishop had been 'the first trafficker' between him and John Leslie, Bishop of Ross. Another conspirator had told Moon that, during the hearings of the commission, Queen Mary had written to the Bishop of Ross, enclosing a letter to Margaret, and asked him to present it to her and work for a reconciliation between them.[62] This is the first evidence of Mary trying to win over Margaret to her cause.

Margaret was now with the court at Windsor, and from there, on 5 October, she wrote once more to the absent Cecil, revealing how much she had been missing her husband, and showing how friendly and confidential her relations with the Queen had become:

Good Master Secretary,

Being now in court I sought the way how I might visit you with these few lines, not for any fear ye should be won, which, as her Majesty tells me, she did speak to you at your departing, but to let you understand how her Majesty hath had some talks to me touching my lord. She said fault was found for [his] executing those of the Queen of Scots' part [i.e. the Hamilton adherents], howbeit my lord was holden excused and all laid upon the Earl of Morton. The Bishop of Ross did much commend my lord's good nature.

Her Majesty said she remembered how I wept and wished my lord at home when she was at Oatlands. I answered that since that time he had a great burden laid upon him, which made me not to do so now. Her Majesty said that, if it were not for that little one [James], she thought he [Lennox] could not like her [probably a reference to Margaret] being here. Her Majesty says that Queen [Mary] works many worse.

She meant that others had suffered worse than Margaret on Mary's account.

I ensured [assured] her Majesty [that she] was good lady to her [Mary], and better I thought than any other prince would have been if they were in her cause, for she had stayed publishing abroad her ill use, which was manifestly known. More talks there was, but this was the chief.

I long much till your coming home. Much ado I had to get a lodging here, for that I had first was taken from my man.

This I unburden my mind to you as to him whom I trust hath most care of the good estate of the realm and the preservation of the Queen's Majesty, and a friend to me and mine, which is to my power ye shall find, as knoweth God, who send you good return.

From the court at Windsor.

Margaret Lennox.[63]

Margaret's letters to Cecil show that over time there had developed a genuine affection between them, and a satisfactory professional relationship. On 10 October she sent him another letter:

Master Secretary,

I can not but visit you with some lines, my lord's man coming there. I beseech you to remember, next to our sovereign lady, that innocent King of Scotland, that he and her may not be the worse for any treaty. I pray you to make my hearty commendations to Master [Sir Walter] Mildmay,[64] whom I do request for the same. I assure you I find her Majesty well minded for the preservation of him [King James], and those that belongs to him. I travail as I can. God speed me well, and inspire her Majesty's heart to do for her own surety, and then I know the rest shall fare the better. I will not trouble you with a longer letter, but send you my hearty commendations.

From the court at Windsor, this x of October.

Your assured friend, Margaret Lennox.

I pray you, good Master Secretary, certify my lord my husband of his request declared to you by this bearer.[65]

Lennox's regency was marred by strife and internecine warfare in Scotland. Yet it did smooth relations between Scotland and England, for he ruled as a stout Protestant and a loving guardian of his grandson the King; and Margaret's handling of his affairs in London must have helped in no small measure. Lennox was too busy to see James as often as he would have wished, but he had the little boy with him whenever possible, and in 1570, when the King was five, he appointed the brilliant Calvinist scholar George Buchanan, one of his own affinity, as his tutor. Inevitably Buchanan, in line with his master's prejudices, would poison James's mind against his mother, the Queen of Scots, and bring him up to regard her as an adulteress and murderess. Margaret would have been gratified to hear that, but saddened that her grandson was being brought up in the reformed faith. However, she would have applauded Lennox ordering the demolition of the ruinous choir of Holyrood Abbey and the construction of a new royal vault for the remains of Darnley, James V and other kings and queens who had been buried there.

When, on 8 November, Margaret was summoned before Elizabeth, she must have been astonished to be given a letter from the Queen of Scots, addressed 'To my Lady Lennox, my mother-in-law'. It had been sent from Chatsworth, Derbyshire, on 10 July and intercepted. Mary had been concerned about James's safety in Scotland, but she was worried about the consequences if he was brought into England, and would have preferred that he be spirited away to Spain so that he could be brought up a Catholic. Fearing that there was a very real prospect of her son ending up in the Lennox household, Mary had thought it best to court her mother-in-law's support. Her tone, however, was injured, and not likely to arouse Margaret's sympathy.

Madame,

If the wrong and false reports of rebels, enemies well known for traitors to you, and, alas! too much trusted of me, by your advice, had not so far stirred you against my innocency, and I must say against all kindness, that you have not only, as it were, condemned me wrongfully, but so hated me, as some words and open deeds has testified to all the world a manifest misliking in you against your own blood, I would not have omitted thus long my duty in writing to you, excusing me of these untrue reports made of me. But hoping, with God's grace, and time, to have my innocency known to you, as I trust it is already to the most part of all indifferent persons. I thought best not to trouble you for a time, till now that such a matter is moved that toucheth us both, which is the transporting of your little [grand]son, and my only child, into this country; to the which, albeit I were never so willing, yet I would be glad to have your advice therein, as in all other matters touching him.

I have borne him, and God knoweth with what danger to him and to me both, and of you he is descended, so I mean not to forget my duty to you in showing herein any unkindness to you, how unkindly soever ye have dealt by me, but will love you as my aunt, and respect you as my mother-in-law. And if ye please to know farther of my mind in that and all other things betwixt us, my ambassador, the Bishop of Ross, shall be ready to confer with you.

And so, after my hearty commendations, remitting me to my said ambassador, and your better consideration, I commit you to the protection of Almighty God, whom I pray to preserve you and my brother Charles and cause you to know my part better nor ye now do. Your natural good niece and loving daughter-in-law.[66]

Margaret must have seen this extending of the olive branch for the pragmatic move it was. She did not send a reply, probably on the instructions of the Queen or Cecil, which accorded with her own inclinations, but forwarded the letter to Lennox. His response was unequivocal: he reminded Margaret that he had evidence of Mary's guilt 'by her own hand writ, as well as by the confessions of two men gone to the death', henchmen of Bothwell's.

What can I say but that I do not marvel to see her write the best [she] can for herself. It will be long time that is able to put a matter so notorious in oblivion, to make black white, or innocency to appear where the contrary is so well known. The most indifferent, I trust, doubts not of the equity of your and my cause, and of the just occasion of our misliking. Her right duty to you and me were her true confession and unfeigned repentance of that lamentable fact, odious for her to be reported, and sorrowful for us to think of. God is just and will not in the end be abused; but as He has manifested the truth, so will He punish the iniquity.[67]

In December Lennox was unwell.[68] Margaret must have worried constantly about her husband's health and what was happening to him in Scotland. In January 1571 Drury reported that 'the Regent's party decays daily and great weakness is found in him'.[69] On 22 January 1571 Spes reported that the English government was urgently trying 'to find means of assuring the safety of the Earl of Lennox, whose life is in great danger by reason of the executions which he has carried out'.[70] In February Sir Francis Walsingham, Elizabeth's ambassador in Paris, informed Cecil that 'one of those who have the government of the young King of Scots has promised to kill the Earl of Lennox, and prepare an army if they will furnish him with money'.[71]

That month Margaret received £800 (£140,000) 'of the Queen's Majesty's gift',[72] probably in recognition of her good services. On 7 February Kirkcaldy of Grange was informed that 'the Lady Lennox [was] most busy of all' in working against Mary.[73]

In March 1571 Lennox sent Buchanan's brother Thomas to Frederick II, King of Denmark and Norway, to ask that Bothwell be extradited back to Scotland to face interrogation. This, naturally, caused bad blood between him and Morton, who had good reason not to want Bothwell – who had protested Mary's innocence throughout – giving evidence as to who had actually been responsible for Darnley's murder. And what Lennox learned from King Frederick only fed that enmity.[74]

In February Lennox, encouraged by Queen Elizabeth, had gone to war with the Hamiltons. He emerged triumphant, and on 2 April recaptured Dumbarton Castle,[75] which had been held by Mary's supporters. There he found evidence of Mary's treacherous dealings with Spain, of which he immediately informed Queen Elizabeth.

Lurking in the castle was John Hamilton, Archbishop of St Andrews, who had been hiding there ever since Langside, when he had supported Queen Mary's bid to regain her throne and been condemned as a traitor for it. Lennox now took him prisoner and sent him to Stirling, where he was indicted for being 'art and part' of the murders of Darnley and the Regent Moray. On 6 April the Archbishop was hanged in his vestments and quartered.[76]

Lennox fought his way on to Leith, then entered Edinburgh, where in the Canongate he held what became known as 'the Creeping Parliament', because its members had to creep about under fire from Edinburgh Castle, which Grange, Maitland and Mary's other supporters occupied.[77] Lennox had to reconvene Parliament at Stirling, and send one of his English captains to London 'to beg for ten thousand crowns and some artillery and ammunition to batter the castle of Edinburgh'.[78]

Scotland was in turmoil, and there are now fewer references in the beleaguered Lennox's letters to enclosures for Margaret, yet it is clear that the couple were in constant touch, and that Margaret was kept fully informed about affairs in Scotland, and did what she could to further Lennox's interests and aid his supporters. On 11 May payment was made to a boy 'passing the post to Stirling with one mass of close writing that came from my Lady Lennox'.[79] On 26 May Lennox wrote to Cecil, newly ennobled as Lord Burghley, asking him to credit Margaret and the messenger.[80] On 1 June, from Stirling, he sent to Margaret a letter of recommendation for an old acquaintance, the Laird of Galston, who was now in Lennox's service and needed an English passport so that he could travel to France to attend to his private interests there.[81] On 30 June Drury informed Burghley: 'Yesterday letters came hither to the Regent from Lady Lennox.'[82] In September John Case, who appears to have been an English spy, would reveal to Drury that Margaret got to see most of his (Drury's) reports.[83]

On 25 June Margaret's nephew, William, Lord Ruthven,[84] wrote to her from Leith, saying that he 'desires to hear of the welfare of herself and Mr Charles, her son, and wishes that there were such quietness here that she might arrive in this realm. His Majesty (God save him) increases so daily both in growth of person and judgment, that it is a great comfort to all his faithful subjects, and displeasant to the enemies, whom, he doubts not, God will consume in a short time.' Ruthven could not 'half express in writing the good qualities appearing in his Majesty, and the good success that

God of his mercy gives to my lord's Grace [Lennox] daily in all his proceedings'.[85]

On 1 July Drury wrote again to Burghley to say that 'the misliking of the Regent of both parties increases, and if he tarries he will find neither surety or quietness'.[86] A letter sent by Drury to Burghley on 8 July reveals that Margaret was regarded by some as a formidable force in Scottish politics. It contained an enclosure written by one of Mary's supporters, who had warned his correspondent that 'if he writes anything hereof to the court, to be wise that Lady Lennox gets no knowledge thereof'.[87] He was clearly aware that Margaret took care to keep well informed of events, and feared that she might get wind of a plot to restore Mary to liberty and alert Lennox. That the Lennoxes' correspondence was scrutinised is clear from another letter, written by Drury to Burghley on 24 July: 'I received this packet from the Regent for Lady Lennox, accompanied with this letter to me. May it please you to hold the contents of the letter to yourself till you hear from me again.'[88]

For Margaret, the most welcome news from Lennox was of their grandson. On 27 July, for example, a friend of Margaret, Bess of Hardwick, Countess of Shrewsbury, was informed that Lennox had written to his wife that the young King had a birthmark shaped like a lion on his side.[89]

Lennox's position remained perilous. On 12 August Drury noted, 'If the Queen [Elizabeth] do not further countenance the Regent, he must of force leave either Scotland or his life.' He also noted 'my Lady Lennox's advertisements touching Captain Brickwell and John Case', who were shortly to go to Scotland to discover the intentions of Mary's supporters in Edinburgh Castle. Margaret had written warning Lennox that she had heard how deeply resented he was in Scotland, and that Morton was ready to oust him from the regency.[90] That month, clearly concerned about his safety, and hoping that Elizabeth would offer armed support, Margaret wrote to 'the right honourable my good lord and friend, my Lord Burghley', beseeching him 'to move her Majesty for such comfort as my lord looks for, that the action may not quail. Like as I have always made you privy to my letters, so I do now.'[91]

Margaret was now, quite evidently, an influential force in English politics. Even the Queen listened to her. That summer saw the French pressing for a marriage between Elizabeth and King Charles IX's brother, Henry, Duke of Anjou (the future Henry III), but the Queen, as usual, was blowing hot and cold. In some perplexity, the French ambassador, Bertrand de Salignac de la Mothe Fénélon, sought Margaret's support. He reported their conversation to Catherine de' Medici, the Queen Mother of France:

I have entered into some intelligence with the Countess of Lennox by pretending to promise her much on the part of your Majesty for her infant grandson, James of Scotland, if she and the Earl, her husband, would agree with the Queen of Scots; and I have demonstrated to her that the marriage with Monsieur [Anjou] can not be otherwise than advantageous to her; for if the Queen of England should ever have children, the said Lady Lennox ought to wish them to be French, because of the perfect union there would always be between them and her grandson; and if her Majesty should have no issue, still Monsieur would always be found ready to advance the right of her grandson's right to this crown, against all the others who are now pretending to it.

On this the Countess sent to me, that she entreated your Majesty to take her grandson under your protection, and to believe that her husband was as devoted and affectionate a servant to the [French] Crown as any of his predecessors had been; that she, on her part, desired the marriage of Monsieur with her mistress more than any thing in the world; and that, holding the place nearest to her of any one in this realm, she had already counselled and persuaded to it with all affection.

She had given me all the information on this head that she could, but up to the present hour she could only tell me this, that by all the appearances she could observe in the Queen, she seemed to be not only well-disposed, but very affectionately inclined to the marriage; and that she generally talked of nothing but of Monsieur's virtues and perfections; that she dressed herself better, rejoicing herself, and assuming more beauty and sprightliness, on his account; but that she did not communicate much on this subject with her ladies, and seemed as if she reserved it entirely between herself and the Earl of Leicester and Lord Burghley, whom I should consult to be further enlightened. [92]

It was the right, the only diplomatic advice Margaret could have given, but privately she was probably praying that Elizabeth never would bear children, because they would displace James from the succession.

As she was often required to be at court, Margaret had rented Barber's Barn, an old house on Mare Street in Hackney, five miles north-east of London.[93] Hackney was then a country village, and since the thirteenth century had been much sought after by the well-born and the wealthy. It was a rural area distinguished by its red-brick aristocratic residences and pretty gardens with ancient fruit trees and flowering shrubs. Then, as now, gentrified areas ran side by side with less salubrious parts of the urban sprawl, and nearby Hackney Mead (now Hackney Marsh) was the haunt of thieves and highwaymen. Hackney Wick was then a dairy farm.[94]

Once a property of the Knights Templar, and then the Priory of St John of Jerusalem, Barber's Barn had been built on land known as Barbour Berns; in Henry VIII's reign it had been granted to Henry Percy, Earl of Northumberland, on whose death in 1537 it had reverted to the Crown and been known as the King's Hold, before being granted to William Herbert, Earl of Pembroke.[95] In 1549 he sold it to Edward Carew, whose family held it until 1578 and leased it to Margaret. It was described in 1547 as 'a fair house, all of brick, with a fair hall and parlour, a large gallery, a proper chapel, and a proper library to lay books in'.[96]

Margaret was at Hackney when Lennox's messenger, Captain Robert Cunningham, arrived from Scotland on 19 August. Aware that Lennox's need for English support was now urgent, she wrote to Burghley:

This Saturday Cunningham returned from my lord with writings to her Majesty and my lords of the Council, sufficiently instructed to declare the state of my lord and that country, praying your lordship to solicit the Queen's Majesty that he may present his letter and declare his credit to her Highness conformed to her instructions, for now I must trouble your lordship, seeing I am not present with her Majesty; and to the end your lordship may know further hereafter, you shall receive such letters as my lord and others of the Council there have written to me, which I pray you to move her Majesty to peruse, and to consider thereby that the bruits past or otherwise nor was spoken of, as her Majesty will perceive as well by my letters as by the bearer hereof, whom I desire you to credit, and that her Majesty may believe him, for he is instructed to resolve her Highness in anything that is doubted of in that country.

Last of all, I beseech your lordship to be a means that the actions which my lord has in hand be no longer without resolution of sure and speedy comfort, with the bearer to be hasted again to my lord, for the necessity of the time may bide no longer delay, as your lordship shall perceive as well by the letters sent to me as by the bearer's instructions.

Hackney.

Margaret Lennox.[97]

Drury informed Burghley on 22 August that 'Cunningham has brought Lady Lennox divers letters, disproving such reports as have been sent out of Scotland of doubtfulness in friendship betwixt the Regent and others of the nobility of the King's party, which are but raised to diminish his credit'.[98] Thus Margaret was lulled into a sense of false security.

Her cousin Morton had not been well disposed towards Lennox, but now he was assuring Elizabeth that he was willing to work with him, though only for a price, for on 24 August Drury told Burghley that 'Lady Lennox has advertised the Regent that Morton requires a pension, whereof he is very desirous to know'.[99] The next day Lennox informed Elizabeth that 'Morton and his are at his devotion, though he finds in him some haughtiness and self-liking more than needs'. He protested that he himself had 'given no cause to be misliked of the nobility, as most of they have tasted of his liberality', but 'unless he finds the Queen's goodness in helping him to maintain his force of waged men he will have to leave this place shortly'.[100] A letter from Margaret to Lennox reached Drury on 1 September 1571.[101] It was probably the last one she ever sent him.

On 4 September Drury asked Burghley to keep some of John Case's reports from Margaret, 'otherwise I shall not receive such knowledge as I have done'. The reason for this, as Case himself revealed in the enclosure, written at Stirling, was that 'Lady Lennox gets most of your advertisements and writes them to him, which makes him mislike you so much'.[102]

On 5 September Maitland wrote to Mary, Queen of Scots, about Lord Ruthven's younger brother Archibald,[103] Margaret's nephew, who had 'behaved himself very favourably towards us and all your causes'. Maitland had hopes of Ruthven. 'If he can obtain credit with Lady Lennox, indeed he might be steadable to your cause that way.' But he did not hold out much hope of that.[104]

Standing next to his grandfather, the five-year-old King opened Parliament at Stirling Castle on 3 September. Noticing a gap in the slates that roofed the great hall, he piped up, 'This Parliament has got one hole in it.' This was received by the assembled lords not with amusement, but as a sinister omen.[105]

Margaret was at court when, early in September, 'some Scots, continuing their business most vile, did yield me to drink a cup of new care, wherein of sorrow I tasted my share'. For 'traitors, through treason', did beset her 'dear' with violence.[106]

On Tuesday 4 September 1571, Parliament sat again, but during the previous night a force of Mary's supporters, led by Kirkcaldy of Grange and including the vengeful Hamiltons, had marched on Stirling with the intention of ousting Lennox and his party from power. He was lodging in a house on the market place when, around 4 a.m., 'the Earl of Huntly and the Lairds of Ferniehurst and Buccleuch, accompanied with 280 horsemen, and sixty arquebusiers on horseback, came to Stirling and took the Regent and the earls of Glencairn and Eglington, and a great number of others out of their beds before they could be armed'.[107]

By then, according to Grange, 'our party were masters of the town'. Even though there were in Stirling twenty earls and lords spiritual and temporal, and two thousand men, there was no resistance. As soon as Morton surrendered, Lord Claud Hamilton and others advanced on him with drawn swords, intent on killing him because he had allied with Lennox. Morton was placed under house arrest, but his house was soon besieged and set on fire, as the undisciplined soldiers 'fell to spoiling of the town'. But the Hamiltons were bent on avenging the Archbishop's execution. Lennox and the other noblemen were herded into an assembly, 'that all might be carried away together'.

The plan was to take the captives to Edinburgh, but things went badly awry, as 'with his whole company the Earl of Morton rushed down the street towards the port'.[108] With their captors diverted, Lennox, John Cockburn, Laird of Ormiston, and others managed to escape. But as Ormiston 'and some with him were bringing the Earl of Lennox down another street, in the tumult' both Lennox and Ormiston were wounded by a pistol shot 'by some of the adverse faction'. Morton was rescued.

A Captain George Bell was afterwards to claim that he had met Lennox 'coming down the gait' and cried to Ormiston, 'Gang fast with that man or else ye will not get yourself away nor him, for they are all coming down upon us!' Bell led them to a nearby lodging and there left Lennox to save himself, bidding Ormiston 'tarry with him, for he would be the saving of his life'.[109] Under torture Bell changed his story, and admitted that he incited his men to shoot Lennox, and indeed took part himself.[110] Whatever the truth, Lennox was discovered or ambushed by a Captain James Calder, who had been ordered by Lord Claud Hamilton and the Earl of Huntly to slay him. According to Morton, 'the Regent, after he was taken forth of his house and led away more than two flight shots, was shot with a pistol along his bowels'.[111] A correspondent of Drury's informed him that the bullet passed first through Ormiston, then found its mark in Lennox. 'Some say he was shot negligently by some of his own side; others that it is the Hamiltons in revenge for the Bishop's death.'[112]

Too late, the Earl of Mar with 'forty men came out of the castle there and rescued all the nobility of the Regent's party, and danged the others out of the town', but sixteen of Lennox's men were killed in the skirmish, and thirty-seven were injured. Morton was rescued at the port, and 'the lairds of Buccleuch and Ormiston, and Captain Bell, who was the chief adviser of this attempt, are taken. Forty horsemen and arquebusiers of Edinburgh Castle were taken,'[113] as was Captain Calder. Lennox, although badly injured, called for Ormiston to be spared.[114]

Still on horseback, and probably in agony, Lennox was escorted back into the castle, declaring, 'If the bairn's well, all's well.'[115] Only when he was inside the walls did he dismount.[116] James VI, watching in horror, would never forget the sight of his grandfather with his bowels bleeding, and spent the rest of his life in dread of dying violently.

Lennox was helped to bed and a doctor was summoned, who saw that nothing could be done for him. As he lay dying he looked back over his life, forgave his enemies, and begged the lords gathered around him to protect his grandson. He said to his friend Mar and those around him: 'I am now, my lords, to leave you at God's good pleasure, to go to a world where there is rest and peace. Ye know that it was not my ambition, but your choice, which brought me to the charge I have this while sustained, which I undertook the more willingly because I was assured of your assistance in the defence of the infant King, whose protection, by nature and duty, I could not refuse. And now, being able to do no more, I must commend him to the Almighty God and to your care, entreating you to continue in the defence of his cause, wherein, I do assure you, in God's name, of your victory, and make choice of some worthy person, fearing God and affectionate to the King, to succeed in my place.'[117] Another account states that Lennox declared he had urged the lords 'to favour the revenge of my son, the late King, his death and murder, [and] the welfare of your natural prince'.[118]

As death approached, Lennox's thoughts were of Margaret; he charged Mar and the rest: 'And I must likewise commend unto your favour my servants, who never have received benefit at my hands, and desire you to remember my love to my wife, Meg, whom I beseech God to comfort.' Having commended her to 'the goodness of God',[119] he took leave of them all, one by one, and asked them to join him in his prayers, which he continued for some hours.[120] 'The Regent lived after his hurt till towards night, exhorting all men still to follow the action for maintaining the King.' At four o'clock that afternoon[121] he 'departed to God very peacefully, exhorting all men to follow still the action for the maintenance of the King'.[122]

'He might have lived in England with great ease, were not he was sent about by great men of this realm to accept one charge upon him that he was not able to perform or guide,' observed a contemporary.[123] But the Scottish divine David Calderwood remembered Lennox as a man with 'noble qualities, tried with both fortunes, and if he had enjoyed a longer and more peaceable time, he had doubtless made the kingdom happy by his government'.[124]

19

'Treason Bereft Me'

On 5 September Drury forwarded to Burghley a report that Lennox had been killed, adding, 'If it be true, the Queen's Majesty hath received a great loss, the like in affection she will never find of a Scottish man born.'[1] Elizabeth was at Leez Priory in Essex as the guest of Robert, Lord Rich, when the report arrived three days later. Burghley was with her and immediately informed the Privy Council, but charged them to 'otherwise disperse it not, lest it be not true that he is dead; and I would not have knowledge come to Lady Lennox before she shall have it from the Queen's Majesty'.[2]

When confirmation did come, Elizabeth herself undertook the dreadful task of breaking to Margaret the news that her husband had been killed.[3] After twenty-six years of marital happiness, tragically marred by the loss of seven children and long separations, Margaret, at fifty-six, now found herself facing a bleak widowhood. She was quite devastated with a grief that was 'poignant and perpetual'.[4] 'My anguish was such as to bear was too great, yet to God, by prayer, I still made my way. Thus treason bereft me of my son and mate.' She longed to ask those 'rebels ruthless and falsely forsworn, what meant ye my son and husband to kill? Would God, I wish it, ye had never been born. Woe worth you rebels, chief cause of all my trouble!' She appealed to Heaven that, 'for these great injuries unto me done, God's vengeance in time no doubt will be won'.[5]

Lennox had never been popular in Scotland, where he would be remembered disparagingly as 'the English Regent'.[6] Within twenty hours of his passing it had been agreed that the Earl of Mar should assume the office of regent in his stead.[7] It was arranged that Lennox

should be buried in the Chapel Royal at Stirling Castle, a fitting
sepulchre for one with Stewart blood.[8] Here Margaret built a 'sumptuous sepulchre' to his memory.[9] The chronicler Holinshed recorded
the epitaph she placed there, and possibly composed herself, and in
no sense could it be said to have been written in the spirit of
forgiveness:

> Lo here a prince and potentate, whose life to understand,
> Was godly, just, and fortunate, though from his native land
> His enemies thrice did him out thring [throw], he thrice
>   returned again,
> Was lawful tutor to the King, and regent did remain:
> Where he with rigor rebels racked, the right for to defend,
> Till enemies old through tyrants tracked, did work his
>   fatal end.
> Lo thus respects the death no wight,
> When God permits the time,
> Yet shall the vengeance on them light that wrought that
>   cursed crime.

The tomb also bore 'heroical verses' in which Margaret's love for
her husband shines forth. If she had seen no wrong in him in life,
in death she was determined to proclaim him a paragon – with just
the slightest emphasis on her own royal descent:

> Behold herein interred is Matthew, of Lennox earl,
> Who long of late in Britain's soil, did live a peerless pearl;
> And as he was of royal blood, by royal progeny,
> From Stewart's stock of ancient time, princes of Albany,
> His fortune was even so to match, with passing virtuous
>   wight,
> Whose race derived from famous kings, of wide renowned
>   might.
> His mother[-in-law] queen of Scotland was, and eldest
>   daughter dear,
> Of Henry Seventh, English King, a princely mirror clear.
> Her father earl of Angus was, she Lady Margaret hight
>   [named],
> The only heir of Angus lands, and all his fathers' right.
> Thus did King Brutus blood conjoin, for both by grace divine

Are come of North Wales princes hault [high], which were of
   Trojans' line.[10]
And divers goodlie imps there were, that issued from them
   twain:
Charles; James, now king . . . , of them doth still remain.
King Henry, father to this King, their first-begotten son:
Oh cruel fates! the which so soon, his vital thread unspun;
By whose demise the grandsire came, lord regent in this land:
And nobly bare the regal sword of justice in his hand,
Whereby he did, in tender age of the Kings Majesty,
This realm protect with fortitude, prudence and equity.
But now Dame Fame with flickering wings withouten
   any let,
Shall spread abroad this worthy man, and through the world
   him set;
And tearing time shall not consume, nor wear the same away,
But with the worthiest reckoned be, until the latter day,
After which time, eternity doth triumph then by right,
Where he with angels shall rejoice, in God's eternal sight.[11]

The collegiate chapel at Stirling dated from 1110 and had been
beautified by several Scottish monarchs, but it had been neglected
during the Reformation of the 1560s and was already in poor struc-
tural condition when Lennox's monument was erected. It was
demolished when Margaret's grandson, James VI, built a new one
in 1594 for the baptism of his son, Henry, named for Lord Darnley.
At that time Lennox's tomb was lost, but his bones still rest some-
where beneath the floor.

On 5 and 6 September Captain Bell was interrogated. He recounted
how he had helped Lennox to hide with Ormiston, and admitted
that he had been ordered 'only to take the Regent and the rest';[12]
but his accusers chose to believe that he had deliberately lured
Lennox into a trap, and 'was the chief deviser of this attempt'.[13]
Having finally confessed that 'he was the special deviser of this
enterprise', he was 'put to pains', or tortured, and declared that he
came 'running down the gait' crying, 'Shoot the Regent, the traitors
is coming upon us and ye will not get him away!' Lord Claud
Hamilton had commanded him 'to follow the Regent and slay him,
which he obeyed'.[14]

On 6 September Captain Calder was examined and 'confessed that he slew the Regent by Huntly's and Lord Claud's procurement'.[15] He had 'shot the Regent (which he has taken upon his soul) with his own hand, also that the Earl of Huntly and the whole of the Hamiltons were utterly bent to have slain them both'. Calder had obviously been tortured too, as his confession was signed 'with my hand laid on the pen because I cannot write'.[16]

That day Grange and Maitland, the perpetrators of the plot, wrote to Drury from the safety of Edinburgh Castle: 'We regret most the slaughter of Lennox, because thereby the adverse faction have obtained what they have long sought by many means – that is, to be rid of him.'[17] Mary's supporters were 'very well satisfied at Lennox's death', but 'they go in great fear that the Queen of England will send an army into this country, under pretext of revenging herself for the death of the said Lennox, to win the country, which is already at her commandment outside this town and castle'.[18]

On 13 September Mar, who had been good friends with Lennox, wrote to Elizabeth: 'The whole country is troubled.' He told her he had written Margaret a letter, the contents of which she would declare to the Queen.[19]

Calder and Bell were to be the scapegoats for their masters and shoulder all the blame. On 13 September they were savagely executed, 'Calder after the manner of France, arms and legs broken and set upon a wheel'.[20]

Mar sent two letters of condolence to Margaret, neither of which appears to have been the one he had asked her to show Elizabeth. In the first he wrote that he could not but 'marvel to hear how dolorously you take the loss of your husband', having apparently thought her a woman of strong character who would bear her bereavement stoically. He beseeched her 'to take the least of evils, and to follow forth the likeliest and best apparent course for the comfort, weal, and safety of yourself, the King, and your only child now living, Mr Charles, in which last two you may repose your trust'. Mar's letter was entrusted to Laurence Nesbit, 'who served your husband truly, having put some order in the late Regent's private matters, [and] returns to your Grace, to whose sufficiency I commit the report of all the matters'.[21] Evidently Margaret did not know all the details of Lennox's end, as in the second letter Mar remitted 'the manner of the unhappy accident to the report of the bearer, your servant, who, being present, heard and saw the whole. No doubt there was over-little care taken. The chief loss is fallen on your Grace.'

Mar begged Margaret 'not to let your accustomed care and favour un-like toward that cause and action which your husband had in hand'. He 'sent some new instructions to be used by your Grace's advice, and have also written to her Majesty'. He prayed Margaret 'to give knowledge of your pleasure as to your husband's affairs in Scotland, which, to my best, shall be furthered and used to your contentment'.[22] This letter, with 'a packet', was forwarded to Margaret by Drury.[23]

On 20 September Spes sent King Philip what he described as 'a true relation of the death of the Earl of Lennox, which certainly has been a most successful enterprise. The only one who paid the penalty of his bad government was Lennox. They have appointed in the meanwhile for governor the Earl of Mar, who has the Prince in his possession, and holds the castle of Stirling. This Earl is bringing up the Prince without any religion, or rather with the bad instead of the good one. One of the worst evils connected with such a bringing up is that the Prince should be fed upon such vile milk as this.'[24]

Margaret had to accept that she now had little prospect of ever being involved in the rearing of her grandson.

On 29 September Spes informed his master of 'a letter which was found in Scotland, written by the Queen of England to the Earl of Lennox, directing him and his party to demand the surrender to them of the Queen of Scotland in the interests of peace, to which demand the Queen of England promised she would accede if she were asked, and almost commanded him to have the Queen of Scotland killed when they got possession of her; but Lennox himself was killed on the very day that he received the letter'.[25] Delivering Mary into the hands of Lennox would have been one way for Elizabeth to get rid of her, and of course she could not be held responsible for what the Scottish Regent decided to do with her. But Spes's information may not have been reliable, and all Elizabeth's efforts so far had been made to protect Mary from execution at the hands of her enemies.

On 2 October Elizabeth wrote to Mar recommending 'the Lady Lennox's causes to his favour', and saying she thought it 'reasonable to remind him that all who have been parties to the death of Lennox may be punished with all severity'.[26] Neither she nor Margaret was satisfied that the true culprits had been brought to justice.

Margaret herself wrote to Mar two days later:

Though perversed fortune has been such towards me in that realm that I have lost my choicest comforts, having cause sufficient thereby that the remembrance of the country should be grievous unto me, yet the natural love that I bear to the young King, with your lordship's friendly dealings and last letter – of which I am informed, though I saw it not – are some comfort to me. I will do all I can in the advancement of the King's actions. Whereas your lordship offers to advance the House [of Lennox] again to the ancient estate, whensoever I hear that the same is done, it will be to my comfort. There is money owing to servants and poor men, which I wish you to discharge. The Earl of Lennox meant to recompense such gentlemen and others who served him, but had not time. I commend them to your lordship to be good unto them, and especially the bearer. Hackney.[27]

She was keeping herself busy with hawking, a sport much favoured by aristocrats of both sexes. On 15 October she asked Mar that 'a cast of falcons may be sent to Berwick, where a man from me tarries to receive them'.[28]

On 23 October Mar replied to Margaret, thanking her for the letter she had sent on the 4th:

None can marvel that you take the remembrance of this country grievously, having lost your chiefest earthly comforts therein, and for my own part I find nothing but cares, restless business and daily danger to such as occupy this charge of government which now is laid upon my shoulder, and which no respect would have caused me to take on hand were it not for the preservation of the innocent person of the King, your nephew [*sic*], being subject to such present danger after the murders of his goodsire and others his dear friends, if some present remedy had not been found by placing another in the regiment.

I understand that your travails, nothwithstanding this dolorous season, have greatly furthered the King's actions, wherein he beseeches you to continue your earnestness and former affection, for that the troubles here still last and it has no appearance of sudden end.

The only remedy would be the intervention of Queen Elizabeth, with English aid.

Mar explained that there was no money to pay the debts and outstanding wages of Lennox's servants; 'the same inability remains as in the life of his Grace'. However, when the time was right, that would be 'considered and remembered'.[29]

Margaret was now lodging at Islington, then a village north of London. In Tudor times, like Stepney and Hackney, it was a rural place favoured by the nobility for country residences. Many were built on former monastic land, and it was probably in one of these, Canonbury Place (or Canonbury House, now called Canonbury Tower), that Margaret was staying[30] as the guest of a wealthy merchant, Sir John Spencer, the future Lord Mayor of London, who had acquired the house and its surrounding land in 1570. A difficult and truculent, even cruel, man, he was no friend to Catholics, but had apparently been willing to offer a grieving widow a refuge at this sad time.

Built before 1373 by the canons of St Bartholomew's Priory, Smithfield, after whom it was named, Canonbury Place was reconstructed by Prior William Bolton between 1509 and 1532, and after the Dissolution was owned in succession by Thomas Cromwell, John Dudley, Duke of Northumberland, and Thomas, Lord Wentworth. Margaret stayed there until at least January 1572.[31]

She was now coming to terms with widowhood, and realising that she had a problem on her hands. As she had done with Darnley, she had over-indulged her fourteen-year-old son Charles – probably all the more so recently, as he had lost his father and she had been trying to cope with her grief. He was now proving a great trial to her and was in need of a firm hand, as she had lost any authority over him. Had he been the son of an English peer, he would, upon his father's death, being a minor, have become subject to the Court of Wards, but Charles was the son of a Scottish lord, so he had remained under his mother's jurisdiction.

Lord Burghley was Master of the Court of Wards. He had in his own household a number of royal wards and noblemen's sons, for whom he had taken on the responsibility for their upbringing and education. He looked after his charges well, and personally saw to it that they were well taught. Places in his household were therefore sought after, and Margaret wanted one for Charles. On 4 October, in some desperation, she dictated a letter to Burghley:

My very good lord,
    Entering into considerations with myself of the many ways I have approvedly found your lordship most friendly to me and mine, I could not long delay to betray unto you a special grief which long time, but chiefly of late, hath grown upon me through the bringing up of my only son, Charles, whose well-doing and prosperity in all things comely for his calling should

be my greatest comfort, so the contrary I might not avoid to my greatest dolour. And having awakened myself lately, I have found that his father's absence so long time in his riper years hath made him lack to be in divers ways that were answerable in his brother, whose education and bringing up, living only at home with his father and me, at his coming to court I suppose was not misliked of.

Burghley may have paused here to reflect that there was much in Darnley that had been misliked of by many people, and that, had he been better disciplined in youth, he might not have come to such a grim end. And now here was Charles, seemingly set to turn out in the same mould. Margaret went on:

And though the good hap of this Lord Charles hath not been to have had that help of his father's company that his brother had, whereby at these years he is somewhat unfurnished in qualities needful, and I, being now a lone widow, am less able to have him well reformed at home than before. Yet the especial care I have that he might be able to continue a worthy member of his father's House and to serve his Prince and country hereafter (to my joy, if God lend me life) hath enforced me for redress to desire your good lordship, above all the pleasures that ever you did me, to accept my said son into your house, to be brought up and instructed as the wards be, so long time as shall be needful, in which doing you shall not only bind me but him and his friends to pray for your lordship and be yours assured during life, as knoweth the Almighty, to Whose protection I commit your lordship. From Islington, this 4 of November.

Your lordship's assured loving friend, Margaret Lennox.[32]

Margaret must have accepted that in Burghley's household Charles would have been brought up in the Protestant religion. Her amenability to that, and the hospitality shown to her by the Puritan Sir John Spencer, suggest that she had reverted to her former pragmatism in regard to religion. Given her reduced circumstances, she had probably had no choice. As Spes had said, she dared not speak openly of her faith.[33]

Burghley, probably loath to take into his household a difficult young man with such contentious royal blood, and possibly fearing that Charles might act as a spy for Margaret,[34] replied that already there were twenty young gentlemen being educated in his house. Instead he recommended a Swiss tutor, Peter Malliet, for Charles. Malliet had recently come to England from Paris, and although he was a follower of the Protestant reformer Huldrych Zwingli, Margaret did not demur. She duly engaged him, and Charles was sent to live with Malliet in his 'hostel' at Gray's Inn, London.[35] Gray's Inn was then flourishing as the largest of London's Inns of Court and enjoyed the special patronage of the Queen, which is probably how Burghley had secured lodgings there for Malliet. A portrait dated 1573[36] shows Charles to have been a handsome, fair-haired youth, in whom the resemblance to his dead brother is striking.

On 26 May 1572 Malliet wrote from Gray's Inn to the reformer Heinrich Bullinger:

> I undertook the office of tutor and governor to the Earl of Lennox, the brother of the King of Scots who was murdered, and uncle of the present one, not without a great deal of trouble and hindrance to my studies. But, induced by the entreaties and promises of the principal personages of this kingdom, I could not decline to undertake this burden for a limited time, since I am at full liberty to leave this place whenever I choose. The youth is just entering upon his sixteenth year, and gives great promise of hope for the future. For in case the present King, his nephew, should die without lawful issue, he is the sole successor by hereditary right to the crown of Scotland, and is entitled to be placed at the head of the kingdom and empire. So also no one is more nearly allied to the royal blood of England, after the death of the present Queen, than his mother, to whom her only son is the heir.[37]

Malliet's assessment of his pupil was encouraging to Margaret. Evidently the tutor continued to give satisfaction, and decided that he liked working for the Lennoxes, as he was to serve in her household for many years.

Lennox's death had left Margaret the poorer. She had no right to the properties settled on her and her husband by Henry VIII as they were entailed upon her son Charles. Fortunately the Queen permitted her to continue using them and their revenues during his minority. As for the Scottish lands that Lennox had settled upon her before their marriage, when she responded to Mar on 20 November from Islington, she asked for his help in regard to some of these. She thanked him 'for the continuance of your most noble and friendly mind towards me and mine. I am determined ere long to send some [i.e. similar goodwill] to your lordship, with instructions for such affairs as I must be bold to trouble you with.' She asked him to order that officials of the bishopric of Glasgow, which was at the heartland of Lennox territory, 'be employed in the redeeming of the earldom of Lennox' out of pledge. She knew that her brother-in-law, the Bishop of Caithness, was struggling to hold on to the priory of St Andrews, which Lennox had given him, and she asked Mar 'earnestly to extend your favour to him that he may enjoy that benefice wholly for his portion, paying all such sums as said is for his brother's sake, the rather at my request, and for your honourable offer for advancing my son Charles [to] the earldom of Lennox. I request that you will cause the Isle of Inchinnan,[38] appointed for my dowry, to be kept by Robert Cunningham to my use. I request you to be good to certain musicians there [and] commend poor Robert Nesbit to you.'[39]

On 24 November Elizabeth wrote to Mar in favour of the Countess of Lennox's suits in Scotland:

> Like as by your own letters we perceive your good inclination to further with your favour all the causes of our right dear cousin, the Lady Margaret, Countess of Lennox, so we understand by herself that she esteems the favour to be the more amply and effectuously offered to her for our sake, and for that purpose we have thought it very convenient both to give you our most hearty thanks, and to require you to continue your goodwill, not only as her causes shall require, but also according to the particular affection which she bears towards her late husband's kin and family, that you will show favour to the Bishop of Caithness, brother to the said Earl her husband, that he may enjoy still the priory of St Andrews which was bestowed on him in recompense of another benefice that he left, and that the intention of the late Regent might be fulfilled in the bestowing of the bishopric of Glasgow towards the redemption of the lands of the earldom of Lennox, which were mortgaged by the said Earl by occasion of his service in that realm.[40]

On 31 January 1572 Margaret wrote from Islington to tell Mar that she had 'received his most friendly letter, and is informed thereby of the King's prosperous increase. [She] shall be glad to further all things that concern his Majesty's causes in these parts,' and desired Mar 'to continue his good mind toward her'.[41]

Margaret's ambition was now vested in her only surviving child, Charles, who was the most viable heir to the Scottish throne until such time as James VI had children. But she was more immediately concerned about Charles inheriting his father's title, so that they could live off the revenues of the earldom, even though its lands were all mortgaged.[42] James VI had succeeded his grandfather as earl of Lennox, but the Regent was looking into the possibility that Charles 'might be rewarded for the loss of his father and brother by having the earldom of Lennox given him, by which means the King hereafter should have a good [main]stay of a near kinsman, and the House [of Lennox] thereby preserved to do more service to the crown'. Mar was also going to 'further the Countess of Lennox's reasonable suits for her dower'.[43]

It was probably early in her widowhood that Margaret leased from her landlord, the antiquary Richard Carew,[44] another of his properties, the King's Place in Hackney, and moved there from Barber's Barn. Better known, from around 1621, as Brooke House, it was part of a two-hundred-acre manor once belonging to Margaret's great-grandmother, Elizabeth Wydeville, the queen of Edward IV,[45] and stood where Lower Clapton Road and Kenninghall Road meet today.

There had probably been a house on the site since 1439 or earlier – it is first documented in 1476. Henry VIII had acquired it by an exchange of lands with the penurious Henry Percy, Earl of Northumberland, in 1535. That year Henry granted it to Thomas Cromwell, who never lived there and who in 1536 surrendered it to the King. Henry VIII had come there that summer with Jane Seymour to be reconciled with his daughter Mary. On Henry's death in 1547 the house had been given to Sir William Herbert (later earl of Pembroke), who sold it that year to Sir Ralph Sadler, the builder of nearby Sutton House. Sadler in turn sold the property to Sir Wymond Carew, whose family owned it until 1578. They did not live there but leased it out.[46]

Herbert's lease of 1547 described the King's Place as 'a fair house', with a hall, parlour, kitchen, 'pastory [patisserie?]', dry larder, buttery, pantry 'and all other houses of office necessary and many fair chambers', including a long gallery, a chapel and a closet, with a great chamber above, and 'a proper library to lay books in'. There was a barn in which 'to lay hay' and a stable. The house was 'enclosed on the back side with a great broad ditch', and beyond that was a large fenced garden; at the further end of the house were fifty-one acres of orchard 'having but few trees of fruit therein', and in front of it, 'coming from London, is a fair large garden ground enclosed with a brick wall'.[47]

A survey of the ruined house made in the 1950s reveals that it had been built in the medieval collegiate style around two courtyards; the ground floor was of brick, and the upper was timbered. It had turrets, gables, brick chimney stacks and mullioned windows. Traces of the foundations of the medieval house were found beneath Tudor and later remains. Despite the rebuilding of Tudor times, the south and west fronts were reminiscent of late-fifteenth-century architectural styles. There was probably a long gallery in the west range in Margaret's day,[48] which may have been the footprint of the 150-foot-long gallery built by Lord Hunsdon, who bought the house in 1578.

After two hundred years in use as an asylum, little survived of the original interiors, and there were no large rooms, only small ones, with some opening off narrow corridors, suggesting that the original chambers were partitioned at some date. Badly mutilated wall paintings featuring St Peter, sunbursts, flowers, birds and scrolled foliage were found in a lofty room with the remains of a Purbeck marble floor, which was probably the chapel. Its decorations included a foot-high frieze with armorial shields, Tudor roses and chevrons, dating from the late fifteenth century.

Mary, Queen of Scots, had now been a prisoner in England for nearly four years. Infuriated at Elizabeth's recent assertion that she had enticed Darnley 'out of England and married him against the Queen's Majesty's goodwill, thereby to nourish division in England',[49] she replied on 14 February 1572 that she would 'make the Countess of Lennox, his mother, judge who pursued and caused her [Mary] to be pursued since her return to Scotland', for it would not be found that she, Mary, had had or sought 'practice [action or advice] or greater amity in England' by Darnley's means or his mother's.[50] In other words, it had been Margaret who had brought about her marriage to Darnley and had been out for Mary's ruin ever since, and neither Margaret nor her son had helped Mary's cause in England.

On 28 March Elizabeth declared that she had 'just cause to defer the delivery of the Queen of Scots and her restitution to the crown of Scotland'. Among other reasons, she could not

with honour or conscience show any favour to her that in
former times the proximity of blood or the equality of her
state, having been born to be a queen, might have required,
for that she has been so notoriously charged, and never probably purged of the devising, working, and consenting to the
horrible strange murder of her husband, who was the next
kinsman of the royal blood of England that her Majesty had,
and also her Majesty's born subject, yea he was also the next
kinsman of the Queen of Scots of the father's side; the avenge
of whose death, upon the complaint of the Earl of Lennox, the
father, and the mother, the Lady Margaret, to her Majesty, did
and doth belong to her Majesty by the law of God and the
laws of the realm of England.[51]

On 18 April, thanks to Mar, the earldom of Lennox was settled
upon Charles Stuart and his heirs in perpetuity, and without restric-
tion, and this was afterwards ratified by the Scottish Parliament.[52]
On 2 May a grateful Elizabeth, spared the need to help Margaret
financially, wrote to Mar:

Right trusty and well-beloved cousin, whereas we understand
by our dear cousin the Countess of Lennox the favour and
goodwill you bear towards her and all such as belong to her
house, and her late husband, and especially towards her second
son, our cousin Charles, unto whom we hear that by your good
means the title, name, and livelihood of the earldom of Lennox
is granted to him, like as we cannot but very much commend
this your favourable dealing towards the only son of the said
Lady Lennox, manifesting thereby plainly the good regard you
have of the father, who spent his blood and life in the service
of the King and that realm, so have we thought good to give
you our most hearty thanks for your benefits bestowed on them.[53]

Charles was tardy in expressing his own thanks to the lords of
the Scottish Council. It was not until 20 May that – prodded perhaps
by his mother or his tutor – he sent them an apologetic letter:

Having received advertisement of your lordships' friendly dealings
in procuring, or so willingly consenting, to my advancement to
honour, it had been my duty ere this to have showed myself
thankful. I shall, therefore, right effectuously desire your lordships'

pardon my long silence, and to receive by these my lines my most hearty commendations, and condign thanks for your good deeds towards me, unknown to you – or to the most number of you. For which benefit received, I shall not be, God willing, ungrateful; but shall endeavour to requite your lordships, or any of you, in what I possibly can do.

From my chamber at Gray's Inn.

Charles Lennox.[54]

Margaret still had a significant role to play in Scottish politics, for her grandson was king and she was known to have influence with Queen Elizabeth. She remained in correspondence with Mar. On 6 July he prayed her 'not to take in evil part my delay in writing nor my present shortness. The order of our late proceedings and present state I have sent to Mr Randolph, whereby you will perceive the true report of things.' He trusted 'to write more at length soon'.[55] His letter of 6 August to Randolph reveals that Margaret was kept abreast of affairs and sent copies of important letters.[56]

On 4 September Mar wrote at length 'to the right honourable and my very good lady, the Countess of Lennox, her Grace':

Madame,

Since the receipt of your last letter I never found a proper commodity to write unto your Grace, saving a very short letter, which I trust come to your Grace's hands by the means of Master Randolph, and the discourse of things then past. Since which time matters have proceeded here in reasonable quietness.

He recounted in depth how Queen Mary's partisans in Edinburgh Castle had reneged on a two-month abstinence of hostilities that he had agreed with them, his discovery of proofs that Drury was in league with them, and their machinations to have Randolph recalled. It was clear that he wanted Margaret to make plain to Elizabeth his opinion of her servants.

Whom her Majesty's pleasure is to employ, must be to us acceptable; yet, having such cause and interest, I cannot dissemble to your Grace our misliking, which we wish might come to the knowledge of her Majesty's self and such of her Council as might help to amend it. For surely we all think, if her

Highness – as we doubt not – would have matters to proceed
here well and sincerely to her Majesty's satisfaction and the
continuance of the amity betwixt the realms, some better
affected minister, in our opinion, were meet to be employed.
The greater that the credit, gravity, and experience of the
personage were, the better should all things succeed. Further,
may it please your Grace to understand that we have not yet
accorded upon any place of the general meeting of the whole
Estates for deliberating upon the pacification, but what falls out
thereupon, your Grace shall shortly hear. The King's Majesty,
our sovereign, your Grace's nephew [sic], praised be God, is in
good health and like shortly to speak for himself.[57]

We do not know if Margaret conveyed to Elizabeth Mar's dissatisfac-
tion with Drury. What is more important is that he thought she had
sufficient influence to persuade the Queen to replace him.

Drury soon got wind that something was up. On 1 October he
told Burghley he perceived 'that something concerning him has been
written by Lord Morton to Lady Lennox', and prayed 'that his doings
may have trial'.[58]

Margaret lost a good friend in Scotland when, on 29 October
1572, the Regent Mar died unexpectedly, having suffered only a
short illness. Her cousin Morton felt that he should be given the
governorship in Mar's place. On 6 November Killigrew informed
Sir Thomas Smith that Morton

has written his mind to Lady Lennox touching the state of this
country, and what he supposes fit to be done by the Queen's
Majesty. [He] has named great personages in this letter, which
may peradventure move him to think that it will be hard to
establish a Regent, for though the voices of the King's party
are three to one of the other, yet no honest and worthy
nobleman of that party will take the charge unless encouraged
by the Queen. There is a proposal to appoint four nobles to
guard the King.[59]

Morton was elected regent on 24 November. He proved a competent administrator, even if he did take advantage of his position to
enrich himself. Like Mar, he recognised Margaret's importance, and
continued to keep her apprised of events at the highest level.

★

In May 1578 Mary, Queen of Scots, was to write of Margaret to James Boyd, Archbishop of Glasgow:

> This good lady was, thanks to God, in very good correspondence with me these five or six years bygone, and has confessed to me, by sundry letters under her hand, which I carefully preserve, the injury she did me by the unjust pursuits, which she allowed to go out against me in her name, through bad information, but principally, she said, through the express orders of the Queen of England and the persuasion of her Council, who also took much solicitude that she and I might never come to good understanding together. But how soon she came to know of my innocence, she desisted from any further suit against me; nay, went so far as to refuse her consent to anything they should act against me in her name.[60]

It was politic for Margaret to blame Elizabeth and her Council for coercing her in her efforts to bring Mary to justice, but it was a blatant manipulation of the truth.[61]

Mary's letter places the reconciliation between her and Margaret in 1572–3. It has been said that in the wake of the notorious Ridolfi plot to put Mary on Elizabeth's throne – a plot in which Mary was complicit – Margaret began to realise what the consequences would be for herself if Mary succeeded in England, and that from early 1573, increasingly concerned that Mary might be restored to power in Scotland,[62] she decided that the safest course was to ally herself with her daughter-in-law. Yet the likelihood of Mary becoming queen of either country was fairly remote; as an alien, she had no legal claim under the Act of Succession or Henry VIII's will; and because she was a Catholic she could command only limited support. Indeed, in the wake of the plot, there were many to revile her. Above all, Margaret's hatred of Mary had been such that it is inconceivable that, believing that she had colluded in Darnley's murder, she would have contemplated lending her any support.

It has been suggested[63] that it was not until 1575 that Margaret became convinced of Mary's innocence of the murder of Darnley, after she had read a testament supposedly written that year by Bothwell, in which he stated that Mary 'did never know nor consent to the death of the King; but he and his friends by his appointment and device' had brought it about. Said to have been made when

Bothwell was 'sick unto death in the castle of Malmö' in Denmark, this 'confession' was almost certainly a forgery; it was 'signed' by witnesses who were already dead, and states that he had died at Malmö, when in fact he had left that place in 1573 and would die at Dragsholm Castle in 1578; it also asserts, incorrectly, that Kirkcaldy of Grange, Lord Boyd and Lennox's brother, the Bishop of Caithness, were among Darnley's murderers, which Bothwell is hardly likely to have alleged, since he would have known they were not. Probably it was written by an adherent of Mary.[64]

Abstracts of the confession were in circulation in 1575, and it has been suggested that it was after seeing one[65] that Margaret wrote to Mary that year: 'I can but wish and pray God for your Majesty's long and happy estate, till time I may do your Majesty better service . . . I beseech your Highness pardon these rude lines and accept the good heart of the writer, who loves and honours your Majesty unfeignedly.'[66] But it is clear from Mary's letter of March 1578 that the two women had been reconciled at least two years prior to 1575, so it cannot have been the testament that changed Margaret's mind, although seeing it probably helped to convince her that Bothwell was the guilty party. On 6 January 1577 Mary informed Archbishop Boyd, that the King of Denmark had sent Bothwell's testament to Queen Elizabeth, but that she had secretly suppressed it.[67] This document, which does not survive, may have been a different testament from the one allegedly made at Malmo, and Margaret could not have seen it; even if she had, it would not account for her change of heart in 1572–3.

Possibly Margaret had learned more details of Darnley's end from members of his household,[68] although enquiries would surely have been made of his servants very early on. It is more likely that by 1572–3, through her many contacts in Scotland and England, she had been offered compelling evidence to convince her that Mary was innocent. By the 1570s many people had a shrewd idea of who had murdered Darnley, although there were those in Scotland who had a vested interest in concealing the truth.

It is clear that Margaret never found out that it was her own kinsmen, the Douglases, who had killed her son. To the end of her days she would believe that Bothwell had murdered him. That is evident in Phillips's *Commemoration*:

But yet remember thou and thy train,
Offenders most vile, wicked and ill,

> Doth God not traitors hate and disdain?
> We read in His wrath, destroy them He will.
> Esteem that His justice lots them to spill.
> Look with thy consorts from the East to the West,
> Your guile is offended, God doth you detest.

The initial letters of the first six lines in this verse read 'BODWEL'. There follow several lines vehemently damning him for his most cruel crimes, as a person 'past grace' who should prepare to face God's wrath.

It must have been mortifying for Margaret to realise that she had done her daughter-in-law a great wrong. It may be that it was she herself who gave instructions for the damning inscriptions and scenes in the Darnley Memorial to be obliterated. Morton, who had more reason than most to fear the truth coming out, got wind of the rapprochement early on, and it was possibly because he feared that Margaret would make an alliance with Mary that on 16 August 1574 he asked Killigrew 'that he may be certified of the Countess of Lennox's and her son's present condition and affairs'.[69]

It has been stated too that Margaret continued to make a show of reviling Mary at Elizabeth's court.[70] Mary's letter appears to contradict this, although there is no evidence of Margaret ever speaking out in Mary's favour. Yet her reconciliation with the woman she had vilified as her son's murderess must in time have cast doubt in the minds of many – as indeed it must today – as to the veracity of the official version of what had happened at Kirk O'Field. It is one of the strongest proofs of Mary's innocence.

In January 1573 the Scottish Parliament 'confirmed the earldom of Lennox to the Lord Charles'.[71] On 5 February Killigrew reported that the Regent Morton had desired him 'to procure some public witness' who would testify to Queen Elizabeth's opinion as to who had murdered Lennox and Moray. Failing that, Morton would proceed against the Hamiltons.[72]

In the interests of peace and concord, Elizabeth had been manoeuvring to bring about a rapprochement between Morton and the lords who had murdered Lennox, although that was not meant to exempt the latter from paying the penalty for it. On 23 February Huntly and the Hamiltons formally submitted 'to the King's obedience and government of his Regent, James Earl of Morton', and confessed 'that all things done or assisted unto by them in name or by colour of any other authority has been unlawful'; but the lords conceded that 'it shall be decreed by Act of Parliament that all penalties arising therefrom against certain members of the House of Hamilton and others since the 15th June 1567 shall be void and of none effect'. However, this did not extend to the murders of Moray and Lennox, 'which is a matter of such weight and importance that the Regent cannot conveniently of himself remit them; yet the matter of the remission of the murders being moved to the Queen of England, whatever she shall advise and counsel the Regent, with consent of Parliament, will perform and observe'.[73]

Margaret had evidently been pressing for the Hamiltons to be brought to justice. On 14 March Killigrew wrote to Burghley 'that in his poor opinion the Queen may in honour consent' to spare them 'to save the kingdom from shipwreck. If Lady Lennox be not satisfied, it would be asked whether war would make the matter better or worse, and whether it be not more necessary to preserve him that is alive than to continue the danger of his life in seeking a revenge for the dead; yet if she were to persuade the Queen to send the Regent means to win the castle [of Edinburgh], she could not be better revenged, nor do the Queen and this young babe greater service.' In a postscript he recommended that Margaret be persuaded to make John Cunningham, Laird of Drumquhassle and Captain of Dumbarton, 'receiver and overseer of the earldom of Lennox during the Earl's minority, and make yearly account thereof, which will be a small matter by reason that the land is all mortgage, which he must unmortgage with his own money and policy'.[74]

On 29 March Killigrew informed Burghley: 'The young King and the Countess of Mar write to the Queen of England [and] to the Countess of Lennox, who has the delivery of them; the King's letter contains thanks, with desire of aid of her as the princess under God whom he most leaneth unto for help.'[75] Nesbit was also sending Margaret news from Scotland.[76]

Elizabeth had sent a force to aid the regency government against Mary's supporters, and in June Morton sent Margaret the momentous news that Edinburgh Castle had fallen to the besiegers. Maitland, 'the fountain of all the mischief', had 'departed this life', probably by his own hand. Morton went on:

I will require your Grace to give your most hearty thanks to my lord of Leicester and my Lord Treasurer [Burghley] for their great goodwill declared in the advancement of this action by furthering of her Majesty's aid and forces, whereby this troublesome castle is recovered, and peace restored to our country.

I might also forewarn your Grace to be wary and circumspect with the Marshal of Berwick's [Drury's] information, for that he is undoubtedly a secret friend to our enemies. Yet were it most convenient that he were removed from his charge at Berwick, and that if your Grace's talk might anywise procure that Mr Killigrew should be returned hither, who has done notable good service and is able to do further if he were here employed, and that also he were made governor of Berwick, which, in my own opinion, would be a great advancement to her Majesty's service and both the countries, knowing him so well as I do to be faithful to his mistress and his country, and so well beloved here for the good parts found in him, that I think none can travail in the like service that shall acquire greater benevolence and reputation. And in the meantime I will pray your Grace to give him hearty thanks, which assuredly he has well deserved.[77]

It is clear from Morton's letter that Margaret still had influence at the English court.

On 5 August 1573 he informed her that, two days earlier, Grange had been executed. In the same letter Morton accused Drury of appropriating some of the Scottish crown jewels that had been left in the castle, and asked Margaret, since Drury was now at the English court, to request their return.[78] That same day he prayed Killigrew to advise her 'in what order it is best to handle the matter'.[79] On 19 August Morton thanked Margaret 'for the great care and goodwill you show to the furtherance of the King your dearest nephew's [sic] affairs there' and wished 'that you may long continue in good health, and so be able to stand him in good stead there, as you have always heretofore'. He also wanted to know what progress she had made with Drury, 'trusting shortly to understand from you what you have done in that behalf'.[80] But in the end it was discovered that Drury had been the victim of a malicious allegation, and had not had the jewels at all.[81]

Morton had asked Margaret to use her influence to get Killigrew sent back to Scotland, but that did not happen until May 1574; the lapse of nine months suggests that Margaret had not been behind his appointment. In fact she was probably at Settrington, for between January 1573 and February 1574 we find her leasing land, meadows and farms to her tenants there.[82] She was also at Temple Newsam in the summer of 1574,[83] and it was soon after that that the last great drama of her life would be played out.

20

'The Hasty Marriage'

By November 1573 the likelihood of the forty-year-old Queen Elizabeth marrying and bearing an heir was becoming increasingly remote. As Margaret knew from bitter experience, many children died young, and she had only the one grandson, James VI, in line for the English succession. It was therefore important to secure a suitable, and preferably rich, bride for her son Charles, now sixteen. It has been suggested that Charles may have been manifesting symptoms of the tuberculosis that was to kill him, and that Margaret was perhaps aware that it was imperative that he marry and beget an heir as soon as possible.[1]

Margaret herself was fifty-eight, and given the tragedies that had wrecked her life, it might have been expected that she would have retired from the political arena for a quieter existence; but ambition was still lively in her, and by that November, in pursuance of a marriage for Charles, she had involved herself in yet another fateful and potentially dangerous intrigue, and was plotting with two old acquaintances. One was that redoubtable matriarch and arch-intriguer, Bess of Hardwick, Countess of Shrewsbury, one of the wealthiest women in the kingdom and in high favour with the Queen, who once said of her, 'there is no lady in this land that I better love and like'.[2] The other was Katherine Willoughby, the Dowager Duchess of Suffolk. The three of them were intent on a match between Charles and Elizabeth Cavendish, aged eighteen, Bess's remaining marriageable daughter from her second marriage, to Sir William Cavendish. Elizabeth had recently been disappointed by the latest in a line of suitors, Peregrine Bertie, the Duchess of Suffolk's son by her second marriage,[3] who had preferred another lady.[4]

(*Left*) Elizabeth I. Margaret praised her as 'a Princess of Peace who excelled the Muses and the Graces', but she posed a dangerous dynastic threat to the Queen, and relations between the two cousins were turbulent.

(*Right*) William Cecil, later Lord Burghley, Margaret's 'assured loving friend', who for many years saw her as an enemy.

(*Below*) Robert Dudley, Earl of Leicester, who interceded for Margaret when he could, and remained a good friend to her.

The former Charterhouse at Sheen, where Margaret was imprisoned for a year from 1562–3. 'I assure you I am weary of this life, for, as methink, we have had punishment enough for a great offence.'

Margaret's sons had strong claims to the crowns of England and Scotland. These double portraits of Henry, Lord Darnley, and Charles Stuart were painted as baits for Mary, Queen of Scots.

(*Above left*) Margaret's unnamed daughters, all of whom had died young by 1565. 'Six of our children away from us bent, in tender youth.'
(*Above right*) The Lennoxes' house at Whorlton. Tradition has it that Margaret was here when she first proposed to Queen Mary a marriage with Darnley.

The Lennox Jewel, obverse and reverse. 'What we resolve, only death shall dissolve.'

(*Above left*) Mary, Queen of Scots, Margaret's daughter-in-law. Mary was to incur Margaret's virulent hatred. (*Above right*) Henry, Lord Darnley, King of Scots. 'It was not possible to see a more beautiful prince.'

The Lieutenant's Lodging (now the Queen's House) in the Tower of London, where Margaret was imprisoned for two years from 1565–7, and again, briefly, in 1574–5.

Cecil's spy's drawing of the murder scene at Kirk O'Field, Edinburgh, 10 February 1567. 'The case is a very strange one.'

(*Left*) The decaying Coldharbour, London, where the Lennoxes lived in 1567. Here 'my lady wept bitterly, my lord sighed deeply'.

(*Below*) Somerset Place, Strand, London. Elizabeth I allowed Margaret to lodge in the magnificent mansion built by Protector Somerset.

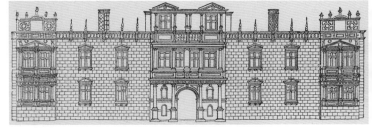

'Arise, Lord, and avenge the innocent blood of the King my father!'

The Darnley Memorial: the famous 'vendetta picture'.

The Darnley Memorial: the undefaced copy at Goodwood House.

SIR WILLIAM ST LOE OF GLOWCESTERSHIRE
HUSBAND TO THE COUNTESS OF SHREWSBURY

(*Above left*) Lennox was regent of Scotland from 1570–1. 'The burden which is laid on my shoulders is weighty and dangerous.'

(*Above right*) John Erskine, Earl of Mar, who was a good friend to the Lennoxes.

(*Left*) Margaret's cousin, James Douglas, Earl of Morton, 'the wicked Regent', who was to be executed for Darnley's murder.

Stirling Castle, where Lennox was carried bleeding, after being rescued from his enemies. 'Remember my love to my wife, Meg,' he enjoined Mar.

Barber's Barn, Hackney, where Margaret lived during her early widowhood. Her grief was 'poignant and perpetual'.

(*Above left*) Brooke House in 1920. (*Above right*) Brooke House in 1642. When Margaret leased the property in the 1570s it was known as the King's Place, having once been owned by Henry VIII.

The chapel at Brooke House in 1642.

One of the early sixteenth-centur wall paintings in the chapel.

Margaret's son Charles as a child.
'He is somewhat unfurnished
in qualities needful.'

Charles Stuart, Earl of Lennox.
He was 'inclined to love with a few days'
acquaintance', with disastrous results.

The redoubtable Bess of Hardwick,
Countess of Shrewsbury, whose intrigues with
Margaret provoked the wrath of the Queen.

Margaret's granddaughter, Arbella Stuart,
aged two. The portrait shows her
as countess of Lennox.

(*Above left*) 'A Scottish lady at length in mourning habit', who may be Margaret. (*Above right*) Margaret's grandson, James VI, King of Scots. In her later years all her dynastic hopes were invested in him.

(*Below*) Margaret's tomb in Westminster Abbey, showing the kneeling figures of her sons, Henry, Philip, Charles and Darnley, with the crown of Scotland suspended above his head. (*Right*) Margaret's tomb effigy, completed by October 1578. Her epitaph calls her 'a lady of most pious character, invincible spirit and matchless steadfastness'.

Referring on 5 November 1574 to the marriage being planned by Margaret, Bess and Lady Suffolk, Bess's fourth husband, George Talbot, Earl of Shrewsbury, stated that it 'hath been in talk betwixt them more than a year past'. By his own admission, he was well aware of what was being discussed, and in favour of the match, having done what he could to further it.[5]

The two matriarchs, Margaret and Bess, had strong motives for forging this union. Bess wanted all her children to marry well, and Charles, with his royal blood, was highly eligible, of greater birth than the 'sundry' young men[6] who had rejected the hand of Elizabeth Cavendish; moreover, he had claims to both the English and Scottish thrones. No wonder the ambitious Bess wanted him as a son-in-law. She too may have suspected that Charles might not live long,[7] and she undoubtedly foresaw the heady possibility of her grandchild one day wearing two crowns.

Elizabeth Cavendish was not as suitable a bride for Charles as many girls of higher birth: his great-grandfather had been a king, hers a clerk of the Exchequer, his father an earl, hers a knight.[8] But she had apparently wealthy parents who could be expected to provide a substantial dowry, which must have brought a gleam to the penurious Margaret's eye. As her letter to Leicester quoted below shows, she had hoped for a better match, but financial need was a deciding factor. Yet in this she was ultimately destined to be disappointed, and it was Bess who got the better bargain.

The Duchess of Suffolk visited Bess at Chatsworth in the spring of 1573, when the marriage would almost certainly have been discussed. She probably felt obliged to help with finding another husband for Elizabeth Cavendish, given that her own son would not wed the girl. But there was more to the matter than that, for it has been suggested that the Queen of Scots herself was involved in the marriage negotiations. Elizabeth Cavendish was close to Queen Mary, and a marriage between the two young people would ally Margaret to Mary's cause and open up a channel of communication between them. Margaret, of course, was unable to contact Mary openly, and was probably concerned to maintain the pretence that they were still enemies. But if Mary was instrumental in bringing the marriage about, she may have hoped that it would be seen as tangible evidence that Margaret no longer believed that she had murdered Darnley, and was now her friend.[9]

What is incredible is that, according to Shrewsbury, this marriage that might have produced new heirs to the throne was 'not thought of as a matter worth her Majesty's hearing'.[10] Margaret, who has been described as 'a survivor of nearly sixty years of intrigue and catastrophe',[11] had seemingly learned little from her previous experiences, and not given sufficient thought to the consequences of committing what was, after all, a crime. As she should have known – for it was her misconduct that had led to the passing of the Act of Attainder in 1536 – arranging the marriage of a youth of royal blood without the permission of the Crown might well have been construed as high treason. It was a debatable matter whether Charles Stuart came under the remit of the Act – cousins of the sovereign were not specified – but at the very least Margaret must have realised that the Queen would almost certainly have forbidden the match. Elizabeth did not like her heirs marrying and having children who could challenge her throne; Margaret had only to remember what had happened to her cousin, Katherine Grey, dead these five years after spending her life in captivity, separated from her husband and one of her sons. But, heedless as ever of the consequences, she pressed ahead with her plans.

Conveniently, in the autumn of 1574, Margaret's hopes of rearing her eight-year-old grandson James sprang anew. The Council had 'unanimously agreed' that the sons of Katherine Grey were illegitimate, and that the lawful heir to Queen Elizabeth was James VI. They were therefore putting great pressure on the Scots to send the boy to be raised in England, having 'adopted the expedient of giving him up to the Countess of Lennox, his grandmother'.[12] Never one to waste an opportunity, Margaret decided that she and Charles would travel north at once, so that she could be at hand to welcome James. She asked for Elizabeth's permission to go, saying that she also needed to visit her estates in Yorkshire. The French ambassador, Fénélon, who had not been informed of the reason for her journey, suspected 'that she has no other purpose than to transfer the little Prince into England'.[13] But he was wrong.

Elizabeth gave her permission, but then Margaret told her that she might visit her friend, the Duchess of Suffolk, at Chatsworth. 'At my coming from her Majesty,' Margaret wrote later to Leicester, 'I perceived that she misliked of my lady of Suffolk being at Chatsworth'[14] – and no wonder, for the Queen of Scots was then staying there, in Shrewsbury's custody. By September 1574 Elizabeth had heard rumours of the détente between the two great protagonists, Margaret and Mary, and her suspicions were now further aroused.

It seemed inconceivable that Margaret, who had so vehemently demanded vengeance on Mary, should secretly have been reconciled to her. Was Margaret plotting against Elizabeth once more?

The Council concluded that Mary was seeking to appease Margaret by offering to broker an advantageous marriage for Charles Stuart. Elizabeth feared that Margaret might collude in Mary's endless plotting. As Margaret recounted to Leicester, 'I asked her Majesty, if I were bidden thither [to Chatsworth], for that had been my wonted way before, if I might go. She prayed me not, lest it should be thought I should agree with the Queen of Scots. And I asked her Majesty if she could think so, for I was made of flesh and blood and could never forget the murder of my child; and she said, marry, by her faith, she could not think so, that ever I could forget it, for if I would I were a devil.'[15]

Margaret kept her word; like Elizabeth, she was never to meet Mary. Yet her journey was not to be uneventful, and its outcome would prove to be almost as dangerous as conspiring with the Queen of Scots.

On 4 October the Council arranged for 'the taking up of two teams of horses or oxen, with their furniture, for the moving of the Lady Lennox's stuff from Hackney unto her manor of Temple Newsam in Yorkshire'.[16] Margaret left London on 9 October and 'was already on the road to receive' her grandson as soon as Morton and the Scottish Council agreed to give him up when she learned that they had refused. 'The Scotch people were so much disturbed at this, that they were already crying out that, if the Prince is surrendered to the English, they will murder all the nobles, as the only object is to kill the Prince and his mother.'[17] Margaret must have been deeply disappointed. She had never set eyes on her grandson, and doubtless longed to do so.

On the road towards Yorkshire, Margaret came to Grimsthorpe Castle, the Lincolnshire seat of Lady Suffolk.[18] Here, needing to rest her mules,[19] she sought the Duchess's hospitality. But Lady Suffolk had already informed Bess that Lady Lennox 'meant to come to her house in the north, and that she would bring her to Chatsworth if she could entreat her to, but if she could not, herself would [i.e. go to Chatsworth]'. Since Queen Mary was at Chatsworth, the Shrewsburys 'thought better' that Margaret and Charles should visit them at their house, Rufford Abbey, in Sherwood Forest, 'and made that home ready'.[20]

What happened next was to be related by Margaret and others at a time when she and Bess were suspected of conspiring treason, and were therefore concerned to portray their actions as innocent. On the face of it these accounts suggest that Margaret was unwittingly bounced into a situation in which she could not but consent to her son's marriage – but we know, of course, that she had been planning it for nearly a year. It is likely therefore that when she travelled north, she had already arranged for her son to be married, and how this was to be achieved, but that the fallout from the marriage made her tell a different story.

Margaret was to recount that when she and Charles left Grimsthorpe, the Duchess 'friendly brought me on the way to Grantham, and so departed home again'.[21] Margaret and Charles stayed for at least one night at Grantham,[22] then Margaret seems to have gone ahead alone to Newark.[23] Possibly Charles was unwell, and she was seeking out a suitable lodging. Bess, meanwhile, was now 'by chance' installed with her daughter thirty miles away at Rufford Abbey, and hearing (no doubt from Lady Suffolk) 'of their being at Grantham, sent the next day' her servant, Henry Camen, 'to desire them both to come to Rufford'. At Grantham Camen found Charles alone and 'loth to come', and it took great persuasion to get him to consent.[24] Probably he had wanted to wait for his mother's sanction for the diversion.

Camen and the reluctant Charles caught up with Margaret at Newark[25] and pressed her to break her journey and stay a night with Bess at Rufford Abbey, or at least to travel by a route that lay within a mile of it, which Camen said was a better way north. Apparently undecided, Margaret took that road, but then, as she later recalled to Leicester, there was Bess herself, riding forward to greet her. Having been 'very earnestly requested, and the place not one mile distant out of my way, yea, and a much better way, as is well to be proved, and my lady meeting me herself along the way, I could not refuse, it being near upon thirty miles from Sheffield. And as it was well known to all the country thereabouts that great provision was there made both for my Lady Suffolk and me.'[26] In referring to 'all the country', Margaret probably meant all the landed families in the county – people who would have known Bess and taken an interest in her doings. Shrewsbury even informed Burghley of Margaret's visit.[27]

It was the middle of October when Bess brought Margaret and Charles to Rufford Abbey, a former Cistercian monastery owned and converted into a fine residence by the Shrewsburys.[28] There, Shrewsbury was to recount, Margaret was 'sickly' and rested for five days, keeping mostly to her chamber; and while she was doing so, Charles fell into 'such liking' with Elizabeth Cavendish that Bess was prompted to tell her husband that there was no doubt of a match between them. In fact Charles and Elizabeth had 'so tied', or precontracted, themselves that they 'cannot part'. Charles was 'so far in love that belike he is sick without her'.[29]

Margaret was also to assert, in similar terms, that the young couple had fallen headily in love, but the two countesses had clearly colluded to bring together their unsupervised children, who must have been given their instructions. Probably Bess had made herself busy – and scarce – looking after her ailing guest, and so Charles and Elizabeth had plenty of scope for trysting: a sheriff of Nottingham described Rufford as 'a confused labyrinth, underneath all vaults, above entries, closets, oratories . . . I was never so puzzled in my life.'[30] It has been pointed out that had Bess not wanted her daughter to marry Charles, her chaperonage would have been 'Argus-eyed'.[31] Indeed, as Margaret later wrote (see below), Charles had so 'entangled himself that he could have none other' – no doubt as he had been told to do. Possibly, on the strength of the precontract, he had relieved Elizabeth of her virginity. Either way, marriage was now a necessity.

If love had flowered, which is by no means certain, it was the perfect outcome to what the two matriarchs had contrived, and they proceeded to the marriage. Rapid secret negotiations ensued, in which the Queen of Scots may have involved herself, writing at this time, and possibly seeking foreign support, to the Bishop of Ross, Antonio de Guaras (a Spanish merchant and banker resident in London, who had been acting as *chargé d'affaires* at the Spanish embassy after Spes had been expelled from England in 1572 for his involvement in the Ridolfi plot), and Antonio Fogaza, a Portuguese spy with connections to the Spanish embassy.[32]

If, when she learned of the marriage, the Queen expressed concern, the intention was to present it as the necessary consequence of a love affair that had gone too far. The wedding took place soon after 5 November[33] in the chapel of Rufford Abbey, with only a handful of witnesses present.[34] Shrewsbury, the bride's stepfather, was not among them; he only learned of the marriage after it was a *fait accompli*, but he was pleased to see his stepdaughter so well matched, and later stated that he was 'well at quiet, for there is few noblemen's sons in England that she hath not prayed me to deal for at one time or other; so did I for my Lord Rutland, my Lord Sussex, for my Lord Wharton and sundry others'.[35]

Margaret was probably dismayed to discover that her new daughter-in-law brought with her no dowry after all. Shrewsbury was perennially short of funds, having had largely to finance his royal prisoner out of his own pocket, and Bess was land-rich but cash-poor, as what she owned was vested in her sons. The best she could give Margaret was a loan. When Bess did eventually insist that her husband provide a dowry, he protested that, as he had known nothing of the marriage, he should not have to pay anything. At length, 'by brawling', Bess got him to agree to bestow £3,000 (£520,600), although there is no record of it ever being paid.[36] But that was the least of Margaret's troubles.

Predictably news of the marriage provoked the Queen's wrath, for if Elizabeth Cavendish bore a son he would have a sounder claim than the alien James VI to the English succession.[37] The Queen felt threatened; she was convinced that the marriage had been part of a sinister conspiracy against her throne, and expressed her belief that the Queen of Scots had been 'a party to the treason'.[38] On 17 November Margaret was summoned immediately to London with her son and his bride to answer for their actions.

Realising the enormity of what she had done, Margaret was in great fear, and Shrewsbury nearly fainted when he learned of the Queen's displeasure. Early in November he sent a letter seeking the Earl of Leicester's support, and on the 5th he wrote to Burghley, in fear that he and Bess would be arrested, 'for that my wife sought the marriage of her daughter, as oft she before hath done'. He recounted how Margaret had come to be at Rufford, and reminded Burghley that

> when we heard that the lady of [Lennox] was coming to Grimsthorpe, I made a full account of both their comings, and took occasion of small matter to write unto your lordship. As for the motion of marriage between the Duchess' [*sic*] son and my wife's daughter, it was not [blank] nor hid from the world. It hath been in talk betwixt them more than a year past, and not thought of as a matter worth her Majesty's hearing. To be plain with your lordship, I wished the match, and put to my helping hand to further it, and was contented, by my Lady Suffolk's great entreat[ing], to suffer my wife for that purpose to accompany her to Grimsthorpe; and at her return she thought

it in good forwardness, and so hoped . . . and this is all the dealing I know of that Lord [Charles].

Shrewsbury went on to describe in detail what had happened at Rufford. It had been no more than an innocent love affair that had led to a necessary wedding. 'And now this comes unlooked-for and without thanks to me. Thus have I at large particularly made account of these ladies and their dealings at my houses, for your lordship's full knowledge.' He had been 'tedious' in relating everything he knew 'concerning those ladies', hoping that Burghley would 'as friendly satisfy her Majesty in all these things', and he ended by saying that he and Bess wished his lordship 'heartily well'.[39]

Her Majesty was not friendly or satisfied. News of the marriage had caused a sensation at court, and enemies of the protagonists were ready to pounce. It is clear that there was a whispering campaign aimed at bringing down the Shrewsburys, if not Margaret too. By 2 December the Earl was beginning to panic. He wrote again to Burghley: 'I am advised that the late marriage of my wife's daughter is not well taken in the court, and there are some conjectures, more than well brought to her Majesty's ears, in ill part against my wife.' He asked Burghley to counter such talk.[40]

Margaret's journey south to London was terrible, as her little party battled gales, sleet and floods. Even so, they were in no hurry to reach their destination, for Margaret was deeply fearful of what the Queen might do next. On 3 December, marooned at Huntingdon, she wrote to Leicester, who had been sympathetic towards her in the past but had now sent her 'a letter of small comfort':

My very good lord,
    The great unquietness and trouble that I have had with passing these dangerous waters [floods], which hath many times enforced me to leave my way, which hath been some hindrance unto me that hitherto I have not answered your lordship's letters chiefly on that point wherein your lordship, with other my friends (as your lordship says) seems ignorant how to answer for me. And being forced to stay this present Friday in Huntingdon, somewhat to refresh myself and my over-laboured mules, that are both crooked and lame with their extreme labour by the way, I thought good to lay open before your

lordship, in these few lines, what I have to say for me touching my going to Rufford to my lady of Shrewsbury.

She told Leicester how Bess had pressed her to stay, and how she had been unable to refuse, and insisted that neither she nor Lady Suffolk had known of Bess's invitation 'till the morning after I came to Newark. And as I meant simply and well, so did I least mistrust that my doings should be taken in evil part.' Here she related the interview she had had with the Queen before her journey.

Now, my lord, for the hasty marriage of my son, after he had entangled himself so that he could have none other, I refer the same to your lordship's good consideration whether it was not most fitly for me to marry them, he being mine only son and comfort that is left me. Your lordship can bear me witness how desirous I have been to have had a match for him other than this. And the Queen's Majesty, much to my comfort, to that end gave me good words at my departure.

She ended by craving 'some comfort from her Majesty to help to lighten me of the heavy burden of this most wearisome journey' and begged for Leicester's 'kind influence in her favour'.[41]

Margaret also wrote that day to Burghley:

My very good lord,

Assuring myself of your friendship, I will use but few words at this present other than to let you understand of my wearisome journey and the heavy burthen of the Queen's Majesty's displeasure, which I know well I have not deserved, together with a letter of small comfort that I received from my lord of Leicester, here enclosed, the copy of my letter now sent to my lord of Leicester; and I beseech you to use your friendship towards me as you see time. Thus with my hearty commendations I commit you to Almighty God, Whom I beseech to send you long life to your heart's desire.

Your lordship's assured loving friend, Margaret Lennox.[42]

Fearful of the Queen's displeasure, most of Margaret's friends had abandoned her, but Leicester interceded with Elizabeth on her behalf, and let Margaret know that he had done so.[43] Yet surely she did not expect either Leicester or Burghley to believe that she was so naïve as to have overlooked the need to inform the Queen of Charles's proposed marriage.

On 4 December Shrewsbury wrote nervously to Elizabeth, still trying to make the affair sound as innocent as possible, and to exonerate himself:

> May it please your Majesty,
>
> I understand of late your Majesty's displeasure is set against my wife for the marriage of her daughter to my lady of Lennox's son. I must confess to your Majesty, as true it is, that it was dealt in suddenly and without my knowledge, but as I dare undertake and ensure to your Majesty for my wife, she finding her daughter disappointed of young Bertie, whereof she hoped, and that the other young gentleman [Charles] was inclined to love with a few days' acquaintance, did her best to further her daughter to that match, without having therein any other intent or respect than with reverent duty thought towards your Majesty.

In other words, Bess had despaired of finding a husband for her daughter, and had merely seized this unlooked-for opportunity. Shrewsbury went on:

> I wrote of this matter to my good lord of Leicester a good while ago at great length. I hid nothing from him I knew was done about the same, and thought it not meet to have troubled your Majesty therewith, because I took it not to be of any such importance as to write of, till now that I am urged by such as I see will not forbear to speak and devise what may procure any suspicion or doubtfulness of my service here. But as I have always found your Majesty my good and gracious sovereign, so do I comfort myself that your wisdom can find out right well what causes there are that move them thereunto, and therefore I [am] not afraid of any doubtful opinion or displeasure to remain with your Majesty of my wife or me, whom your Highness and your Council, as good cause is, have tried many ways in most dangerous times. We never had thought or respect but as your Majesty's most true and faithful servants, and so do truly serve and faithfully love and honour your Majesty.[44]

Margaret's bedraggled and exhausted party arrived in London on 10 December. They had received orders to go to Hackney, there to remain under house arrest pending official inquiries. On the Queen's command, the newly married couple were separated.[45]

That day, as soon as she arrived at Hackney, Margaret wrote to thank Leicester for presenting her excuse to the Queen. She again justified her visit to the Countess of Shrewsbury at Rufford, saying she had had no idea that it would offend the Queen, whose command she had obeyed. 'I neither went to Chatsworth, which was the place her Majesty did mislike of, nor yet near Sheffield, by thirty miles at the least.' As for consenting to the 'marriage of my son with the daughter of the Countess of Shrewsbury, surely my lord, as touching the marriage, other dealing or longer practice was there none, but the sudden affection of my son, as heretofore I have written unto your lordship to be a mean unto her Majesty to pity my cause and painful travel, and to have compassion on my widowish estate, being aged and of many cares'.[46] But Shrewsbury had already said that the two countesses had been planning the marriage for a year, which proved that Margaret was lying. As far as the Queen was concerned, that smacked of a treasonable conspiracy.[47]

On 12 December Fénélon reported to King Henry III of France: 'Lady Lennox came this day to court. She fears greatly the indignation of Queen Elizabeth, and that she will send her to the Tower on account of the marriage of her son. Still she relies on friends, who she hopes will save her from this blow.'[48] The next day Margaret was summoned to appear before the Queen.[49] There is no record of what took place at the audience, but certainly Elizabeth was not interested in her excuses. Like her father, Henry VIII, in 1536, she had every right to be angry, for she felt that her prerogative had been usurped, and that in doing so Margaret had committed treason. But for now the Queen stayed her hand and allowed her to go home to Hackney. Margaret, Charles and Elizabeth were ordered, on pain of close imprisonment, not to stir from their abode, and not to speak to anyone save those persons whom the Privy Council permitted to listen to them.[50]

The Queen now commanded that a commission of inquiry be set up under the direction of Sir Francis Walsingham, her new principal Secretary of State, to establish how the marriage had come about. Henry Hastings, Earl of Huntingdon, in whose house Margaret and Bess had first met years before, was ordered to question both of them, and every servant in their households. Both the Queen of Scots and Shrewsbury hated Huntingdon – Mary feared him because he was a staunch Puritan and a threat to her with his rival claim to the throne, and there was rivalry between the two earls.[51] Bess was placed under house arrest at Rufford pending the outcome of the inquiry.

The government clearly suspected a far-ranging conspiracy. Huntingdon was to begin by questioning Margaret's servants. On 22 December Walsingham informed him that the Queen's pleasure was that Thomas Fowler and Charles's former tutor, Malliet, be examined. Before Fowler was questioned he was to be kept in close custody for four or five days, and warned that 'unless he shall dutifully confess what he knows, he is like to incur some greater peril. Some such kind of persuasion cunningly used may, perhaps, breed such fear and deep conceit in him as may cause him to utter such truth as otherwise may hardly be drawn out of him.' As for Malliet, if there was no cause to detain him, he could be set at liberty.

Walsingham informed Huntingdon that the Queen had lately learned 'by secret means that the Bishop of Ross and a Scotsman called the Laird of Kilsyth, about half a year past, who remained in London well near six months, pretending to be enemies to the Queen of Scots, have had before their departure out of England some secret access to the Lady Margaret's house at Hackney'. This would not have been surprising, because Sir William Livingston, Laird of Kilsyth, was of the Lennox affinity; he had been a friend of Darnley's, and remained a friend of Queen Mary. Anyone trying to communicate with Mary was suspect, and a compromising letter from Kilsyth had been intercepted. Walsingham had liked Kilsyth, and was appalled to think that the Laird had been playing a double game. As a result of English pressure, Kilsyth was banished from Scotland for seven years. Possibly he had helped to convince Margaret that Mary was innocent of Darnley's murder. In 1581 he would be on the jury that condemned Morton to death for it.[52]

Huntingdon was also told that Antonio de Fogaza had conveyed letters to Sheffield and was 'acquainted with the Lady Lennox, and, as is informed, some of her household'; and that Antonio de Guaras had, 'since the late marriage, and especially since the Lady Lennox has been commanded to the keeping of her house, showed himself so inquisitive and fearful touching her case, as though some part of her dealings, not yet discovered, might reach unto himself, upon these advertisements her Majesty'. These two were to be closely examined. Fogaza and Guaras hated each other, but both represented Catholic powers that supported the Queen of Scots, and 'Mr Guaras was a friend of hers and bore affection to her'.[53]

Worse still, he was conniving in a plot to rescue Margaret. Walsingham revealed that Guaras had 'enquired often whether the Lady Lennox shall not be committed to the Tower, and seeks to have a vessel in readiness, as it is secretly informed, for the transportation of some whomsoever upon the sudden and need be'. Walsingham also knew of one of Charles's servants called Wendslow, a cousin to the Archbishop of Canterbury's steward, but 'by former profession a Popish massing priest. What ill instruments such disguised men of his calling oftentimes have been, and are in these days most like to be, your lordship knows or may easily conjecture.'[54]

In the event Walsingham himself interrogated Fowler. He fired numerous questions at him, most crucially 'whether about midsummer last he was not sent to his mistress' house at Temple Newsam', and if so, for what cause. When he was there, had he gone to meet Bess at Sheffield or Rufford, how often, and on what 'special matters'? Had he known, 'or at least had some conjecture', of Charles's projected marriage?[55]

Fowler was also questioned by Burghley as to whether, during Lennox's regency in Scotland, there had been talk of plans for the English succession. Clearly the government feared that the Lennox marriage was part of a much wider conspiracy, almost certainly involving the Queen of Scots.[56] Despite these close interrogations, the faithful Fowler revealed nothing of any import, and was soon released.

Margaret fared far worse. On 27 December, after what must have been a tense and dismal Christmas, she was imprisoned in the Tower. There she was accommodated in the Lieutenant's Lodging, where she had been confined in 1565–7, and once again she lost control of her lands and property. Wendslow, who had confessed to encouraging Charles to marry Elizabeth Cavendish, was also sent to the Tower.[57]

Prior to her arrest, Margaret had sent a desperate appeal to Shrewsbury, who did not delay in speaking up for her. On 27 December he informed Burghley that

upon my Lady Lennox's earnest request, I have written to my lords of the Council all I can find out of her behaviour towards this Queen [Mary] and dealing when she was in these north parts; and if some disallowed of my writing (as I look they will, because they would have it thought that I should have enough to do to answer for myself), let such reprove. I take it that Lady

Lennox be a subject in all respects worthy of her Majesty's favour, and for the duty I bear to her Majesty I am bound, methinks, to commend her as I find her, yea, and to entreat you and all my lords of the Council for her, to save her from blemish, if no offence can be found in her against her Majesty. I do not, nor can, find in the marriage of that lady's son to my wife's daughter can any way be taken, with indifferent judgement, [to] be any offence or contemptuous to her Majesty.

It was but a right that 'any subject may by law claim'.

Shrewsbury shrewdly perceived that it was not so much the marriage that was exercising the minds of the Queen and her Council as the political agenda that might lie behind it. 'But I must be plain with your lordship. It is not the marriage matter, nor the hatred some bear to my Lady Lennox, my wife or to me that makes this great ado and occupies heads with so many devices. It is a greater matter, which I leave to conjecture, not doubting your lordship's wisdom has foreseen it.' He would not have her Majesty imagine that there had been any 'liking or insinuation' with Mary, Queen of Scots, which was at the hub of official fears – nor would he hide such for Margaret's sake or his wife's.[58] He must also have been alluding to the dynastic possibilities of the marriage, a subject too dangerous to speak of openly.

Late in January 1575 Bess was also summoned to London, and it has often been stated that she too was sent to the Tower, but there is no record of it, or of her coming south. It is likely that Elizabeth spared her imprisonment because she knew that there was no reason to doubt her loyalty,[59] and because of the trust the Queen reposed in Shrewsbury.[60] It would have been a political embarrassment to have the wife of the Queen of Scots' gaoler in prison for intriguing against the Queen.[61] It was Margaret, with her royal blood and her infuriating maternal ambition, whom Elizabeth regarded as by far the more dangerous conspirator.

During her imprisonment Margaret sent Mary a gift of a square of *point tressé* lace worked from her own white hairs 'when she was in the Tower'. It was found among the possessions Mary left behind at Chartley Castle after her arrest in 1586, along with an ivory miniature of Margaret.[62]

On 18 and 20 February, during examinations of persons suspected of abetting the Queen of Scots, it emerged that in a letter to her supporters sent in November or December, Mary had been 'desirous to know how the Queen's Majesty of England liked of the marriage between Lord Lennox and Lady Shrewsbury's daughter'; and that Mary had been informed that 'it was thought that she was the deviser of that marriage', to which she made no comment.[63] This looked like proof that the government had been right to suspect that Charles's marriage was part of a greater conspiracy, but for all its diligence it could uncover no evidence of one. That it had not taken seriously the protestations of Margaret and Shrewsbury that the marriage had been purely the result of a love affair is evident from its failure to question the Duchess of Suffolk. But soon afterwards the commission concluded that there was no evidence to support formal charges of 'large treasons'.[64]

Elizabeth was still angry with Margaret, but she did sanction her release from the Tower. We do not know the date, but it was probably in the early months of 1575, as on 19 April (and also on 13 October) Margaret leased land to a tenant at Settrington.[65] On 14 May 1575 Bess's stepson, Gilbert Talbot, informed her that recently his bearer, Master Tyndall, 'was at Hackney, where he found them there well. And I trust very shortly that the dregs of all misconstruction will be wiped away, that their abode there after this sort will be altered.'[66] Yet although Margaret had been freed, it seems that the family were still living under a cloud of displeasure, and it was not until October that the Queen finally decided that 'money [was] at the ground of it' (i.e. the marriage between Charles and Elizabeth) and there was no other motive 'that may cause twitch',[67] and Margaret was exonerated.

There was more good news to come. On 9 June 1575, at Edinburgh, Margaret was designated as the nearest lawful heir after Archibald Douglas to her grandfather, George, Master of Angus.[68]

By then, she had become a grandmother once again. Elizabeth had gone home to Chatsworth and there borne Charles a daughter.[69] Now at last Margaret had cause to rejoice: 'God, to my comfort, list to provide a young tender infant, mine heart for to cheer.' 'That young lady fair'[70] was given the medieval Scottish name Arbella, which, perhaps intentionally, had no obvious royal connections but was a variant on Annabella, meaning 'graceful and beautiful'; in the fourteenth century there had been a queen of Scotland by that name, Annabella Drummond, the wife of Robert III. The christening may have been held at Edensor parish church, where other Cavendish babies had been baptised. Queen Mary, who had consented to be godmother but was not allowed to attend, sent a present for Arbella. Margaret was not among the sponsors, but she must have been delighted when the young parents returned to Hackney with her granddaughter, even if she had been disappointed that the baby wasn't a boy. Even so, there were now three royal heirs of the Lennox line.

Arbella's arrival seems to have cemented the reconciliation between Margaret and Queen Mary, who was thrilled by the birth of her niece and sent Arbella more gifts.[71] There was a gift for Margaret too, enclosed with a letter. Margaret's reply, dated 10 November 1575, leaves us in no doubt that the two women were fully reconciled. It is inconceivable that she would have written in such loving fashion if she still believed Mary to be Darnley's murderess. Her letter reveals that she knew how much Mary loved the child she had not seen since he was an infant, and who had been brought up to regard her as the personification of wickedness.

It may please your Majesty, I have received your token and mind [remembrance] both by your letter and other ways, much to my comfort, specially perceiving what zealous natural care your Majesty has of our sweet and peerless jewel [James VI] in Scotland, not little to my content. I have been no less fearful than careful as your Majesty of him, that the wicked governor [Morton] should not have power to do ill to his person, whom God preserve from his enemies.

We may infer from this that Margaret had found out that Morton had been one of the prime movers in the plot to murder Darnley, his own kinsman; small wonder then that she feared for James's safety. She went on:

Nothing I neglected, but presently, upon the receipt of your Majesty's [letter], the court being far off, I sent one trusty [Fowler?], who had done so much as if myself had been there, both to understand the state present and for prevention of evil to come. He has dealt with such as both may and will have regard for our jewel's preservation, and will use a bridle to the wicked when need requires.

I beseech your Majesty fear not, but trust in God that all there shall be well. The treachery of your traitor is known better than before. I shall always play my part to your Majesty's content, willing God, so that [it] may tend to both our comforts.

And now must I yield your Majesty my most humble thanks for your good remembrances and bounty to our little daughter here, Arbella, who some day may serve your Highness.

Almighty God grant unto your Majesty an happy life.

Hackney, this 10th of November.

Your Majesty's most humble and loving mother and aunt, M. L.[72]

Elizabeth Lennox added a postscript:

I most humbly thank your Majesty that it has pleased your Highness to remember me, your poor servant, both with a token and in my lady's Grace's letter [i.e. from Mary to Margaret], which is not little to my comfort. I can but wish and pray God for your Majesty's long and happy estate till time I may do your Majesty better service, which I think long to do, and shall always be as ready thereto as any servant your Majesty hath, according as by duty I am bound. I beseech your Highness pardon these rude lines, and accept the good heart of the writer, who loves and honours your Majesty unfeignedly.

Your Majesty's most humble and lowly servant during life, E. Lennox.[73]

Inevitably – for Margaret was probably still under surveillance – the letter was intercepted and brought to Burghley, and it may never have been received by Mary, for in the nineteenth century Agnes Strickland found it among government documents in the State Paper Office in London.[74]

21

'Till Death Do Finish My Days'

Until the spring of 1576 Margaret, Charles, Elizabeth and baby Arbella lived together at Hackney.[1] Margaret's life was not easy at this time; she was deeply in debt and Charles was suffering from tuberculosis, that scourge of Tudor males. Margaret's uncle, Arthur Tudor, Prince of Wales, her cousin, Edward VI, and her grandfather, Henry VII, had all succumbed to it, Arthur and Edward at just fifteen years of age. Margaret was 'reft' when Charles died, probably at Hackney, in April 1576, at the tender age of nineteen, and she was left 'his loss to lament with tears'. 'Thus Fortune still bent my joys to diminish, [and] in this mortal life my cares did augment.'[2] All her children were now dead.

She arranged for Charles to be buried temporarily in St Augustine's, the early-sixteenth-century parish church of Hackney,[3] then a fashionable place of worship among the local elite. She then commissioned a tomb for him and herself in Westminster Abbey. The sculptor is unknown, but work began on it at once, under the direction of Thomas Fowler, and was 'almost perfected' in her lifetime.[4] She did not choose to spend eternity lying beside Lennox, clearly feeling that her rightful resting place was among the kings her forefathers at Westminster.

Margaret wanted the earldom of Lennox to descend to Charles's daughter Arbella, not only because she felt that was Arbella's right, but because she herself had come to depend on its revenues. On 24 April she wrote from Hackney to Lord Ruthven:

My good lord and nephew, I have received your most natural and friendly letter, which showeth to me you fail not your friend for no adversity. I take no small comfort at your friendly remembrance of me at this time, and specially to hear of my sweet jewel, the King's Majesty, who the Almighty preserve. This is the first that I have written to any since my son's death, for I have small care of worldly matters. Yet have I been persuaded by some friends here, ere now, to have sent to some friend of mine there, to know how the state standeth of the earldom of Lennox, because my son hath left a daughter behind him. And having my most special trust in your lordship, these are to desire the same advertisement from you so soon as ye may, whether his daughter be heritable to the land or not, and what your advice is for me to do I will follow (God willing), and till I have received the same I will not write to the Regent nor other there. Always for my own part my lord my husband made good assurance to me in dower for the most part of the lands of Lennox and Darnley. I pray you also procure and send me a perfect pedigree of the descent of the earls of Lennox from the first of the House, with arms and matches in marriage, for I am about a monument which requires the help thereof.

This was almost certainly a reference to the tomb she was planning for Charles and herself. She ended: 'Thus being bold to trouble you, as him whom in those parts I have my chiefest trust in, I commit you to God's Almighty protection. Your lordship's most assured loving aunt and friend.'[5]

It was an opening salvo, signalling Margaret's relentless determination to devote her formidable energies to the interests of Arbella, in whom, with James of Scotland, were now vested the Lennox claims to the crown. James VI was male and had the prior claim, but he was an alien; Arbella had been born in England. Margaret's chief hope lay in James, but whatever happened, it looked as if one of her grandchildren was destined to sit on the English throne.

Margaret was convinced it would be James. She wrote assuring him that he was her chief hope for the future.[6] She sent him books on history, which stood him in good stead in later life, and hunting gloves embroidered with pearls.[7] But she was fiercely protective of Arbella's interests too. With Bess, the child's other grandmother, she worked tirelessly to secure for her the earldom of Lennox.

It seems that Burghley granted Margaret the wardship of her granddaughter, since the Shrewsburys were to apply for it later.[8] Wardships could be profitable, but there was as yet no money in Arbella's, and Margaret was poor. From now on she would marshal her considerable energy and powers of persuasion to protect Arbella's interests. It was probably soon after Charles's death that she and Bess agreed that Arbella and her mother should leave Hackney to live with Bess at Sheffield Castle. Bess had the wherewithal to raise the child in the manner to which the Countess of Lennox should have been accustomed, and maybe the widowed Elizabeth just wanted to go home to her mother. It has been asserted that Margaret was stricken with 'a languishing decay' after Charles's death,[9] but she seems to have been active enough in the two years that followed it.

Left alone at Hackney, Margaret probably missed Elizabeth and Arbella greatly, but she continued to focus her energies on securing her granddaughter's inheritance and her own dower lands. She asked Thomas Randolph to lay Arbella's case before the Regent Morton, arguing that, Mar having granted the earldom to Charles in 1572, it should now pass to Arbella by right of descent. Morton was obdurate, arguing that Arbella was too young to inherit the earldom, and that it must revert to King James until she was eighteen; in any case, since James had been a minor at the time the earldom had been conferred on Charles, 'it may by the King be revoked at any time'.[10] Morton himself was clearly against it being held by an alien: 'he had rather the King should make choice, whom of his so near himself he would prefer'.[11] Of course, if James reserved the earldom to himself, Margaret would lose most of her income.

Indignantly Margaret wrote to the Queen, begging her to bring pressure to bear on Morton:

> 1st. How the dower can be avoided by their laws. 2nd. How the Regent can disinherit the daughter of Charles Stuart, if he will not permit the dower to be answered. 3rd. If he will not permit the dower to be answered. 4th. If he will delay the admittance of Lady Arbella as heir to her father, then to demand that Lady Margaret have the right of the land of the Lennox during the King's minority in right of wardship for her son's child, etc., and her wages.[12]

Elizabeth responded with a terse letter to Morton: 'The Queen finds it very strange that any disposition should be intended of the earldom to the prejudice of the only daughter of the late Earl of Lennox.'[13] But Morton remained impervious.

Margaret was at Settrington on 18 August 1576, when she granted tenants a lease,[14] but she and her cousin, Lady Mary Grey, were at court at Christmas, and their names head the list of those giving presents to the Queen.[15] On New Year's Day 1577 Elizabeth gave Margaret a small silver-gilt gift.

Queen Elizabeth's approach to Morton having failed, Margaret appealed to Queen Mary, who was sympathetic and in February 1577 added a codicil to her will:

> I give to my niece Arbella the earldom of Lennox, held by her late father, and enjoin my son, as my heir and successor, to obey my will in this particular. And I restore to my aunt of Lennox all the rights that she can pretend to the earldom of Angus, previously to the grant made by commandment [in 1565] between my said aunt of Lennox and the Earl of Morton, seeing that it was then made by the late King, my husband, and me, on the promise of his [Morton's] faithful assistance, if he [Darnley] and me were in danger and required his aid, which promise he broke by his secret understanding with our enemies and rebels that made the enterprise against his [Darnley's] life, and also took up arms and bore banners displayed against us.

In this will, drawn up the year before, Mary had left her right to the English succession to Charles Lennox 'or Claud Hamilton, whichever shall serve us faithfully and be most constant in religion, should our son, James, persist in his heresy'.[16] But Mary was no longer queen in Scotland so the document had no force whatsoever in law, and Morton ignored it.

Margaret continued to put pressure on the Scottish government. On 15 February the English Council issued a passport to Thomas Helforth 'to pass into Scotland in her affairs, and to return again', and authorised the provision of 'two geldings for him and his man', on condition that he brought back 'the said geldings at his return, and that the Marshal of Berwick shall take bonds of him for that purpose'.[17] Helforth's mission was almost certainly to gain support for Arbella's claim to the earldom of Lennox.[18] At this time Margaret was probably at Settrington, where on 19 April 1577 she granted another lease. She is not recorded there after this,[19] although she may have stayed on for a few more months, as she was next recorded at Hackney in November.

In late July Leicester, taking the waters at Buxton, met with Queen Mary and Bess at Chatsworth. Pressed by Bess, he promised to use his influence with the Queen on Arbella's behalf.[20] There hangs at Hardwick Hall an exquisite portrait of the two-year-old Arbella, a grave, lavishly dressed little girl holding a doll and looking very much like her grandmother Margaret. Painted in the late summer or early autumn of 1577, it was almost certainly commissioned by Bess, who had it boldly inscribed *Arabella Comitessa Levinae*. Around the child's neck is a triple gold chain with a pendant shield bearing a countess's coronet and the Lennox motto, *To achieve, I endure*, in French. The portrait may have been intended to impress Leicester, or to be displayed at court when Bess and Elizabeth travelled south to London in September to press Arbella's claim to the earldom of Lennox.[21]

That July the Scottish Parliament finally ruled on 'the dower of the Countess of Lennox in Scotland'. The lords recalled how in 1544 Lennox had promised to endow her with various parcels of land in Scotland; but now these lands had descended to the King with the earldom of Lennox. Margaret had demanded that Morton return them, but 'he denies the same'. The Regent's objections 'against the right of the dower' were that 'the covenant was made in England, and the Earl [Lennox] was banished' at the time, and that it was 'against the common weal of Scotland'.[22]

The lords then pronounced on Arbella's title to the earldom of Lennox. Mar had given it to 'Charles, late Earl of Lennox, and to his heirs for ever', and Margaret had argued that after his death, 'by reason of the said gift', it should pass to Arbella. Morton had been asked to grant the wardship of the lands to Margaret, yet he 'not only denied the same, but also denied to allow the lady [Arbella] as heir to the earldom; so that the Regent [Morton] will not permit her Grace to deal with the earldom either in her own right as for her dower, or in right of the young lady, as tutrix or guardian to her'.[23] In this case Morton objected on the grounds that the earldom of Lennox, having been confirmed to Charles by the Earl of Mar, could be revoked by the King. If Morton allowed Arbella's claim, 'and the King hereafter should mislike, how should the Regent discharge himself?'[24]

To be on the safe side, Morton had the earldom declared extinct, which meant that all the lands attached to it reverted to the Scottish Crown. He refused to grant Elizabeth Cavendish any dower or allow her to act in Scotland as Arbella's guardian. She appealed to Burghley and then Leicester, but neither was in a position to help her.[25] Queen Elizabeth expressed indignation at the disinheriting of Arbella, while Queen Mary was gratified that Margaret had now come to see how perfidious Morton could be.[26]

Margaret's efforts had been in vain. They were all gone now, the Lennoxes – Matthew, Darnley and Charles – and she was to remain in penury for the rest of her life, heavily encumbered with debt. Northumberland, who had been beheaded in 1572 for his part in the Northern Rising, had lent her money, and on his attainder, repayment had become due to the Crown. Bess had also made a loan to her, on which the interest was costing Margaret £500 (£74,650) a year.[27] The Queen informed James VI that it was his responsibility to meet his grandmother's debts, and that he could afford to do so now that he was in the possession of the Lennox estates. This fell on deaf ears.[28] All Margaret now had to live on, and meet her debts, were some rents that had once been paid to Charles: 'the old Lady Lennox before her death said that she was yearly satisfied for all that was due to her son Charles, late Earl of Lennox'.[29]

In regard to Arbella, Margaret did not go down without a fight. She protested to Burghley, who on 30 January 1578 instructed Randolph 'to recommend Lady Lennox's causes to the Regent to be considered of, as in law and equity may be thought fit, in which she hopes he will be answerable to the care she has to right the subjects of Scotland who have sustained any loss by any of hers'.[30] But it was a vain hope, and it has rightly been said that the struggle for Arbella's inheritance overshadowed the twilight years of Margaret's life.[31]

In October 1577 Margaret was sixty-two. Phillips implies that she was worn down by the loss of her husband and children, and must have been lonely. Although in poor straits financially, she was still entertaining guests. On 5 November 1577 it was noted that 'my lady of Essex came to Hackney a week past'.[32] Lettice Knollys, the Dowager Countess of Essex, was the Queen's cousin. Her late husband, Walter Devereux, Earl of Essex, had died the previous year, and rumour had linked the Countess's name to that of the Earl of Leicester, whom she would secretly marry the following year. Margaret may have been aware of the affair, as Leicester was her friend. The Countess brought with her to Hackney her two daughters, Penelope and Dorothy; all three were bound for the court to celebrate the Queen's Accession Day, which by now had become an annual festival. Given Leicester's connections with Margaret, it is possible that they visited her on the way.[33]

Both Margaret and Queen Mary had been concerned that James VI, now eleven, was being brought up as a Calvinist, and to believe that his mother was an adulteress and a murderess. Mary had never recognised him as king in her stead, and in her will of 1577 she had bequeathed him her throne on condition that he become a Catholic. If he persevered in his 'heresy', her crown was to descend to Philip of Spain. In order to save James from being disinherited, and to boost her own cause, Mary wanted to have him spirited away to Spain, and in 1577–8 she corresponded secretly with Margaret to this end.[34] But the plan, unrealistic and impractical as it was, came to nothing.

Margaret was probably at court on New Year's Day 1578, when she gave the Queen 'a casting bottle of agate, garnished with gold and set with stone, with sparks of rubies, and a woman holding in her hand a scroll written with the word Abundancia'.[35] In 1584, after Margaret's death, Queen Mary, having fallen out with Bess (whom she blamed for spreading rumours that Mary had borne Shrewsbury a child), drafted what has become notorious as the 'scandal letter' to Elizabeth, telling her how Bess had spread disparaging gossip about the Queen, and how she had ridiculed Elizabeth for having such a good opinion of her own beauty, as if she were 'some goddess' and 'glorious as the sun'. Mary recounted how, 'in her last visit to you, [Bess] and the late Countess of Lennox, while speaking to you, dared not look at one another for fear of bursting out laughing at the tricks she was playing on you'. Worse still, Margaret and Bess had asserted that the Queen was 'not as other women'.[36] But it is highly unlikely that the letter was ever sent (or possibly it was intercepted by Walsingham or Burghley), since there were no repercussions from it.[37] Mary may have been referring to Margaret's visit to court that New Year. One can imagine that, after the Queen had deprived her of her lands and income, Margaret did not feel very kindly disposed towards her.

She could no longer afford to live in, or keep up, her Yorkshire mansions. On 20 February 1578, to augment her income, she leased the house at Settrington to Thomas Fowler, in consideration of his 'good, long and faithful service'. After her death it was noted 'what state the house was left' and that much of it was decayed. She had stipulated that it be left in the care of Laurence Nesbit and two other tenants, Simon Dodsworth and Rowland Fothergill, who remained in charge of it for four years, whereupon Fowler took possession again.[38]

On 26 February she made her will,[39] bequeathing her soul 'unto Almighty God', and directing that her body be buried in 'the great church of Westminster, in the monument, sepulchre or tomb already bargained for, and appointed to be made and set up in the said church. Also I will that the body of my son Charles shall be removed from the church of Hackney and laid with mine both in one vault or tomb in the said church of Westminster.' She bequeathed £1,200 (£180,000) for her funeral and burial, to be raised from the sale of her 'plate, household stuff and movables'. She wanted £40 of that money to be distributed to the poor 'on the day of my burial', and more allocated for the provision of gowns for a hundred poor women to wear as mourners, a visual testimony to her charity.

She left James VI, 'for a remembrance of me, his grandmother, my new field bed [a four-poster bed with an arched canopy] of black velvet embroidered with flowers of needlework, with the furniture thereunto belonging, as curtains, quilt and bedstead, but not any other bedding thereunto' – possibly because it was too worn. These were to be delivered to James within six months of her death.

Margaret left £50 (£7,470) to Margaret Wilton, 'my woman (if she be with me in service at the time of my death)'; and to every other servant of hers, male and female, a year's wages. She bequeathed to 'old Mompesson, my servant', £20 (£2,990). These bequests were to be funded from the sale of the household stuff from all Margaret's houses, after her funeral and burial expenses had been paid.

'For his good and faithful service done to me and mine many years past' Thomas Fowler was to receive all Margaret's flocks of sheep, to the number of 'eight hundred at six score to the hundred'. These sheep were then grazing at Settrington in the charge of Laurence Nesbit, Simon Dodsworth and Rowland Fothergill. The will mentions that Margaret owed Fowler £778.15s. (£116,280), and that was to be paid out of the proceeds of the sale of her 'goods, chattels, plate and jewels'. She left him 'all my clocks, watches, dials, with their furniture', and appointed him joint executor of her will together with John Kaye of Hackney, Esquire, who was clerk of the greencloth in the royal household. Kaye was to be given £40 from the money raised, 'for his pains'.

Margaret appointed Burghley and Leicester overseers of her will. To Burghley she left 'my ring with four diamonds set square therein, black enamelled', and to Leicester 'my chain of pomander beads netted over with gold, and my tablet with the picture of King Henry the Eight therein' – a small portrait painted on a 'table' or board, which perhaps had sentimental value for her.[40]

The rest of her possessions – whatever was left after her expenses and bequests had been met – were to go to her granddaughter

Arbella. She directed that her worldly goods be entrusted to Fowler's safe keeping until such time as they were sold or disposed of, and 'sundry bonds and covenants of warranties' had been made good; those intended for Arbella were to remain in his hands until she married or attained the age of fourteen.

'In witness whereof, and that this is my lawful last will and testament,' Margaret concluded, 'made and determined advisedly by good deliberation and upon good considerations, I, the said Lady Margaret, being in good and perfect mind and remembrance, and in good health of body (thanks be to Almighty God), have put hereunto my hand and seal of arms.'[41]

Although she had stated in her will that she was in good health, it must have been obvious that Margaret was failing. On 5 March Shrewsbury was sufficiently concerned to apply for Arbella's wardship; clearly he and Bess feared that Margaret's death might lead to their losing control over their granddaughter. In the event, the Queen was to make Arbella her own ward.[42]

Margaret's last illness was sudden and short. On the evening of 7 March 1578 she entertained the Earl of Leicester to dinner at her house at Hackney. After he left she became seriously ill. According to John Phillips, as her sickness increased, her strength began to fail; no medicine could restore her to health, 'for Death against life [be]gan to prevail'.[43] On the evening of 10 March[44] she died peacefully, aged sixty-two. She made a 'godly end', bidding her last farewell to the noble persons who were present at the hour of her death,[45] and embracing death 'most joyfully', according to her tomb epitaph.

Phillips states that she was 'lastly so supported with truth' that her misfortunes seemed 'incredible' – he could not believe that one so serene could have suffered so much. Coming from a Puritan preacher, this statement might suggest that on her deathbed Margaret may have embraced the Protestant religion; yet that cannot have been the case, for in the *Commemoration* Margaret states that 'even till Death do finish my days, nor pain nor cross could my faith remove'; and if being 'supported with truth' reflects her staunch Catholic faith, then Phillips was a man of generous heart. While he 'lamented her estate', he 'triumphed in her'. And yet she had stood for much of which he could not have approved.

Margaret's last illness had come on suddenly, and in 1584, in a notorious hostile Catholic libel, a printed tract entitled *Leicester's Commonwealth*, it was asserted that Leicester, who had once been suspected of murdering his wife, Amy Robsart, had poisoned

Margaret. Such rumours often attached to the sudden death of great personages,[46] and the anonymous author of this libel was out to vilify Leicester in every respect. He asserted that in 1571 the Earl had poisoned Sir Nicholas Throckmorton at dinner; in the seventeenth century there was a persistent belief in the family that 'when Sir Nicholas Throckmorton was poisoned and lay upon his death bed, he called one of his own gentlemen privately to him and charged him, "When I am dead and gone, tell that rogue Leicester that I say he hath poisoned me, but that I hope my daughter[47] will outlive him and, when he is also dead and gone, will lift up her farthingale and piss upon his grave, and tell her from me that I charge her to do so!"'[48]

Gossip credited Leicester with poisoning several people.[49] According to *Leicester's Commonwealth*, he had two Italian physicians in his household, both 'poisoners so subtle that they can make a man die in what manner or show of sickness as long after as they like'. It was alleged that he had poisoned Odet de Coligny, Cardinal of Châtillon, in 1571, and Walter Devereux, Earl of Essex, in 1576; in the first case, the Cardinal's servant had probably been the culprit; in the second, an autopsy revealed nothing sinister, which suggests that the cause had been dysentery. Leicester would also be accused of trying to murder a French envoy, Jean Simier, later in 1578, and of poisoning Thomas Radcliffe, Earl of Sussex, in 1583.[50] His mistress, Douglass Howard, Lady Sheffield, would claim many years later that he had tried to poison her, and centuries afterwards it was asserted that her hair and nails had fallen out as a result.[51] These allegations should be treated with the contempt they deserve, since there is no contemporary evidence to support them.

In *Leicester's Commonwealth* the author states:

It hath been told me also by some of the servants of the late Lady Lennox, who was of the blood royal by Scotland, as all men know, and consequently little liked, that a little before her death or sickness, my lord took the pains to come and visit her, with extraordinary kindness, at her house at Hackney, bestowing long discourses with her in private, but as soon as he was departed the good lady fell into such a flux [diarrhoea or dysentery] as by no means could be stayed so long as she had life in her body, whereupon both she herself and all such as were near about her and saw her disease and ending-day, were fully of opinion that my lord had procured her dispatch at his being there. Whereof let the women that served her be examined, as also Fowler, that then had the chief doings in her affairs, and since hath been entertained by my lord of Leicester. Malliet also, a stranger born, then was about her, a sober and zealous man in religion, and otherwise well qualified, can say somewhat in this point, as I think, if he were demanded.[52]

There is no proof to support this story, or any other in the libel, although whoever wrote it was well informed about Margaret's household, which suggests unfounded servants' gossip. After her death Fowler did become steward to the Earl of Leicester.[53] It has been suggested that Leicester employed him because he had access to Margaret's papers, in which there might have been proof that Mary, Queen of Scots, was innocent of Darnley's murder, in which case Leicester envisaged that, should Mary ever become Queen, he would be the one to vindicate her;[54] or that he could destroy the evidence of Margaret's rapprochement with Mary.[55] But this is pure speculation.

Fowler's record of service to the Lennoxes had been exemplary, and his son William would be a staunch supporter of Arbella Stuart. Fowler did stand – as he thought – to inherit a lot of money on Margaret's death, but it is hard to believe that he would have connived with Leicester to do away with her. And what would Leicester have gained? A pomander and a portrait were hardly sufficient reasons to commit murder. The days were past when Margaret posed a threat to the state, when Leicester would – if he were so moved, in the Queen's interests – have had far more reason to remove her. Moreover, he had long been a friend to her, even when there had been nothing in it for him.

If Margaret's last illness was as described in *Leicester's Commonwealth*, it could have resulted from food poisoning, which might well have seemed to observers to be of sinister origin. In January 1568 she had complained of her 'old colic', which had perhaps been a chronic condition engendered by stress; in the intervening years no more is heard of it, and it probably had no connection with her last illness. Had it been symptomatic of something more sinister, there would surely be more evidence that Margaret was in failing health.

Possibly, having 'passed a life of stress and agitation',[56] she died of a heart attack or stroke; her mother, Margaret Tudor, had been felled by a stroke at the age of fifty-two.

★

Margaret's will was sealed on 11 March, the day after her death, and proved by Fowler on 27 March in London before William Drury. Then Fowler and Kaye began winding up her estate. But Fowler soon had to inform the Queen that his mistress had died so poor that there was not even enough money to pay for her funeral. Indeed, she had 'died in so great debt, and her goods so far unable to answer the same, that the Queen's Majesty of natural favour, pity, and honour to her cousin, bestowed the charges of all her funerals, which were as honourably done as could belong to her degree'.[57] Elizabeth, to her chagrin, had had no choice, Margaret being her cousin, yet she did allow her a state funeral complete with heralds and trappings. On 19 June, to recoup the outlay, the Queen seized Margaret's English estates, on account of the debt that the Crown had acquired from the estate of the Earl of Northumberland. However, she thereafter used the rents to maintain Charles's widow, Elizabeth, and Arbella.[58]

In March Burghley confirmed 'the proceeding at the funeral of the Countess of Lennox', in which her noble pedigree in the form of the arms of the great marriages of her forebears was to be displayed in banners, from James Douglas, Earl of Angus, and Isabella, daughter of Robert II, King of Scots, to Angus and Margaret Tudor; Margaret's own arms would be prominent.[59]

The funeral took place on 3 April. The coffin was borne in solemn procession to Westminster Abbey. 'First, two yeomen conductors with black staves', followed by 'the priests and clerks, the poor women, the great banner borne by a knight, gentlemen mourners in gowns'. Margaret's servants were at the front with her chaplains, secretaries and executors following, then 'the preacher alone, the steward, treasurer, and comptroller' of her household, Clarencieux Herald and Garter King of Arms, 'having on each side of him a gentleman usher'. Then came 'the corpse borne by eight gentlemen', and in its wake 'four barons, assistants to the body, six heralds bearing the six banner rolls above the corpse, two gentlemen ushers, the principal mourner assisted by the Lord Treasurer and the Earl of Leicester'. Next came 'a baroness to bear the train', assisted by Margaret's chamberlain, 'ten other mourners, all other ladies and gentlemen according to their degrees, two yeoman ushers in their coats, the yeomen of the household [and] all other yeomen, wearing black'.[60] Prominent among the mourners was Bess of Hardwick, who had hastened to London to take part in the obsequies,[61] which were conducted with Protestant rites.[62]

Margaret was 'most honourably buried',[63] as she had planned, in the same vault as her son Charles in Westminster Abbey,[64] in the south aisle of the soaring Lady Chapel built by her grandfather, Henry VII, where the fine tomb she had wanted was nearly finished.[65] It was another 'sumptuous sepulchre' such as the one she had erected for her husband. 'Thomas Fowler executor to the said Lady Margaret, did with the goods of the said lady erect a costly and stately tomb of rich stone and curious workmanship, with the picture[66] of that lady, as lively and as well coloured as art might afford it, about which monument is graven [a] memorable epitaph declaring her nobility.'[67] Built of different-coloured marbles, the tomb had obelisks at each corner, of which two survive.[68] The life-like painted and gilded alabaster effigy of Margaret, which was in place by the following October, had probably been sculpted by someone who had seen her. It portrays her in her robes of state: a red mantle lined with ermine over a gown of blue and gold with a ruff, and her golden countess's coronet upon a white French cap. A crowned lion rests at her feet.[69] At the sides of the tomb are weepers: the kneeling figures of her four sons – Darnley in armour and an ermine-lined mantle, having a crown above his head, as he was never crowned king of Scots – and her four daughters, all looking like young women in their Venetian gowns, paned sleeves and embroidered caps.[70] On the chest are sculpted and painted coats of arms: Darnley impaling Scotland, a lozenge of Angus and Douglas, and Lennox impaling Angus and Douglas.

This was a fitting resting place for one who had had a strong claim to the Tudor throne. At the further end of the chapel stood the fine Renaissance tomb of Margaret's great-grandmother, Margaret Beaufort, Countess of Richmond and Derby, who had died in 1509; Margaret's was the first burial in the south aisle since then. The space between their tombs would, from 1612, be occupied by the grand monument of Mary, Queen of Scots, placed there by James I to underline her – and therefore his – legitimate descent from Henry VII.[71]

On the ledge of Margaret's tomb chest at the east end is a Latin inscription, which translates as: 'This work was completed at the charge of Thomas Fowler, the executor of this lady, 24 October 1578.' At the west end is the epitaph referred to by Holinshed, also in Latin, and perhaps composed by the faithful Fowler:

Sacred to the memory of Margaret Douglas, wife of Matthew Stuart, Earl of Lennox, granddaughter to Henry VII, King of

England, by his daughter; joined by the closest ties of kinship to most puissant kings, grandmother to James VI of Scotland; a lady of most pious character, invincible spirit and matchless steadfastness. She died the tenth of March, year of Our Lord 1577 [*sic*]. Margaret, mighty in virtue, mightier yet in lineage: ennobled by kings and by her forebears, descended from Scottish and English princes, she was also a progenitor of princes. Those things that belong unto death she released to death most joyfully, and sought God, for she belonged to God before.

A later inscription on the side panels reads:

Here lieth the noble Lady Margaret, Countess of Lennox, daughter and sole heir of Archibald, Earl of Angus, by Margaret, Queen of Scots, his wife, that was eldest daughter to King Henry the 7; who bare unto Matthew, Earl of Lennox, her husband, four sons and four daughters. This lady had to her great-grandfather King Edward the 4, to her grandfather King Henry the 7, to her uncle King Henry the 8, to her cousin germane King Edward the 6, to her brother King James of Scotland the V, to her son King Henry the First, to her grandchild King James the 6. Having to her great-grandmother and grandmother two queens, both named Elizabeth, to her mother Queen Margaret of Scots, to her aunt Mary, the French Queen, to her cousins germanes Mary and Elizabeth, queens of England, to her niece and daughter-in-law Mary, Queen of Scots. Henry, second son to this lady, was king of Scots and father to James the 6, now king. This Henry was murdered at the age of 21 years. Charles, her youngest son, was earl of Lennox, father to the Lady Arbell[a]. He died at the age of 21 years, and is here entombed.

This inscription must have been added after 1603, in the reign of Margaret's grandson, James I.

Over the centuries Margaret's tomb suffered the depredations of souvenir hunters and other damage. A Westminster Abbey guidebook of 1953 refers to it being 'once painted and gilt' and to the crown above Darnley's head being broken. It was restored and re-coloured in 1957–60, when Darnley's crown was replaced, but since then there has been further damage: the hands of two of the weepers are missing, the heraldic unicorn devices have lost their horns, and Darnley's crown has lost its cross.[72]

Yet it is another, greater memorial in Westminster Abbey that bears testimony to Margaret's dynastic importance, for on the canopy surmounting the joint tomb of Elizabeth I and Mary I is a shield bearing her arms impaled with those of Lennox, set between those of Margaret Tudor and James IV, and those of Mary, Queen of Scots, and Margaret's son, Lord Darnley, all of them proclaiming the right line of succession.[73]

Given her many intrigues and treasonable activities, her closeness to the throne, and Queen Elizabeth's suspicions of her, it is surprising that Margaret Douglas lived so long. There had been occasions on which the Queen would have had every justification for sending her to the block, yet there is no evidence that Elizabeth ever contemplated such an extreme punishment.[74] Although she feared the dynastic pretensions of her female cousins, and imprisoned them for it, she was not in favour of executing them, even Mary, Queen of Scots, over the signing of whose death warrant she agonised for three months. Possibly, despite all the bad blood between them, she came to like and admire Margaret, a strong character like herself. Maybe she recognised that her subversive activities had been driven to a great extent by her love and ambition for her children, as Margaret herself once admitted.

William Camden, writing in 1615, declared: 'She was a matron of singular piety, patience and modesty, who was thrice cast into the Tower (as I have heard her say herself) not for any crime of treason but for love matters: first, when Thomas Howard, falling in love with her, died in the Tower of London; then for the love of Henry, Lord Darnley, her son, to Mary, Queen of Scots; and lastly for the love of Charles, her younger son, to Elizabeth Cavendish, mother of the Lady Arbella.'[75] Love had been the great blessing and the great curse of Margaret's life, for she had truly suffered for it, and in the end had lost all those who were dear to her, including her adored husband and son, to violent deaths. She of all people should have learned that love and politics make dangerous bedfellows, but that seems to have eluded her, which shows that she had allowed her heart to rule her head.

In his *Commemoration*, published in London soon after her death, John Phillips referred to Margaret's 'goodly life', 'her constancy in suffering' and 'her constant and perfect patience in time of misfortune', which was a 'bulwark against the brunts of fickle Fortune'. Since infancy Margaret had been 'tossed with both fortunes, sometime in adversity, and sometime in prosperity'.[76] She had been 'a noble lady compassed with care' and 'pursued by dolour', who had 'felt the fullness of Fortune's fallacies'. Yet, from being 'drowned in griefs', she had come to be 'comforted by hope'. Some might argue that misfortune had been her destiny. Her royal blood had been a dangerous inheritance. It had inescapably drawn her into the politics and controversies of her day; it had brought danger and tragedy in her youth, when she had attempted to marry for love; and it had fuelled her perilous, driving ambition to secure a crown for her descendants,[77] which in its turn brought even more tragedy.

Although life had dealt with her harshly,[78] in some ways she was luckier than her cousins.[79] Her marriage had been an enduring and successful love match, unlike those of poor Katherine and Mary Grey, who had been cruelly parted from the husbands they had loved and secretly wed, or Lady Jane Grey, who had been forced against her will to marry Guildford Dudley. Margaret had had the joy of bringing up two beloved sons, whereas Katherine's elder son had been taken from her and she had died before she could see the younger grow up. Like all her cousins, Margaret was a victim of Queen Elizabeth's animosity towards her female heirs; like them, she was imprisoned, but, unlike them, she was freed. Despite everything, she had managed to retain her position at court through four turbulent reigns, a lucky survivor in the brutal world of sixteenth-century politics.[80] Furthermore, she died in her bed, not by the axe like Jane Grey or Mary, Queen of Scots, or in prison like Katherine and Mary Grey; and she lived out what her contemporaries would have seen as her allotted span. Perhaps that is why her story is more obscure than theirs – and that is one of many reasons why it needs to be told.

22

'A Progenitor of Princes'

'The Countess of Lennox, my mother-in-law, died about a month ago,' the Queen of Scots wrote to James Boyd, Archbishop of Glasgow, in May 1578. It was in this letter that she recalled how she and Margaret had been reconciled 'these five or six years bygone'. She also informed the Archbishop that 'the Queen of England has taken into care her ladyship's granddaughter'.[1]

That month James VI, now twelve, sent Robert Pitcairn, the benefice holder, or Commendator, of Dunfermline, on an embassy to London. The Spanish ambassador reported:

> The principal cause of their coming is to claim the inherit-
> ance of the Countess of Lennox, grandmother of the King
> of Scotland, and when this is obtained the King would claim
> to be the heir to this throne. It is asserted that his succession
> is barred by a law made by Henry III or Henry IV, and
> confirmed by Henry VIII, by which an alien cannot inherit
> property here; but as the words used in the Act are *in partibus
> ultramarines* [in the regions beyond the sea] it appears that
> Scotsmen are not debarred, as they are born in the same
> island, and the kings of Scotland formerly possessed the county
> of Huntingdon.[2]

James argued that he was not 'the first born in Scotland, nor the first Scottish king, that hath succeeded to lands in England, respecting that this objection of foreign birth could have no place against the Countess of Lennox nor her son, both born in England, if they were alive'.[3] But that was still regarded as highly debatable, and Queen

Elizabeth 'would not give ear to those who affirmed that the Lady Arbella was next heir to the lands in England'.[4]

On 17 June 1578 Pitcairn was instructed by James VI 'to enquire the state and order of his dearest grandmother's the Countess of Lennox's will, who were her executors with her jewels, plate, and movables; what order is taken for the payment of her creditors, *etc.*' He was also to enquire about the livings and rents that Margaret and Lennox had held in England, for James had been 'instructed of his right thereto in succession'. The Commendator was 'to crave of the Queen and her Council that the same may be preserved to him', and in aid of that he was to 'speak with some of our grandmother's servants that were privy and skilful in her affairs as ye ride up through Yorkshire, or at London for your better information, before passing to the court'.[5] But two days later Elizabeth revoked Margaret's lands, having no intention of allowing James to claim them, and they reverted to the Crown. Three months after Margaret's death her landlord, Richard Carew, sold the King's Place at Hackney to Lord Hunsdon.[6]

In a letter of 1603 Arbella wrote of her hopes of having 'recovered a little land which a most noble great-great uncle of mine [Henry VIII] gave his niece [Margaret] when he bestowed on her a noble exiled gentleman',[7] meaning Lennox. As it turned out, of her grandmother's properties, she was permitted to retain only the manor of Smallwood, Cheshire, which yielded an annual income of about £900 (£112,760) in rent. It was not listed in the grant of lands given by Henry VIII to the Lennoxes on their marriage, so was probably acquired by Margaret during her widowhood. It was to be the subject of a number of lawsuits between Arbella and her tenant before she sold it in 1607.[8]

Margaret had died believing that she had left much in the way of worldly goods to her granddaughter, as well as something of worth and sentimental value, namely her jewels. There survives a letter from Fowler, her treasurer, dated April 1590, stating that 'my Lady Margaret's Grace committed her casket with jewels into the hands of Mr Thomas Fowler to be delivered to the Lady Arbella at the age of fourteen'.

Fowler itemised the contents of the casket. This fascinating list shows that although the widowed Margaret had always worn black, she had been very richly adorned with jewels, namely:

A jewel set with a fair table diamond.

A table ruby and an emerald with a fair great pearl.

A cross all set with fair table diamonds with a square-linked chain.

A jewel set with a balas [a red or orange semi-precious stone] and a fair table diamond set beneath it.

A 'H' of gold set with a rock ruby.[9]

A burnish[ed] set with a fair diamond.

A rose set with fair diamonds.

A carcanet [necklace] set with table diamonds.

A girdle set with table diamonds.

A border set with table diamonds.

A border set with table rubies.

A border set with rock emeralds.

A table [tablet], the head of gold set with diamonds.

A fair pearl chain.

A chain set with rock rubies, pillar-wise.

A chain of small turquoise set upon a three-square pillar.

A clock set in crystal with a wolf[10] of gold upon it.

Buttons of rock rubies to set on a gown.

Table diamonds to set upon a sleeve.

Two tablets of gold, the one with two agates with divers small turquoise, the other enamelled [in] the form of a globe.

Bracelets, two pair, one of agate, and the other of plain gold, with other things that be not yet in memory.[11]

It has been suggested that the Lennox Jewel was left by Margaret to Arbella,[12] but it does not feature on this list. Another theory is that Margaret left the jewel to her daughter-in-law, Elizabeth Cavendish, who in turn, on her death in 1582, bequeathed it to Elizabeth I. Elizabeth Cavendish did leave a 'poor remembrance' to the Queen, but that would hardly have described the Lennox Jewel, and there is nothing else to support this theory.[13] The Jewel probably passed to James VI, and thus came into the Royal Collection.

On 19 September 1578 the Queen of Scots issued a warrant requiring Thomas Fowler, 'sole executor to our dearest mother-in-law and aunt, the Lady Margaret, Countess of Lennox, deceased, to deliver into the hands and custody of our right well beloved cousin, Elizabeth, Countess of Shrewsbury, all and every such jewels as the said Lady Margaret before her death delivered and committed in charge to the said Thomas Fowler for the use of the Lady Arbella Stuart, her grand-child, if God send her life till fourteen years of age; if not, then for the use of our dear son, the Prince of Scotland'.[14] But Fowler, respecting Margaret's wish that the jewels remain in his possession until Arbella reached fourteen, held them in safe keeping until he travelled north to Scotland to take up service with James VI. On the way they were stolen from him during an ambush by Francis Stewart, Earl of Bothwell, who entrusted them to King James; but James gave them as securities to his creditors. When Arbella reached the age of fourteen in 1589, Burghley made representations to him for their return, and he was still making them after Fowler died in 1590, when James claimed the jewels 'in recompense' for the legacy he had not received from his grandmother. In June 1590 Sir Robert Bowes informed Burghley, 'I am still deferred that, upon sight of the Lady Margaret's will, the King will take order in all these things.'

It is possible that Arbella eventually received at least some of her legacy: the long rope of fine pearls that she wears in several portraits may have been Margaret's 'fair pearl chain'; in one portrait she is holding what may possibly be the clock set in crystal, and in another there hangs around her neck a cross, which might be the one Margaret bequeathed her.[15]

Margaret's death brought Arbella a step nearer to the throne. Queen Mary had appealed to James Boyd, Archbishop of Glasgow, to press the child's claim to the earldom of Lennox, but on 16 June 1578 Morton, in King James's name, conferred it on Margaret's brother-in-law, Robert Stewart, Bishop of Caithness, the next male heir.[16] It has been noted[17] that Morton did not take this decision until Margaret was no longer alive to contest it, which is a measure of how formidable an opponent he had accounted her. James VI would always maintain that he himself, as Darnley's heir, was the rightful inheritor of the earldom of Lennox.[18]

All the Lennox claims to the throne and the lands of the earldom were now vested in Arbella, and Bess of Hardwick informed the Queen of Scots that Arbella had a better claim than she did.[19] Elizabeth chose to ignore the entail that had been attached to the Lennox inheritance, and took up the cudgels on Arbella's behalf in regard to the earldom of Lennox. On 30 July she informed the Scottish ambassador: 'Her Majesty finds it very strange that any disposition should be intended of the earldom to any other to the prejudice of the young lady, only daughter and heir of Charles, late Earl of Lennox, who had that estate assured to him and his heirs of his body generally; whereof it is great reason, for justice sake, that the King be made privy, that by ignorance he be not counselled to do any open wrong to an infant, a lady, and one of his next cousins in blood.'[20]

On 28 July the Commendator of Dunfermline requested 'that the King of Scots may have the lands and living in England sometime appertaining to the Earl of Lennox and the Lady Margaret, his wife, now falling to his Highness by just title of order and lawful succession'. James had been much offended by Elizabeth's revocation of those lands, 'wherefore his Highness would never think that her Majesty – who otherwise has been so careful and favourable a mother to him – will in this point suffer him to be frustrate of his right by the rigour of any such law'. But 'this persuasion availed nothing'.[21]

James's final attempt to obtain the Lennox lands was made in 1583, but again Elizabeth refused him.[22] It was in that year that the Lord Chancellor, Sir Walter Mildmay, described the seven-year-old Arbella as 'a very proper child, and to my thinking will be like her grandmother, my old Lady Lennox'.[23] After Mary, Queen of Scots, was executed at Fotheringhay Castle in 1587, Bess anticipated that 'Arbell', as she called her granddaughter, would be chosen as Elizabeth's successor – a view shared by many – and commanded family members to curtsey to her. There was a time when Elizabeth dropped heavy hints that Arbella would indeed be her successor, but it was James VI who succeeded in 1603, and like his predecessor he did not trust his heirs or approve of them marrying without his consent. He saw Arbella, as Elizabeth had seen Margaret, as a threat to his security.

Arbella seems to have inherited Margaret's impulsiveness, and her talent for ruffling the feathers of those in power, and in the end it was her own conduct that brought her to a tragic fate. In 1610, continuing a tradition set by her mother, her grandmother, Margaret, and her great-grandmother, Margaret Tudor, she made a secret marriage. But in her case it was with a man who had his own claim to the throne, William Seymour, the grandson of the Earl of Hertford who had rashly taken Katherine Grey as his wife. For this crime James I invoked the 1536 law that had been passed in the wake of

Margaret's marriage to Thomas Howard,[24] and Arbella was imprisoned in the Tower, where she apparently starved herself to death in 1615 at the age of forty. She was buried in Mary, Queen of Scots' vault in Westminster Abbey.

In 1683 the vault below Margaret's tomb,[25] which led off the much larger one of Mary, Queen of Scots, was broken into, and the shrivelled body of Charles Stuart was visible in its broken coffin. In 1868 the vault was again opened and three coffins were found lying on top of one another. Margaret's lay on that of Charles, and on top of hers was the coffin of Esmé Stuart, Duke of Richmond, who died in 1624.[26]

Margaret did not live to see her dynastic ambitions brought to fruition. How she would have exulted to see her grandson ascend the English throne as James I, first monarch of the House of Stuart, uniting the kingdoms of England and Scotland under one ruler. It is what she had hoped and schemed for all her life. And it is her blood, not that of Henry VIII or her rival, Elizabeth I, that has flowed in the veins of every sovereign since.[27]

Appendix 1

Margaret's Portraiture

The portraiture of Margaret Douglas has been much debated by historians and in many online forums. With a dearth of authenticated portraits, and the one that is unquestionably authentic (in the Darnley Memorial of 1568) showing her later in life, there has been an understandable quest for hitherto-unidentified likenesses among the many that survive of anonymous, undocumented sitters. A portrait of Margaret is recorded in Lord Lumley's inventory of 1590, and another in the 1601 inventory of Bess of Hardwick's collection at Hardwick Hall.[1] Both are presumed lost.

In the Darnley Memorial, dating from 1568, Margaret bears a resemblance to her cousin, Mary Tudor, although the facial structure suggests that in youth she was as attractive as she was reputed to be. At fifty-two she had a snub, slightly uptilted nose, inherited from her mother, heavy-lidded, deep-set eyes, a strong jaw, a pointed chin and a small mouth with upturned lips. There is also a hint of her Plantagenet ancestry when one compares her portrait to those of King Edward IV, her Yorkist great-grandfather. The fact that she is middle-aged in this portrait makes it hard to draw comparisons with portraits of younger women who might be her.

Unfortunately we have no certain portrait of Margaret in her youth, although we know that she gave one to Thomas Howard in 1535–6; it may even have been painted or drawn by Hans Holbein, who was working for Henry VIII at that time. A three-quarter-length of a young woman, inscribed 'A. W. // pingebat [painted by A. W.], 1536', originally in the collection of Arthur, Viscount Lee of Fareham, and now in the collection of the Courtauld Institute of Art, was once identified as Margaret. She does wear clothing identical to that which Henry VIII ordered for his niece in 1531: a black gown with a low, square, richly bordered neckline, with a high-necked ruffled chemise or smock beneath it, covered with a semicircular black partlet with a stand-up collar. Her kirtle and undersleeves are of rose or red silk and she wears a French hood. 'HIS' is engraved on one of her rings, and there is a heavy gold chain around her waist; she holds a white flower and her other hand rests upon the base of an elaborate gold cup. High-necked, frilled chemises like this can be seen in Holbein's drawings of Mary Howard, Duchess of Richmond, the Duchess of Suffolk and at least six more of his female sitters. Partlets with stand-up collars appear in his portraits of the 1530s, as in the drawing of Elizabeth Jenks, Lady Rich. French hoods of this style feature in Holbein's sketches of *c.*1533–6 of Mary Zouche and Grace Parker. The date of the portrait is therefore authentic, but the sitter has a longer nose than Margaret's as it appears in the Darnley Memorial, and her tomb effigy.

The engraved letters HIS are not a christogram, nor can they be initials, as middle names were unknown in early Tudor England. They might be the initials of a motto, or simply the word 'his', denoting belonging. If this is Margaret – although the evidence for the identification is very slender – then they might be a discreet allusion to her love for Thomas Howard.

I support Leanda de Lisle's suggestion[2] that a much-debated portrait of a young woman in the collection of Shaun Agar, 6th Earl of Normanton, at Somerley, Hampshire – thought by some, on no evidence at all, to be Anne Boleyn – might be Margaret. The buttons at her cuff are engraved with an M and a D. The jewel, or flower, at her breast is a daisy, or marguerite. Facially there is a resemblance to later portraits, and the face shape is similar to that of her mother, Margaret Tudor.[3] The portrait is attributed to a follower of Raphael, Luca Penni (*c.*1504–56), a Florentine artist of the School of Fontainebleau, but there is no record of his ever working in England. However, the attribution is by no means certain, although it is likely that the artist who painted the Somerley portrait had worked at the French court, and we know that Italian artists also worked at Henry VIII's court. Possibly the portrait was painted in 1534 or 1538 in connection with Henry VIII's plans to marry Margaret to an Italian prince.

This may also have been a marriage portrait. The costume is French in style; thanks to the 'Auld Alliance' and cultural links with France, French Renaissance influence was strong in Scotland, where

French fashions were worn at court. Margaret would have grown up wearing such fashions, and her husband Lennox would have been accustomed to seeing women dressed similarly in France and Scotland. The style of dress in the portrait was still worn in France in the mid-1540s, and it would have been a nod to Margaret's birthright, and to her new husband, for her to have been painted wearing French attire, especially if this was a marriage portrait.

It has been suggested that three Holbein portraits that almost certainly depict Katherine Howard are of Margaret.[4] There is no certain portrait of Katherine Howard, although a good case can be made for identifying these three – two miniatures and a half-length panel portrait – as her. The existence of two versions of the same miniature suggests that the sitter was a lady of some prominence,[5] and her cloth-of-gold bodice, rich jewels and fur sleeves show her to have been of high rank. One version, dating from *c.*1540, is in the Royal Collection. It was first said to be Katherine Howard around 1837, but may perhaps be identified with one of a group of miniatures at Lee Priory, Kent, that were described by George Vertue in the 1730s as being of Anne of Cleves,[6] Jane Seymour and Katherine Howard. On the back of the miniature is engraved an inscription, probably dating from the nineteenth century: *Catherine Howard, Queen of Henry 8th by Hans Holbein.*

The other version of the miniature, signed by Holbein, was in the collection of Katherine's relative, Thomas Howard, Earl of Arundel, in the early seventeenth century, and was engraved in 1645 by Wenceslaus Hollar without any identifying inscription. In 1743 it was engraved by Jacobus Houbraken as being Katherine Howard, which, together with Vertue's identification of the first miniature as Katherine in the 1730s, suggests that this portrait type was accepted as her likeness by 1730. The second miniature was acquired by Horace Walpole in the eighteenth century, although he believed that it probably portrayed Mary Tudor, Queen of France. It was sold to Walter Montagu-Douglas Scott, 5th Duke of Buccleuch, in 1842, and is still owned by the present Duke. The original miniature has been trimmed, as the hands are cropped.

Both miniatures show a young woman with dark auburn hair wearing a tawny-gold gown with a deep jewelled border at the neckline, a French hood, and an ouche and a pearl necklace that can be seen in portraits of Jane Seymour and Katherine Parr. Only recently have several portraits once thought to be of Lady Jane Grey been identified, on the evidence of jewellery, as Katherine Parr, and prior to that there were theories that Jane Seymour may have given away those jewels, perhaps to Mary Brandon, Lady Monteagle, who was possibly the sitter in these miniatures.[7] But Katherine Parr is wearing the ouche in two portraits in the National Portrait Gallery, and the necklace in a portrait at Seaton Delaval Hall. Since the Queen's jewels were handed down from consort to consort, the sitter in the miniatures is almost certainly Katherine Howard; furthermore the 'square of jewels' edging the neckline of her bodice and the rich habiliments in the hood have been identified with wedding gifts given to Katherine by Henry VIII, the border being described in an inventory of her jewels as a 'square containing xxiii diamonds and lx rubies with an edge of pearl containing xxiii'. As has been observed, the identification as Margaret cannot explain why she is wearing the royal jewels.[8] It is hard to understand why, given the evidence of jewellery, historians have been reluctant to accept these miniatures as Katherine Howard. David Starkey, Alasdair Hawkyard and Bendor Grosvenor have collectively stated that 'a comparison between the sitter's jewellery and the inventory of jewels presented to Katherine on her marriage demonstrates beyond doubt that the sitter is Henry's fifth queen'.[9]

Holbein's portrait of a young woman 'in her twenty-first year' (according to the Latin inscription), painted around 1540, almost certainly features the same sitter. The original hangs in the Toledo Museum of Fine Arts, Ohio, and there are copies in the National Portrait Gallery and at Hever Castle (formerly at Trentham Hall); the latter has been tree-ring-dated to the middle of the sixteenth century.[10] The rich clothing and jewellery show that she is of high rank. The Toledo portrait was not said to be Katherine Howard until 1898, so historians have long questioned the identification. It descended in the Cromwell family, and in 1969 Roy Strong suggested that the lady was Jane Seymour's sister Elizabeth, who married Gregory, Thomas Cromwell's only son. But the costume does seem rather lavish for the daughter of a knight and wife of a gentleman, and more recently, Dr David Starkey has identified the sleeves and jewels in the Hever Castle version with items in Katherine Howard's inventory. That evidence, the existence of three versions, and the resemblance of the lady to the sitters in the miniatures and engravings all suggest that the Toledo portrait is of Katherine Howard, whose image was at one time in demand. Lisle doubts that people would have kept portraits of a disgraced queen – none survive from Anne Boleyn's lifetime, for example – but these particular paintings have emerged from an obscurity in which they were kept for centuries.

The Toledo portrait dates from *c.*1540; Margaret was in her twenty-first year in 1536. The sitter in this and the miniature bears no resemblance to her as she appears in the Darnley Memorial. The nose, again, is too long. Comparing portraits on appearance alone is a subjective approach, however, and one must look for other evidence. In regard to all these Holbein portraits, there is none to link any of them with Margaret Douglas, and much to connect them with Katherine Howard.

A drawing by Holbein at Windsor, which has no inscription but has sometimes been said to portray Katherine Howard, does not appear to be the same sitter as the lady in the portraits just discussed. If the Somerley portrait is not Margaret, this may just possibly be her, as it bears a resemblance to her in later years. Although this sitter is fuller-faced, that may be down to her being about thirty years younger.

A sitter who is perhaps an older Margaret may appear in a little-known but fine portrait of a lady with a black hood and a fox fur around her neck, painted between 1544 and 1555. In 1956–7, when it was displayed at the Royal Academy's 'British Portraits' exhibition, it was attributed to Hans Eworth. Prior to that it was thought to be by Hans Holbein. In 2009 Ludwig Meyer attributed it to Guillaume Scrots, who worked at the English court from 1545 until 1550.[11] The sitter is clearly a lady of high rank, as denoted by her embroidered cuffs and furs, and her loose black gown suggests that she is pregnant, as Margaret was so often in this period. The headdress resembles the ones worn by Elizabeth Stonor, Lady Hoby and Margaret Wyatt, Lady Lee, in portraits executed by Holbein before 1544. There is a resemblance to the later portrait of Margaret, and to her tomb effigy. The portrait, formerly in a Welsh private collection, was sold at Christie's, London, in 2011.

A full-length portrait of the 1550s of a lady in black, formerly at Sawston Hall, Cambridgeshire, and attributed to Guillaume Scrots, has traditionally been identified as Mary I, who took refuge from Northumberland's pursuers at Sawston after Edward VI's death. However, in recent years the identity of the sitter has been the subject of much debate, as she bears little resemblance to other portraits of Mary. Mary's biographer Linda Porter was so convinced that this is Mary that she chose the painting for her book jacket. But Sir Roy Strong has never been convinced of this identification, and Dr Tarnya Cooper, Sixteenth Century Curator at the National Portrait Gallery, has stated: 'We concluded that, while it is undoubtedly a very interesting and important painting, it cannot represent Mary I mainly because of facial dissimilarity with other authentic portraits of her. It is more likely to be a member of the nobility, possibly from within Princess Mary's circle.' Professor John Scarisbrick asserts: 'There was nobody outside the royal family important enough for such a lavish full-length painting – and if it isn't Mary, who is it?'[12]

Professor John Guy has argued that it is Margaret Douglas.[13] However, the painting is far more likely to portray Margaret Howard (c.1515–71), sister of Katherine Howard and wife of Katherine Parr's chancellor, Sir Thomas Arundell, who was executed in 1552. Before it came to Sawston Hall in 1918, the portrait was at Sutton Place, Surrey, where it was recorded by George Vertue in 1733.[14] Lady Arundell's daughter, Dorothy, married Henry Weston of Sutton Place in 1559.

Another portrait that has tentatively been identified as Margaret is a three-quarter-length of a lady by Hans Eworth in the Fitzwilliam Museum, Cambridge, painted around 1556. Again, she was once thought to be Mary I, but that was questioned by Strong as long ago as 1965. The history of the picture is unknown before 1856. She has the snub nose, wide cheekbones, upturned mouth and pointed chin seen in the portrait of Margaret in the Darnley Memorial; she has red hair and she wears a black gown with a stand-up collar over a rose-pink kirtle and undersleeves, a square French hood and jewellery rich enough to mark her out as someone of high rank. The ornamental prayer book hanging from her girdle is embossed with the letter D. However, she is unlikely to be Margaret Douglas, because the jewel at her breast depicts the maiden Esther kneeling before King Ahasuerus, which almost certainly indicates that the sitter is unmarried.[15]

The Victoria and Albert Museum holds in storage a miniature of a lady by the court artist Levina Teerlinc, which was formerly in the collection of the dukes of Beaufort. The sitter wears a square-shaped French hood and bonnet with a jewelled brooch and a black feather, a black gown with a high furred collar, a small ruff and a crucifix, which suggests that she was Catholic. There is a marked resemblance between her features and Margaret Douglas's in the Darnley Memorial and her tomb effigy, and although she looks older than in the Memorial, that may be because Teerlinc, who came to England in

1545 and was appointed painter to Henry VIII, was not the most accomplished of artists. She served as a gentlewoman in the households of Mary I and Elizabeth I, and painted miniatures of Elizabeth I, Lady Katherine Grey and Katherine Parr, among others. Her style is exemplified by female sitters with stick-thin arms.

This miniature has been dated to *c.*1560. The square-shaped version of the French hood is first seen in the mid-1540s, when it appears in two portraits of Katherine Parr, who was also painted wearing a feathered bonnet on top of a circular pearl-edged pleated coif, not unlike the one the sitter wears in the Teerlinc miniature, although the latter is a squarer shape. Such bonnets also feature in portraits of the 1530s. The square hood gained popularity and is familiar in portraits of Mary I (reigned 1553–8); it remained in fashion until around 1567. It is extremely rare to find examples of it surmounted by a cap such as the Teerlinc sitter wears. The furred collar and the high-necked ruff appear in portraits of the 1550s–60s, although there are examples of the latter in Holbein's drawings of the 1530s. Allowing for the fact that some portraits show older women wearing the outdated fashions of their youth, the miniature probably dates from around 1550 to 1565. The fact that Teerlinc painted this sitter at all strongly suggests that the lady was at court and of high rank. Given that, the jewellery and the facial similarities, it may portray Margaret, but there is also a facial resemblance to Bess of Hardwick as she appears in two portraits at Hardwick Hall.[16]

In the National Portrait Gallery there is a half-length portrait by an unknown artist, dating from *c.*1560–5, of an unknown woman who was identified in 1866 as Margaret solely on the grounds of similarity with the portrait of her in the Darnley Memorial. In fact there is little resemblance at all, the sitter in this portrait being older, more angular and thinner-faced than Margaret appears in the Memorial. The painting's history before 1866 is unknown.[17]

There are several portraits said to portray Margaret in her widowhood. The most important is a full-length by an unknown artist in the Royal Collection at the Palace of Holyroodhouse, which depicts a woman in black mourning wearing a white cap. It bears a framed inscription: 'THE LADY MARGARET. HIR GRACE / LATE WIFE TO MATHEW ERLLE / OF LENNOX REGENT OF SCOTLANDE / AND MOTHER TO HENRY KINGE / OF SCOTLAND / Aetatis 55 Aí Dni. 1572'. It was first recorded in the Royal Collection in 1639, in the Queen's Gallery at Greenwich,[18] when it was described merely as 'a Scottish lady at length in mourning habit and a clock upon the table in a gilded frame',[19] but ten years later it was sold as 'The Lady Margaret at length, wife to ye Regent of Scotland'. It would appear that the inscription was added sometime between 1639 and 1649, otherwise the sitter would surely have been named in the earlier inventory. Doubts have been expressed about her identity: the portrait was not known to be of Margaret in 1639; the features do not tally with Margaret's in the Darnley Memorial, and the age is given incorrectly:[20] Margaret had reached fifty-five in October 1570. After 1660 the portrait was returned to the collection of Charles II.[21] It may well have been the one recorded as hanging in the Queen's Privy Chamber at Hampton Court in the reign of George I.[22] The panel has been extended on all four sides.

The sitter wears a heavy wide-skirted black overgown over a black gown trimmed with fur at the neckline and down the front, and carries a pair of leather gloves trimmed with the same black bows that adorn the dress; a thin scarf knotted at the ends hangs almost to the length of her hem. The dark background is plain, but she stands on a rich Turkey carpet, proclaiming to the world her high status, as such carpets were costly and were usually draped on tables to preserve them from wear and tear. At her feet prances a griffon, a toy dog from Flanders of a breed that was popular among the English aristocracy. It was believed that griffons mated for life and never sought a new partner after one had died. Behind the sitter is a finely turned side table covered with a black cloth with a fringe or border, on which the sitter rests her hand. Upon the table stands a gold clock in the form of a *tempietto* – a small round chapel – with a dial surmounted by a hound and a shield bearing what may be the royal arms of Scotland. The sitter is clearly of high status, and if the arms are royal, then she probably is Margaret. That being so, the portrait was either appropriated by Elizabeth after her death, or came by descent to her grandson James.[23] A nineteenth-century copy by Rhoda Sullivan hangs in the Darnley Room at Temple Newsam, a companion full-length to one of Mary, Queen of Scots. Both are in the collection of Leeds Museums and Art Galleries.[24]

The Royal Collection Trust has another portrait that might be Margaret. It was bought by Queen Victoria in 1843 from John Ponsonby, 4th Earl of Bessborough, as a portrait of Mary I. Later it was identified as Margaret Douglas, but that was disputed by Oliver Millar. It is said to date from *c.*1575, and is probably by an English artist, but has been damaged and overpainted.[25] Given the distinctive nose and deep-set eyes, it is possible that the identification was correct, but without further investigation it is impossible to tell. If it is Margaret, it must date from early in her widowhood, as her hair has not yet gone grey and she is wearing deeper mourning than in her other portraits from the 1570s.

A half-length portrait of Margaret, similar to the full-length in the Royal Collection, was owned by the earls of Morton and once hung at Dalmahoy House near Edinburgh. Its present location is uncertain, but it was described by Strickland, and is known from a nineteenth-century engraving by Gourlay Steell.[26] The portrait was inscribed 'The Lady Margaret, her Grace, The Countess of Levenax, Aetatis sue 50'. The sitter wears black damask, which was not necessarily mourning, as deep black dye was costly and therefore black was a high-status colour; she has a white ruff, and the same thin scarf and white hood with a cornette as in the Royal Collection portrait. This headdress may be similar to the one provided for Margaret in the Tower in 1565. The only jewellery is a balas ruby brooch with a pendant pearl. The frame is enamelled in black and white on gold and adorned with marguerites.[27] If this was painted when Margaret was in her fiftieth year, it must have been done between October 1564 and April 1565, before she was placed under arrest. But she looks older and plumper than in the Darnley Memorial of 1568, so the Dalmahoy portrait was probably painted later, in which case the age given in the inscription is incorrect.

A miniature of 1575 by Nicholas Hilliard, also showing an ageing woman in black, in the collection of the Rijksmuseum, Amsterdam, is also said to portray Margaret. The sitter has grey hair; in the Darnley Memorial, painted seven years earlier, Margaret's was dark brown, so if this is her she had aged considerably during those sad years. Yet this sitter has a distinctive hooked nose, unlike Margaret's in the Darnley Memorial or her tomb effigy, and one eye partially closed, suggesting some facial paralysis or possibly a stroke. This miniature was perhaps the one recorded in Charles I's inventory in 1639: 'The picture . . . being upon blue grounded-card written about the year of Our Lord with gold letters 1575, and also her age, 53, being the Lady Margaret Douglas, aunt to Queen Mary of Scotland, in a black and white mourning widow's habit [and] a little plain ruff.' The miniature has since been cut down, so the age is missing, but in October 1575 Margaret was fifty, not fifty-three. There is another version, damaged, with the face entirely repainted, dated 1576 and called 'Anne [Morgan], Lady Hunsdon', in the Fitzwilliam

Museum, Cambridge, but it is impossible to say for certain that it is by Hilliard.[28]

A painted genealogy dating from *c.*1603 is at Parham Park, Sussex, and shows the ancestry of James I. The royal figures in the genealogy are based on known portraits, but those from which the images of Margaret and Lennox originate are unknown, and probably lost. An engraving of Margaret dating from *c.*1603 is in Benjamin Wright's *The Royal Progeny of King James*, and again is based on an unknown portrait, although the snub nose and pointed chin are evident.[29]

Leanda de Lisle suggests on her website that a portrait of a woman of *c.*1560 in the Royal Collection may be Margaret Douglas. The sitter has traditionally been identified as her cousin, Frances Brandon, Duchess of Suffolk, but bears no resemblance to Frances's tomb effigy, or to Margaret in the Darnley Memorial, and there is no evidence to support the identification as either of them.

A portrait by George Gower, published in 1911 as 'Lady Katherine Grey' in *Davey's The Sisters of Lady Jane Grey*, was then in the possession of Mary Wright Biddulph. Nowadays it appears on the internet, apparently on no authority, as Margaret Douglas. The sitter, who wears rich costume of the 1560s–70s, is probably Isabel Gifford, wife of Sir Francis Biddulph, in whose family the portrait remained until 1931. The portrait was sold by the Weiss Gallery to a private collector in 2001.[30]

An engraving said to be of Margaret[31] based on a miniature in the collection of David Douglas-Home, 15th Earl of Home, depicts a lady in mid-seventeenth-century dress, who cannot be Margaret. On page 511 of his book *Tudor Costume and Fashion* (1938), Herbert Norris reproduced a drawing based on 'a three-quarter portrait of Margaret Douglas', but the portrait is in fact that of Mary, Queen of Scots, and Lord Darnley, which hangs in Hardwick Hall.

To conclude, there is still only one certain portrait of Margaret, that in the Darnley Memorial.

Appendix II

Miscellaneous Poems Copied by Margaret Douglas into the Devonshire Manuscript

The poems below[1] cannot be related to any known events in Margaret's life. They are copied in her hand, and may not necessarily have been composed by her.

No. 59

[To a faithless lover. Margaret is not known to have been jilted by any suitor.]

Thy promise was to love me best
And that thy heart with mine should rest,
And not to break this thy behest.
Thy promise was, thy promise was.

Thy promise was not to acquit
My faithfulness with such despite,
But recompense it if thou might.
Thy promise was, thy promise was.

Thy promise was, I tell thee plain,
My faith should not be spent in vain,
But to have more should be my gain.
Thy promise was, thy promise was.

Thy promise was to have observed
My faith like as it hath deserved,
And not causeless thus to a-swerved.
Thy promise was, thy promise was.

Thy promise was, I dare avow,
But it is changed, I wot well how.
Though then were then and now is now,
Thy promise was, thy promise was.

But since to change thou dost delight,
And that thy faith have ta'en his flight,
As thou deservest I shall thee quit,
I promise thee, I promise thee.

No. 60

[To a lover who has grown cold and loves another.]

I see the change from that that was,
And how thy faith hath ta'en his flight,
But I with patience let it pass
And with my pen this do I write
To show thee plain by proof of sight
I see the change.

I see the change of wearied mind
And slipper hold, hath quit my hire.
Lo! How by proof in thee I find
A burning faith in changing fire.
Farewell my part, proof is no liar:
I see the change.

I see the change of chance in love;
Delight no longer may abide.
What should I seek further to prove?
No, no, my trust, for I have tried
The following of a false guide.
I see the change.

I see the change, as in this case,
Has made me free from mine avow,
For now another has my place
And, ere I wist, I wot ne'er how.
It happened thus as ye hear now.
I see the change.

I see the change, such is my chance
To serve in doubt and hope in vain,
But since my surety so doth glance,
Repentance now shall quit thy pain,
Never to trust the like again.
I see the change.

Finis.

No. 63

[The poem is in a man's voice.]

To my mishap, alas, I find
That happy hap is dangerous,
And fortune works but her kind
To make the joyful dolorous.
But all too late it comes in mind
To wail the want which made me blind,
So often warned.

Amidst my mirth and pleasantness
Such chance is chanced suddenly,
That in despair to have redress
I find my chiefest remedy.
No new kind of unhappiness
Should thus have left me comfortless,
So often warned.

Who could have thought that my request
Should have brought forth such bitter fruit?
But now is happed that I feared least
And all this grief comes by my suit;

For where I thought me happiest
Even there I found my chiefest unrest,
So often warned.

In better case was never none,
And yet unawares thus I am trapped.
My chief desire doth cause me moan,
And to my pain my wealth is happed.
Was never man but I alone,
That had such hap to wail and groan,
So often warned?

Thus am I taught for to beware
And not to trust such pleasant chance.
My happy hap has bred this care
And turned my mirth to great mischance.
There is no man that hap will spare,
But when she list our wealth is bare.
Thus am I warned.

No. 64

[A faithless poet overhears her lover's lament.]

'How should I
Be so pleasant
In my semblant
As my fellows be?'

Not long ago
It chanced so
As I walked alone
I heard a man
That now and then
Himself did thus bemoan:

'Alas!' he said,
'I am betrayed
And utterly undone.
Whom I did trust
And think so just,
Another man has won.

'My service due
And heart so true
On her I did bestow.
I never meant
For to repent
In wealth nor yet in woe.

'Love did assign
Her to be mine
And not to love none new,
But who can bind
Their fickle kind
That never will be true?

'The western wind
Has turned her mind
And blown her clean away,
Whereby my wealth,
My mirth, my health,
Is turned to great decay.

'Where is the truth?
Where is the oath
That ye to me did give?
Such crafty words
And wily boards [assaults]
Let no man believe.

'How should I
Be so pleasant
In my semblant
As my fellows be?'

No. 65

[The poet laments that his/her love now belongs to someone else.]

What needeth life when I require
Nothing but death to quench my pain?
Fast flyeth away that I desire
And double sorrows return again.

By proof I see before mine eyen
Another hath that once was mine.

That I was wont to have in hold
Is slipped away full suddenly,
And craftily I am withhold
From all my life and liberty,
So that I see before mine eyen
Another hath that once was mine.

It is no news to find, I know,
For faithfulness to find untruth,
But I perceive the wind doth blow
A crafty way to cloak the truth.
By which I see before mine eyen
Another hath that once was mine.

A proverb old I have heard oft,
That a light love lightly doth go.
Now am I low that was aloft,
That was my friend is now my foe.
So that I see before mine eyen
Another hath that once was mine.

Since right with wrong hath his reward,
And feigned faith doth true oppress,
I let it pass, and it regard
As I have cause, no more or less,
Because I see before mine eyen
Another has that once was mine.

What heart could think more than was thought,
Or tongue could speak more that was spoke?
Yet what for that? All was for naught,
For he is gone and slipped the knot,
Whereby I see before mine eyen
Another has that once was mine.

Chief Dramatis Personae

Margaret Douglas and her close relations

Margaret Douglas (1515–78): daughter of Archibald Douglas, 6th Earl of Angus, by Margaret Tudor, daughter of Henry VII, King of England, by Elizabeth of York.

Archibald Douglas, 6th Earl of Angus (c.1489–1557): son of George Douglas, Master of Angus, by Elizabeth Drummond. Father of Margaret Douglas. Married (1) Margaret Hepburn (d.1513); precontracted to Jane Stewart of Traquair; married (2) Margaret Tudor (1489–1541) and (3) Margaret Maxwell (d.1594).

Margaret Tudor (1489–1541): daughter of Henry VII, King of England, by Elizabeth of York. Mother of Margaret Douglas. Married (1) James IV, King of Scots (1473–1513); (2) Archibald Douglas, 6th Earl of Angus (c.1489–1557) and (3) Henry (Harry) Stewart, Lord Methven (c.1495–1552).

Lord Thomas Howard (c.1511–37): son of Thomas Howard, 2nd Duke of Norfolk, by Agnes Tilney. Precontracted to Margaret Douglas.

Matthew Stuart, 4th Earl of Lennox (1516–71): son of John Stewart, 3rd Earl of Lennox. Husband of Margaret Douglas. The spelling of his surname was changed when he lived in France. Regent of Scotland 1570–1.

Children of Margaret Douglas and Matthew Stuart, Earl of Lennox

Henry Stuart, Lord Darnley (b. & d.1545)

Henry Stuart, Lord Darnley (1546–67): married Mary, Queen of Scots (1542–87). Parents of James VI and I, King of Scots and King of England (1566–1625). Murdered.

Unnamed daughter (b.1552; d. by 1565)

Philip Stuart (b.1554/5; d. by 1562)

Three unnamed daughters (d. young by 1562–5)

Charles Stuart, 6th Earl of Lennox (1557–76): married Elizabeth Cavendish (1555–82). Parents of Arbella Stuart (1575–1615). Died of tuberculosis.

Scottish Kings and Queens: House of Stewart/Stuart

James IV (1473–1513): married Margaret Tudor (1489–1541), daughter of Henry VII, King of England, by Elizabeth of York, and sister of Henry VIII, King of England. She married secondly Archibald Douglas, 6th Earl of Angus, and by him was the mother of Margaret Douglas.

James V (1512–42): son of James IV and Margaret Tudor. Half-brother of Margaret Douglas. Married (1) Madeleine of France (1520–37) and (2) Marie de Guise (1515–60), who was Regent of Scotland from 1554 to 1559 for their daughter, Mary, Queen of Scots.

Mary, Queen of Scots (1542–87): daughter of James V by Marie de Guise. Niece and daughter-in-law of Margaret Douglas. Married (1) Francis II, King of France (1544–60); (2) Henry Stuart, Lord Darnley (1546–67), son of Margaret Douglas; and (3) James Hepburn, 4th Earl of Bothwell (c.1535–78). Deposed 1567.

James VI (1566–1625): son of Mary, Queen of Scots, by Henry Stuart, Lord Darnley. Grandson of Margaret Douglas. Became James I of England at the Union of the Crowns in 1603.

Scottish royal family

Alexander, Duke of Ross (1514–15): youngest son of James IV and Margaret Tudor. Half-brother of Margaret Douglas.

James Stewart, Earl of Moray (*c.*1531–70): bastard son of James V by Margaret Erskine; half-brother of Mary, Queen of Scots; nephew of Margaret Douglas. Married Agnes Keith (*c.*1540–88). Protestant reformer and Regent of Scotland 1567–70. Murdered.

English Kings and Queens

House of York (Plantagenet) 1461–85

Edward IV, King of England (1442–83): married Elizabeth Wydeville (1437–92). Great-grandparents of Margaret Douglas.

Richard III, King of England (1452–85): killed at the Battle of Bosworth.

House of Tudor 1485–1603

Henry VII (1457–1509): married Elizabeth of York (1466–1503). Grandparents of Margaret Douglas.

Henry VIII (1491–1547): son of Henry VII by Elizabeth of York. Uncle of Margaret Douglas. Married (1) Katherine of Aragon (1485–1536); (2) Anne Boleyn (*c.*1501–36); (3) Jane Seymour (*c.*1508–37); (4) Anne of Cleves (1515–57); (5) Katherine Howard (*c.*1519–42); and (6) Katherine Parr (1512–48).

Edward VI (1537–53): son of Henry VIII by Jane Seymour. First cousin of Margaret Douglas.

Mary I (1516–58): daughter of Henry VIII by Katherine of Aragon. First cousin of Margaret Douglas. Married Philip II, King of Spain (1527–98).

Elizabeth I (1533–1603): daughter of Henry VIII by Anne Boleyn. First cousin of Margaret Douglas.

English royal family

Margaret Beaufort, Countess of Richmond and Derby (1443–1509): descended from King Edward III through John of Gaunt, Duke of Lancaster. Married Edmund Tudor, Earl of Richmond (1430–56), by whom she was the mother of Henry VII, King of England (1457–1509). Great-grandmother of Margaret Douglas.

Arthur Tudor, Prince of Wales (1486–1501): son of Henry VII by Elizabeth of York. Uncle of Margaret Douglas. Married Katherine of Aragon (1485–1536).

Henry Fitzroy, Duke of Richmond and Somerset (1519–36): bastard son of Henry VIII by Elizabeth Blount (c.1489–1540). First cousin of Margaret Douglas. Married Mary Howard (1519–57).

Arthur Plantagenet, Viscount Lisle (d.1542); bastard son of Edward IV. Constable of Calais. Married Honor Grenville (c.1493–1566).

Margaret Pole, Countess of Salisbury (1473–1541): daughter of George Plantagenet, Duke of Clarence, brother of Edward IV and Richard III. Married Sir Richard Pole (d.1505). Governess to the future Mary I and probably to Margaret Douglas also.

Reginald Pole, Archbishop of Canterbury (1500–58): son of Margaret Pole, Countess of Salisbury.

Arthur Pole (1531–70) and Edmund Pole (1541–70): grandsons of Margaret Pole, Countess of Salisbury. Pretenders to the throne.

Henry Hastings, 3rd Earl of Huntingdon (c.1535–95): son of Francis Hastings, 2nd Earl of Huntingdon, by Katherine Pole, granddaughter of Margaret Pole, Countess of Salisbury, through whom Hastings derived his claim to the throne. President of the Council of the North.

English royal family: House of Suffolk

Mary Tudor (1496–1533): daughter of Henry VII, King of England, by Elizabeth of York. Aunt of Margaret Douglas. Married (1)

Louis XII, King of France (1462–1515) and (2) Charles Brandon, Duke of Suffolk (c.1484–1545).

Frances Brandon (1517–59): elder daughter of Charles Brandon, Duke of Suffolk, by Mary Tudor. First cousin of Margaret Douglas. Married (1) Henry Grey, Marquess of Dorset, later Duke of Suffolk (1517–54) and (2) Adrian Stokes (1519–86).

Eleanor Brandon (1519–47): younger daughter of Charles Brandon, Duke of Suffolk, by Mary Tudor. First cousin of Margaret Douglas. Married Henry Clifford, 2nd Earl of Cumberland (1517–70).

Henry Brandon, 1st Earl of Lincoln (c.1523–34): son of Charles Brandon, Duke of Suffolk, by Mary Tudor. First cousin of Margaret Douglas.

Jane Grey (1536–54): eldest daughter of Henry Grey, Duke of Suffolk, by Frances Brandon. Second cousin of Margaret Douglas. Married Lord Guildford Dudley (c.1535–54). Reigned as 'Queen Jane' for nine days in 1554.

Katherine Grey (1540–68): second daughter of Henry Grey, Duke of Suffolk, by Frances Brandon. Second cousin of Margaret Douglas. Married (1) Henry Herbert, 2nd Earl of Pembroke (c.1538–1601) and (2) Edward Seymour, 2nd Earl of Hertford (1539–1621), by whom she was the mother of Edward Seymour, Viscount Beauchamp (1561–1612) and Thomas Seymour (1563–1619).

Mary Grey (1545–78): third daughter of Henry Grey, Duke of Suffolk, by Frances Brandon. Second cousin of Margaret Douglas. Married Thomas Keyes (c.1524–71).

Mary Brandon (1510–44?): daughter of Charles Brandon, Duke of Suffolk, by his second wife, Anne Browne. Married Thomas Stanley, 2nd Baron Monteagle (1507–60).

Katherine Willoughby (1519–80): daughter of William, 11th Baron Willoughby d'Eresby, by Maria de Salinas. Second wife of Charles Brandon, Duke of Suffolk (c.1484–1545). She married (2) Richard Bertie (c.1517–82), by whom she was the mother of Peregrine Bertie,

13th Baron Willoughby d'Eresby (1555–1601) and others. Friend of Margaret Douglas.

French Kings and Queens: House of Valois

Louis XII, King of France (1462–1515): married, as his third wife, Mary Tudor (1496–1533), sister of Henry VIII, King of England.

Francis I, King of France (1494–1547): cousin and son-in-law of Louis XII, whom he succeeded.

Henry II, King of France (1519–59): son of Francis I. Married Catherine de' Medici (1519–89).

Francis II, King of France (1544–60): eldest son of Henry II and Catherine de' Medici. Married Mary, Queen of Scots (1542–87).

Charles IX, King of France (1550–74), previously Duke of Orléans: third son of Henry II and Catherine de' Medici.

Henry III, King of France (1551–89), previously Duke of Anjou: fourth son of Henry II and Catherine de' Medici.

French Ambassadors

Claude d'Annebault, Admiral of France (1495–1552), ambassador to Henry VIII.

Michel de Castelnau, Sieur de la Mauvissière (c. 1520–92), ambassador to Elizabeth I.

Louis de Perreau, Sieur de Castillon, ambassador to Henry VIII.

Henry Cleutin, Sieur d'Oysel (1515–66), ambassador to Scotland 1546 to 1560.

Philibert du Croc, ambassador to Scotland 1575 to 1572.

Bertrand de Salignac de la Mothe Fénélon (1523–89), ambassador to Elizabeth I.

Paul de Foix (1528–84), ambassador to Elizabeth I.

Antoine de Noailles (1504–62), ambassador to Mary I.

Spanish and Imperial royal family: House of Hapsburg

Charles I, King of Spain; also Charles V, Holy Roman Emperor (1500–58).

Philip II, King of Spain (1527–98): son of Charles I/V.

Don Carlos, Prince of Asturias (1545–68): eldest son of Philip II.

Charles of Hapsburg, Archduke of Austria (1540–90): third son of the Holy Roman Emperor Ferdinand I, and nephew of Charles I/V. Suitor to both Elizabeth I and Mary, Queen of Scots.

Spanish and Imperial Ambassadors

Eustache Chapuys (1489–1556), ambassador to Henry VIII.

Juan Esteban, Duke of Najera (1504–58), ambassador to Henry VIII.

Gómez Suárez de Figueroa y Córdoba, Count (later Duke) of Feria (1520–71): ambassador to Mary I and Elizabeth I. Married Jane Dormer (1538–1612), a maid-of-honour to Mary I.

Antonio de Guaras (1520–79), ambassador to Elizabeth I.

Alvaro de Quadra, Bishop of Aquila (d.1564), ambassador to Elizabeth I.

Simon Renard (1513–73), ambassador to Mary I.

Jehan Scheyfve (*c.*1515–81), ambassador to Edward VI and Mary I.

Diego Guzman de Silva (*c.*1520–77), ambassador to Elizabeth I.

Guerau de Spes (1524–72), ambassador to Elizabeth I.

Scottish Nobility

Cunningham

William Cunningham, 4th Earl of Glencairn (*c.*1480–1548): ally of Lennox, with whom he later fell out.

Alexander Cunningham, 5th Earl of Glencairn (d.1574)

Douglas

Archibald 'Bell-the-Cat' Douglas, 5th Earl of Angus (1449–1513): great-grandfather of Margaret Douglas.

George Douglas, Master of Angus (1469–1513): eldest son of Archibald 'Bell-the-Cat' Douglas, 5th Earl of Angus. Grandfather of Margaret Douglas.

Archibald Douglas, 6th Earl of Angus (*c.*1489–1557): son of George Douglas, Master of Angus, by Elizabeth Drummond. Father of Margaret Douglas. Married (1) Margaret Hepburn (d.1513); precontracted to Jane Stewart of Traquair; married (2) Margaret Tudor (1489–1541) and (3) Margaret Maxwell (d.1594).

Margaret Douglas (1515–78): daughter of Archibald Douglas, 6th Earl of Angus, by Margaret Tudor, daughter of Henry VII, King of England, by Elizabeth of York.

James Douglas, Master of Angus (d. young 1548): son of Archibald Douglas, 6th Earl of Angus, by Margaret Maxwell. Half-brother of Margaret Douglas.

George Douglas, Bishop of Moray (d.1589): bastard son of Archibald Douglas, 6th Earl of Angus.

Sir George Douglas of Pittendreich (d.1552): second son of George Douglas, Master of Angus, and younger brother of Archibald Douglas, 6th Earl of Angus. Uncle of Margaret Douglas.

William Douglas, Prior of Coldingham (*c.*1495–1528): third son of George Douglas, Master of Angus, and younger brother of Archibald Douglas, 6th Earl of Angus. Uncle of Margaret Douglas.

Janet Douglas, Lady Glamis (d.1537): daughter of George Douglas, Master of Angus, by Elizabeth Drummond, and sister of Archibald Douglas, 6th Earl of Angus. Aunt of Margaret Douglas. Married John Lyon, 6th Lord Glamis (d.1528).

James Douglas, 7th Lord of Drumlanrig (d.1578): husband of Margaret Douglas, daughter of George Douglas, Master of Angus, by Elizabeth Drummond, and sister of Archibald Douglas, 6th Earl of Angus. Uncle and aunt of Margaret Douglas.

David Douglas, 7th Earl of Angus (c.1515–58): elder son of George Douglas of Pittendreich. First cousin of Margaret Douglas.

James Douglas, Master of Morton, later 4th Earl of Morton (c.1516–81): younger son of George Douglas of Pittendreich. First cousin of Margaret Douglas. Regent of Scotland 1572–81.

Archibald Douglas, 8th Earl of Angus, 5th Earl of Morton (1555–88): son of David Douglas, 7th Earl of Angus. Second cousin of Margaret Douglas.

Sir Archibald Douglas, Laird of Glenbervie (1513–70): son of Sir William Douglas of Glenbervie (c.1473–1513), second son of Archibald 'Bell-the-Cat' Douglas, 5th Earl of Angus.

Sir Archibald Douglas, Laird of Kilspindie (c.1475–c.1536): fourth son of Archibald 'Bell-the-Cat' Douglas, 5th Earl of Angus. Great-uncle of Margaret Douglas. Married Isobel Hoppar (b. c.1490; d. after 1538), who served as waiting woman and possibly governess to Margaret Douglas.

Archibald Douglas, Parson of Douglas (c.1540–c.1587): from the Whittinghame branch of the Douglas family. Ambassador to Elizabeth I.

Erskine

John Erskine, 1st Earl of Mar (d.1572): Regent of Scotland 1571–2.

Gordon

Katherine Gordon (c.1474–1537): daughter of George Gordon, 2nd Earl of Huntly, wife to the pretender Perkin Warbeck, and chief lady of the Princess Mary's privy chamber.

George Gordon, 4th Earl of Huntly (1514–62)

George Gordon, 5th Earl of Huntly (c.1535–76): son of the 4th Earl.

John Gordon, 11th Earl of Sutherland (1525–67): cousin of the earls of Huntly. Married Lennox's sister Helen. Margaret's brother- and sister-in-law.

Hamilton

James Hamilton, 1st Earl of Arran (c.1475–1529)

James Hamilton, 2nd Earl of Arran (c.1516–75): son of James Hamilton, 1st Earl of Arran, Duke of Châtelherault, Regent of Scotland 1542–54.

James Hamilton, 3rd Earl of Arran (c.1532–1609): eldest son of James Hamilton, 2nd Earl of Arran, Duke of Châtelherault.

Claud Hamilton, 1st Lord Paisley (1546–1621): younger son of James Hamilton, 2nd Earl of Arran, Duke of Châtelherault.

John Hamilton, Archbishop of St Andrews (1512–71): bastard son of James Hamilton, 1st Earl of Arran.

Hepburn

Margaret Hepburn (d.1513): daughter of Patrick Hepburn, 1st Earl of Bothwell. First wife of Archibald Douglas, 6th Earl of Angus.

Patrick Hepburn, 3rd Earl of Bothwell. Mooted as a husband for Margaret Douglas.

James Hepburn, 4th Earl of Bothwell, 1st Duke of Orkney (c.1534–78): married (1) Jean Gordon (1546–1629) and (2) Mary, Queen of Scots (1542–87).

Alexander Hepburn, Laird of Riccarton: cousin of James Hepburn, 4th Earl of Bothwell.

Home

Alexander, 3rd Lord Home (d.1516): married Agnes Stewart.

Sir David Home of Wedderburn (1489–1524): from a cadet branch of the Home family. Married Alison Douglas, sister of Archibald Douglas, 6th Earl of Angus. Uncle and aunt of Margaret Douglas.

Lennox Stewart/Stuart

John Stewart, 3rd Earl of Lennox (1490–1526): father of Matthew Stuart, 4th Earl of Lennox, and father-in-law of Margaret Douglas.

Matthew Stuart, 4th Earl of Lennox (1516–71): eldest son of John Stewart, 3rd Earl of Lennox. Married Margaret Douglas (1515–78). The spelling of his surname was changed when he lived in France.

John Stuart, 5th Seigneur d'Aubigny (*c.*1519–67): second son of John Stewart, 3rd Earl of Lennox. Brother of Matthew Stuart, 4th Earl of Lennox, and brother-in-law of Margaret Douglas.

Robert Stewart, Bishop of Caithness, 6th Earl of Lennox, 1st Earl of March (*c.*1522–86): third son of John Stewart, 3rd Earl of Lennox. Brother of Matthew Stuart, 4th Earl of Lennox, and brother-in-law of Margaret Douglas.

Henry Stuart, Lord Darnley (1546–67): eldest surviving son of Matthew Stuart, 4th Earl of Lennox, by Margaret Douglas. Married Mary, Queen of Scots (1542–87). Parents of James VI and I, King of Scots and King of England (1566–1625).

Charles Stuart, 6th Earl of Lennox (1557–76): fourth surviving son of Matthew Stuart, 4th Earl of Lennox, by Margaret Douglas. Married Elizabeth Cavendish (1555–82). Parents of Arbella Stuart (1575–1615).

James Stewart, Laird of Cardonald: distant cousin of Matthew Stuart, 4th Earl of Lennox.

Maxwell

Robert, 5th Lord Maxwell (1493–1546): father-in-law of Archibald Douglas, 6th Earl of Angus.

Robert, Master of Maxwell (d.1554): son of Robert, 5th Lord Maxwell, and brother-in-law of Archibald Douglas, 6th Earl of Angus.

Margaret Maxwell (d.1594): daughter of Robert, 5th Lord Maxwell, third wife of Archibald Douglas, 6th Earl of Angus, and stepmother of Margaret Douglas.

Melville

Sir Robert Melville, later 1st Lord Melville (1547–1621): brother of Sir James Meville, ambassador to Elizabeth I.

Ruthven

Patrick, 3rd Lord Ruthven (c.1520–66): married Janet Douglas (d. c.1552), bastard daughter of Archibald Douglas, 6th Earl of Angus, and half-sister of Margaret Douglas.

William, 4th Lord Ruthven (c.1541–84): son of Patrick, 3rd Lord Ruthven, and nephew of Margaret Douglas.

English Nobility

Boleyn

Thomas Boleyn, Earl of Wiltshire and Ormond (c.1477–1539): married Elizabeth Howard (c.1480–1538), daughter of Thomas Howard, 2nd Duke of Norfolk.

Mary Boleyn (c.1498–1543): elder daughter of Thomas Boleyn, Earl of Wiltshire and Ormond, by Elizabeth Howard. Married William Carey (1496?–1528). Mistress of Henry VIII.

Anne Boleyn (c.1501–36): younger daughter of Thomas Boleyn, Earl of Wiltshire and Ormond, by Elizabeth Howard. Second wife of King Henry VIII and mother of Queen Elizabeth I.

George Boleyn, Viscount Rochford (*c.*1503–36): son of Thomas Boleyn, Earl of Wiltshire and Ormond, by Elizabeth Howard. Married Jane Parker (d.1542).

Mary Shelton (*c.*1510–*c.*1571): daughter of Sir John Shelton by Anne Boleyn, sister of Thomas Boleyn, Earl of Wiltshire. Married Sir Anthony Heveningham (1507–57). Mistress of Henry VIII. Friend of Margaret Douglas. Sister of Thomas Shelton, a groom porter at the Tower of London.

Carey

Henry Carey, 1st Lord Hunsdon (1525–96): son of William Carey by Mary Boleyn.

Katherine Carey (1524–69): officially the daughter of William Carey by Mary Boleyn, but probably Mary's bastard daughter by Henry VIII. Probably first cousin to Margaret Douglas. Married Sir Francis Knollys (1514?–96).

Dudley

John Dudley, Duke of Northumberland (1504–53): Lord Admiral, Lord Great Chamberlain, Lord President of the Council. Ruler of England 1549–53 during the minority of Edward VI. Married Jane Guildford (*c.*1508–55).

Lord Guildford Dudley (*c.*1535–54): sixth son of John Dudley, Duke of Northumberland. Married Lady Jane Grey (1536–54).

Lord Robert Dudley, later Earl of Leicester (*c.*1532–88): fifth son of John Dudley, Duke of Northumberland. Master of the Horse, Lord Steward of the Royal Household and Privy Councillor under Elizabeth I. Favourite of Elizabeth I. Married (1) Amy Robsart (1532–60) and (2) Lettice Knollys (1543–1634).

Robert Dudley, Lord Denbigh (1581–4): son of Robert Dudley, Earl of Leicester, by Lettice Knollys.

Grey

William, 13th Lord Grey de Wilton (*c.*1508–62): Governor of Berwick and Warden of the Marches towards Scotland.

Herbert

William Herbert, 1st Earl of Pembroke (*c.*1501–70)

Howard

Thomas Howard, 2nd Duke of Norfolk (1443–1524): son of John Howard, 1st Duke of Norfolk (*c.*1425–85). Married (1) Elizabeth Tilney (*c.*1445–97) and (2) Agnes Tilney (*c.*1477–1545).

Thomas Howard, 3rd Duke of Norfolk (1473–1554): son of Thomas Howard, 2nd Duke of Norfolk, by Elizabeth Tilney. Married (1) Anne of York (1475–1511), daughter of Edward IV, and (2) Elizabeth Stafford (*c.*1497–1558).

Lord Edmund Howard (*c.*1478–1539): younger son of Thomas Howard, 2nd Duke of Norfolk, by Elizabeth Tilney. Married Joyce Culpeper (*c.*1480–1531).

Muriel Howard (*c.*1485–1511): daughter of Thomas Howard, 2nd Duke of Norfolk, by Elizabeth Tilney. Married Sir Thomas Knyvett. Mother of Sir Henry Knyvett (d. *c.*1546).

Lord William Howard, later 1st Baron Howard of Effingham (*c.*1510–73): eldest son of Thomas Howard, 2nd Duke of Norfolk, by Agnes Tilney. Married Margaret Gamage (d.1581).

Lord Thomas Howard (*c.*1511–37): second son of Thomas Howard, 2nd Duke of Norfolk, by Agnes Tilney. Precontracted to Margaret Douglas.

Henry Howard, Earl of Surrey (*c.*1516–47): son of Thomas Howard, 3rd Duke of Norfolk, by Elizabeth Stafford.

Mary Howard (1519–57): daughter of Thomas Howard, 3rd Duke of Norfolk, by Elizabeth Stafford. Married Henry Fitzroy, Duke of Richmond and Somerset (1519–36), bastard son of Henry VIII. Friend of Margaret Douglas.

Margaret Howard (*c.*1515–71): daughter of Lord Edmund Howard by Joyce Culpeper. Married Sir Thomas Arundell (*c.*1502–52).

Sir Charles Howard (d.1544?): son of Lord Edmund Howard by Joyce Culpeper.

Katherine Howard (c.1519–42): daughter of Lord Edmund Howard by Joyce Culpeper. Married Henry VIII, King of England (1491–1547) as his fifth wife.

Thomas Howard, 4th Duke of Norfolk (1536–72): son of Henry Howard, Earl of Surrey. Married (1) Mary Fitzalan (1540–57); (2) Margaret Audley (1540–64) and (3) Elizabeth Leyburne (1536–67).

Manners

Henry Manners, 2nd Earl of Rutland (1526–63)

Neville

Henry Neville, 5th Earl of Westmorland (1525–64): adherent of Margaret Douglas.

Parr

William Parr, Marquess of Northampton (1513–71): brother of Queen Katherine Parr.

Percy

Thomas Percy, 7th Earl of Northumberland (1528–72)

Sackville

Sir Richard Sackville (c.1507–66): son of Sir John Sackville by Margaret Boleyn. Married Winifred Bridges (d.1586).

Thomas Sackville, Lord Buckhurst, later 1st Earl of Dorset (1536–1608): son of Sir Richard Sackville by Winifred Bridges. Married Cicely Baker (1535–1615).

Anne Sackville (d.1595): daughter of Sir Richard Sackville by Winifred Bridges. Married Gregory Fiennes, 10th Lord Dacre (1539–94).

Seymour

Edward Seymour, 1st Earl of Hertford, 1st Duke of Somerset (*c.*1500–52): oldest surviving son of Sir John Seymour and brother of Queen Jane Seymour. Married (1) Katherine Fillol (*c.*1507–*c.*1535) and (2) Anne Stanhope (*c.*1510–87). Lord Protector of England from 1547 to 1549 during the minority of Edward VI.

Jane Seymour (*c.*1508–37): daughter of Sir John Seymour. Third wife of King Henry VIII and mother of King Edward VI.

Lord Thomas Seymour of Sudeley (*c.*1508–49): fourth son of Sir John Seymour and brother of Queen Jane Seymour. Married Queen Katherine Parr (1512–48) after the death of King Henry VIII.

Edward Seymour, 2nd Earl of Hertford (1539–1621): son of Edward Seymour, 1st Earl of Hertford, 1st Duke of Somerset. Married Lady Katherine Grey (1540–68).

Edward Seymour, Viscount Beauchamp (1561–1612): elder son of Edward Seymour, 2nd Earl of Hertford, by Katherine Grey. Married Honora Rogers.

Thomas Seymour (1563–1619): younger son of Edward Seymour, 2nd Earl of Hertford, by Katherine Grey.

William Seymour, 2nd Duke of Somerset (1588–1660): son of Edward Seymour, Viscount Beauchamp, by Honora Rogers. Married Arbella Stuart (1575–1615), granddaughter of Margaret Douglas.

Talbot and Cavendish

George Talbot, 4th Earl of Shrewsbury (1468–1538)

Francis Talbot, 5th Earl of Shrewsbury (1500–60)

George Talbot, 6th Earl of Shrewsbury (1528–90): married Elizabeth (Bess of) Hardwick (*c.*1527–1608). Custodian of Mary, Queen of Scots.

Elizabeth (Bess of) Hardwick (*c.*1527–1608): married (1) Robert Barley (d.1544); (2) Sir William Cavendish (*c.*1505–57); (3) Sir William

St Loe (1518–65) and (4) George Talbot, 6th Earl of Shrewsbury (1528–90).

Elizabeth Cavendish (1555–82): daughter of Sir William Cavendish by Elizabeth (Bess of) Hardwick. Married Charles Stuart, 6th Earl of Lennox (1557–76). Parents of Arbella Stuart (1575–1615).

Gilbert Talbot, later 7th Earl of Shrewsbury (1552–1616)

Wharton

Thomas, 1st Lord Wharton (1495–1568): associate of Matthew Stuart, 4th Earl of Lennox.

Philip, 3rd Lord Wharton (1555–1625): grandson of Thomas, 1st Lord Wharton.

Scottish Politicians

Sir James Balfour (c.1525–83): judge and one of the Protestant Lords of the Congregation.

Cardinal David Beaton, Archbishop of St Andrews (c.1494–1546): Keeper of the Privy Seal. Committed to preserving Scotland's alliance with France.

James Beaton, Archbishop of Glasgow (c.1517–1603): loyal to Mary, Queen of Scots.

George Buchanan (1508–82): Protestant, humanist scholar, Moderator of the Church of Scotland and tutor to James VI.

Sir William Kirkcaldy of Grange (c.1520–73): Lord High Admiral of Scotland; Captain of Edinburgh Castle.

Sir William Maitland of Lethington (1525–73): Protestant reformer and Secretary of State.

David Rizzio (c.1533–66): Italian-born French secretary to Mary, Queen of Scots.

John Stewart, 2nd Duke of Albany (*c.*1481–1536): grandson of King James II of Scots. Regent of Scotland during the minority of King James V.

Scottish Ambassadors

Sir James Melville (1535–1617), ambassador to Elizabeth I.

Sir Adam Otterbourne (d.1548), ambassador to Edward VI.

English Politicians

Sir Nicholas Bacon (1510–79): Lord Keeper of the Great Seal under Elizabeth I.

Sir William Cecil, 1st Lord Burghley (1520–98): Lord Privy Seal, Secretary of State and Lord Treasurer under Elizabeth I. Married Mildred Cooke (1526–89).

Thomas, Lord Dacre of Gilsland (1467–1525): Warden General of the Marches towards Scotland.

Sir William Drury (1527–79): Marshal of Berwick and later Lord Justice of Ireland under Elizabeth I.

Thomas Cromwell, Earl of Essex (1485–1540): Chancellor of the Exchequer, Master of the Rolls, Secretary of State, Lord Privy Seal and Lord Great Chamberlain under Henry VIII.

Sir Francis Jobson (*c.*1509–73): Master of the Jewel House; Lieutenant of the Tower.

Sir William Paget, later 1st Lord Paget (1506–63): Privy Councillor, Secretary of State and Lord Privy Seal.

William Paulet, 1st Marquess of Winchester (*c.*1483–1572): Privy Councillor, Lord Chamberlain, Lord High Treasurer of England.

Thomas Radcliffe, 3rd Earl of Sussex (*c.*1525–83): Lord Lieutenant of Ireland, Lord Chamberlain and President of the Council of the North under Elizabeth I.

Francis Russell, 2nd Earl of Bedford: Governor of Berwick.

Sir Ralph Sadler (1507–87): Privy Councillor and Secretary of State.

Sir Francis Walsingham (1532–90): Principal Secretary of State to Elizabeth I, and her 'spymaster'.

Cardinal Thomas Wolsey, Catholic Archbishop of York (1473–1530): Lord Chancellor under Henry VIII.

English Ambassadors

Sir Thomas Challoner (1521–65), ambassador to Spain.

Sir Henry Killigrew (c.1528–1603), ambassador to Scotland.

Thomas Magnus (c.1453–1550), ambassador to Scotland.

Sir Henry Norris (1525–1601), ambassador to France.

Thomas Randolph (1523–90), ambassador to Scotland.

Sir Thomas Smith (1513–77), ambassador to France.

John Tamworth (or Thornworth) (c.1524–69), ambassador to Mary, Queen of Scots.

Sir Nicholas Throckmorton (c.1515–71), ambassador to France and Scotland.

Sir Francis Walsingham (1532–90), ambassador to France.

Sir Thomas Wyatt (1503–42), poet; ambassador to France and Italy.

Royal Household

Thomas Alsopp, physician to Henry VIII.

Thomas Aske, apothecary to Henry VIII.

Walter Cromer, physician to Henry VIII.

Alice Davy, former nurse to Margaret Tudor, possibly nurse to Margaret Douglas.

Robert Huicke (d.1581?), physician to Henry VIII and Elizabeth I.

John Kaye, Clerk of the Greencloth, Margaret's executor.

Margaret's Household

John Baily, Margaret's servant.

Thomas Bishop (b. *c.*1518; d. by 1511): Lennox's secretary. Married Janet Stirling and had three sons, Francis (d. by 1611), Thomas (d.1570) and Richard.

Thomas Blackmore, Lennox's servant.

Elizabeth Chamberlain, Margaret's servant.

Charles, Margaret's chaplain at the court of Henry VIII.

Christian, waiting woman to Margaret.

Captain Robert Cunningham, Lennox's servant.

Sir John Dixon, priest, secretary to Margaret Douglas.

Robert Dolman, steward to the Lennoxes.

Thomas Dolman, steward to the Lennoxes.

John Elder, tutor to Lord Darnley.

Mabel Fortescue, Margaret's servant.

Thomas Fowler (d.1590), clerk of the kitchen, secretary, treasurer and executor of Margaret Douglas.

Harvey, Margaret's servant at the court of Henry VIII.

Thomas Helforth, Margaret's servant.

John Hume, Lennox's servant.

Elizabeth Hussey, Margaret's servant.

William Knockes, Lennox's falconer.

Ralph Lacy, Margaret's servant.

Arthur Lallard, tutor to Lord Darnley.

Peter, groom of the wardrobe to Margaret at the court of Henry VIII.

Peter Malliet, tutor to Lord Charles Stuart.

Margaret Maxton, Margaret's serving woman.

William Mompesson, Lennox's servant.

John Moon, Lennox's servant.

Wat Nepe, Margaret's falconer.

Laurence Nesbit, Lennox's servant.

Richard Norton, steward to the Lennoxes.

William Paterson, Lennox's servant.

Robert Portinger, Margaret's servant.

Rigg, Margaret's footman.

William Robinson, Margaret's servant.

Mary Silles, Margaret's servant.

Robert Thwaites, Lennox's servant.

Edward Vane, Margaret's servant.

Henry Whitreason, receiver to the Lennoxes.

Margaret Wilton, Margaret's gentlewoman.

John Wood, Lennox's servant.

Priests receiving stipends from Margaret

Sir John Cancefeld

Sir John Dixon

Sir Peter Glentham

Sir John Kay

Sir Thomas Middelton

Sir Thomas Swadale

Sir Richard Waddell

Sir Martin Wardman

Sir John Wilde

Sir William of Malton

Adherents and agents of Margaret Douglas and Matthew Stuart, Earl of Lennox

Hugh Allen

Mr Brinklow

George Chamberlain

Sir Richard Chamberlain, Keeper of Scarborough Castle.

Sir Richard Cholmeley (*c.*1516–83), Keeper of Scarborough Castle.

Sir Marmaduke Constable

John Elder, former tutor to Lord Darnley.

Sir John Foster (1520–1602), Warden of the Middle Marches.

Henry Gwyn

Thomas Kelly

Ralph Lacy, Margaret's servant.

Arthur Lallard (d.1565), tutor to Lord Darnley.

Sir William Livingston, Laird of Kilsyth (d. c.1596).

John Lockhart, Laird of Barr.

Wat Nepe, Margaret's falconer.

Laurence Nesbit, Lennox's servant.

Rigg, Margaret's footman.

Anthony Standen

Thomas Stewart, Laird of Galston, cousin of Lennox.

Dr Turner

Peter Vavasour, solicitor to the Lennoxes.

Francis Yaxley (d.1565)

Agents of the English Government

Thomas Bishop

John Case

William Forbes

John Moon, Lennox's servant.

Alexander Pringle, formerly an adherent of the Douglases
William Rogers.

Agents of Mary, Queen of Scots

Andrew Abercrombie

Antonio Fogaza, Portuguese spy.

Clergy

William Barlow, Protestant Bishop of Chichester (d. 1568).

Thomas Cranmer, Protestant Archbishop of Canterbury
(1489–1556).

Gabriel Goodman, Protestant Dean of Westminster (1528–1601).

John Jewel, Protestant Bishop of Salisbury (1522–71).

John Knox (*c.*1514–72), Protestant founding father of the Scottish
Reformation.

John Leslie, Catholic Bishop of Ross (1527–96), supporter of Mary,
Queen of Scots.

Matthew Parker, Protestant Archbishop of Canterbury (1504–75).

Cardinal Reginald Pole, Catholic Archbishop of Canterbury
(1500–58).

Thomas Robertson, Catholic Dean of Durham (d. after 1559).

Cuthbert Tunstall, Catholic Bishop of Durham (1474–1559).

Cardinal Thomas Wolsey, Catholic Archbishop of York (1473–1530).

Thomas Young, Protestant Archbishop of York (1507–68).

Government Commissioners for the management of the Lennox estates:

Sir Thomas Gargrave (1495–1579)

Henry Gates (c.1515–89)

John Vaughan (d.1577), Justice of the Peace, Married to Anne Pickering, Lady Knyvett.

Other

Scotland

Sir John Borthwick (d.1566): Scottish reformer who defected to Elizabeth I but then changed sides.

Captain James Calder (d.1571), adherent of the Hamiltons.

England

Sir Francis Bigod (1507–37), a Protestant who led a revolt against Henry VIII at the time of the Pilgrimage of Grace. Builder of Settrington House.

Sir Christopher Garnish, gentleman usher to Henry VIII, envoy to Margaret Tudor.

Sebastian Giustinian, Venetian ambassador to the court of Henry VIII.

Roger Lascellesy, steward of Norham Castle.

Sir Thomas Strangeways, comptroller of the household of Cardinal Wolsey; Captain of Berwick.

Sir Edward Warner (1511–65), Lieutenant of the Tower of London.

Sir Thomas Wyatt the Younger (1521–54), son of the poet and ambassador Sir Thomas Wyatt. Led a rebellion against Mary I.

Bibliography

Primary Sources

Abell, Adam: *The Roit ir Quheill of Tyme* (see A. M. Stewart, 'Final Folios
    of the Roit ir Quheill of Tyme', in *Stewart Style* (ed. Janet Hadley
    Williams, East Linton, 1996)
Accounts of the Lord High Treasurer of Scotland (12 vols., ed. T. Dickon
    et al., Edinburgh, 1877–1970)
Acts of the Parliaments of Scotland, 1124–1707 (12 vols., ed. Thomas
    Thompson and Cosmo Innes, Edinburgh, 1814–75)
Acts of the Privy Council of England, 1542–1631 (vols. 1 to 10 of 45, ed.
    John Roche Dasent, E. G. Atkinson, J. V. Lyle, R. F. Monger and
    P. A. Penfold, London, 1890–1964)
Additional MSS (The British Library)
Ambassades de MM. de Noailles en Angleterre (5 vols., ed. R. A. Vertot and
    C. Villaret, Leyden, 1763)
Archaeologia, or Miscellaneous Tracts relating to Antiquity (Society of
    Antiquaries, London, 1910)
Arundel MSS (The British Library)
Ascham, Roger: *The Schoolmaster* (London, 1570; London, 1909)

*Batman vpon Bartholome, his book De Proprietatibus rerum, newly corrected,
    enlarged, and amended* (compiled Steven Batman; translated by John
    Trevisa, London, 1582)
Bickham, George: *Deliciae Brittanicae* (London, 1742)
Buck, Samuel and Nathaniel: *Buck's Antiquities or Venerable Remains of
    Above 400 Castles, &c., in England and Wales, with near 100 Views of
    Cities* (London, 1774)

Calderwood, David: *The True History of the Church of Scotland from the
    beginning of the Reformation unto the end of the Reign of King James VI*

(8 vols., ed. Thomas Thomson and David Laing, Wodrow Society, Edinburgh, 1842–9)

Calendar of the Cecil Papers in Hatfield House, Vol. 1, 1306–1571, Vol. 2, 1572–1582 (Calendar of the Manuscripts of the Most Honourable The Marquess of Salisbury, Historical Manuscripts Commission, 24 vols., London, 1883–1976; www.british-history.ac.uk)

Calendar of Letters, Despatches and State Papers relating to Negotiations between England and Spain, preserved in the Archives at Simancas and Elsewhere (13 vols., ed. G. A. Bergenroth, P. de Goyangos, Garrett Mattingley, R. Tyler *et al.*, HMSO, London, 1862–1965; www.british-history.ac.uk)

Calendar of Letters and State Papers relating to English Affairs, preserved principally in the Archives of Simancas (4 vols., ed. Martin A. S. Hume, London, HMSO, 1892; www.british-history.ac.uk)

Calendar of the manuscripts of the Most Honourable the Marquess of Salisbury . . . preserved at Hatfield House, Hertfordshire (24 vols., Historical Manuscripts Commission, London, 1883–1976)

A Calendar of the Shrewsbury and Talbot Papers in Lambeth Palace Library and the College of Arms (2 vols., ed. Catherine Jamison, revised by E. G. W. Bill, Historical Manuscripts Commission, London, 1966, 1972).

Calendar of State Papers Domestic: Vol. I: Edward, Mary and Elizabeth, 1547–80 (ed. Robert Lemon, London, 1856; www.british-history.ac.uk)

Calendar of State Papers, Foreign: Edward VI, 1547–1553 (ed. William B. Turnbull, London, 1861; www.british-history.ac.uk)

Calendar of State Papers, Foreign: Elizabeth (vols. 1–13, ed. Joseph Stevenson and A. J. Crosby *et al.*, London, 1863–1980; www.british-history.ac.uk)

Calendar of State Papers, Foreign: Mary, 1553–1558 (ed. William B. Turnbull, London, 1861; www.british-history.ac.uk)

Calendar of State Papers and Manuscripts existing in the Archives and Collections of Milan, 1385–1618 (ed. Allen B. Hinds, London, 1912; www.british-history.ac.uk)

Calendar of State Papers and Manuscripts relating to English Affairs preserved in the Archives of Venice and in the other Libraries of Northern Italy (vols. 2 and 7, ed. L. Rawdon-Brown, Cavendish Bentinck *et al.*, London, 1864–1947; www.british-history.ac.uk)

Calendar of State Papers and Manuscripts relating to English Affairs in the Vatican Archives, Vol. 1 (ed. J. M. Rigg, London, 1916; www.british-history.ac.uk)

Calendar of the State Papers relating to Scotland and Mary, Queen of Scots, 1547–1603 (vols. 1–5, ed. Joseph Bain, W. K. Boyd and M. S. Giuseppi, Edinburgh, 1898–1969; www.british-history.ac.uk)

Cambridge University Library MSS

Camden, William: *Annales rerum Anglicarum et Hibernicarum regnante Elizabetha* (London, 1615)

Cavendish-Talbot MSS (Folger Shakespeare Library)

Chapters in the History of Yorkshire, being a Collection of Original Letters, Papers and Public Documents illustrating the State of that County during the Reigns of Elizabeth I, James I and Charles I (ed. J. J. Cartwright, Wakefield, 1872)

The Chronicle of Calais in the Reigns of Henry VII and Henry VIII, to the year 1540 (attributed to Richard Turpin; ed. J. G. Nichols, Camden Society, 25, 1846)

The Chronicle of Queen Jane and of Two Years of Queen Mary, written by a Resident in the Tower of London (ed. John Gough Nichols, Camden Society, London, 1850)

Cobbett's Complete Collection of State Trials, Vol. 1 (London, 1809)

A Collection of Letters, and State Papers, From the Original Manuscripts of Several Princes and Great Personages in the Two Last Centuries (ed. Leonard Howard, London, 1765)

A Collection of State Papers, relating to affairs in the reigns of King Henry VIII, King Edward VI, Queen Mary and Queen Elizabeth, from the year 1542 to 1570. Transcribed from original letters and other authentick memorials (ed. Samuel Haynes, London, 1740)

A Collection of State Papers relating to affairs in the Reign of Queen Elizabeth, from the year 1571 to 1596, translated from the original papers in the Library of Hatfield House (ed. William Murdin, London, 1759)

Correspondence Diplomatique Angleterre (Archives des affaires étrangères)

Cotton MSS (The British Library)

Crossley, E. W.: 'A Temple Newsam Inventory, 1565' (*Yorkshire Archaeological Journal*, 25, 1918–20)

The Devonshire Manuscript: A Women's Book of Courtly Poetry, by Lady Margaret Douglas and Others (ed. Elizabeth Heale, Toronto, 2012)

A diurnal of remarkable occurrents that have passed within Scotland since the death of King James IV till the year MDMLXV (ed. Thomas Thomson, Edinburgh, 1833)

Doleman, R.: *A Conference about the Next Succession to the Crown of England* (Antwerp, 1594)

The Douglas Book (4 vols., ed. William Fraser, Edinburgh, 1885)

The Earl of Warwick's MSS at Warwick Castle, Class OG.308

Early Modern Women Poets (1520–1700): An Anthology (ed. Jane Stevenson and Peter Davidson, Oxford, 2001)

Ecclesiastical Memorials (3 vols., ed. John Strype, Oxford, 1822)

Edward VI: *The Chronicle and Political Papers of King Edward VI* (ed. W. K. Jordan, London, 1966)

Edward VI: *England's Boy King: The Diary of Edward VI, 1547–1553* (ed. Jonathan North, Welwyn Garden City, 2005)

Egerton MSS (The British Library)

Elder, John: *The Copy of a Letter sent into Scotland of the Arrival and Landing and Marriage of Philip, Prince of Spain to the Princess Mary, Queen of England* (London, 1555)

Erskine, John Francis, and Paton, Henry: *Report on the Manuscripts of the Earl of Mar and Kellie, preserved at Alloa House, N.B.* (Historical Manuscripts Commission No. 60, 1904)

Fénélon, Bertrand de Salignac de la Mothe: *Correspondence diplomatique de Bertrand de Salignac de la Mothe Fénélon: ambassadeur de France en Angleterre de 1568 à 1575* (7 vols., ed. Alexandre Teulet, Paris and London, 1838–40)

Folger Shakespeare Library MSS (Washington DC)

Foxe, John: *The Acts and Monuments of John Foxe* (8 vols., ed. Stephen Reed Cattley, London, 1853–70; The Acts and Monuments Online, www.johnfoxe.org)

Fuller, Thomas: *The Church History of Britain* (London, 1655; 6 vols., ed. J. S. Brewer, Oxford, 1845)

Goodare, Julian: 'Queen Mary's Catholic interlude' (in *Mary Stewart: Queen in Three Kingdoms*, ed. Michael Lynch, Oxford, 1988)

The Great Wardrobe Accounts of Henry VII and Henry VIII (ed. Maria Hayward, London Record Society, 2012)

Hall, Edward: *The Union of the Two Noble and Illustre Families of Lancaster and York* (ed. H. Ellis, London, 1809; published in facsimile 1970)

Harleian MSS (The British Library)

Herbert, Edward, 1st Baron Herbert of Cherbury: *The Life and Raigne of King Henry the Eighth* (London, 1649, reprinted London, 1870)

The Historie and Life of King James the Sext (Bannatyne Club, 13, Edinburgh, 1825)

Holinshed, Raphael: *The Chronicles of England, Scotland and Ireland* (2 vols., London, 1577; ed. Henry Ellis, 6 vols., London, 1807–8)

Knox, John: *The Works of John Knox* (6 vols., ed. David Laing, Bannatyne Society, Edinburgh, 1846–64)

Lansdowne MSS (The British Library)

The Last Testament of the Earl of Bothwell (transcribed by Eileen Santen, ed. Prue Mosman, www.mariestuart.co.uk)

Latymer, William: 'William Latymer's Chronicle of Anne Boleyn' (ed. Maria Dowling, *Camden Miscellany*, 30, Camden Society 4th Series 39, 1990)

Leicester's Commonwealth (ed. Nina Green, 2002, www.oxford-shakespeare.com)

Leland, John: *Antiquarii de Rebus Brittanicis Collectanea* (London, 1612; 6 vols., ed. Thomas Hearne, Chetham Society, Oxford, 1715, London, 1774)

Leland, John: *The Itinerary of John Leland in or about the years 1535–1543* (5 vols., ed. Lucy Toulin Smith, London, 1906–10)

The Lennox Narrative (Cambridge University Library, Oo.vii.47; reproduced in R. H. Mahon: *Mary, Queen of Scots: A Study of the Lennox Narrative*, Cambridge, 1924)

Lesley (or Leslie), John: *De origine, moribus, ac rebus gestis Scotiae libri decem* (10 vols., Rome, 1578; published as *The history of Scotland, from the death of King James I in the year M.CCCC.XXXVI to the year M.D.LXI, ed. Thomas Thomson, Bannatyne Club, Edinburgh, 1830)

The Letters of King Henry VIII (ed. Muriel St Clare Byrne, London, 1936)

Letters and Papers, Foreign and Domestic, of the Reign of Henry VIII (21 vols. in 33 parts, ed. J. S. Brewer, James Gairdner, R. Brodie *et al.*, 1862–1932)

Letters of the Queens of England, 1100–1547 (ed. Anne Crawford, Stroud, 1994)

Letters of Royal and Illustrious Ladies of Great Britain (3 vols., ed. Mary Anne Everett Green, London, 1846)

Lettres, Instructions et Mémoires de Marie Stuart, Reine d'Écosse (7 vols., ed. Alexandre Labanoff, London, 1844)

Lindsay, Robert, of Pitscottie: *The History and Chronicles of Scotland, 1436–1565* (Laing MS. 218, University of Edinburgh; ed. Aeneus Mackay, Scottish Texts Society, Edinburgh, 1899)

Loke, William: 'Account of Materials furnished for the use of Anne Boleyn and Princess Elizabeth, 1535–6' (*Miscellanea of the Philobiblion Society*, VII, 1862)

Melville, Sir James: *Memoirs of Sir James Melville of Halhill* (ed. A. Francis Steuart, London, 1929)

National Archives: C.: Chancery Records
National Archives: E.: Exchequer Records
National Archives: PROB: Records of the Prerogative Court of Canterbury
National Archives: SP: State Papers
National Archives: SPD: State Papers Domestic
National Archives of Scotland: GD: Gifts and Deeds

National Records of Scotland: PC: Privy Council

Naunton, Sir Robert: *Fragmenta Regalia* (London, 1653; ed. Edward Arber, London, 1879, 1896)

Original Letters Illustrative of English History (11 vols. in 3 series, ed. Sir Henry Ellis, London, 1824, 1827 and 1846)

Papiers d'état, pièces et documents inédits ou peu connus, relatifs a l'histoire de l'Écosse au XVIe siècle, tirés des bibliothèques et des archives de France (3 vols., ed. A. Teulet, Bannatyne Club of Edinburgh, Paris, 1852)

Peck, Francis: *New Memoirs of the Life and Poetical Works of Mr John Milton* (London, 1740)

Pepys Library, Cambridge MSS (Magdalene College, Cambridge)

Phillips, John: *A Commemoration of the Right Noble and virtuous Lady Margaret Douglas's good Grace, Countess of Lennox* (London, 1578)

Privy Purse Expenses of Henry VIII, 1529–1532 (ed. Nicholas Harris Nicolas, London, 1827)

Privy Purse Expenses of the Princess Mary, daughter of King Henry the Eighth, afterwards Queen Mary, with a memoir of the Princess, and notes (ed. Frederick Madden, London, 1831)

Records of the Court of Augmentations and the Augmentation Office (The National Archives)

Register of the Privy Council of Scotland (14 vols., ed. J. H. Burton and D. Masson, Edinburgh, 1877–98)

Register of the Privy Seal of Scotland (4 vols., ed. M. Livingstone, D. H. Fleming and J. Beveridge, Scottish Record Office, 1908)

Regnans in Excelsis: Excommunicating Elizabeth I of England (www.papalencyclicals.net)

Relations Politiques de la France et de l'Espagne avec l'Ecosse au XVIième Siècle (5 vols., ed. J. A. B. Teulet, Paris, 1862)

The Scottish Correspondence of Mary of Lorraine: Including Some Three Hundred Letters from 20th February 1542–3 to 15th May 1560 (ed. Annie I. Cameron, Edinburgh, 1927)

Secret Writing in the Public Records, Henry VIII–George II (ed. Sheila R. Richards, London, 1974)

Selections from unpublished manuscripts in the College of Arms and the B.M. illustrating the reign of Mary, Queen of Scotland, 1543–68 (ed. J. Stevenson, Maitland Club, 42, Glasgow, 1837)

Sloane MSS (The British Library)

Spottiswood, John: *The History of the Church and State of Scotland* (London, 1655)

State Papers of the Reign of Henry VIII (11 vols., Records Commissioners, 1830–52)

Statutes of the Realm (11 vols., ed. A. Luders *et al.*, London, 1810–28)

Stow, John: *A Survey of London* (London, 1598; Stroud, 1994)

Stowe MSS (The British Library)

A Survey of the Manor of Settrington (ed. H. King and A. Harris, Yorkshire Archaeological Society, CXXVI, Wakefield, 1962)

Talbot MSS (Lambeth Palace Library and College of Arms)

Tottel, Richard: *Songs and Sonnets, Written by the Right Honourable Lord Henry Howard, late Earl of Surrey, and Other* (London, 1557, ed. Edward Arber, London, 1870)

Two Missions of Jacques de la Brosse (ed. Gladys Dickinson, Scottish History Society, 1942)

Udall, William: *History of the Life and Death of Mary Stuart, Queen of Scotland* (London, 1636)

University of Nottingham MSS

Vergil, Polydore: *The Anglica Historia of Polydore Vergil, A.D. 1485–1573* (trans. and ed. D. Hay, Camden Series, 1950; www.philological.bham.ac.uk)

Weever, John: *Ancient Funeral Monuments within the United Monarchies of Great Britain, Northern Ireland and the Islands Adjacent* (London, 1631)

Wright, Benjamin: *The Royal Progeny of King James* (1603; London, 1619)

Wriothesley, Charles, Windsor Herald: *A Chronicle of England in the Reigns of the Tudors from 1485 to 1559* (2 vols., ed. William Douglas Hamilton, Camden Society, 2nd Series, X and XX, 1875, 1877)

The Zurich Letters, or the Correspondence of Several English Bishops and Others with the Helvetian Reformers during the Reign of Queen Elizabeth, Vol. 1 (ed. Hastings Robinson, The Parker Society, Cambridge, 1846)

Secondary Sources

Abernethy, Susan: 'Margaret Douglas, Countess of Lennox' (www. saintssistersandsluts.com, 2012; www.earlymodernengland.com, 2013)

Adams, Simon: 'The release of Lord Darnley and the failure of amity' (*Innes Review*, 38, 1987)

Armstrong-Davison, M. H.: *The Casket Letters* (London, 1965)

Arnold, Janet: *Princely Magnificence: Court Jewels of the Renaissance, 1500–1630* (exhibition catalogue, Victoria and Albert Museum, 1980)

Arnold, Janet: *Queen Elizabeth's Wardrobe Unlock'd* (Leeds, 1988)

The Art of Jewellery in Scotland (ed. R. Marshall and G. Dalgleish, Edinburgh, 1991)

Ashdown, Dulcie M.: *Ladies in Waiting* (London, 1976)

Ashdown, Dulcie M.: *Royal Murders* (Stroud, 1998)

Ashdown, Dulcie M.: *Tudor Cousins: Rivals for the Throne* (Stroud, 2000)

Ashdown-Hill, John: 'The Opening of the Tombs of the Dukes of Richmond and Norfolk, Framlingham, April 1841: the Account of the Reverend J. W. Darby' (*The Ricardian*, 18, 2008)

Ashley, Mike: *British Monarchs* (London, 1998)

Aveling, J. C. H.: 'Catholic Households in Yorkshire, 1580–1603' (*Northern History*, 16, 1980)

Aveling, J. C. H.: 'Some Aspects of Yorkshire Catholic Recusant History, 1558–1791' (*Studies in Church History*, IV, London, 1967)

Bagley, J. J.: *Henry VIII and his Times* (London, 1962)

Baldwin, David: *Henry VIII's Last Love: The Turbulent, Tragic Life of Katherine Willoughby, Duchess of Suffolk, 1519–1580* (Stroud, 2015)

Barber, P. M.: 'Mapping Britain from Afar' (*Mercator's World*, 3, 1998)

Baron, Helen: 'Mary (Howard) Fitzroy's Hand' (*The Review of English Studies,* New Series, 45, no. 179, August 1994)

Baron, Helen: 'Women and the Courtly Love Lyric: The Devonshire MS. (B. L. Additional 17492)' (*Modern Language Review*, 90, 1995)

Bastow, Sarah L.: '"Worth Nothing, but very Wilful": Catholic Recusant Women of Yorkshire' (*Recusant History*, 25, 2001)

Bell, Doyne C.: *Notices of the Historic Persons Buried in the Chapel of St Peter ad Vincula in the Tower of London* (London, 1877)

Bindoff, S. T.: *The History of Parliament: The House of Commons, 1509–1558* (3 vols., London, 1982)

Bingham, Caroline: *Darnley: A Life of Henry Stewart, Lord Darnley, Consort of Mary, Queen of Scots* (London, 1995)

The Bishop Family of Pocklington (www.pocklingtonhistory.com)

Black, J. B.: *The Reign of Elizabeth, 1558–1603* (Oxford, 1959)

Bond, Edward A.: 'Wyatt's Poems' (*The Athenaeum*, 2274, 1874)

Borman, Tracy: *Elizabeth's Women: The Hidden Story of the Virgin Queen* (London, 2009)

Boulter, W. C.: 'Court Rolls of some East Riding Manors 1565–1573' (*Yorkshire Archaeological Journal*, 10, London, 1889)

Bowen, Marjorie: *Mary, Queen of Scots* (London, 1934)

Bowle, John: *Henry VIII* (London, 1965)

Brenan, Gerald, and Statham, Edward Phillips: *The House of Howard* (2 vols., London, 1907)

Bridgeman: Portrait of a Lady in Black (www.bridgemanart.com)

Brigden, Susan: 'Henry Howard, Earl of Surrey, and the "Conjured League"' (*Historical Journal*, 37, 3, Cambridge, 1994)

Brigden, Susan: *Thomas Wyatt: The Heart's Forest* (London, 2012)

Brooke House (www.hackney.gov.uk)

Buchanan, Patricia: *Margaret Tudor, Queen of Scots* (Edinburgh, 1985)

The Buildings of Settrington (2012, www.maltonbuildingsgroup.com)

Burke's Guide to the Royal Family (Burke's Peerage Ltd, London, 1973)

Burke's Peerage, Baronetage & Knightage, 107th edition, 3 volumes (ed. Charles Mosley, Burke's Peerage (Genealogical Books) Ltd, 2003)

Cameron, James: *James V, the Personal Rule, 1528–1542* (ed. Norman Mcdougall, East Linton, 1998)

Campling, Arthur: *The History of the Family of Drury in the Counties of Suffolk and Norfolk from the Conquest* (London, 1937)

Cannon, John, and Hargreaves, Ann: *The Kings and Queens of Britain* (Oxford, 2001)

Carleton Williams, Ethel: *Bess of Hardwick* (London, 1959)

Castelli, Jorge H.: Margaret Douglas (www.tudorplace.com)

Chalfant, Frank C.: *Ben Jonson's London: A Jacobean Placename Dictionary* (Georgia, 1978)

Chalmers, George: *The Life of Mary, Queen of Scots, drawn from the State Papers* (3 vols., London, 1818)

Chapman, Hester W.: *The Sisters of Henry VIII* (London, 1969)

Chapman, Hester W.: *Two Tudor Portraits* (London, 1960)

Childs, Jessie: *Henry VIII's Last Victim: The Life and Times of Henry Howard, Earl of Surrey* (London, 2006)

'Cistercians "depopulated land" to found Jervaulx' (*British Archaeology*, 50, December 1999, News)

Claremont, Francesca: *Catherine of Aragon* (London, 1939)

Clarke, Siobhan: Dangerous Inheritance: Lady Margaret Douglas, 1515 to 1578 (unpublished lecture, 2013)

Cliffe, J. T.: *The Yorkshire Gentry from the Reformation to the Civil War* (London, 1969)

Cloake, John: *Palaces and Parks of Richmond and Kew* (Chichester, 1995)

The Complete Peerage (6 vols., ed. G. H. White *et al.*, St Catherine's Press, 1910–59, Stroud, 1982)

Darnton Index (www.darnton.info)

Davey, Richard: *The Pageant of London* (2 vols., London, 1906)

Davey, Richard: *The Sisters of Lady Jane Grey and their Wicked Grandfather* (London, 1911)

Denny, Joanna: *Anne Boleyn* (London, 2004)

Denny, Joanna: *Katherine Howard* (London, 2005)

The Devonshire Manuscript: General Introduction (www.wikibooks.org, 2013)

Dictionary of National Biography (22 vols., ed. Sir Leslie Stephen and Sir Sidney Lee, 1885–1901; Oxford, 1998 edition)

Dixon, William Hepworth: *Her Majesty's Tower* (London, 1869)

Donaldson, Gordon: *All the Queen's Men* (London, 1983)

Donaldson, Gordon: *The First Trial of Mary, Queen of Scots* (London, 1969)

Donaldson, Gordon: *Mary, Queen of Scots* (London, 1974)

Donaldson, Gordon: *Scotland: James V to James VII* (Edinburgh, 1965)

Dootson, Shelley: Community Dig at Stepney City Farm (www.dayofarchaeology.com)

Doran, Susan: *Mary, Queen of Scots: An Illustrated Life* (The British Library, London, 2007)

The Douglas Archives (www.douglashistory.co.uk)

Dunn, Jane: *Elizabeth and Mary: Cousins, Rivals, Queens* (London, 2003)

Durant, David N.: *Arbella Stuart: A Rival to the Queen* (London, 1978)

Eden, W. A., Draper, Marie P. G., and Williams, Audrey: 'Brooke House, Hackney' (*Survey of London*, vol. 28, English Heritage, 1960)

Eleftheriou, Krista: Volunteers to Unearth London's History (www.crossrail.co.uk)

Emerson, Kate: *A Who's Who of Tudor Women* (www.kateemersonhistoricals.com)

English Heritage: The National Heritage List for England (www.list.english-heritage.org.uk)

Evans, Victoria Sylvia: *Ladies-in-Waiting: Women Who Served at the Tudor Court* (CreateSpace, 2014)

Fielding, J: 'Barber's Barn, Hackney' (*The European Magazine and London Review*, 59, 1811)

The Fitzwilliam Museum (www.fitzmuseum.cam.ac.uk)

Foister, Susan: *Holbein in England* (London, 2006)

Fraser, Antonia: *King James VI of Scotland, I of England* (London, 1974)

Fraser, Antonia: *Mary, Queen of Scots* (London, 1969)

Fraser, Antonia: *The Six Wives of Henry VIII* (London, 1992)

Fraser, William: *The Lennox* (2 vols., Edinburgh, 1874)

Friedmann, Paul: *Anne Boleyn* (2 vols., London, 1884)

Froude, James Anthony: *The History of England from the Fall of Wolsey to the Death of Elizabeth* (12 vols., London, 1856–70)

Fry, Plantagenet Somerset: *Castles* (Newton Abbot, 2005)

Furtado, Peter; Harris, Nathaniel; Harrison, Hazel, and Pettit, Paul: *The Country Life Book of Castles and Houses in Britain* (London, 1986)

Gayley, Charles Mills: *Francis Beaumont, Dramatist, With Some Account of His Circle, Elizabethan and Jacobean, and of His Association With John Fletcher* (London, 1914)

A Genealogical History of the Royal Families of England from William the Conqueror to the present Royal Grand Childen . . . Collected from Mr Rapin and other authentic Historians (anonymous, London, 1753)

Glenne, Michael: *King Harry's Sister: Margaret Tudor, Queen of Scotland* (London, 1952)

Goodall, John: *The English Castle* (New Haven and London, 2011)

Graham, Roderick: *An Accidental Tragedy: The Life of Mary, Queen of Scots* (Edinburgh, 2008)

Green, Mary Anne Everett: *Lives of the Princesses of England, from the Norman Conquest* (6 vols., London, 1857)

Gristwood, Sarah: *Arbella, England's Lost Queen* (London, 2003)

Guy, John: *The Children of Henry VIII* (Oxford, 2013)

Guy, John: Historical Report on a Panel Painting: A full length portrait of a Lady in Black (unpublished report for Sothebys Auction House, 1 May 2010)

Guy, John: *My Heart is My Own: The Life of Mary, Queen of Scots* (London 2004)

Hamilton, The Duke of: *Maria R.: Mary, Queen of Scots: The Crucial Years* (Edinburgh, 1991)

Handbook of British Chronology (ed. F. Maurice Powicke and E. B. Fryde, Royal Historical Society, London, 1961)

Handover, P. M.: *Arbella Stuart: Royal Lady of Hardwick and Cousin to King James* (London, 1957)

Hans Eworth and the London Stranger Painters (www.hanseworth.com)

Harbottle (www.northumberlandnationalpark.org.uk)

Harbottle Castle (www.rothbury.co.uk)

Hardy, Blanche C.: *Arbella Stuart: A Biography* (London, 1913)

Harrier, Richard: 'A Printed Source for "The Devonshire Manuscript"' (*Review of English Studies*, 11, 1960)

Harris, Barbara J.: *English Aristocratic Women, 1450–1550* (Oxford, 2002)

Hayward, Maria: *Dress at the Court of King Henry VIII* (Leeds, 2007)

Head, David M.: '"Beyn Ledde and Seduced by the Devyll": The Attainder of Lord Thomas Howard and the Tudor Law of Treason' (*Sixteenth-Century Journal*, 13, 4, 1982)

Head, David M.: *The Ebbs and Flows of Fortune: The Life of Thomas Howard, Third Duke of Norfolk* (Georgia, 1995)

Heale, Elizabeth: 'Women and the Courtly Love Lyric: The Devonshire MS. (B. L. Additional 17492)' (*Modern Language Review*, 92, 2, 1995)

Hearn, Karen: *Nicholas Hilliard* (London, 2005)

Henderson, Thomas Finlayson: 'Lady Margaret Douglas, Countess of Lennox' (*Dictionary of National Biography*, vol. 5, Oxford, 1895–1901)

The Herald and Genealogist, Vol. 8 (ed. John Gough Nichols, London, 1874)

Hibbert, Christopher: *Tower of London* (London, 1971)

A History of the County of Renfrew from the Earliest Times (www.electricscotland.com)

The History Today Who's Who in British History (ed. Juliet Gardiner, London, 2000)

Holbein and the Court of Henry VIII: The Queen's Gallery, Buckingham Palace (exhibition catalogue, London, 1978)

Howard Family of Anne Arundel, County Maryland (www.netcom.com/howard)

Howard, Maurice: *The Early Tudor Country House: Architecture and Politics, 1490–1550* (London, 1987)

Huggett, Jane: *The Language of Lust: The Sexual Vocabulary of the 16th and 17th Centuries* (Bristol, 1999)

Hume, Martin A. S.: *The Wives of Henry the Eighth* (London, 1905)

Hurren, Elizabeth T.: 'Cultures of the Body, Medical Regimen, and Physic at the Tudor Court' (in *Henry VIII and the Court: Art, Politics and Performance* (Farnham, 2013)

Hutchinson, Robert: *House of Treason: The Rise and Fall of a Tudor Dynasty* (London, 2009)

Hutchinson, Robert: *The Last Days of Henry VIII* (London, 2005)

Irish, Bradley J.: 'Gender and Politics in the Henrician Court: The Douglas-Howard Lyrics in the Devonshire Manuscript (B.L. Add. 17492)' (*Renaissance Quarterly*, 64, 1, Spring 2011)

It's About Time: 1500s Woman Artist – Flemish-born Levina Bening Teerlinc *c.*1510–76 (www.bjws.blogspot.co.uk)

Ives, Eric: *Anne Boleyn* (Oxford, 1986)

Ives, Eric: *The Life and Death of Anne Boleyn* (Oxford, 2004)

Jacques, D.: 'Observations on a picture representing the cenotaph of the Lord Darnley' (in *A Visit to Goodwood*, London, 1822)

James, Susan: *Catherine Parr* (Stroud, 2008)

James, Susan: 'Lady Margaret Douglas and Sir Thomas Seymour by Holbein: two miniatures re-identified' (*Apollo*, 147, May 1998)

Jenkins, Elizabeth: *Elizabeth the Great* (London, 1958)

Jenkins, Elizabeth: *Elizabeth and Leicester* (London, 1961)

Jones, Norman: *The Birth of the Elizabethan Age: England in the 1560s* (Oxford, 1993)

Joynes, Nora Elaine: The History of Carlton in Coverdale, 1086–1910 (D.Phil. thesis, University of Leeds, 2006)

Keay, Anna: *The Elizabethan Tower of London* (London, 2001)

Keith, Robert: *History of the Affairs of Church and State in Scotland, from the beginning of the reformation to the Retreat of Queen Mary into England, anno 1568* (Edinburgh, 1734; 3 vols., ed. J. P. Lawson, Spottiswoode Society, 1844–50)

Kendall, Alan: *Robert Dudley, Earl of Leicester* (London, 1980)

Kilsyth, A Parish History (www.electricscotland.com)

Kitson, Sydney D., and Pawson, Edmund D.: *Temple Newsam* (Leeds, 1929)

Lane, Henry Murray: *The Royal Daughters of England* (2 vols., London, 1910)

Lefuse, M.: *The Life and Times of Arabella Stuart* (London, 1913)

Lemprière, J.: *Universal Biography* (New York, 1810)

Lenz-Harvey, Nancy: *The Rose and the Thorn: The Lives of Mary and Margaret Tudor* (London and New York, 1975)

Lerer, Seth: *Courtly Letters in the Age of Henry VIII: Literary Culture and the Arts of Deceit* (Cambridge, 1997)

Levine, Mortimer: *The Early Elizabethan Succession Question, 1558–1568* (Stanford, 1966)

Lisle, Leanda de: The Lady Jane Grey Reference Guide (www. ladyjanegrey.info)

Lisle, Leanda de: 'King Henry's Niece' (*History Today*, August 2013)

Lisle, Leanda de: *The Sisters Who Would Be Queen: The Tragedy of Mary, Katherine and Lady Jane Grey* (London, 2008)

Lisle, Leanda de: *Tudor: The Family Story* (London, 2013)

Lisle, Leanda de: King Henry's Niece (www.queenanneboleyn.com, 2014)

Lloyd, Christopher, and Remington, Vanessa: *Portrait Miniatures in the Collection of Her Majesty the Queen* (London, 1996)

Loades, David: *Elizabeth I* (London, 2003)

Loades, David: *Mary Tudor* (Oxford, 1989)

Lost Faces (ed. Bendor Grosvenor, Philip Mould Ltd, London, 2007)

Lovell, Mary S.: *Bess of Hardwick, First Lady of Chatsworth* (London, 2005)

Lysons, Samuel and Daniel: *The Environs of London* (4 vols., London, 1792–6)

Macauley, Sarah: Matthew Stewart, Fourth Earl of Lennox, and the Politics of Britain, *c.*1543–1571 (D.Phil. thesis, Christ's College, Cambridge, 2005)

Mackay, James: *In My End Is My Beginning: A Life of Mary. Queen of Scots* (Edinburgh, 1999)

Mackie, J. D.: *The Earlier Tudors, 1485–1558* (Oxford, 1952)

MacNalty, Arthur S.: *Mary, Queen of Scots: The Daughter of Debate* (London, 1960)

Mahon, R. H.: *Mary, Queen of Scots: A Study of the Lennox Narrative* (Cambridge, 1924)

Mann, Ernest A.: 'Brooke House, Hackney' (*Survey of London*, monograph 5, English Heritage, 1904)

Marotti, Arthur F.: *Manuscript, Print, and the English Renaissance Lyric* (Cornell University, 1995)

Marshall, P.: 'The Making of the Tudor Judas: Trust and Betrayal in the English Reformation' (*Reformation*, 13, 2008)

Marshall, Rosalind K.: 'Lady Margaret Douglas' (in *Oxford Dictionary of National Biography*, 2004)

Marshall, Rosalind K.: *Mary of Guise* (Glasgow, 1977)

Marshall, Rosalind K.: *Mary, Queen of Scots: Truth or Lies* (Edinburgh, 2010)

Marshall, Rosalind K.: *Queen Mary's Women* (Edinburgh, 2006)

Marshall, Rosalind K.: *Virgins and Viragos: Women in Scotland* (London, 1983)

Martienssen, Anthony: *Queen Katherine Parr* (London, 1975)

Mary Stewart: Queen in Three Kingdoms (ed. M. Lynch, Oxford, 1988)

Maxwell, Sir Herbert: *A History of the House of Douglas* (2 vols., London, 1902)

McInnes, Ian: *Arabella: The Life and Times of Lady Arabella Seymour, 1575–1615* (London, 1968)

McLaren, Moray: *The Shell Guide to Scotland* (London, 1967)

Merriman, Marcus: 'Matthew Stewart, thirteenth or fourth Earl of Lennox (1516–71), magnate and Regent of Scotland' (in *Oxford Dictionary of National Biography*, 2004)

Merriman, Marcus: *The Rough Wooings: Mary, Queen of Scots, 1542–1551* (East Linton, 2000)

Millar, Oliver: *The Queen's Pictures* (London, 1977)

Millar, Oliver: *The Tudor, Stuart and Early Georgian Pictures in the Collection of Her Majesty the Queen* (2 vols., London, 1963)

Miller, Lee: *Roanoke: Solving the Mystery of a Lost Colony* (London, 2001)

Minney, R. J.: *Hampton Court* (London, 1972)

Minney, R. J.: *The Tower of London* (London, 1970)

Moorhouse, Geoffrey: *The Pilgrimage of Grace* (London, 2002)

Morpeth Castle (www.landmarktrust.co.uk)

'Morpeth in the Middle Ages – And a Royal Visitor Calls' (*Morpeth Herald*, 21 July 2013)

Moss, James E.: *Providence, Ye Lost Town at Severn in Maryland* (Washington, 1976)

Mumby, Frank Arthur: *The Fall of Mary Stuart: A Narrative in Contemporary Letters* (London, 1921)

Murphy, Beverley A.: *Bastard Prince: Henry VIII's Lost Son* (Stroud, 2001)

Murphy, Beverley A.: 'Fitzroy, Mary, Duchess of Richmond (c.1519–1555?)' (Oxford Dictionary of National Biography, 2004)

Musgrave, Ernest I.: Temple Newsam House (Leeds, 1951)

Neale, J. E.: Elizabeth I (London, 1934, reprinted London, 1998)

Newton, William: London in Olden Time (London, 1855)

Nichols, John, and Gough, Richard: The Progresses and Public Processions of Queen Elizabeth (3 vols., London, 1788–1805)

A Noble Visage: Early Portraiture 1545–1660 (The Weiss Gallery, London, 2001)

Norrington, Ruth: In the Shadow of the Throne: The Lady Arbella Stuart (London, 2002)

Norris, Herbert: Tudor Costume and Fashion (London, 1938)

Norton, Elizabeth: The Boleyn Women (Stroud, 2013)

The Oxford Handbook of Witchcraft in Early Modern Europe and Colonial America (ed. Brian P. Levack, Oxford, 2013)

Pailthorpe, Richard; Martyn, Topher; Shrimpton, Colin, and Baxter, Claire: Syon (Derby, 2003)

Panton, Kenneth: London: A Historical Companion (Stroud, 2001)

Pastscape: Jervaulx Abbey, North Yorkshire (www.pastscape.org)

Pepys, Walter Courtenay: The Church of St Dunstan, Stepney (London, 1905)

Perry, Maria: Sisters to the King: The Tumultuous Lives of Henry VIII's Sisters – Margaret of Scotland & Mary of France (London, 1998)

Perry, Maria: The Word of a Prince: A Life of Elizabeth I (Woodbridge, 1990)

Petrina, Alessandra: Machiavelli in the British Isles (Farnham, 2009)

Phillips, G.: The Anglo-Scots Wars, 1513–1550: A Military History (Woodbridge, 1999)

Plowden, Alison: The House of Tudor (London, 1976)

Plowden, Alison: Lady Jane Grey and the House of Suffolk (London, 1985)

Plowden, Alison: Two Queens in One Isle (Brighton, 1984; Stroud, 2010)

Pollitt, Ronald: 'An "Old Practizer" at Bay: Thomas Bishop and the Northern Rebellion' (Northern History, 16, 1980)

Porter, Linda: Crown of Thistles: The Fatal Inheritance of Mary, Queen of Scots (London, 2013)

Porter, Linda: Katherine the Queen: The Remarkable Life of Katherine Parr (London, 2010)

Porter, Linda: Mary Tudor: The First Queen (London, 2007)

Portrait of an Unknown Woman (www.vam.ac.uk)

Portrait of a Woman in Black (www.tudorhistory.org, 2009)

Prebble, John: The Lion in the North: One Thousand Years of Scotland's History (London, 1971)

Read, Conyers: *Mr Secretary Walsingham and the Policy of Queen Elizabeth* (2 vols., Oxford, 1925)

Remley, Paul G.: 'Mary Shelton and Her Tudor Literary Milieu' (in *Rethinking the Henrician Era*, ed. Peter C. Herman, Illinois, 1994)

Renn, Derek: *Norman Castles in Britain* (London, 1968)

Reynolds, Graham: *The Sixteenth and Seventeenth-Century Miniatures in the Collection of Her Majesty the Queen* (London, 1999)

Richards, Judith M.: *Mary Tudor* (Abingdon, 2008)

Ridley, Jasper: *Elizabeth I* (London, 1987)

Ridley, Jasper: *Henry VIII* (London, 1984)

Ridley, Jasper: *The Life and Times of Mary Tudor* (London, 1973)

The Ringing Isle: Lady Margaret Douglas: The Vivacious Tudor Cousin (www.the-ringing-isle.blogspot.co.uk)

Riordan, Michael: 'Lord Thomas Howard' (*Oxford Dictionary of National Biography*, 2004–14)

Rivals in Power: Lives and Letters of the Great Tudor Dynasties (ed. David Starkey, London, 1990)

Robert Howard (www.genealogy.com/howard)

Roberts, Jane: *Holbein and the Court of Henry VIII* (National Galleries of Scotland, Edinburgh, 1993)

Roberts, Marilyn: Trouble in Paradise (www.queens-haven.co.uk)

Robertson, William: *The History of Scotland during the Reigns of Queen Mary and James VI* (2 vols., London, 1759; in *The Works of William Robertson*, 9 vols., London, 1820)

Robinson, William: *History and Antiquities of the Parish of Tottenham* (2 vols., London, 1840)

Ross, Josephine: *The Tudors: England's Golden Age* (London, 1979)

Roulstone, Michael: *The Royal House of Tudor* (St Ives, 1974)

Rowse, A. L.: *Raleigh and the Throckmortons* (London, 1962)

Rowse, A. L.: *The Tower of London in the History of the Nation* (London, 1972)

Royal Collection Trust: Lady Margaret Douglas, Countess of Lennox (1515–78) (www.royalcollection.org.uk)

Royal Treasures (ed. Jane Roberts, The Royal Collection, London, 2002)

Ryrie, Alec: *The Sorcerer's Tale: Faith and Fraud in Tudor England* (Oxford, 2008)

Sandeford, Marie: *Long-Lived Ladies* (Great Glen, 2012)

Scarisbrick, J. J.: *Henry VIII* (London, 1968)

Schutte, Kimberley: *A Biography of Margaret Douglas, Countess of Lennox, 1515–1578: Niece of Henry VIII and Mother-in-Law of Mary, Queen of Scots* (New York, 2002)

Scott Giles, C. W.: *Heraldry in Westminster Abbey* (London, 1954)

Scott, Kenneth: *St James's Palace: A History* (London, 2010)

Scottish Monarchs: Lady Margaret Douglas (www.englishmonarchs.co.uk)

The Scottish Nation: Lennox (www.electricscotland.com)

Seaton, Ethel: 'The Devonshire Manuscript and its Medieval Fragments' (*Review of English Studies*, 7, 1956)

Sessions, William A.: *Henry Howard, The Poet Earl of Surrey: A Life* (Oxford, 1999)

Sitwell, Edith: *The Queens and the Hive* (London, 1963)

Skidmore, Chris: *Death and the Virgin: Elizabeth, Dudley and the Mysterious Fate of Amy Robsart* (London, 2010)

Skipper, Lesley: *The Castle on the Hill: Memories of Whorlton Castle* (Stockton-on-Tees, 2009)

Smith, Lacey Baldwin: *A Tudor Tragedy: The Life and Times of Catherine Howard* (London, 1961)

Somerset, Anne: *Ladies in Waiting* (London, 1984)

Southall, Raymond: 'The Devonshire Manuscript Collection of Early Tudor Poetry, 1532–41' (*Review of English Studies*, 15, 1964)

Stanley, Arthur Penrhyn: *Historical Memorials of Westminster Abbey* (London, 1886)

Starkey, David: *Six Wives: The Queens of Henry VIII* (London, 2003)

Stedall, Robert: *The Challenge to the Crown* (Brighton, 2012)

Stedall, Robert: *The Survival of the Crown* (Brighton, 2014)

Steel, David and Judy: *Mary Stuart's Scotland: The Landscapes, Life and Legends of Mary, Queen of Scots* (London, 1987)

Strickland, Agnes: *Lives of the Queens of England* (12 vols., London, 1840–8; digital version, Cambridge, New York, 2010)

Strickland, Agnes: *Lives of the Queens of Scotland and English Princesses Connected with the Regal Succession of Great Britain* (London, 1851; 3 vols., Memphis, 2012)

Strickland, Agnes: *Lives of the Tudor Princesses, including Lady Jane Grey and her Sisters* (London, 1868)

Strong, Roy: *Artists of the Tudor Court: The Portrait Miniature Rediscovered, 1520–1620* (London, 1983)

Strong, Roy: *The English Icon: Elizabethan and Jacobean Portraiture* (London, 1969)

Strong, Roy: *The English Renaissance Miniature* (London, 1983)

Strong, Roy: *Hans Eworth: A Tudor Artist and his Circle* (London, 1965)

Strong, Roy: *Tudor and Jacobean Portraits* (2 vols., London, 1969)

Survey of London, Vol. 23 (ed. Howard Roberts and Walter H. Godfrey, London, 1951)

Sutherland, N. M.: *Princes, Politics and Religion, 1547–89* (London, 1984)

Tait, H.: 'Historiated Tudor Jewellery' (*The Antiquities Journal*, 42, 1962)

Temple Newsam (Leeds Museums and Galleries, undated)

Thomson, George Malcolm: *The Crime of Mary Stuart* (London, 1967)

Thoresby, Ralph: *Ducatus Leodiensis, or the Topography of the antient and populous Town and Parish of Leedes and parts adjacent in the West Riding of the County of York* (London, 1715; 2 vols., ed. Thomas Dunham Whitaker, Leeds, 1816)

Thornbury, Walter: *Old and New London* (6 vols., London, 1878)

Thurley, Simon: *Hampton Court: A Social and Architectural History* (New Haven and London, 2003)

Treasures: The Royal Collection (ed. Jane Roberts, London, 2008)

Trowles, Tony: *Treasures of Westminster Abbey* (London, 2008)

Tudor Hackney (www.thenationalarchives.gov.uk)

Tytler, Fraser: *Historical Notes on the Lennox or Darnley Jewel, the Property of the Queen* (London, 1843)

Varlow, Sally: *The Lady Penelope* (London, 2007)

Victoria County Histories (www.britishhistory.ac.uk)

The Visitation of Norfolk (ed. Walter Rye, Harleian Society Publications 32, London, 1891)

Waldman, Milton: *The Lady Mary* (London, 1972)

Warnicke, Retha: *The Rise and Fall of Anne Boleyn* (Cambridge, 1989)

Warnicke, Retha: *Wicked Women of Tudor England: Queens, Aristocrats, Commoners* (New York, 2012)

Weir, Alison: *Children of England: The Heirs of King Henry VIII* (London, 1996)

Weir, Alison: *Elizabeth the Queen* (London, 1998)

Weir, Alison: *Elizabeth of York, the First Tudor Queen* (London, 2013)

Weir, Alison: *Henry VIII, King and Court* (London, 2001)

Weir, Alison: *Mary, Queen of Scots, and the Murder of Lord Darnley* (London, 2003)

Weir, Alison: *The Six Wives of Henry VIII* (London, 1991)

Westhorpe (www.pevsnersuffolk.co.uk)

The Westminster Abbey Guide (London, 1953)

Westminster Abbey: Official Guide (Norwich, 1966)

West Scrafton Manor House (www.geograph.org.uk)

Whitelock, Anna: *Elizabeth's Bedfellows: An Intimate History of the Queen's Court* (London, 2013)

Wilkinson, James: *Henry VII's Lady Chapel in Westminster Abbey* (London, 2007)

Willey, Russ: *Chambers' London Gazetteeer* (Edinburgh, 2007)

Williams, Neville: *All The Queen's Men* (London, 1972)

Williams, Neville: *Elizabeth I, Queen of England* (London, 1967)

Williams, Neville: *Henry VIII and His Court* (London, 1971)

Williams, Neville: *The Life and Times of Elizabeth I* (London, 1972)

Williams, Neville: *A Tudor Tragedy: Thomas Howard, Fourth Duke of Norfolk* (London, 1964)

Wilson, Derek: *At the Lion's Court: Ambition, Power and Sudden Death at the Court of Henry VIII* (London, 2001)

Wilson, Derek: *The Uncrowned Kings of England: The Black Legend of the Dudleys* (London, 2005)

Wodderspoon, John: *Historic Sites and Other Remarkable and Interesting Places in the County of Suffolk* (Ipswich, 1839)

Women and Power in the Middle Ages (ed. Mary Erler and Maryanne Kowaleski, Georgia, 1988)

Younghusband, George: *The Tower of London from Within* (London, 1918)

Notes and References

Abbreviations

APC	*Acts of the Privy Council of England, 1542–1631*
Cecil Papers	*Calendar of the Cecil Papers in Hatfield House*
CP	*The Complete Peerage*
CSP Haynes	*A Collection of State Papers, relating to affairs in the reigns of King Henry VIII, King Edward VI, Queen Mary and Queen Elizabeth, from the year 1542 to 1570. Transcribed from original letters and other authentick memorials*
CSP Milan	*Calendar of State Papers and Manuscripts existing in the Archives and Collections of Milan, 1385–1618*
CSP Murdin	*A Collection of State Papers relating to affairs in the Reign of Queen Elizabeth*
CSP Scotland	*Calendar of the State Papers relating to Scotland and Mary, Queen of Scots, 1547–1603*
CSP Simancas	*Calendar of Letters and State Papers relating to English Affairs, preserved principally in the Archives of Simancas*
CSP Spain	*Calendar of Letters, Despatches and State Papers relating to Negotiations between England and Spain, preserved in the Archives at Simancas and Elsewhere*
CSP Vatican	*Calendar of State Papers and Manuscripts relating to English Affairs in the Vatican Archives*
CSP Venice	*Calendar of State Papers and Manuscripts relating to English Affairs preserved in the Archives of Venice and in the other Libraries of Northern Italy*

CSPD	*Calendar of State Papers Domestic*
CSPF	*Calendar of State Papers Foreign*
CUL	Cambridge University Library
GWA	*The Great Wardrobe Accounts of Henry VII and Henry VIII*
LP	*Letters and Papers, Foreign and Domestic, of the Reign of Henry VIII*
LQS	*Lives of the Queens of Scotland*
LRIL	*Letters of Royal and Illustrious Ladies of Great Britain*
NA	National Archives
NAS	National Archives of Scotland
ODNB	*Oxford Dictionary of National Biography*
PPE Henry VIII	*Privy Purse Expenses of Henry VIII, 1529–1532*
PPE Mary	*Privy Purse Expenses of the Princess Mary, daughter of King Henry the Eighth, afterwards Queen Mary, with a memoir of the Princess, and notes*
SP	*State Papers of the Reign of Henry VIII*
VCH	*Victoria County Histories*

Where more than one book by an author is listed in the bibliography, the work is indicated by initial letters after the author's name.

Introduction

1 John Phillips

Prologue

1 Leland ARBC 4, 258–62
2 Vergil, online edition, XXVII
3 LP 2, Preface, Section 4
4 LP 2, 1113
5 LP 2, Preface, Section 4
6 Ibid.
7 LP 2, 1350
8 CSP Venice 2, 667
9 Harbottle; Harbottle Castle; Goodall; Renn. Harbottle Castle was crumbling and uninhabitable by 1541, and only a few ruins remain today.
10 Chapman SHVIII, 99
11 LP 2, Preface, Section 4, 1672, 1380, 1294

1 'A Fair Young Lady'

1   William Fraser 4, 171
2   Lindsay, 120
3   Prebble, 140
4   LRIL 1, 107
5   LRIL 1, 150
6   LP 2, Preface, Section 4; LP 2, 846, 885
7   LRIL 1, 151; LP 2, 885
8   LP 2, Preface, Section 4; LP 2, 833; LP 2, 872
9   LP 2, Preface, Section 4
10 LRIL 1, 146; LP 2, Preface, Section 4
11 LRIL 1, 151
12 LP 2, Preface, Section 4
13 LRIL 1, 151
14 Cotton MS. Caligula B.VI, f.81; LP 2, 885
15 Cotton MS. Caligula B.VI, f.14
16 LP 2, Preface, Section 4; LP 2, 885
17 LP 2, Preface, Section 4; LP 2, 885
18 *Original Letters* 1, 265–7; LP 2, 1044
19 LP 2, 1044
20 John Phillips
21 Henderson; LRIL 2, 283–4
22 *Original Letters* 1, 265–7
23 Levine, 105
24 LP 2, 1011
25 LP 2, 1011, 1027
26 LP 2, Preface, Section 4
27 *Original Letters* 1, 265–7
28 LP 2, Preface, Section 4
29 Ibid.
30 Morpeth Castle. Morpeth Castle was ruinous by 1600, and today
    only its gatehouse and part of the curtain wall survive.
31 LRIL 1, 151; LP 2, Preface, Section 4; LP 2, 885
32 LP 2, 1672
33 Cotton MS. Caligula B.VI, f.59
34 LP 2, 1672
35 Vergil, online edition, XXVII
36 Ibid.
37 Ibid.
38 LP 2, Preface, Section 4
39 LP 2, 1350
40 LP 2, 1387

41 LP 2, 1380; CSP Venice 2, 671

42 LP 2, Preface, Section 4

43 LP 2, 1672

44 Cotton MS. Caligula B.VI, f.272

45 Cotton MS. Julius A.XVI, f.266

46 Hall

47 Green 4, 238

48 Cotton MS. Caligula B.III, f.32

49 Demolished between 1608 and 1660, it stood in the grounds of the present Jacobean Forty Hall; the royal apartments were excavated in the 1960s.

50 The remains of his house are the earliest surviving parts of Bruce Castle, which was named after the family of Robert the Bruce, King of Scots, who owned the land in the Middle Ages; it was also known as Lordship House.

51 Thomas Allen to the Earl of Shrewsbury, 6 May 1516, Talbot MS. A, f.31, College of Arms; *A Calendar of the Shrewsbury and Talbot Papers in Lambeth Palace Library and the College of Arms*

52 Newton; Stow; Panton; Davey: *The Pageant of London*; Thornbury. Margaret Tudor was the last royal personage to live in Scotland Yard. After she left, Henry VIII allowed it to fall into decay and it was turned into tenements in Elizabethan times. Ruinous by the seventeenth century, most of it was demolished after the Act of Union of 1707, to make way for Whitehall offices. In the early nineteenth century only a few arches and turrets survived, but they have long vanished. After 1829 the site became famous as the headquarters of London's Metropolitan Police, which was moved further along the Thames embankment in 1890, and to Broadway, off Victoria Street, in 1967.

53 Weir EY, 284

54 LP 3, 524

55 LRIL 1, 154; LP 2, Preface, Section 4

56 LP 2, 3136

57 Cotton MS. Titus D.X, f.92b

58 LP 2, Preface, Section 4

59 LP 4, 4969

2   'Disdained with Dishonour'

1 CSP Scotland 3, 508

2 A condensed version, his *Epitaph*, appeared in print at the same time.

3 LP 3, 1, 166, 373

4 Perry SK, 171

5   Cotton MS. Caligula B.I, f.157
6   Cotton MS. Caligula B.III, f.110b
7   James CP, 136; Marshall MQSTL, 39; Bingham, 16; Schutte, 16
8   LP 4, 792
9   LP 4, 1004
10 LP 4, 835
11 LRIL 1, 234
12 SP 4, 272
13 Chapman SHVIII, 136
14 LRIL 1, 249
15 Herbert, 133
16 Lindsay, 133
17 William Fraser 1, xx
18 LP 4, 4130
19 Perry SK, 171
20 Strickland LQS 2, 66
21 *Cecil Papers* 1, 848
22 Strickland LQS 2, 78
23 Cotton MS. Caligula B.VI, f.194; LP 4, 4131
24 Strickland LQS 2, 66; Schutte, 17
25 Lisle TFS, 177; Lisle KHN
26 The actual spelling is 'disherest'. It is unlikely to mean diseased, as
    in LRIL 1, 252, listed incorrectly under 1525.
27 Strickland LQS 2, 66; Marshall MQSTL, 39; Schutte, 12
28 Cotton MS. Caligula B.II, f.368
29 Reduced by Oliver Cromwell's troops in 1651 and abandoned by
    the end of the seventeenth century, Tantallon is now an impressive
    ruin, its remaining three towers still nearly eight feet high; the
    Douglas Tower survives, but its west side has collapsed.
30 Strickland LQS 2, 66; Schutte, 12; Lefuse, 6. Dalkeith Palace, as it
    later became known, was largely rebuilt in 1702.
31 Strickland LQS 2, 67
32 Lefuse, 7
33 LP 20, Part 1, 210 (2)
34 Strickland LQS 2, 67
35 McLaren
36 LP 2, 779. Isobel's surname is sometimes given as 'Hopper'.
37 LP 4, 539–40, 567
38 Abell
39 LP 4, 4709
40 *Register of the Privy Seal of Scotland* 1, 4060, 4077, 4082
41 LP 4, 4830
42 Strickland LQS 2, 67

43 His son, James, would become the 4th Earl of Bothwell and marry Mary, Queen of Scots.

44 Ashdown RT, 11

45 *Cecil Papers* 1, 848, 1562

46 SP 5, 4; LP 4, 4830. The timescale suggests that Margaret had gone to Coldingham with Angus and been left there. There is no evidence to support a tale that she had insisted on accompanying her father on the forays he made through the Borders at this time.

47 Strickland LQS, 67

48 LP 2, 861

49 Strickland LQS 2, 68

50 Lisle TFS, 178

51 LP 4, 4923–5

52 Porter CT, 240

53 The castle fortifications and ramparts were later massively extended under Elizabeth I, but the ruins of the original castle where Margaret stayed still survive.

54 LRIL 2, 283–4; LP 4, 5794

55 LP 4, 6586

56 In August 1531 Strangeways was obliged to send a reminder to Thomas Cromwell, the man who had replaced the Cardinal in the King's counsels, reminding him of the '£700 which should have been paid me by my Lord Cardinal, whose soul Jesu pardon'. But if the King should be pleased to pay for the completion of the Hospital of Jesus Christ at Bradford, Northumberland, 'I shall also consider myself to be well paid for my costs in bringing up to London and long keeping of my Lady Margaret, daughter to the Queen of Scots.' (LP 5, 365)

57 Strickland, LQS 2, 69, states that she came by invitation of her aunt, Henry VIII's sister, Mary Tudor, Queen Dowager of France, but there is no evidence for that.

58 LP 5, 365

59 GWA, 197; NA E.101/420, f.14

3 'The Princess of Scotland'

1 George Buchanan, cited by Strickland LQS 2, 81

2 Fraser SW, 204; Murphy BP, 167–8

3 For a discussion of Margaret's portraiture, see Appendix 1.

4 See Appendix 1.

5 John Phillips

6 Ibid.; Strickland LQS 2, 69, 70; Hardy, 6; Claremont, 158; Martienssen, 16; Norrington, 16; Bingham, 18. Ashdown RT, 13, on the incorrect assumption that Margaret journeyed to London late

in 1529, states that she stayed with Mary Tudor until Christmas. It has also been asserted that Margaret was placed in the household of her godfather, Cardinal Wolsey, but in the months before his death Wolsey had been in no position to make provision for her, for he was living in disgrace at Esher when she arrived in London, and then retired to his archdiocese of York, dying in November 1530 on his way south to the Tower and, probably, the block; there can have been no question of his taking a practical fatherly interest in his royal godchild. Even had he still been in favour, a cardinal's household could not have accommodated a young girl.

7 Martienssen, 51. He goes on to say (p.69) that Margaret remained there until after Mary Tudor's death in June 1533, when Anne Boleyn had 'little difficulty in persuading Margaret to rejoin her at court', but sound evidence places Margaret in the Princess Mary's household from 1530 to 1533.

8 Wodderspoon; Westhorpe; Baldwin, 13. All that remains of Westhorpe is a three-arched Tudor bridge that once spanned the moat. The present Westhorpe Hall is a care home.

9 John Phillips

10 Ibid.

11 PPE Mary, various entries; Arundel MS. 97, ff.77, 40b

12 Loades MT, 71; Porter MT, 77; LP 6, 1199. Porter states that Mary Tudor, Duchess of Suffolk, used her influence to promote Margaret's appointment.

13 GWA, 197

14 PPE Henry VIII, 98

15 LP 6, 1199

16 GWA, 197

17 A decorative trimming for a hood.

18 LP 5, 498; NA E.101/421, f.3

19 LP 21, Part 1, 1410; GWA, 243

20 Clarke; Porter MT, 77

21 John Phillips

22 LP 5, 686. Her gift is not described; there is a blank after her name, whereas the other ladies' gifts are described after theirs.

23 LP 5, 1710

24 PPE Henry VIII, 281

25 I can find no evidence to support the claim made by Schutte, 30, that Margaret was probably among the ladies who accompanied Anne Boleyn to Calais in October 1532. At that time Margaret was still in the Princess Mary's household.

26 Schutte, 33, asserts that Margaret 'had an important role to play in the coronation', and that she was probably one of the four ladies of great estate who, dressed in crimson velvet, were in the second chariot in

the Queen's procession, but the chronicler Edward Hall identifies them
as four ladies of the bedchamber, a post that Margaret did not occupy.

27 Fraser SW, 204

28 LP 6, 1199

29 Ibid.

30 Strickland LQS 2, 70; Hardy, 6; Clarke; Fraser SW, 204; Weir
HVIIIKC, 350; Wilson ALC, 392; Ashdown RT, 34; Richards, 57;
Norrington, 16; Buchanan 255; Bingham, 19; Denny AB, 208
(although on the next page she states that Margaret served Anne
Boleyn)

31 Porter MT, 95

32 LP 7, 9

33 John Phillips

34 LP 7, 9

35 LP 7, appendix 13

36 PPE Mary, 86; LP 11, 1473; Strickland LQS 2, 69

37 Warnicke AB, 134

38 John Phillips

39 She was the daughter of Charles Brandon, Duke of Suffolk, by his
second wife, Anne Browne, stepdaughter of his third wife, Mary
Tudor, and therefore only the King's step-niece.

40 Paris Bibliothèque Nationale MS. Français 5499, ff.191–6; LP 7,
appendix 13; Brenan and Statham, 191

41 Marshall ODNB; Schutte, 13, states that Margaret showed an
interest in the work of humanist scholars attached to the court, but
cites no source and gives no further details. Her poems reveal
humanist influence.

42 Warnicke AB, 139; *Women and Power*, 192. Honor Grenville was the
wife of the King's cousin, Arthur Plantagenet, Viscount Lisle, a
bastard son of King Edward IV.

43 LP 8, 1028

44 Meerson

45 LP 6, 613

46 Additional MS. 17,492. For the Devonshire Manuscript see Baron
(both titles); Irish; Bond; Ives AB, 87–8; Ives LDAB, 72; Southall;
Brigden HH; Heale; Marotti; Remley; Seaton; Harrier; Lerer; *Early
Modern Women Poets.*

47 Latymer, 62

48 Murphy BP, 221

49 The hands of Margaret and the two Marys were first identified by
Helen Baron in 1994. Baron MHFH; Heale, 3; Irish, who compared
this writing with a holograph letter of Margaret's in Cotton
Vespasian MS. 188, f.13.

50 Heale, 10, 25

51 Heale, 19

52 Heale, 1, 9; Baron MHFH, 327. The transcriptions of the poems in
    this chapter come mainly from Heale. A poem by Margaret's son,
    Henry, Lord Darnley, who was not born until 1546, was the last to
    be added, in the early 1560s, which shows that the manuscript was
    still in Margaret's possession many years later. The initials 'S. E.'
    stamped on the binding may suggest that Margaret later gave the
    manuscript to her younger son, Charles Stuart, Earl of Lennox, and
    daughter-in-law, Elizabeth Cavendish, as a wedding gift, the initials
    standing for 'Stuart' and 'Elizabeth' (Southall), and it is likely that it
    was inherited by Margaret's granddaughter, Arbella Stuart. This
    would explain how it came to be in the Devonshire Library at
    Chatsworth, where it was first recorded in 1816 and remained until
    being acquired by the British Museum in 1848.

53 John Phillips

54 Bond

54 Heale

4   'Suffering in Sorrow'

1 Heale, 23

2 Riordan

3 Hutchinson HT, 276, n.3

4 Hall, 806

5 LP 11, 48

6 Abernethy

7 Poems by Margaret that do not have an apparent link to events in
   her life are printed in Appendix 2.

8 Strickland LQS 2, 70; Sessions, 117; Lisle TFS, 201; Riordan;
   Bingham, 19, states that Henry even permitted the pair to be
   betrothed.

9 Sessions, 117

10 LP 11, 293

11 LP 11, 48. Norton, 206, suggests that this Lady Boleyn was
    Elizabeth Wood, the wife of Sir James Boleyn, Anne Boleyn's uncle.

12 LP 11, 48

13 LP 10, 913; Loke

14 Lisle TFS, 209

15 *Statutes of the Realm* 3, 28 Hen. VIII, c.24. Lisle TFS, 200, says they
    were betrothed on Easter Sunday, which fell on 16 April, two days
    after the King had blessed the cramp ring, but LP 11, 48, makes it
    clear that a betrothal was first discussed, not entered into, at Easter,

and the Act of Attainder passed against Thomas Howard (*Statutes of the Realm* 3, 28 Hen. VIII, c.24) reveals that the couple became precontracted after 7 June.

16 Herbert, 585
17 *Statutes of the Realm* 3, 28 Hen. VIII, c.24
18 CSP Spain 5, 2, 77; LP 11, 147
19 LP 11, 48. Irish mistakenly assumes that they were witnesses. Lord William Howard's daughter Douglass, born in 1542/3, would be named in Margaret's honour.
20 John Phillips
21 LP 11, 147
22 Clarke
23 Hamilton, 245
24 Lefuse, 6
25 Wilson UKE, 285
26 Starkey, 736
27 Wriothesley, 48
28 LP 12, Part 2, 973
29 *Statutes of the Realm* 3, 28 Hen. VIII, c.7
30 *Statutes of the Realm* 3, 28 Hen. VIII, c.24; Hutchinson HT, 78
31 Head EFF, 132
32 Murphy BP, 168; Ashdown RT, 41
33 Denny KH, 93
34 Herbert, 585–6
35 Clarke
36 Herbert, 586
37 *Statutes of the Realm* 3, 28 Hen. VIII, c.24
38 Ibid.
39 It has been stated that Lord William Howard was sent to Scotland by Henry to seek evidence of Margaret's illegitimacy (Strickland LQS 2, 76; Ashdown RT, 42–3; Bingham, 24; Buchanan, 257). He had actually been sent there in 1534–5 with William Barlow, later Bishop of Chichester, to persuade Margaret Tudor to renounce Methven and return to Angus (CSPF 6, 483). Lord William remained in Scotland until May 1536, and did not return there for many years. Much later, asked if he had learned anything in Scotland that had a bearing on Margaret's legitimacy, he stated 'that, from all he could gather there, the marriage between the Lady Margaret's father and his Majesty's sister, Queen Margaret, was not a lawful one'. (Strickland LQS 2, 76)
40 *Statutes of the Realm* 3, 28 Hen. VIII, c.7
41 Wriothesley 1, 54

42 LP 11, 48. Lisle TFS, 210, citing Baron, states that Thomas confessed to calling Margaret 'his sweet wife', and also says that Margaret described the gifts that Thomas had given her.

43 LP 10, 740; Ashdown RT, 41

44 *Statutes of the Realm* 3, 28 Hen. VIII, c.24

45 LP 11, 48. Schutte, 52, identifies Thomas Smyth with the keeper of the stables to the Lady Mary and a page of the King's household.

46 Herbert, 586

47 LP 11, 147; CSP Spain 5, Part 2, 77 (10)

48 CSP Milan, 971

49 John Phillips

50 Younghusband

51 LP 14, Part 2, 287

52 He is perhaps to be identified with John Astley, the older half-brother of the courtier Sir John Astley (d.1596) who married Katherine Champernowne, later governess to Anne's daughter Elizabeth. The Astleys were connections of Anne Boleyn; the elder John came to court at the age of twelve and was later in the household of Prince Edward.

53 Noted in margin '8 July'.

54 LP 11, 48

55 Castelli

56 Childs, 111

57 *Statutes of the Realm* 3, 28 Hen. VIII, c.24; Hutchinson HT, 78

58 LP 11, 147; CSP Spain 5, Part 2, 77 (10)

59 CSP Milan, 971

60 LP 11, 376

61 John Phillips

62 LP 11, 147; CSP Spain 5, Part 2, 77 (10)

63 LP 11, 294

64 John Phillips

65 LP 11, 147; CSP Spain 5, Part 2, 77 (10)

66 For which they had been obliged to petition Cromwell (LP 11, 1473)

67 LP 11, 294

68 Herbert, 586

69 Ibid.

70 LP 11, 293. This letter is listed in LP under 1537, but it cannot have taken over a year for news of her daughter's disgrace and imprisonment to reach Margaret Tudor in Perth, so it must belong to 1536.

71 LP 11, 815

72 LP 11, 1373

73 LP 11, 1396

5   *'Now May I Mourn'*

1   Remley

2   The handwriting has been given the identification TH2. There is
     no way of checking whether or not it was Thomas Howard's
     because no example of his handwriting is extant (Bond; Heale, 13;
     Seaton; Harrier; Lerer, 143–60). There is another sequence of poems
     in the manuscript – numbers 67 to 70 – that has been attributed
     to Thomas Howard, but is written in a different hand, called TH1.
     There are similarities in that handwriting to TH2, and in both to
     the hand that has written on the flyleaf 'Marayg' and 'Th.h' (the
     page is torn here), which may denote joint ownership by the
     couple (Heale, 14).

3   Remley; *Visitation*, 247; Norton, 215. Remley also states that in the
     mid-1530s Sir John Shelton, the father of Margaret's friend, Mary
     Shelton, was in command of some of the palace guards, but from
     July 1536 Shelton was governor of the combined household of the
     Lady Mary and the Lady Elizabeth, and in command of their
     guards, who were not stationed at the Tower.

4   Batman

5   In Greek mythology Argus was a giant with a hundred eyes. After
     he was killed in her service, Hera, the wife of the god Zeus, caused
     his eyes to be placed in the tail of the peacock.

6   These are perilous quicksands off the Kent coast.

7   Several poems in the manuscript by TH2 reveal a detailed
     knowledge of Chaucer's works as published by William Thynne in
     1532 (Bond; Heale, 13; Seaton; Harrier; Lerer, 143–60).

8   Remley

9   The first three verses also appear in the manuscript as poem 99,
     also in Margaret's hand.

10   There is a story that Margaret bore Thomas a child, Robert, during
     their captivity. This Robert Howard is said to have been delivered
     in secret on 1 January 1537 at Syon Abbey, Middlesex, and was
     supposedly taken away to be brought up by relations. The birth of
     a son to Margaret and Thomas Howard, a traitor convicted of
     aiming at the throne, at a time when Henry VIII was hoping for
     an heir of his body from Jane Seymour, would surely have alarmed
     the King. Their child might well have rivalled his own offspring for
     the crown; his parents having being precontracted before witnesses,
     Robert would have been accounted legitimate (although Henry
     VIII had the prerogative to declare the union illegal), and some
     might have thought he had a better claim to the throne than
     Margaret's later issue, and – because he was born in England – than

her grandson, James I, although he would never have become king as he died around 1598.

Robert Howard certainly existed, but the theory that Margaret and Thomas were his parents was put forward only in the 1970s by James Moss, an American novelist, and it has been much debated since. But there are serious drawbacks to it. Apart from Chapuys' evidence that the couple had not had sex, Margaret was in the Tower in January 1537, and was not sent to Syon until November; and in her letter to Cromwell, sent in August 1536, she describes herself as 'being a maid' (LP 11, 294). The pedigree in the College of Arms that Moss cited actually stated that Robert Howard was born around 1530 at Brockdish, Norfolk. Moss's theory rests entirely on his claim that a coat of arms granted to Howard's descendants in 1714 included a mullet (or star), a Douglas emblem, suggesting to him that information about Robert Howard's true birth had been handed down secretly in the family.

Actually the ancient Douglas arms bear three mullets and a crowned heart on an azure field, so if the theory is true, the 1714 arms should have borne three mullets, not one between cinquefoils, and the arms of both ancestral families shown impaled; moreover, a mullet is often a symbol showing cadence, or steps of descent. Finally, the grant of arms itself would have recognised the family as a cadet branch of the Howard family. Thus there is no evidence to connect Robert Howard of Brockdish with Margaret Douglas and Thomas Howard (Howard Family of Anne Arundel; Robert Howard).

11 LP 12, Part 1, Preface
12 LP 12, Part 1, 532
13 LP 12, Part 1, 533
14 Martienssen, 101
15 Moorhouse, 206
16 Chapman SHVIII, 150
17 LP 12, Part 1, 1198
18 The speed with which Margaret was released after Prince Edward's birth argues that the King had already planned to set her free.
19 John Phillips
20 Gristwood, 17
21 Wriothesley, 70
22 John Phillips
23 Cotton MS. Vespasian f.13
24 LP 12, Part 2, 1023
25 Ashdown RT, 44

26 The King's Book of Payments, f.6, cited in LRIL 2, 194–5; PPE Mary, 228

27 Hutchinson HT, 78

28 LRIL 2, 194

29 The King's Book of Payments, f.6, cited in LRIL 2, 195; PPE Mary, 228; Strickland LQS 2, 73

30 LP 12, Part 2, 1023

31 Wriothesley, 70

32 Hutchinson HT, 100

33 Tottel, 219

34 LRIL 2, 195; LP 12, Part 2, 1013

35 Wriothesley, 70

36 When the priory was dissolved in 1540 some of the Howard tombs, and Richmond's, were removed to a new chancel in the church of St Michael and All Angels at Framlingham (VCH Norfolk 2, 19) or to the Howard chapel in St Mary's Church, Lambeth. Other remains, including those of Thomas's father, the 2nd Duke of Norfolk, were apparently left undisturbed among the ruins. (Ashdown-Hill) What happened to Thomas Howard's remains is not known.

37 Wriothesley, 70

38 John Phillips

39 LRIL 2, 196; LP 11, 994, listed incorrectly under 1536.

40 LP 14, Part 2, 781, from a list of the King's Payments in Arundel MS. 97, f.82: payments from 1 January 28 Hen. VIII (1536–7), i.e. from 1 January 1537. This, and Wriothesley's chronicle, cited in the text, prove that Margaret was taken to Syon in November 1537, not 1536, as suggested by the incorrect listing of LP 11, 994 under 1536 and by Lisle THS, 212; Schutte, 56, and Irish. Margaret could not therefore have attended Jane Seymour's funeral, as Schutte, 61, and Bingham, 25, state; they also say that she was named among the mourners as 'Lady Margaret Howard, the King's niece', but the reference is to Margaret Gamage, the wife of Lord William Howard; Margaret is not mentioned in the official account of the funeral in LP 12, Part 2, 1060.

41 Willey

42 Strickland LQS 2, 74

43 Pailthorpe *et al.* Only the brick undercroft beneath the great hall remains of the fifteenth-century convent in which Margaret stayed. It was largely demolished when Edward Seymour, Duke of Somerset, built Syon House around 1550, partly on the site of the abbey church; his house was remodelled by Robert Adam in the eighteenth century (Howard).

According to Strickland, LQS 2, 74, and Bingham, 25, the Abbess was dismayed at the large train of servants that Margaret brought with her, as well as the number of visitors she was allowed to receive, and voiced her complaints in a letter to Cromwell, which prompted him to send a rebuke to Margaret. Both these writers assumed that Margaret's letter of August 1536, reproduced in the text, was sent from Syon in response to this. However, Margaret was not at Syon in August 1536 or August 1537, nor did she go there until November 1537, and there is no record of the Abbess making any complaint to Cromwell.

44 NA SP 1/241, f.262
45 LP 13, Part 1, 877
46 Ashdown RT, 46
47 LP 13, Part 2, 1280
48 PPE Mary, 72; Strickland LQS 2, 76
49 GWA, 206
50 Heale

6 'Beware the Third Time'

1 LP 13, Part 1, 1419
2 LP 13, Part 2, 622
3 Brigden TW, 403; P. Marshall
4 LP 13, Part 2, 622
5 Scarisbrick, 361n.
6 I can find no evidence to support Schutte's statement (p.62, citing no source) that in 1538 Margaret was 'at the centre of intense speculation' because the government was seeking to prove her illegitimate.
7 Brigden HH, 521
8 LP 14, Part 2, 572
9 LP 15, 21
10 LP 14, part 2, 572; *Chronicle of Calais*, 170
11 PPE Mary, 86
12 LP 15, 138. In LP the reference is to the 'Prince's lodging', but it should almost certainly read 'Princess's lodging', meaning Mary's, as Prince Edward's was off Chapel Court. Strickland, LQS 2, 77, states that Margaret's lodging was at the foot of the spiral stairs that led up behind the chapel to the Queen's gallery, but that is nowhere near the Inner Court.
13 The Second Court was the Green Court (the present Fountain Court) to the east, and the Outer Court was the present Base Court.

14 The lodgings of Sir Anthony Denny and Sir Thomas Heneage, the
    two chief gentlemen of the Privy Chamber, can still be identified
    in the south range of Clock Court, opposite the Great Hall;
    Cromwell's were probably in that range too. These apartments all
    survive today (Thurley, 76–7).

15 Thurley, 21

16 Wriothesley, 110; Hall

17 Strickland LQE 3, 49

18 PPE Mary, 88

19 *Letters of the Queens of England*, 207; Weir HVIIIKC, 440

20 LP 15, 996

21 LP 16, 380

22 LP 16, 1389

23 LP 17, 267

24 Margaret Pole did not, as is so often asserted, refuse to lay her head
    on the block, crying, 'So should traitors do, but I am none!' Nor
    did the hangman chase her around the scaffold with the axe. These
    are later stories reported by Herbert. Chapuys described her
    execution thus: 'She was told to make haste and place her neck on
    the block, which she did. But as the ordinary executor of justice
    was absent doing his work in the north, a wretched and blundering
    youth was chosen, who literally hacked her head and shoulders to
    pieces in the most pitiful manner' (CSP Spain 6, Part 1, 166).

25 Brenan and Statham, 295

26 Perry SK, 221. Ashdown, RT, 49, says she declared that her
    marriage to Angus had been valid, and Margaret was therefore truly
    legitimate.

27 LP 16, 1307. A Scottish mark was the equivalent of an English
    shilling, so Queen Margaret left about £37,680 in today's values.

28 Buchanan, 270

29 LP 16, 1328

30 LP 16, 678, no. 38; Head EFF, 183; Schutte, 72

31 Warnicke, 73

32 It is unlikely that it relates to Thomas Howard's arrest, as has been
    suggested, because it is lacking in emotion and betrays uncertainty
    as to her lover speaking in her favour.

33 LP 16, 1332

34 Ashdown, RT, 48, states incorrectly that he was imprisoned, but then
    freed, and then went to fight the Turks, returning after a year, late in
    1542, to find Margaret interested in another man. But there is no
    record of her having another suitor before the summer of 1543.

35 Schutte, 73; Brenan and Statham, 305–7

36 Heale, 155, states that 'thing' then meant either 'object' or 'genitals', and according to Huggett, 3, it is a contemporary term for a penis, but given that Margaret did not give herself to Thomas Howard but kept herself chaste until they could be properly married, and that neither she nor Charles Howard was punished severely for their involvement, I do not think that meaning is intended here. In this context, 'thing' probably means love.

37 LP 16, 1331

38 LP 16, 1332

39 Deriving from Strickland LQS 2, 77

40 Although Charles, not being the son of a peer, was not entitled to this courtesy title, he and his siblings were styled 'Lord' and 'Lady' after his sister's marriage to the King.

41 LRIL; LP 16, 1333

42 Underneath the poem another hand has added: 'Hap have bidden/ My hap a-wanting/*Madame/Madame d/Madame Margaret/et Madame de Richemont/Je voudrais bien qu'il fut*' (I really would that it was).

43 LP 16, 1342

44 Meerson

45 Howard

46 Most of Kenninghall was demolished between 1650 and 1751, but the two-storey brick service range survives as a private house.

47 *Survey of London*, 137–40; Roberts TP

48 LP Addenda 1, 2, 1573

49 Hayward, 202–3

50 LP 17, 896

51 LP 18, Part 2, 190

52 Strickland LQS 2, 78; Ashdown RT, 50

53 PPE Mary, 96

54 Brother of the future Queen Katherine Parr.

55 LP 18, Part 1, 467

56 CP 1, 157

57 Hutchinson LDHVIII, 59; LP 18, Part 1, 873

58 James CP, 199

59 Porter MT, 144

60 James CP, 136

7 'A Strong Man of Personage'

1 The original Gaelic form of the name Lennox was Levenach, which was still sometimes in use, usually as 'Levenax', in sixteenth-century sources.

2 Mary, daughter of James II, had had, by her second husband, James, Lord Hamilton, a daughter, Elizabeth, who married Lennox's grandfather, Matthew Stewart, 2nd Earl of Lennox, who had fallen at Flodden in 1513.

3 Macauley, 9

4 Macauley, 10, 21, 22

5 Merriman ODNB; Porter CT, 309

6 Through James II's daughter Mary's son by James, Lord Hamilton.

7 Ridley HVIII, 379

8 Mahon, 120

9 Merriman ODNB

10 Additional MS. 32,649, f.126

11 Steel, 43

12 Additional MS. 32,650, f.73; Guy MHIMO, 31

13 Macauley, 29

14 CSP Scotland 1, 343

15 Porter CT, 312

16 LP 18, Part 1, 810

17 Additional MS. 32,651, f.85

18 LP 18, Part 1, 880

19 Marshall MG, 136; *The Scottish Correspondence of Mary of Lorraine*, 31

20 Additional MS. 32,652, f.114; Macauley, 42

21 LP 18, Part 2, 202

22 Additional MS. 32,652, f.159

23 Merriman ODNB

24 LP 18, Part 2, 257; Additional MS. 32,652, f.182

25 *Two Missions of Jacques de la Brosse*, 19; Marshall MG, 137–8

26 Guy MHIMO, 31

27 A History of the County of Renfrew from the Earliest Times

28 LP 18, Part 2, 269

29 LP 18, Part 2, 275

30 Additional MS. 32,652, ff.203–4

31 LP 18, part 2, 281

32 LP 18, Part 2, 282

33 LP 18, Part 2, 302

34 Additional MS. 32,652, f.247

35 Macauley, 49

36 LP 18, Part 2, 439

37 LP 18, Part 2, 527

38 Additional MS. 32,653, f.105

39 LP 19, Part 1, 30, 33

40 LP 19, Part 1, 33

41 PPE Mary, 135, 136, 143, 146; Strickland LQS 2, 79

42 LP 19, Part 1, 296

43 Fraser SW, 375

44 LP 19, Part 1, 136

45 *Statutes of the Realm* 3, 35 Hen. VIII, c.1

46 Williams EQE, 96

47 Lisle TFS, 229

48 Probably Darlington, County Durham, or Darrington in North Yorkshire (Darnton Index).

49 LP 19, Part 1, 143

50 LP 19, Part 1, 180

51 NA SP 2/1

52 *Cecil Papers* 1, 231, 42

53 Guy MHIMO, 32

54 NA E.39/2

55 LP 19, Part 1, 243; *The Letters of King Henry VIII*, 347–8

56 LP 19, Part 1, 314

57 Additional MS. 32,654, f.88

58 LP 19, Part 1, 343

59 LP 19, Part 1, 33, 51, 58

60 LP 19, Part 1, 522, 337

61 *Cecil Papers* 1, 172

62 CSP Spain 7, 124

63 Lindsay, 182

64 Spottiswood, 257

65 John Phillips

66 LRIL 3, 167

67 LP 19, Part 1, 812, no. 86

68 LP 21, Part 2, 768v

69 CSP Spain 7, 149

70 Probably Crookston.

71 A pound Scots was then worth about a quarter of a pound sterling. The properties Lennox settled on Margaret were Glenrinnie, Balloch and Auchtintorlies in the earldom of Lennox and the sheriffdom of Dumbarton; the lands and baronies of Cruckisfew, Inchinnan, Craig of Neilstoun and Tarbolton in the lordships of Darnley and the sheriffdom of Renfrew, and the lands of Errol in the sheriffdom of Perth (LP 19, Part 1, 779, 878; CSP Scotland 2, 636; Macauley, 81).

72 LP 19, Part 1, 779, 878; CSP Scotland 2, 636; Macauley, 81

73 Porter CT, 208

74 Herbert, 688. He was referring to the first Stuart kings, James I and Charles I.

75 LP 19, Part 1, 781; Starkey, 736

8 *'This Happy Match'*

1 As, for example, in *Burke's Guide to the Royal Family*.

2 CSP Spain 7, 149

3 CSP Spain 7, 138; LP 19, Part 1, 799

4 Scott. The ceiling and the perpendicular windows remain, but the rest of the chapel has been subject to many changes over the centuries. On the day of the wedding, the King is said to have made a speech in which he declared to Margaret that 'in case his own issue failed, he would be right glad if some of her body succeeded to the crown' (Fuller 3, 232), but this is so at variance with his wishes as recently expressed in the Act of Succession as to be dismissed as a myth. It was written after the Stuarts had succeeded to the throne, and naturally it was an inspired idea on Thomas Fuller's part to show Henry VIII approving of that.

5 Schutte, 102; Perry WP, 27

6 PPE Mary, 175, 177, 192, 193, 198

7 John Phillips

8 CSP Haynes, 443

9 Strickland LQS 2, 96

10 Merriman ODNB

11 Boulter. The list of estates granted to 'Matthew, Earl of Lennox, and Dame Margaret his wife' was as follows: 'the castle, lordship and manor of Whorlton; the manors of [New] Brighton and Greenhow, which belonged to Sir James Strangeways; the manors of Temple Hirst, Temple Newsam, Silkstone and Beckhay, which belonged to Thomas, Lord Darcy, attainted; the lordship and manor of Settrington, which belonged to Sir Francis Bigod, attainted; the manor of Hunmanby [which became known as Lennox Manor] and manors of Kirk Leavington, Wansford, Gembling and Nafferton, which belonged to Henry, late Earl of Northumberland; the manor and grange of Scrafton and the grange called Carleton Grange, which belonged to Sir Arthur Darcy, with lands in [blank], called Arundale House and Slappgill House, and a messuage [a dwelling house with outbuildings] in Caldbergh; the site &c., of the late monastery of Jervaulx and the lordships and manors of East Witton, Finghall, Wensleydale and Horton [in Ribblesdale], and the granges and farms called Jervaulx Grange, Newhouse, Akebar [Aysgarth], Haslingden, Rookwith, Kilgramhow, Heyne, Lazenby, Newstead, Elfa Hall, Riswicke, Diderston and Tunstall, which belonged to Jervaulx monastery; and all appurtenances of the premises in Whorlton, [New] Brighton, Greenhalgh, Temple Hirst, Temple Newsam, Silkstone, Beckhay, Settrington, Hunmanby, Kirk

Leavington, Wansford, Gembling, [West] Scrafton, Carleton, Caldbergh, Nafferton, Jervaulx, New House, Akebarth [Aysgarth], Haslingden, Rookwith, Kilgramhow, Heyne, Lazenby, Gollinglith [Foot], East Witton, Newstead, Elfa Hall, Hutton Hang, Riswicke, Finghall, Thornton Steward, Newton-le-Willows, Richmond borough, Widderston, Whixley, Wensleydale, [Low] Ellington, [North] Ferriby, Harmby, Estmeryforth within Rokewyk, Gilling, Hartforth, [West] Felton, Melsonby, Milby, Burton Constable, Hunton, Brompton Patrick [now Patrick Brompton], Welburn, Hartlepool, Bellerby, Colburn, Tunstall, Ellingstring and Horton in Ribblesdale' (LP 19, Part 1, 900, 1035 (96); *VCH North Riding of Yorkshire*, 2; Boulter; Bingham, 40; Strickland LQS 2, 81–2).

12 Schutte, 100

13 LP 19, Part 1, 900, 1035 (96); *VCH North Riding of Yorkshire,* 2; Boulter; Bingham, 40; Strickland LQS 2, 81–2

14 *A Survey of the Manor of Settrington.* He was probably English, although it has been suggested that he was related to the Scottish poet and courtier William Fowler of Edinburgh (Petrina, 69, 84; Read 2, 377), yet there is no evidence for it.

15 NA SP 12/51, f.198

16 NA SP 15/12, f.175; CSP Haynes, 183

17 CSP Scotland 1, 1076

18 Pollitt; Strickland LQS 2, 82

19 CSP Scotland 2, 333; Cotton MS. Caligula B.VIII, 184–5

20 CSP Scotland 1, 1076

21 Cotton MS. Caligula B.VIII, 165–8; Lisle TFS, Appendix 2; Ashdown RT, 61. For Thomas Bishop's career, see *The Herald and Genealogist.*

22 Hayward, 203

23 NA SP 49/7

24 Holinshed, 5

25 Additional MS. 32,656, f.191

26 Additional MS. 27, 402, ff.39–40

27 LP 19, Part 2, 201

28 Originally Stebbenhithe or Stebunheath, or 'Stikoneth', as Stow called it in 1598.

29 There were two other great houses in the village. Bishopshall, the Bishop of London's manor house of Stepney and Hackney, had been in existence prior to the Domesday survey of 1086, and stood to the north of the parish; Edward I had held a parliament there in 1299. It was in the possession of the bishops until 1550, when Edward VI granted it to the Wentworth family. South-west of the church was the timber-framed Mercers' Great Place, which had been, until his fall and execution in 1540, in the possession of

Thomas Cromwell. During his lifetime it was occupied by Sir Thomas Alleyn, and on Cromwell's attainder it was granted to Cromwell's nephew, Sir Richard Williams, who took his uncle's surname.

30 *VCH Middlesex* 11

31 Strickland LQS 2, 82

32 The house was rebuilt or extensively remodelled when it was purchased in 1597 by Edward Somerset, Earl of Worcester, and renamed Worcester House. Part of the building blew down in a storm in 1800, but the rest – including a 'fine hall and chapel' (Strickland LQS 2, 82) – survived until 1863, when it was destroyed by fire.

33 *VCH Middlesex* 11; Dootson; Eleftheriou

34 NA E.314/22, ff.22, 29; James CP, 136

35 Bowle, 277

36 CP 3, 598

37 Harleian MS. 289, f.73

38 Porter CT, 313

39 LP 19, Part 2, 618

40 LP 19, Part 2, 719

41 LP 21, Part 2, 768v

42 John Phillips

43 Lane. Warnicke, 198, n.72, states that Margaret had a miscarriage in the spring of 1545 and delivered her second son, another Lord Darnley, in December, but the death of the first Lord Darnley is recorded in November 1545, and as will be seen, the second son was not born until December 1546.

44 Schutte, 104–5

45 Schutte, 104–5, suggests that Margaret could have conceived two months before her marriage, because it was quite permissible for couples to cohabit after betrothal, but the Lennoxes were not betrothed until 13 June, and a conception on or soon after that date would have made little difference to the length of the pregnancy.

46 PPE Mary, 198

47 CSPF 5, 27

48 Schutte, 107, states that Margaret accompanied him on his campaign of 1545, but I can find no evidence for this.

49 Macauley, 83, 102

50 Leland IJL. Wressle would fall into decay by the end of the Tudor period.

51 LP 20, Part 1, 210 (2)

52 LP 21, Part 2, 768v

53 LP 20, Part 1, 563

54 LP 20, Part 2, 824

55 Weever; Strickland LQS 2, 82–3

56 Pepys

57 CSPF 5, 26

58 Strickland LQS 2, 83; Schutte, 105

59 LP 21, Part 2, 768v

60 NA E.314/22, ff.22, 29, 47–8, 51–3; James CP, 237

61 James CP, 237

62 LP 21, Part 1, 969

63 LP 21, Part 1, 1384

64 Foxe 5, 553–61

65 LP 21, Part 2, 768v. The items prescribed for her were 'cons, prunes, berberis [used like citrus peel in cooking] and roses', diaciton, '*manus Christi* with cinnamon', 'penettes' (barley sugar), '*pulles pectoralis*' (a herbal infusion), senna 'cods', kidney plasters, an ointment, 'a roll of plaster', and quinces. In November she was given 'bengemyn' – possibly benzoin from a Benjamin tree, which was used to make perfumes and incense.

66 LP 21, Part 2, 181

67 Furtado *et al.*; *Temple Newsam*. The estate buildings of the preceptory stood south of the present house near the River Aire, and were excavated in the 1980s.

68 Howard; Furtado *et al.*

69 At the south wing's west end today is the dining room (which did not exist in the Lennoxes' day), in which there are coats of arms copied from Margaret's tomb in Westminster Abbey, with the motto *Avant, Darnley, jamais derrière* (Forward, Darnley, never be behind), all dating from the 1890s. Above the dining room is a room known as Lord Darnley's Chamber, after Margaret's second son, although it too dates only from the seventeenth century. In 1929 the Darnley Room, as it is now called, contained portraits associated with Henry Stuart, Lord Darnley; his mother, Margaret herself – a version of the full-length portrait in the Royal Collection; his son, James VI and I; his wife, Mary, Queen of Scots; and a small picture of Darnley himself with his younger brother Charles. In 1951 the only portrait in the room connected with Darnley was of his niece, Arbella Stuart. The present décor dates from 1897.

70 There was a Langstroppe family in Leeds, who were probably connected with Temple Newsam. The baptism register for Leeds parish church shows that a John Langstroppe was baptised there in 1584.

71 Howard; Crossley; Kitson and Pawson; Musgrave; Bingham, Chapter 2; Furtado *et al.*; *Temple Newsam*. The earliest known

illustration of Temple Newsam dates from 1699. For nearly sixty years after 1565 the house was allowed to fall into disrepair. On his accession to the English throne in 1603, James I granted it to his favourite, Ludovic Stuart, Duke of Lennox, whose heirs sold it in 1622 to Sir Arthur Ingram. Between 1622 and 1637 the east wing was demolished and the north and south wings rebuilt in the Tudor style by Ingram, whose descendants lived at Temple Newsam until 1922, when it was sold to Leeds City Council. It is now a magnificent mansion and museum containing a great collection of furniture, paintings and ceramics.

72 Crossley; Kitson and Pawson; Bingham, 43

73 There have been erroneous claims that Darnley was born at Settrington. The parish registers survive from 1559, and no children of Margaret and Lennox are recorded in them. A local tradition has it that Darnley was born in the manor house at West Scrafton in Coverdale, where Lennox owned five granges (West Scrafton Manor House). However, these were all leased out (Joynes), indicating that the Earl and Countess never lived there.

74 Mackay, 128

75 Crossley

76 Three, on good evidence, were his bastards, Elizabeth Tailboys, Katherine Carey and Etheldreda Malte. I am grateful to Elizabeth Norton for the information pointing to Elizabeth Tailboys being Henry's child.

77 John Phillips

78 CSP Scotland 1, 1076. The grant of land cannot have been that of the manor of Pocklington, which was given to Bishop by Henry VIII in 1544, since Bishop was away in Scotland with Lennox after the Lennoxes' wedding at that time, and there would have been no opportunity for enmity to build up between him and Margaret.

79 Porter MT, 432, n.13; Schutte, 108; Bingham, 47, who suggests that Bishop was about to denounce Margaret as a Papist and only Henry's death saved her from the Tower. But there is no evidence for this.

80 Cotton MS. Caligula B.VIII, f.165

81 Lisle KHN

82 Lisle TFS, 236; Lisle KHN

83 For example, Ashdown RT, 64

84 Lisle, KHN, states that it gave the impression that she was a woman whose poor judgement led to her diminished political importance, and that the mud has stuck to her name ever since, but there is little in the secondary sources to support that, and as far back as the nineteenth century Strickland applauded Margaret's stand against the

'relentless fiend' Bishop: 'It is to the honour of the Lady Margaret
that she was the constant theme of Tom Bishop's abuse' (LQS 2, 85).

85 Lisle TFS, 236
86 Plowden LJGHS, 51
87 Bingham, 47
88 LP 21, Part 2, 634

9 'Great Unnaturalness'

1   Porter MT, 155; Strickland LQS 2, 84
2   Strickland LQS 2, 84
3   Foxe, online edition, Book 9, 1321
4   Edward VI EBK, 115–16, CPP, 93–4
5   Merriman ODNB; Lisle TFS, 255
6   CSP Scotland 1, Introduction
7   CSP Scotland 1, 55; Ashdown RT, 61
8   CSP Scotland 1, 100
9   CSP Scotland 1, 1076
10 Holinshed 2, 473; Bingham, 48. Strickland, LQS 2, 84, embellished
    the tale, claiming that eleven of the hostages, all young boys, were
    hanged. She describes Sir John Maxwell – who was supposedly
    spared the rope at the last minute by a remorseful hangman – as a
    very young boy, when in fact he was thirty-six.
11 Merriman ODNB; CSP Scotland 1, 181; NA SP 15/2, f.47v
12 NA SP 15/2, f.47v
13 It has been stated that in 1547 the King granted the Lennoxes a
    house at Hackney, east of London, that had been confiscated from
    the Percys after the Pilgrimage of Grace (Bingham, 48; Strickland
    LQS 2, 86; Ashdown RT, 61), but the manor of Hackney had
    reverted to the Crown on the death without issue of Henry Percy,
    Earl of Northumberland, in 1537, and in 1547 Edward VI granted
    it to Sir William Herbert, later Earl of Pembroke. It would be
    leased by Margaret in the 1570s.
14 Macauley, 83
15 Porter CT, 347
16 NA SP 50/1, f.86
17 William Fraser 4, 171
18 CSP Scotland 1, 261
19 NA SP 15/2, f.47v
20 NA SP 15/3, f.8
21 In a letter dated 10 March 1549 (reproduced in the text) Margaret
    refers to 'all' Angus's legitimate sons, which implies that there were
    more than two.

22 *Selections from unpublished manuscripts*, 52–3; Cotton MS. Caligula B.VII, f.436

23 Cotton MS. Caligula B.VIII, f.446

24 Leland IJL

25 Between Edward VI and Mary, Queen of Scots.

26 Another of Margaret's uncles, James Douglas, 7th Lord of Drumlanrig, who had helped to wrest James V from the dominance of Angus in 1528.

27 CSP Scotland 1, 343, where the letter is incorrectly dated 10 March; LRIL 3, 167

28 APC 3, 118

29 APC 3, 126

30 Edward VI CPP, 62

31 CSP Spain 10, June 1551; Edward VI CPP, 62

32 Lisle TFS, 490, citing Edward VI's journal, states that, anxious to dissociate himself from the affair, and fearful for his neck, Lennox publicly relinquished his claim to the throne of Scotland, saying he had no desire for it; but I can find nothing about this in either Jordan's edition or North's.

33 Macauley, 89

34 Edward VI EBK, 115, CPP, 93–4

35 CSPF, Edward VI, 477

36 Edward VI EBK, 115–6, CPP, 93–4

37 Edward VI EBK, 116

38 CSPD Edward VI 14, 18; Strickland LQS 2, 90

39 Strickland LQS 2, 89

40 CSPD Edward VI 14, 10, 15, 70

41 Strickland LQS 2, 90

42 APC 4, 250

43 APC 4, 251; CSPF 5, 27

44 William Fraser 1, 428

45 CSPF 5, 27

46 See next chapter.

10 'The Person Best Suited to Succeed'

1 Ashdown RT, 107, says she was absent because she was expecting a child, but she was recorded at court on 17 October.

2 CSPF 5, 27

3 Richards, 154

4 Ashdown RT, 107

5 He must have been referring to Margaret. Elsewhere he calls her the Countess 'Durcley' and her father as the 'Count of Durcley', which is close to 'Doubley'. CSP Spain 11, 28 November.

6 CSP Spain 11, 19 October

7 *Ambassades de MM. de Noailles en Angleterre* 2, 209–12; Marshall MG, 196–7

8 CSP Spain 11, 28 November; Guy CHVIII, 164

9 Loades EI, 90

10 CSP Spain 11, 28 November

11 *Ambassades de MM. de Noailles en Angleterre* 2, 273

12 NA SP 12/22, f.77

13 Ibid.; Marshall ODNB; Bingham, 56

14 CSPD Elizabeth 12, 22: 'What my Lady Lennox had in Queen Mary's Days'; William Fraser 1, 429

15 Merriman ODNB

16 Marshall QMW, 110

17 In 1555 Lennox's servants, Robert Thwaites and Thomas Blackmore, were committed to the Marshalsea Prison for making an affray at Brentford (APC 5, 159; *VCH Middlesex*).

18 CSPD Elizabeth 12, 22; Marshall ODNB; Ashdown RT, 108

19 Strickland, LQS 2, 90, says they were at Temple Newsam, but this seems unlikely as Margaret was at court at Christmas and when Elizabeth was brought to Whitehall late in February.

20 CSPD Elizabeth 22, 48; Froude 7, 396

21 CSPD Elizabeth 22, 48

22 *Original Letters* 2, 335; William Fraser 1, 430

23 CSP Spain 12, 3 April; Correspondence Diplomatique Angleterre 12, 204

24 Ibid. (both)

25 *The Chronicle of Queen Jane and of Two Years of Queen Mary*, 169

26 Schutte, 130

27 William Fraser 1, 429

28 Marshall ODNB; Ashdown RT, 106

29 Crossley

30 Strong EI, 9, 345

31 Now in the National Galleries of Scotland; formerly in the Royal Collection until at least 1714.

32 Strong EI, 88

33 Mahon, 120, 122

34 Schutte, 148–9

35 Merriman ODNB

36 Elder; Boulter; Strickland LQS 2, 86, 92

37 Bingham, 61

38 Elder

39 Cotton MS. Vespasian F.III, f.378; Schutte, 135

40 Bingham, 125

41 CSP Simancas 1, 357

42 CSPF Mary, 523

43 Macauley, 104; Schutte, 138

44 CSPF 5, 26, 412

45 Cecil Papers 1, 848; CSP Haynes, 381; CP, 158. Dixon is sometimes spelt Dicconson.

46 *Relations Politiques de la France et de l'Espagne avec l'Ecosse au XVIième Siècle* 1, 289–90. Angus was buried with his forefathers in the collegiate church of Abernethy, Perthshire, one of the lordships attached to his earldom. The last remains of the church were demolished in 1802.

47 Porter CT, 279

48 CSP Haynes, 381; William Fraser 1, 431; Strickland LQS 2, 92; Marshall QMW, 112

49 Schutte, 137

50 LRIL 3, 239–40; CSP Scotland 1, 415

51 CSP Spain 13, Miscellaneous, 24 March 1557

52 Margaret's tomb epitaph describes him as the youngest son.

53 Lane. In a letter dated 25 May 1572, Charles's tutor, Peter Malliet, wrote that the boy was 'just entering upon his sixteenth year', meaning he had recently turned fifteen, which places his birth in 1557 (*Zurich Letters*, 231). Margaret's tomb epitaph gives Charles's age in April 1576 as twenty-one, implying a date of birth in 1555, but it is incorrect, and also gives the year of Margaret's death incorrectly. Some historians, following the epitaph, state that Charles was perhaps born in 1554, but Margaret had given birth to his brother Philip sometime after the Queen's wedding in July 1554, probably in the winter following. The inscription giving Charles's age as six on the Eworth portrait of him and his brother Darnley, dated 1562, must be incorrect, although the inscription on the 1563 copy correctly gives his age as six.

54 Ashdown RT, 106; Lisle, TFS, 502, states that he was named 'after the new King of France', Charles IX, but the latter did not succeed until 1560.

55 Strickland LQS 2, 94

56 CSP Spain 13, 417

57 Ross; Bingham, 63

58 CSPF 5, 27

59 CSP Scotland 1, 1076

60 NA E.318/Box 6/222; C.1/1492, 67; E.318/Box 28/1599; C.66, 25; *VCH East Riding of Yorkshire* 3, 133–40. Pollitt says his estates had been re-granted to Northumberland, but it appears that Bishop's ownership of Pocklington was continuous.

61 APC 6, 218

62 Macauley, 96
63 Strickland LQS 2, 94
64 LRIL 3, 248–9
65 CSPD Mary 1, 11, 13
66 Ashdown RT, 109; Strickland LQS 2, 95

11 'The Second Person in the Kingdom'

1 Marshall ODNB; Fraser 1, 432; Strickland LQS 2, 95
2 Ashdown RT, 112
3 Leland ARBC; *Ecclesiastical Memorials* 3, 2 (142)
4 Schutte, 142
5 CSP Scotland 1, 597
6 CSP Venice 7, 10
7 Strickland LQS 2, 95, 105; CSPF 5, 421
8 Schutte, 142
9 Handover, 40
10 Marshall ODNB; Macauley, 123
11 CSPF 5, 26
12 Lefuse, 14
13 Neale, 133
14 Froude 1, 328
15 Hamilton, 245
16 Macauley, 83
17 Marshall QMW, 112
18 The Buildings of Settrington; *A Survey of the Manor of Settrington*.
   By 1599 the manor house was Crown property; according to the
   survey made that year, 'Lawrence Nesbit, Simon Dodsworth and
   Rowland Fothergill did leave the possession of the said manor
   house [to] her Majesty'. By the late eighteenth century it was
   ruinous, and it was demolished when the present Settrington
   House was built adjacent to the site in 1793. See The Buildings of
   Settrington. The nearby village, which was larger in Margaret's day,
   was rebuilt during the nineteenth century.
19 Pastscape: Jervaulx Abbey
20 'Cistercians "depopulated land" to found Jervaulx'; English Heritage:
   The National Heritage List for England
21 *Zurich Letters* 1, 125
22 Strickland LQS 2, 70
23 Perry, 221. There are no visible remains of the Charterhouse today,
   although a blue stone marks the site of Queen Margaret's tomb.
24 Macauley, 113; Aveling: 'Catholic Households in Yorkshire', 88;
   Bastow, 593

25　CSP Scotland 2, 333, from Cotton MS. Caligula B.VIII, ff.184–5; CSPF 5, 26

26　CSP Venice 7, 45

27　Ryrie; Hurren

28　CSPF 5, 26

29　LQS 2, 89

30　NA SP 15/12, ff.174–5

31　Cliffe, 168

32　NA SP 15/12, f.175

33　Ibid.; *Chapters in the History of Yorkshire*, 68

34　Macauley, 107

35　Henderson

36　Bingham, 69

37　National Records of Scotland PC 5/2, f.12, 1565

38　CSPF 5, 26

39　CSP Simancas 1, 139

40　CSPF 5, 26

41　NA SP 12/22, f.23

42　Strickland LQS 2, 98

43　CSP Simancas 1, 122

44　Ibid.

45　CSP Simancas 1, Introduction. There is no evidence that, on Dudley's advice, he arranged for Thomas Bishop and William Forbes to spy on the Lennoxes, as Strickland suggested (Strickland LQS 2, 98; Macauley, 121).

46　CSPF 5, 26

47　CSPF 1, 868

48　Strickland LQSEP 2, 340

49　Harleian MS. 289, ff.73–4

50　Barber, 25; Strickland LQS 2, 96

51　NA SPD Elizabeth 1, 12/23, ff.10–15

52　CSPF 5, 26

53　Ibid.

54　Neale, 132

55　CSPF 2, footnote to 524

56　Strickland LQS 2, 96

57　Ibid.

58　*Cecil Papers* 1, 582; CSPF 2, 422; CSP Haynes, 213

59　*Cecil Papers* 152, f.89v; *Cecil Papers* 1, 583; CSP Simancas 1, 85; CSPF 2, 467

60　CSPF 2, footnote to 524

61　Additional MS. 33,592, ff.214–16

62　Strickland LQS 2, 97

63 Macauley, 18
64 CSPF 2, 499
65 *Cecil Papers* 1, 596; CSPF 2, 577
66 NA SP 52/1, f.314
67 *Cecil Papers* 1, 596; CSPF 2, 577
68 CSPF 2, 579; CSP Scotland 1, 610
69 CSPF 5, 26
70 CSP Scotland 1, 612
71 CSPF 2, 634
72 CSP Simancas 1, 85
73 CSP Simancas 1, 84
74 CSP Simancas 1, 154
75 CSPD Elizabeth 11, 18
76 Henry, Lord Hastings, later earl of Huntingdon. He was descended from the Plantagenets through the Pole family.
77 CSP Simancas 1, 92
78 CSP Simancas 1, 93
79 CSPF 5, 34
80 Knox 2, 135; William Fraser 1, 434
81 Macauley, 109
82 CSP Simancas 1, 120
83 CSP Simancas 1, 121
84 CSPF 3, 752; CSP Scotland 1, 923
85 CSPD Elizabeth 14, 51; NA SP 12/14, f.100; NA SP 12/16, f.38; Strickland LQS 2, 99

12 'Her Son Should Be King'

1 Dating from the early twelfth century, Whorlton had been largely rebuilt in the fourteenth, and consisted of a keep and a rectangular gatehouse; the latter survives today, an atmospheric ruin, along with the remains of the undercroft of the keep. Possibly because the castle itself was in a decaying state, the Lennoxes built a substantial house of two storeys with a steeply pitched roof with gabled dormer windows against the north-west end of the gatehouse, as can be seen in a drawing of 1725 by Samuel Buck; but no trace of it remains today (Skipper; Buck). Camden, writing not long after Margaret's death, describes Whorlton as 'old and ruinous'. The village that surrounded the castle has long been abandoned, and the castle ruins have been vandalised in recent years.
2 CSP Scotland 1, 922
3 CSP Scotland 1, 929; CSPF 3, 795
4 CSP Scotland 1, 930; CSPF 3, 806

5 CSPF 3, 805

6 CSPF 3, 818

7 Macauley, 136

8 CSP Scotland 2, 333, from Cotton MS. Caligula B.VIII, ff.184–5; Pollitt, 61–2. Bishop has been called a professional spy (Lisle TFS, 326); in 1566 he admitted that his previous master, Sir John Stirling of Stirling, had 'used me as a spy here' in England (CSP Scotland 2, 334).

9 NA SP 12/23, ff.17–18

10 Harleian MS. 289, ff.73–4

11 CSP Simancas 1, 123

12 Now in the Scottish National Portrait Gallery.

13 CSP Scotland 1, 964

14 William Fraser 1, 469

15 Merriman ODNB

16 CSPF 4, 39; CSP Scotland 1, 975

17 NA SP 52/6, f.70; CSP Scotland 1, 974; CSPF 4, 40

18 Sometimes spelt Latye.

19 CSPF 5, 26

20 Ibid.; Strickland LQS 2, 99

21 William Fraser 1, 469

22 Lisle TFS, 317

23 John Gordon, 11th Earl of Sutherland.

24 CSPF 5, 26, 34

25 Ibid.

26 CSP Scotland 1, 1076; Harleian MS. 289, ff.73–4

27 CSPF 4, 402

28 CSPF 5, 26

29 Ibid.

30 Porter CT, 407

31 CSPF 5, 26

32 CSPF 5, 34

33 CSPF 5, 26

34 Ibid.

35 Ibid.

36 *Lettres* 4, 33

37 CSPF 4, 582

38 CSPF 5, 26

39 CSPF 4, 644

40 CSPF 4, 720

41 CSP Simancas 1, 144

42 Lisle KHN states that Elizabeth invited Margaret to spend Christmas at court.

43 CSPF 5, 26

44 CSPF 4, 720

45 Knox 2, 336

46 CSPF 4, 855; CSP Scotland 1, 1071

47 Lisle KHN. It has been stated that royal messengers and guards arrived at Settrington shortly before Christmas and arrested the Lennoxes, their children and their servants (William Fraser 1, 436; Bingham, 76; Strickland LQS 2, 101). But this is at variance with other evidence, and neither Lennox nor Margaret were arrested until the following year; proceedings against them did not commence until the middle of January.

48 CSP Simancas 1, 139

49 CSPF 5, 26

50 Lisle, KHN, states that while Margaret was at court, she saw one of Bishop's servants there. Immediately her suspicions were aroused, and she and Lennox came to the realisation that Bishop had betrayed them. Together they devised a means of discrediting him, and soon afterwards laid a complaint against him before the Council, accusing him of causing dissension between them, cowardice, sexual immorality and thievery. However, their complaint (in Cotton MS. Caligula B.VIII, ff.184–5) is endorsed by Cecil: 'V February 1565 [1566]. Contra Tho. Bishop.' That date can be confirmed by Bishop's reference in his defence to the murder of William Stirling, Captain of Dumbarton, having taken place '31 years since'; Stirling had died at Easter 1534 (Cotton MS. Caligula B.VIII, ff.165). The new year of 1534 did not officially begin until Lady Day, 25 March, hence the date 1565.

51 CSPF 4, 777

52 CSPF 4, 801

53 CSPF 4, 803

54 This portrait came via the collections of John, Lord Lumley (in which it was recorded in 1590) and the Cecils of Hatfield House (recorded 1629) to that of Charles I. Today it is in the Royal Collection at the Palace of Holyroodhouse (Strong EI, 102).

55 Schutte, 160

56 CSP Simancas 1, 149

57 Ibid.

58 CSPF 4, 851; CSP Scotland 1, 1071

59 CSPF 4, 855; CSP Scotland 1, 1071

60 CSP Simancas 1, 150

61 CSP Simancas 1, 154

62 CSP Simancas 1, 150

63 CSP Simancas 1, 151

64 *Zurich Letters* 1, 125
65 CSP Scotland 1, 1076; Harleian MS. 289, ff.73–4
66 CSP Scotland 1, 1076; NA SP 12/23, ff.14–15
67 *Cecil Papers* 1, 848; CSP Haynes, 381–2
68 CSP Scotland 1, 1077, 1089; CSPF 4, 883
69 CSPF 4, 971
70 CSP Scotland 1, 1076; Harleian MS. 289, ff.73–4
71 Skidmore, 130; CSPD Elizabeth 21, 55; Bindoff 1, 681
72 Cotton MS. Caligula B.VIII, f.299. Laurence Nesbit was released from the Tower. Margaret later rewarded him for his good service with farmland, property and tenements at Settrington. He died in 1587 (*A Survey of the Manor of Settrington*).
73 CSPD Elizabeth 22, 48
74 CSP Simancas 1, 153; Williams TT, 82–3
75 CSP Simancas 1, 159
76 CSP Simancas 1, 154
77 Additional MS. 48,023, f.362
78 CSP Simancas 1, 154
79 CSP Simancas 1, 155
80 CSP Simancas 1, 156

13 'Indignation and Punishment'

1 William Fraser 1, 436; Bingham, 76; Strickland LQS 2, 101
2 Strickland LQS 2, 101
3 CSPF 4, 980; Lisle TFS, 326
4 It is clear from this that Margaret's son Philip had died by this time, otherwise Quadra would surely have referred to three sons. Schutte, 162, states that Quadra was expecting Margaret to arrive from Sheen, destined for the Tower, but in a letter dated 22 August 1562 Margaret herself refers to having come down from Settrington (CSPF 5, 516; CSPD Elizabeth 24, 17; Strickland LQS 2, 106).
5 CSP Simancas 1, 157
6 CSP Simancas 1, 159. Hertford could only have claimed the throne in right of his wife, Katherine Grey, and since both were in the Tower, Elizabeth was hardly likely to have sanctioned that.
7 William Fraser 1, 436; Bingham, 76; Strickland LQS 2, 101
8 Margaret's letter in CSPF 5, 516, and CSPD Elizabeth 24, 17, mentions her being imprisoned with her children, in the plural, but Darnley had escaped and Charles was still in York.
9 Ascham, 71
10 Cloake

11 By 1769 all that remained of Sheen was a gateway, which was demolished that year.

12 CSPF 5, 121; NA SP 12/23, f.78

13 NA SP 52/7, f.58

14 *Cecil Papers* 1, 848

15 Ibid.; CSP Haynes, 381–2

16 NA SP Foreign 70/36, ff.178–80; CSPF 4, 1073; Sitwell, 155; Sutherland, 95

17 CSPD Elizabeth 23, 6

18 Ibid.

19 CSPF 5, 26

20 Ibid.; Knox 2, 336

21 CSPF 5, 26. The Court of Star Chamber was the ancient high court of England, made up of Privy Councillors and judges and under the control of the monarch. Its name derived from the decorative pattern of stars on the ceiling of the chamber in the Palace of Westminster where the court sat.

22 CSPF 5, 27

23 Bingham, 70. Lallard's commentary does not survive.

24 Schutte, 158, 159

25 CSP Simancas 1, 144

26 CSPF 5, 34

27 Jones, 38

28 NA SP 12/23, f.48; CSPF 5, 59; CSPD Elizabeth 23, 17

29 CSPF 5, 80; NA SP 12/23, f.62; CSPD Elizabeth 23, 25

30 CSPF 5, 91

31 CSPF 5, 121; NA SP 12/23, f.78

32 CSPF 5, 122

33 NA SP 12/23, f.30

34 NA SP 12/23, ff.80–1

35 NA SP 59/6, ff.3, 17. George Norton was the son of the Lennoxes' steward, Richard Norton, and Mr Constable is probably to be identified with Marmaduke Constable.

36 NA SP 59/6, f.106

37 CSP Simancas 1, 168. Not surprisingly, Quadra fell out with Venturini after what he saw as a gross betrayal, and Venturini resigned from his service soon afterwards.

38 CSPF 5, 168. On 10 May the Archbishop of Canterbury had ruled that their union had been no marriage.

39 CSPF 5, 170

40 A discharge of mucus from the eyes and nose.

41 CSPF 5, 181; NA SP 12/23, f.87; CSPD Elizabeth 23, 37

42 CSPF 5, 219; NA SP 12/23, f.103

43 CSPF 5, 295

44 Margaret, Regent of the Netherlands, the bastard daughter of the Emperor Charles V.

45 CSP Simancas 1, 169

46 CSPF 5, 223; CSPD Elizabeth 23, 45

47 CSPF 5, 258

48 NA SP 12/23, f.111

49 CSP Simancas 1, 173

50 CSPF 5, 295; NA SP 12/23, f.119

51 CSPF 5, 332

52 CSPF 5, 343; NA SP 12/23, f.132. The date is given as 24 June in CSPD Elizabeth 23, 58, but it is listed incorrectly under 24 July.

53 Strickland LQS 2, 84

54 William Fraser 1, 387

55 CSPF 5, 362; NA SP 12/23, f.134

56 CSPF 5, 412, 464; Additional MS. 35,831, ff.55–7, 65; NA SP 59/6, f.109; Macauley, 122

57 CSPF 5, 421; Strickland LQS 2, 105

58 CSPF 5, 464

59 CSPF 5, 468

60 The children Margaret refers to must have been her son Charles and probably her two daughters.

61 CSPF 5, 516; CSPD Elizabeth 24, 17; Strickland LQS 2, 106

62 CSPD Elizabeth 24, 40

63 Strickland LQS 2, 106; Sitwell, 204

64 CSP Simancas 1, 189

65 CSPF 5, 912

66 Sheen was six miles from Hampton Court.

67 CSPF 5, 1037

68 CSP Simancas 1, 198

69 CSPF 5, 1123; CSPD Elizabeth 25, 63; Strickland LQS 2, 106

70 CSP Simancas 1, 199

71 CSPD Elizabeth 27, 7; Strickland LQS 2, 106–7

72 Strickland LQS 2, 106–7

73 This probably refers to a land dispute in 1553. After the Pilgrimage of Grace the Strangeways family had been dispossessed of lands that were now owned by the Lennoxes.

74 CSPD Elizabeth 27, 17; Strickland LQS 2, 107

75 Strickland LQS 2, 107

76 CSP Simancas 1, 304

77 Macauley, 126

78 *Cobbett's Complete Collection of State Trials*, 1199

79 Clarke

80 Merriman ODNB

81 CSPD Elizabeth 27, 50

82 CSP Simancas 1, 211

83 CSP Simancas 1, 216

84 CSPF 6, 483; CSP Scotland 1, 1175

85 CSPF 6, 485; CSP Scotland 1, 1179

86 Schutte, 174

87 CSP Scotland 1, Introduction. The issue of her legitimacy never entirely went away. In 1593, some years after her death, a Jesuit tract, *A Conference about the Next Succession to the Crown of England*, by R. Doleman, asserted that she was doubly illegitimate, with a view to undermining the claim of her Protestant heir, Arbella Stuart.

14 'Lady Lennox's Disgrace'

1 William Fraser 1, 440; Strickland LQS 2, 107

2 CSPF 6, 743

3 CSP Simancas 1, 218

4 CSPF 6, 905; CSP Scotland 2, 15

5 Macauley, 133–4

6 Loades EI, 154

7 CSP Simancas 1, 233

8 CSP Simancas 1, 234

9 CSPF 6, 1027

10 CSPF 6, 1211

11 CSP Vatican, 282

12 It has been said that it descended from Margaret to James VI (Strong EI, 96), but James may have inherited it from Mary. It is now in the Royal Collection at Windsor. A later copy by Rhoda Sullivan, dating from *c.*1897, is at Temple Newsam in the collection of Leeds Museums and Galleries.

13 NA SP 52/9, f.30

14 NA SP 52/9, f.51

15 NA SP 52/9, f.53

16 NA SP 52/9, ff.55–6

17 NAS GD 220/2, 152

18 NA SP 52/25, f.209; Macauley, 137

19 CSP Scotland 2, 70

20 Porter CT, 407

21 Merriman ODNB

22 *Lettres* 1, 216

23 NA SP 52/9, f.59

24 NA SP 52/9, f.63

25 CSPF 7, 367; CSP Scotland 2, 72; NA SP 52/9, f.57

26 CSP Scotland 2, 72

27 CSP Simancas 1, 262

28 CSP Simancas 1, 251

29 CSP Simancas 1, 253

30 Nichols and Gough 1; Bingham, 83

31 NA SP Scotland, MQS 53/9, ff.187–8; Macauley, 140

32 CSP Simancas 1, 262; NA SP 59/9, f.93

33 CSPF 7, 556

34 NA SP 52/9, f.63

35 CSPF 7, 557

36 CSPF 7, 591

37 CSP Simancas 1, 262

38 Egerton MS. 1818, f.31

39 CSP Simancas 1, 262

40 William Fraser 1, 441; Melville's brother William was married to
    Margaret's distant cousin, another Margaret Douglas, the daughter
    of Thomas Douglas of Lochleven.

41 CSP Simancas 1, 240

42 CSP Simancas 1, 265

43 NA SP 52/9, f.109

44 CSPF 7, 699

45 CSPF 7, 700; CSP Scotland 2, 98

46 CSPF 7, 704; CSP Scotland 2, 99

47 Melville, 83

48 Melville, 92

49 Melville, 99

50 Melville, 92

51 Melville, 82

52 Melville, 99

53 Tait; Antonia Fraser MQS, 271. Now on display at the Palace of
    Holyroodhouse, the Lennox Jewel was formerly in the collection of
    Horace Walpole at Strawberry Hill, and was purchased by Queen
    Victoria in 1842. Its earlier history is unknown, as Walpole would
    never reveal where he acquired it. In 1843 Queen Victoria
    commissioned an account of the Jewel from the antiquarian Fraser
    Tytler.

54 Henderson, who claims that Margaret wore the Jewel constantly
    around her neck or at her girdle.

55 Tait; Antonia Fraser MQS, 271

56 Tait

57 Guy MHIMO, 199; NA SP 52/8, 75–6

58 Marshall QMW, 115

59 *Treasures: The Royal Collection*, 133

60 For the Lennox Jewel see Tytler; Marshall ODNB; *Treasures: The Royal Collection*, 133; Lisle TFS, 346; *Royal Treasures*, Chapter 9; Macauley, 143; Tait; Antonia Fraser MQS, 271. Stedall, CC, plate section, states that the Jewel may have been one of the two gold brooches with large sapphires that were given by Mary Tudor to Margaret on her marriage, but it is clearly a pendant and not a brooch, and would surely have merited a more detailed description. Stedall also states that Margaret gave Mary, Queen of Scots, the Jewel when she married Darnley, which seems unlikely, given the imagery.

61 Melville, 101

62 Williams ATQM, 86

63 NA SP 70/74, f.152

64 CSP Scotland 2, 108

65 Guy MHIMO, 199; NA SP 52/8, ff.75–6

66 CSPF 7, 772

67 CSP Simancas 1, 273

68 CSPF 7, 855

69 NA SP 52/9, ff.172–3

70 CSP Simancas 1, 280; NA SP 52/9, f.153

71 CSPF 7, 757, 859; CSP Scotland 2, 110

72 CSPF 7, 866

73 CSPF 7, 960

74 NA SP 52/10, f.33; Camden, 60

75 Macauley, 148

76 Melville, 101–2

77 Macauley, 164

78 Keith 2

79 Strickland LQS 2, 108

80 CSP Simancas 1, 296

81 *Papiers d'état* 2, 192

82 CSP Scotland 2, 166

83 CSPF 7, 958; CSP Scotland 2, 141; Pollitt, 65; Macauley, 146

84 Heale, 147

85 Melville, 107

86 CSPF 7, 1000

87 CSPF 7, 1008

88 NA SP 52/10, f.37

89 CSPF 7, 1029; CSP Scotland 2, 154

90 CSPF 7, 1017

91 CSPF 7, 1043

92 CSPF 7, 1079

93   CSP Simancas 1, 290

94   CSP Simancas 1, 292

95   CSP Simancas 1, 284

96   CSPF 7, 1105

97   Mahon, 120

98   CSP Scotland 2, 166

99   CSP Simancas 1, 286

100 William Fraser 1, 444. Strickland, LQS 2, 109, states that Margaret
     had been at Settrington and received a summons to come to
     London, but the evidence shows that she was already at court.

101 CSP Simancas 1, 295

102 Holinshed 5; William Fraser 1, 441

103 CSP Simancas 1, 296

104 CSPF 7, 1120

105 CSP Scotland 2, 170

106 CSP Simancas 1, 296

107 CSP Simancas 1, 297

108 CSPF 7, 1123

109 CSPF 7, 1125

110 CSPF 7, 1140

111 CSPF 7, 1141

112 CSP Scotland 2, 186

113 Melville, 99

114 CSPF 7, 1189; CSP Scotland 2, 185; NA SP 52/10, f.129

115 NAS GD 220/3, 155; Pollitt, 65

116 CSPF 7, 1129

117 CSPF 7, 1224; CSP Scotland 2, 194. The fact that only Charles was
     mentioned strongly suggests that Margaret's other children had all
     died.

118 CSP Simancas 1, 300

119 Holinshed 5

120 CSP Simancas 1, 301, 302

121 CSP Simancas 1, 320

122 CSPF 7, 1279

123 Ibid.

124 CSP Simancas 1, 304, 25 June

15 'Strait Imprisonment'

1   CSP Simancas 1, 304, 25 June. William Fraser, 1, 445, Marshall,
    ODNB, and Henderson, relying on an inscription in the Tower,
    state that Margaret was taken there on 20 June; Lisle, TFS, 337,
    gives 22 June, citing CSP Simancas 1, 296, which was written on

26 April and refers to Margaret being placed under house arrest; Strickland, LQS 2, 109, and Schutte, 195, also give 22 June, Dunn, 292, 25 June.

2 Dunn, 293

3 Marshall ODNB

4 Keay, 39

5 Ibid.; Bell, 64; Handover, 51

6 William Fraser 1, 445. The inscription was uncovered in 1834 during renovations to what was then the Deputy Governor's dressing room.

7 Strickland LQS 2, 110; Dixon, 162–3

8 Hibbert

9 Hardy, 10. In 1611 Margaret's granddaughter, Arbella Stuart, would be imprisoned in this same room, which is supposedly haunted by her ghost.

10 Keay, 39

11 William Fraser 1, 444–5; Keith 2, 161

12 CSPF 7, 1251

13 CSP Simancas 1, 304

14 NA SP 15/12, f.175

15 NA SP 15/12, f.172; CP 3, 600

16 CSPF 7, 1271

17 CSP Simancas 1, 442

18 Strickland LQS 2, 109

19 William Fraser 1, 446

20 Keith 2, 161

21 CSP Simancas 1, 305

22 CSP Simancas 1, 307

23 CSP Simancas 1, 308

24 CSPF 7, 1313; CSP Scotland 2, 213

25 CSP Simancas 1, 409

26 CSPD Elizabeth 37, 25

27 Keith 2, 161

28 CSP Simancas 1, 310

29 CSP Simancas 1, 311

30 CSP Simancas 1, 312

31 Keith 2, 347

32 Macauley, 130

33 CSPF 7, 1333; NA SP 52/11, ff.1–4

34 CSPF 7, 1511

35 CSP Simancas 1, 313

36 CSP Scotland 2, 229; CSPF 7, 1381

37 CSP Scotland 2, 230; CSPF 7, 1383

38 CSP Simancas 1, 314

39 CSP Simancas 1, 316
40 Crossley; Furtado *et al.*; NA SP 15/12, f.175
41 CSPD Elizabeth 37, 36
42 Hardy, 10; CSPD Elizabeth 37, 67
43 Macauley, 84
44 Strickland LQS 2, 111
45 Stedall CC, 225
46 NA SP 52/11, f.87
47 CSPF 7, 1441; CSP Scotland 2, 242
48 Sutton-on-Derwent, where the Vaughans lived, was twenty-seven miles away.
49 Vaughan had married Anne Pickering, the widow of Sir Henry Knyvett.
50 CSPD Elizabeth 37, 25; Strickland LQS 2, 110; Hardy, 10; Ashdown RT, 142. The Knyvetts were related to Elizabeth I on her mother's side through the Howards. Margaret's granddaughter, Arbella Stuart, would later be placed in the charge of the Knyvett family.
51 CSP Simancas 1, 319
52 CSP Simancas 1, 320
53 A rectangular visor attached to the French hood, overshadowing the forehead.
54 A stiffened underskirt.
55 Lengths of heavy cotton twill fabric.
56 Decorative cloths laid on top of cupboards, on which to display plate.
57 Shallow bowls with handles.
58 A double tripod for toasting bread before the fire.
59 CSPD Elizabeth 37, 39
60 Ibid.; Strickland LQS 2, 111
61 Strickland LQS 2, 113
62 Lansdowne MS. 102, 64; NA SP 52/11, f.62; NA SP 52/11, f.75
63 NA SP 52/11, f.299; NA SP 52/11, f.181
64 CSPF 7, 1510
65 CSP Scotland 2, 261; CSPF 7, 1514
66 CSP Simancas 1, 327
67 CSP Scotland 2, 288
68 CSP Simancas 1, 329
69 CSP Simancas 1, 331

16 'In Great Trouble'

1 Mahon, 121
2 Macauley, 155; Robertson 1, 276
3 NA SP 52/11, f.217

4　Macauley, 156

5　CSPF 7, 1510

6　Knox 2, 507

7　CSP Scotland 2, 318

8　Knox 2, 192

9　CSP Haynes, 443

10　*Cecil Papers* 3, 72

11　CSPF 8, 1

12　Pepys Library, Cambridge MS. 2502, f.493

13　CSP Simancas 1, 335

14　Cesar Adelmare of Treviso, physician successively to Mary I and Elizabeth I.

15　CSP Scotland 5, 22. This is listed under July 1574, and is endorsed by Cecil, 'The examination of Fowler, 1564', but its content shows that it belongs to January 1565.

16　CSPF 8, 90; CSP Scotland 2, 340

17　CSP Scotland 2, 332

18　CSP Simancas 1, 336

19　CSP Scotland 2, 333, from Cotton MS. Caligula B.VIII, ff.184–5

20　Macauley, 156

21　CSP Scotland 2, 333, from Cotton MS. Caligula B.VIII, ff.184–5. The reference is to Patrick Hepburn, 3rd Earl of Bothwell, who had died in 1556.

22　CSP Scotland 2, 334, from Cotton MS. Caligula B.VIII, f.165

23　On 24 June 1567 Melville would report to Cecil that he had 'spoken with Master Bishop to know if he will go with my lord of Lennox to Scotland, who answered he would be directed by your Honour. He may serve to good purpose both for experience of the country, and for religion, as well as to keep friendship between Lennox and his friends there. I know Moray has a good opinion of him, and he will employ his service to withdraw us from France. How he is in my Lord and Lady Lennox's favour, I am not certain' (CSP Scotland 2, 530). There is no evidence that Bishop went north with Lennox. He could talk himself out of a difficult situation, and his honeyed tongue may have accounted for him being spoken highly of by Moray and Melville (*The Herald and Genealogist*; The Bishop Family of Pocklington).

24　CSP Simancas 1, 337

25　CSPF 8, 90; CSP Scotland 2, 340. *Lettres* 1, 313. Maitland had already written to Cecil on 9 February asking him to take pity on Fowler and spare him (CSP Scotland 2, 336).

26　Goodare, 167; Macauley, 157

27　CSPF 8, 134; CSP Scotland 2, 346

28 CSP Simancas 1, 342
29 Merriman ODNB
30 CSPF 8, 165
31 CSP Simancas 1, 349
32 Knox 2, 179–80
33 CSP Simancas 1, 349
34 Calderwood 2, 312
35 CSPF 8, 205
36 Macauley, 158
37 CSPF 8, 208
38 NA SP 52/12, ff.180–1
39 CSP Scotland 2, 464; CSPF 8, 894
40 Cotton MS. Caligula B.IV, f.254
41 Additional MS. 35, 831, f.243
42 CSP Simancas 1, 344
43 Randolph refers to it as 'the Abbey', the name by which Holyrood Palace was then known.
44 CSP Scotland 2, 371
45 CSP Simancas 1, 350
46 CSP Simancas 1, 353
47 CSPD Elizabeth 39, 68
48 CSP Simancas 1, 357
49 CSPF 8, 414
50 CSP Scotland 2, 390
51 CSP Simancas 1, 361
52 CSP Simancas 1, 362
53 CSPF 8, 498
54 CSPF 8, 552; NA SP 52/12, ff.180–1
55 Lisle TFS, 339
56 CSPF 8, 706
57 CSP Simancas 1, 365
58 CSP Simancas 1, 366
59 NA SP 52/12, ff.180–1
60 This information was divulged some months later by William Rogers, and reported by Randolph to Cecil on 15 January 1567 (NA SP 52/12, f.122).
61 Macauley, 177
62 CSP Simancas 1, 367
63 CSP Simancas 1, 368
64 Keith 2, 448–52, 467
65 NAS GD 220/1, 194
66 CSP Simancas 1, 386
67 CSP Simancas 1, 402

68 CSPF 8, 885
69 Mahon, 124
70 NA SP 52/13, f.5
71 CSP Simancas 1, 405
72 CSPF 8, 960
73 Mumby, 157

17 'Horrible and Abominable Murder'

1 For a full account of the murder of Darnley, see my *Mary, Queen of Scots, and the Murder of Lord Darnley.*
2 *Register of the Privy Council of Scotland* 1, 498
3 CSP Simancas 1, 407
4 CSPF 8, 977
5 CSP Simancas 1, 408
6 *Cecil Papers*, Cecil to Sir Henry Norris, 20 February 1567; CSP Simancas 1, 408
7 Ibid. (both sources)
8 Ibid.
9 Ibid.
10 CSP Venice 7, 383
11 CSP Venice 7, 384
12 CSP Scotland 2, 478
13 NA SP 59/12, f.202
14 *Cecil Papers*, Cecil to Sir Henry Norris, 20 February 1567; Fraser 1, 447; Marshall QMW, 117
15 Cloake
16 CSP Simancas 1, 408
17 Dunn, 350; Bingham, 184
18 CSPF 8, 953
19 CSP Simancas 1, 408
20 John Phillips
21 NA SP 52/13, f.30
22 Cotton MS. Caligula B.X, f.408
23 CSP Haynes, 177
24 CSP Scotland 2, 477
25 CSP Scotland 2, 488
26 CSP Simancas 1, 413
27 Cotton MS. Caligula B.X, f.410
28 CSP Simancas 1, 409
29 CSPF 8, 997
30 CSP Scotland 2, 481; CSPF 8, 1001
31 CSPD Elizabeth 42, 12

32 Gayley
33 CSPF 8, 1061
34 CSP Scotland 2, 488
35 Cotton MS. Caligula B.X, f.412
36 Merriman ODNB
37 Sloane MS. 3199, ff.8–9
38 Macauley, 182
39 CSPF 8, 1061
40 CSPF 8, 1059
41 CSPF 8, 1079
42 Calderwood 2, 349
43 Calderwood 2, 350
44 CSPF 8, 1097; CSP Simancas 1, 417
45 CSP Scotland 2, 488
46 NA SP 52/13, f.76; Macauley, 185
47 CSP Simancas 1, 417
48 CSP Simancas 1, 418, 422
49 CSPF 8, 1100
50 CSP Scotland 2, 495. Loch Gairloch is on the River Clyde.
51 Sitwell, 252
52 CSP Simancas 1, 420
53 CSP Simancas 1, 422
54 Ibid.
55 CSP Scotland 2, 513; CSPF 8, 1277
56 CSP Simancas 1, 426
57 Ibid.
58 CSP Simancas 1, 427
59 The first reference to this is dated 6 August, but the Lennoxes were
    certainly in residence by the end of June (NA SP 12/43, f.79;
    Marshall ODNB).
60 Thornbury; Weir EY. Coldharbour was burned down in 1666
    during the Great Fire of London. Its site is now occupied by 89
    Upper Thames Street.
61 CSPF 8, 1340
62 NA SP 52/13, ff.139, 148
63 CSP Simancas 1, 428
64 CSP Simancas 1, 429
65 CSP Scotland 2, 543; CSPF 8, 1379
66 CSPD Elizabeth 43, 22
67 CSP Venice 7, 395
68 Elizabeth I was entertained at Corney House in 1602. It was sold
    by the Russells in the 1660s, when it was rebuilt. The later house
    was demolished in 1832 (*VCH Middlesex*).

69 CSP Simancas 1, 434

70 CSPD Elizabeth 43, 37

71 CSP Simancas 1, 438

72 Macauley, 194

73 Now in the Royal Collection at the Palace of Holyroodhouse, Edinburgh.

74 Ashdown TR, picture caption

75 Marshall QMW, 118

76 Strickland, LQS 2, 119, suggests that the setting is the Catholic chapel at Settrington, but the Lennoxes had not yet returned there when the picture was painted.

77 There is an eighteenth-century engraving of it by George Vertue in West Sussex Record Office at Chichester (Goodwood MS. PD/85).

78 Stowe MS. 157, ff.16, 28; West Sussex Record Office, Goodwood MS. PD/85; Macauley, 188; Millar TSEGP, 75; Marshall QMW, 118–19; Bingham, 194

79 It is inscribed as Sir William St Loe, but the sitter is plainly Lennox. His appearance matches the likeness in the Darnley Memorial, having the same balding head and pale red beard.

80 CSPD Elizabeth 44, 38

81 CSPF 8, 1902

82 CSPF 8, 1875

83 CSPD Elizabeth 46, 11; Strickland LQS 2, 115. Norrington, 30, places this letter in January 1564.

84 Stedall SC, 44

85 CSP Murdin, 764; Macauley, 195

86 Camden, 91; Strickland LQS 2, 115; Marshall QMW, 119; Borman, 286

87 It survives in draft, partly in Lennox's hand, as CUL Oo.vii.47; the text is printed as an appendix in Mahon.

88 Macauley, 196

89 NAS GD 406/1, 26

90 Warden of the Middle Marches.

91 CSP Scotland 2, 677

92 *Cecil Papers* 1, 1186; *Lettres* 2, 102–3, 106

93 CSP Scotland 2, 771

94 CUL DdIII, ff.17–18; Macauley, 200. There was to be a third version, too, *A Remembrance after what sort the late King of Scots, son to me, the Earl of Lennox, was used by the Queen his wife* (CUL Oo. vii.47, ff.30–1), a far more concise document than its predecessors, which presents a much better case.

95 *Relations Politiques de la France et de l'Espagne avec l'Ecosse au XVIieme Siecle* 2, 390–1

96 CSP Scotland 2, 832
97 CSP Scotland 2, 850
98 CSP Simancas 2, 52
99 CSPF 8, 1812
100 CSP Scotland 2, 894
101 CSP Scotland 2, 906
102 John Phillips

18 'Business Most Vile'

1 CSPF 9, 68
2 Ashdown RT, 149; Strickland LQS 2, 116
3 Perry WP, 149–50
4 *Cecil Papers* 1, 1377
5 Schutte, 214
6 CSPF 9, 507
7 CSPF 9, 513
8 CSP Simancas 2, 174
9 *Cecil Papers* 1, 1469
10 CSP Scotland 3, 95
11 CSPF 9, 655
12 Strickland LQS 2, 116
13 Stow. What became known as Old Somerset House was demolished in 1775 and replaced with the present Somerset House.
14 CSP Scotland 3, 110; *Original Letters* 2, 333–4
15 *Regnans in Excelsis*
16 CSP Simancas 2, 180
17 CSPF 9, 713
18 Ridley EI, 172
19 CSPF 9, 818
20 CSPF 9, 839
21 Cannon and Hargreaves
22 Merriman ODNB
23 Hardy, 11, states that she served as Elizabeth's chief lady, but I can find no contemporary evidence to support this.
24 CSPF 9, 855
25 CSP Scotland 3, 195
26 CSP Scotland 3, 196
27 CSPF 9, 870; CSP Scotland 3, 207
28 CSP Scotland 3, 228; CSPF 9, 910
29 CSPF 9, 911; CSP Scotland 3, 230
30 NA SP 52/18, f.41
31 CSP Scotland 3, 214, 215

32 CSP Simancas 2, 198

33 CSPF 9, 918

34 CSP Scotland 3, 244

35 *Cecil Papers* 1, 1490

36 His heir, Francis, having died, his third son, Richard, inherited Pocklington, which was later purchased by the Dolmans, whose forebears had also served the Lennoxes.

37 CSPF 9, 1026

38 CSP Scotland 3, 289, 304

39 CSP Scotland 3, 340

40 CSP Scotland 3, 344, 350

41 CSP Scotland 3, 356

42 CSP Scotland 3, 402

43 CSPF 9, 1097

44 Tytler

45 Schutte, 216

46 CSPF 9, 1149

47 CSP Scotland 3, 415

48 CSP Simancas 2, 209

49 CSP Scotland 3, 437

50 CSPF 9, 1206

51 Macauley, 223

52 CSP Scotland 3, 434

53 CSP Scotland 3, 446; NA SP 53/5, f.128; William Fraser 1, 450

54 CSP Scotland 3, 468, 469; CSPF 9, 1266; NA SP 52/19, f.98

55 William Fraser 1, 451

56 CSPF 9, 1262; CSP Scotland 3, 465

57 William Fraser 1, 450–1

58 Additional MS. 19,401, f.105

59 CSP Scotland 3, 478

60 CSP Scotland 3, 496

61 CSPF 9, 1286

62 CSPF 9, 1328; CSP Scotland 3, 519

63 CSP Scotland 3, 508

64 Chancellor of the Exchequer.

65 CSPD Elizabeth 74, 9

66 NAS GD 149/265, f.1; CSP Scotland 3, 349; endorsed, 'Delivered to her in presence of the Queen of England viij[vo] No[bris] 1570; Robertson 3, 237–8

67 Robertson 3, 238

68 CSP Scotland 3, 584

69 CSPF 9, 1525

70 CSP Simancas 2, 233

71 CSPF 9, 1572
72 CSPD Elizabeth 77, 39
73 CSP Scotland 3, 627
74 Strickland LQS 2, 118
75 CSP Simancas 2, 247; CSPF 9, 1638
76 CSP Simancas 2, 247; CSPF 9, 1647
77 Merriman ODNB
78 CSP Simancas 2, 273
79 *Accounts of the Lord High Treasurer of Scotland* 12, 240
80 CSP Scotland 3, 764
81 CSP Scotland 3, 777; CSPF 9, 1759
82 CSP Scotland 3, 821
83 CSPF 9, 1985
84 His mother had been Margaret's bastard half-sister, Janet Douglas.
85 CSP Scotland 3, 816; CSPF 9, 1819
86 CSPF 9, 1841
87 CSPF 9, 1847
88 CSP Scotland 3, 841
89 Strickland LQS 2, 118
90 CSPF 9, 1908, 2080, 2085
91 CSP Scotland 3, 856; CSPF 9, 1909
92 Fénélon 4, 180
93 Mann
94 Willey
95 Fielding
96 Records of the Court of Augmentations and the Augmentation
    Office. Barber's Barn was later demolished and replaced by a three-
    storeyed gabled house built around 1590–1 (Lysons). That house was
    demolished probably in the 1790s.
97 CSP Scotland 3, 884
98 CSPF 9, 1936; CSP Scotland 3, 888
99 CSPF 9, 1943
100 CSPF 9, 1945
101 CSP Scotland 3, 904
102 CSP Scotland 3, 911
103 He was a younger son of Patrick, Lord Ruthven, who had taken
    part in the murder of Rizzio and died in exile in 1566.
104 CSP Scotland 3, 917
105 Strickland LQS 2, 118
106 John Phillips
107 CSPF 9, 2027; CSP Scotland 3, 921
108 CSP Scotland 3, 921; CSPF 9, 2026
109 Ibid.

110 CSPF 9, 2027
111 CSPF 9, 2014; CSP Scotland 3, 912, 921
112 CSPF 9, 1983, 1997; CSP Scotland 3, 913; NA SP 52/21, f.69
113 CSP Scotland 3, 912, 921
114 William Fraser 1, 416
115 William Fraser 1, 416; Lisle TFS, 347; Guy MHIMO, 508
116 Strickland LQS 2, 118
117 Spottiswood 2, 166
118 *The Historie and Life of King James the Sext*, 93
119 Spottiswood 2, 166; William Fraser 1, 416; Marshall ODNB;
    Merriman; Schutte, 222
120 William Fraser 1, 417
121 Ibid.
122 CSPF 9, 2010
123 *A diurnal of remarkable occurrents*, 249
124 Calderwood 3, 139

19 'Treason Bereft Me'

1 William Fraser 1, 418
2 William Fraser 1, 453; Strickland LQS 2, 119
3 Ibid.
4 CSP Scotland 4, Appendix, 7; Stedall SC, 135
5 John Phillips
6 NA SP 52/21, f.184
7 CSPF 9, 1997
8 Merriman ODNB
9 Holinshed 5; Marshall ODNB
10 It was then believed that the legendary Brutus of Troy had founded
   the ancient kingdom of Britain and was the ancestor of all its
   kings.
11 Holinshed 5
12 CSPF 9, 2026
13 CSPF 9, 1989
14 CSPF 9, 2027
15 CSPF 9, 2023
16 CSPF 9, 2028
17 CSP Scotland 3, 921
18 CSP Scotland 3, 924
19 CSP Scotland 4 Appendix, 3
20 CSPF 9, 2023
21 CSP Scotland 4 Appendix, 7
22 CSP Scotland 4 Appendix, 8

23 CSPF 9, 2051; CSP Scotland 3, 956

24 CSP Simancas 2, 279

25 CSP Simancas 2, 280

26 CSPF 9, 2059; CSP Scotland 4, 2

27 CSP Scotland 4 Appendix, 10

28 CSP Scotland 4 Appendix, 15

29 CSP Scotland 4 Appendix, 26

30 Chalfant; Strickland LQS 2, 120

31 Canonbury Tower was rebuilt by Spencer in the 1580s and '90s. Sir Francis Bacon, Oliver Goldsmith and Washington Irving were among the famous persons who later lived there. In 1795 the house was again largely rebuilt and the south range of Prior Bolton's building was demolished. It served as the Tower Theatre from 1953 to 2003, and is now a masonic research centre. Only parts of the walls survive from the house Margaret knew. The tower and three-storey wing to the south date from *c.*1580.

32 CSPD Elizabeth 83, 5; Strickland LQS 2, 120

33 CSP Simancas 2, 279

34 Schutte, 222–3

35 CSP Scotland 4, 326

36 Reproduced in Durant and credited to the National Portrait Gallery, although it cannot be traced there.

37 *Zurich Letters*, 231; CSP Scotland 5, 89; Ashdown RT, 165; Hardy, 12

38 Not an island, but perhaps regarded as one because of its situation on the banks of the Clyde.

39 CSP Scotland 4 Appendix, 36

40 CSP Scotland 4, 61; CSPF 9, 2136

41 CSP Scotland 4 Appendix, 57

42 CSPF 10, 824

43 CSP Scotland 4, 122; CSPF 10, 99

44 NA C.142/165/126; Erskine and Paton

45 Mann

46 By 1758 the east side of the southern courtyard of Brooke House was derelict; it was rebuilt and became a mental asylum. The house was bombed in the Blitz of 1940, and the east range of the northern courtyard, comprising a range of what were probably Tudor offices, was destroyed. The remains of Brooke House were acquired by the London County Council in 1944, but deemed too damaged to be restored. After a careful record was made of what survived, the house was demolished in 1954–5. Hackney Community College now stands on the site (Brooke House; Tudor Hackney; Eden *et al.*).

47 Tudor Hackney

48 Eden *et al.*
49 CSP Scotland 4, 127
50 CSP Scotland 4, 139
51 CSP Scotland 4, 211
52 CSPF 10, 253; Hardy, 21
53 CSP Scotland 4, 299; CSPF 10, 329
54 CSP Scotland 4, 326
55 CSP Scotland 4 Appendix, 61
56 CSP Scotland 4 Appendix, 71
57 CSP Scotland 4, 428
58 CSP Scotland 4, 448
59 CSP Scotland 4, 474; CSPF 10, 632
60 *Lettres* 5, 31
61 Sitwell, 354; Jenkins EL, 199
62 CSP Scotland 5, Introduction
63 Lisle TFS, 350; Guy MHIMO, 382; Stedall CC, 433
64 *The Last Testament of the Earl of Bothwell*
65 Guy MHIMO, 382
66 NA SP 53/10, f.71
67 Chalmers 2, 243
68 MacNalty, 145
69 CSP Scotland 5, 38
70 Sitwell, 354
71 CSPF 10, 738
72 CSPF 10, 754
73 CSPF 10, 780
74 CSPF 10, 824
75 CSP Scotland 4, 596
76 CSP Scotland 4, 605
77 CSP Scotland 4, 703
78 CSP Scotland 4, 713; CSPF 10, 1119
79 CSPF 10, 1117
80 CSP Scotland 4, 720; CSPF 10, 1133; Campling
81 *Register of the Privy Council of Scotland* 2, 247, 330
82 *A Survey of the Manor of Settrington*
83 CSP Scotland 5, 21

20 'The Hasty Marriage'

1 Lovell, 259
2 Lovell, 200
3 CSP Scotland 5, 66
4 Lovell, 240

5 *A Collection of Letters, and State Papers*, 255–7
6 Ibid.
7 Durant, 8
8 Handover, 48
9 Lisle TFS, 349; Ashdown RT, 169–70; Hardy, 14
10 *A Collection of Letters, and State Papers*, 255–7
11 Gristwood, 16
12 CSP Simancas 2, 403
13 Ashdown RT, 167; Hardy, 16
14 CSPD Elizabeth 99, 12
15 Ibid.
16 APC 8, 293
17 CSP Simancas 2, 403
18 *A Collection of Letters, and State Papers*, 255–7
19 CSPD Elizabeth 99, 12; Sandeford, 143; Strickland LQS 2, 122–3
20 *A Collection of Letters, and State Papers*, 255–7
21 CSPD Elizabeth 99, 12; Strickland LQS 2, 122–3
22 Lovell, 242
23 CSPD Elizabeth 99, 12; Strickland LQS 2, 122–3
24 *A Collection of Letters, and State Papers*, 255–7
25 CSPD Elizabeth 99, 12; Strickland LQS 2, 122–3
26 Ibid.
27 *A Collection of Letters, and State Papers*, 255–7
28 What remains of the house and abbey after much of it was demolished in the 1950s is an imposing ruin set in a country park.
29 *A Collection of Letters, and State Papers*, 255–7
30 Cited Gristwood, 12–13
31 Jenkins EL, 201
32 Hardy, 14
33 Handover, 50
34 In the 1950s, before Rufford Abbey was partly demolished, the chapel was still hung with tapestries and contained armorial glass commemorating the marriage.
35 *A Collection of Letters, and State Papers*, 255–7
36 Durant, 6–7, 14–15
37 Norrington, 24
38 MacNalty, 145
39 *A Collection of Letters, and State Papers*, 255–7
40 Lovell, 245–6
41 CSPD Elizabeth 99, 12; Strickland LQS 2, 122–3
42 Ibid.
43 CSPD Elizabeth 99, 13
44 CSP Scotland 5, 66; Hardy, 18

45 CSP Simancas 2, 408
46 CSPD Elizabeth 99, 13
47 Lovell, 247
48 Strickland LQS 2, 123
49 Durant, 9; Lovell, 247
50 Strickland LQS 2, 123; Lefuse, 14
51 Hardy, 19
52 For Sir William Livingston, see Kilsyth, a Parish History. Morton was found guilty and beheaded on 'the Maiden', an early guillotine he had himself introduced into Scotland.
53 CSP Scotland 5, 89
54 CSP Scotland 5, 68
55 CSP Scotland 5, 21. Fowler's interrogation by Walsingham is listed under July 1574, but it clearly took place after Charles Stuart's marriage, probably in December.
56 Ashdown RT, 171
57 Strickland LTP, 94
58 Hardy, 125; Gristwood, 15; Lefuse, 15–16
59 Lovell, 249
60 Borman, 295, 296
61 Gristwood, 19
62 *Lettres* 7, 243
63 CSP Scotland 5, 89, 94
64 Gristwood, 19; Lefuse, 17
65 *A Survey of the Manor of Settrington*
66 Cavendish-Talbot MS. X.d.428, f.108; Hardy, 19
67 *Cecil Papers* Addenda, 123
68 William Fraser 1, 459
69 Harleian MS. 289, ff.200, 202; *Archaeologia* 32, 81; Strickland LTP, 94; Hardy, 19
70 John Phillips
71 CSP Scotland 5, 210
72 This was the first recorded mention of Arbella in contemporary sources (Durant, 10).
73 CSP Scotland 5, 210
74 Ashdown RT, 172; Strickland LTP, 95

21 'Till Death Do Finish My Days'

1 Strickland LTP, 94
2 John Phillips
3 NA PROB 12 Langley. Most of the church was demolished in 1798, and only the tower survives.

4   Holinshed 5
5   CSP Scotland 5, 227; CSPF 11, 755
6   Clarke; Borman, 297
7   Lisle TFS, 352; Marshall QMW, 122; Schutte, 233
8   Durant, 15
9   Strickland LQS 2, 124 (no source cited)
10 Hardy, 22
11 Harleian MS. 289, f.202; Macauley, 86
12 Harleian MS. 289, f.202
13 Harleian MS. 289, f.198
14 *A Survey of the Manor of Settrington*
15 Davey SLJG, 286
16 Strickland LTP, 95; Robertson 2, Appendix
17 APC 10, 161
18 Schutte, 232
19 *A Survey of the Manor of Settrington*
20 Durant, 14
21 Strickland LTP, 95; Durant, 14
22 CSP Scotland 5, 290
23 CSP Scotland 5, 277, 290
24 CSP Scotland 5, 291
25 Strickland LTP, 96
26 *Lettres* 4, 397–8
27 Durant, 14; Lisle TFS, 352
28 Hardy, 24
29 CSP Scotland 5, 370
30 CSP Scotland 5, 295
31 Norrington, 25
32 Folger Shakespeare Library L.a.249
33 Varlow, 54
34 MacNalty, 153
35 Nichols 2, 522. A casting bottle was used for sprinkling scented
    water.
36 *Lettres* 6, 51–7
37 Lovell, 314–15; Borman 314–15
38 *A Survey of the Manor of Settrington*
39 NA PROB 11/60/174. The will is dated 1577, but the new year of
    1578 did not officially begin until Lady Day, 25 March.
40 It has been suggested that the tablet given to Leicester is perhaps
    to be identified with a girdle book containing a portrait of the
    King now in the British Library (Stowe MS. 956) and once in the
    possession of the descendants of William Seymour, Duke of
    Somerset, the man Arbella married; and that Arbella was briefly

betrothed to Leicester's heir, the 'noble imp', Robert Dudley, Lord Denbigh, in childhood; and that the tablet came to her at this time (Lisle TFS, 414), but there is no proof of the betrothal.

41 Eden *et al.*; NA PROB 11/60/174. The will was witnessed and sealed by Dr Robert Huicke, the Queen's physician, Dr Richard Caldwell, Sir Robert Bowes, N. Paine, Robert Weldoms, Margery Williams, John Wolfe, Laurence Nesbit and William Mompesson, in the presence of William Drury, Doctor of Law and commissary of the Prerogative Court of Canterbury.

42 Durant, 15; Lovell, 275

43 John Phillips

44 The date is given in her tomb epitaph and by Holinshed, although John Phillips gives 9 March.

45 John Phillips

46 Marshall ODNB

47 Elizabeth Throckmorton, wife of Sir Walter Raleigh.

48 Peck

49 Miller, 143

50 Naunton; Sitwell, 101; Jenkins EL, 293

51 Lemprière, 446

52 Leicester's Commonwealth, 18

53 Following Leicester's death in 1588, he entered the service of James VI. He died in 1590 in Edinburgh.

54 Ashdown RT, 174

55 Stedall SC, 138

56 Lefuse, 6

57 CSP Scotland 5, 368

58 CSP Scotland 5, 368; NA C.66, 1170; Macauley, 84; Durant, 18. Mann says that Margaret was first buried in Hackney Church with Charles, and was moved to Westminster by James I, but this is not supported by the other evidence.

59 CSP Scotland 5, 328

60 Ibid.

61 Lovell, 276

62 Lisle TFS, 353

63 Holinshed 5

64 Stow

65 Holinshed 5

66 Meaning a representation or model, in this case almost certainly an effigy.

67 Holinshed 5

68 Strong TJP, 199

69 An electrotype of the effigy is in the National Portrait Gallery.

70 Arnold QEWU, 128, 152
71 Whitelock, 353
72 For the tomb, see The Douglas Archives; Wilkinson
73 Scott Giles
74 Borman, 298
75 Camden, 277
76 Holinshed 5
77 Clarke
78 Gristwood, 17
79 Clarke
80 Ibid.

22 'A Progenitor of Princes'

 1 Keith 3, 307; Hardy, 13
 2 CSP Simancas 2, 493
 3 NA SP 52/27, f.120v
 4 Gristwood, 29
 5 CSP Scotland 5, 356
 6 Eden *et al.*
 7 *Original Letters* 2, 60
 8 Hardy, 33; Gristwood, 51; University of Nottingham MS.
    Mi6/1/173/242
 9 Possibly the H stood for Henry Darnley or Henry VIII.
10 Darnley's emblem.
11 Hardy, 25; Lefuse, 26–7
12 Tytler
13 *Royal Treasures*
14 Hardy, 25–6
15 Ashdown RT, 177–8; Hardy, 55
16 *Acts of the Parliaments of Scotland* 3, 154–7; CSP Scotland 5, 365
17 Macauley, 86
18 NA SP 52/31, f.2
19 Somerset
20 CSP Scotland 5, 368
21 CSP Scotland 5, 369
22 NA SP 52/31, f.5
23 CSP Scotland 6, 505
24 Schutte, 53
25 The head of the vault is in fact two or three feet to the south of
    the tomb.
26 Stanley, 510–11. The discovery of Richmond's body in this vault left
    Stanley baffled as to why it should be there when his heart was

encased in an urn near his son's magnificent monument in the Henry VII Chapel.

27 Clarke

Appendix 1: Margaret's Portraiture

1 Strong EI, 44; Strong TJP, 200
2 Lisle, interview for the Lady Jane Grey Reference Guide
3 I am grateful to Siobhan Clarke, a guide lecturer at Historic Royal Palaces, who guides in costume as Margaret Douglas, for this comparison.
4 Marshall ODNB; Lisle, interview for the Lady Jane Grey Reference Guide; James, in *Apollo*; Porter CT, 312
5 Strong ERM, 47
6 Now in the Victoria and Albert Museum.
7 Lloyd and Remington, 1538
8 Denny KH, 175; *Holbein and the Court of Henry VIII*, 126–7; James, in *Apollo*; *Treasures: The Royal Collection*, 61; Reynolds, 50–2; Arnold PM, 5; Jane Roberts, 126; Foister, 102
9 *Lost Faces*, 72
10 *Lost Faces*, 74
11 Information from www.christies.com
12 Portrait of a Woman in Black; Hans Eworth and the London Stranger Painters
13 Guy HRPP
14 Bridgeman; Hans Eworth and the London Stranger Painters
15 Strong HE; Hans Eworth and the London Stranger Painters
16 It's About Time; Portrait of an Unknown Woman
17 Strong TJP, 199
18 Millar QP, 23
19 Millar TSEGP, 77; Strong TJP, 200
20 Millar TSEGP, 77
21 Ibid.
22 Thurley
23 Royal Collection Trust: Lady Margaret Douglas, Countess of Lennox
24 Kitson and Pawson
25 Millar TSEGP, 73
26 Scan kindly sent to me by Sally E. Douglas of The Douglas Archives.
27 Strickland LQS 2, 112
28 Reynolds, 304; Strong ATC, 65; Hearn, 36; The Fitzwilliam Museum

29 Strong TJP, 200
30 *A Noble Visage*
31 Scan kindly sent to me by Sally E. Douglas of The Douglas
    Archives.

Appendix II: Miscellaneous Poems Copied by Margaret Douglas into the Devonshire Manuscript

1 Additional MS. 17,492; Heale

Index

www.vintage-books.co.uk